COMPENSATION

Third Canadian Edition
McGraw-Hill Ryerson Series in Human Resource Management

George T. Milkovich
Cornell University

Jerry Newman
State University of New York—Buffalo

Nina Cole
Ryerson University

McGraw-Hill
Ryerson
Connect. Learn. Succeed.

The McGraw-Hill Companies

McGraw-Hill Ryerson
Connect. Learn. Succeed.

Compensation
Third Canadian Edition

ISBN-13: 978-0-07-096742-7
ISBN-10: 0-07-096742-3

3 4 5 6 7 8 9 10 WEB 1 9 8 7 6 5 4 3 2

Printed and bound in Canada.

Care has been taken to trace ownership of copyright material contained in this text; however, the publisher will welcome any information that enables them to rectify any reference or credit for subsequent editions.

Vice-President and Editor-in-Chief: Joanna Cotton
Senior Sponsoring Editor: Kim Brewster
Marketing Manager: Cathie Lefebvre
Developmental Editor: Lori McLellan
Senior Editorial Associate: Christine Lomas
Supervising Editor: Jessica Barnoski
Copy Editor: Michael Kelly
Team Lead, Production: Paula Brown
Cover Design: Katherine Strain
Cover Image: Christopher Leggett/Getty Images
Interior Design: Greg Devitt Design
Page Layout: Greg Devitt Design
Printer: Transcontinental Printing Group

Library and Archives Canada Cataloguing in Publication

Milkovich, George T.
    Compensation / George T. Milkovich, Jerry M.
Newman, Nina Cole. -- 3rd Canadian ed.

Includes bibliographical references and indexes.
ISBN 978-0-07-096742-7

    1. Compensation management--Textbooks.
I. Newman, Jerry M. II. Cole, Nina D. (Nina Dawn) III. Title.

HF5549.5.C67M54 2010   658.3'2   C2009-907143-6

ABOUT THE AUTHORS

George T. Milkovich is the M.P. Catherwood Professor at the ILR School, Cornell University. He studies and writes about how people get paid and what difference it makes. People's compensation has been his interest for over 30 years. His research has resulted in numerous publications. Four have received national awards for their contributions. His books, *Compensation*, co-authored with Jerry Newman, now in its 8th edition, and *Cases in Compensation*, co-authored with Carolyn Milkovich, are the most widely adopted text and cases about pay in the world. His current research examines the globalization of compensation and reward systems.

Milkovich received the Keystone Award from the World at Work Association (formerly the American Compensation Association) for lifetime achievement. He also received the Distinguished Career Contributions Award from the Academy of Management HR Division, and is a Fellow in both the Academy of Management and the National Academy of Human Resources. He chaired the National Academy of Sciences Committee on Performance and Pay, and the Federal Joint Labor-Management Committee on Pay and Performance.

He has received three Outstanding Teacher Awards and is also on the faculties of Zhejiang University in China and Ljubljana University in Slovenia. He has served as a Visiting Professor at several leading international universities, including London Business School, Hong Kong University of Science and Technology, Charles University in Prague, Comenius University in Bratislava, and University of California in Los Angeles.

Jerry Newman (B.A., U of Michigan; M.A., Ph.D., U of Minnesota) is Distinguished Professor of Organization and Human Resources at the State University of New York at Buffalo. His research and teaching interests are in the areas of compensation, team effectiveness, and performance management. When not working he definitely does not sky dive.

Nina Cole is Associate Professor of Organizational Behaviour and Human Resources Management at Ryerson University in Toronto. Prior to her academic career, she spent 12 years in the business world—eight years as a human resources consultant, and four years as a human resources manager. The last 20 years have been spent as an academic, teaching and conducting research on the application of organizational justice theories to human resource management. Nina has published articles in both academic journals and industry publications, and has led seminars to assist managers with meeting the challenges of managing human capital. She has spoken and written on these topics on numerous occasions, and also has co-authored textbooks on human resources management and organizational behaviour.

BRIEF CONTENTS

CONTENTS

PART I   32

Internal Alignment: Determining the Structure

6 Person-Based Pay Structures 105

PART II   130

External Competitiveness: Determining the Pay Level

7 Defining Competitiveness 133

Contents

8 Designing Pay Levels, Mix, and Pay Structures   156

9 Employee Benefits   184

Contents

PART III   210

Employee Contributions: Determining Individual Pay

10 Pay for Performance: Performance Appraisal and Plan Design   212

11 Pay-for-Performance Plans   241

Contents

PART IV   270

Managing the System

12   The Role of Government and Unions in Compensation   272

13   Compensation Budgets and Administration   291

Contents

Appendix: International Pay Systems   314

PREFACE

A few books can change your life. This is probably not one of them. However, if you read it, you will better understand that pay matters. For example, if you are a Russian cosmonaut, you can earn a bonus of $1,000 for every space walk (technically known as "extravehicular activity," or EVA), up to three, per space trip. A contract listing specific tasks to be done on a space mission permits you to earn up to $30,000 above the $20,000 you earn while you are on the ground. (In contrast to the Russian cosmonauts, wealthy Americans are lining up to pay $15 million [plus an additional $20 million airfare] to the Russian Space Agency for their own personal EVA.) Conclusion: Pay matters.

Such problems are global. A British telephone company paid a cash bonus based on how fast operators completed requests for information. Some operators discovered that the fastest way to complete a request was to give out a wrong number or—even faster—just hang up on the caller. "We're actually looking at a new bonus scheme," says an insightful company spokesperson. Conclusion: What you pay for matters.

In this book, we strive to cull beliefs from facts, wishful thinking from demonstrable results, and opinions from research. Yet when all is said and done, managing compensation is an art. As with any art, not everything that can be learned can be taught.

The third Canadian edition of the Milkovich/Newman/Cole compensation text continues to respond to the demand on the part of Canadian faculty and students for a Canadian version of the unique perspective on compensation taken by Milkovich/Newman/Cole.

This textbook is based on the strategic choices in managing compensation. These choices, which confront managers in Canada and around the world, are introduced in the total compensation model in Chapter 1. This model provides an integrating framework that is used throughout the book. Major compensation issues are discussed in the context of current theory, research, and practice. The practices illustrate new developments as well as established approaches to compensation decisions.

Each chapter contains a Web exercise to point you to some of the vast compensation information on the Internet. The case at the end of each chapter asks the student to apply the concepts and techniques discussed in the chapter. For example, the case in Chapter 11: Pay-for-Performance Plans guides the student through several exercises designed to explain how stock options work and how to value them. It also connects the student to real-time stock prices for up-to-date stock option valuations.

WHAT'S NEW IN THE THIRD CANADIAN EDITION

All chapters of this edition have been completely revised. This edition gives greater emphasis to the importance of total compensation. It reinforces our conviction that beyond how much, *how* people are paid really matters. Chapter 2 tells how to craft a total compensation strategy and examines the research on best practices. The chapters on performance-based pay dig into all forms of variable pay, such as stock options, profit sharing, gain sharing, and team-based approaches. Person-based plans are contrasted with job-based plans, including recent developments in skill and competency approaches. Changes in competitive market analysis caused by the focus on total compensation are covered, as well as the increased use of market pricing and broadbanding.

The employee benefits chapter has been expanded and updated. A broader discussion of board of director compensation and executive compensation has been added. We have always used international examples in every section; we have also completely revised the appendix on global compensation. Many of the Web exercises, cases, and .Net Worth features have been updated or replaced.

The book includes a margin icon next to material that is directly relevant to the Required Professional Capabilities that are covered in the National Knowledge Exam, one of the requirements for the Certified Human Resources Professional (CHRP) designation from the Canadian Council of Human Resources Associations.

ORGANIZATION OF THE CANADIAN EDITION

Compensation, Third Canadian Edition, is divided into four parts:

1. **Part I Internal Alignment: Determining the Structure**
2. **Part II External Competitiveness: Determining the Pay Level**
3. **Part III Employee Contributions: Determining Individual Pay**
4. **Part IV Managing the System**

The "meat" of each chapter in these parts (13 chapters in total) is interspersed with and followed by additional material provided to supplement the chapter's contents and provide both context and relevance:

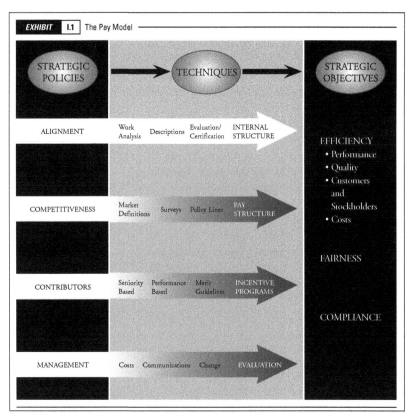

EXHIBIT 1.1 The Pay Model

The Pay Model: The unique Milkovich Pay Model around which the text is based is introduced right up front and is integrated throughout all subsequent chapter discussions.

LEARNING OUTCOMES

- Describe how compensation is viewed differently by society, stockholders, managers, and employees in Canada and around the world.
- Define the term *compensation*.
- Discuss major components of total rewards.
- Identify and explain the three strategic objectives of compensation.
- Describe the four strategic policies in the pay model and the techniques associated with them.

CHAPTER SUMMARY

1. Job analysis is the systematic process of collecting information about the nature of specific jobs. Job analysis data are used in virtually every major HR function, including recruiting and selection, training, compensation, and so on.
2. There is a six-step approach to job analysis: develop preliminary job information; conduct initial tour of work site; conduct interviews; conduct second tour of work site; consolidate job information; and verify job description.
3. The information that must be collected for job analysis includes job identification data, job content data, and data on qualifications necessary to do the job. Job content data are the heart of job analysis, and include the tasks involved, their purpose, reporting relationships, working conditions, and other specific job information. Conventional methods of collecting job analysis data such as questionnaires and interviews are being replaced by online questionnaires because they are more objective and less time-consuming.
4. Job descriptions provide a written summary of a job, including responsibilities, qualifications, and relationships. Job specifications are the qualifications required to be hired for a job, and may be included in the job description.

Learning Outcomes have been highlighted at the beginning of each chapter, and the **Chapter Summary** relating to these learning objectives is included at the end of the chapter.

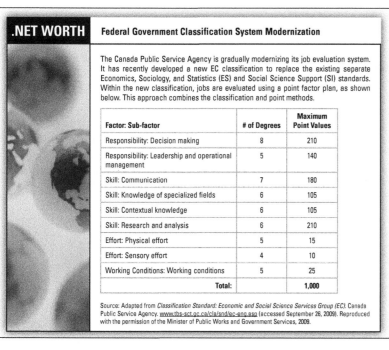

.NET WORTH **Federal Government Classification System Modernization**

The Canada Public Service Agency is gradually modernizing its job evaluation system. It has recently developed a new EC classification to replace the existing separate Economics, Sociology, and Statistics (ES) and Social Science Support (SI) standards. Within the new classification, jobs are evaluated using a point factor plan, as shown below. This approach combines the classification and point methods.

Factor: Sub-factor	# of Degrees	Maximum Point Values
Responsibility: Decision making	8	210
Responsibility: Leadership and operational management	5	140
Skill: Communication	7	180
Skill: Knowledge of specialized fields	6	105
Skill: Contextual knowledge	6	105
Skill: Research and analysis	6	210
Effort: Physical effort	5	15
Effort: Sensory effort	4	10
Working Conditions: Working conditions	5	25
Total:		**1,000**

Source: Adapted from *Classification Standard: Economic and Social Science Services Group (EC)*. Canada Public Service Agency. www.tbs-sct.gc.ca/cla/snd/ec-eng.asp (accessed September 26, 2009). Reproduced with the permission of the Minister of Public Works and Government Services, 2009.

Each chapter includes a **.Net Worth** boxed feature, which highlights a comprehensive, real-world example of the material in the chapter.

Definitions of Key Terms highlighted in each chapter are provided in the margins, and a list of these terms with page references is provided at the end of the chapter.

job structure
hierarchy of all jobs based on value to the organization; provides the basis for the pay structure

EXHIBIT **II.1** Who Makes How Much?

Sidney Crosby	Pittsburgh Penguins hockey player	$9,000,000
Michaëlle Jean	Governor General of Canada	$117,950
Katherine Caldwell	Ontario provincial court judge	$225,234
Shinzo Abe	Prime Minister of Japan	$174,000*
Adam Bartkowski	Software engineer, Krakow, Poland	$39,800*
Elvis Presley	Entertainer (deceased)	$52,000,000*
Roger Martin	Dean, Rotman School of Management, University of Toronto	$371,250
Robert Hinrichs	Vice president and chief actuary, Workplace Safety and Insurance Board	$280,761
Frank Mahovlich	Member, Senate of Canada	$130,400
Wang Yang	HR supervisor, Shanghai	$5,806*

Exhibits are interspersed throughout the text to illustrate concepts and provide a visual framework for students.

REVIEW QUESTIONS

1. Read again the values statements in Exhibit 2.6. Discuss how, if at all, these values might be reflected in a compensation system. Are these values consistent with "letting the market decide"?
2. What are the three tests used to determine whether a pay strategy is a source of competitive advantage? Discuss whether these three tests are difficult to pass. Can compensation really be a source of competitive advantage?
3. Contrast the essential difference between the "best fit" (strategic business-based) and "best practice" perspectives on compensation.

EXPERIENTIAL EXERCISES

1. Interview a compensation specialist about his or her organization's compensation strategy, specifically the five issues—objectives, alignment, competitiveness, employee considerations, and management. How does this organization compare to Google? To Whole Foods? What business strategy does it seem to fit (i.e., cost cutter, customer-centred, innovator, or something else)?
2. Set up a debate over the following proposition: "Best practices" is superior to the "best fit" approach when designing a compensation system.
3. Survey ten people about their total rewards preferences. What conclusions can you draw from the results?

WEB EXERCISE

Compensation Consultants on the Web

Compensation consultants are major players, and practically every organization uses at least one for data and advice. So, learning more about services these consultants offer is useful. Go to the Web site of at least two of the following consulting firms, or find others.

Towers Watson: www.towerswatson.com/canada-english

Hay Group: www.haygroup.ca

Review Questions and **Experiential Exercises** are suggested at the end of each chapter. In response to instructor suggestions, these real-life exercises require the application of learned concepts and techniques.

A **Web Exercise** at the end of each chapter will familiarize the student with the wealth of compensation-related material available on the Internet. Also included at the end of each chapter is a comprehensive **Case** requiring application of the chapter material.

REQUIRED PROFESSIONAL CAPABILITIES®

As of March 2003, provincial human resources associations throughout Canada have successfully agreed on a framework for achieving the designation of Certified Human Resources Professional (CHRP). This national accreditation process was launched by the Canadian Council of Human Resources Associations (CCHRA). Go to www.cchra.ca; click on CHRP Certification, then Required Professional Capabilities. The national CHRP certification program has raised the bar for HR practitioners across the country. HR practitioners must now meet an even more demanding set of professional performance standards and acquire knowledge and skills covering a wide range of Required Professional Capabilities (RPCs).

Look to the inside front cover of this text to see the conveniently located set of the specific RPCs required for Compensation. You will see these referenced throughout the chapter with the icon displayed to the left here. Whenever you see this icon in the margin beside chapter content, simply look to the inside front cover to link to the required competency. Please note that for the sake of brevity and simplicity, we have included only the Total Compensation competencies for which the student will be responsible in the CHRP exams; these RPCs are not cross-referenced to other functional areas.

INSTRUCTOR AND STUDENT SUPPORT

Integrated Learning System

Great care was used in the creation of the supplemental materials to accompany *Compensation*, Third Canadian Edition. Whether you are a seasoned faculty member or a newly minted instructor, you will find the support materials to be comprehensive and practical.

Instructor and Student Online Learning Centres—www.mcgrawhill.ca/olc/milkovich

This Online Learning Centre is a text Web site that follows the textbook material chapter-by-chapter. Students will find custom quizzes for chapter content and a searchable glossary. Instructors will find downloadable supplements, including the instructor's manual, computerized test bank, and PowerPoint Presentations.

WebCT/BlackBoard

This text is available in two of the most popular course-delivery platforms—WebCT and BlackBoard—for more user-friendly and enhanced features. Contact your local McGraw-Hill *i*Learning Sales Specialist for more information.

iLearning Sales Specialist

Your Integrated Learning Sales Specialist is a McGraw-Hill Ryerson representative who has the experience, product knowledge, training, and support to help you assess and integrate any of the above-noted products, technology, and services into your course for optimum teaching and learning performance. Whether it's how to use our test bank software, helping your students improve their grades, or how to put your entire course online, your *i*Learning Sales Specialist is there to help. Contact your local *i*Learning Sales Specialist today to learn how to maximize all McGraw-Hill Ryerson resources!

iLearning Services Program

McGraw-Hill Ryerson offers a unique *i*Services package designed for Canadian faculty. Our mission is to equip providers of higher education with superior tools and resources required for excellence in teaching. For additional information, visit **www.mcgrawhill.ca/highereducation/iservices/**.

ACKNOWLEDGEMENTS

Many people have contributed to our understanding of compensation and to the preparation of this textbook. In particular, we thank the following instructors whose comments and suggestions throughout the review and development process greatly added to the value of this third Canadian edition:

Jody Merritt, St. Clair College
Suzanne Payette, University of Ottawa
Carol Ann Samhaber, Algonquin College of Applied Arts and Technology
Linda Eligh, University of Western Ontario
Indira Somwaru, Seneca College of Applied Arts and Technology
David McPherson, Humber College Institute of Technology & Advanced Learning
David Morrison, Durham College
Wenlu Feng, Centennial College
John Hardisty, Sheridan Institute of Technology and Advanced Learning
Anna Bortolon, Conestoga College
Anne Hardacre, St. Lawrence College
Sean MacDonald, University of Manitoba
Don Schepens, Grant MacEwan University
Julie Bulmash, George Brown College
Jeffrey Young, Mount Saint Vincent University
Susan Quinn, Mount Royal University
Jeff Ryan, Grant MacEwan University

Finally, we thank the McGraw-Hill Ryerson publishing team: Kim Brewster, *Senior Sponsoring Editor*; Lori McLellan, *Developmental Editor*; Jessica Barnoski, *Supervising Editor*; Paula Brown, *Team Lead, Production;* and Mike Kelly, *Copy Editor*, for their dedicated work in this collaborative undertaking.

THE PAY MODEL

LEARNING OUTCOMES

- Describe how compensation is viewed differently by society, stockholders, managers, and employees in Canada and around the world.
- Define the term *compensation*.
- Discuss major components of total rewards.
- Identify and explain the three strategic objectives of compensation.
- Describe the four strategic policies in the pay model and the techniques associated with them.

In the touring company of the musical *Cats,* there are two performers called "swings" who sit backstage during each performance. Swings must learn five different lead roles in the show. During the performance, a swing sits next to a rack with five different costumes, as well as make-up for each of the five roles. If a performer gets hurt during a dance number, he or she signals to someone offstage, and by the time they finish the number, the swing is dressed, in makeup, and out on stage for the next scene.

Actors are paid $2,000 per week for playing one of the cats in the show. They are expected to do a certain number of performances and a certain number of rehearsals per week. Swings get paid $2,500 per week, whether they perform 20 shows that week or none. They are paid for knowing the five roles, whether they play them or not.

Think of all the other employees, in addition to the performers, required to put on a performance of *Cats.* Electricians, trombonists, choreographers, dressers, janitors, nurses, vocal coaches, accountants, stagehands, payroll supervisors, ushers, lighting technicians, ticket sellers—the list goes on. Consider the array of wages paid to these employees. Why does a swing get paid more than other performers? Why does a performer get paid more (or less) than the trombonist? How are these decisions made, and who is involved in making them? Compensation questions engage our attention. Does the compensation received by all the people connected with *Cats* matter? Most employers believe that how employees are paid affects their behaviour at work, which affects an organization's chances of success. Compensation systems can help an organization achieve and sustain competitive advantage.[1]

COMPENSATION

How people view compensation affects how they behave at work. It does not mean the same thing to everyone. Views differ depending on whether one looks at compensation from the perspective of a member of society, a stockholder, a manager, or an employee. Therefore it is important to recognize different perspectives.

Society

Some people view pay as a measure of justice. For example, a comparison of earnings of women with those of men highlights inequity in pay decisions. The gender pay gap in Canada for full-time, full-year workers narrowed from 42 percent in 1967 to 28.6 percent in 2007.[2] Despite this narrowing, and despite pay equity legislation, the gap persists, and always to the detriment of women. The latest studies show that because women often withdraw temporarily from the labour force for family-related reasons, the resulting reduction in their experience has a serious impact on pay over the long term. For workers with less than two years' experience, the gap is only 4 percent, but it still exists.[3] However, a large portion of the wage gap still has yet to be explained.

Sometimes, differences in compensation between countries are listed as a cause of loss of North American jobs to less developed economies. For example, labour costs in Mexico are about 13 percent of those in Canada. However, when differences in productivity (the relative output for each dollar of pay) are factored in, the wage advantage is reduced considerably because Mexican productivity is only 39 percent of the Canadian level.[4]

Voters may see compensation, pensions, and health care for public employees as the cause of increased taxes. Public policymakers and legislators may view changes in average pay as guides for adjusting eligibility for social services (provincial health care plans, welfare assistance, and the like).

Consumers sometimes see compensation as the cause of price increases. They may not believe that higher labour costs are to their benefit. Yet, other consumers have lobbied universities to insist on higher wages for labourers in Guatemala who sew shirts and caps bearing the university logo.[5]

Stockholders

To stockholders, executive pay is of special interest. In Canada, pay for executives is supposed to be tied to the financial performance of the company. When executive pay is excessive relative to company performance, profits are diverted away from stockholders to the executives. Stockholders may suffer further if excessive executive pay also tarnishes corporate reputation and sends negative signals to stock markets.[6]

Managers

Managers also have a stake in compensation: It directly influences their success in two ways. First, it is a major expense. Competitive pressures, both internationally and domestically, force managers to consider the affordability of their compensation decisions. Studies show that in many enterprises, labour costs account for more than 50 percent of total costs.[7] In some industries, such as financial or professional services, or in public employment such as education and government, this figure can be even higher. However, even within an industry (e.g., automotive manufacturing, financial services), labour cost as a percentage of total costs varies among individual firms.

In addition to treating pay as an expense, a manager uses it to influence employee behaviours and to improve organization performance. The way people are paid affects the quality of their work, their attitude toward customers, their willingness to be flexible or learn new skills or suggest innovations, and even their interest in unions or pursuing legal action against their employer. This potential to influence employees' behaviours, and subsequently the productivity and effectiveness of the organization, is an important reason to be clear about the meaning of compensation.[8]

Employees

The pay that individuals receive in return for the work they perform is usually the major source of their financial security. Hence, pay plays a vital role in a person's economic and social well-being. Employees may view compensation as the return in an exchange between their employer and themselves, as an entitlement for being an employee of the company, or as a reward for a job well done. Compensation can be all of these things.

Describing pay as a reward may sound far-fetched to anyone who has reluctantly rolled out of bed to go to work. Even though writers and consultants use the term reward, no one ever says, "They gave me a reward increase," or "Here is my weekly reward cheque." Yet, if people view their pay as the return for their contributions and investments rather than as a reward, and if writers and consultants persist in trying to convince them that pay is a reward, then there is a disconnect that misleads both employees and managers. Employees invest in education and training; they contribute their time and energy at the workplace. Compensation is their return on those investments and contributions.[9]

Employees in large, state-owned countries (e.g., China) and in highly regulated countries (e.g., Sweden) sometimes believe their pay is an entitlement—their due, regardless of their performance or that of their employers. It is not uncommon for political leaders, trade unions, and employer federations in countries such as Sweden and Germany to negotiate compensation policies that are supportive of their country's sociopolitical as well as economic priorities.[10]

Global Views

In English, "compensation" means to counterbalance, to offset, to make up for. However, by looking at the origin of the word in different languages, a sense of the richness of its meaning becomes apparent. It combines entitlement, return, and reward.

In China, the traditional characters for compensation are based on the signs for logs and water—compensation provides the necessities in life. In today's China, however, the reforms of the last decade have led to use of a new word, *dai yu,* which refers to how one is treated or taken care of. When people talk about compensation, they ask each other, "How about the *dai yu* in your company?" rather than about wages. Benefits and training opportunities are considered very important.

Compensation in Japanese is *kyuyo,* which is made up of two separate characters (*kyu* and *yo*), both meaning "giving something." *Kyu* is an honorific used to indicate that the person doing the giving is of high rank, for example a feudal lord, emperor, or Samurai leader. Traditionally, compensation is thought of as something given by one's superior. Today, business consultants in Japan try to substitute the word *hou-syu,* which means reward and has no association with notions of superiority. The many allowances that are part of Japanese compensation systems translate as *teate,* which means "taking care of something." *Teate* is regarded as compensation that takes care of employees' financial needs. This concept is consistent with the family, housing, and commuting allowances still used in many Japanese companies.[11]

These contrasting perspectives on compensation—societal, stockholder, managerial, employee, and even global—add richness to the topic. But these perspectives can also cause confusion unless everyone is talking about the same thing, so a clear definition of compensation or pay (the words are used interchangeably in this book) is essential. **Compensation** refers to all forms of financial returns and tangible services and benefits that employees receive as part of an employment relationship.

compensation
all forms of financial returns and tangible services and benefits that employees receive as part of an employment relationship

FORMS OF PAY

relational returns

psychological returns employees believe they receive in the workplace

total rewards

all rewards received by employees, including cash compensation, benefits, and relational returns

Exhibit 1.1 shows the variety of returns people receive from work. They are categorized as total compensation and relational returns. The **relational returns** (development opportunities, status, opportunity to belong, challenging work, and so on) are the psychological returns people believe they receive in the workplace.[12] Total compensation is more transactional and includes pay received directly as cash (e.g., base, merit increases, incentives, cost-of-living adjustments) and indirectly as benefits (e.g., pensions, medical insurance, programs to help balance work and life demands). This book focuses on **total rewards**, which includes cash compensation, benefits, and relational returns.

Cash Compensation: Base

wage

pay calculated at an hourly rate

salary

pay calculated at an annual or monthly rate

Base **wage** is the cash compensation an employer pays for the work performed. Base wage tends to reflect the value of the work or skills and generally ignores differences attributable to individual employees. For example, the base wage for machine operators may be $12 an hour. However, some individual operators may receive more because of their experience and/or performance. Some pay systems set base wage as a function of the skill or education an employee possesses; this is common for engineers and schoolteachers. A distinction is often made between a wage and a **salary**, with salary referring to pay that is calculated at an annual or monthly rate rather than hourly.

Cash Compensation: Merit Increases and Cost-of-Living Adjustments

merit increase

increment to base pay in recognition of past work behaviour

cost-of-living adjustment

percentage increment to base pay provided to all employees regardless of performance

Almost all Canadian firms use merit pay increases.[13] **Merit increases** are given as increments to the base pay in recognition of past work behaviour. Some assessment of past performance is made, with or without a formal performance evaluation program, and the size of the increase is varied according to performance. Thus, outstanding performers could receive an 8 to 10 percent merit increase 8 months after their last increase, whereas an average performer might receive a 4 to 5 percent increase after 12 or 15 months. By contrast, a **cost-of-living adjustment** gives the same percentage increase to everyone regardless of performance in order to maintain pay levels relative to increases in the cost of living.

Cash Compensation: Incentives

incentives (variable pay)

one-time payments for meeting previously established performance objectives

Incentives tie pay increases directly to performance. However, incentives differ from merit adjustments. First, incentives do not increase the base wage, and so must be re-earned each pay period. Second, the potential size of the incentive payment generally will be known beforehand. Whereas merit pay programs evaluate the past performance of an individual and then decide on the size of the increase, the performance objective for incentive payments is specified ahead of time. For example, an auto sales agent knows the commission on a BMW versus the commission on a Honda prior to making the sale. Thus, although both merit pay and incentives can influence performance, incentives do so by offering pay to influence future behaviour. Merit, on the other hand, recognizes and rewards past behaviours. The distinction is a matter of timing.

Incentives can be tied to the performance of an individual employee, a team of employees, a total business unit, or some combination of individual, team, and unit. The performance objective may be expense reduction, volume increases, customer satisfaction, revenue growth, return on investments, or increases in total shareholder value—the possibilities are endless.[14]

Because incentives are one-time payments, they do not have a permanent effect on labour costs. When performance declines, incentive pay automatically declines, too. Consequently, incentives are frequently referred to as variable pay.

EXHIBIT **1.1** Total Rewards

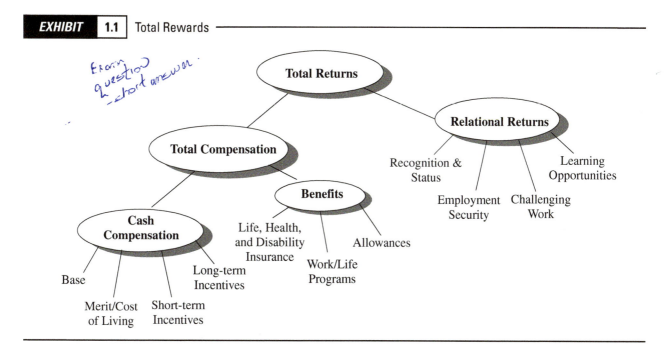

Long-Term Incentives

Incentives may be short or long term. Long-term incentives are intended to focus employee efforts on multi-year results. Typically they are in the form of stock ownership or options to buy stock at specified, advantageous prices. The idea behind stock options is that giving employees a financial stake in the organization's performance will focus them on such long-term financial objectives as return on investment, market share, return on net assets, and such. Magna International grants shares of stock to selected key employees who have made outstanding contributions to the firm's success. Some companies have extended stock ownership beyond the ranks of managers and professionals. Sun Microsystems, Google, and Starbucks offer stock options to all their employees. These companies believe that having a stake in the company supports a culture of ownership. They hope that employees will behave like owners.[15]

Benefits: Insurance and Pensions

Exhibit 1.1 shows that employee benefits, including life, health, and disability insurance; work/life programs; and allowances, are also part of total compensation. Some insurance programs are required by law. For example, employers must make contributions to the Canada/Quebec Pension Plan, Employment Insurance, and Workers' Compensation. Different countries have different mandatory benefits.

Health insurance, dental insurance, pensions, and life insurance are common benefits. They help protect employees from the financial risks inherent in daily life. Often, companies can provide these protections to employees more cheaply than employees can obtain them for themselves. Because the cost of providing benefits has been rising, they are regarded as an increasingly important form of pay.[16]

Benefits: Work/Life Programs

Work/life programs that help employees better integrate their work and life responsibilities include time away from work (e.g., vacations, jury duty), access to services to meet specific needs

work/life programs

programs that help employees better integrate their work and life responsibilities

(e.g., drug counselling, financial planning, referrals for child and eldercare), and flexible work arrangements (e.g., telecommuting, non-traditional schedules, non-paid time off). Responding to the tight labour market for highly skilled employees and the changing demographics of the workforce (e.g., two-income families who demand employer flexibility so that family obligations can be met), many Canadian employers are giving higher priority to these forms of benefits. Buffett Taylor & Associates, a leading wellness consulting firm in Whitby, Ontario, follows its own advice by offering a best-in-class wellness program in its own workplace.[17]

Benefits: Allowances

allowances

compensation to provide for items that are in short supply

Allowances often grow out of whatever is in short supply. In Vietnam and China, housing (dormitories and apartments) and transportation allowances frequently are part of the pay package. Some Japanese companies continue to offer a "rice allowance" based on the number of dependents an employee has, a practice that grew out of post–World War II food shortages. Almost all companies starting operations in China soon discover that housing, transportation, and other allowances are expected. Companies that resist these allowances must come up with other ways to attract and retain talented employees. In many European countries, managers expect a car to be provided. The issue then becomes which make and model.

Total Earnings Opportunities: Present Value of a Stream of Earnings

Up to this point compensation has been treated as something paid or received at a moment in time. But compensation decisions have a temporal effect. If an employee with a job offer of $50,000 stays with the firm for five years and receives an annual increase of 4 percent, he or she will be earning $58,493 in the fifth year. The total dollars paid out in cash and benefits costs over the five years based on the decision to hire turns out to be over $382,061 ($50,000 base compounded by 4 percent for five years, plus benefits equal to 30 percent of base).

A present value perspective shifts the choice from comparing today's initial offers to consideration of future bonuses, merit increases, and promotions. Some employers claim that their relatively low starting offers will be overcome by larger future pay increases. In effect, they are selling the present value of the future stream of earnings. But potential employees should apply that same analysis in calculating the future increases required to offset the lower initial offers.

Relational Returns from Work

employee engagement

a level of connection employees feel to their employer that results in them giving full discretionary effort on a sustained basis above and beyond specific job requirements

Why do Google millionaires still show up for work every morning? There is no doubt that non-financial returns from work create intrinsic motivation that has a substantial effect on employees' behaviour. Exhibit 1.1 includes recognition and status, employment security, challenging work, and opportunities to learn. Other relational forms might include personal satisfaction from successfully facing new challenges, teaming with great co-workers, and the like. Such factors are part of the total rewards, which is a broader umbrella than total compensation. So, although this book is about total compensation, let's not forget that compensation is only one of many factors affecting people's decisions about work.

Relational returns affect **employee engagement**—a level of connection employees feel to their employer that results in them giving full discretionary effort on a sustained basis above and beyond specific job requirements. Research has shown that organizations with a highly engaged workforce have superior operating income, profits, and earnings per share.[18] The .Net Worth box provides an example of the importance of relational returns in employee engagement.

.NET WORTH **Employee Engagement Driven by Relational Returns**

Findings of the *2007–2008 Global Workforce Study* by compensation consultants Towers Watson illustrate the importance of relational returns to employee engagement—commitment to giving full discretionary effort to the job. The top driver of engagement worldwide is sincere interest on the part of senior management in employee well-being. While pay and benefits are important in attracting employees to an organization, relational returns become more important to retaining them in the organization and to motivating and engaging them in their work.

Other top drivers of engagement on the part of employees include knowing that they have improved their skills and abilities each year, the organization's reputation for social responsibility, input into decision making in their department, and the quick resolution of customer concerns by the organization.

Source: *2007–2008 Global Workforce Study.* Towers Watson.

The Organization as a Network of Returns

Sometimes it is useful to think of an organization as a network of returns created by all these different forms of pay, including total compensation and relational returns. The challenge is to design this network so that it helps the organization to succeed. As in the case of rowers pulling on their oars, success is more likely if all are pulling in unison rather than working against one another. In the same way, the network of returns is more likely to be useful if bonuses, development opportunities, and promotions all work together. Even though this book focuses on total compensation, it is important to remember that compensation is only one of many factors affecting people's decisions about work.

■ A PAY MODEL

The pay model shown in Exhibit 1.2 serves as both a framework for examining current pay systems and as a guide to most of this book. It contains three basic building blocks: (1) the strategic compensation objectives, (2) the strategic policies that form the foundation of the compensation system, and (3) the techniques of compensation. Because objectives drive the system, they are discussed first.

Strategic Compensation Objectives

Pay systems are designed and managed to achieve certain strategic objectives. The basic objectives, shown at the right side of the pay model in Exhibit 1.2, include efficiency, fairness, and compliance with laws and regulations. Efficiency can be stated more specifically: (1) improving performance and quality, delighting customers and stockholders; and (2) controlling labour costs. Compensation objectives at Medtronic and Whole Foods are contrasted in Exhibit 1.3. Medtronic is the medical technology company that pioneered cardiac pacemakers. Its compensation objectives emphasize performance, business success, and salaries that are competitive with other companies whose financial performance matches Medtronic's. Whole Foods is a large organic- and natural-foods grocer. Its markets are "a celebration of food": bright, well-stocked,

---

EXHIBIT | **1.2** | The Pay Model

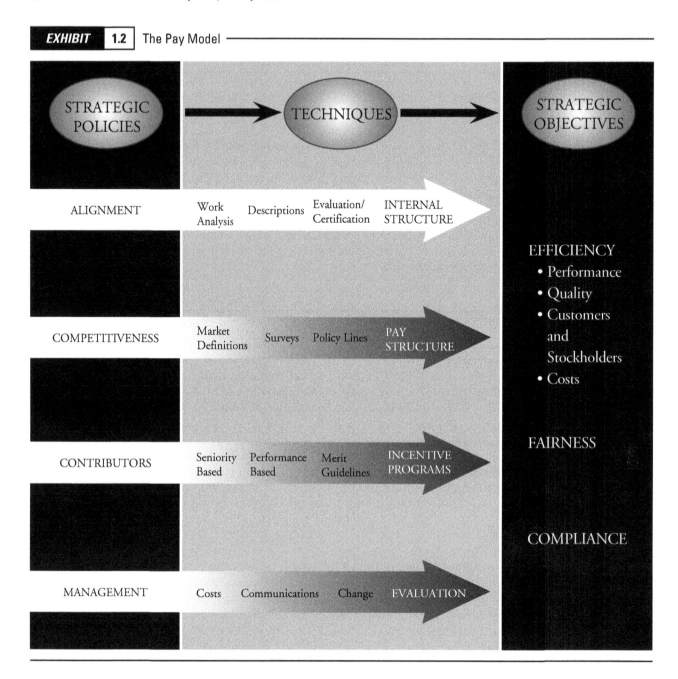

and well-staffed.[19] The company describes its commitment to offering the highest quality and least processed foods as a shared responsibility. Its first compensation objective is "… committed to increasing shareholder value."

Fairness is a fundamental objective of pay systems. In Medtronic's objectives, fairness is reflected in "ensure fair treatment" and "recognize personal and family well-being." Whole Foods' pay objectives discuss a "shared fate." In their egalitarian work culture, pay beyond base wages is linked to team performance, and employees have some say about who is on their team. The fairness objective calls for fair treatment for all employees by recognizing both employee contributions (e.g., higher pay for greater performance, experience, training) and employee needs (e.g., a fair wage as well as fair procedures). **Procedural fairness** is concerned with the processes used to

procedural fairness
fairness of the process used to make a decision

EXHIBIT 1.3 Comparison of Pay System Objectives at Medtronic and Whole Foods

Medtronic	Whole Foods
Support Medtronic mission and increased complexity of business.	We are committed to increasing long-term shareholder value.
Minimize increases in fixed costs.	Profits are earned every day through voluntary exchange with our customers.
Attract and engage top talent.	Profits are essential to create capital for growth, prosperity, opportunity, job satisfaction, and job security.
Emphasize personal, team, and Medtronic performance.	Support team member happiness and excellence.
Recognize personal and family total well-being.	We share together in our collective fate.
Ensure fair treatment.	

make decisions about pay.[20] It suggests that the way a pay decision is made may be as important to employees as the result of the decision.

Compliance as a pay objective involves conforming to various federal, provincial, and territorial compensation laws and regulations. As these laws and regulations change, pay systems may need to be adjusted to ensure continued compliance.

There probably are as many statements of pay objectives as there are employers. In fact, highly diversified firms such as George Weston Ltd. and Onex Corp., which compete in multiple lines of business, may have different pay objectives for different business units. Objectives at these companies emphasize the increased complexity of the business and importance of integrity (customers, quality), competitiveness (costs), ability to attract and retain quality people (performance), and having fun.

Objectives serve several purposes. First, they guide the design of the pay system. Consider the employer whose objective is to reward outstanding performance. That objective will determine the pay policy (e.g., pay for performance) as well as the elements of pay plans (e g., merit increases and/or incentives). Another employer's objectives may be to develop a flexible, continuously learning workforce through job design, training, and team-building techniques. A pay system that is aligned with this employer's objectives may have a policy of paying salaries at least equal to those of competitors and that go up with increased skills or knowledge. This pay system could be very different from our first example in which the focus is on performance. Thus, different objectives guide the design of different pay systems. Policies and techniques are the means to reach the objectives.

Ethics

Asian philosophy includes the concepts of yin and yang—complementary opposites rather than substitutes or trade-offs. It is not yin or yang; part of yin is in yang, and part of yang is in yin. So it is with objectives in the pay model. All three must be achieved. It is not efficiency versus fairness versus compliance. Rather, it is all three simultaneously. The tension of working toward all objectives at once creates fertile grounds for ethical dilemmas.

Ethics means the organization cares about how its results are achieved. Scan the Web sites or lobby walls of corporate headquarters and you will inevitably find statements of "key behaviours," "our values," and "codes of conduct." The challenge is to put these statements into daily practice.

Because it is so important, it is inevitable that managing pay sometimes creates ethical dilemmas. Manipulating results to ensure executive bonus payouts, misusing (or failing to understand) statistics used to measure competitors' pay rates, re-pricing or backdating stock options to increase their value, encouraging employees to invest a portion of their wages in company stock while executives are bailing out, offering just enough pay to get a new hire in the door while ignoring the relationship to co-workers' pay, and shaving the hours recorded in employees' time cards are all too common examples of ethical lapses.

Some, but not all, compensation professionals and consultants remain silent during ethical misconduct and outright malfeasance. Absent a professional code, compensation managers must look to their own ethics—and the pay model, which calls for combining the objectives of efficiency and fair treatment of employees as well as compliance.[21]

So, objectives guide the design of pay systems. They also serve as standards for judging the success of the pay system. If the objective is to attract and retain the best and the brightest, yet skilled employees are leaving for higher-paying jobs elsewhere, the system may not be performing effectively. Although there may be many non-pay reasons for turnover, objectives provide standards for evaluating the effectiveness of a pay system.[22]

Four Policy Choices

Every employer must address the strategic policy decisions shown on the left side of the pay model in Exhibit 1.2: (1) internal alignment, (2) external competitiveness, (3) employee contributions, and (4) administration of the pay system. These policies form the foundation on which pay systems are built. They also serve as guidelines for managing pay in ways that accomplish the system's objectives.

internal alignment

pay comparisons between jobs or skill levels inside a single organization

Internal Alignment   **Internal alignment** refers to pay comparisons between jobs or skill levels inside a single organization. Jobs and people's skills are compared in terms of their relative contribution to the organization's objectives. For example, how does the work of the programmer compare to the work of the systems analyst, the software engineer, or the software architect? Does one contribute more than another to providing solutions to customers and satisfying shareholders? Does one require more knowledge or experience than another? Internal alignment refers to the pay rates both for employees doing equal work and for those doing dissimilar work. In fact, determining what is an appropriate difference in pay for people performing different work is a key challenge facing managers.

Internal alignment policies affect all three compensation objectives. Pay relationships within the organization affect employee decisions to stay with the organization, to become more flexible by investing in additional training, or to seek greater responsibility. By motivating employees to choose increased training and greater responsibility in dealing with customers, pay relationships indirectly affect the capabilities of the workforce and hence the efficiency of the entire organization. Fairness is determined by employees' comparisons of their pay to the pay of others in the organization. Basic fairness is provided by Canadian human rights laws, which make discrimination on the basis of race, gender, age, and other grounds illegal.

external competitiveness

comparison of compensation with that of competitors

External Competitiveness   **External competitiveness** refers to compensation relationships external to the organization (i.e., compared with competitors). How should an employer position its pay relative to what competitors are paying? How much should one employer pay accountants in comparison to what other employers pay them? What mix of pay forms—base, incentives, stock, benefits—will help achieve the compensation objectives? Employers have several policy options. Whole Foods combines base pay and team incentives to offer higher pay if team performance warrants. Medtronic sets its base pay to match its competitors but ties bonuses to performance. It offers stock to all its employees based on company performance.[23] Further, Medtronic believes that its benefits, particularly its emphasis on programs that balance work and life, make it a highly attractive place to work. It believes that how pay is positioned and what forms it uses creates an advantage over competitors.

Many organizations claim their pay systems are market-driven, i.e., based on what competitors pay. However, "market-driven" gets translated into practice in different ways. Some employers set their pay levels higher than their competition, hoping to attract the best applicants. Of course, this assumes that someone is able to identify and hire the "best" from a pool of applicants.

External competitiveness decisions—both how much, and what forms—have a twofold effect on objectives: (1) they ensure that the pay is sufficient to attract and retain employees—if employees do not perceive their pay as competitive with what other organizations are offering for similar work, they may leave—and (2) they control labour costs so that the organization's prices of products or services can remain competitive. Thus, external competitiveness directly affects both efficiency and fairness. And the organization must respond in a way that complies with relevant legislation.

Employee Contributions   The policy on employee contributions refers to the relative emphasis placed on performance. Should one programmer be paid more than another because of better performance or greater seniority? Should all employees share in the organization's financial success (or failure) via incentives based on profit? Should more productive teams of employees be paid more than less productive teams?

The degree of emphasis placed on performance is an important policy decision, because it directly affects employees' attitudes and work behaviours. Employers with strong pay-for-performance policies place greater emphasis on incentives and merit pay. Starbucks emphasizes stock options and sharing the success of corporate performance with its employees. General Electric emphasizes performance at the unit, division, and company-wide level. Recognition of contributions also affects fairness, because employees must understand the basis for judging performance in order to conclude that their pay is fair.

Management   A policy regarding management of the pay system is the last building block in the pay model in Exhibit 1.2. Although it is possible to design a system that is based on internal alignment, external competitiveness, and employee contributions, nevertheless the system will not achieve its objectives unless it is managed properly.

The ground under compensation management is shifting. While not yet an earthquake, the tremors are there. The traditional focus on how to administer various techniques is long gone, replaced by more strategic thinking—managing pay as part of the business. The coming jolt will go beyond simply managing pay as an expense to better understanding and analyzing the impact of pay decisions on people's behaviours and organizations' success. The impact of pay decisions on expenses is one result that is easily measured and well understood. But other measures such as pay's impact on attracting and retaining the right people, and engaging these people productively, are not yet widely used in the management of compensation. Efforts to do so are increasing and the perspective is shifting from "how to" toward trying to answer the "so what" question.

Pay Techniques

The remaining portion of the pay model in Exhibit 1.2 shows the pay techniques. The exhibit provides an overview only; pay techniques are discussed throughout the rest of the book. Techniques tie the four basic policies to the pay objectives. Uncounted variations in pay techniques exist; many are examined in this book. Surveys report differences in compensation policies and techniques among firms. Indeed, many consulting firms have Web sites in which they report their survey results. Updated information on various practices can be obtained simply by surfing the Web.

■ BOOK PLAN

Compensation is such a broad and compelling topic that several books could be devoted to it. The focus of this book is on the design and management of compensation systems. To aid in understanding how and why pay systems work, our pay model, which emphasizes the key strategic objectives, policies, and techniques, also provides the structure for much of the book.

Chapter 2 discusses how to formulate and implement a compensation strategy. It analyzes what it means to be strategic about how people are paid and how compensation can help achieve and sustain an organization's competitive advantage. The pay model plays a central role in formulating and implementing an organization's pay strategy. The pay model identifies four basic policy decisions that are the core of the pay strategy.

After strategy is discussed, the next sections of the book will examine each basic policy decision in detail. The first, internal alignment (Chapters 3 through 6), examines pay relationships within a single organization. The next section (Chapters 7 and 8) examines external competitiveness—the pay relationships among competing organizations—and analyzes the influence of market-driven forces.

Once compensation rates and structures are established, other issues emerge. How much should each employee be paid? How much and how often should an employee's pay be increased, and on what basis—experience, seniority, or performance? Should pay increases be contingent on the organization's and/or the employee's performance? How should the organization share its success (or failure) with employees? Stock awards, profit-sharing, bonuses, merit pay? These are examples of employee contributions, the third building block in the model (Chapters 9 and 10). After that, employee services and benefits will be examined (Chapter 11). The role of governments and unions in compensation is explored in Chapter 12. The concluding topic is management of the compensation system (Chapter 13), which includes planning, budgeting, evaluating, and communicating. More detail on global compensation systems is provided in the Appendix.

Although the book is divided into sections that reflect the pay model, pay policies and decisions are not discrete. In fact, all policy decisions are interrelated. Together, they influence employee behaviours and organization performance, and can be a source of competitive advantage.

Conclusion

The model presented in this chapter provides a structure for understanding compensation systems. The three main components of the model include the objectives of the pay system, the policy decisions that provide the system's foundation, and the techniques that link policies and objectives. The following sections of the book examine each of the four policy decisions—internal alignment, external competitiveness, employee contributions, and administration—as well as techniques, new directions, and related research.

Two questions should constantly be in the minds of managers and readers of this text. First, why do it this way? There is rarely one correct way to design a system or pay an individual. Organizations, people, and circumstances are too varied. But a well-trained manager can select or design a suitable approach.

Second, so what? What does this technique do for us? How does it help achieve our organization goals? If good answers are not apparent, there is no point to the technique. Adapting the pay system to meet the needs of the employees and help achieve the goals of the organization is what this book is all about.

The basic premise of this book is that compensation systems have a profound impact. Yet, too often, traditional pay systems seem to be designed in response to some historic but long-forgotten problem. The practices continue, but the logic underlying them is not always clear or even relevant.

CHAPTER SUMMARY

1. Compensation is viewed by society as a measure of justice as well as a cause of increased taxes and price increases. Stockholders are concerned with executive pay relative to company performance. Managers view compensation as a major expense and a means to influence employee behaviour. Employees view compensation as a return in an exchange with their employer, an entitlement, or a reward. In other countries, compensation relates to being taken care of.

2. The two major components of total rewards are total compensation and relational returns. Total compensation is composed of cash compensation (base pay and incentives) and benefits. Relational returns include psychological aspects of work such as recognition and status, challenging work, and learning opportunities.

3. The strategic objectives of compensation are (1) efficiency in performance and quality, satisfying customers and stockholders, and controlling costs; (2) fairness; and (3) compliance with laws and regulations.

4. The four strategic policies in the pay model are internal alignment, external competitiveness, employee contributions, and management. The internal structure techniques associated with alignment are job analysis, descriptions, and evaluation/certification. The pay structure techniques associated with competitiveness are market definitions, surveys, and pay policy lines. The incentive program techniques associated with contributions are seniority-based, performance-based, and merit guidelines. The evaluation techniques associated with management are planning, budgeting, and communication.

KEY TERMS

REVIEW QUESTIONS

1. How do differing perspectives affect our views of compensation?
2. How does the pay model help organize one's thinking about compensation?
3. What can a pay system do for an organization? For an employee? Are these mutually exclusive?

EXPERIENTIAL EXERCISES

1. What is your definition of compensation? Which meaning of compensation seems most appropriate from an employee's view—return, reward, or entitlement? Compare your ideas with someone who has more experience, with someone from another country, with someone from another field of study.

2. List all the forms of pay you receive from work. Compare to someone else's list. Explain any differences.

3. Answer the two questions in this chapter's "Conclusion," above (Why do it this way? So what?), for any study or business article that tells you how to pay people. Such articles can be found in the *WorldatWork Journal* or *Compensation and Benefits Review*.

WEB EXERCISE

Compensation on the Web

The WorldAtWork Web site at www.worldatwork.org provides information on its compensation-related journals and special publications, as well as short courses aimed at practitioners. The Canadian Council of Human Resource Associations (CCHRA) at www.cchra.ca provides links to provincial human resources (HR) associations that offer compensation-related information as well as more general human resource management (HRM) information. Some provinces have job boards for HR association members, including students. Both sites are good sources of information for people interested in careers in HRM. The Employee Benefits Research Institute (EBRI) includes links to other benefits sources on its Web site at www.ebri.org. Using the WorldAtWork and EBRI sites as a starting point, search for a list of five or more compensation magazines and journals.

CASE

Inside Internships

Many students work as unpaid interns as they begin their careers. Career Edge is a private Canadian organization that arranges youth internships. The Career Edge internship program provides meaningful entry-level work experience for Canadian graduates. It is designed to help recent graduates launch careers in their chosen field. For employers, Career Edge offers 10,000 candidates in its online database for 6-, 9-, or 12-month internships. For a very reasonable salary, these interns can help with special projects, add diversity to company operations, and cover leaves of absence. Interns gain practical work experience, develop employability skills such as teamwork and critical thinking, benefit from networking, and get paid.

Kim Burgess, a business analyst at Bell Systems & Technology, benefitted tremendously from Career Edge. She says, "After taking a year off work to return to school, re-entering the workforce was difficult. Career Edge gave me the opportunity I needed to apply my new skill set and learn within a working environment. Your internship is what you make of it and Career Edge will provide exactly what you need to excel!"

Questions

1. What do employers receive from summer interns? What returns do students get from the opportunities?

2. Should summer interns be paid? If so, how much? How would you recommend an employer decide the answers to both these questions?

3. What added information would you like to have before you make your recommendations? How would you use this information?

Source: "Inside Internships" at www.careeredge.ca/testimonials.asp (September 18, 2008).

 **Visit the Online Learning Centre at**
www.mcgrawhill.ca/olc/milkovich

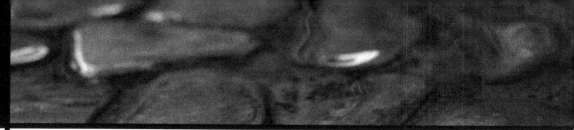

STRATEGY: THE TOTALITY OF DECISIONS

LEARNING OUTCOMES

- Explain the four steps to develop a total compensation strategy.
- Explain why managers should tailor their pay systems to support the organization's strategy.
- Describe the three tests used to determine whether a pay strategy is a source of competitive advantage.
- Contrast the "best fit" perspective on compensation with the "best practices" perspective.

Some employers avoid the formation and implementation of a compensation strategy by just paying the market rate. Unfortunately, a dose of reality quickly reveals that employers cannot behave so simply.

SIMILARITIES AND DIFFERENCES IN STRATEGIES

In Exhibit 2.1, compensation strategies at Google and Medtronic are compared. Google is a popular Internet search engine company; Medtronic is a pioneer in implantable medical devices such as pacemakers and stents. Both are innovators in their industry. Their decisions on the five dimensions of compensation strategy are both similar and different. Both formulate their pay strategy to support their business strategy. Both emphasize outstanding employee performance and commitment. However, there are major differences.

Google positions itself as still being the feisty start-up populated by nerds and math whizzes. It offers all its employees such generous stock options that many of them have become millionaires. Its benefits are "way beyond the basics" compared to its competitors. (Yes, there is a free lunch, a gym, a grand piano, and roller hockey in the parking lot.) Google downplays cash compensation (base plus bonuses), but it does match its competitors on these pay forms.

At Medtronic, the office holiday party includes invited guests whose lives have been prolonged thanks to Medtronic medical devices. The yearly gathering brings alive to employees that what they are doing makes a real difference. So it is not surprising that Medtronic's pay strategy seeks employees' "Total Well Being"—programs designed to ensure that employees are "fully present at their work and in their personal lives" in order to focus on the customer. Additionally there is a strong emphasis on performance-based pay that is based on individual, team, and organization accomplishments. These programs offer Medtronic employees the opportunity to earn well above what they would earn at competitors.

EXHIBIT 2.1 Strategic Perspectives toward Total Compensation

	Google	Medtronic
Objectives	• Emphasis on innovation • Commitment to cost containment • Recognize contributions • Attract and reward the best	• Focus on customers • Fully present at work and in personal lives • Recognize personal accomplishment and share success • Attract and engage top talent • Control costs
Internal Alignment	• Minimize hierarchy • Everyone wears several hats • Emphasize collaboration	• Reflect job responsibilities • Support promotional growth opportunities • Foster team culture
Externally Competitive	• Explore novel ideas in benefits and compensation • Generous, unique benefits	• Market value of jobs establishes overall pay parameters • Choices in benefits
Employee Contributions	• Recognize individual contributions • Unrivaled stock programs	• Incentives directly tied to business goals • Opportunity to earn above-market pay • Recognition of individual and team performance
Management	• Love employees, want them to know it • Technology support	• Clearly understood; open • Technology support • Employee choice

These two companies are in very different businesses facing different conditions, different customers, and different talent. So the differences in their pay strategies may not be surprising. Pay strategies can also differ among companies competing for the same talent and similar customers.[1]

Different Strategies within the Same Industry

Google, Microsoft, and SAS all compete for software engineers and marketing professionals. In its earlier years, Microsoft adopted a very similar strategy to Google's, except its employees accepted less base pay to join a company whose stock value was increasing exponentially.[2] But when its stock quit performing so spectacularly, Microsoft shifted its strategy to increase base and bonus to the 65th percentile from the 45th percentile of competitors' pay. It still retained its strong emphasis on stock ownership, and its benefits continue to lead the market. It also replaced its stock options with stock awards, which further reduced the riskiness of their pay plans.

SAS Institute, the world's largest privately owned software company, takes a very different approach. It emphasizes its work/life programs over cash compensation and gives only limited bonuses and no stock awards. SAS headquarters in Cary, North Carolina, includes free on-site child care centres, subsidized private schools for children of employees, two doctors on site for free medical care, plus recreation facilities.[3] Working more than 35 hours per week is discouraged. By removing as many of the frustrations and distractions of day-to-day life as possible, SAS, like Medtronic, believes people will focus on work when they are at work and won't burn out. Google so far retains the excitement of a start-up, Microsoft has morphed into "the new Boeing—a solid place to work for a great salary,"[4] and SAS emphasizes its work/family programs.

These examples illustrate the variance in strategic perspectives among companies in different industries and even among companies in the same industry.

Different Strategies within the Same Company

strategic perspective

a focus on compensation decisions that help the organization gain and sustain competitive advantage

Sometimes different business units within the same corporation will have very different competitive conditions, adopt different business strategies, and thus fit different compensation strategies. The Korean company SK Group has a wide variety of business units. They include a gasoline retailer, a cellular phone manufacturer, and SK Construction. SK has different compensation strategies aligned to each of its very different businesses.[5]

Thus a strategic perspective on compensation is more complex than it first appears. Taking a **strategic perspective** requires a focus on compensation decisions that help the organization gain and sustain competitive advantage.

▦ STRATEGIC CHOICES

strategy

the fundamental business decisions that an organization has made in order to achieve its strategic objectives, such as what business to be in and how to obtain competitive advantage

competitive advantage

a business practice or process that results in better performance than one's competitors

Strategy refers to the fundamental business decisions that an organization has made in order to achieve its strategic objectives. An organization defines its strategy through the trade-offs it makes in choosing what (and what not) to do.[6] Exhibit 2.2 relates these strategic choices to the quest for competitive advantage, or better performance than one's competitors. At the corporate level, the fundamental strategic choice is: *What business should we be in?* At the business unit level, the choice shifts to: *How do we gain and sustain competitive advantage in this business?* At the functional level, the strategic choice is: *How should total compensation help this business gain and sustain competitive advantage?* The ultimate purpose is to gain and sustain **competitive advantage**.[7]

In a recent survey of 122 Canadian organizations by Watson Wyatt, the majority (74 percent) reported that they have a clearly articulated cash compensation strategy. However, only 34 percent said that they had a formalized and documented total rewards strategy, suggesting that more work is required in strengthening the strategic impact of non-cash rewards. Just over half (51 percent) indicated that their reward system was closely linked to their business strategy.[8]

▦ SUPPORT BUSINESS STRATEGY

A currently popular theory found in almost every book and consultant's report tells managers to tailor their pay systems to align with the business strategy. The rationale is based on contingency notions. That is, differences in a firm's strategy should be supported by corresponding differences in its human resource strategy, including compensation. The underlying premise is that the greater the alignment, or fit, between the organization and the compensation system, the more effective the organization.

Exhibit 2.3 gives an example of how compensation systems might be tailored to three general business strategies.[9] The innovator stresses new products and short response times to market trends. A supporting compensation approach places less emphasis on evaluating skills and jobs and more

EXHIBIT **2.2** | Strategic Choices

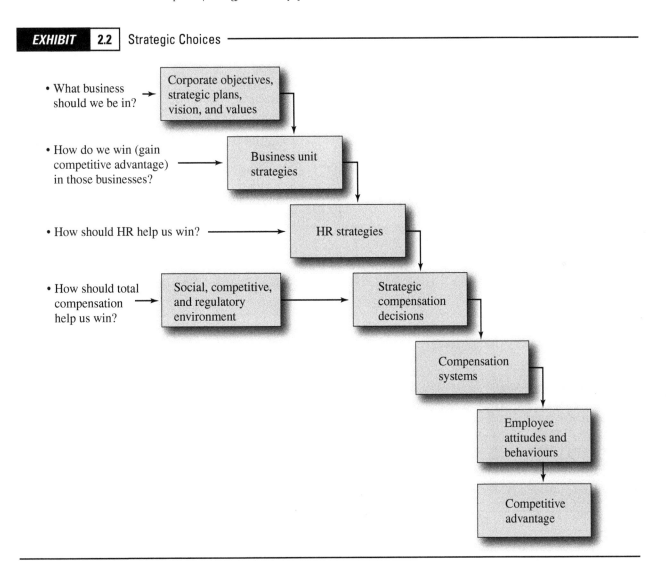

- What business should we be in? → Corporate objectives, strategic plans, vision, and values

- How do we win (gain competitive advantage) in those businesses? → Business unit strategies

- How should HR help us win? → HR strategies

- How should total compensation help us win? → Social, competitive, and regulatory environment → Strategic compensation decisions

Compensation systems

Employee attitudes and behaviours

Competitive advantage

emphasis on incentives designed to encourage innovations. The cost cutter's efficiency-focused strategy stresses doing more with less by minimizing costs, encouraging productivity increases, and specifying in greater detail exactly how jobs should be performed. The customer-focused business strategy stresses delighting customers and bases employee pay on how well they do this.

It also follows that when business strategies change, pay systems should change too. A classic example is IBM's strategic and cultural transformation. IBM's emphasis on internal alignment (e.g., well-developed job evaluation plan, clear hierarchy for decision making, work/life balance benefits, policy of no layoffs) had served it well during the decades when the company dominated the market for high-profit, mainframe computers. But it did not provide flexibility to adapt to industry changes in the 1990s. A redesigned IBM now provides advanced information technology, including hardware, software, services, and research. A new business strategy requires a new compensation strategy. At IBM, this meant streamlining the organization by cutting layers of management, redesigning jobs to build in more flexibility, increasing incentive pay to more strongly differentiate on performance, and keeping a constant eye on costs. IBM changed its pay strategy and system to support its changed business strategy.

EXHIBIT 2.3 | Tailor the Compensation System to the Strategy

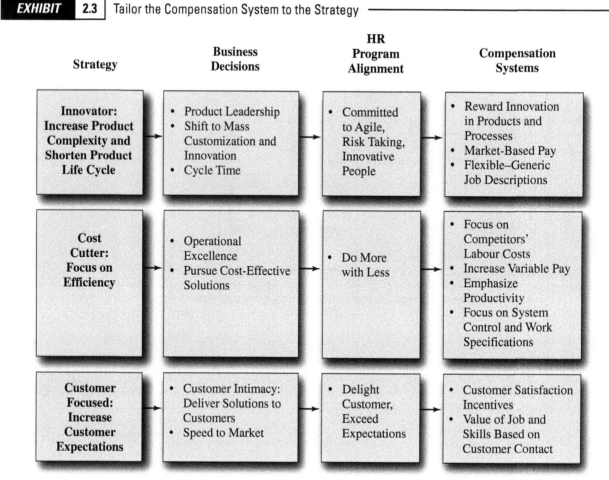

Strategy	Business Decisions	HR Program Alignment	Compensation Systems
Innovator: Increase Product Complexity and Shorten Product Life Cycle	• Product Leadership • Shift to Mass Customization and Innovation • Cycle Time	• Committed to Agile, Risk Taking, Innovative People	• Reward Innovation in Products and Processes • Market-Based Pay • Flexible–Generic Job Descriptions
Cost Cutter: Focus on Efficiency	• Operational Excellence • Pursue Cost-Effective Solutions	• Do More with Less	• Focus on Competitors' Labour Costs • Increase Variable Pay • Emphasize Productivity • Focus on System Control and Work Specifications
Customer Focused: Increase Customer Expectations	• Customer Intimacy: Deliver Solutions to Customers • Speed to Market	• Delight Customer, Exceed Expectations	• Customer Satisfaction Incentives • Value of Job and Skills Based on Customer Contact

■ THE PAY MODEL GUIDES STRATEGIC PAY DECISIONS

Whole Foods was introduced in the previous chapter. Its competitive advantage is apparent with the first visit to one of its grocery stores, described as "a mouth-watering festival of colors, smells, and textures; an homage to the appetite."[10] Whole Foods has grown from a small supermarket to the world's leading natural and organic foods supermarket. Along the way, the company has designed a total compensation system to support the company's phenomenal growth while remaining true to the founder's vision.

Using the pay model, the five strategic compensation decisions facing Whole Foods managers can be considered.

1. **Objectives:** How should compensation support the business strategy and be adaptive to the cultural and regulatory pressures in a global environment? (Whole Foods objectives: Increase shareholder value through profits and growth; go to extraordinary lengths to satisfy and delight customers; seek and engage employees who are going to help the company make money—every new hire must win a two-thirds vote from team members before being given a permanent position.)

2. **Internal alignment:** How differently should the different types and levels of skills and work be paid within the organization? (Whole Foods: Store operations are organized around eight

to ten self-managed teams; egalitarian, shared-fate philosophy means that executive salaries do not exceed 14 times the average pay of full-time employees; all full-time employees qualify for stock options; and 94 percent of the company's options go to non-executive employees.)

3. **External competitiveness:** How should total compensation be positioned against competitors? (Whole Foods: Offer a unique deal compared to competitors.) What forms of compensation should be used? (Whole Foods: Provide health insurance for all full-time employees and 20 hours of paid time per year to do volunteer work.)

4. **Employee contributions:** Should pay increases be based on individual and/or team performance, on experience and/or continuous learning, on improved skills, on changes in cost of living, on personal needs (e.g., housing, transportation, health services), and/or on each business unit's performance? (Whole Foods: A shared fate—every four weeks, assess the performance of each team. Top teams get an extra $1.50 to $2.00 an hour in the next pay period. [This is one reason why staffers are given some say in who gets hired—co-workers want someone who will help them make money!])

5. **Management:** How open and transparent should the pay decisions be to all employees? Who should be involved in designing and managing the system? (Whole Foods: No secrets approach—every store has a book listing the previous year's pay for every employee including executives; employees make decisions—they voted to pick their health insurer rather than having one imposed by management.)

These decisions, taken together, form a pattern that becomes an organization's compensation strategy.

Stated versus Unstated Strategies

All organizations that pay people have a compensation strategy. Some may have written, or stated, compensation strategies for all to see and understand. Others may not even realize they have a compensation strategy, claiming that "We do whatever it takes." Their compensation strategy emerges from the pay decisions they have made. Unstated compensation strategy is inferred from compensation practices.[11] The point is that managers in all organizations make the five strategic decisions discussed earlier. Some do it in a rational, planned way; others do it more chaotically—as ad hoc responses to pressures from the economic, socio-political, and regulatory context in which the organization operates. But in any organization that pays people, there is a compensation strategy at work.

◼ DEVELOPING A TOTAL COMPENSATION STRATEGY: FOUR STEPS

Developing a compensation strategy involves four simple steps, shown in Exhibit 2.4. While the steps are simple, executing them is complex. Trial and error, experience, and insight play major roles. Research evidence can also help.[12]

Step 1: Assess Total Compensation Implications

The factors in the business environment that have contributed to a company's success and that are likely to become more (or less) important as the company looks ahead are classified in Exhibit 2.4. They are: competitive dynamics, culture/values, social and political context, employee/union needs, and other HR systems.

Competitive Dynamics—Understand the Business   This first step includes an understanding of the industry in which the organization operates and how it plans to compete. To cope with

EXHIBIT | **2.4** | Key Steps to Formulate a Total Compensation Strategy

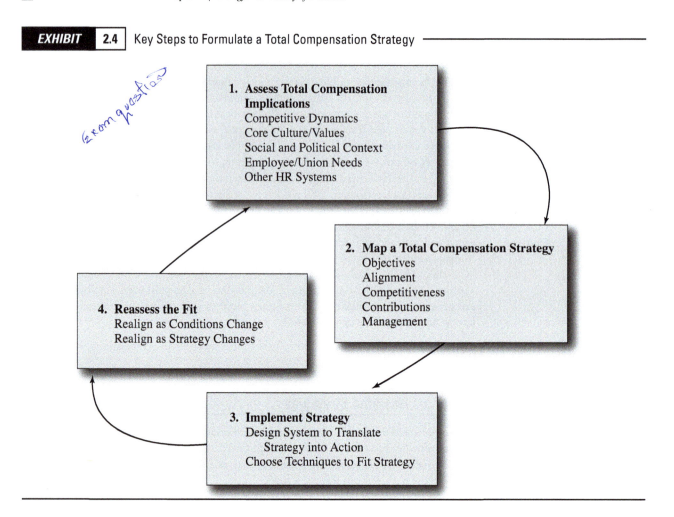

Exam question [handwritten annotation]

1. Assess Total Compensation Implications
Competitive Dynamics
Core Culture/Values
Social and Political Context
Employee/Union Needs
Other HR Systems

2. Map a Total Compensation Strategy
Objectives
Alignment
Competitiveness
Contributions
Management

4. Reassess the Fit
Realign as Conditions Change
Realign as Strategy Changes

3. Implement Strategy
Design System to Translate
Strategy into Action
Choose Techniques to Fit Strategy

turbulent, competitive dynamics, focusing on factors in the business environment (i.e., changing customer needs, competitors' actions, changing labour market conditions, changing regulations, globalization) is important today. What will be important in the future?

It is important to learn to sense or read the underlying dynamics in a business, such as its business strategy, and to consider how the compensation system should change to support and be part of that strategy.. Fitting different compensation strategies to different business strategies—cost-cutter, customer-centred, and innovator (see Exhibit 2.3)—has already been discussed. But reality is more complex and chaotic. Organizations are not necessarily innovators, cost cutters, or customer-centred. Instead, they are some of each, and more. So the rational, planned, and orderly image conveyed in Exhibit 2.3 does not adequately capture the turbulent and chaotic, competitive dynamics underlying this process.[13]

Competitive dynamics can be assessed globally.[14] However, comparing pay between countries is complex. In Chapter 1, differences in hourly labour costs and productivity (output per dollar of wages) between countries were noted. Countries also differ in the average length of the workweek, the average number of paid holidays, the kinds of social support programs, and even on how wages are set.[15] Different global competitors use different pay systems. Exhibit 2.5 describes Toshiba's total cash compensation for its managers. Thirty-seven percent of a Toshiba manager's pay is in the form of bonuses. Because they are paid out twice a year rather than in a biweekly paycheque, bonuses give Toshiba a cash flow advantage. In addition, because bonuses are not added into the employee's base pay, they do not become fixed costs. Japan levies payroll taxes on base wages only (in the exhibit,

EXHIBIT 2.5   Toshiba's Managerial Compensation Plan Annual Amount

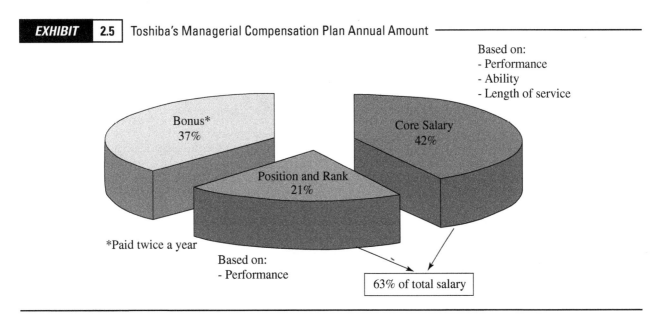

core salary), not on bonuses or allowances. Hence, the mix of forms at Toshiba (and most Japanese employers) emphasizes bonuses and allowances rather than core salary. A common misperception is that Japanese pay systems are based solely on seniority, but Toshiba's managers' pay depends on educational level (i.e., ability), experience (i.e., seniority), and performance. Toshiba's use of performance-based pay is not unique in Japan. Toyota, Mitsubishi, and other traditional Japanese firms are also increasing their performance-based plans.[16]

Culture/Values   A pay system reflects the values that underlie an employer's treatment of its employees. In many organizations, core values guide employees' business behaviours and are reflected in the pay systems. The pay system mirrors the company's image and reputation. Exhibit 2.6 shows Medtronic's values. The fifth value recognizes employees' worth by fostering "personal satisfaction in work accomplished, security, advancement opportunity, and means to share in the company success." Its compensation strategy reflects this value by including work/life balance programs for security, incentives, and stock options to share in the company's success.

But there are some skeptics out there. One study described mission statements as "an assemblage of trite phrases which impressed no one." On the other hand, Johnson and Johnson views its statement as "the glue that holds our corporation together."[17]

Social and Political Context   *Context* refers to a wide range of factors, including legal and regulatory requirements, cultural differences, changing workforce demographics, expectations, and so on. In the case of Whole Foods, business is very people-intensive. Consequently, Whole Foods managers expect that an increasingly diverse workforce and increasingly diverse forms of pay (child care, chemical dependency counselling, educational reimbursements, employee assistance programs) may add value and be difficult for competitors (other grocery outlets) to imitate.

Governments are major stakeholders in determining compensation. Hence, government relations to influence laws and regulations may also be part of compensation strategies. For example, the European Union's "social contract" becomes a matter of interest to managers.[18] And in China, many companies have discovered that building relationships with government officials is essential. So from a strategic perspective, managers of compensation may try to shape the socio-political environment as well as be shaped by it.

EXHIBIT | **2.6** | Medtronic Mission and Values

Medtronic Values

Medtronic's mission imparts stability and provides a firm foundation for the company's growth. Written more than 30 years ago, our mission statement gives purpose to our work, describes the values we live by, and is the motivation behind every action we take.

1. To contribute to human welfare by application of biomedical engineering in the research, design, manufacture, and sale of instruments or appliances that alleviate pain, restore health, and extend life.
2. To direct our growth in the areas of biomedical engineering where we display maximum strength and ability; to gather people and facilities that tend to augment these areas; to continuously build on these areas through education and knowledge assimilation; to avoid participation in areas where we cannot make unique and worthy contributions.
3. To strive without reserve for the greatest possible reliability and quality in our products; to be the unsurpassed standard of comparison and to be recognized as a company of dedication, honesty, integrity, and service.
4. To make a fair profit on current operations to meet our obligations, sustain our growth, and reach our goals.
5. To recognize the personal worth of employees by providing an employment framework that allows personal satisfaction in work accomplished, security, advancement opportunity, and means to share in the company's success.
6. To maintain good citizenship as a company.

Employee Preferences The simple fact that employees differ is too easily overlooked in formulating a compensation strategy. Individual employees join the organization, make investment decisions, design new products, assemble components, and judge the quality of results. Individual employees receive the pay. A major limitation of contemporary pay systems is the degree to which individual attitudes and preferences are ignored. Offering more choice is one approach. Older, highly paid workers may wish to defer taxes by putting their pay into retirement funds, whereas younger employees may have high cash needs to buy a house, support a family, or finance an education. Dual-career couples who are overinsured medically may prefer to use more of their combined pay for child care, automobile insurance, financial counselling, or other benefits such as flexible schedules. Employees who have young children or dependent parents may desire dependent care coverage.[19] However, preferences are notoriously unstable, changing according to the economic and personal conditions people face.

Choice is Good. Yes, No, Maybe?[20] Many contemporary benefit plans do offer some choice. Flexible benefits and choices among investment funds for retirement plans are examples. This approach adds value and is difficult for other companies to imitate—it is a source of competitive advantage.

Some studies have found that employees do not always choose well. They do not always understand the alternatives, and too many choices simply confuse them. Thus the value added by offering choices and satisfying preferences may be offset by the expense of communicating and simply confusing people.[21]

Union Preferences Pay strategies also need to be adapted to the nature of the union–management relationship.[22] Union influence on pay systems in Canada remains significant. In 2007, unionized workers at Loblaws in Ontario approved pay cuts for one-third of their members in order to remain competitive with Walmart.[23] Bombardier employees represented by the International Association of Machinists and Aerospace Workers recently negotiated a flexible benefits plan for their members.[24] Union preferences for different forms of pay and their concern with job security also affect pay strategy. Internationally, the role of unions in pay determination varies greatly.[25] In Europe, unions are major players in all strategic pay decisions. The point here is that union interests are part of the environmental pressures that help shape compensation strategies.

Prominence of Pay in Overall HR Strategy: Supporting Player or Catalyst for Change? The pay strategy is also partially influenced by how well it fits with other HR systems in the organization. A highly centralized and confidential pay system controlled by a few people in a corporate unit will not support a highly decentralized, flexible, open organization.

The importance of fit between pay programs and other HR management processes is illustrated in "high-performance" systems. High-performance systems generally include three features: (1) high skill/knowledge requirements (selective hiring), (2) work designed so that employees have discretion and opportunities to collaborate with others (teams) and continue to learn (training and development), and (3) performance-based pay systems. Whatever the overall HR strategy, a decision about the prominence of pay in that HR strategy is required. Pay can be a supporting player, as in the high-performance approach, or it can take the lead and be a catalyst for change. Whatever the role, compensation is embedded in the total HR approach.[26]

In sum, assessing the compensation implications of many factors—including the organization's business strategy, the global competitive dynamics, its culture and values, the socio-political context, employee needs, unions, and how pay fits with other HR systems—is necessary to formulate a compensation strategy.

Step 2: Decide on a Total Compensation Strategy

The compensation strategy is made up of the five decisions outlined in the pay model: set objectives and specify the four policies on alignment, competitiveness, contributions, and management. This is Step 2 in developing a compensation strategy. It requires compensation decisions that fit the organization's business and environment. As already noted, compensation decisions support different business strategies. The organization's objective is to make the right compensation decisions based on how the organization decides to compete. The .Net Worth box illustrates this concept.

The rest of the book discusses these compensation decisions in detail. It is important to realize, however, that the decisions made on these five issues together form the compensation strategy.

Steps 3 and 4: Implement and Reassess

Step 3 is to implement the strategy through the design of the compensation system. The compensation system translates strategy into practice. Employees infer the underlying strategy based on how they are treated by the compensation system.

Step 4, reassess and realign, closes the loop. This step recognizes that the compensation strategy must change to fit changing conditions. Thus, periodic reassessment of the fit is needed to continuously learn, adapt, and improve. Managing the links between the compensation strategy (grand policy decisions) and the pay system (procedures for paying people) as well as to people's perceptions and behaviours is vital to implementing a pay strategy.

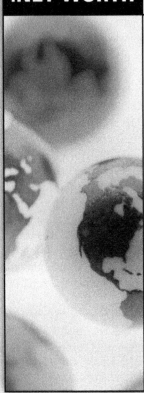

.NET WORTH

Netflix—Freedom and Responsibility in Rewards

Netflix is an online DVD-rental service offering millions of U.S. subscribers access to 100,000 titles. Their strategy is all about innovation, and their corporate culture is defined as freedom and responsibility. The strategy requires a high-performance workforce, and therefore, they "hire adults and expect adult behaviour." The company has no formal structure, no career paths, no health club, no ping-pong tables, no recognition program, and no performance bonuses. Benefits are traditional.

When it comes to rewards, freedom and responsibility rule. The company considers the opportunity to do challenging work to be the greatest reward. Compensation is very generous (90th percentile). Employees decide at the beginning of each year how to split their compensation between cash and immediately vested stock options. Up to 15 percent of compensation can be used to buy deeply discounted, immediately vested stock through the employee stock purchase plan.

Employees can take as much vacation time as they want as long as their manager and team members agree. Turnover is considered a good thing because they don't want employees to stay with the company unless they really want to be there.

The Netflix approach to total rewards is closely aligned with their strategy, and the results have been excellent. The company has been rated the #1 Web site for customer satisfaction five times and their stock price has held strong in the volatile high-tech sector.

Source: C. Fuoco-Karasinski, "Netflix Bucks Traditional Total Rewards," *Workspan*, August 2007, pp. 38–42; www.netflix.com (accessed November 9, 2008).

◼ SOURCE OF COMPETITIVE ADVANTAGE: THREE TESTS

Designing and implementing a pay strategy that is a source of competitive advantage is easier said than done. Not all compensation decisions are strategic nor a source of competitive advantage. Three tests determine whether a pay strategy is a source of competitive advantage: (1) Does it align? (2) Does it differentiate? and (3) Does it add value?[27]

Does the Pay Strategy Align?

Alignment of the pay strategy includes three aspects: (1) alignment with the business strategy, (2) alignment externally with the economic and socio-political conditions, and (3) alignment internally with the overall HR system. Alignment is probably the easiest test to pass.

Does the Pay Strategy Differentiate?

Some people believe that the only thing that matters about a strategy is that it be different from everyone else's.[28] If a pay system is relatively simple for a competitor to copy, then it cannot be a source of competitive advantage. The answer, according to advocates of the strategic approach, is that sustained competitive advantage derives from the way in which the pay system is managed. This rhetoric is appealing, but the evidence is slim.

A pay strategy is woven into the fabric of the company's overall HR strategy. Copying another strategy means ripping apart the overall approach and patching in a new one. So in a sense, the alignment test (weaving the fabric) helps ensure passing the differentiation test. Microsoft's use of stock awards for all employees, often worth considerably more than base pay, is difficult for its competitors to copy. The Medtronic and SAS work-family balance and total-presence-at-the-workplace strategies are difficult to copy. It may be relatively easy to copy a single thing a competitor does (e.g., grant stock options to more employees, offer more choice in benefits). But the idea of a strategic perspective implies that the way programs fit together and fit the organization will be difficult to copy. Simply copying others—blindly benchmarking and following so-called best practices—amounts to trying to stay in the race, not win it.

Does the Pay Strategy Add Value?

Organizations today look for the return they are getting from their incentives, benefits, and even base pay. Compensation often is a company's largest controllable expense. Because consultants and some researchers treat different forms of pay as investments, the task becomes to come up with ways to calculate the return on those investments (ROI). But this is a difficult proposition. Costs are easy to fit into a spreadsheet, but any value created as a result of those costs is difficult to specify, much less measure.[29]

Trying to measure an ROI for a compensation strategy implies that people are "human capital," just like other factors of production. Many people find this view dehumanizing. They argue that viewing pay as an investment with measurable returns diminishes the importance of treating people fairly.[30] Of the three tests of strategy—align, differentiate, add value—the last is the most difficult.

Regarding advantages of an innovative compensation strategy, it is known that in products and services, first movers (innovators) have well-recognized advantages that can offset the risks involved—high margins, capturing market share and mindshare (brand recognition).[31] But it is not known whether such advantages accrue to innovators in total compensation such as Microsoft (one of the first to offer very large stock options to all employees) or American Express (among the first to offer flexible benefit programs in Canada) now that many competitors are doing the same thing It is not known whether a compensation innovator attracts more and better people, induces people to stay and contribute, or provides cost advantages. Studies are needed to find the answers.

■ "BEST FIT" VERSUS "BEST PRACTICES"

The basic underlying premise of any strategic perspective is that if managers align pay decisions with the organization's strategy and values, are responsive to employees and union relations, and are globally competitive, the organization will be more likely to achieve competitive advantage.[32] The challenge is to design the "fit" with the environment, business strategy, and pay plan. The better the fit, the greater the competitive advantage.

But not everyone agrees. In contrast to the notion of strategic fit, some believe that (1) a set of best pay practices exists, and (2) these practices can be applied universally across situations. Rather than a better fit between business strategy and compensation plans yielding better performance, they say a set of best practices yields better performance with almost any business strategy.[33] The challenge here is to select from various recommended lists that are "the" best practices. Research from the past few years is beginning to provide some answers.

Guidance from the Evidence

There is consistent research evidence that the following practices do matter to the organization's objectives.

- *Internal alignment:* Both smaller and larger pay differences among jobs inside an organization can affect results. Smaller internal pay differences and larger internal pay differences can both be a "best" practice. Which one depends on the context, including the fit with business strategy, other HR practices, and organizational culture.[34]

- *External competitiveness:* Paying higher than the average paid by competitors can affect results. Is higher competitive pay a "best" practice? Again, it depends on the context.[35]
- *Employee contributions:* Performance-based pay can affect results. Are performance incentives a "best" practice? Once again it depends on the context.[36]
- *Managing compensation:* Rather than focusing on only one dimension of the pay strategy, such as pay for performance or internal pay differences, all dimensions need to be considered together.[37]
- *Compensation strategy:* Finally, embedding compensation strategy within the broader HR strategy affects results. Compensation does not act alone; it is part of the overall HR approach.[38]

So, specific pay practices appear to be more beneficial in some contexts than in others.[39] Thus best practices versus best fit does not appear to be a useful way to frame the question. A more useful question is: *What practices pay off best under what conditions?* Much of the rest of this book is devoted to exploring this question.

CONCLUSION

Managing total compensation strategically means fitting the compensation system to the business and environmental conditions. The best way to proceed is to start with the pay model—the objectives and four policy choices—and then take the steps discussed in this chapter: (1) assessing environmental conditions, (2) deciding on the best strategic choices following the pay model (objectives, alignment, competitiveness, contributions, and management), (3) implementing the strategy through the design of the pay system, and (4) reassessing the fit by comparing results against the pay objectives. The major challenge in managing total compensation is to understand how the pay system can add value and make the organization more successful. Research is beginning to offer some evidence-based guidance, with the promise of more to come.

CHAPTER SUMMARY

1. The four steps to develop a total compensation strategy are: (1) assess total compensation implications, including competitive dynamics, culture/values, social and political context, employee needs for flexibility, unions, and the role of pay in overall HR strategy; (2) create a total compensation strategy from the five decisions in the pay model; (3) implement the compensation strategy; and (4) reassess and realign the strategy.
2. Alignment of the compensation strategy to the business strategy is expected to improve organizational effectiveness.
3. The three tests used to determine whether a pay strategy is a source of competitive advantage are (1) Does it align? (2) Does it differentiate? and (3) Does it add value?
4. The "best fit" perspective on compensation suggests that compensation be aligned, or fit, with the specific business strategy adopted by the organization, given its environment, in order to maximize competitive advantage. The "best practices" perspective suggests there is one set of best pay practices that can be applied universally across situations and strategies, attracting superior employees who then create a winning strategy. A better approach appears to be: *What practices pay off best under what conditions?*

Key Terms

Review Questions

1.   Read again the values statements in Exhibit 2.6. Discuss how, if at all, these values might be reflected in a compensation system. Are these values consistent with "letting the market decide"?

2.   What are the three tests used to determine whether a pay strategy is a source of competitive advantage? Discuss whether these three tests are difficult to pass. Can compensation really be a source of competitive advantage?

3.   Contrast the essential difference between the "best fit" (strategic business-based) and "best practice" perspectives on compensation.

EXPERIENTIAL EXERCISES

1.   Interview a compensation specialist about his or her organization's compensation strategy, specifically the five issues—objectives, alignment, competitiveness, employee considerations, and management. How does this organization compare to Google? To Whole Foods? What business strategy does it seem to fit (i.e., cost cutter, customer-centred, innovator, or something else)?

2.   Set up a debate over the following proposition: "Best practices" is superior to the "best fit" approach when designing a compensation system.

3.   Survey ten people about their total rewards preferences. What conclusions can you draw from the results?

WEB EXERCISE

Compensation Consultants on the Web

Compensation consultants are major players, and practically every organization uses at least one for data and advice. So, learning more about services these consultants offer is useful. Go to the Web site of at least two of the following consulting firms, or find others.

Towers Watson: www.towerswatson.com/canada-english

Hay Group: www.haygroup.ca

Mercer: www.mercer.com (click on Mercer Human Resources Consulting)

1. Compare Web sites. From their Web sites, construct a chart comparing these consulting firms' stated core values and culture and their business strategy, and highlight the services offered.

2. Critically assess whether their strategies and services are unique and/or difficult to imitate. Which one would you select (based on the Web information) to help you formulate a company's total compensation strategy?

3. Based on the Web information, which one would you prefer to work for? Why?

4. Be prepared to share this information with others in class.

Result: If everyone does a great job on this exercise, you will have useful information on consultants.

CASE

Difficult to Copy?

One of the best ways to maintain strategic competitive advantage is to have a strategy that is difficult for competitors to copy. The more that different aspects of a strategy are interrelated or interconnected, the more difficult it becomes for others to replicate. Consider the compensation strategy at Netflix, discussed in the .Net Worth feature on page 26. On the face of it, this strategy appears easy to copy (or at least to articulate). But determining which compensation strategy best fits an organization's business strategy and culture as well as the external pressures it faces may make the strategy more difficult to imitate. It is the relationship, the fit, the way a pay system works with other aspects of the organization that makes it difficult to imitate and adds value. It is not the techniques themselves, but their interrelationships that make a strategic perspective successful.

Questions

1. Spend some time looking at the Web site for Netflix. What can you infer about the business strategy and the organizational culture?

2. Find some information on the DVD-rental industry. What are the external pressures Netflix is facing?

3. After you have a sense of what Netflix is like, decide whether you think its compensation strategy fits its business strategy, organizational culture, and external pressures.

4. How would you change compensation at Netflix?

Visit the Online Learning Centre at

www.mcgrawhill.ca/olc/milkovich

PART I

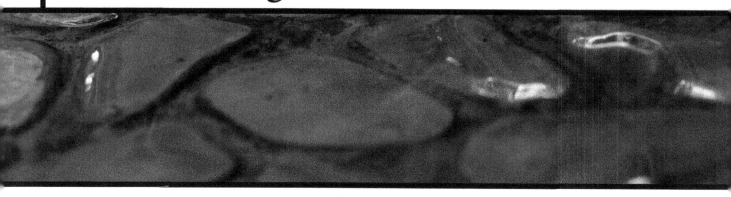

Internal Alignment: Determining the Structure

Nothing is routine at a *CSI* crime scene. And nothing is routine during the creation of the hit TV series. Nine writers struggle to come up with a plot for the season finale that will ensure that the 28 million viewers will tune in again next season.

Carol Mendelsohn, one of three executive producers and also the "show runner" (the ultimate decision maker), leads the team of creative writers and manages the cast, support crew, and production crew. In addition to the writers and actors, jobs on the series include director of photography, editor (2), story editor, executive story editor (also 2), gaffers, and special effects makeup (severed heads and other body parts?), among others.

What determines the pay for all the different types of work involved in creating *CSI*? Executive story editors Andrew Lipsitz and Josh Berman get paid more than editors Alec Smight and Augie Hess. How much more? Does it matter? Can an editor be promoted to the executive story editor for this or some other series? Writers can become producers—Ms. Mendelsohn started her career as a writer—but can stunt coordinators become producers? Is the editor paid more than the stunt coordinator or the gaffer? And what's a gaffer anyway?

What criteria are used to set pay—the content of the work itself, the value of what is contributed to each episode, the person's skill/experience/reputation? Perhaps the ratings for the show? How do pay differences between jobs in the organization affect behaviour? Do they support the organization's business strategy? Do they help attract and retain employees? Do they motivate employees to do their best work? Or are the pay procedures bureaucratic burdens that drive away creative talent?

So many questions! Two of them lie at the core of compensation management: (1) How is pay determined for the wide variety of work performed in organizations? and (2) How do the pay differences affect employees' attitudes and work behaviours? These questions are examined within the framework of the pay model introduced in Chapter 1 and shown again in Exhibit I.1. The focus in this part of the book is *within* the organization. Chapter 3 examines internal alignment, what affects it, and what is affected by it. Chapter 4 looks at how to assess the similarities and differences in work content. Chapters 5 and 6 look at various approaches to value those similarities and differences and use them to determine internal pay structures.

exam?,

EXHIBIT | **I.1** | The Pay Model

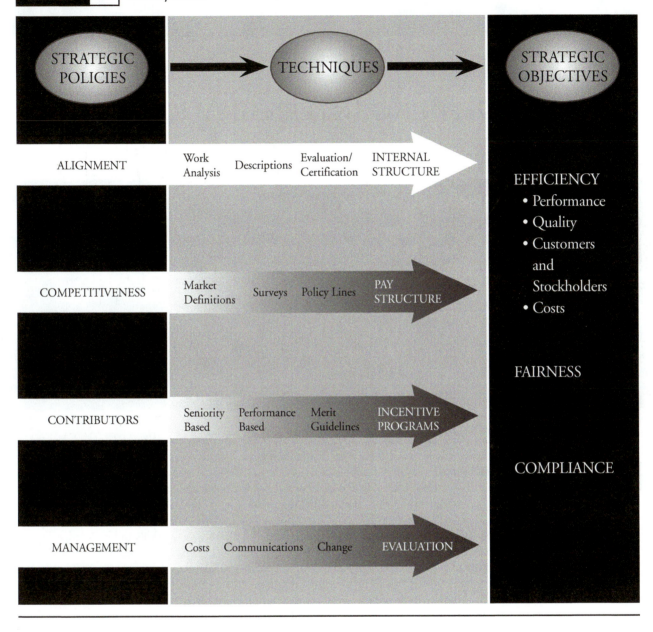

Defining Internal Alignment

LEARNING OUTCOMES

- Define what is meant by internal alignment and pay structure.
- Describe the three factors that determine how internal pay structures are designed.
- Describe the factors that shape internal structure.
- Explain the two strategic choices involved in designing internal pay structures.
- Explain three theoretical approaches to determining which pay structure is best for an organization.
- Describe three consequences of an internally aligned pay structure.

An ancient parable describes a vineyard owner hiring labourers throughout the day and then paying them equally at the end of the day. The labourers hired at the beginning of the day question the fairness of those hired at the end of the day being paid the same amount for fewer hours of work.[1]

This parable raises age-old questions about internal alignment and pay structures within a single organization.[2] The labourers felt that those who worked all day in the hot sun should be paid more than those who worked fewer hours. But apparently the householder was looking at an individual's needs. He ignored (1) the content of the work, (2) the skills and knowledge required to perform it, and (3) its relative value for achieving the organization's objectives. These three are common bases for today's pay structure. And if the procedures to determine the structure are not acceptable to the parties involved, today's employees murmur too. That murmuring translates into turnover, an unwillingness to try new technologies, even indifference to the quality of the grapes or the customer's satisfaction with them. This chapter examines internal alignment and its consequences.

■ COMPENSATION STRATEGY: INTERNAL ALIGNMENT

internal alignment (internal equity)

the pay relationships between the jobs/skills/competencies within a single organization

Setting objectives was our first pay policy issue in a strategic approach. **Internal alignment** (or, **internal equity**), our second, addresses relationships *inside* the organization. How do the responsibilities of a vine fastener, pruner, or weeder relate to each other? How do they relate to the responsibilities of the cook, the wine steward, or the accountant employed in the same household? The relationships among different jobs inside an organization form a job structure that should *support the organization's strategy, support the workflow,* and *motivate behaviour* toward organization objectives.

pay structure

the array of pay rates for different work or skills within a single organization; the number of levels, differentials in pay between the levels, and the criteria used to determine these differences create the structure

Exhibit 3.1 shows a job structure for the engineering and scientific work at an engineering company. The structure includes six levels that range from entry to consultant, as evidenced by the relationships among the titles for each level of work. Deciding how much to pay the six levels creates a **pay structure**.

Supports Organization Strategy

The organization's strategy indicates how it plans to achieve its purpose. Internal job structures that are aligned to the strategy help to achieve it. The engineering company decided that six levels of engineering work would support the company's strategy of researching, designing, and developing advanced technology systems.

Supports Workflow

workflow

process by which goods and services are delivered to the customer

Workflow refers to the process by which goods and services are created and delivered to the customer. The structure should support the efficient flow of that work and the design of the organization.[3] For example, drug companies traditionally base the size of their sales force on the number of physicians to be called on per day and the number of working days per year. The drug manufacturer Merck decided to take a non-traditional approach to organizing sales and marketing. Merck's analysis indicated that the ability of physicians to choose specific drugs was being constrained by government regulations and company health plan restrictions that control access to products for their members. With physicians no longer the sole decision makers, Merck created sales teams

---

EXHIBIT 3.1 | Job Structure at an Engineering Company

Entry Level

Engineer
Limited use of basic principles and concepts. Develops solutions to limited problems. Closely supervised.

Senior Engineer
Full use of standard principles and concepts. Provides solutions to a variety of problems. Under general supervision.

Systems Engineer
Wide applications of principles and concepts, plus working knowledge of other related disciplines. Provides solutions to a wide variety of difficult problems. Solutions are imaginative, thorough, and practicable. Works under only very general direction.

Lead Engineer
Applies extensive expertise as a generalist or specialist. Develops solutions to complex problems that require the regular use of ingenuity and creativity. Work is performed without appreciable direction. Exercises considerable latitude in determining technical objectives of assignment.

Advisor Engineer
Applies advanced principles, theories, and concepts. Contributes to the development of new principles and concepts. Works on unusually complex problems and provides solutions that are highly innovative and ingenious. Works under consultative direction toward predetermined long-range goals. Assignments are often self-initiated.

Consultant Engineer
Exhibits an exceptional degree of ingenuity, creativity, and resourcefulness. Applies and/or develops highly advanced technologies, scientific principles, theories, and concepts. Develops information that extends the existing boundaries of knowledge in a given field. Often acts independently to uncover and resolve problems associated with the development and implementation of operational programs.

Recognized Authority

consisting of account executives, client representatives, and medical information scientists to serve a broader clientele of insurance companies and physicians. A cross-functional team responsible for a distinct geographic area (rather than a list of physician-clients) provides a relationship-building approach to selling products. Rather than handing out free samples, the Merck teams got to know the clients and provided them with up-to-date information about trends and research. They became a source of knowledge useful to the physicians and the insurance companies. The teams keep clients apprised of regulations and cover drugs for a wider range of medical conditions. One team even translated brochures that explain a course of treatment into Chinese, Russian, and Spanish for a physician whose patients included non-English-speaking immigrants. (Of course, the recommended treatment did include Merck products.) Such a response would have been beyond the resources of a single sales representative under Merck's old approach.

To support these new work teams, Merck designed a new compensation structure. Pay differences between account executives, customer representatives, and medical information scientists who served on the same teams were a major issue—just as they had been for the vineyard owner described in the parable, just as they are for the engineers.

Motivates Behaviour

line-of-sight

link between an individual employee's work and the achievement of organizational objectives

Internal pay structures influence employees' behaviour by providing pay increases for promotions, more challenging work, and greater responsibility as employees move up in the structure. The criteria or rationale on which the structure is based should make clear the relationship between each job and the organization's objectives.[4] This is an example of **line-of-sight**. Employees should be able to "see" or understand links between their work, the work of others, and the organization's objectives. Internal alignment in pay structures helps create that line-of-sight.

◼ STRUCTURES VARY BETWEEN ORGANIZATIONS

An internal pay structure is defined by (1) the number of *levels* of work, (2) the pay *differentials* between the levels, and (3) the *criteria* used to determine those levels and differentials. These are the factors that a manager may vary to design a structure that supports the workflow and directs employee behaviours toward objectives.

Levels

One feature of any pay structure is its hierarchical nature—the number of levels and reporting relationships. Because pay structures typically reflect the flow of work in the organization, some are more hierarchical with multiple levels, others are compressed with few levels.[5] As noted earlier, in comparison to the engineering company's six levels for a single job group (Exhibit 3.1), a plastics company uses five broad levels, described in Exhibit 3.2, to cover all professional and executive work.

Differentials

differentials

pay differences between job levels

The pay differences between levels are referred to as **differentials**. If an organization has a compensation budget of a set amount to distribute among its employees, there are a number of ways to do so. It can divide the budget by the number of employees, giving everyone the same amount. But few organizations in the world are so egalitarian, and in most, pay varies among employees.

Work that requires more human capital—knowledge, skills, abilities, is performed under less desirable working conditions, and/or whose results are more valued—is usually paid more than

| EXHIBIT | 3.2 | Managerial/Professional Levels at a Plastics Company |

Level	Description
Executive	Provides vision, leadership, and innovation to major business segments or functions
Director	Directs a significant functional area or smaller business segment
Leadership	Individual contributors leading projects or programs with broad scope and impact, or managers leading functional components with broad scope and impact
Technical/managerial	Individual contributors managing projects or programs with defined scope and responsibility, or first-tier management of a specialty area
Professional	Supervisors and individual contributors working on tasks, activities, and/or less complex, shorter duration projects

work with lesser requirements.[6] Exhibit 3.3 shows the differentials attached to the engineering company's pay structure. One intention of these differentials is to motivate people to strive for promotion to a higher-paying level.

Criteria: Content and Value

Work content and work value are the most common bases for determining internal structures. *Content* refers to the work performed in a job and how it gets done (tasks, behaviours, knowledge required, and so on). *Value* refers to the worth of the work: its relative contribution to the organization objectives. A structure based on content typically ranks jobs based on skills required, complexity of tasks, and/or responsibility. By contrast, a structure based on the value of the work focuses on the relative contribution of the skills, tasks, and responsibilities of a job to the organization's goals. Although the resulting structures may be the same, there are some important differences. In addition to including relative contribution, value may also include external market pressures (such as what competitors pay for this level of contribution). Or value may include rates that have been agreed upon through collective bargaining or even legislation (e.g., minimum wage). Job values across all organizations in Cuba are set by a government agency. The universal structure dictates 8 levels for industrial workers, 16 levels for technical and engineering workers, and 26 levels for government employees.

Use value reflects the value of goods of services an employee produces in a job. Exchange value is whatever wage the employer and employee agree on for a job. Jobs such as software engineer may have the same use value but different exchange values, if, for example, one job is located in Bangalore and the other in New York.

Job- and Person-Based Structures A *job-based structure* looks at work content—tasks, behaviours, responsibilities. A *person-based structure* shifts the focus to the employee: the *skills*, *knowledge*, or *competencies* the employee possesses, whether or not they are used on the particular job the employee is doing.[7] The engineering structure (Exhibit 3.1) uses the work performed as the criterion. The plastics structure (Exhibit 3.2) uses the competencies that are required at each level of work.

EXHIBIT | **3.3** | Engineering Pay Structure

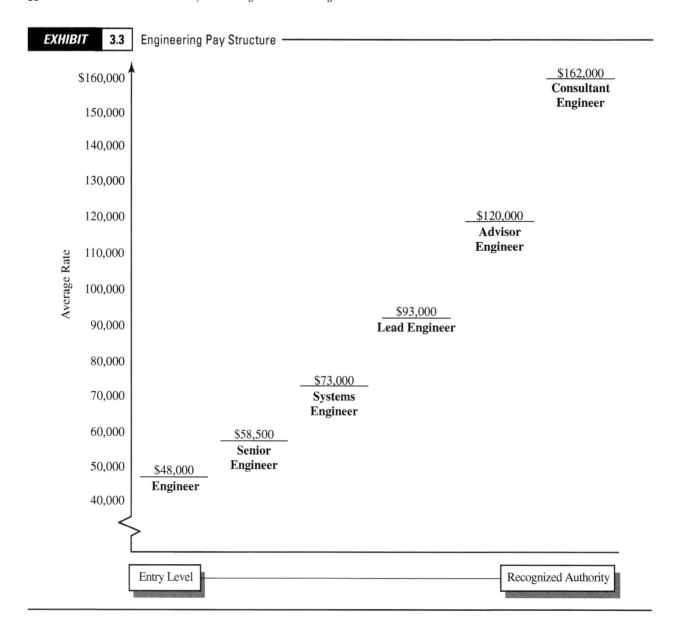

In the real world, it is hard to describe a job without reference to the job holder's knowledge and skills. Conversely, it is hard to define a person's job-related knowledge or competencies without referring to work content. So rather than a job- or person-based structure, reality includes both job and person.

WHAT FACTORS SHAPE INTERNAL STRUCTURES?

The major factors—both external and internal organization factors—that shape internal structures are shown in Exhibit 3.4. The various factors might better be represented as a web, with all factors connected and interacting. Exactly how these factors interact is not well understood. No single theory accounts for all factors. Some theories emphasize certain factors, others omit competing factors.

EXHIBIT | **3.4** | What Shapes Internal Structures?

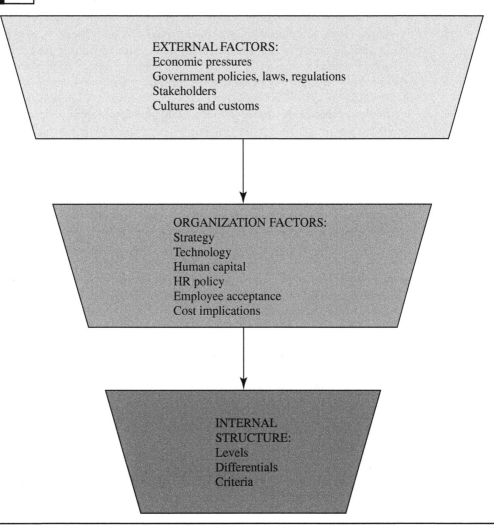

EXTERNAL FACTORS:
Economic pressures
Government policies, laws, regulations
Stakeholders
Cultures and customs

ORGANIZATION FACTORS:
Strategy
Technology
Human capital
HR policy
Employee acceptance
Cost implications

INTERNAL STRUCTURE:
Levels
Differentials
Criteria

Economic Pressures

Adam Smith was an early advocate of letting economic market forces influence pay structures. Smith ascribed to human resources both an exchange value and a use value. Exchange value is whatever wage the employer and the employee agree on. Use value reflects the value of the goods or services labour produces. New technologies associated with the Industrial Revolution increased the use value of labour without a corresponding increase in exchange value.

Karl Marx accused capitalistic economic systems of basing pay structures on exchange value.[8] He said that employers unfairly pocketed the surplus value created by the difference between what owners were willing to pay workers and what owners earned from workers' efforts. He urged workers to overthrow capitalistic systems in order to reap the benefits of their labour and become owners themselves. In some sense, broad-based stock ownership by employees is following Marx's suggestion that employees become owners.

In the face of rising wages in the last half of the 19th century, new theories began to examine the demand for labour. **Marginal productivity theory** says that employers do in fact pay use value.[9] Unless an employee can produce a value equal to the value received in wages, it will not be

marginal productivity theory

unless an employee can produce something of value from his/her job equal to the value received in wages, it will not be worthwhile for an employer to hire that employee worthwhile for the employer to hire that worker. Pay differences among the job levels reflect differences in use value associated with different jobs. One job is paid more or less than another because of differences in relative productivity of the job and/or differences in how much a consumer values the output. Hence, differences in productivity provide a rationale for the internal pay structure.

In addition to supply and demand for labour, supply and demand for products and services also affects internal structures. Rapid, often turbulent changes, in either competitors' products and/or services (as in the rise of the Internet for making purchases) or in customers' tastes (as in the popularity of fuel-efficient vehicles) means organizations must be able to redesign workflow and employees must continuously learn new skills. Turbulent, unpredictable external conditions require pay structures that support agile organizations and flexible people.[10]

Government Policies, Laws, and Regulations

In Canada, human rights legislation forbids pay systems that discriminate on the basis of gender, race, religion, sexual orientation, national origin, and many other grounds. Therefore, a benefit plan that provides benefits only to males over the age of 35 is illegal. Pay equity acts require "equal pay for work of equal value," based on skill, effort, responsibility, and working conditions. For example, male-dominated police jobs and female-dominated nursing jobs have often been found to require equal skill, effort, responsibility, and working conditions, and the nurses' pay has been increased to the same level as that of police officers. An internal structure may contain any number of levels, with differentials of any size, as long as the criteria for setting them do not include gender, race, religion, or national origin.

Much pay-related legislation attempts to regulate economic forces to achieve social welfare objectives. The most obvious place to affect an internal structure is at the minimums (minimum wage legislation) and maximums (special reporting requirements for executive pay). But legislation also aims at the differentials. Most countries have various legal standards regulating pay structures. Whatever they are, organizations operating within these countries must abide by them.[11]

External Stakeholders

Unions, stockholders, and even political groups have a stake in establishing internal pay structures. Unions are the most obvious case. Most unions seek smaller pay differences among jobs as well as seniority-based promotions in order to promote solidarity among members. At a minimum, unions seek to ensure that the interests of their members are well represented in decisions about structures. Years of union negotiations between the CAW and GM resulted in extremely high average compensation of $69 per hour. When the company was facing bankruptcy in 2009, major reductions in compensation were necessary to save the company, as described in the .Net Worth box.

Stockholders also pay attention to executive pay. Research is beginning to document its effects on employees' behaviours and performance, and consequently, organization performance.

Cultures and Customs

Culture is the mental programming for processing information that people share in common.[12] Such shared mindsets within a society may form a judgment of what size of pay differential is fair. In ancient Greece, Plato declared that societies are strongest when the richest earned a maximum of four times the lowest pay. Aristotle favoured a five-times limit.

Historians describe how in 14th-century Western Europe, the church endorsed a "just wage" doctrine, a structure of wages that supported the existing class structure in the society. The doctrine was an effort to end the economic and social chaos resulting from the death of one-third of the population from bubonic plague. The shortage of workers that resulted from the devastation

.NET WORTH

Auto Union to Freeze Pay at GM

GM of Canada Ltd. and the Canadian Auto Workers announced on March 8, 2009, that they had negotiated significant concessions affecting employees and retirees that will freeze their wages and pensions, increase personal expenses for health care benefits, reduce employee holidays, and eliminate annual bonuses.

The cuts, which could mean hundreds of millions of dollars in additional savings for GM until the fall of 2012, are critical for the company's survival plan and to qualify for loans from the federal and provincial governments.

CAW senior economist Jim Stanford said the deal will cut labour costs by "several dollars" an hour and retain the competitive edge of GM workers in Canada over other auto employees in the U.S. under a range of currency rates between the two countries.

Average wages and benefits currently total about $69 an hour per GM worker.

The deal would extend the current three-year contract by a year to September 2012 and freeze wages and quarterly cost-of-living allowance for almost the entire term. Production technicians now earn about $34 an hour in wages.

Furthermore, workers would lose one more week of special holidays a year and a $1,700 annual bonus. The company will divert that money to pay for retiree health care costs.

Workers and retirees under 65 would pay a $360-a-year premium for health care for the first time plus contribute more for benefits such as dental services under the deal.

More than 30,000 retirees and surviving spouses would also face a freeze in monthly pensions and cost-of-living protection. Those older than 65 would have to pay a $180 annual premium for health care plus contribute more for long-term care and other benefits.

Source: T. Van Alphen, "Auto Union to Freeze Pay at GM," *Toronto Star,* March 9, 2009. www.thestar.com/News/Canada/article/598763 (accessed August 15, 2009).

---

led nobles and landholders to bid up the wages for surviving craftspeople. By allowing the church and royalty to determine wages, market forces such as scarcity of skills were explicitly denied as appropriate determinants of pay structures.

Even today cultural factors continue to shape pay structures around the world. Pay equity is a Canadian example in which advocates have been changing societal judgments about what constitutes a just wage. These judgments change in response to pressure. For example, many traditional Japanese employers emphasize seniority in their internal pay structures. But pressures from global competitors and an aging workforce have made age-based pay structures very expensive. Consequently, some Japanese employers are shifting older employees to lower-paying business units, emphasizing performance, and downplaying seniority.[13]

Organization Strategy

The last chapter explained that organization strategies influence internal pay structures. Different business strategies may require different pay structures to support them. The basic belief of a strategic perspective is that pay structures that are not aligned with the organization strategy may become obstacles to the organization's success.

Organization's Human Capital

Human capital—the education, experience, knowledge, abilities, and skills that people possess—is regarded as a major influence on internal structures.[14] The stronger the link between these skills and experience and an organization's strategic objective, the more pay these skills will command. The engineering structure in Exhibit 3.1 results in paying consultant engineers more than lead engineers or senior engineers because the human capital of consultant engineers brings a greater return to the company. It is more critical to the organization's success.

Technology and Work Design

Technology used in producing goods and services influences the organizational design, the work to be performed, and the skills/knowledge required to perform the work. Thus, the technology employed is another critical organization factor influencing the design of pay structures.[15] These differences contribute to the different structures in Exhibits 3.1 and 3.2.

The design of organizations is undergoing profound changes. A lot of people who work in organizations are not employees of these organizations. They may be employed by either a supplier (such as an IT supplier) or perhaps a temporary staff supplier (such as Manpower Services). Or they may be working under a temporary contract for a limited amount of time or on a limited project. The security guards, software engineers, or accountants may be supplied by outsourcing specialists. Pay for these people is based on the internal structure of their own employer.

Another major work design change is delayering. Entire levels of work have disappeared at HP because of complaints about sluggish response to customer needs. Levels of management were cut from 11 to 8, and customers immediately applauded the reduce response time.[16] Delayering can reduce unnecessary work that does not contribute to strategic objectives. It can also add work to other jobs, enlarging them. Through the use of self-managed work teams in production work, entire levels of supervisory jobs are removed and the responsibility for their decisions is delegated to the teams.[17] This changes the value of jobs on the team and hence changes the job structure.

Overall HR Policies

The organization's other human resource policies also influence pay structures. Most organizations tie money to promotions to induce employees to apply for higher-level positions.[18] If an organization has more levels, it can offer more promotions, but there may be smaller pay differentials between levels. The belief is that more frequent promotions (even without significant pay increases) offer a sense of career progress to employees.[19]

Internal Labour Markets: Combining External and Organizational Factors

Internal labour markets combine both external and organizational factors. Internal labour markets refer to the rules and procedures that (1) determine the pay for the different jobs within a single organization, and (2) allocate employees to those different jobs.[20] As depicted in Exhibit 3.5, individuals tend to be recruited and hired only for specific entry-level jobs (an engineer would be hired right out of university; a senior engineer would have a few years' experience), and are later allocated (promoted or transferred) to other jobs. Because the employer competes in the external market for people to fill these entry jobs, their pay is linked to the external market. It must be high enough to attract a qualified pool of applicants. By contrast, pay for non-entry jobs (those staffed internally via transfer and promotions) is buffered from external forces and is more heavily influenced by internal factors such as the organization's strategy, technology, human capital required, and other HR systems. External factors are dominant influences on pay for entry jobs, but the differences for non-entry jobs tend to reflect the organization's internal factors.

| EXHIBIT | 3.5 | Illustration of an Internal Labour Market

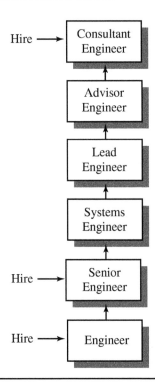

Employee Acceptance: A Key Factor

Employees judge the fairness of their pay through comparisons with the compensation paid others for work related in some fashion to their own.[21] Accordingly, an important factor influencing the internal pay structure is its acceptability to the employees involved.[22] Employees make multiple pay comparisons to assess the fairness of an internal pay structure. They compare their pay to that for other jobs in the same internal job structure and to the pay for their job in the external market at competing employers.[23]

procedural justice

fairness of a process by which a decision is reached

distributive justice

fairness of a decision outcome

Two aspects of fairness are important: the procedures for determining the pay structure, called procedural justice, and the results of those procedures—the pay structure itself—called distributive justice. **Procedural justice** refers to the process by which a decision is reached. **Distributive justice** refers to the fairness of the decision outcome. Researchers report that employees' perceptions of procedural fairness significantly influence their acceptance of the results. Employees are more willing to accept lower pay if they believe that the way the decision was made was fair. The research also suggests that pay procedures are more likely to be perceived as fair if (1) they are consistently applied to all employees, (2) employees participate in the process (although recent research suggests an exception when wages are very low[24]), (3) appeals procedures are included, and (4) the data used are accurate.

Applied to internal structures, procedural justice addresses how design and administration decisions are made and whether procedures are applied in a consistent manner. Distributive justice addresses whether the actual pay differences among employees are acceptable.

Pay Structures Change

As previously noted, pay structures change in response to changing external pressures such as skill shortages. Over time, the distorted pay differences become accepted as equitable and customary;

efforts to change them are resisted. Thus, pay structures established for organizational and economic reasons at an earlier time may be maintained for cultural or other political reasons. It may take another economic jolt to overcome the cultural resistance. Then, new norms for employee acceptance are formed around the new structure. This "change and congeal" process does not yet support the continuous change occurring in today's economy. New norms for employee acceptance probably will need to include recognition that people must get used to constant change, even in internal pay relationships.

The pay for airport security screeners relative to other airport jobs illustrates the change and congeal process. Prior to 9/11, airport screeners were paid minimum wage with no benefits. Today, wages are comparable to police and fire protection jobs. Employees in other airport jobs had to revise their comparisons to the security jobs.[25]

■ STRATEGIC CHOICES IN DESIGNING INTERNAL STRUCTURES

Internally aligned pay structures support the way the work gets done, fit the organization's business strategy, and are fair to employees. Greater internal alignment—fit—is more likely to lead to success. Misaligned structures become obstacles. They may motivate employee behaviour that is inconsistent with the organization's strategy. But what does it mean to fit or tailor the pay structure to be internally aligned? Two strategic choices are involved: (1) how tailored to organization design and workflow to make the structure, and (2) how to distribute pay throughout the levels in the structure.

Tailored versus Loosely Coupled

tailored structure

pay structure for well-defined jobs with relatively small differences in pay

A low-cost, customer-focused business strategy such as that followed by McDonald's or Walmart may be supported by a closely **tailored structure**. Jobs are well defined, with detailed tasks or steps to follow. You can go into a McDonald's in Vancouver, Prague, or Shanghai and find they all are very similar. Their pay structures are, too. The customer representative and the food preparation jobs are very well defined in order to eliminate variability in how they are performed. The amount of ketchup that goes on the burger is pre-measured, even the keys on the cash register are labelled with menu items rather than prices. And the difference in pay between jobs is relatively small.

loosely coupled structure

pay structure for jobs that are flexible, adaptable, and changing

In contrast to McDonald's, 3M's business strategy requires constant product innovation and short product design-to-market cycle times. Companies like 3M need to be very agile, constantly innovating and adapting. The competitive environment these organizations face is turbulent and unpredictable. Their engineers may work on several teams developing several products at the same time. 3M's pay system needs to accommodate this flexibility. Hence, they need a more **loosely coupled structure** in order to facilitate constant change.

Egalitarian versus Hierarchical

Pay structures can range from egalitarian at one extreme to hierarchical at the other. Egalitarian structures have fewer levels and smaller differentials between adjacent levels and between the highest- and lowest-paid workers. Exhibit 3.6 shows some variations in structures. Structure A has eight different levels, with relatively small differentials in comparison to structure B, which has only three levels. Structure A is hierarchical in comparison to the egalitarian structure of B; the multiple levels typically include detailed descriptions of work done at that level and delineate who is responsible for what. Hierarchical structures are consistent with a belief in the motivational effects of frequent promotion. Hierarchies value the differences in individual employee skills, responsibilities, and contributions to the organization.[26]

| EXHIBIT | 3.6 | Structures Vary in Number of Levels |

Structure A Layered	Structure B Delayered
Chief Engineer	Chief Engineer
Engineering Manager	
Consulting Engineer	
Senior Lead Engineer	
Lead Engineer	Consulting Engineer
Senior Engineer	
Engineer	
Engineer Trainee	Associate Engineer

Structure B can also be characterized as "de-layered," or compressed. Several levels of responsibility and supervision are removed so that all employees at all levels become responsible for a broader range of tasks, but also have greater freedom to determine how best to accomplish what is expected of them. An egalitarian structure implies a belief that more equal treatment will improve employee satisfaction, support cooperation, and therefore improve workers' performance.[27]

Yet, more egalitarian structures are not problem-free, either. For example, Ben and Jerry's Homemade, a purveyor of premium ice cream, tried to maintain a ratio of only 7 to 1 between its highest-paid and lowest-paid employee. The relatively narrow differential reflected the company's philosophy that the prosperity of its production workers and its management should be closely linked. The compressed structure also generated a great deal of favourable publicity. However, it eventually became a barrier to recruiting. Ben and Jerry's was forced to abandon this policy in order to hire an accounting manager and a new CEO. And only when the company was acquired by Unilever, a Dutch multinational, did the press publicize the fact that the value of stock increased the total compensation for founders Ben Cohen and Jerry Greenfield to much more than the 7 to 1 ratio.

There are drawbacks to this approach. Equal treatment can result in more knowledgeable employees with more responsible jobs (stars) going unrecognized and unrewarded, which may cause them to leave the organization. They may leave physically for another job, or they may simply slack off or tune out and refuse to do anything not specifically required of them. Their change in behaviour will lower overall performance. So a case can be made for both egalitarian and hierarchical structures.

Exhibit 3.7 clarifies the differences between egalitarian and hierarchical structures. Keep in mind, though, the choice is not either/or. Rather, the differences are a matter of degree. So levels

| EXHIBIT | 3.7 | Strategic Choice: Hierarchical versus Egalitarian |

	Hierarchical	Egalitarian
Levels	Many	Fewer
Differentials	Large	Small
Criteria	Person or Job	Person or Job
Fit	Tailored	Loosely Coupled
Supports	Individual Performers	Teams
Fairness Criterion	Performance	Equal Treatment
Behaviour Rewarded	Opportunities for Promotion	Cooperation

can range from many to few, differentials can be large or small, and the criteria can be based on the job, the person, or some combination of the two. The question to be resolved is: What size should the pay differentials be between the adjacent engineering levels? Exhibit 3.8 shows that the differentials between engineering jobs range from $10,500 (Engineer to Senior Engineer) to $42,000 (Advisor to Consultant). Both the amount and the percentages increase at each level.

GUIDANCE FROM THE EVIDENCE

Before managers recommend which pay structure is best for their organizations, we hope they will look not only at the factors in their organization, such as workflow, what is fair, and how to motivate employee behaviour, but also look to theory and research for guidance. Both psychologists and economists have something to tell us about the effects of various structures.

Equity Theory: Fairness

As noted earlier, employees judge the fairness or equity of their pay by comparing it to that for other jobs at their own employer (internal equity) and to that for jobs at other employers (external equity).[28] A recent study of 2,000 teachers found that those who were higher up in the internal pay structure perceived that the structure was fair, and that lower-paid teachers perceived that the structure was fair if they worked in a highly paid school district. The results from these comparisons depend in part on the accuracy of employee knowledge of other employees' jobs, internal structures, and external pay levels.[29] Teachers' pay schedules are generally public knowledge, but this is seldom the case in private organizations. Past research has shown that employees

EXHIBIT 3.8 | Pay Differentials

Job	Dollars (bonus + base)	Differential	
		Dollars	Percentage
Consultant	$162,000		
		$42,000	35
Advisor Engineer	$120,000		
		$27,000	29
Lead Engineer	$93,000		
		$20,000	27
Systems Engineer	$73,000		
		$14,500	25
Senior Engineer	$58,500		
		$10,500	22
Engineer	$48,000		

are often misinformed about their relative standing in the pay structure.[30] Thus, equity theory could support either egalitarian or hierarchical structures, depending on the comparisons and the accuracy of information about them.

Tournament Theory: Motivation and Performance

Economists have focused more directly on the motivational effects of structures. Their starting point is a golf tournament at which the prizes total, say, $100,000. How that $100,000 is distributed affects the performance of all players in the tournament. Consider three prizewinners, with the first-place winner getting over half the purse, versus ten prizewinners, with only slight differences in the size of the purse among the ten. According to tournament theory, all players play better in tournaments where the prize differentials are sizable.[31] Some research supports tournament theory. Raising the total prize money by $100,000 in the Professional Golf Association tournament improved each player's score.[32] And the closer the players got to the top prize, the more their scores improved.

Applying these results to organizations, the greater the differential between an employee's present salary and his or her boss's salary, the harder the employee (and everyone else) will work. Suppose that the engineering structure contains ten advisor engineers at the second-to-the-top level, each making $120,000, and each competing for two consultant positions, where the pay is $162,000. A tournament model says that if the consultants instead are paid $200,000, everyone will work even harder. Rather than resenting the big bucks paid to the consultants, engineers at all levels in the structure will be motivated by the greater differential to work harder to "win" the promotion to the next level.

But most work is not a round of golf, nor does it lead to the company presidency. Virtually all the research that supports hierarchical structures and tournament theory takes place in situations where individual performance matters most (e.g., auto racing, bowling, golf tournaments), or at best where the demand for cooperation among a small group of individuals is relatively low (e.g., professors, stockbrokers). In contrast, team sports provide a setting where both individual players' performance and the cooperative efforts of the entire team make a difference.[33] Using eight years of data on major league baseball, one study found that teams with egalitarian structures (practically identical player salaries) did better than those with hierarchical structures (very large differentials between players). In addition to affecting team performance (e.g., games won, gate receipts, franchise value, total income), internal structures had a sizable effect on players' individual performance (e.g., batting averages, errors, runs batted in). It may also be that the egalitarian pay structure reflects a more flexible, supportive organizational culture where players are given the training and support they need.

Another study looked at pay differentials between members of 460 organizations' executive teams.[34] It found that members of executive leadership teams were twice as likely to leave companies with larger pay differentials, and concluded that if executives need to cooperate, then an egalitarian structure is a better fit.

Institutional Theory: Copy Others

Internal pay structures are sometimes adopted because they have become so-called "best practices."[35] Organizations simply copy what others are doing. Recent examples of such "benchmarking" behaviour include outsourcing and competency-based pay systems adopted without regard to whether these practices fit the organization or its employees and whether they add value. Institutional theory predicts that very few firms are "first movers." Instead they copy innovative practices after innovators have learned how to make the practices work. The copiers have little concern for alignment and even less for innovative pay practices.

(More) Guidance From the Evidence

Exhibit 3.9 summarizes the effects attributed to internally aligned structures.

- More hierarchical structures are related to greater performance when the workflow depends more on individual contributors (e.g., consulting and law practices, surgical units, stockbrokers, even university researchers).
- High performers quit less under more hierarchical systems when pay is based on performance rather than seniority and when people have knowledge of the structure.
- More egalitarian structures are related to greater performance when close collaboration and sharing of knowledge is required (e.g., fire fighting and rescue squads, manufacturing teams, hotel customer service staff, global software design teams). The competition fostered in "winner-take-all" tournament hierarchies appears to have negative effects on performance when the workflow and organization design require teamwork.
- The impact of any internal structure on organization performance is affected by the other dimensions of the pay model: pay levels (competitiveness), employee performance (contributions), and employee knowledge of the pay structure (management).

Beyond these points, much remains to be studied. There is practically no research on the optimal size of the promotional increase or its effects on behaviours, satisfaction, or performance. Nor is much known about whether smaller, more frequent promotions are better (or worse) than fewer, larger, less frequent promotions. Perhaps informal expectations are developed at each workplace. ("You can expect to be promoted here after about three years, and a 10 percent raise usually goes with it.") At universities, promotion from assistant to associate professor tends to occur after six years, although there is no norm for promotion pay increases. In Japanese pay structures, promotion from associate to *kakaricho* occurs after five years in a company. Similar norms exist in the military. Little is known about how these rules developed and what the original logic was. But they do matter. Promotions sooner (or later) than expected, accompanied by a larger (or smaller) pay increase send a powerful message.

So what size should the pay differentials be between the adjacent levels within the engineering company? To answer this question, it is necessary to understand how differentials within the career path support the business strategy and workflow, motivate engineers to contribute to the company's success, and are considered fair by the engineers. The next several chapters discuss how to manage these internal structures.

EXHIBIT   3.9   Some Organizational Outcomes of Internally Aligned Structure

Undertake training

Increase experience

Reduce turnover

Pay structure — Facilitate career progression

Facilitate performance

Reduce pay-related grievances

Reduce pay-related work stoppages

■ CONSEQUENCES OF STRUCTURES

The "so what?" question and the pay model: Why worry about internal alignment at all? Why not simply pay employees whatever it takes to get them to take a job and show up for work every day? Why not let external market forces and what competitors are paying determine internal wage differentials? Or why not let a government agency decide?

Efficiency

Research shows that an aligned pay structure can lead to better organization performance.[36] If the structure does not motivate employees to help achieve the organization's objectives, then it is a candidate for redesign. Internal pay structures imply future rewards. The size of the pay differential between the entry level and the highest level in the structure may induce employees to remain with the organization, increase their experience and training, cooperate with co-workers, and seek greater responsibility.[37] Thus, the number of levels and titles in a career path may be rewarding beyond the pay attached to the titles. Microsoft added a "distinguished engineer" title to its structure. The consulting firm McKinsey and Company added an "associate partner." Their rationale was that employees are motivated by frequent steps in the career ladder. These are new titles and levels that are not yet reflected in the external market.

Fairness

Writers have long agreed that departures from an acceptable wage structure will result in higher turnover, grievances, and diminished motivation.[38] But that is where the agreement ends. One group argues that if fair (i.e., sizable) differentials between jobs are not paid, individuals may harbour ill will toward the employer, resist change, change employment if possible, become depressed, or "lack that zest and enthusiasm which makes for high efficiency and personal satisfaction in work."[39] Others, including labour unions, argue for small differentials, in the belief that more egalitarian structures support team cooperation, high commitment to the organization, and improved performance.

Legal Compliance

As with any pay decision, the design and management of internal pay structures must comply with the regulations of the countries in which the organization operates. Although the research on internal alignment is informative, there is still a lot that is not known. What about the appropriate number of levels, the size of the differentials, and the criteria to advance employees through a structure? It is believed that the answers lie in understanding the factors discussed in this chapter: the organization's strategic intent, organization design and workflow, human capital, and the external conditions, regulations, and customs it faces. It is also believed that aligning the pay structures to fit the organization and the surrounding conditions is more likely to lead to competitive advantage for the organization and a sense of fair treatment for employees.

CONCLUSION

This chapter discusses the strategic policy of internal alignment and how it affects employees, managers, and employers. Internal alignment refers to the pay relationships among jobs, skills, and competencies within a single organization. The potential consequences of internal pay structures are vital to organizations and individuals. Recent research and experience offer guidance concerning the design and management of internal pay structures.

Pay structures—the array of pay rates for different jobs within an organization—are defined by levels, differentials, and the criteria for determining these. Pay structures are shaped by societal, economic, organizational, and other factors. Employees judge the fairness of pay structures by comparing their pay to other jobs within the organization and to what competitors pay for jobs similar to theirs. Acceptance by employees of pay differentials between jobs is a key test of an equitable pay structure. Pay structures are part of the network of returns offered by organizations. They offer career paths to higher-paying jobs and a sense of achievement.

The goals of the entire compensation system must be kept in mind when thinking about internal pay structures. Widespread experience and, increasingly, research support the belief that differences in internal pay structures, particularly employee career paths, influence people's attitudes and work behaviours, and therefore the success of organizations.

CHAPTER SUMMARY

1. Internal alignment refers to the pay relationships between jobs, skills, and competencies within a single organization. The relationships form a structure that supports organizational strategy, supports the workflow, and motivates employee behaviour toward organization objectives. A pay structure is the array of pay rates for different work or skills.
2. The three types of factors that define how internal pay structures are designed are: (1) the number of levels of work, (2) the pay differentials between the levels, and (3) the criteria used to determine these levels and differentials.
3. The factors that shape internal pay structures are: (1) external factors such as economic pressures; government policies, laws, and regulations; and culture; and (2) organizational factors such as strategy, human capital, work design, and employee acceptance.
4. The two strategic choices involved in designing internal pay structures are: (1) how closely to link the pay structure to organization design and workflow (tailored or loosely coupled), and (2) how to distribute pay throughout the levels in the structure (egalitarian or hierarchical).
5. Three theoretical approaches to determining which pay structure is best for an organization are equity theory, tournament theory, and the institutional model. Equity theory focuses on how employees compare their work, qualifications, and pay to those of others. Tournament theory suggests that the greater the differences between salaries in the pay structure, the harder employees will work. Institutional theory suggests that organizations copy the "best practices" of others.
6. Three consequences of an internally aligned pay structure are efficiency, fairness, and legal compliance.

KEY TERMS

REVIEW QUESTIONS

1. Why is internal alignment an important compensation policy? What happens when a compensation policy is not internally aligned?
2. Based on your own experience, which factors shaped the internal pay structure at your most recent employer? Provide examples that support your choice.
3. Would Research In Motion, makers of the BlackBerry, be better served by a tailored pay structure or a loosely coupled pay structure? Explain your answer.
4. Explain the consequences of internal alignment for competitive advantage, fairness to employees, and legal compliance.

EXPERIENTIAL EXERCISES

1. Look into any organization—your university/college, workplace, or the grocery store where you shop. Describe the flow of work. How is the job structure aligned with the organization's business, the workflow, and the organization objectives? How do you think it influences employee behaviours?

2. Prepare a list of at least five Canadian laws at various levels of government that impact pay rates.

3. Illustrate the internal labour market for faculty at your university/college, using Exhibit 3.5 as a guide.

WEB EXERCISE

Assessing Differentials in Major League Baseball

Go to the Web site www.sportscity.com and click on "Salaries" to check salaries for all the players on all the teams in your favourite major league sport.

1. Pick some of your favourite teams and compare the highest- and lowest-paid player on the team.

2. Based on the differentials, which teams do the models and research discussed in this chapter predict will have the better record?

3. Go back to the home page and click on "Standings" and check it out. Suggestion: Don't bet your tuition on the relationship between player salary differentials on a team and the team's performance.

CASE

The Orchestra

Orchestras employ skilled and talented people, joined together as a team to create products and services. Job descriptions for orchestras look simple: Play the music. Violins play violin parts; trumpets play trumpet parts. Yet one study reported that orchestra players' job satisfaction ranks below that of prison guards. (Nevertheless, orchestra players were more satisfied than operating room nurses or hockey players.)

The pay structure for a regional chamber orchestra is shown below. The pay covers six full orchestra concerts, one Carolling by Candlelight event, three Sunday Chamber Series Concerts, several Arts in Education elementary school concerts, two engagements for a flute quartet, and one "Ring in the Holidays" brass event, as well as regularly scheduled rehearsals.

Orchestra Compensation Schedule

Instrument	Pay
Violin, Concertmaster	$6,790
Principal Bass and Conductor	$5,070
Principal Viola	$5,036
Principal Flute	$4,337
Principal Trumpet	$4,233
Principal Cello	$4,181
Principal Clarinet	$4,146
Trumpet	$3,638
Principal Oboe	$3,615
Principal Violin II	$3,488
Principal Horn	$3,390
Keyboard I	$3,361
Cello	$3,228
Principal Percussion	$3,049
Violin I	$2,899
Cello	$2,882
Principal Bassoon	$2,824
Violin I	$2,685
Violin I	$2,483
Violin I	$2,483
Violin I	$2,483
Violin II	$2,483
Violin II	$2,483
Viola	$2,483
Viola	$2,212
Oboe	$2,206
Trombone	$2,137
Viola	$2,033
Violin II	$1,975
Violin II/Viola	$1,784
Cello	$1,634
Clarinet	$1,548
Horn	$1,548
Flute	$1,455
Keyboard II	$1,392
Bassoon	$1,265
Violin II	$1,178

Questions

1. Describe the orchestra's pay structure in terms of levels, differentials, and job- or person-based.

2. Discuss which factors may explain the structure. Why does violinist I receive more than the oboist or trombonist? Is it because the violins play more notes? Why does the principal trumpet player earn more than the principal cellist and clarinetist, but less than the principal viola and flute players? What explains these differences? How does the relative supply versus demand for violinists compare to the supply versus demand for trombonists?

3. How well do equity and tournament models apply?

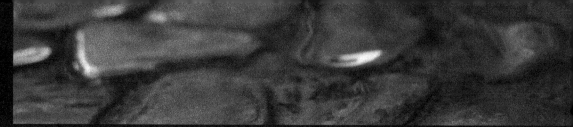

JOB ANALYSIS

LEARNING OUTCOMES

- Explain job analysis and why it has been called the cornerstone of human resources management.
- Describe the step-by-step approach to conducting conventional job analysis.
- Describe the information that must be collected for job analysis and explain recent changes in how this information is collected.
- Discuss the differences between job descriptions and job specifications.
- Explain the pros and cons of job analysis and different ways to judge job analysis.

Three people sit in front of their keyboards scanning their monitors. One is a sales representative in Montreal, checking the progress of an order for four dozen picture cellphones from a retailer in Vancouver, who has just placed the four dozen into his shopping cart on the company's Web site. A second person is an engineer, logging in to the project design software for the next generation of these picture cellphones. Colleagues in China working on the same project last night (day in China) sent some suggestions for changes in the new design; the team in Canada will work on the project today and have their work waiting for their Chinese colleagues when they come in to work in the morning. A third employee, in Ireland, is using business software recently installed worldwide to analyze the latest sales reports. In today's workplace, people working for the same company need no longer be down the hallway from one another. On-site or overseas, networks and business software link them all. And all these jobs are part of the organization's internal structure.

If pay is to be based on work performed, some method is needed to discover and describe the differences and similarities among these jobs—observation alone is not enough. Job analysis is that systematic method.

▪ STRUCTURES BASED ON JOBS, PEOPLE, OR BOTH

Exhibit 4.1 outlines the process for constructing a work-related internal pay structure. No matter the approach, the process begins by looking at people at work. Job-based pay structures look at the tasks the people are doing and the expected outcomes; skill- and competency-based pay structures look at the person. However, the underlying purpose of each phase of the process (shown in the left-hand column of Exhibit 4.1) remains the same for both job- and person-based pay structures: (1) collect and summarize information that identifies similarities and differences, (2) determine what is to be valued, (3) quantify the relative value, and (4) translate relative value into an internal pay structure. (The blank boxes for the person-based pay structure will be filled in when we get to Chapter 6.) This chapter and the next focus on the job-based pay structure.[1]

JOB-BASED APPROACH: MOST COMMON

job analysis

the systematic process of collecting information about the nature of specific jobs

Exhibit 4.2 shows how job analysis and the resulting job description are the first steps in the process of creating an internal pay structure. Each step is defined and related to designing the structure. **Job analysis** provides the underlying information for preparing job descriptions and evaluating jobs. The content of the job is identified via job analysis; this content serves as input for describing and valuing work.

Exhibit 4.2 also lists the major decisions in designing a job analysis: (1) Why are we collecting job information? (2) What information do we need? (3) How should we collect it? (4) Who should be involved? (5) How useful are the results?

EXHIBIT 4.1   Many Ways to Create Internal Structure

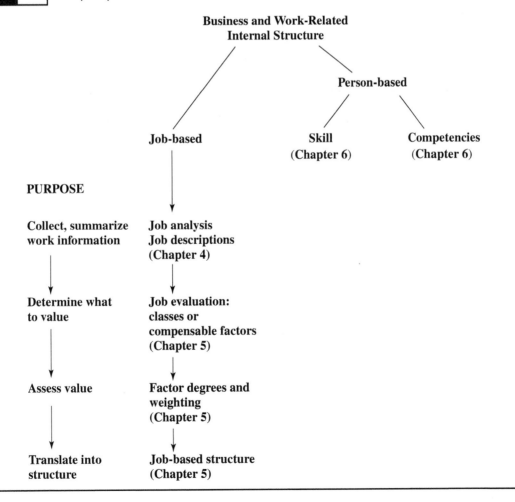

Business and Work-Related Internal Structure

Person-based

Job-based

Skill
(Chapter 6)

Competencies
(Chapter 6)

PURPOSE

Collect, summarize work information → **Job analysis Job descriptions (Chapter 4)**

Determine what to value → **Job evaluation: classes or compensable factors (Chapter 5)**

Assess value → **Factor degrees and weighting (Chapter 5)**

Translate into structure → **Job-based structure (Chapter 5)**

Exam·

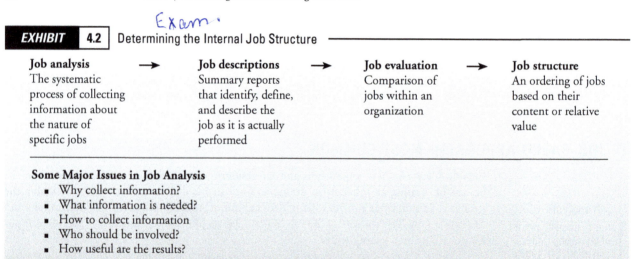

EXHIBIT   4.2 Determining the Internal Job Structure

Job analysis →	**Job descriptions** →	**Job evaluation** →	**Job structure**
The systematic process of collecting information about the nature of specific jobs	Summary reports that identify, define, and describe the job as it is actually performed	Comparison of jobs within an organization	An ordering of jobs based on their content or relative value

Some Major Issues in Job Analysis
- Why collect information?
- What information is needed?
- How to collect information
- Who should be involved?
- How useful are the results?

Why Perform Job Analysis?

Potential uses for job analysis have been suggested for every major human resources function.[2] The type of job analysis data needed varies according to function. For example, job analysis identifies the skills and experience required to perform the work, which clarifies hiring and promotion standards. Training programs may be designed with job analysis data; jobs may be redesigned based on such data. In performance evaluation, both employees and supervisors look to the required behaviours and results expected in a job to help assess performance.

An internal structure based on job-related information provides both managers and employees with a work-related rationale for pay differences. Employees who understand this rationale can better direct their behaviour toward organization objectives. Job analysis data also help managers defend their decisions when they are challenged.

In compensation, job analysis has two critical uses: (1) It establishes similarities and differences in the content of jobs, and (2) it helps establish an internally fair and aligned job structure. If jobs have equal content, then in all likelihood, the pay established for them will be equal. If, on the other hand, the job content differs, then those differences, along with the market rates paid by competitors, are part of the rationale for paying jobs differently.

The key issue for compensation decision makers is still to ensure that the data collected serve the purpose of making decisions and are acceptable to the employees involved. As the arrows in Exhibit 4.2 indicate, collecting job information is only an interim step, not an end in itself.

■ JOB ANALYSIS PROCEDURES

Exhibit 4.3 summarizes some job analysis terms and their relationship to one another. Job analysis usually collects information about specific tasks or behaviours. A group of tasks performed by one person makes up a position. Identical positions make a job, and broadly similar jobs combine into a job family.[3]

Large organizations, often the biggest users of job analysis data, usually follow a step-by-step approach to conducting conventional job analysis.[4] Standard procedures, shown in Exhibit 4.4, include developing preliminary information, interviewing job holders and supervisors, and then using the information to create and verify job descriptions. The picture that emerges from the exhibit is of a stable workplace where the division from one job to the next is clear, with little overlap. In this workplace, jobs follow a steady progression in a hierarchy of increasing responsibility, and the relationship between jobs is clear. So is how to qualify for promotion into a

EXHIBIT | **4.3** | Job Analysis Terminology

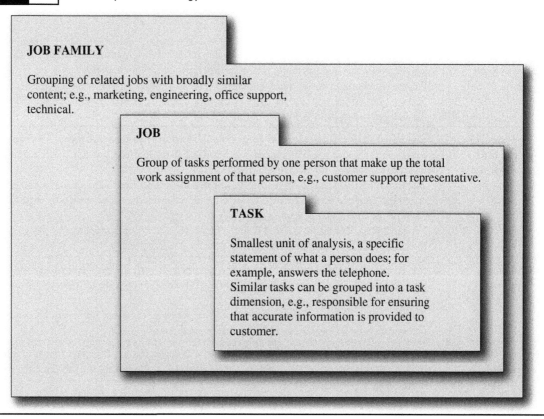

JOB FAMILY

Grouping of related jobs with broadly similar content; e.g., marketing, engineering, office support, technical.

JOB

Group of tasks performed by one person that make up the total work assignment of that person, e.g., customer support representative.

TASK

Smallest unit of analysis, a specific statement of what a person does; for example, answers the telephone. Similar tasks can be grouped into a task dimension, e.g., responsible for ensuring that accurate information is provided to customer.

higher-level job. Although some argue that such a traditional, stable structure is a shrinking part of the workplace landscape, such structures nevertheless persist, in varying degrees, in many large organizations.[5] Thus, this depiction of conventional job analysis provides a useful description of the process.

WHAT INFORMATION SHOULD BE COLLECTED?

As Exhibit 4.4 suggests, a typical analysis starts with a review of information already collected in order to develop a framework for further analysis. Job titles, major duties, task dimensions, and workflow information may already exist. However, this information may no longer be accurate. So the analyst must clarify existing information, too.

Generally, a good job analysis collects sufficient information to adequately identify, define, and describe a job. Exhibit 4.5 lists some of the information that is usually collected. The information is categorized as "related to the job" or "related to the employee."

Job Data: Identification

Job titles, departments, and the number of people who hold the job are examples of information that identifies a job. Although a job title may seem pretty straightforward, it may not be. For example, the Canadian federal government has hundreds of job titles, some of which are hard to interpret, such as Specialist, Oral Literature; Detachment Quality Representative; Photogrammetrist; FRED Plan Administrator; and so on.[6]

EXHIBIT   **4.4**   General Procedures for Conventional Job Analysis

Step	Things to Remember or Do
1. Develop preliminary job information	a. Review existing documents in order to develop an initial "big-picture" familiarity with the job—its main mission, its major duties or functions, workflow patterns. b. Prepare a preliminary list of duties which will serve as a framework for conducting the interviews. c. Make a note of major items that are unclear or ambiguous or that need to be clarified during the data-gathering process.
2. Conduct initial tour of work site	a. The initial tour is designed to familiarize the job analyst with the work layout, the tools and equipment that are used, the general conditions of the workplace, and the mechanics associated with the end-to-end performance of major duties. b. The initial tour is particularly helpful for those jobs where a first-hand view of a complicated or unfamiliar piece of equipment may save the interviewee the thousand words required to describe the unfamiliar or technical. c. For continuity, it is recommended that the first level supervisor-interviewee be designated as the guide for the job-site observations.
3. Conduct interviews	a. It is recommended that the first interview be conducted with the first-level supervisor who is considered to be in a better position than the job holders to provide an overview of the job and how the major duties fit together. b. For scheduling purposes, it is recommended that no more than two interviews be conducted per day, each interview lasting no more than three hours.
Notes on selection of interviewees	a. The interviewees are considered subject matter experts by virtue of the fact that they perform the job (in the case of job incumbents) or are responsible for getting the job done (in the case of first-level supervisors). b. The job incumbent to be interviewed should represent the *typical* employee who is knowledgeable about the job (*not* the trainee who is just learning the ropes *or* the outstanding member of the work unit). c. Whenever feasible, the interviewees should be selected with a view towards obtaining an appropriate diversity mix.
4. Conduct second tour of work site	a. The second tour of the work site is designed to clarify, confirm, and otherwise refine the information developed in the interviews. b. As in the initial tour, it is recommended that the same first-level supervisor-interviewee conduct the second walk-through.
5. Consolidate job information	a. The consolidation phase of the job study involves piecing together into one coherent and comprehensive job description the data obtained from several sources—supervisor, job holders, on-site tours, and written materials about the job. b. Past experience indicates that one minute of consolidation is required for every minute of interviewing. For planning purposes, at least five hours should be set aside for the consolidation phase. c. A subject matter expert should be accessible as a resource person to the job analyst during the consolidation phase. The supervisor-interviewee fills this role. d. Check your initial preliminary list of duties and questions—all must be answered or confirmed.
6. Verify job description	a. The verification phase involves bringing all the interviewees together for the purpose of determining if the consolidated job description is accurate and complete. b. The verification process is conducted in a group setting. Typed or legibly written copies of the job description (narrative description of the work setting *and* list of task statements) are distributed to the first-level supervisor and the job incumbent interviewees. c. Line by line, the job analyst goes through the entire job description and makes notes of any omissions, ambiguities, or needed clarifications. d. Collect all materials at the end of the verification meeting.

| EXHIBIT | 4.5 | Typical Data Collected for Job Analysis |

Data Related to Job

Job identification	*Job content*
Title	Tasks and activities
Department in which job is located	Effort (physical, mental, emotional)
Number of people who hold job	Constraints on actions
	Performance criteria
	Critical incidents
	Conflicting demands
	Working conditions
	Roles (e.g., negotiator, monitor, leader)
	Responsibility

Data Related to Employee

Employee characteristics	*Internal relationships*	*External relationships*
Professional/technical knowledge	Boss and other superiors	Suppliers
Manual skills	Peers	Customers
Verbal skills	Subordinates	Regulatory
Written skills		Professional/industry
Quantitative skills		Community
Mechanical skills		Union/employee groups
Conceptual skills		
Managerial skills		
Leadership skills		
Interpersonal skills		

Job Data: Content

This is the heart of job analysis. Job content data involve the elemental tasks or units of work, with emphasis on the purpose of each task. An excerpt from a job analysis questionnaire that collects task data is shown in Exhibit 4.6. The inventory describes the job aspect of "Communication" in terms of actual tasks, for example, "read technical publications" and "consult with co-workers." The inventory takes eight items to cover "obtain technical information" and another seven for "exchange technical information." In fact, the task inventory from which the exhibit is excerpted contains 250 items and covers only systems and analyst jobs. New task-based questions need to be designed for each new set of jobs.

In addition to the emphasis on the task, the other distinguishing characteristic of the inventory in the exhibit is the emphasis on the objective of the task, for example, "read technical publications to keep current on industry" and "consult with co-workers to exchange ideas and techniques." Task data reveal the actual work performed as well as its purpose or outcome.

In Canada, it is very important to collect information relating to pay equity legislation. In particular, thorough information about the skill, effort, responsibility, and working conditions of each job is essential.

Employee Data

Once we have specified the tasks and outcomes, we can look at the kinds of behaviours that will result in the outcomes. Exhibit 4.5 categorizes employee data as employee characteristics, internal relationships, and external relationships. Exhibit 4.7 shows how "Communications" can be

EXHIBIT   4.6   Communications: Task-Based Data

1. Mark the circle in the "Do This" column for tasks that you currently perform.

2. At the end of the task list, write in any unlisted tasks that you currently perform.

3. Rate each task that you perform for relative time spent by marking the appropriate circle in the "Time Spent" column.

   Please use a No. 2 pencil and fill all circles completely.

Time spent in current position

Do This / Very small amount / Much below average / Below average / Slightly below average / About average / Slightly above average / Above average / Much above average / Very large amount

PERFORM COMMUNICATIONS ACTIVITIES		
Obtain technical information		
421. Read technical publications about competitive products.	○	①②③④⑤⑥⑦⑧⑨
422. Read technical publications to keep current on industry.	○	①②③④⑤⑥⑦⑧⑨
423. Attend required, recommended, or job-related courses and/or seminars.	○	①②③④⑤⑥⑦⑧⑨
424. Study existing operating systems/programs to gain/maintain familiarity with them.	○	①②③④⑤⑥⑦⑧⑨
425. Perform literature searches necessary to the development of products.	○	①②③④⑤⑥⑦⑧⑨
426. Communicate with system software group to see how their recent changes impact current projects.	○	①②③④⑤⑥⑦⑧⑨
427. Study and evaluate state-of-the-art techniques to remain competitive and/or lead the field.	○	①②③④⑤⑥⑦⑧⑨
428. Attend industry standards meetings.	○	①②③④⑤⑥⑦⑧⑨
Exchange technical information		
429. Interface with coders to verify that the software design is being implemented as specified.	○	①②③④⑤⑥⑦⑧⑨
430. Consult with co-workers to exchange ideas and techniques.	○	①②③④⑤⑥⑦⑧⑨
431. Consult with members of other technical groups within the company to exchange new ideas and techniques.	○	①②③④⑤⑥⑦⑧⑨
432. Interface with support consultants or organizations to clarify software design or courseware content.	○	①②③④⑤⑥⑦⑧⑨
433. Attend meetings to review project status.	○	①②③④⑤⑥⑦⑧⑨
434. Attend team meetings to review implementation strategies.	○	①②③④⑤⑥⑦⑧⑨
435. Discuss department plans and objectives with manager.	○	①②③④⑤⑥⑦⑧⑨

| **EXHIBIT** | **4.7** | Communications: Behaviour-Based Data (from the Position Analysis Questionnaire) |

Section 4 Relationships with Others
This section deals with different aspects of interaction between people involved in various kinds of work.

Importance to this Job (1)

N Does not apply
1 Very minor
2 Low
3 Average
4 High
5 Extreme

4.1 Communications
Rate the following in terms of how important the activity is to the completion of the job. Some jobs may involve several or all of the items in this section.

4.1.1 Oral (communicating by speaking)

99 _____ Advising (dealing with individuals in order to counsel and/or guide them with regard to problems that may be resolved by legal, financial, scientific, technical, clinical, spiritual, and/or professional principles)

100 _____ Negotiating (dealing with others in order to reach an agreement or solution, for example, labour bargaining, diplomatic relations, etc.)

101 _____ Persuading (dealing with others in order to influence them toward some action or point of view, for example, selling, political campaigning, etc.)

102 _____ Instructing (the teaching of knowledge or skills, in either an informal or a formal manner, to others, for example, a public school teacher, a machinist teaching an apprentice, etc.)

103 _____ Interviewing (conducting interviews directed toward some specific objective, for example, interviewing job applicants, census taking, etc.)

104 _____ Routine information exchange: job related (the giving and/or receiving of *job-related* information of a routine nature, for example, ticket agent, taxicab dispatcher, receptionist, etc.)

105 _____ Nonroutine information exchange (the giving and/or receiving of *job-related* information of a nonroutine or unusual nature, for example, professional committee meetings, engineers discussing new product design, etc.)

106 _____ Public speaking (making speeches or formal presentations before relatively large audiences, for example, political addresses, radio/TV broadcasting, delivering a sermon, etc.)

4.1.2 Written (communicating by written/printed material)

107 _____ Writing (for example, writing or dictating letters, reports, etc., writing copy for ads, writing newspaper articles, etc.: does *not* include transcribing activities described in item 4.3, but only activities in which the incumbent creates the written material)

Source: E. J. McCormick, P. R., Jeanneret, and R. C. Mecham, *Position Analysis Questionnaire*, copyright © 1969 by Purdue Research Foundation, West Lafayette, IN 47907. Reprinted with permission.

described with verbs (e.g., negotiating, persuading). The verbs chosen are related to the employee characteristic being identified (e.g., bargaining skills, interpersonal skills). The rest of the statement helps identify whether the behaviour involves an internal or external relationship.

Position Analysis Questionnaire (PAQ)

a structured job analysis questionnaire used for analyzing jobs on the basis of 194 job elements that describe generic work behaviours

The excerpt in Exhibit 4.7 is from the **Position Analysis Questionnaire (PAQ),** which groups work information into seven basic factors: information input, mental processes, work output, relationships with other persons, job context, other job characteristics, and general dimensions. Similarities and differences among jobs are described in terms of these seven factors, rather than in terms of specific aspects unique to each job.[7] The communications behaviour in this exhibit is part of the "relationships with other persons" factor.

The entire PAQ consists of 194 items. Its developers claim that these items are sufficient to analyze any job. However, you can see from Exhibit 4.7 that the reading level is quite high. Many employees will need help to get through the whole thing.

However appealing it may be to rationalize job analysis as the foundation of all HR decisions, collecting all of this information for so many different purposes is very expensive. In addition, the resulting information may be too generalized for any single purpose, including compensation. If the information is to be used for multiple purposes, the analyst must be sure that it is accurate and sufficient for each use. Trying to be all things to all people often results in being nothing to everyone.

Level of Analysis

The job analysis terms defined in Exhibit 4.3 are arranged in a hierarchy. The level in this hierarchy where an analysis begins may influence whether the work is similar or dissimilar. At the job family level, bookkeepers, tellers, and accounting clerks may be considered similar, yet at the job level, they are very different. An analogy might be looking at two grains of salt under a microscope versus looking at them as part of a serving of french fries. If job data suggest that jobs are similar, then the jobs must be paid equally; if jobs are different, they can be paid differently. In practice, many employers are finding it difficult to justify the time and expense of collecting task level information, particularly for flexible jobs with frequently changing tasks. They may collect only job-level data and emphasize comparisons in the external market in setting wages.

Many managers are increasing their organization's flexibility by adopting broad, generic descriptions that cover a large number of related tasks closer to the job family level in Exhibit 4.3. Two employees working in the same broadly defined job may be doing entirely different sets of related tasks. But for pay purposes, they are doing work of equal value. Employees working in very broadly defined jobs can easily be switched to other tasks that fall within the broad range of the same job, without the bureaucratic burden of making job transfer requests and wage adjustments. Thus, employees can more easily be matched to changes in the workflow. Recruiter, compensation analyst, and training specialist could each be analyzed as a separate, distinct job, or could all be combined more broadly in the job "HR Associate."

Still, a countervailing view deserves consideration. More specific distinctions among jobs represent career paths to employees. Reducing the number of levels in a structure may reduce the opportunity for recognition and advancement. Reducing titles or labelling all employees as "associates" may signal an egalitarian culture. But it also may sacrifice a sense of advancement and opportunity.[8]

■ HOW CAN THE INFORMATION BE COLLECTED?

Conventional Methods

The most common way to collect job information is to ask the people who are doing a job to fill out a questionnaire. Sometimes an analyst will interview the job holders and their supervisors to be sure they understand the questions and that the information is correct. Or the analyst may observe the person at work and take notes on what is being done. Exhibit 4.8 shows part of a job analysis questionnaire. Questions range from "Give an example of a particularly difficult problem that you face in your work. Why does it occur? How often does it occur? What special skills and/ or resources are needed to solve this difficult problem?" to "What is the nature of any contact you have with individuals or companies in countries other than Canada?" These examples are drawn from the Complexity of Duties section of a job analysis questionnaire used by 3M. Other sections of the questionnaire are Skills/Knowledge Applied (19 to choose from), Impact This Job Has on 3M's Business, and Working Conditions. The job analysis questionnaire concludes by asking respondents how well they feel the questionnaire has captured their particular job.

The advantage of conventional questionnaires and interviews is that the involvement of employees increases their understanding of the process. However, the results are only as good as the people involved. If important aspects of a job are omitted, or if the job holders themselves either do not realize or are unable to express the importance of certain aspects of the job, the resulting job descriptions will be faulty. Considering the number of jobs in an organization, it is unrealistic to expect a single analyst to understand all the different types of work and the

| EXHIBIT | 4.8 | 3M's Structured Interview Questionnaire |

I. Job Overview

| **Job Summary** | What is the main purpose of your job? (Why does it exist and what does the work contribute to 3M?)
Examples: To provide secretarial support in our department by performing office and administrative duties.
    To purchase goods and services that meet specifications at the least cost.
    To perform systems analysis involved in the development, installation, and maintenance of computer applications.

Hint: It may help to list the duties first before answering this question. |

| **Duties and Responsibilities** | What are your job's main duties and responsibilities? (These are the major work activities that usually take up a significant amount of your work time and occur regularly as you perform your work.)

In the spaces below, list your job's five most important or most frequent duties. Then, in the boxes, estimate the percentage of the time you spend on each day.
1. | Percentage of Time Spent (Total may be less than but not more than 100%) |

II. Skills/Knowledge Applied

| **Formal Training or Education** | What is the level of formal training/education that is needed to start doing your job?
Example: High School, college diploma in Data Processing, Bachelor of Science in Chemistry.
In some jobs, a combination of education and job-related experience can substitute for academic degrees.
Example: Bachelor's Degree in Accounting or completion of 2 years of general business plus 3–4 years' work   experience in an accounting field. |

| **Experience** | Months: Years: None |

| **Skills/ Competencies** | What important skills, competencies, or abilities are needed to do the work that you do? (Please give examples for each skill that you identify.)
A. Coordinating Skills (such as scheduling activities, organizing/maintaining records)
Are coordinating skills required? ☐Yes ☐No   If yes, give examples of specific skills needed
Example |

III. Complexity of Duties

| **Structure and Variation of Work** | How processes and tasks within your work are determined, and how you do them are important to understanding your work at 3M. Describe the work flow in your job. Think of the major focus of your job or think of the work activities on which you spend the most time.
1. From whom/where (title, not person) do you receive work?
2. What processes or tasks do you perform to complete it? |

| **Problem Solving and Analysis** | 3.
Give an example of a particularly difficult problem that you face in your work.
Why does it occur?
How often does it occur?
What special skills and/or resources are needed to solve this difficult problem? |

VI. General Comments

| **General Comments** | What percentage of your job duties do you feel was captured in this questionnaire?
☐ 0–25%   ☐ 26–50%   ☐ 51–75%   ☐ 76–100%
What aspect of your job was not covered adequately by this questionnaire? |

importance of all job aspects. Different people have different perceptions, which may result in differences in interpretation or emphasis. The whole process is open to bias and favouritism.[9] As a result of this potential subjectivity, as well as the huge amount of time the process takes, conventional methods have given way to more quantitative (and systematic) data collection.

Quantitative Methods

Increasingly, an analyst will direct job holders to a Web site where they complete a questionnaire online. Such an approach is characterized as quantitative job analysis, because the results can be analyzed arithmetically. A quantitative questionnaire typically asks job holders to assess whether each item is or is not part of their job. If it is, they are asked to rate how important it is, and the amount of job time spent on it. The results can be machine scored like a multiple-choice test (except there are no wrong answers), and the results can be used to develop a profile of the job. Exhibit 4.9 shows part of an online job analysis questionnaire used by a United Kingdom consulting firm.[10] Questions are grouped around five compensable factors (discussed in Chapter 5): knowledge, accountability, reasoning, communications, and working conditions. Knowledge is further subcategorized as range of depth, qualifications, experience, occupational skills, management skills, and learning time. Assistance is given in the form of prompting questions and a list of jobs that have answered each question in a similar way. Results can be used to prepare a job profile based on the compensable factors. If more than one person is doing a particular job, results of several people in the job can be compared or averaged to develop the profile. Profiles can be compared across job holders in the same or in different jobs. Exhibit 4.10 is a job profile prepared from the results of the questionnaire used in Exhibit 4.9. Exhibits 4.6 and 4.7 are also excerpts from quantitative questionnaires.

Some consulting firms have developed quantitative inventories they can tailor to the needs of a specific organization or to a specific family of jobs, such as data/information processing jobs. Many organizations find it practical and cost effective to modify these existing inventories rather than develop their own analysis from ground zero. Turning over the analysis to a consulting firm does not mean that the organization and its employees are not involved in the process, both as sources of information and as consumers who want to be sure the results are useful. The advantage of quantitative data collection is that more data can be collected faster. But keep in mind that the results are only as good as the items in the questionnaire, and the conscientiousness of employees who complete them.[11]

EXHIBIT 4.9   Online Job Analysis Questionnaire ───────────────────

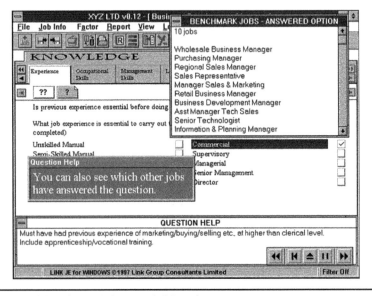

Source: Link Group Consultants, Limited. Used by permission. www.hrlink.co.uk

EXHIBIT | **4.10** | Online Job Profile

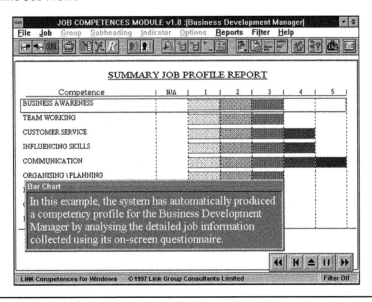

Source: Link Group Consultants, Limited. Used by permission. www.hrlink.co.uk.

Who Collects the Information?

Collecting job analysis information through one-on-one interviews can be a thankless task. No matter how good a job you do, not everyone will be happy with the resulting job descriptions. Although organizations frequently assign the task to a new employee (often justifying the assignment on the grounds that it will help the new employee become familiar with the company's jobs), the analysis is better done by someone thoroughly familiar with the organization and its jobs, and trained in how to do the analysis properly.[12]

Who Provides the Information?

The decision regarding the source of the data (job holders, supervisors, and/or analysts) hinges on how to ensure consistent, accurate, and acceptable data. Expertise about the work resides with the job holders and supervisors; hence, they are the principal sources. For key managerial/professional jobs, supervisors two levels above have also been suggested as valuable sources because they may have a more macro view of the way jobs fit in the overall organization. In other instances, subordinates and employees in other jobs that interface with the job under study also may be involved.

The number of incumbents per job from which to collect data probably varies with the stability of the job, as well as with the ease of collecting the information. An ill-defined or changing job will require either the involvement of more respondents or a more careful selection of respondents. Obviously, the more people involved, the more time-consuming and expensive the process (although computerization mitigates these objections).

What about Discrepancies?

What happens if the supervisor and the employees present different pictures of the job? Although in theory, supervisors ought to know the jobs well, they may not, particularly if the jobs are changing or ill-defined. People actually working in a job may change it, perhaps by finding ways to do things more efficiently, or perhaps because they may not realize that certain tasks are supposed to be part of their job. The crossfire from differing perspectives on the nature of a job indicates why conducting a job analysis can be a dangerous activity for a brand-new HR employee.

3M had an interesting problem when it collected job information from a group of engineers. The engineers listed a number of responsibilities they viewed as part of their jobs; however, the manager realized that those responsibilities actually belonged to a higher level of work. The engineers had enlarged their jobs beyond what they were being paid to do. No one wanted to tell this highly productive group of employees to throttle back and slack off, so instead 3M looked for ways to recognize and reward them.

What should the manager do if employees and their supervisors do not agree on what is part of the job? The answer is: Collect more data. Enough data are required to ensure consistent, accurate, and acceptable results. In general, the more unusual the job, the more sources of data required. Discussing discrepancies with everyone, then asking both employees and supervisors to sign off on the proposed analysis will help ensure agreement, or at least understanding, of the results.

Top Management (and Union) Support Is Critical   In addition to involvement by analysts, job holders, and their supervisors, support of top management and unions is essential. They must be alerted to the cost of a thorough job analysis, its time-consuming nature, and the fact that changes may result after it is completed. For example, jobs may be combined or pay rates adjusted. If top management and unions are not willing to carry through, or at least to seriously weigh, any changes suggested by the job analysis, the process probably will not be worth the bother and expense.

JOB DESCRIPTIONS SUMMARIZE THE DATA

job description

written summary of a job, including responsibilities, qualifications, and relationships

So, now the job information has been collected, maybe even organized. But it still must be summarized in a way that will be useful for HR decisions, including job evaluation (Chapter 5). That summary of the job is the **job description**. The job description provides a word picture of the job. Exhibit 4.11 is part of a job description for a registered nurse. Trace the connection between different parts of the description and the job analysis data collected. The job is identified by title and its relationships to other jobs. The relationships demonstrate where the job fits into the organization—whom is supervised by this job holder, who supervises this job holder, and the nature of any internal and external relationships. A job summary consists of a short paragraph that provides an overview of the job. The section on essential responsibilities elaborates on the summary. It includes the tasks. Related tasks may be grouped into task dimensions.

job specifications

qualifications required to be hired for a job; may be included in the job description

This particular job description also includes very specific standards for judging whether an essential responsibility has been met (for example, "Provides a written assessment of patient within one hour of admission and at least once a shift"). A final section lists the qualifications necessary to be hired for the job. These are the **job specifications** that can be used as a basis for hiring—the knowledge, skills, and abilities required to adequately perform the tasks. But keep in mind that the summary must be relevant to pay decisions and therefore must focus on similarities and differences in content.

Describing Managerial/Professional Jobs

In addition to defining and describing jobs, descriptions of managerial/professional jobs often include more detailed information about the nature of the job, its scope, and accountability. One challenge is that an individual manager may influence the job content.[13] This is a classic example of how job-based and person-based approaches blend in practice, even though the distinctions are easy to make in a textbook. Professional/managerial job descriptions must capture the relationship between the job, the person performing it, and the organization objectives—how the job fits

| **EXHIBIT** | **4.11** | Contemporary Job Description for Registered Nurse |

Job Title
Registered Nurse

Job Summary
Accountable for the complete spectrum of patient care from admission through transfer or discharge through the nursing process of assessment, planning, implementation, and evaluation. Each R.N. has primary authority to fulfill responsibility of the nursing process on the assigned shift and for projecting future needs of the patient/family. Directs and guides patient teaching and activities for ancillary personnel while maintaining standard of professional nursing.

Relationships
Reports to: Head Nurse or Charge Nurse.
Supervises: Responsible for the care delivered by L.P.N.'s, nursing assistants, orderlies, and transcribers.
Works with: Ancillary Care Departments.
External relationships: Physicians, patients, patients' families.

Qualifications
Education: Graduate of an accredited school of nursing.
Work experience: Critical care requires one year of recent medical/surgical experience (special care nursing preferred), medical/surgical experience (new graduates may be considered for noncharge positions).
Licence or registration requirements: Current R.N. licence or permit in the Province of Alberta.

Physical requirements: A. Ability to bend, reach, or assist to transfer up to 23 kilos.
B. Ability to stand and/or walk 80 percent of 8-hour shift.
C. Visual and hearing acuity to perform job-related functions.

Essential Responsibilities
1. Assess physical, emotional, and psycho-social dimensions of patients.
   Standard: Provides a written assessment of patient within one hour of admission and at least once a shift. Communicates this assessment to other patient care providers in accordance with hospital policies.

2. Formulates a written plan of care for patients from admission through discharge.
   Standard: Develops short-term and long-term goals within 24 hours of admission. Reviews and updates care plans each shift based on ongoing assessment.

3. Implements plan of care.
   Standard: Demonstrates skill in performing common nursing procedures in accordance with but not limited to the established written R.N. skills inventory specific to assigned area. Completes patient care activities in an organized and timely fashion, reassessing priorities appropriately.

Note: Additional responsibilities omitted from exhibit.

into the organization, the results expected, and what the person performing it brings to the job. Someone with strong information systems and computer expertise performing the compensation manager's job will probably shape it differently, based on this expertise, than someone with strong negotiation and/or counselling expertise. Exhibit 4.12 excerpts this scope and accountability information for a nurse manager. Rather than emphasizing the tasks to be done, this description focuses on the responsibilities (e.g., "responsible for the coordination, direction, implementation, evaluation and management of personnel and services; provides leadership; participates in strategic planning and defining future direction").

EXHIBIT 4.12 Job Description for a Manager ──────────────────────

Title: Nurse Manager

Department: ICU

Date Posted:

Status: Open

Position Description:
Under the direction of the Vice President of Patient Care Services and Directors of Patient Care Services, the Nurse Manager assumes 24-hour accountability and responsibility for the operations of defined patient specialty services. The Nurse Manager is administratively responsible for the coordination, direction, implementation, evaluation, and management of human resources and services. The Nurse Manager provides leadership in a manner consistent with the corporate mission, values, and philosophy and adheres to policies and procedures established by Saint Joseph's Hospital and the Division of Patient Care Services. The Nurse Manager participates in strategic planning and defining future direction for the assigned areas of responsibility and the organization.

Qualification:
Education: Graduate of accredited school of nursing. A bachelor's degree in Nursing or related field required. Master's degree preferred. Current licence in the Province of Nova Scotia as a Registered Nurse. Experience: A minimum of three year's clinical nursing is required. Minimum of two year's management experience or equivalent preferred.

Verify the Description

The final step in the job analysis process is to verify the accuracy of the resulting job descriptions (Step 6 in Exhibit 4.4). Verification often involves the interviewees as well as their supervisors to determine whether the proposed job description is accurate and complete. The description is discussed, line by line, with the analyst, taking note of any omissions, ambiguities, or needed clarifications (often an excruciating and thankless task). Outside sources of job descriptions, such as the National Occupational Classification profiled in the .Net Worth box can be used for reference.

It would have been interesting to hear the discussion between our nurse from 100 years ago, whose job is described in Exhibit 4.13, and her supervisor. The job description paints a vivid picture of expectations at that time. It is unlikely that she would have had much opportunity for input 100 years ago.

■ JUDGING JOB ANALYSIS

Beyond beliefs about its usefulness, or lack thereof, for satisfying both employees and employers, there are several ways to judge job analysis.

Reliability

If something is measured tomorrow and the results are the same as those from today, the measurement is considered to be reliable. This doesn't mean it is right—only that repeated measures give the same result. **Reliability** is a measure of the consistency of results if the same measure is repeated many times.

reliability
consistency of results from repeated applications of a measure

Research findings on employee and supervisor agreement on the reliability of job analysis information are mixed. For instance, experience may change an employee's perception of a job—he/she may have found new ways to do it or may have added new tasks to it. The supervisor may not realize the extent of change. In such cases, the job the employee is actually doing may

| **EXHIBIT** | **4.13** | Job Description for Nurse 100 Years Ago |

In addition to caring for your 50 patients, each nurse will follow these regulations:

1. Daily sweep and mop the floors of your ward, dust the patient's furniture and window sills.
2. Maintain an even temperature in your ward by bringing in a scuttle of coal for the day's business.
3. Light is important to observe the patient's condition. Therefore, each day, fill kerosene lamps, clean chimneys, and trim wicks. Wash the windows once a week.
4. The nurse's notes are important in aiding the physician's work. Make your pens carefully; you may whittle nibs to your individual taste.
5. Each nurse on the day duty will report every day at 7 a.m. and leave at 8 p.m. except on the Sabbath, on which day you will be off from 12:00 noon to 2:00 p.m.
6. Graduate nurses in good standing with the director of nurses will be given an evening off each week for courting purposes, or two evenings a week if you go regularly to church.
7. Each nurse should lay aside from each pay day a goodly sum of her earnings for her benefits during her declining years, so that she will not become a burden. For example, if you earn $30 a month you should set aside $15.
8. Any nurse who smokes, uses liquor in any form, gets her hair done at a beauty shop, or frequents dance halls will give the director good reason to suspect her worth, intentions, and integrity.
9. The nurse who performs her labours and serves her patients and doctors faithfully and without fault for a period of five years will be given an increase by the hospital administration of five cents a day, provided there are no hospital debts that are outstanding.

not be the same as the job originally assigned by the supervisor. Obviously, the way to increase reliability in a job analysis is to reduce the sources of variance. Quantitative job analysis helps reduce variance. But we need to be sure that we do not eliminate the richness or the nuances of a job while eliminating the variance.

Validity

validity
accuracy of a measure

Does the analysis create an accurate portrait of the work? There is almost no way of showing statistically the extent to which an analysis is accurate, particularly for complex jobs. Consequently, **validity** examines convergence of results among different sources of data and methods. If several job incumbents respond in similar ways to questionnaires, then it is considered more likely that the information given is valid. However, a sign-off on the results does not guarantee validity. It may only mean everyone was sick to death of the process and wanted to get rid of the analyst so that they could get back to work.

Acceptability

If job holders and managers are dissatisfied with the initial data collected or with the process, they are not likely to buy into either the resulting job structure or the pay rates that eventually are attached to that structure. An analyst collecting information through one-on-one interviews or observation is not always accepted because of the potential for subjectivity and favouritism. However, more quantitative approaches also may run into difficulty, especially if they give in to the temptation to try to collect too much information for too many purposes.

Usefulness

Usefulness refers to the usefulness of the information collected. For pay purposes, job analysis provides work-related information to help determine how much to pay for a job—it helps determine

.NET WORTH

National Occupational Classification

In Canada, many companies turn to the federal government's National Occupational Classification (NOC) for reference when preparing job descriptions. The NOC is an excellent source of standardized job information, based on systematic field research by Human Resources and Skills Development Canada. It contains comprehensive descriptions and qualifications for over 30,000 occupations. NOC information is available online at www5.hrsdc.gc.ca/NOC/English/NOC/2006/Welcome.aspx.

The NOC classifies occupations in Major Groups based on two key dimensions: skill level and skill type. The Major Groups, which are identified by two-digit numbers, are then broken down further into Minor Groups, with a third digit added, and Unit Groups, at which a fourth digit is added. For example, Major Group 12: Skilled Administrative and Business Occupations includes Minor Group 122: Administrative and Regulatory Occupations, which includes Unit Group 1223: Personnel and Recruitment Officers.

1223 Personnel and Recruitment Officers

Personnel and recruitment officers identify and advertise job vacancies, recruit candidates, and assist in the selection and reassignment of employees. They are employed throughout the private and public sectors. Personnel and recruitment officers perform some or all of the following duties:

- Identify current and prospective staffing requirements, prepare and post notices and advertisements, and collect and screen applications

- Advise job applicants on employment requirements and on terms and conditions of employment

- Review candidate inventories and contact potential applicants to arrange interviews and arrange transfers, redeployment and placement of personnel

- Recruit graduates of colleges, universities and other educational institutions

- Co-ordinate and participate in selection and examination boards to evaluate candidates

- Notify applicants of results of selection process and prepare job offers

- Advise managers and employees on staffing policies and procedures

- Organize and administer staff consultation and grievance procedures

- Negotiate settlements of appeals and disputes and co-ordinate termination of employment process

- Determine eligibility to entitlements, arrange staff training and provide information or services such as employee assistance, counselling and recognition programs

- May supervise personnel clerks performing filing and record-keeping duties

Source: Human Resources and Social Development Canada, National Occupation Classification. Reproduced with the permission of the Minister of Public Works and Government Services Canada, 2009.

whether the job is similar or dissimilar to other jobs. If job analysis does this in a reliable, valid, and acceptable way, then the technique is of practical use.[14]

As we have noted, some see job analysis information as useful for multiple purposes, such as hiring and training. But multiple purposes may require more information than is required to assess pay. The practical utility of all-encompassing quantitative job analysis plans, with their complex procedures and analysis, remains in doubt. Some advocates are so taken with their statistics and computers that they ignore the role that human judgment must continue to play in job analysis. A statement made 25 years ago still holds today: "I wish to emphasize the central role played in all these procedures by human judgment. I know of no methodology, statistical technique or objective measurements that can negate the importance of, nor supplement, rational judgment."[15]

A Judgment Call

In the face of all the difficulties, time, expense, and dissatisfaction, why on earth would you as a manager recommend that your employer bother with job analysis? Because work-related information is needed to determine pay, and differences in work determine pay differences. There is no satisfactory substitute that can ensure that the resulting pay structure will be work related or will provide reliable, accurate data to make and explain pay decisions.

If work information is required, then the real issue should be: How much detail is needed to make these pay decisions? The answer is: enough to help set individual employees' pay, encourage continuous learning, increase the experience and skill of the workforce, and minimize the risk of pay-related grievances. The risk of omitting this detail is dissatisfied employees who drive away customers with their poor service, complain about management's inability to justify their decisions, or file lawsuits. The response to inadequate analysis should not be to dump the analysis; rather, the response should be to do more useful analysis.

CONCLUSION

Encouraging employee behaviours that help achieve an organization's objectives and fostering a sense of fairness among employees are two hallmarks of a useful internal pay structure. One of the first strategic pay decisions is how much to align a pay structure internally as opposed to aligning it to external market forces. Do not be misled. The issue is not achieving internal alignment versus alignment with external market forces. Both are required. Rather, the strategic decision focuses on sustaining the optimal balance of internally aligned and externally responsive pay structures that help the organization achieve its mission. This section of the book is about one of the first decisions you will face in designing pay systems: how much to emphasize pay structures that are internally aligned with the work performed, the organization's structure, and its strategies. Whatever the choice, it needs to support (and be supported by) the organization's overall human resource strategy.

Next, managers must decide whether job and/or individual employee characteristics will be the basic unit of analysis supporting the pay structure. This is followed by deciding what data will be collected, what method(s) will be used to collect them, and who should be involved in the process.

A key test of an effective and fair pay structure is acceptance of results by managers and employees. The best way to ensure acceptance of job analysis results is to involve employees as well as supervisors in the process. At a minimum, all employees should be informed of the purposes and progress of the activity.

Although almost everyone agrees about the importance of job analysis, that does not mean that everyone does it. Unfortunately, job analysis can be tedious and time-consuming. Often, the job is given to newly hired compensation analysts, ostensibly to help them learn about the organization, but there may also be a hint of "rite of passage" in such assignments.

Alternatives to job-based structures, such as skill-based or competency-based systems, are being experimented with in many firms. The premise is that basing structures on these other criteria will encourage employees to become more flexible, and fewer workers will be required for the same level of output. But as experience increases with these alternatives, managers are discovering that they can be as time-consuming and bureaucratic as job analysis. Bear in mind that job content remains the conventional criterion for structures.

CHAPTER SUMMARY

1. Job analysis is the systematic process of collecting information about the nature of specific jobs. Job analysis data are used in virtually every major HR function, including recruiting and selection, training, compensation, and so on.
2. There is a six-step approach to job analysis: develop preliminary job information; conduct initial tour of work site; conduct interviews; conduct second tour of work site; consolidate job information; and verify job description.
3. The information that must be collected for job analysis includes job identification data, job content data, and data on qualifications necessary to do the job. Job content data are the heart of job analysis, and include the tasks involved, their purpose, reporting relationships, working conditions, and other specific job information. Conventional methods of collecting job analysis data such as questionnaires and interviews are being replaced by online questionnaires because they are more objective and less time-consuming.
4. Job descriptions provide a written summary of a job, including responsibilities, qualifications, and relationships. Job specifications are the qualifications required to be hired for a job, and may be included in the job description.
5. The benefit of traditional job analysis is that it provides the basis for defensible job-related decisions, and establishes a foundation for career paths. However, it is sometimes considered too rigid for today's more flexible organizations with fluid work assignments. Job analysis can be judged based on reliability (consistency) of the information obtained, validity (accuracy) of the information obtained, acceptability of the data and the process by employees and managers, and practicality (usefulness) of the information collected.

KEY TERMS

REVIEW QUESTIONS

1. What are the two critical uses of job analysis for compensation decisions?
2. Describe the major decisions involved in job analysis.
3. Distinguish between task and behavioural data.
4. How should discrepancies between job analysis information provided by employees and supervisors be resolved?

EXPERIENTIAL EXERCISES

1. Talk to several managers and find one who claims to have never heard of job analysis. Ask the manager how job descriptions (if there are any) in the organization are developed. Ask whether there are any problems because of jobs that overlap, problems with performance evaluations, and problems with concerns about pay fairness. How might these problems be related to the lack of job analysis information?

2. a) Think of a specific job you presently hold or have held in the past (including a part-time job or volunteer work). Use the information in this chapter to develop a job analysis questionnaire that you believe would adequately capture all relevant information about that job. Then complete the questionnaire for your specific job.

   b) Pick a teammate (or the instructor will assign one) and exchange questionnaires with your teammate.

   c) Write a job description for your teammate's job. Does the questionnaire give you sufficient information? Is there additional information that would be helpful?

   d) Exchange descriptions. Critique the job description written by your teammate. Does it adequately capture all the important job aspects? Does it indicate which aspects are most important?

WEB EXERCISE

Job Analysis and Online Job Postings

The number of online job boards has been expanding exponentially. Many companies post a sample of job openings on their Web sites. Compare the job postings from Workopolis.com, Monster.ca, and several companies. How complete is the job description included with the posting? Are job titles specific or generic? Can you get any sense of a company's culture from its job postings?

CASE

The Customer Service Agent

Read the following article on a day in the work life of Bill Ryan. Then write a job description for the job of customer service agent. Use the exhibits in this chapter to guide you in deciding what information in the story is relevant for job analysis.

1. Does the day diary include sufficient information?
2. Identify the specific information in the article that you found useful.
3. What additional information do you require? How would the information help you?

Pick a teammate (or the instructor will assign one) and exchange job descriptions with your teammate.

1. How similar/different are the two descriptions? You and your teammate started with exactly the same information. What might explain any differences?
2. What process would you go through to understand and minimize the differences?
3. What are some of the relational returns of the job?

Bill Ryan often deals with difficult people. It's what he gets paid for. He's one of 30 customer service agents at Half.com, an online marketplace owned by eBay Inc., the Internet auction company. Like eBay, Half.com attempts to match buyers and sellers in a vast flea market featuring millions of products ranging from trading cards to camcorders. But unlike eBay, there's no bidding. Half.com lists items only at a fixed price. If you see something you like, pay the price and it's yours.

The other big difference from eBay is that for most products listed on Half.com, there's no way for buyers and sellers to interact directly. Usually there's no need to. To make a purchase, buyers use their credit cards or chequing accounts to pay Half.com, which then automatically credits the amount to the seller's card or account, minus a transaction fee. Once the payment is made, the seller ships the product.

Despite a well-oiled system, however, questions arise. Things can go wrong. A purchased item doesn't arrive, or isn't in the condition the buyer expected. Or maybe an interesting product is listed but its description isn't clear. And that's where Ryan and his colleagues come in, handling the buckets of e-mail and intermittent phone calls from curious, addled, and upset users. They pass information between buyers and sellers, answer questions, and resolve the occasional dispute. Half.com says that fewer than 1 percent of the site's transactions require customer service involvement. But with more than 15 million items for sale—well, you do the math.

In fact, the customer service department receives about 1,500 to 2,000 e-mails per day, of which nearly a third are complaints about transactions. The rest are mostly questions about the goods and how the site works. Ryan himself on a typical day fields between 60 and 100 e-mails and half a dozen phone calls. The calls are the most stressful. "People panic and they want answers," says Ryan. "If they are calling, they're not happy."

For Half.com—as well as for most other e-commerce companies—customer service agents like Ryan are the crucial link between the faceless Web site and the consumer. And how they deal with the public can make or break a business. As Half.com's vice president for operations says, "It costs too much to get a new customer only to fumble the relationship away." Half.com won't discuss salaries, but Ryan and his colleagues, who are split into two shifts covering 8 a.m. to midnight, seven days a week, say they're satisfied with their wages, which include quarterly bonuses.

What he likes about his work, Ryan says, is the kind of customer problem that requires research and deep digging to find the resolution. What he sometimes doesn't like about his work are the routine questions that generate stock responses. Here's a day in Ryan's work life:

The Answer Man

8:00 a.m.: Ryan strolls into the Half.com office in Lethbridge, Alberta, a short drive from his home. The company's single-storey grey building is a former tire factory in this Colonial-era industrial town in the south of Alberta. Ryan works in a low-slung black cubicle toward the back of the office, his space sparsely decorated. The atmosphere at Half.com is decidedly young and casual. Jeans are the uniform. Ryan certainly fits in, although at 32 he's a few years older than most of his cubicle mates.

He started doing strictly customer service, answering customer e-mails. Now he also does what the company calls "trust and safety work": investigating fraud and looking for things on the site that are "funky." For instance, when Half.com receives a complaint from a buyer about a seller, it's Bill Ryan's job to contact both parties and make sure there is no fraud occurring.

This day, because the site has received a high volume of e-mails, he's on regular customer service duty. After checking the few internal e-mail messages he receives each day, he gets right to work. Ryan downloads his first batch of 10 e-mails for the day. He says it usually takes him about an hour to get through 10 messages.

8:10 a.m.: The first e-mail is from a woman interested in buying back an audio book on CD that she saw listed on the site. She wants to know whether the CD will work on her DVD player. But because she doesn't specify the exact listing, Ryan is stuck. He can't search for it among all the listings or contact the seller. The best he can do is suggest that she send him an item number so that he can contact the seller with her question.

8:15 a.m.: The next e-mail comes from a user who sold the Diana Krall CD, "When I Look in Your Eyes," but lost the buyer's shipping information. The seller is concerned that a delay in her shipment will give the buyer reason to give her a negative rating on the site. After each purchase is made, the buyer gets a chance to rate the seller's performance on a scale from 1 to 5—"poor" to "excellent." Every rating sellers collect is displayed along with their user name next to subsequent items they list. Just one negative rating can ruin a seller's reputation, depending on how many sales he or she has made overall.

Ryan tracks down the details on this particular transaction in the Half.com user database. He identifies the buyer and writes an e-mail to explain that the seller lost the shipping address and "wants to let you know they are sorry for the inconvenience." He then e-mails the buyer's shipping address to the seller.

Ryan says he doesn't find the e-mails tedious. "There is such a variety of topics to respond to," he says. "I never get 50 of the same questions in a row." But a few e-mails later, he shrugs with disapproval. The user's question could easily have been answered by going to the help section of the Web site: "Do I include shipping in the sale price or is it added later?"

Says Ryan, "It's a general question. I like the detailed research questions." He pastes in an answer from a database of stock responses the customer service team has put together. He then tacks onto the end of the e-mail a salutation that he draws from a list of suggested message closers provided by Half.com. The list, the company says, makes it easier for the agents to write so many e-mails. For this message, Ryan chooses, "It was my pleasure to assist you."

Got Juice

9:30 a.m.: After answering a few more messages, it's time for a coffee break. Ryan says he drinks two cups of coffee a day, a habit he picked up since starting at Half.com. "A year ago I wouldn't have touched the stuff," he says. He heads to the kitchen, which is just down the hall from his desk. The well-lit room is stocked with free cappuccino, juice, pop, cereal, cookies, and other munchies. The cafeteria also doubles as a lounge, with a satellite television playing TSN, a Foosball table, and a ping-pong table. This early in the morning, however, most people are interested in the coffee.

9:48 a.m.: An e-mail arrives from a Half.com colleague in charge of the stock answer database. He writes that a response Ryan submitted on how users can sign up for direct deposit—linking their Half.com transactions with their chequing account—would be included in the database. "There are so many things we don't have responses to," Ryan says. "It makes everyone's life easier to have the database."

10:00 a.m.: The first 10 e-mails are done. Ryan downloads 10 more. One is from a father who several days earlier ordered the latest Sony PlayStation for his son's birthday and is concerned because it hasn't arrived yet. Half.com's policy is that if a buyer hasn't received an item within 30 days of purchase, he or she can lodge an official complaint. The PlayStation seller is thus a long way from the delivery deadline. Nevertheless, as a courtesy, Ryan sends the seller and e-mail asking whether he can provide a shipping date and tracking number that Ryan can pass on to the restless father.

Half.com believes that help like this—beyond the requirements of its own rules—separates its customer service approach from that of other companies. When the company was starting out, says training supervisor Ed Miller, customer service tried to respond to as many messages as it could, as fast as possible. What the company learned, however, is the "customers don't mind if you take a little more time to answer their specific question." Instead of just firing off e-mails, Half.com now sees it as important to personalize each message. Even with the personalization, Half.com says it responds to most messages within 24 hours. Communications with customers have a consistent and pleasant tone. E-mail messages conform to the "grandmother rule." Each message should "make sense to my grandmother."

10:10 a.m.: Washroom break.

10:15 a.m.: "All right," Ryan says eagerly, returning to his desk. He cracks his knuckles and starts typing. A buyer who purchased a video game two months ago but never received it writes to thank Half.com for "hounding" the seller to send him the item. But he wants a refund. Ryan verifies the buyer's version of events in Half.com's records, then refunds the buyer's money and charges the seller's account for the amount of the sale. Ryan sends e-mails to both parties informing them of his action. Half.com's rules say that when an official complaint has been lodged, the other party has five days in which to respond. In this case, the seller didn't respond, so the buyer won the dispute by default.

10:25 a.m.: Snack time. Ryan breaks into a high-energy Balance bar—a little nourishment to get him ready for what comes next.

Wrecking Crew

10:30 a.m.: Time to knock down some walls. Lively human resources worker Alicia Di Ciacco invites Ryan and his colleagues to pick up sledgehammers and knock through a wall at the end of the office. Half.com's staff has doubled in the past year, and the company is expanding into adjacent space in the old tire factory. Everyone in the office takes turns whacking at the wall. Some of the younger males dish out screams of "I'm not going to take it anymore!" and "Where's the Pink Floyd?"—a reference to the 1970s rock album "The Wall" by Pink Floyd.

Ryan eats up the office energy. "It's exciting to work here," he says. "We're growing. We had the second launch of the site. (Half.com expanded the product line in April.) We're doing construction. It's good to come to work when the company is doing well."

11:15 a.m.: Finished with a batch of 10 e-mails, Ryan downloads 10 more, including two separate queries from customers who can't redeem special introductory coupons Half.com offers to new users.

11:47 a.m.: Ryan gets an e-mail from a seller responding to a message from Half.com. A potential buyer has asked Half.com whether the seller's 75-cent copy of Carolyn Davidson's Harlequin romance *The Midwife* is a paperback or hardcover. Half.com forwarded the question to the seller, who now is writing back to say it's a paperback. Ryan sends two e-mails: one to the buyer, answering his question, and one to the seller, thanking him for the information.

12:10 p.m.: Ryan eats his turkey wrap in the company cafeteria with some colleagues and heads back to his desk by 1 p.m.

1:06 p.m.: E-mail from a user who can't find the new Stephen King novel on Half.com. The site is supposed to list all new books from major publishers, even if no one is selling them. That way, if a user is interested, he or she can put it on a wish list and the site will automatically e-mail him or her when a copy has been posted for sale. Ryan searches for the book meticulously, checking by title, author, and publisher's ISBN number. Once he's sure the book isn't listed, he e-mails Matt Walsh, who is in charge of fixing catalogue errors. Ryan then e-mails the user and instructs him to check back at the site soon.

1:21 p.m.: First phone call of the day. Because Half.com prefers to conduct customer service on e-mail, to keep its costs down, it doesn't display its phone number on its Web site. Still, persistent users get the number through directory assistance or other sources. This caller, an agitated buyer of the video *Valley Girl,* a 1983 comedy starring Nicolas Cage, says she received a damaged tape. She has lodged an official complaint against the seller on the Web site, but the seller hasn't responded. Ryan tells her that the five days the seller has to respond aren't up yet. He assures her that if the seller doesn't respond within the allotted time, he will refund her money and charge the seller's account. Until then, there's nothing Ryan can do except comfort the caller with apologies and explanations.

In the event that the seller disputes the buyer's claim about the tape, Half.com is still likely to grant a refund, especially on such an inexpensive item. Half.com makes it clear, however, that its customer service team keeps a close watch on users' complaints, looking out for fraudulent refund requests. If Half.com suspects foul play, it doesn't grant refunds so easily.

2:02 p.m.: A seller of the video *I Know What You Did Last Summer* got the package returned, marked address unknown. Ryan looks up the buyer's information in the user database and e-mails him, asking for an updated address to forward to the seller. He then e-mails the seller, telling him the address should be on its way shortly.

2:21 p.m.: Ryan downloads 10 more e-mails.

Home Stretch

2:30 p.m.: The day is starting to get long, at least to an observer. But Ryan says sitting still all day doesn't cramp his style. "Sometimes it's tough to work at a desk, but it doesn't really bother me," he says. "I work out after work, and that really loosens things up."

3:00 p.m.: Washroom break.

3:15 p.m.: With the clock ticking toward quitting time, Ryan works on finishing his last batch of e-mails. It's more of the same: a user unsure how Half.com works; a seller who wants to list a 1976 edition of *The Grapes of Wrath* but can't figure out where to put it on the site; a buyer who wants a book shipped second-day air, even though the order was already placed.

3:30 p.m.: A call from a buyer interrupts Ryan's streak of dispensing e-mails. The buyer felt that the quality of a book she bought was not up to snuff. The book, a $2 copy of Danielle Steel's *Secrets* apparently had a torn cover. The buyer is upset, but Ryan remains calm, calling on skills he learned in a one-day seminar called "Dealing With Difficult People." In the class, which he took before coming to Half.com, he learned to paraphrase what the customer is saying to make sure he understands the complaint. Ryan also takes care to speak clearly with a strong sense of empathy. At one point he says, "I understand your frustration." When he explains that the buyer will have to wait some time for a final resolution of the matter, he makes sure to preface it with a heartfelt "I'm sorry to let you know..." An observer listening to Ryan gets the sense that he is not acting.

"If you don't understand what they are saying, then you have a problem," he says. Though he can't satisfy this customer then and there, he promises to talk to his supervisor and to call her back tomorrow with more information.

4:00 p.m.: The day is done. Ryan finishes his last e-mail, closes up his desk, and heads home. A new shift of workers picks up where Ryan left off, toiling from 4 p.m. to midnight. When they finish, the customer service staff in eBay's facility in Salt Lake City will take over. Tomorrow, Ryan will be back on duty at 8 a.m., downloading his first 10 e-mails.

Source: Alex Frangos, *The Wall Street Journal*, July 16, 2001.

Visit the Online Learning Centre at

www.mcgrawhill.ca/olc/milkovich

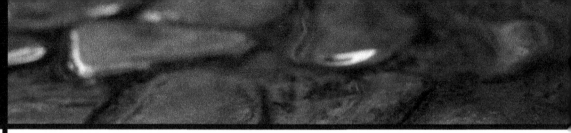

CHAPTER 5

EVALUATING WORK: JOB EVALUATION

LEARNING OUTCOMES

- Define job evaluation and explain the different perspectives regarding this activity.
- Describe the ranking method of job evaluation and explain two specific methods of ranking.
- Discuss the classification method of job evaluation and how benchmark jobs are used in this method.
- Explain the six steps involved in the point method of job evaluation and describe the three common characteristics of point plans.
- Discuss who should be involved in job evaluation.

How does any organization go about valuing work? At a supermarket, there are many types of work: store manager, produce manager, front-end manager, deli workers, butchers, stock clerks, check-out people, bakers—the list is long, and the work surprisingly diverse. Specifically, what techniques are used to value work, and would the techniques really matter?

This chapter and the next discuss techniques used to value work. Both chapters focus on the "how to"—the specific steps involved. Job evaluation techniques are discussed in this chapter; person-based techniques, both skill-based and competency-based, are discussed in Chapter 6. The objective of all the techniques is an internally aligned pay structure. Ultimately, the pay structure helps the organization sustain its competitive advantage by influencing employee behaviours.

■ JOB-BASED STRUCTURES: JOB EVALUATION

job structure

hierarchy of all jobs based on value to the organization; provides the basis for the pay structure

job evaluation

the process of systematically determining the relative worth of jobs to create a job structure for the organization

Exhibit 5.1 is an elaboration of Exhibit 4.1 in the previous chapter. It describes the process of building a job structure and the techniques for building a job-based structure. Job analysis and job descriptions (Chapter 4) collected and summarized work information. In this chapter, the focus is on how to determine what to value in the jobs, how to quantify that value, and how to translate that value into a **job structure**. **Job evaluation** is the process of determining and quantifying value. The potential to blend internal forces and external market forces is both a strength and a challenge for job evaluation.

Exhibit 5.2 shows how job evaluation fits into the process of determining the internal structure. The process begins with a job analysis, in which information on jobs is collected, and then job descriptions summarize this information and serve as input for the evaluation. The exhibit calls out some of the major decisions in the job evaluation process.

EXHIBIT 5.1 Many Ways to Create Internal Structure ——————————

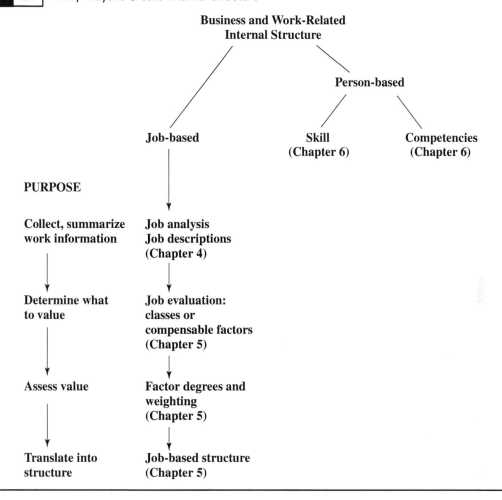

Business and Work-Related
Internal Structure

Person-based

Job-based

Skill
(Chapter 6)

Competencies
(Chapter 6)

PURPOSE

Collect, summarize
work information

Determine what
to value

Assess value

Translate into
structure

Job analysis
Job descriptions
(Chapter 4)

Job evaluation:
classes or
compensable factors
(Chapter 5)

Factor degrees and
weighting
(Chapter 5)

Job-based structure
(Chapter 5)

■ DEFINING JOB EVALUATION: CONTENT, VALUE, AND EXTERNAL MARKET LINKS

Job Content and Job Value

Perspectives differ on whether job evaluation is based on job content or job value. A structure based on job content refers to the skills required for the job, its duties, and its responsibilities. A structure based on job value refers to the relative contribution of the skills, duties, and responsibilities of a job to the organization's goals. But can this structure translate directly into pay rates, without regard to the external market, government regulations, or any individual negotiation process? Most people think not. Recall that internal alignment is just one of the building blocks of the pay model. Job characteristics matter, but they are not the only basis for pay. Job value may also include its value in the external market and/or its relationship to some other set of rates that has been agreed upon through collective bargaining or other negotiation process or to government legislation (minimum wage).

Not only may the content be described and valued differently by different observers, but the value added by the same work may be more or less in one organization than in another. It was observed in Chapter 3 that the value added to a firm by a compensation specialist whose earnings are generated through sales of manufactured goods or engineering expertise may differ from the value

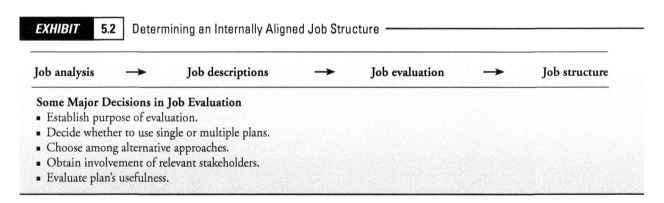

EXHIBIT 5.2   Determining an Internally Aligned Job Structure

Job analysis → Job descriptions → Job evaluation → Job structure

Some Major Decisions in Job Evaluation
- Establish purpose of evaluation.
- Decide whether to use single or multiple plans.
- Choose among alternative approaches.
- Obtain involvement of relevant stakeholders.
- Evaluate plan's usefulness.

added by a specialist to a consulting firm whose revenues come through the sale of compensation expertise. So, although internal job value (contributions to organization objectives) may be equivalent, external market value may differ. There is not a one-to-one correspondence with pay rates.

Linking Content with the External Market

Some see job evaluation as a process that links job content with external market rates. Aspects of job content (e.g., skills required and customer contacts) take on value based on their relationship to market wages. Because willingness to work more closely with customers or higher skill levels usually command higher wages in the labour market, the nature of customer contacts and skill level become useful criteria for establishing differences between jobs. If some aspect of job content, such as working conditions, is not related to wages paid in the external labour market, then that aspect is excluded in the job evaluation. According to this perspective, the value of job content is based on what it can command in the external market; it has no intrinsic value.[1]

But not everyone agrees. A developer of the Hay job evaluation plan (widely used by large corporations) states that the "measures are independent of the market and encourage rational determination of the basis for pricing job content."[2] Hay claims that job evaluation establishes the relative value of jobs based on their content, independent of any link to the market.

Different Perspectives on Job Evaluation

Researchers, too, have their own perspective on job evaluation. Some say that if job value can be quantified, then job evaluation takes on the trappings of measurement (objective, numerical, generalizable, documented, and reliable) and can be judged according to technical standards. Just as with employment tests, the reliability and validity of job evaluation plans can be compared; research will be able to tell us if ten compensable factors is too many, or if three is too few.

Those involved in actually making pay decisions have a different view. They see job evaluation as a process that helps gain acceptance of pay differences between jobs—an administrative procedure through which the parties become involved and committed. The process invites give and take—an exchange of views. Employees, union representatives, and managers haggle over "the rules of the game" for determining relative worth. As in sports and games, we are more willing to accept the result if we accept the rules and believe they are applied fairly.[3] This interpretation is consistent with the history of job evaluation, which was begun as a way to bring labour peace and order to the wage-setting process.

Some say the content of jobs has intrinsic value that the evaluation will uncover; others that the only fair measure of job value is found in the external market. Although some claim contemporary job evaluation practices are just and fair, others say they are just fair. "Beneath the superficial orderliness of job evaluation techniques and findings, there is much that smacks of chaos."[4] All these perspectives will be captured in this chapter.[5]

■ "HOW TO": MAJOR DECISIONS

The major job evaluation decisions are depicted in Exhibit 5.2. They are: (1) establish the purpose(s), (2) decide on single versus multiple plans, (3) choose among alternative methods, (4) obtain involvement of relevant stakeholders, and (5) evaluate the usefulness of the results.

Establish the Purpose(s)

Job evaluation is part of the process for establishing an internally aligned pay structure. Recall from Chapter 2 that an internally aligned pay structure supports organizational strategy, supports the workflow, is fair to employees, and directs their behaviour toward organization objectives.

Supports Organizational Strategy   Job evaluation aligns with the organization's strategy by stating what it is about a job that adds value (i.e., contributes in pursuit of the organization's objectives). Job evaluation helps answer the question: How does this job add value?[6]

Supports Workflow   The job evaluation process supports workflow by aligning each job's pay with its relative contribution to the organization and by setting pay for new, unique, or changing jobs.

Is Fair to Employees   Job evaluation can reduce disputes and grievances over pay differences between jobs by establishing a workable, agreed-upon structure that reduces the role that chance, favouritism, and bias may play in setting pay.

Motivates Behaviour toward Organization Objectives   Job evaluation spells out for employees what it is about their work that the organization values, and what it is they do that supports the organization's strategy and promotes its ultimate success. Job evaluation also can help employees adapt to change by improving their understanding of what is valued in their assignments and how that value might change.

If the purpose of the evaluation is not spelled out, it becomes easy to get lost in complex procedures, negotiations, and bureaucracy. The job evaluation process becomes an end in itself, instead of a means to achieve an objective. Establishing the objectives can help ensure that the evaluation actually is the rational and systematic process it is meant to be.

Single versus Multiple Plans

Rarely will an employer evaluate all jobs in the organization at the same time. More typically, a related group of jobs, for example, production, engineering, or marketing, will be the focus. Many employers design different evaluation plans for different types of work because they believe the work content is too diverse to be evaluated adequately by a single plan. For example, production jobs may vary in terms of working conditions, manipulative skills, knowledge of statistical control, and working conditions But these tasks may not be relevant to engineering, and marketing jobs do not vary on these factors, nor are these factors particularly important in finance jobs. Instead, the nature of contacts with customers may be relevant. Consequently, a single, universal plan may not be acceptable to employees if the work covered is highly diverse. Even so, there are some plans that have been successfully applied across a wide breadth and depth of work. The most prominent examples include the Hay plan and the Position Analysis Questionnaire.

Benchmark Jobs

To be sure that all relevant aspects of work are included in the evaluation, an organization may start with a sample of benchmark jobs. In Exhibit 5.3, benchmark jobs would be identified for as

EXHIBIT **5.3** Perspectives on Job Evaluation

Job evaluation is:	Assumption
A measure of job content	Content has innate value outside of external market.
A measure of relative value	Relevant groups can reach consensus on relative value.
A link with external market	Job worth cannot be specified without external market information.
A measurement device	Honing instruments will provide objective measures.
Negotiation	Puts face of rationality onto a social/political process. Establishes rules of the game. Invites participation.

many levels in the structure and groups of related jobs (office, production, engineering) as possible. The heavy shading in the exhibit indicates the benchmark jobs.

A **benchmark job** has the following characteristics:

benchmark job

a job whose contents are well-known, relatively stable, and common across different employers

- Its contents are well known and relatively stable over time.
- The job is common to a number of employers; i.e., it is not unique to a particular employer.
- A reasonable proportion of the workforce is employed in this job.

A representative sample of benchmark jobs includes the entire domain of work being evaluated—office, production, engineering, and so on—and captures the diversity of the work within that domain. Diversity in the work can be thought of in terms of depth (vertically) and breadth (horizontally). The depth of work in most organizations ranges from strategic leadership jobs (e.g., CEOs, general directors) to filing and mail distribution tasks in entry-level office jobs. Horizontally, the breadth of work depends on the nature of the business. Relatively similar work can be found in specialty consulting firms (e.g., compensation or executive search firms). The breadth of work performed in some multinational conglomerates such as General Electric mirrors the occupations in an entire nation. GE includes jobs in businesses spanning financial services, entertainment (NBC), aircraft engines, medical instruments, power systems, and home appliances.

Typically, a job evaluation plan is developed using benchmark jobs, and then the plan is applied to the remaining, non-benchmark jobs. Selecting benchmark jobs from each level ensures coverage of the entire work domain, thus helping to ensure the accuracy of the decisions based on the job evaluation.

The number of job evaluation plans used hinges on how detailed an evaluation is required to make pay decisions and how much it will cost. There is no ready answer to the question of "one plan versus many." Current practice (not always the best answer for the future, since practice is based on the past) is to use separate plans for major domains of work: top executive/leadership jobs, managerial/professional jobs, operational/technical jobs, and office/administrative jobs. Some organizations, however, have additional plans for sales, legal, engineers/scientists, and skilled trades. The costs (including time) associated with these plans give impetus to the push to simplify job structures (i.e., reduce titles and levels).

Choose between Methods

Ranking, classification, and point method are the most common job evaluation methods, though uncounted variations exist. Research over 40 years consistently finds that different job evaluation plans generate different pay structures, so the method chosen matters.[7] Exhibit 5.4 compares the methods. All begin by assuming that an accurate job analysis has been translated into useful job descriptions.

EXHIBIT **5.4**	Comparison of Job Evaluation Methods	
	Advantage	**Disadvantage**
Ranking	Fast, simple, easy to explain.	Cumbersome as number of jobs increases. Basis for comparisons is not called out.
Classification	Can group a wide range of work together in one system	Descriptions may leave too much room for manipulation.
Point	Compensable factors call out basis for comparisons. Compensable factors communicate what is valued.	Can become bureaucratic and rule-bound.

RANKING

ranking

job evaluation method that ranks jobs from highest to lowest based on a global definition of value

Ranking simply orders the job descriptions from highest to lowest based on a global definition of relative value or contribution to the organization's success. Ranking is the simplest, fastest, easiest method to understand and explain to employees, and the least expensive method, at least initially. However, it can create problems that require difficult and potentially expensive solutions because it doesn't tell employees specifically what in their jobs is important.

alternation ranking method

ranking the highest- and lowest-valued jobs first, then the next highest- and lowest-valued jobs, repeating the process until all jobs have been ranked

Two ways of ranking are common: alternation ranking and paired comparison. The **alternation ranking method** orders job descriptions alternately at each extreme. Agreement is reached among evaluators on which jobs are the most and least valuable, then the next most and least valuable, and so on, until all jobs have been ordered. The **paired comparison method** uses a matrix to compare all possible pairs of jobs. The higher-ranked job is entered in the cell of the matrix. When all comparisons have been completed, the job most frequently judged "more valuable" becomes the highest-ranked job, and so on.

paired comparison method

listing all jobs across columns and down rows of a matrix, comparing the two jobs in each cell and indicating which is of greater value, then ranking jobs based on the total number of times each is ranked as being of greater value

Alternation ranking and paired comparison methods may be more reliable (produce similar results more consistently) than simple ranking. Nevertheless, ranking has drawbacks. The criteria on which the jobs are ranked usually are so poorly defined—if they are specified at all—that the evaluations become subjective opinions that are impossible to justify in work-related terms. Furthermore, evaluator(s) using this method must be knowledgeable about every single job under study. The numbers alone turn what should be a simple task into a formidable one—50 jobs require 1,225 comparisons—and as organizations change, it is difficult to remain knowledgeable about all jobs. Some organizations try to overcome this difficulty by ranking jobs within single departments and merging the results. However, even though ranking appears simple, fast, and inexpensive, in the long run, the results are difficult to defend, and costly solutions may be required to overcome the problems created.

CLASSIFICATION

classification

job evaluation method based on job class descriptions into which jobs are categorized

Picture a bookcase with many shelves. Each shelf is labelled with a paragraph describing the kinds of books on that shelf and, perhaps, one or two representative titles. This same approach describes the **classification** system of job evaluation. A series of classes covers the range of jobs. Class descriptions are the labels. A job description is compared to the class descriptions to decide which class is the best fit for that job. Each class is described in such a way that it captures sufficient work detail, yet is general enough to cause little difficulty in slotting a job description into its appropriate "shelf" or class. The classes may be described further by including titles of benchmark jobs that fall into each class.

.NET WORTH | Federal Government Classification System Modernization

The Canada Public Service Agency is gradually modernizing its job evaluation system. It has recently developed a new EC classification to replace the existing separate Economics, Sociology, and Statistics (ES) and Social Science Support (SI) standards. Within the new classification, jobs are evaluated using a point factor plan, as shown below. This approach combines the classification and point methods.

Factor: Sub-factor	# of Degrees	Maximum Point Values
Responsibility: Decision making	8	210
Responsibility: Leadership and operational management	5	140
Skill: Communication	7	180
Skill: Knowledge of specialized fields	6	105
Skill: Contextual knowledge	6	105
Skill: Research and analysis	6	210
Effort: Physical effort	5	15
Effort: Sensory effort	4	10
Working Conditions: Working conditions	5	25
Total:		**1,000**

Source: Adapted from *Classification Standard: Economic and Social Science Services Group (EC)*. Canada Public Service Agency. www.tbs-sct.gc.ca/cla/snd/ec-eng.asp (accessed September 26, 2009). Reproduced with the permission of the Minister of Public Works and Government Services, 2009.

Writing class descriptions can be troublesome when jobs from several job families are covered by a single plan. For example, class definitions written with sales jobs in mind may make it difficult to slot office or administrative jobs and vice versa. An examination of the group definition for the Economic and Social Science Services Group of the federal government's classification system in Exhibit 5.5, indicates that the vagueness of the descriptions seems to leave a lot of room for judgment. Including titles of benchmark jobs for each class helps make the descriptions more concrete. So, in practice, the job descriptions are compared not only to the four compensable factors, standard class descriptions, and benchmark jobs, but they also can be compared to one another to ensure that jobs within each class are more similar to each other than to jobs in adjacent classes. The final result is a series of classes with a number of jobs in each. The jobs within each class are considered to be equal (or similar) work and will be paid equally. Jobs in different classes should be dissimilar and may have different pay rates. The .Net Worth box illustrates the use of classification by the federal government, and the combination of this method with the point method, described next, in evaluating jobs within each classification.

| **EXHIBIT** | **5.5** | Economic and Social Science Services Group Description |

The Economics and Social Science Services Group comprises positions that are primarily involved in the conduct of surveys, studies and projects in the social sciences; the identification, description and organization of archival, library, museum and gallery materials; the editing of legislation or the provision of advice on legal problems in specific fields; and the application of a comprehensive knowledge of economics, sociology or statistics to the conduct of economic, socio-economic and sociological research, studies, forecasts and surveys; the research, analysis and evaluation of the economic or sociological effects of departmental or interdepartmental projects, programs and policies; the development, application, analysis and evaluation of statistical and survey methods and systems; and the development, analysis and interpretation of qualitative and quantitative information and socio-economic policies and recommendations.

Inclusions

Notwithstanding the generality of the foregoing, for greater certainty, it includes positions that have, as their primary purpose, responsibility for one or more of the following activities:

1. the conduct of surveys, studies, projects and tests requiring a practical knowledge of a specialized field such as economics, history, law or psychology and requiring the development of specialized techniques and procedures, or the development and use of related processing applications, or the interpretation of findings;
2. the identification, description, classification, organization and location of archival, gallery, library or museum materials; or the creation, manipulation, verification, analysis and transmission of descriptive records pertaining to such materials, both of which require a practical knowledge of the subject matter;
3. the editing of legislation or the conduct of studies in matters such as land conveyancing, expropriation, litigation and labour relations requiring a practical knowledge of the specific legal area to interpret findings or prepare submissions;
4. the application of a practical knowledge of a specialized field such as economics, history, law or psychology to the use and modification or adaptation of computer systems, utilities or software;
5. the application of a comprehensive knowledge of economics, sociology or statistics to economic, socio-economic or sociological studies, forecasts and surveys in a variety of subject areas in domestic and/or international settings;
6. the application of a comprehensive knowledge of economics, sociology or statistics to the development, application and evaluation of statistical and survey methods and indicators for use in natural or social science research projects, or in the planning of surveys and censuses or in the determination of statistical measures and techniques for data analysis and reporting;
7. the provision of advice in the fields of economics, sociology and statistics; and
8. the leadership of any of the above activities.

Exclusions

Positions excluded from the Economics and Social Science Services Group are those whose primary purpose is included in the definition of any other group or those in which one or more of the following activities is of primary importance:

1. the operation, scheduling or controlling of the operations of electronic equipment used in the processing of data for the purpose of reporting, storing, extracting and comparing information or for solving formulated problems according to prescribed plans;
2. the collecting, recording, arranging, transmitting and processing of information, the filing and distribution of information holdings, and the direct application of rules and regulations;
3. the planning, development, delivery or management of policies, programs, services or other activities directed to the public or to the Public Service;
4. the explanation, promotion and publication of federal government programs, policies and services;
5. the application of a comprehensive knowledge of mathematics to the development or application of mathematical and analytical methods, including those of mathematical statistics; and
6. the planning, development, delivery and management of economic development policies, programs, services and other activities designed to promote the establishment, growth and improvement of industry, commerce and export trade and the regulation of trade and commerce.

Source: *Classification Standard: Economic and Social Science Services Group (EC).* Canada Public Service Agency. www.tbs-sct.gc.ca/cla/snd/ ec-eng.asp (accessed September 26, 2009). Reproduced with the permission of the Minister of Public Works and Government Services, 2009.

POINT METHOD

point method

job evaluation method that assigns a number of points to each job, based on compensable factors that are numerically scaled and weighted

compensable factors

characteristics of the work that the organization values, that help it pursue its strategy, and that achieve its objectives

Point methods have three common characteristics: (1) compensable factors, with (2) numerically scaled factor degrees, and (3) weights reflecting the relative importance of each factor.[8] Each job's relative value, and hence its location in the pay structure, is determined by the total points assigned to it.

Point plans are the most commonly used approach to establish pay structures in Canada due to pay equity legislation requirements for the evaluation of skill, effort, responsibility, and working conditions in jobs. They represent a significant change from ranking and classification methods in that they make explicit the criteria for evaluating jobs—compensable factors.

Compensable factors are defined on the basis of the strategic direction of the business and how the work contributes to that strategy. The factors are scaled to reflect the degree to which they are present in each job, and weighted to reflect their overall importance to the organization. Points are then attached to each factor weight. The point total for each job determines its position in the job structure.

Exhibit 5.6 lists the six steps involved in the design of a point plan.

1. Conduct job analysis.
2. Determine compensable factors.
3. Scale the factors.
4. Weight the factors according to importance.
5. Communicate the plan and train users; prepare manual.
6. Apply to non-benchmark jobs.

The end product of this design process is an evaluation plan that helps develop and explain the pay structure.

EXHIBIT 5.6   The Point Plan Process

Step One: Conduct Job Analysis
- A representative sample of benchmark jobs
- The content of these jobs is basis for compensable factors

Step Two: Determine Compensable Factors
- Based on the work performed (what is done)
- Based on strategy and values of the organization (what is valued)
- Acceptable to those affected by resulting pay structure (what is acceptable)

Step Three: Scale the Factors
- Use examples to anchor

Step Four: Weight the Factors
- Can reflect judgment of organization leaders, committee
- Can reflect a negotiated structure
- Can reflect a market-based structure

Step Five: Communicate the Plan
- Prepare manual
- Train users

Step Six: Apply to Non-benchmark Jobs

---

1. Conduct Job Analysis

Just as with ranking and classification, point plans begin with job analysis. Typically, a representative sample of jobs, that is, benchmark jobs, is drawn for analysis. The content of these jobs serves as the basis for defining, scaling, and weighting the compensable factors.

2. Determine Compensable Factors

Compensable factors play a pivotal role in the point plan. These factors reflect how work adds value to the organization. They flow from the work itself and from the strategic direction of the business. A sample list of compensable factors and subfactors is shown in Exhibit 5.7.

To select compensable factors, an organization asks what it is about the work that adds value. One company chose decision making as a compensable factor. As shown in Exhibit 5.8, the definition of decision making is three-dimensional: (1) the risk and complexity (hence the availability of guidelines to assist in making the decisions), (2) the impact of the decisions, and (3) the time that must pass before the impact is evident.

competitive advantage

a business practice or process that results in better performance than one's competitors

In effect, this firm determined that its **competitive advantage** depends on decisions employees make in their work. And the relative value of the decisions depends on their risk, their complexity, and their impact on the company. Hence, this firm is signalling to all employees that jobs will be valued based on the nature of the decisions required by employees in those jobs. Jobs that require riskier decisions with greater impact have a higher relative worth than jobs that require fewer decisions of relatively little consequence.

EXHIBIT 5.7 Factor Evaluation System (with Subfactors)

Responsibility

1. Information for the Use of Others
2. Well-Being of Individuals
3. Leadership of Human Resources
4. Money
5. Physical Assets and Products
6. Ensuring Compliance

Skill

7. Job Content Knowledge Application
8. Contextual Knowledge
9. Communication
10. Motor and Sensory Skills

Effort

11. Intellectual Effort
12. Sustained Attention
13. Psychological/Emotional Effort
14. Physical Effort

Working Conditions

15. Work Environment
16. Risks to Health

Source: www.tbs-sct.gc.ca/Classification/Tools/FactorElement_e.asp (August 4, 2003).

EXHIBIT 5.8 Example of Compensable Factor Definition: Decision Making ─────────

Compensable Factor Definition: Evaluates the extent of required decision making and the beneficial or detrimental effect such decisions would have on the profitability of the organization.

Consideration is given to the:
- Risk and complexity of required decision making
- Impact such action would have on the company

What type of guidelines are available for making decisions?

_____ 1.   Few decisions are required; work is performed according to standard procedures and/or detailed instructions.

_____ 2.   Decisions are made within an established framework of clearly defined procedures. Incumbent is only required to recognize and follow the prescribed course of action.

_____ 3.   Guidelines are available in the form of clearly defined procedures and standard practices. Incumbent must exercise some judgment in selecting the appropriate procedure.

_____ 4.   Guidelines are available in the form of some standard practices, well-established precedent, and reference materials and company policy. Decisions require a moderate level of judgment and analysis of the appropriate course of action.

_____ 5.   Some guidelines are available in the form of broad precedent, related practices, and general methods of the field. Decisions require a high level of judgment and/or modification of a standard course of action to address the issue at hand.

_____ 6.   Few guidelines are available. The incumbent may consult with technical experts and review relevant professional publications. Decisions require innovation and creativity. The only limitations on course of action are company strategy and policy.

What is the impact of decisions made by the position?

_____ 1.   Inappropriate decisions, recommendations or errors would normally cause minor delays and cost increments. Deficiencies will not affect the completion of programs or projects important to the organization.

_____ 2.   Inappropriate decisions, recommendations or errors will normally cause moderate delays and additional allocation of funds and resources within the immediate work unit. Deficiencies will not affect the attainment of the organization's objectives.

_____ 3.   Inappropriate decisions, recommendations, or errors would normally cause considerable delays and reallocation of funds and resources. Deficiencies will affect scheduling and project completion in other work units and, unless adjustments are made, could affect attainment of objectives of a major business segment of the company.

_____ 4.   Inappropriate decisions, recommendations, or errors would normally affect critical programs or attainment of short-term goals for a major business segment of the company.

_____ 5.   Inappropriate decisions, recommendations, or errors would affect attainment of objectives for the company and would normally affect long-term growth and public image.

The effectiveness of the majority of the position's decisions can be measured within:

_____ 1. One day.   _____ 4. Six months.
_____ 2. One week.   _____ 5. One year.
_____ 3. One month.   _____ 6. More than a year.

Source: Jill Kanin-Lovers, "The Role of Computers in Job Evaluations: A Case in Point," *Journal of Compensation and Benefits* (New York: Warren Gorham and Lamont, 1985).

To be useful, compensable factors should be:

- Based on the strategy and values of the organization.
- Based on the work performed.
- Acceptable to the stakeholders affected by the resulting pay structure.

Based on the Strategy and Values of the Organization   The leadership of any organization is the best source of information on where the business should be going and how it is going to get there. Clearly, leadership's input into factor selection is crucial. So, for example, if the business strategy involves providing innovative, high-quality products and services designed in collaboration with customers and suppliers, then jobs with greater responsibility for product innovation and customer contacts should be valued more highly. Or if the business strategy is more like Walmart's, "providing goods and services to delight customers at the lowest cost and greatest convenience possible," then compensable factors might include impact on cost containment, customer relations, and so on.

Compensable factors reinforce the organization's culture and values as well as its business direction and the nature of the work. If that direction changes, then the compensable factors may also change. For example, strategic plans at many companies call for increased globalization. Both Procter and Gamble (P&G) and 3M include a "multinational responsibilities" factor similar to the one in Exhibit 5.9 in their managerial job-evaluation plan. Multinational responsibilities are defined in terms of the type of responsibility, the percentage of time devoted to international issues, and the number of countries covered.

Factors may also be eliminated if they no longer support the business strategy. One railway company revised its job evaluation plan to omit the factor, "Number of Subordinates Supervised." It decided that a factor that values increases to staff runs counter to the organization's objective of

---

EXHIBIT 5.9   Compensable Factor Definition: Multinational Responsibilities ————————

This factor concerns the multinational scope of the job. Multinational responsibilities are defined as line or functional managerial activities in one or several countries.

1. **The multinational responsibilities of the job can best be described as:**
   A. Approving major policy and strategic plans.
   B. Formulating, proposing, and monitoring implementation of policy and plans.
   C. Acting as a consultant in project design and implementation phases.
   D. Not applicable.

2. **Indicate the percentage of time spent on multinational issues:**
   A. 50%
   B. 25–49%
   C. 10–24%
   D. 10%

3. **The number of countries (other than your unit location) for which the position currently has operational or functional responsibility:**
   A. More than 10 countries
   B. 5 to 10 countries
   C. 1 to 4 countries
   D. Not applicable

reducing bureaucracy and increasing efficiency. Major shifts in the business strategy are not daily occurrences, but when they do occur, compensable factors should be reexamined to ensure they are consistent with the new directions.

Based on the Work Itself   Employees are the experts in the work actually done in any organization. Hence, it is important to seek their answers to what should be valued in the work itself. Some form of documentation (i.e., job descriptions, job analysis, employee and/or supervisory focus groups) must support the choice of factors. Work-related documentation helps gain acceptance by employees and managers, is easier to understand, and can withstand a variety of challenges to the pay structure. For example, managers may argue that the salaries of their employees are too low in comparison to those of other employees, or that the salary offered a job candidate is too low. Union leaders may wonder why one job is paid differently from another. Allegations of pay discrimination may be raised. Employees, line managers, union leaders, and compensation managers must understand and be able to explain why work is paid differently or the same. Differences in factors that obviously are based on the work itself provide that rationale and diminish the likelihood of challenges arising.

Acceptable to the Stakeholders   Acceptance of the compensable factors used to slot jobs into the pay structure may depend, at least in part, on tradition. For example, people who work in hospitals, nursing homes, and child care centres make the point that responsibility for people is used less often, and valued less, than responsibility for property.[9] This deficiency may be a carry-over from the days when nursing and child care services were provided by family members, usually women, without reimbursement. People now doing these jobs for pay say that properly valuing a factor for people responsibility would raise their wages. It is important that the compensable factors be acceptable to all stakeholders.

Adapting Factors from Existing Plans   Although a wide variety of factors are used in standard existing plans, the factors tend to fall into four generic groups: skill, effort, responsibility, and working conditions. These four are required in pay equity legislation across Canada. The *Hay Guide Chart–Profile Method*, used by 5,000 employers worldwide, is perhaps the most widely used. The classic three Hay factors—know-how, problem solving, and accountability—use guide charts to quantify the factors in more detail. In Exhibit 5.10, the Hay factor "Know-How" is measured on three dimensions: scope (practical procedures vs. specialized techniques vs. scientific disciplines); depth (minimal vs. related vs. diverse vs. broad); and human relations skills (basic vs. important vs. critical). The cell that corresponds to the right level of all three dimensions for the job being evaluated is located in the guide chart. The cell gives the points for this factor. In the exhibit, the supervisor keypunch position gets 152 points for know-how because the job has an "advanced vocational" scope, requires "critical" human relations skills, and a "minimal" depth of managerial know-how. The area manager position gets a much higher number of points (700) because the job has a "technical-specialist mastery" scope, requires "critical" human relations skills, and a "diverse" depth of managerial know-how.

How Many Factors?   A remaining issue to consider is how many factors should be included in the plan. Some factors may have overlapping definitions or may fail to account for anything unique in the criterion chosen. One writer calls this the "illusion of validity"—we want to believe that the factors are capturing divergent aspects of the job and that all are important.[10]

Another problem is called "small numbers."[11] If even only one job in our benchmark sample has a particular characteristic, we tend to use that factor for the entire work domain. A common example is unpleasant working conditions. If even one job is performed in unpleasant working conditions, it is tempting to make it a compensable factor and apply it to all jobs. Once a factor is part of the system, others are likely to say their job has it, too. For example, office staff may feel that ringing telephones or leaky toner cartridges constitute unpleasant or hazardous conditions.

EXHIBIT **5.10** Hay Guide Chart–Profile Method of Job Evaluation

KNOW-HOW DEFINITIONS

DEFINITION: Know-How is the sum total to every kind of skill, however acquired, required for acceptable job performance. This sum total which comprises the overall savvy has 3 dimensions–the requirements for:

1 Scope: Practical procedures, specialized techniques, and scientific disciplines.

2 Human Relations Skills: Know-How of integrating and harmonizing the diversified functions involved in managerial situations occurring in operating, supporting, and administrative fields. This Know-How may be exercised consultatively (about management) as well as executively, and involves in some combination the areas of organizing, planning, executing, controlling, and evaluating.

3

Depth: Active, practising, face-to-face skills in the area of human relationships (as defined at right).

MEASURING KNOW-HOW: Know-How has both scope (variety) and depth (thoroughness). Thus, a job may require some knowledge about a lot of things, or a lot of knowledge about a few things. The total Know-How is the combination of scope and depth. This concept makes practical the comparison and weighing of the total Know-How content of different jobs in terms of "how much knowledge about how many things."

2 HUMAN RELATIONS SKILLS

1. **BASIC:** Ordinary courtesy and effectiveness in dealing with others.

2. **IMPORTANT:** Understanding, influencing, and/or serving people are important, but not critical, considerations.

3. **CRITICAL:** Alternative or combined skills in understanding, selecting, developing, and motivating people are important in the highest degree.

KNOW-HOW 1 Scope 2 Human Relations Skills ➡ 3 Depth ➡	MANAGERIAL KNOW-HOW											
	I. MINIMAL			II. RELATED			III. DIVERSE			IV. BROAD		
	1	2	3	1	2	3	1	2	3	1	2	3
A. PRIMARY	50	57	66	66	76	87	87	100	115	115	132	152
	57	66	76	76	87	100	100	115	132	132	152	175
	66	76	87	87	100	115	115	132	152	152	175	200
B. ELEMENTARY VOCATIONAL	66	76	87	87	100	115	115	132	152	152	175	200
	76	87	100	100	115	132	132	152	175	175	200	230
	87	100	115	115	132	152	152	175	200	200	230	264
C. VOCATIONAL	87	100	115	115	132	152	152	175	200	200	230	264
	100	115	132	132	152	175	175	200	230	230	264	304
	115	132	152	152	175	200	200	230	264	264	304	350
D. ADVANCED VOCATIONAL	115	132	(152)	152	175	200	200	230	264	264	304	350
	132	152	175	175	200	230	230	264	304	304	350	400
	152	175	200	200	230	264	264	304	350	350	400	460
E. BASIC TECHNICAL-SPECIALIZED	152	175	200	200	230	264	264	304	350	350	400	460
	175	200	230	230	264	304	304	350	400	400	460	528
	200	230	264	264	304	350	350	400	460	460	528	608
F. SEASONED TECHNICAL-SPECIALIZED	200	230	264	264	304	350	350	400	460	460	528	608
	230	264	304	304	350	400	400	460	528	528	608	700
	264	304	350	350	400	460	460	528	608	608	700	800
G. TECHNICAL-SPECIALIZED MASTERY	264	304	350	350	400	460	460	528	608	608	700	800
	(304)	350	400	400	460	528	528	608	(700)	700	800	920
	350	400	460	460	528	608	608	700	800	800	920	1056
H. PROFESSIONAL MASTERY	350	400	460	460	528	608	608	700	800	800	920	1056
	400	460	528	528	608	700	700	800	920	920	1056	1216
	460	528	608	608	700	800	800	920	1056	1056	1216	1400

Left margin labels: SCIENTIFIC DISCIPLINES / SPECIALIZED TECHNIQUES / PRACTICAL PROCEDURES

KH	PS	AC	TOTAL
152			

SUPERVISOR KEY PUNCH

KH	PS	AC	TOTAL
304			

ACTUARIAL SPECIALIST RESEARCH ASSOCIATE

KH	PS	AC	TOTAL
700			

AREA MANAGER

In one plan, a senior manager refused to accept a job evaluation plan unless some kind of working conditions factor was included. The plan's designer, a recent university graduate, showed through statistical analysis that working conditions did not vary enough between 90 percent of the jobs to have a meaningful effect on the resulting pay structure. Nevertheless, the manager rejected this argument, pointing out that the plan designer had never worked in the plant's foundry, where working conditions mattered. In order to get the plan and pay decisions based on it accepted by the foundry workers, the plan was redesigned to include working conditions.

This situation is not unusual. In one study, a 21-factor plan produced the same job structure that could have been generated using only 7 of the factors. In fact, the jobs could be correctly slotted into classes using only three factors. Yet the company decided to keep the 21-factor plan because it was "accepted and doing the job." Research as far back as the 1940s demonstrates that the skills dimension explains 90 percent or more of the variance in job evaluation results; three factors generally account for 98 to 99 percent of the variance.[12] But, as we have seen, other factors often are included to ensure the plan's acceptance.

3. Scale the Factors

factor degree/level

description of several different degrees or levels of a factor in jobs; a different number of points is associated with each degree/level

Once the factors are chosen, scales reflecting the different degrees within each factor are constructed. Each degree may be anchored by the typical skills, tasks, and behaviours taken from the benchmark jobs that illustrate each **factor degree/level**. Exhibit 5.11 shows the federal government's scaling for the subfactor "Physical Effort" of the factor "Effort" for employees in the Economic and Social Science Services group.

A major problem in determining degrees is whether to make each degree equidistant from the adjacent degrees (interval scaling) in terms of the number of points for each level or degree. The following criteria for scaling factors have been suggested: (1) limit the degrees to the number necessary to distinguish between jobs, (2) use understandable terminology, (3) anchor degree definitions with benchmark job titles, and (4) make it apparent how the degree applies to the job. Using too many degrees makes it difficult for evaluators to accurately choose the appropriate degree. This in turn reduces the acceptability of the system.

EXHIBIT   5.11   Subfactor Degrees: "Physical Effort" in General Labour and Trade (GL) Group ——————

In rating positions under the Physical Effort element, raters are to consider the fatigue caused by the kind, frequency, intensity, and duration of muscular exertion; the work positions; and the weight of objects handled. When rating positions under this element, raters are to consider only the general or "on average" requirement. An occasional or infrequent requirement should not be credited as it cannot be considered as contributing to fatigue.

Degree	Physical Effort	Points
1	The work generally requires some physical effort, such as intermittent standing or walking, or handling of light-weight objects or controls.	15
2	The work generally requires moderate physical effort, such as standing or walking where only limited periods of relief are possible, or handling of moderate-weight objects or controls.	30
3	The work generally requires considerable physical effort, such as frequent climbing, working from ladders, working in difficult positions, or handling of medium-weight objects.	45
4	The work generally requires great physical effort, such as frequent handling of heavy-weight objects.	60
5	The work generally requires extreme physical effort, such as continual handling of heavy-weight objects.	75

Source: *Classification Standard*: General Labour and Trade Group. Treasury Board of Canada Secretariat. www.tbs-sct.gc.ca/gui/csnc/gl_e.pdf (accessed September 26, 2009). Reproduced with permission of the Minister of Public Works and Government Services, 2009.

4. Weight the Factors According to Importance

factor weights

weighting assigned to each factor to reflect differences in importance attached to each factor by the employer

Once the degrees have been assigned, the **factor weights** must be determined. Different weights reflect differences in importance attached to each factor by the employer. Weights often are determined through an advisory committee that allocates 100 percent of the value among the factors.[13] In the illustration in Exhibit 5.12, a committee allocated 40 percent of the value to skill, 30 percent to effort, 20 percent to responsibility, and 10 percent to working conditions. Each factor has two subfactors, each with five degrees. For the bookstore manager, the subfactor "Mental Skill" gets half the 40 percent given to "Skill"; four degrees of "Mental Skill" times 20 equals 80 points, and three degrees of the subfactor "Experience" times 20 equals another 60 points. "Effort" is weighted 30 percent, so two degrees of physical effort times 15 gives 30 points, and four degrees of mental effort times 15 gives 60 points, and so on.

Select Criterion Pay Structure Contemporary job evaluation often supplements committee judgment regarding weights with statistical analysis.[14] The committee recommends the *criterion pay structure* they wish to duplicate with the point plan. The criterion structure may be the current rates paid for benchmark jobs, market rates for benchmark jobs, rates for predominantly male jobs (in an attempt to eliminate gender bias), or union-negotiated rates.[15] Once a criterion structure is agreed on, statistical modelling techniques such as regression analysis are used to determine the weight of each factor that will best reproduce the chosen structure. The statistical approach is often labelled *policy capturing* to contrast it to the *committee judgment* approach. Not only do the weights reflect the relative importance of each factor, but research

EXHIBIT 5.12 Job Evaluation Form

Job	**bookstore manager**			
Check one:	X Administrative			
	☐ Technical			

Compensable Factors	Degree	x	Weight	=	Total
	1 2 3 4 5				
Skill: (40%)					
Mental	X (degree 4)		20%		80
Experience	X (degree 3)		20%		60
Effort: (30%)					
Physical	X (degree 2)		15%		30
Mental	X (degree 4)		15%		60
Responsibility: (20%)					
Effect of Error	X (degree 4)		10%		40
Inventiveness/ Innovation	X (degree 3)		10%		30
Working Conditions: (10%)					
Environment	X (degree 1)		5%		5
Hazards	X (degree 1)		5%		5
					(310)

(Handwritten margin notes: "4 compensable — short answer." / "Group Project from ENRON — pick person & score." / "Add sub factors" / "350 m pg 119")

clearly demonstrates that the weights influence the resulting pay structure.[16] Thus, selecting the appropriate pay rates to use as the criteria is critical. The job evaluation results are based on it.[17]

Perhaps the clearest illustration can be found in the criterion structures used in municipalities. If only market rates were used, firefighters would be paid much less than police. Yet many firefighters' unions have successfully negotiated a link between their pay and police rates. Hence, the negotiated pay structure deviates from a market structure.

5. Communicate the Plan and Train Users

Once the job evaluation plan is designed, a manual is prepared so that other people can apply the plan. The manual describes the method, defines the compensable factors, and provides enough information to permit users to distinguish varying degrees of each factor. The point of the manual is to allow users who were not involved in the plan's development to apply the plan as its developers intended.. Users will require training on how to apply the plan, and background information on how the plan is integrated with the organization's total pay system. An appeals process may also be included so that employees who feel that their jobs are unfairly evaluated have some recourse. Employee acceptance of the process is crucial if the organization is to have any hope that employees will accept the resulting pay as fair. In order to build this acceptance, communication to all employees whose jobs are part of the process used to build the structure is required. This communication may be done through informational meetings, Web sites, or other methods. In some cases, the entire job evaluation process is carried out online.

6. Apply to Non-benchmark Jobs

Recall that the compensable factors and weights were derived using a sample of benchmark jobs. The final step in the point plan process is to apply the plan to the remaining jobs. To do so, usually a manual is written that describes the method, defines the compensable factors, and provides enough information to permit users to distinguish varying degrees of each factor. The point of the manual is to allow users who were not involved in its development to apply the plan. Users require training and background information on the total pay system.

◼ WHO SHOULD BE INVOLVED?

If the internal structure's purpose is to aid managers, and if ensuring high involvement and commitment from employees is important, all those managers and employees with a stake in the results should be involved in the process of designing it. A common approach is to use committees, task forces, or teams that include representatives from key operating functions, including non-managerial employees. In some cases, the group's role is advisory only; in others, it designs the evaluation approach, chooses compensable factors, and approves all major changes. Organizations with unions often find it advantageous to include union representation as a source of ideas and to help promote acceptance of the results. However, some union leaders believe that philosophical differences prevent their active participation. They take the position that collective bargaining yields more equitable results. As a result, the extent of union participation varies. No single perspective exists on the value of active participation in the process, just as no single management perspective exists.

The Design Process Matters

Research suggests that attending to the fairness of the design process and the approach chosen (job evaluation, skill/competency-based plan, and market pricing) rather than focusing solely on the results (the internal pay structure) is likely to achieve employee and management commitment, trust, and acceptance of the results.[18] The absence of participation makes it easier for employees and managers to imagine ways in which the structure could have been rearranged to their personal liking. If employees do not participate in decisions, they can easily assume that things would have been better if they had.

Additional research is needed to ascertain whether the payoff from increased participation offsets the potential cost (e.g., time involved to reach consensus, potential problems caused by disrupting current perceptions). For example, in multinational organizations the involvement of both corporate compensation and country managers raises the potential for conflict due to their differing perspectives. Country managers may wish to focus on the particular business needs in their country, whereas corporate managers may want a system that operates equally well (or poorly) across all countries. The country manager has operating objectives, does not want to lose key individuals, and views compensation as a mechanism to help accomplish these goals. Corporate managers, on the other hand, adopt a worldwide perspective and focus on ensuring that decisions are consistent with the organization's overall global strategy.

Appeals/Review Procedures

No matter the technique, no job evaluation plan anticipates all situations. It is inevitable that some jobs will be evaluated incorrectly, or at least that employees and managers may suspect that they were. Consequently, review procedures to handle such cases and to help ensure procedural fairness are required. Often the compensation manager handles reviews, but peer or team reviews are increasingly being used. Sometimes these reviews take on the trappings of formal grievance procedures (e.g., documented complaints and responses and levels of approval). Problems may also be handled by managers and employee relations generalists through informal discussions with employees.[19]

Once the evaluations are completed, approval by higher levels of management usually is required. An approval process helps ensure that any changes that result from evaluating work are consistent with the organization's operations and directions.

Political Influences

A recent study found that more powerful departments in a university were more successful in using the appeals process to change the pay or the classification of a job than were weaker departments.[20] This result is consistent with other research that showed that a powerful member of a job evaluation committee could sway the results.[21] Consequently, procedures should be judged for their susceptibility to political influences. "It is the decision-making process, rather than the instrument itself that seems to have the greatest influence on pay outcomes," writes one researcher.[22]

◼ THE FINAL RESULT: JOB STRUCTURE

The final result of the job analysis-job description-job evaluation process is a job structure, a hierarchy of work. This hierarchy translates into practice the employer's internal alignment policy. Exhibit 5.13 shows four hypothetical job structures within a single organization. These structures were obtained via different approaches to evaluating work. The jobs are arrayed within four basic functions: managerial, technical, manufacturing, and administrative. The managerial and administrative structures were obtained via a points-based job evaluation plan, and technical and manufacturing work via two different person-based plans (Chapter 6); the manufacturing plan was negotiated with the union. The exhibit illustrates the results of evaluating work—structures that support a policy of internal alignment.

EXHIBIT **5.13** | Resulting Internal Structures—Job-, Skill-, and Competency-Based

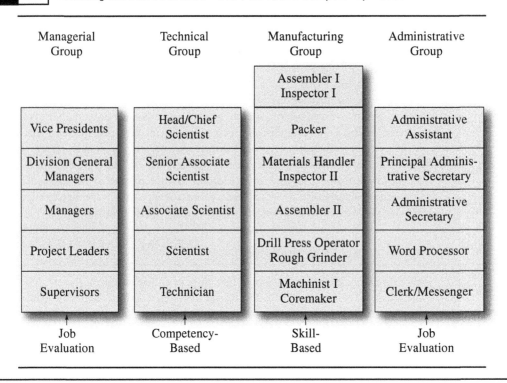

Managerial Group	Technical Group	Manufacturing Group	Administrative Group
		Assembler I Inspector I	
Vice Presidents	Head/Chief Scientist	Packer	Administrative Assistant
Division General Managers	Senior Associate Scientist	Materials Handler Inspector II	Principal Administrative Secretary
Managers	Associate Scientist	Assembler II	Administrative Secretary
Project Leaders	Scientist	Drill Press Operator Rough Grinder	Word Processor
Supervisors	Technician	Machinist I Coremaker	Clerk/Messenger
↑ Job Evaluation	↑ Competency-Based	↑ Skill-Based	↑ Job Evaluation

Organizations commonly have multiple structures derived through multiple approaches that apply to different functional groups or units. Although some employees in one structure may wish to compare the procedures used in another structure to their own, the underlying premise in practice is that internal alignment is most influenced by fair and equitable treatment of employees doing similar work in the same skill/knowledge group.

BALANCING CHAOS AND CONTROL

Looking back at the material that has been covered in the past three chapters (determining internal alignment, job analysis, job evaluation), it is clear that a lot of time and money has been spent to develop some complex techniques. But it is still not clear how much to pay each employee. Why bother with all this? Why not just pay whatever it takes and get on with it?

Prior to the widespread use of job evaluation in the 1930s and 1940s, employers had irrational pay structures, the legacy of decentralized and uncoordinated wage-setting practices. Pay differences were a major source of unrest among workers. Employment and wage records were rarely kept; only the foreman knew with any accuracy how many workers were employed in his department and the rates they received. Foremen were thus "free to manage," often using wage information to vary the day rate for favoured workers or to assign them to jobs where piece rates were loose.

Job evaluation, with its specified procedures and documentable results, helped to change that. The technique provided work-related and business-related order and logic. At the same time, the world of work is changing. The work of most people now requires that they figure out what to do in a given situation instead of simply performing a canned routine. They must identify problems and opportunities, make decisions, plan courses of action, marshal support, and, in general, design their own work methods, techniques, and tools. The challenge is to ensure that job-evaluation plans allow for the flexibility to adapt to changing conditions.

Some balance between chaos and control is required. History suggests that when flexibility without guidelines exists, chaotic and irrational pay rates frequently result. Removing inefficient bureaucracy is important, but balanced guidelines are necessary to ensure that employees are treated fairly and that pay decisions help the organization achieve its objectives.

Conclusion

The differences in the rates paid for different jobs and skills affect the ability of managers to achieve their business objectives: Differences in pay matter. They matter to employees, because their willingness to take on more responsibility and training, to focus on adding value for customers and improving quality of products, and to be flexible enough to adapt to change all depend at least in part on how pay is structured for different levels of work. Differences in the rates paid for different jobs and skills also influence how fairly employees believe they are being treated. Unfair treatment ultimately is counterproductive.

So far, the most common approach to designing pay differences for different work has been examined: job evaluation. In the next chapter, we will examine several alternative approaches. However, any approach must be evaluated according to how well it will help design an internal pay structure that is based on the work, that will help achieve the business objectives, and that is acceptable to key stakeholders.

Job evaluation has evolved into many forms and methods. Consequently, wide variations exist in its use and in the way in which it is perceived. This chapter discussed some of the many views concerning the role of job evaluation and reviewed the criticisms levelled at it. No matter how job evaluation is designed, its ultimate use is to help design and manage a work-related, business-focused, and agreed-upon pay structure.

Chapter Summary

Job evaluation is the process of determining and quantifying the value of jobs. Different perspectives regarding job evaluation include the following:

- Job evaluation can determine the innate value of jobs.
- Job evaluation can determine the relative value of jobs.
- It is not possible to value jobs without external market information.
- Job evaluation is dependent on objective measurement instruments.
- Job evaluation should be conducted participatively through a process of negotiation.

The ranking method of job evaluation rank orders the jobs from highest to lowest based on a global definition of value. Two methods of ranking are: (1) alternation ranking, in which the most- and least-valued jobs are selected first, then the next most- and least-valued jobs, and so on; and (2) paired comparison, in which each job is ranked against all other jobs.

The classification method of job evaluation uses class descriptions to categorize jobs. Descriptions of benchmark jobs (those that are well known, relatively stable, and common across different employers) are used as part of the class descriptions for clarification. The final result is a series of classes with a number of jobs in each.

The six steps involved in the point method of job evaluation are:

- Conduct job analysis
- Determine compensable factors
- Scale the factors

- Weight the factors according to importance
- Communicate the plan
- Apply the plan to non-benchmark jobs

The three common characteristics of point plans are compensable factors, numerically scaled factor degrees/levels, and weights reflecting the importance of each factor.

Committees, task forces, or teams including non-managerial employees should be involved in job evaluation in an advisory or decision-making capacity. Union participation may also be desirable.

KEY TERMS

REVIEW QUESTIONS

1. How does job evaluation translate internal alignment policies (loosely coupled versus tight fitting) into practice? What do (a) organizational strategy, (b) flow of work, (c) fairness, and (d) motivating employee behaviour have to do with job evaluation?
2. Why are there different approaches to job evaluation? Think of several employers in your area (e.g., hospital, Walmart, manufacturing plant, bank, university/college). What approach would you expect each of them to use? Why?
3. What are the advantages and disadvantages of using more than one job evaluation plan in any single organization?
4. Why bother with job evaluation? Why not simply market price? How can job evaluation link internal alignment and external market pressures?

EXPERIENTIAL EXERCISES

1. Consider your university or college. Develop compensable factors for your institution to evaluate jobs. Would you use one job evaluation plan or multiple plans? Should the school's educational mission be reflected in your factors? Or are generic factors okay? Discuss. Ask your professor to help you identify the actual factors used (this likely will involve contacting the HR department compensation staff).

2. You are the manager of 10 people in a large organization. All become suspicious and upset when they receive a memo from the HR department saying their jobs are going to be evaluated. What would you say to try to reassure them?

WEB EXERCISE

The Correctional Services and Foreign Service Classification Standard

The Canadian federal government has recently reformed several classification standards (job evaluations). Go to the classification standard for the Foreign Service Group (www.tbs-sct.gc.ca/gui/csnc/FS_e.pdf) and for the Correctional Services Group (www.tbs-sct.gc.ca/gui/csnc/CX_e.pdf). Compare the new standard for Foreign Service jobs with the older standard for Correctional Services jobs on the basis of aligning with organizational strategy, supporting workflow, fairness to employees, and motivating behaviour toward organizational objectives. Which standard matches more closely the point method of job evaluation described in the text? What is missing from the Correctional Services job evaluation plan?

CASE

Job Evaluation at Whole Foods

Rather than wait until you are next in a supermarket to check out the different types of work, we brought some of the jobs at Whole Foods to you. Now that you have some background in job evaluation, it is time to try it out. As a first step, Whole Foods has conducted job analysis and prepared job descriptions. The results are shown below. Now a job structure is needed. The manager has assigned this job to you.

1. Divide into teams of four to six students each. Each team should evaluate the nine jobs and prepare a job structure based on its evaluation. Assign titles to each job, and list your structure by title and job letter. A broad hint: Remember from our discussion of Whole Foods' business and pay strategy in Chapter 2 that teams play an important role.

2. Each team should describe the process the group went through to arrive at that job structure. Job evaluation techniques and compensable factors used should be described, and the reasons for selecting them should be stated.

3. Each team should give each job a title and put its job structure on the board. Comparisons can then be made between the job structures of the various teams. Does the job evaluation method used appear to affect the results? Do the compensable factors chosen affect the results? Does the process affect the results?

4. Evaluate the job descriptions. What parts were most useful? How could they be improved?

Job A

Kind of Work Provide excellent customer service. Follow and comply with all applicable health and sanitation procedures. Prepare food items: make sandwiches, slice deli meats and cheeses. Prepare items on station assignment list and as predetermined. Stock and rotate products; stock supplies and paper goods in a timely basis; keep all utensils stocked. Check dates on all products in stock to ensure freshness and rotate when necessary. Use waste sheets properly, as directed. Operate and sanitize all equipment in a safe and proper manner. Comply with and follow Whole Foods Market Safety Procedures. Follow established Weights and Measures procedures. Answer the phone and pages to department quickly and with appropriate phone etiquette. Practise proper use of knives, slicer, trash compactor, box baler, and all other equipment used during food preparation and cleanup. Perform other duties as assigned, and follow through on supervisor requests in a timely manner.

Requirements

- Some deli experience preferred
- Clear and effective communicator
- Patient, enjoys working with and mentoring people
- Ability to perform physical requirements of position
- Ability to learn proper use of knives, slicer, box baler (must be 18 years of age or older), and all other equipment used during food preparation and cleanup
- Ability to work well with others as a team
- Knowledge of all relevant Whole Foods Market policies and standards
- Understands and can communicate quality goals to customers

Job B

Kind of Work Assist and focus on customers during entire checkout process. Perform all cash register functions according to established procedures. Maintain a positive company image by providing courteous, friendly, and efficient customer service. Check out customer groceries efficiently and accurately. Pass entry-level PLU code test. Maintain a professional demeanour at all times. Stock registers with supplies as needed. Follow proper cheque-receiving procedure. Clean, stock, and detail front-end area with special attention to own register. Change journal tapes and ribbon as needed. Walk produce department at the beginning of every shift to identify and learn new produce codes. Comply with all posted provincial health and safety codes.

Requirements

- Excellent communication skills necessary for good customer and team relations
- Ability to work well with others
- Ability to learn proper use of box baler (must be 18 years of age or older)
- Desire to learn and grow
- Ability to work in a fast-paced environment, with a sense of urgency
- Understanding the importance of working as a team
- Good math skills
- Patience

Job C

Kind of Work   Reports to store team leader and to associate store team leader. Provides overall management and supervision of Prepared Foods Department. Responsible for team member hiring, development, and termination. Also responsible for profitability, expense control, buying/merchandising, regulatory compliance, and special projects as assigned. Complete accountability for all aspects of department operations. Consistently communicate and model Whole Foods' vision and goals. Interview, select, train, develop, and counsel team members in a manner that builds and sustains a high-performing team and minimizes turnover. Make hiring and termination decisions with guidance of store team leader. Establish and maintain a positive work environment. Manage inventory to achieve targeted gross profit margin. Manage the ordering process to meet Whole Foods Market quality standards. Maintain competitive pricing and achieve targeted sales. Establish and maintain positive and productive vendor relationships. Develop and maintain creative store layout and product merchandising in support of regional and national vision. Establish and maintain collaborative and productive working relationships. Model and cultivate effective inter-department and inter-store communication. Provide accurate, complete information in daily, weekly, monthly, annual, and ad hoc management reports. Maintain comprehensive knowledge of, and ensure compliance with, relevant regulatory rules and standards.

Requirements

- Two years relevant experience as a team leader, assistant team leader, supervisor, or buyer
- Thorough knowledge of products, buying, pricing, merchandising, and inventory management
- Excellent verbal and written communication skills
- Strong organizational skills
- Knowledge of all relevant Whole Foods Market policies and standards
- Computer skills

Job D

Kind of Work   Perform all duties and responsibilities of Prepared Foods team member. Provide excellent customer service. Assist team leader in nightly team operations. Report all actions of team members that violate policies or standards to the team leader or associate team leader. Mentor and train team members. Maintain quality standards in production and counter display. Comply with all applicable health and safety codes. Help implement and support all regional programs.

Requirements

- Minimum six months retail food production experience or equivalent
- Overall knowledge of both front and back of the house operations
- Comprehensive product knowledge
- Comprehensive knowledge of quality standards
- Excellent organizational skills
- Excellent interpersonal skills and ability to train others
- Demonstrated decision-making ability and leadership skills
- Ability to perform physical requirements of position

Job E

Kind of Work   Performs all duties related to dishwashing: unloading kitchen deliveries and cleaning all dishes, utensils, pots, and pans. May be prep work. Maintain food quality and sanitation in kitchen. Maintain a positive company image by being courteous, friendly, and efficient. Wash and sanitize all dishes, utensils, and containers. Assist with proper storage of all deliveries. Rotate and organize products. Perform prep work as directed. Provide proper ongoing maintenance of equipment. Maintain health department standards when cleaning and handling food. Perform deep-cleaning tasks on a regular basis. Take out all of the garbage and recycling materials. Sweep and wash floors as needed.

Requirements

- Entry-level position
- Ability to perform physical requirements of job
- Practises safe and proper knife skills
- Ability to work box baler (must be 18 years of age or older)
- Works well with others and participates as part of the team

Job F

Kind of Work   Performs all functions related to breaking down deliveries and moving back stock to floor. Assists in organizing and developing promotional displays; maintaining back room; training entry-level grocery clerks. Trained and capable of operating any of the sub-departments as needed. Maintains and ensures retail standards during shift. Responsible for implementing team's break schedule. Performs all duties and responsibilities of grocery team member. Builds displays and requests appropriate signage. Supervises shift to ensure standards are maintained. Implements break schedule for shift. Responsible for problem solving in team leader or associate team leader's absence. Fully responsible for completion of all opening or closing checklists. Responsible for checking in deliveries.

Requirements

- Minimum one year retail grocery experience or equivalent
- Proficient in math skills (addition, subtraction, multiplication, and division)
- Ability to perform physical requirements of position
- Ability to properly use box baler (must be 18 years of age or older)
- Ability to direct team members and implement break schedule
- Ability to work well with others

Job G

Kind of Work   Reports directly to Prepared Foods team leader. Assists in overall management and supervision of the Prepared Foods Department. Can be responsible for team member hiring, development, and termination. Also responsible for profitability, expense control, buying/merchandising, regulatory compliance, and special projects as assigned. Complete accountability for all aspects of department operations. Consistently communicate and model Whole Foods' vision and goals. Assist in the interview, selection, training, development, and counselling of team members in a manner that builds and sustains a high-performing team and minimizes turnover. Discuss hiring and termination decisions with guidance of others. Establish and maintain a positive work environment. Manage inventory to achieve targeted gross profit margin. Manage the ordering process to meet Whole Foods Market quality standards, maintain competitive pricing, and achieve targeted sales. Develop and maintain creative store layout and product merchandising in support of regional and national vision. Establish and maintain collaborative and productive working relationships. Model and cultivate effective inter-department and inter-store communication. Provide accurate, complete information in daily, weekly, monthly, annual, and ad hoc management reports. Maintain comprehensive knowledge of, and ensure compliance with, relevant regulatory rules and standards.

Requirements

- Over two years of department experience or industry equivalent
- Analytical ability and proficiency in math needed to calculate margins, monitor profitability, and manage inventory
- Clear and effective communicator
- Patient and enjoys working with and mentoring people
- Strong organizational skills
- Knowledge of all relevant Whole Foods Market policies and standards
- Computer skills

Job H

Kind of Work Rotate among stores. Assist and support the store team leader with all store functions. Interview, select, evaluate, counsel, and terminate team members. Coordinate and supervise all store products and personnel. Follow through on all customer and team member questions and requests. Evaluate customer service and resolve complaints. Operate the store in an efficient and profitable manner. Have a firm understanding of store financials and labour budgets. Establish and achieve sales, labour, and contribution goals. Review department schedules and research productivity improvements. Order store equipment and supplies in a timely manner. Enforce established food safety, cleaning, and maintenance procedures. Inspect store, ensure cleanliness, visit off-hours for consistency. Maintain accurate retail pricing and signage. Ensure that product is cross-merchandised in other departments. Coordinate, supervise, and report physical inventory. Analyze product transfers, waste, and spoilage. Manage expenses to maximize the bottom line. Provide, maintain, and safety-train team members on all equipment and tools. Resolve safety violations and hazards immediately. Maintain store security and ensure that opening and closing procedures are followed. Show EVA improvement over a designated period. Leverage sales growth to improve store profitability. Assist in handling liability claims and minimize their occurrence. Establish and maintain good community relations. Create a friendly, productive, and professional working environment. Communicate company goals and information to team members. Ensure and support team member development and training. Evaluate team member duties, dialogues, raises, and promotions. Keep regional leadership informed of all major events that affect the store. Ensure that store policies and procedures are followed. Visit the competition on a regular basis and react to current industry trends.

Requirements

- A passion for retailing
- Complete understanding of Whole Foods Market retail operations
- Strong leadership and creative ability

- Management and business skills with financial expertise
- Well organized with excellent follow-through
- Detail oriented with a vision and eye for the big picture
- Self-motivated and solution oriented
- Excellent merchandising skills and eye for detail
- Ability to delegate effectively and use available talent to the best advantage
- Strong communicator and motivator; able to work well with others and convey enthusiasm
- Ability to maintain good relationships with vendors and the community
- Can train and inspire team members to excellence in all aspects of the store
- Ability to make tough decisions
- Love and knowledge of natural foods
- Strong computer skills

Job I

Kind of Work   Performs all functions related to breaking down deliveries and moving back stock to floor. May assist in organizing and developing promotional displays; maintains back room. Stock and clean grocery shelves, bulk bins, frozen and dairy case. Maintain back stock in good order. Sweep floors and face shelves throughout the store. Comply with all applicable health and safety codes. Provide excellent customer service. Log and expedite customers' special orders. Retrieve special orders for customers by request and offer service out to car. Respond to all grocery pages quickly and efficiently. Build displays and request appropriate signage.

Requirements

- Retail grocery or natural foods experience a plus
- Proficient in math skills (addition, subtraction, multiplication and division)
- Ability to learn basic knowledge of all products carried in department
- Ability to perform physical requirements of position
- Proper and safe use of box cutter, baler, and all equipment
- Ability to work well with others

Visit the Online Learning Centre at

www.mcgrawhill.ca/olc/milkovich

PERSON-BASED PAY STRUCTURES

LEARNING OUTCOMES

- Explain the difference between skill-based pay plans and competency-based pay plans, and describe the types of jobs to which each is commonly applied.
- Describe the four basic steps in skill analysis.
- Define competency, and explain what is meant by core competencies, competency sets, and competency indicators.
- Explain why employee acceptance is crucial for person-based pay plans, and how this acceptance can be obtained.
- Describe two potential sources of bias in internal pay structures.

Historians say that some form of job evaluation was in use when the pharaohs built the pyramids. Chinese emperors managed the Great Wall construction with the assistance of job evaluation. The logic underlying today's job-based pay structures flows from scientific management, championed by Frederick Taylor in the early 1900s. Work was broken into a series of steps and analyzed so that the "one best way"—the most efficient way—to perform every element of the job (right down to how to shovel coal), could be specified. Strategically, Taylor's approach fit with mass production technologies that were beginning to revolutionize the way work was done.

But in today's work culture, employees are told they must go beyond the tasks specified in their job descriptions. They must know more, think more on the job, and take personal responsibility for their results. Pay systems that support continuous learning and improvement, flexibility, participation, and partnership are essential to achieving competitive advantage today. Person-based pay structures hold out that promise. The logic supporting person-based approaches is that structures based on differences in people's skills or competencies will be more flexible and thus encourage agility.

Person-based approaches are the topic of this chapter. At the end of this chapter, the usefulness of the various approaches—job- and person-based—for determining internal pay structures will be discussed.

Exhibit 6.1 points out the similarities in the logic underlying job-based and people-based approaches. No matter the basis for the structure, a way is needed to (1) collect and summarize information about the work, (2) determine what is of value to the organization, (3) quantify that value, and then (4) translate that value into internal structure. The previous two chapters discussed the process for job-based structures (job analysis and job evaluation). This chapter discusses the process for person-based structures.

EXHIBIT **6.1** Many Ways to Create Internal Structure

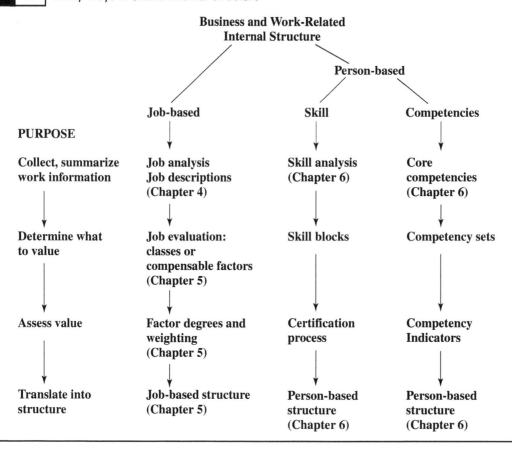

■ PERSON-BASED PAY STRUCTURES: SKILL PLANS

Skill-based pay plans are usually applied to so-called blue-collar work and competency-based plans to so-called white-collar work. The distinctions are not hard-and-fast. However, the majority of applications of skill-based pay have been in manufacturing and assembly work where the work can be specified and defined. The advantage of a **skill-based pay structure** is that people can be deployed in a way that better matches the flow of work, thus avoiding bottlenecks as well as idle hands.[1] Structures based on skill pay individuals for all the skills for which they have been certified regardless of whether the work they are doing requires all or just a few of those particular skills. By contrast, a job-based plan pays employees for the job to which they are assigned, regardless of the skills they possess.

> **skill-based pay structures**
>
> link pay to the depth or breadth of the skills, abilities, and knowledge a person acquires that are relevant to the work

Types of Skill Plans

Skill plans can focus on depth (e.g., specialists in corporate law, finance, or welding and hydraulic maintenance) or breadth (generalists with knowledge in all phases of operations including marketing, manufacturing, finance, and human resources).

Specialist: Depth   The pay structures for elementary and high school teachers are usually based on their knowledge measured by education level. A typical teacher's contract specifies a series of steps, with each step corresponding to a level of education. A bachelor's degree in education is step one and is the minimum required for hiring. To advance a step to higher pay requires additional education. For example, the salary schedule included in the case at the end of this chapter requires 15 additional credits beyond the bachelor's degree to move to a higher step. Each year of seniority also is associated with a pay increase. The result can be that two teachers may receive different pay rates for doing essentially the same job—teaching English to high school students. The pay is based on the knowledge of the individual doing the job (measured by the number of university credits and years of teaching experience) rather than on job content or output (performance of students).[2] The presumption is that teachers with more knowledge are more effective and more flexible—able to teach many grades.

Generalist/Multiskill-Based: Breadth   As with teachers, employees in a multiskill system earn pay increases by acquiring new knowledge, but the knowledge is specific to a range of related jobs. Pay increases come with certification of new skills, rather than with job assignments. Employees then can be assigned to any of the jobs for which they are certified, based on the flow of work.[3] An example from Balzer's Tool Coating (a global tool manufacturer) makes the point. This company coats cutting tools by bombarding them with, among other things, titanium nitrate ions. This coating makes the sharp edge last much longer. Originally, eight different jobs were involved in the coating process. Everyone started at the same rate, no matter the job to which they were assigned. Employees received cross-training in a variety of jobs, but without a specific training path or level. Different locations started new people in different jobs. In order to put some order into its system and make better use of its employees, Balzer moved to a skill-based plan for all its hourly workers, including administrative and sales employees. Its new structure includes four different levels, from Fundamental to Advanced. Exhibit 6.2 shows the new structure and the skill blocks in each level. New employees are hired into the Fundamental level. Fundamental skills include familiarity with company forms and procedures, basic product knowledge, safety, basic computer usage, and so on.

EXHIBIT 6.2   Proposed Skill Ladder at Balzer Tool Coating

Skill-Based Salary Grades

| | Skill Path | | | | | |
Grade	*Admin*	*Sales*	*Tool*	*Machine*	*Grade min*	*Grade max*
Advanced					$10.50	$13.50
Advanced						
Advanced						
Advanced						
Advanced						
Advanced				Service		
Advanced	Office Admin	Inside Sales	Incoming Ins	Arc Tech	$9.50	$12.50
Intermed						
Intermed						
Intermed	Blueprint	Cust Serv	Outgoing Ins	Evap Tech		
Intermed	Expediting	Pricing- B	Shipping	Coating	$7.50	$11.50
Basic	Software	Van Driver	Receiving	Degas		
Basic	Pricing	Licensing	Racking	Stripping		
Basic	File/route	Packing	Packing	Cleaning		
Basic	Gen Office	Courier	Fixturing	Blasting		
Entry	Fundamental	Fundamental	Fundamental	Fundamental	$7.00	$7.50
# of skills	7	7	7	8	$0.50 per skill	

Source: Diana Southall, HR Foundations, Inc.

Once they have been certified in all the skills at the Fundamental level, employees receive a pay increase of $0.50 an hour and move to the Basic skill level. Certification in each of the four skill blocks (blasting, cleaning, stripping, and degas) in this level is worth an additional $0.50 an hour. Basic level employees can be assigned to any of the tasks for which they are certified; they will be paid whatever is their highest certification rate. The same approach is used to train and certify employees at the Intermediate and Advanced levels. A person certified at the very top of the structure, who earns at least $10.50 an hour, could be assigned to any of the tasks in the structure. The advantage to Balzer is workforce flexibility and, hence, staffing assignments that can be better matched to the workflow.[4] The advantage to employees is that the more they learn, the more they earn.

The system at Balzer differs from the system for teachers in that the responsibilities assigned to an employee in a multiskill system can change drastically over a short period of time, whereas teachers' basic job responsibilities do not vary on a day-to-day basis. Additionally, Balzer's system is designed to ensure that all the skills are clearly job related. Training improves skills that the company values. In contrast, a school district has no guarantee that courses taken actually improve teaching skills.

Purpose of the Skill-Based Structure

To evaluate the usefulness of skill-based structures, we shall use the objectives already specified for an internally aligned structure: supports the organization's strategy, supports workflow, is fair to employees, and motivates their behaviour toward organization objectives. How well do skill-based structures perform?

Supports the Strategy and Objectives   The skills on which a structure is based should be directly related to the organization's objectives and strategy. In practice, however, the "line of sight" between changes in the specific work skills (Fundamental to Advanced) required to operate the titanium nitrate ion coaters and increased shareholder returns is difficult to make clear. In some sense, we know that these operating skills matter, but the link to the plant's performance is clearer than is the link to corporate goals.

Supports Workflow   One of the main advantages of a skill-based plan is that it can more easily match people to a changing workflow.[5] For example, one national hotel chain moves many of its people to the hotel's front desk between 4 and 7 p.m., when the majority of guests check in. After 7 p.m., these same employees move to the food and beverage service area to match the demand for room service and dining room service. By ensuring that guests do not have to wait long to check in or to eat, the hotel provides a high level of service with fewer staff. (The tastiness of the resulting food is another matter, reinforcing the point that skill-based systems focus on inputs, not results.)

Is Fair to Employees Employees like the potential of higher pay that comes with learning. And by encouraging employees to take charge of their own development, skill-based plans may give them more control over their work lives. However, favouritism and bias may play a role in determining who gets first crack at the training necessary to become certified at higher paying skill levels. Employees complain that they are forced to pick up the slack for those who are out for training. And the courts have not yet been asked to rule on the legality of two people doing the same task for different (skill-based) pay.

Motivates Behaviour toward Organization Objectives   Person-based plans have the potential to clarify new standards and behavioural expectations. The fluid work assignments that skill-based plans permit encourage employees to take responsibility for the complete work process and its results, with less direction from supervisors.[6]

■ "HOW TO": SKILL ANALYSIS

skill analysis

a systematic process to identify and collect information about skills required to perform work in an organization

Exhibit 6.3 depicts the process for determining a skill-based structure. It begins with a **skill analysis**, which is similar to the task statements in a job analysis. Related skills can be grouped into a skill block; skill blocks can be arranged by levels into a skill structure. To build the structure, a process is needed to describe, certify, and value the skills.

Exhibit 6.3 also identifies the major skill analysis decisions: (1) What information should be collected? (2) What methods should be used? (3) Who should be involved? (4) How useful are the results for pay purposes? These are exactly the same decisions managers face in job analysis.

What Information to Collect?

There is far less uniformity in the use of terms in person-based plans than in job-based plans. FMC (a global chemical company with a manufacturing facility in Prince George, British Columbia) assigns points and groups skills as foundation, core electives, and optional electives. FMC's plan for technicians is more fully developed in Exhibit 6.4.

- *Foundation skills* include a quality seminar, videos on materials handling and hazardous materials, a three-day safety workshop, and a half-day orientation. All foundation skills are mandatory and must be certified to reach the Technician I rate ($11 per hour).
- *Core electives* are necessary to the facility's operations (e.g., fabrication, welding, painting, finishing, assembly, inspection). Each skill is assigned a point value.
- *Optional electives* are additional specialized competencies ranging from computer applications to team leadership and consensus building.

To reach Technician II ($12 per hour), 40 core elective points (of 370) must be certified in addition to the foundation competencies. To reach Technician III, an additional 100 points of core electives must be certified plus three optional electives.

A fully qualified Technician IV (e.g., certified as mastering foundations, 365 points of core electives, and 5 optional electives) is able to perform all work in a cell at the facility. Technician IVs earn $17 per hour no matter the task they are doing. FMC's approach should look familiar to any college and university student: required courses, required credits chosen among specific categories, and optional electives.

The FMC plan illustrates the kind of information that underpins the skill-based plans, i.e., very specific information on every aspect of the production process. This makes the plans particularly suited for continuous flow technologies where employees work in teams.

EXHIBIT 6.3 Determining the Internal Skill-Based Structure ————————

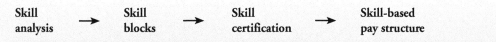

Skill analysis → Skill blocks → Skill certification → Skill-based pay structure

Basic Decisions:
- What is the objective of the plan?
- What information should be collected?
- What methods should be used to determine and certify skills?
- Who should be involved?
- How useful are the results for pay purposes?

EXHIBIT 6.4 FMC Technician Skill-Based Structure

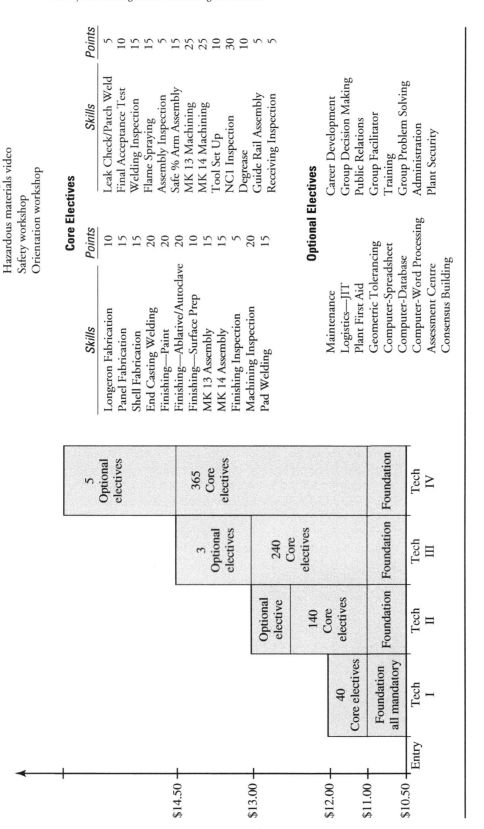

Foundations

- Quality course
- Shop floor control
- Materials handling
- Hazardous materials video
- Safety workshop
- Orientation workshop

Core Electives

Skills	Points	Skills	Points
Longeron Fabrication	10	Leak Check/Patch Weld	5
Panel Fabrication	15	Final Acceptance Test	10
Shell Fabrication	15	Welding Inspection	15
End Casting Welding	20	Flame Spraying	15
Finishing—Paint	20	Assembly Inspection	5
Finishing—Ablative/Autoclave	20	Safe % Arm Assembly	15
Finishing—Surface Prep	10	MK 13 Machining	25
MK 13 Assembly	15	MK 14 Machining	25
MK 14 Assembly	15	Tool Set Up	10
Finishing Inspection	5	NC1 Inspection	30
Machining Inspection	20	Degrease	10
Pad Welding	15	Guide Rail Assembly	5
		Receiving Inspection	5

Optional Electives

Maintenance	Career Development
Logistics—JIT	Group Decision Making
Plant First Aid	Public Relations
Geometric Tolerancing	Group Facilitator
Computer-Spreadsheet	Training
Computer-Database	Group Problem Solving
Computer-Word Processing	Administration
Assessment Centre	Plant Security
Consensus Building	

Pay scale (from chart): $10.50, $11.00, $12.00, $13.00, $14.50

	Entry	Tech I	Tech II	Tech III	Tech IV
Optional electives			Optional elective	3 Optional electives	5 Optional electives
Core electives		40 Core electives	140 Core electives	240 Core electives	365 Core electives
Foundation		Foundation all mandatory	Foundation	Foundation	Foundation

Whom to Involve?

Employee involvement is almost always built into skill-based plans. Employees are the sources of information for defining the skills, arranging them into a hierarchy, bundling them into skill blocks, and certifying whether a person actually possesses the skills. At Balzer and FMC, a committee composed of managers from several sites developed, with input from employees, the skill listing and certification process for each of the four skill ladders.

Establish Certification Methods

Practices for certifying that employees possess the skills and are able to apply them vary widely. Some organizations use peer review, on-the-job demonstrations, and tests for certification, similar to the traditional apprentice/journeyman/master path. Honeywell evaluates employees during the six months after they have learned the skills. Again, leaders and peers are used in the certification process. Still others require successful completion of formal courses. However, we do not need to point out to a student that sitting in the classroom doesn't guarantee that anything is learned. School districts address this issue in a variety of ways. Some are more restrictive than others about which courses will increase teachers' pay. Some will certify for any courses; others only for courses in the teacher's subject area. However, no districts require evidence that the course makes any difference to results.

Newer skill-based applications appear to be moving away from an on-demand review and toward scheduling fixed-review points during the year. Scheduling makes it easier to budget and control payroll increases. Other changes include ongoing recertification, which replaces the traditional one-time certification process and helps ensure that skills are kept fresh, and removal of certification (and the accompanying pay) when a particular skill is deemed obsolete.[7] (This is the case with the national Certified Human Resources Professional designation in Canada.) However, it can be difficult to change certification procedures once a system is in place. TRW faced this problem when using formal classes for its airbag facility. TRW felt that some employees were only putting in "seat time." Yet no one was willing to take responsibility for refusing to certify, because an extra signoff beyond classroom attendance was not part of the original system design.

Many plans require that employees be recertified, because skills can get rusty when not used frequently. Airplane pilots, for example, must go through an emergency-landing simulation every 12 months. Similarly, the introduction of new skill requirements and the obsolescence of previous skills require recertification. At its Ome facility in Tokyo, Toshiba requires all team members to recertify their skills every 24 months. Those who fail have the opportunity to retrain and attempt to recertify before their pay rate is reduced. However, the pressure to keep up to date and avoid obsolescence is intense.

Skill-based plans become increasingly expensive as the majority of employees become certified at the highest pay levels. As a result, the employer may have an average wage higher than competitors who are using conventional job evaluation. Unless the increased flexibility permits leaner staffing, the employer may also experience higher labour costs. Some employers are combatting this by requiring that employees stay at a rate for a certain length of time before they can take the training to move to a higher rate. Motorola abandoned its skill-based plan because, at the end of three years, everyone had topped out (by accumulating the necessary skill blocks). TRW, too, found that after a few years, people at two manufacturing plants on skill-based systems all had topped out. They were flexible and well trained. So now what? What happens in the next years out? Does everybody automatically receive a pay increase? In a firm with labour-intensive products, the increased labour costs under skill-based plans may also become a source of competitive disadvantage.

Guidance from the Research on Skill-Based Plans

Skill-based plans are generally well accepted by employees because it is easy to see the connection between the plan, the work, and the size of the paycheque. Consequently, the plans provide strong motivation for individuals to increase their skills. "Learn to earn" is a popular slogan used in these plans. One study connected the ease of communication and understanding of skill-based plans to employees' general perceptions of being treated fairly by the employer.[8] The design of the certification process is crucial in this perception of fairness. Two studies related use of a skills system to productivity. One found positive results, the other did not.[9] Another study found that younger, more educated employees with strong growth needs, organizational commitment, and a positive attitude toward workplace innovations were more successful in acquiring new skills.[10] Nevertheless, for reasons not made clear, the study's authors recommend allocating training opportunities by seniority.

So what kind of workplace seems best suited to a skill-based plan? Early longitudinal research on skill-based plans found that about 60 percent of the companies in their original sample were still using skill-based plans seven years later. One of the key factors that determined a plan's success was how well it was aligned with the organization's strategy. Plans were more viable in organizations following a cost-cutter strategy (focusing on operational efficiency—doing more with less). The reduced numbers of highly trained, flexible employees that skill-based pay promises fit this strategy very well.[11]

A final question is whether a multiskilled "jack-of-all-trades" might really be the master of none. Some research suggests that the greatest impact on results occurs after just a small amount of increased flexibility.[12] Greater increments in flexibility achieve fewer improvements. So, more skills may not necessarily improve productivity. Instead, there may be an optimal number of skills for any individual to possess. Beyond that number, productivity returns are smaller than the pay increases. Additionally, some employees may not be interested in giving up the job they are doing. Such "campers" create a bottleneck for rotating other employees into that position to acquire those skills. Organizations should decide in advance whether they are willing to design a plan to work around campers or force them into the system.

The bottom line is that skill-based approaches may be only short-term initiatives for specific settings. Unfortunately, the longitudinal study did not report on the 40 percent of cases where skill-based pay did not survive beyond six years.

■ PERSON-BASED PAY STRUCTURES: COMPETENCIES

While skill- and job-based systems focus on information about specific tasks, a competency-based approach pays for underlying, broadly applicable knowledge, skills, and behaviours that form the

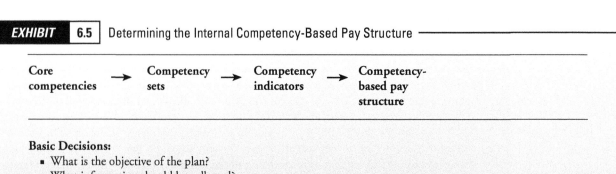

EXHIBIT 6.5   Determining the Internal Competency-Based Pay Structure

Core competencies → Competency sets → Competency indicators → Competency-based pay structure

Basic Decisions:
- What is the objective of the plan?
- What information should be collected?
- Which methods should be used to determine and certify competencies?
- Who is involved?
- How useful for pay purposes?

competencies

underlying, broadly applicable knowledge, skills, and behaviours that form the foundation for successful work performance

competency-based pay structure

links pay to work-related competencies

core competencies

competencies required for successful work performance in any job in the organization

competency sets

specific components of a competency

competency indicators

observable behaviours that indicate the level of competency within each competency set

foundation for successful work performance, called **competencies**. Exhibit 6.5 shows the process of using competencies to address the need for internal alignment by creating a **competency-based pay structure**.

Core competencies are those that form the foundation for successful performance at all jobs in the organization. They are often linked to mission statements that express an organization's philosophy, values, business strategies, and plans.

Competency sets begin to translate each core competency into action. For the core competency of "business awareness," for example, competency sets might be related to organizational understanding, cost management, third-party relationships, and ability to identify business opportunities.

Competency indicators are the observable behaviours that indicate the level of competency within each set. These indicators may be used for staffing and evaluation as well as for pay purposes.

TRW's competency model for its human resource management department, shown in Exhibit 6.6, includes the four core competencies considered critical to the success of the business. All HR employees at TRW are expected to demonstrate some level of these competencies. However, not all would be expected to reach the highest level in all competencies. Rather, the HR function would want to be sure it possessed all levels of mastery of all the core competencies within its HRM group, and individual employees would use the model as a guide to what TRW values and what capacities it wants people to develop.

The competency indicators anchor the degree of a competency required at each level of complexity of the work. Exhibit 6.7 shows five levels of competency indicators for the competency called "Impact and Influence." These behavioural anchors make the competency more concrete. The levels range from "uses direct persuasion" at level 1 to "uses experts or other third parties to influence" at level 5. Sometimes the behavioural anchors include scales of the intensity of action, the degree of impact of the action, its complexity, and/or the amount of effort expended. Scaled competency indicators are similar to job analysis questionnaires and degrees of compensable factors, discussed in previous chapters.

Defining Competencies

Because competencies are trying to get at what underlies work behaviours, there is a lot of fuzziness in defining them. Early conceptions of competencies focused on five areas:[13]

1. Skills (demonstration of expertise)
2. Knowledge (accumulated information)
3. Self-concepts (attitudes, values, self-image)
4. Traits (general disposition to behave in a certain way)
5. Motives (recurrent thoughts that drive behaviours)

As experience with competencies has grown, organizations seem to be moving away from the vagueness of self-concepts, traits, and motives. Instead, they are placing greater emphasis on business-related descriptions of behaviours that excellent performers exhibit much more consistently than average performers. Competencies are becoming "a collection of observable behaviours (not a single behaviour) that require no inference, assumption, or interpretation." A comparison of the behavioural anchors for the competency: "Impact and Influence" in Exhibit 6.7 with compensable factors used in job evaluation such as "Decision Making" (Exhibit 5.8) reveal the greater behavioural orientation of competencies. However, differences can be rather small. For example, "consults" and "uses experts" anchor both the sixth level of the compensable factor and the fifth level of the competency.

EXHIBIT **6.6** **TRW Human Resources Competencies**

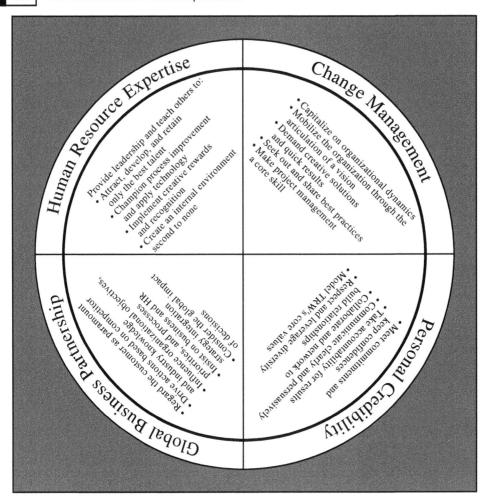

Purpose of the Competency-Based Structure

Do competencies help support an internally aligned structure? Using the by-now familiar yardstick: How well do competencies support the organization's strategy and workflow, treat employees fairly, and direct their behaviour toward organization objectives? The .Net Worth box illustrates how competencies are also used in the management training program of the federal government.

Organization Strategy   Frito-Lay, which has used competency-based structures for over ten years, lists four competencies for managerial work:

1. *Leading for results:* Using initiative and influence with others to drive results and promote continuous improvement
2. *Building workforce effectiveness:* Coaching individual development and building capability of operational, project, or cross-functional teams to achieve business results
3. *Leveraging technical and business systems:* Acquiring and applying a depth and/or breadth of knowledge, skills, and experience to achieve functional excellence
4. *Doing it the right way:* Modelling, teaching and coaching company values

EXHIBIT **6.7** Sample Competency Indicator Description

Impact and Influence: The intention to persuade, convince, or influence to have a specific impact. It includes the ability to anticipate and respond to the needs and concerns of others.

"Impact and Influence" is one of the competencies considered "most critical."

Level	Competency Indicators
0: Not shown	▪ Lets things happen ▪ Quotes policy and issues instruction
1: Direct persuasion	▪ Uses direct persuasion in a discussion or presentation ▪ Appeals to reason; uses data or concrete examples ▪ Does not adapt presentation to the interest and level of the audience ▪ Reiterates the same points when confronted with opposition
2: Multiple attempts to persuade	▪ Tries different tactics when attempting to persuade without necessarily making an effort to adapt to the level or interest of an audience (e.g., making two or more different arguments or points in a discussion)
3: Builds trust and fosters win-win mentality (expected performance level)	▪ Tailors presentations or discussions to appeal to the interest and level of other ▪ Looks for the "win–win" opportunities ▪ Demonstrates sensitivity and understanding of others in detecting underlying concerns, interests, or emotions, and uses that understanding to develop effective responses to objections
4: Multiple actions to influence	▪ Takes more than one action to influence, with each action adapted to the specific audience (e.g., a group meeting to present the situation, followed by individual meetings) ▪ May include taking a well-thought-out unusual action to have a specific impact
5: Influences through others	▪ Uses experts or other third parties to influence ▪ Develops and maintains a planned network of relationships with customers, internal peers, and industry colleagues ▪ When required, assembles "behind the scenes" support for ideas regarding opportunities and/or solving problems

There are three levels of impact for each competency. At the first level, exhibiting the competency affects the team. At the next level, it has an impact across teams. At the highest level, it has an impact on the entire location.[14]

Workflow Competencies are chosen to ensure that all the critical needs of the organization are met. For example, it is common practice to write: "These skills are considered important for all professionals but the weighting of importance and the level of proficiency varies for different positions, organizations, and business conditions." Where skill-based plans are tightly connected to today's work, competencies apply more loosely to work requiring more tacit (implicit or not stated) knowledge and behaviour such as in managerial and professional work.

.NET WORTH

Competencies for Management Trainees in the Federal Government

Competencies often are used, in addition to pay, as the basis for other human resource management initiatives. The Canadian federal government requires specific competencies for its management trainee program. There are 14 competencies in five categories, as follows:

Intellectual competencies
- Cognitive capacity
- Creativity

Future-building competencies
- Visioning

Management competencies
- Action management
- Organizational awareness
- Teamwork
- Partnering

Relationship competencies
- Interpersonal relations
- Communication

Personal competencies
- Stamina / stress resistance
- Ethics and values
- Personality
- Behavioural flexibility
- Self-confidence

Each of these competencies has a specific definition. As an example, *interpersonal relations* is defined as:

> Managers recognize the importance of developing and maintaining positive relationships with others for the productivity and well-being of their unit. They show sensitivity to the concerns and situations of others, and consider the people component of issues and decisions. They accommodate diversity. They actively foster positive relations among their subordinates, dealing with disagreements constructively and fairly before they escalate into conflict.

Six of the fourteen competencies are considered as key competencies. They are most critical because they are the ones for which the most growth is expected and where growth can be demonstrated and measured. In addition, trainees have considerable opportunity to demonstrate them throughout the management training program in progressively more demanding assignments. The key competencies for promotion are:

- Cognitive capacity
- Action management
- Organizational awareness
- Teamwork
- Interpersonal relations
- Communication

Source: Treasury Board of Canada Secretariat, 2009. www.tbs-sct.gc.ca/dev/mtpsg/cmp-eng.asp (accessed September 26, 2009).

Fair to Employees   Advocates of competencies say they can empower employees to take charge of their own development. By focusing on optimum performance rather than average performance, competencies can help employees maintain their marketability.[15] However, critics of competencies worry that the field is going back to the middle of the last century, when basing pay on personal characteristics was standard practice.[16] Basing pay on race or sex seems appalling today, yet it was standard practice at one time. Basing pay on someone's judgment of another person's integrity raises a similar flag. Trying to justify pay differences based on inferred competencies creates risks that need to be managed.

Motivate Behaviour toward Organization Objectives   Competencies provide guidelines for behaviour and keep people focused. They also can provide a common basis for communicating and working together. This latter possibility has become increasingly important as organizations go global, and as employees with widely differing viewpoints and experiences fill leadership positions in these global organizations.

■ "HOW TO": COMPETENCY ANALYSIS

The bottom part of Exhibit 6.5 shows the basic decisions in creating a competency-based structure. The first decision, and by far the most important, is to clarify the objective of the plan.

Objective

competency analysis

a systematic process to identify and collect information about the competencies required for successful work performance

It has already been pointed out that one of the pitfalls of competency systems is trying to do too many things with ill-suited systems. Competencies may have value for personal development and communicating organization direction. However, the vagueness and subjectivity (what exactly are this person's motives?) continue to make competencies a "risky foundation for a pay system."[17] The competency structure may exist on paper by virtue of the competency sets and scaled behavioural indicators, but bear little connection to the work employees do. In contrast, perhaps paying for competencies is the only way to get people to pay attention to them. So the first issue is to conduct a **competency analysis** to clarify the purpose of the competency system.

What Information to Collect?

A number of schemes for classifying competencies have been proposed.[18] One of them uses three groups:

1. *Personal characteristics:* These have the aura of the Boy Scouts about them: trustworthy, loyal, courteous. In business settings, the relevant characteristics might be personal integrity, maturity of judgment, flexibility, and respect for others. Employees are expected to come in the door with these characteristics and then develop and demonstrate them in increasingly complex and ambiguous job situations.
2. *Visionary:* These are the highest level competencies. They might be expressed as possessing a global perspective, taking the initiative in moving the organization in new directions, and being able to articulate the implications for the organization of trends in the marketplace, in world events, and in the local community.
3. *Organization-specific:* Between these two groups are those competencies that are tied specifically to the particular organization and to the particular function where they are being applied. These generally include leadership, customer orientation, functional expertise (e.g., able to leap tall buildings and explain the difference between competencies and compensable factors), and developing others—whatever reflects the company values, culture, and strategic intent.

Exhibit 6.8 shows the leadership competencies that 3M developed internally for its global executives.[19] Behavioural anchors are used to rate an executive on each of these competencies. Exhibit 6.9 shows the behavioural anchors for the "Global Perspective" competency. Executives' ratings on these competencies are used to assess and develop executives worldwide. Because 3M relies heavily on promotion from within, competency ratings help develop executive talent for succession planning. Again, the link to development is clear; the link to pay is less clear.

EXHIBIT | **6.8** | 3M Leadership Competencies

Fundamental

- **Ethics and Integrity**
  Exhibits uncompromising integrity and commitment to 3M's corporate values, human resource principles, and business conduct policies. Builds trust and instills self-confidence through mutually respectful, ongoing communication.
- **Intellectual Capacity**
  Assimilates and synthesizes information rapidly, recognizes the complexity in issues, challenges assumptions, and faces up to reality. Capable of handling multiple, complex, and paradoxical situations. Communicates clearly, concisely, and with appropriate simplicity.
- **Maturity and Judgment**
  Demonstrates resiliency and sound judgment in dealing with business and corporate challenges. Reorganizes when a decision must be made and acts in a considered and timely manner. Deals effectively with ambiguity and learns from success and failure.

Essential

- **Customer Orientation**
  Works constantly to provide superior value to the 3M customer, making each interaction a positive one.
- **Developing People**
  Selects and retains an excellent workforce within an environment that values diversity and respects individuality. Promotes continuous learning and the development of self and others to achieve maximum potential. Gives and seeks open and authentic feedback.
- **Inspiring Others**
  Positively affects the behaviour of others, motivating them to achieve personal satisfaction and high performance through a sense of purpose and spirit of cooperation. Leads by example.
- **Business Health and Results**
  Identifies and successfully generates product, market, and geographic growth opportunities, while consistently delivering positive short-term business results. Continually searches for ways to add value and position the organization for future success.

Visionary

- **Global Perspective**
  Operates from an awareness of 3M's global markets, capabilities, and resources. Exerts global leadership and works respectfully in multicultural environments to 3M's advantage.
- **Vision and Strategy**
  Creates and communicates a customer-focused vision, corporately aligned and engaging all employees in pursuit of a common goal.
- **Nurturing Innovation**
  Creates and sustains an environment that supports experimentation, rewards risk taking, reinforces curiosity, and challenges the status quo through freedom and openness without judgment. Influences the future to 3M's advantage.
- **Building Alliances**
  Builds and leverages mutually beneficial relationships and networks, both internal and external, which generate multiple opportunities for 3M.
- **Organizational Agility**
  Knows, respects, and leverages 3M culture and assets. Leads integrated change within a business unit to achieve sustainable competitive advantage. Utilizes teams intentionally and appropriately.

Source: Margaret E. Allredge and Kevin J. Nilan, "3M's Leadership Competency Model: An Internally Developed Solution," *Human Resource Management* 39, Summer/Fall 2000, pp. 133–45. Reprinted by permission of John Wiley & Sons, Inc.

EXHIBIT 6.9 Competency Indicators for Global Perspectives Competency ─────────

Global Perspective: Behaviours

- Respects, values, and leverages other customs, cultures, and values. Uses a global management team to better understand and grow the total business: Able to leverage the benefits from working in multicultural environments.
- Optimizes and integrates resources on a global basis, including manufacturing, research, and businesses across countries, and functions to increase 3M's growth and profitability.
- Satisfies global customers and markets from anywhere in the world.
- Actively stays current on world economies, trade issues, international market trends and opportunities.

Source: Margaret E. Allredge and Kevin J. Nilan, "3M's Leadership Competency Model: An Internally Developed Solution," *Human Resource Management* 39, Summer/Fall 2000, pp. 133–45. Reprinted by permission of John Wiley & Sons, Inc.

Because they stem from each organization's mission statement or its strategy to achieve competitive advantage, it might be concluded that the core competencies would be unique to each company. In fact, they are not. One analysis showed that most organizations appear to choose from the same list of 20 core competencies (see Exhibit 6.10).[20] So if the competencies do not differ, how can they be a source of competitive advantage? What does appear to differ among organizations is the way in which they operationalize competencies. This parallels an issue related to strategy: There may be only slight differences in the words, but the actions may differ. It is the actions that are the source of competitive advantage.

EXHIBIT 6.10 The Top 20 Competencies ─────────

Achievement orientation
Concern of quality
Initiative
Interpersonal understanding
Customer-service orientation
Influence and impact
Organization awareness
Networking
Directiveness
Teamwork and cooperation
Developing others
Team leadership
Technical expertise
Information seeking
Analytical thinking
Conceptual thinking
Self-control
Self-confidence
Business orientation
Flexibility

Source: Zingheim, Ledford, & Schuster, "Competencies and Competency Models," *Raising the Bar: Using Competencies to Enhance Employee Performance* (Scottsdale, AZ: American Compensation Association, 1996).

Whom to Involve?

Like compensable factors, competencies are derived from the executive leadership's beliefs about the organization and its strategic intent. However, anecdotal evidence indicates that not all employees understand that connection. Employees at one bank insisted that processing student tuition loans was a different competency from processing auto loans. The law department at Polaroid generated a list of over 1,000 competencies they felt were unique to the law department and that created value for the organization.

Exhibit 6.11 shows part of the competencies used by a major toy company. This is one of eight competencies for the marketing department. Other departments have separate competencies. Notice the mind-numbing level of detail. Although this approach may be useful for career development, it is doubtful that all this information is useful, much less necessary, for compensation purposes. The initial promise of simplicity and flexibility in person-based systems remains unfulfilled.

Establish Certification Methods

The heart of the person-based plan is that employees get paid for the relevant skills or competencies they possess, but not necessarily the ones they use. Skill-based plans assume that possessing these skills will make it easier to match workflow with staffing levels, so whether or not an individual is using a particular skill on a particular day is not an issue. Competency-based plans assume . . . what? That all competencies are used all the time? The assumptions are not clear. What is clear, however, is the requirement that when people are paid based on their competency, there must be some way to demonstrate or certify to all concerned that a person possesses that level of competency. While consultants discuss competencies as compatible with 360-degree feedback and personal development, they are quiet about how to objectively certify whether a person possesses a competency.

There is a need for methods that provide a valid assessment of competencies in a way that can be used easily and economically. Simulations and virtual environments are already proving to be cost-effective ways to assess competency. Simulations are being used as a training method in many industries, and Microsoft and Cisco are already using them for technical certification.[21]

Resulting Structure   Recall that internal pay structures are described in terms of the number of levels, pay differentials, and criteria on which the job structure is based. In practice, competency-based structures generally are designed with relatively few levels—four to six—and relatively wide differentials for increased flexibility. A generic structure based on four levels would look as follows:

Level	Phase	Title
4	Expert	Visionary; Champion; Executive
3	Advanced	Coach; Leader
2	Resource	Contributor; Professional
1	Proficient	Associate

Such a generic job structure could be applied to almost any professional work, even the work of university faculty. Consequently, internal alignment using competencies appears loosely linked to the organization's strategy.

Guidelines from the Research on Competencies

Although the notion of competencies may have value in identifying what distinguishes typical from truly outstanding performance, there is debate on whether competencies can be translated into a measurable, objective basis for pay. Competencies often morph into compensable factors. So it is

EXHIBIT 6.11 Product Development Competency for Marketing Department at a Toy Company

Manages the product development process by:

- Analyzing and evaluating marketplace to identify niches/opportunities
- Evaluating product/concepts
- Developing marketing strategies
- Coordinating and evaluating research/testing
- Generating product recommendations and obtaining management support
- Driving product schedules/activities

Phase I: Baseline Expectation	Phase II: Competent/Proficient	Phase III: Advanced/Coach	Phase IV: Expert/Mentor
- Analyzes market/competitive data (e.g., TRST, NPD) and provides top-line trend analysis, with supervision - Evaluates products/concepts (see Toy Viability competency) - Contributes to product brainstorming sessions - Oversees market research activities and ensures timely completion - Obtains Account Management input to the product development effort - Develops and implements marketing strategy, with supervision: product, positioning, pricing/financial, promotion, packaging, merchandising, and advertising - Facilitates cost reductions to achieve price/profit goals; ensures execution of cost meeting next steps - Ensures adherence to product schedules - Coordinates licensor approval of product concept/models	- Monitors and analyzes market/ competitive data (e.g., TRST, NPD) with minimal supervision, and provides recommendations for product development opportunities - Makes substantial contributions in product brainstorming sessions - Analyzes market research results and makes appropriate product recommendations - Partners with Account Management group to obtain their buy-in to the product development effort - Develops and implements marketing strategy, with minimal supervision - Drives cost reductions to achieve price/profit goals - Drives product schedules and resolves product scheduling issues (late delivery, late debug) - Negotiates with licensors to obtain product approvals	- Independently monitors and analyzes market/competitive data (e.g., TRST, NPD), provides recommendations for product development opportunities, and coaches others to do so - Leads and facilitates formal product brainstorming sessions - Coaches others in analyzing market research results and making product recommendations - Develops innovative marketing plans (e.g., new channels of distribution, niche markets) - Independently develops and implements marketing strategy, and coaches others to do so - Identifies/evaluates cost reduction opportunities, and coaches others to do so - Identifies and implements product schedule improvement tactics - Coaches others to manage product schedules - Coaches others in managing licensor relationships - Shares product ideas/strategies with other teams/categories - Reviews/approves	- recommendations for product development opportunities - Provides short- and long-term vision and goals for developing the corporate product portfolio across categories or brands - Reviews/approves marketing strategy, and proactively adjusts strategy in response to internal/ external changes - Approves cost reduction recommendations - Anticipates critical issues that may impact product schedules and develops alternate plans - Ensures on-strategy delivery

not surprising that little empirical research exists. Only one study has analyzed the competencies/performance relationship for managers, and it found that managers' competencies were related to their performance ratings, but that there was no relationship to unit performance level.[22]

An area of research with potential application to competencies deals with intellectual capital and knowledge management.[23] Viewing the competencies of an organization's employees as a portfolio similar to a diversified investment portfolio highlights the fact that not all competencies are unique nor equally valuable strategically.[24] The focus then changes to managing existing competencies and developing new ones in ways that maximize the overall success of the organization. As organizations globalize, they may need to rebalance their values and perspectives to allow a global strategy to function.[25] They seek the right balance between the range and depth of cultural, functional, and product competencies in the global organization. But this is speculative and remains to be translated into pay practices.

The basic question remains whether it is appropriate to pay for what an employee is capable of doing versus what he or she is actually doing? It seems more likely that effectiveness, for pay purposes, relates to focusing on what is easily measurable and directly related to organizational effectiveness (i.e., knowledge and skills that are task/performance related)?[26]

ONE MORE TIME: INTERNAL ALIGNMENT REFLECTED IN STRUCTURES

The purpose of job- and person-based procedures is really very simple—to design and manage an internal pay structure that helps achieve the organization's objectives. As with job-based evaluation, the final result of the person-based plan is an internal structure of work in the organization. This structure should be aligned with the organization's internal alignment policy, which in turn supports its business operations. Furthermore, managers must ensure that the structure remains internally aligned by reassessing work/skills/competencies when necessary. Failure to do so risks structures that lack work- and performance-related logic and opens the door to bias and misdirected behaviours.

MANAGING THE PLAN

Whatever plan is designed, a crucial issue is the fairness of its management. Details of the plan should be described in a manual that includes all information necessary to apply the plan, such as definitions of compensable factors, degrees, or details of skill blocks, competencies, and certification methods. Increasingly, online tools are available for managers to learn about these plans and apply them.[27]

Employee acceptance of the process is just as important here as for job analysis and job evaluation. In order to build this acceptance, communication with all employees whose jobs are part of the process used to build the pay structure is required.

Administrative concerns are the primary reason that people-based plans have been slow to catch on. Two common reasons are a lack of expertise to manage the skills certification process and a means to externally price jobs.[28]

EVIDENCE OF THE USEFULNESS OF THE RESULTS

The criteria for evaluating the usefulness of pay structures, whether job- or person-based, are much the same: how well they achieve their objectives, as well as their reliability and validity. There is vast research literature on job evaluation compared to person-based structures. Most of it focuses on the procedures used rather than its usefulness, its effects on employee behaviours, or its effectiveness in achieving organizational objectives. In virtually all the studies, job evaluation is treated as a measurement device; the research assesses its reliability, validity, and costs, as well as its compliance with laws and regulations. Any value added by job evaluation (e.g., reducing pay dissatisfaction, improving employees' understanding of how their pay is determined) has been largely ignored.[29] In contrast, research on person-based structures tends to focus on their effects on behaviours and organization objectives and ignores questions of reliability and validity.

Reliability of Job Evaluation Techniques

A reliable evaluation would be one where different evaluators produce the same results. Most studies report high agreement when different people rank-order jobs—correlations between 0.85 and 0.96[30] This is important because in practice, several different people usually evaluate jobs. The results should not depend on which person did the evaluation. Reliability can be improved by using evaluators who are familiar with the work and trained in the job evaluation process. Some organizations use group consensus to increase reliability. Each evaluator makes a preliminary independent evaluation. Then, all evaluators in the group discuss their results until consensus emerges. Consensus certainly appears to make the results more acceptable. However, some studies report that results obtained through consensus were not significantly different from those obtained either by independent evaluators or by averaging individual evaluators' results. Others report that a forceful or experienced person on the committee can sway the results. So can knowledge about the job's present salary level.[31]

Validity/Usefulness

Validity refers to the degree to which the evaluation achieves the desired results. Validity of job evaluation has been measured in two ways: (1) by agreement, i.e., the degree of agreement between rankings that resulted from the job evaluation compared to an agreed-upon rank of benchmarks used as the criterion; and (2) by "hit rates," i.e., the degree to which the job evaluation plan matches (hits) an agreed-upon ranking or pay structure for benchmark jobs. In both cases, the predetermined, agreed-upon ranking or pay structure is for benchmark jobs. It can be established by organization leadership or be based on external market data, union negotiations, or the market rates for jobs held predominantly by men (to try to eliminate any general discrimination reflected in the market), or a combination of these.

Many studies report that when different job evaluation plans are compared to each other, they generate very similar rankings of jobs but very low hit rates—they disagree on how much to pay the jobs.[32] One study that looked at three different job evaluation plans applied to the same set of jobs reported similar rank order among evaluators using each plan but substantial differences in the resulting pay.[33]

So it is clear that the definition of validity needs to be broadened to include impact on pay decisions. How the results are judged depends on the standards used. For managing compensation the correct standard is the pay structure—what job holders get paid—rather than simply the jobs' rank order.

Studies of the degree to which different job evaluation plans produce the same results start with the assumption that if different approaches produce the same results, then those results must be "correct," that is, valid. But in one study, three plans all gave the same result (they were reliable) but all three ranked a police officer higher than a detective. They were not valid.[34] What accounts for the reliability of invalid plans? Either the compensable factors did not pick up something deemed important in the detectives' jobs or the detectives have more power to negotiate higher wages. So while these three plans gave the same results, they would have little acceptance among detectives.

Such "details" are very important when an organization is facing challenges by dissatisfied employees or their lawyers. Missing this point can place an organization at risk.[35]

Acceptability

Several devices are used to assess and improve employee acceptability. An obvious one is to include a formal appeals process. Employees who believe their jobs are evaluated incorrectly should be able to request re-analysis and/or skills re-evaluation. Most firms respond to such requests from managers, but few extend the process to all employees, unless those employees are represented by unions who have negotiated a grievance process.[36] Another approach is to use employee attitude surveys to assess their perceptions of acceptability.

■ GENDER BIAS IN INTERNAL PAY STRUCTURES

The continuing differences in jobs held by men and women, and the accompanying pay differences, have focused attention on internal structures as a possible source of discrimination. Much of this attention has been directed at job evaluation as both a potential source of bias against women and a mechanism to reduce bias.[37] It has been widely speculated that job evaluation is susceptible to gender bias; that is, whether jobs held predominantly by women are undervalued relative to jobs held predominantly by men, simply because of the job holder's gender. But evidence does not support the proposition that the gender of an individual job holder influences the evaluation of the job.[38] Additionally, there is no evidence that the job evaluator's gender affects the results.

However, a study found that compensable factors related to job content (such as contact with others and judgment) did reflect bias, but that others pertaining to employee requirements (such as education and experience) did not.[39]

The second potential source of bias affects job evaluation indirectly, through the current wages paid for jobs. In this case, job evaluation results may be biased if the jobs held predominantly by women are underpaid. If this is the case, and if the job evaluation is based on the current wages paid, then the job evaluation results simply mirror any bias in the current pay rates. Considering that many job evaluation plans are purposely structured to mirror the existing pay structure, it should not be surprising that the current wages for jobs influence the results of job evaluation. One study of 400 compensation specialists revealed that market data had a substantially larger effect on pay decisions than did job evaluations or current pay data.[40] This study is a unique look at several factors that may affect pay structures. Several recommendations seek to ensure that job evaluation plans are bias-free, including the following:

1. Define the compensable factors and scales to include the content of jobs held predominantly by women. For example, working conditions should include the noise and stress of office machines and the repetitive movements associated with the use of computers.
2. Ensure that factor weights are not consistently biased against jobs held predominantly by women. Are factors usually associated with these jobs always given less weight?
3. Apply the plan in as bias-free a manner as feasible. Ensure that the job descriptions are bias-free, exclude incumbent names from the job evaluation process, and train diverse evaluators.

At the risk of pointing out the obvious, all issues concerning job evaluation also apply to both skill-based and competency-based plans. For example, the acceptability of the results of skill-based plans can be studied from the perspective of measurement (e.g., reliability, validity) and administration (e.g., costs, simplicity). The various points in skill certification at which errors and biases may enter into judgment (e.g., different views of skill-block definitions, potential favouritism toward team members, defining and assessing skill obsolescence) and whether skill-block points and evaluators make a difference all need to be studied. In light of the detailed bureaucracy that has grown up around job evaluation, we confidently predict a growth of bureaucratic procedures around person-based plans, too. In addition to bureaucracy to manage costs, the whole approach to certification may be fraught with potential legal vulnerabilities if employees who fail to be certified challenge the process. Unfortunately, no studies of gender effects in skill-based or competency-based plans exist. Little attention has been paid to assessor training or validating the certification process. Just as employment tests used for hiring and promotion decisions must be demonstrably free of illegal bias, it seems logical that certification procedures used to determine pay structures should face the same requirement.

■ THREE TYPES OF STRUCTURE

Exhibit 6.12 contrasts job-, skill-, and competency-based approaches. Pay increases are gained via promotions to more responsible jobs under job-based structures or by acquiring more valued skills/competencies under person-based structures. Logically, employees will focus on how to get promoted (e.g., experience, performance) or on how to acquire the required skills or competencies (e.g., training, learning).

EXHIBIT 6.12 Contrasting Approaches

	Job-Based	Skill-Based	Competency-Based
What is valued **Quantify the value**	■ Compensable factors ■ Factor degree weights	■ Skill blocks ■ Skill levels	■ Competencies ■ Competency levels
Mechanisms to translate into pay	■ Assign points that reflect criterion pay structure	■ Certification and price skills in external market	■ Certification and price competencies in external market
Pay structure	■ Based on job performed/ market	■ Based on skills certified/ market	■ Based on competency developed/market
Pay increases	■ Promotion	■ Skill acquisition	■ Competency development
Managers' focus	■ Link employees to work ■ Promotion and placement ■ Control costs via pay for job and budget increase	■ Utilize skills efficiently ■ Provide training ■ Control costs via training, certification, and work assignments	■ Be sure competencies add value ■ Provide competency-developing opportunities ■ Control costs via certification and assignments
Employee focus	■ Seek promotions to earn more pay	■ Seek skills	■ Seek competencies
Procedures	■ Job analysis ■ Job evaluation	■ Skill analysis ■ Skill certification	■ Competency analysis ■ Competency certification
Advantages	■ Clear expectations ■ Sense of progress ■ Pay based on value of work performed	■ Continuous learning ■ Flexibility ■ Reduced workforce	■ Continuous learning ■ Flexibility ■ Lateral movement
Limitations	■ Potential bureaucracy ■ Potential inflexibility	■ Potential bureaucracy ■ Requires costs controls	■ Potential bureaucracy ■ Requires cost controls

Managers whose employers use job-based plans focus on placing the right people in the right job. A switch to skill/competency-based plans reverses this procedure. Now, managers must assign the right work to the right people, that is, those with the right skills and competencies. A job-based approach controls costs by paying only as much as the work performed is worth, regardless of any greater skills the employee may possess. So as Exhibit 6.12 suggests, costs are controlled via job rates or work assignments and budgets.

In contrast, skill/competency-based plans pay employees for the highest level of skill/ competency they have achieved, regardless of the work they perform. This maximizes flexibility. But it also encourages all employees to become certified at top rates. Unless an employer can either control the rate at which employees can certify skill/competency mastery or employ fewer people, the organization may experience higher labour costs than competitors using job-based approaches. The key is to offset the higher rates with greater productivity. One consulting firm claims that an average company switching to a skill-based system experiences a 15 to 20 percent increase in wage rates, a 20 to 25 percent increase in training and development costs, and initial increases in head count to allow people to cross-train and move around.[41] But a research study found that costs were no higher.[42]

In addition to potentially higher rates and higher training costs, skill/competency plans may have the additional disadvantage of becoming as complex and burdensome as job-based plans. Additionally, questions still remain about a skill/competency system's compliance with employment standards legislation. If a female worker has a lower skill-mastery level and lower pay than a male worker who is doing the same work, this would appear to violate the requirement in all Canadian jurisdictions for equal pay for equal work. Similarly, pay equity legislation could be violated if workers in a female-dominated job of equal value to a male-dominated job are not paid equally due to a skill/competency system.

So what is the best approach to pay structures? The answer is that it depends. The best approach may be to permit flexibility to adapt to changing conditions. Too generic an approach may not provide sufficient detail to make a clear link between pay, work, and results; too detailed an approach may become rigid. Bases for pay that are too vaguely defined will have no credibility with employees, will fail to signal what is really important for success, and may lead to suspicions of favouritism and bias.

This chapter concludes our section on internal alignment. Before moving on to external considerations, let's once again address the issue: So what? Why bother with a pay structure? The answer should be: Because it supports improved organization performance. An internally aligned pay structure, whether strategically loosely coupled or tightly fitting, can be designed to (1) help determine pay for the wide variety of work in the organizations, and (2) ensure that pay influences peoples' attitudes and work behaviours and directs them toward organization objectives.

CONCLUSION

This section of the book started by examining pay structures within an organization. The importance placed on internal alignment in the pay structures is a basic strategic issue. The premise underlying internal alignment is that internal pay structures need to be aligned with the organization's business strategy and values, the design of the workflow, and a concern for the fair treatment of employees. The work relationships within a single organization are an important part of internal alignment. Structures that are acceptable to the stakeholders affect satisfaction with pay, the willingness to seek and accept promotion to more responsible jobs, the effort to keep learning and undertake additional training, and the propensity to remain with the employer; they also reduce the incidence of pay-related grievances.

The techniques for establishing internally aligned structures include job analysis, job evaluation, and person-based approaches for skill/competency-based plans. Although viewed by some as bureaucratic burdens, these techniques can aid in achieving the objectives of the pay system when they are properly designed and managed. Without them, the pay objectives of improving competitiveness and fairness are more difficult to achieve.

The first part of the book has now been completed. Strategic perspectives on compensation, the key strategic issues in compensation management, and the total pay model that provides a framework for the book have been discussed. Managing compensation requires creating the pay system to support the organization strategies, its culture and values, and the needs of individual employees. The internal alignment of the pay structure, the techniques used to establish alignment, and the effects on compensation objectives have also been considered. The next section of the book focuses on the next strategic issue in our pay model—external competitiveness.

Chapter Summary

1. Skill-based pay plans and competency-based pay plans are conceptually identical, but skills are very specific and competencies are more general. Skill-based pay plans are usually applied to blue-collar jobs and competency-based plans to white-collar jobs.
2. The four basic steps in skills analysis are: (1) decide what information should be collected, (2) decide what methods should be used to collect the information, (3) decide who should be involved, and (4) ensure that the results are useful for pay purposes by establishing certification methods.
3. The term competency means the underlying, broadly applicable knowledge, skills, and behaviours that form the foundation for successful work performance at any level of job in the organization. Core competencies are competencies that are linked to the mission statement that expresses the organization's philosophy, values, business strategies, and plans. Competency sets translate the core competencies into specific actions. Competency indicators are the observable behaviours that indicate the level of competency in each competency set.
4. Employee acceptance is crucial for person-based plans because it is the key to employees' perceptions of fairness regarding the pay structure. Communication with employees during the building of the structure is the most important step to employee acceptance. Other important actions to enhance acceptability are a formal appeals process, employee attitude surveys, and audits of the pay plan.
5. Two potential sources of bias in internal pay structures are (1) bias in the job evaluation of traditionally female-dominated jobs, and (2) bias in current wages that may be perpetuated when job evaluation plans are structured to mirror existing pay rates.

Key Terms

competencies...113
competency analysis.......................................117
competency-based pay structure....................113
competency indicators 113
competency sets 113
core competencies 113
skill-based pay structures..............................106
skill analysis 109

REVIEW QUESTIONS

1. What are the similarities in the logic underlying job-based and person-based plans?
2. What is the difference between specialist skill plans and generalist skill plans?
3. Why is there not more variation in core competencies between organizations? What does differ?
4. If you were managing employee compensation, how would you recommend that your company evaluate the usefulness of its job evaluation or person-based plans?

EXPERIENTIAL EXERCISES

1. Conduct a skill analysis and design a skill certification plan for payroll administrators.

2. Find the mission statement for an organization with which you are familiar. Define core competencies, competency sets, and competency indicators for this organization.

3. David Tyson, author of the *Canadian Compensation Handbook,* states, "There are a number of problems with skill-based pay. A major one is that, in my opinion, it does not comply with pay equity legislation anywhere in Canada" (pg. 27). Familiarize yourself with the basic components of pay equity legislation by visiting the Ontario Pay Equity Commission Web site (**www.payequity.gov.on.ca**). Survey the human resource management professors at your educational institution on the question, "Do you believe that skill/competency-based pay plans are consistent with pay equity legislation?" Then conduct a debate, starting with a summary of the reasons given on both sides of this issue.

WEB EXERCISE

Leadership Competencies

The Banff Centre for Leadership believes that the three basic requirements of successful leadership are knowledge, competency, and character. They employ a unique competency mapping process (**www.banffcentre.ca/departments/leadership/assessment_tools/ competency_matrix**) using a competency matrix. The matrix contains 24 competencies grouped into six leadership dimensions.

Review the 10 leadership development programs offered by the Banff Centre for Leadership. Compare and contrast the competencies in each. How much overlap is there? What competencies are unique to each of the 10 programs? If these competencies can be applied at any company, how can they be strategic (difficult to imitate or unique)?

CASE

Targeting Teachers' Pay

The pay schedule shown in Exhibit 6.13 is typical of many pay plans for teachers; it contains steps by which a teacher's salary increases with each year of experience as well as with additional university credits beyond a teaching certificate.

Say that Jane begins teaching in September of the current year. She has a bachelor's degree (Group III) and no experience. She will earn $45,969 during the current school year. Next year, she will move up one step in the new schedule and earn $49,056, a raise of $3,087, or 6.7 percent.

Once she has received her Master's degree or qualified as a subject specialist, she will "move over" to the next column (Group IV). Otherwise she will stay in the Group III column and advance one step each year until she reaches step 10 when she "tops out." Note that she will receive the step increase as well as any entire schedule increases that the school board gives each year. So any increase to the entire schedule translates into a larger increase for those teachers currently being paid according to the schedule.

1. Although the stepped salary schedule has many features of a knowledge-based pay system, not everyone agrees. Is this a knowledge-based pay system? How might you change it to make it more like the person-based plans discussed in this chapter? What features would you add/drop?

2. In the pay scale in the exhibit, notice that the column differentials increase with years of experience; for instance, the difference between Group III and Group IV at one year of experience is $2,840, whereas the difference at year 10 is $4,526. What message do these increasing differentials send to teachers? What pay theories address this issue? How would these differentials affect teacher behaviours? How would they affect school district costs?

3. Calculate the size of the pay differential for increased seniority versus increased education. What behaviours do you believe these differentials will motivate; in other words, what pays better, growing older or taking courses?

4. Pay for performance for teachers is a hot topic in many school districts. How might the salary schedule be made compatible with a performance-based pay approach? Evaluate your ideas after you have completed Part III of this book, which discusses employee contributions.

EXHIBIT 6.13 Toronto Teachers' Pay Grid ($) as of February 1, 2008

	Level of Education			
# Years Teaching	*Group I*	*Group II*	*Group III*	*Group IV*
Step 0	$40,612	$42,500	$45,969	$49,225
Step 1	42,757	44,754	49,056	51,896
Step 2	45,245	47,354	52,320	55,073
Step 3	47,731	49,959	55,578	58,261
Step 4	50,563	52,894	59,017	61,959
Step 5	53,388	55,852	62,447	65,658
Step 6	56,217	58,794	65,881	69,351
Step 7	59,054	61,729	69,316	73,057
Step 8	61,884	64,677	72,747	72,747
Step 9	64,712	67,620	76,184	80,449
Step 10	67,544	70,558	79,621	84,147

Source: www.osstfd12.com/artman/documents/resources/2004-2008_coll_agree.pdf (accessed January 25, 2009)

Visit the Online Learning Centre at

www.mcgrawhill.ca/olc/milkovich

PART II

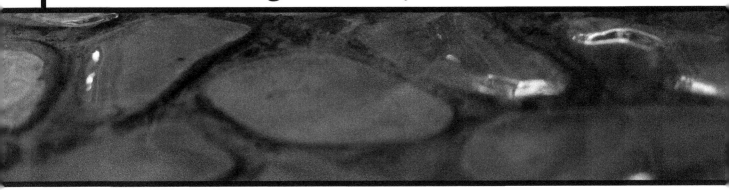

External Competitiveness: Determining the Pay Level

Tiger Woods's golfing prowess is legendary. So are his earnings. In a single year, he won $10 million for playing (playing!) 76 rounds of golf. It took Mr. Woods 5,152 strokes to win this money, or $1,783 per stroke. (*Golf Digest* estimates Mr. Woods's earnings from endorsements at $89 million a year.) One of the fascinations of golf is that the more strokes you take, the less you earn. The number-two person in the PGA ranking, Phil Mickelson, managed to earn $4.8 million, but he got only $856 per stroke. Other pay comparisons are equally fascinating. David Letterman earns $40 million as a talk show host. Katie Couric earns $12 million as a news anchor. Jon Stewart combines both those roles but earns only $4 million. (However, he claims he also gets a discount at Red Lobster.) Compensation managers rarely earn that much, though Dennis M. Donovan earns $5.3 million as executive vice president of HR at Home Depot. A sales associate at Home Depot generally earns $10 to $17 an hour.

The recent earnings for a variety of people are shown in Exhibit II.2. For some people, these examples confirm what they have always suspected: that pay is determined without apparent reason or justice. Nevertheless, there is logic. Mr. Letterman commands $40 million because (1) other networks are also interested in his services, and (2) they believe that his ability to attract young, hip (read "free-spending") viewers will create a stream of earnings for them that will be much greater than his pay. (His agent may also be a better negotiator than Mr. Stewart's.)

External competitiveness is the next strategic decision in the total pay model, as shown in Exhibit II.1. Two aspects of pay translate external competitiveness into practice: (1) how much to pay relative to competitors—whether to pay more than competitors, to match what they pay, or to pay less—and (2) what mix of base, bonus, stock options, and benefits to pay relative to the pay mix of competitors. In a sense, "what forms" to pay (base, bonus, benefits) are the pieces of the pie. "How much" is the size of the pie. External competitiveness includes both questions.

The next two chapters will explain that a variety of answers exist. Chapter 7 discusses choosing the external competitiveness policy, the impact of that choice, and related theories and research. Chapter 8 has two parts: First, it discusses how to translate competitiveness policy into pay level and forms. Second, it discusses how to integrate information on pay levels and forms with the internal structure from Part I.

EXHIBIT II.1 Who Makes How Much?

Sidney Crosby	Pittsburgh Penguins hockey player	$9,000,000
Michaëlle Jean	Governor General of Canada	$117,950
Katherine Caldwell	Ontario provincial court judge	$225,234
Shinzo Abe	Prime Minister of Japan	$174,000*
Adam Bartkowski	Software engineer, Krakow, Poland	$39,800*
Elvis Presley	Entertainer (deceased)	$52,000,000*
Roger Martin	Dean, Rotman School of Management, University of Toronto	$371,250
Robert Hinrichs	Vice president and chief actuary, Workplace Safety and Insurance Board	$280,761
Frank Mahovlich	Member, Senate of Canada	$130,400
Wang Yang	HR supervisor, Shanghai	$5,806*
Wang Ying	Accountant for a Korean company in Shanghai	$3,629*
Zhi Jiang	Analyst and public relations, Shanghai	$8,709*
Monica Jain	Technical team leader, New Delhi	$18,375*
Sandhya Bhatia	Technical team leader, New Delhi	$25,940*

* U.S. dollar

EXHIBIT | **II.2** | The Pay Model

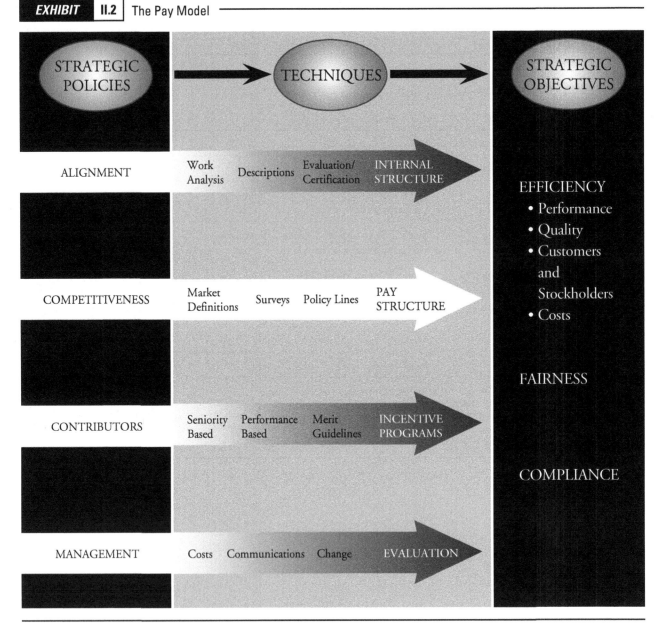

DEFINING COMPETITIVENESS

LEARNING OUTCOMES

■ Describe external competitiveness, and the two specific actions taken in practice that determine external competitiveness.

■ Discuss the three major factors that shape external competitiveness.

■ Discuss three labour demand theories and explain their predictions regarding pay.

■ Discuss two supply-side theories and explain their predictions regarding pay.

■ Explain the three competitive pay policy alternatives.

January is always a good month for travel agents in Montreal, Quebec. In addition to the permanent population eager to flee Montreal's leaden skies, graduating students from Montreal's various universities are travelling to job interviews with employers across the country—at company expense, full fare, no Saturday night stayovers required. When they return from these trips, students compare notes and find that even for people receiving the same degree in the same field from the same university, the offers vary from company to company. What explains the differences?

Location has an effect: Firms in Toronto and New York City make higher offers.[1] The work also has an effect: Jobs in employment pay a little less than jobs in compensation and employee relations. And the industry to which the different firms belong has an effect: Pharmaceuticals, computer software, and petroleum firms tend to offer more than computer hardware, telecommunications, and natural resource firms.

Students would like to attribute these differences to themselves: differences in grades, courses taken, interviewing skills, and so on. But as they accept offers and reject others, many companies whose offers were rejected by their first candidates now extend the identical offer to other students.

So it is hard to make the case that an individual's qualifications totally explain the offers. Why would companies extend identical offers to most candidates? And why would different companies extend different offers? This chapter discusses these choices and what difference they make for the organization.

The sheer number of economic theories related to compensation can make this chapter heavy going. Another difficulty is that the reality of pay decisions doesn't necessarily match the theories. The key to this chapter is to always ask: So what? How will this information help me?

▨ COMPENSATION STRATEGY: EXTERNAL COMPETITIVENESS

pay level

the average of the array of rates paid by an employer: base + bonuses + benefits + options/number of employees

pay forms

the mix of the various types of payments that make up total compensation

In Part I, comparisons *inside* the organization were examined. In external competitiveness, our second pay policy, comparisons *outside* the organization are reviewed—comparisons with other employers who hire the same kinds of employees. A major decision when designing a compensation strategy is whether to mirror what competitors are doing with pay. Or is there an advantage in being different? Competitiveness includes choosing the mix of pay forms (i.e., bonuses, stock options, flexible benefits) that is right for the business strategy.

External competitiveness refers to the pay relationships among organizations—the organization's pay relative to its competitors. It is expressed in practice by (1) setting a **pay level** that is above, below, or equal to competitors; and (2) by considering the mix of **pay forms** relative to those of competitors.

Both pay level and pay forms focus on two objectives: (1) to control costs and (2) to attract and retain employees.[2]

Control Costs

Pay level decisions have a significant impact on expenses. Other things being equal, the higher the pay level, the higher the labour costs:

$$\text{Labour Costs} = \text{Pay Level} \times \text{Number of Employees}$$

Furthermore, the higher the pay level relative to what competitors pay, the greater the relative costs to provide similar products or services. So you might think that all organizations would pay the same job the same rate. However, they do not. A report on graduates of the MBA program at the Rotman School of Management at the University of Toronto in 2008 showed that the average base salary for investment researchers was $85,000. The range of salaries for the same job ran from $65,000 to $125,000. Thus, some investment researchers were making nearly twice what others were paid.[3] The same work *is* paid differently. What could justify a pay level above whatever minimum amount is required to attract and retain financial services staff?

Attract and Retain Employees

One company may pay more because it believes its higher-paid investment researchers are more productive than those at other companies. They may be better trained; maybe they are more innovative in their research. Maybe they are less likely to quit, which saves recruiting and training costs. Different employers set different pay levels; that is, they deliberately choose to pay above or below what others are paying for the same work. That is why there is no single "going rate" in the labour market for a specific job.[4]

Not only do the rates paid for similar jobs vary between employers, a single company may set a different pay level for different job families.[5] The company in Exhibit 7.1 illustrates the point. The top chart shows that this particular company pays about 2 percent above the market for its entry-level engineer. (Market is set at zero in the exhibit.) However, they are 13 percent above the market for most of their marketing jobs and over 25 percent above the market for marketing managers. Office personnel and technicians are paid below the market. So this company uses very different pay levels for different job families.

These data are based on comparisons of base wage. When we look at total compensation in the bottom of the exhibit, a different pattern emerges. The company still has a different pay level for different job families. But when bonuses, stock options, and benefits are included, only marketing managers remain above the market. Every other job family is now substantially below the market. Engineering managers take the deepest plunge, from only 2 percent below the market to over 30 percent below.

EXHIBIT **7.1** One Company's Market Comparison: Base versus Total Compensation ────────

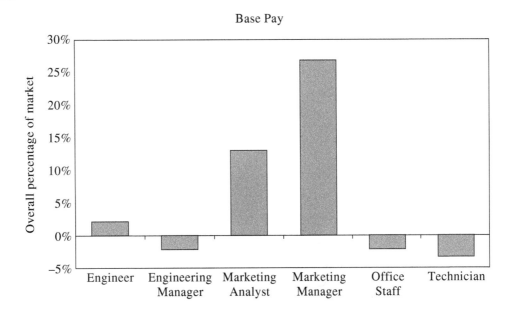

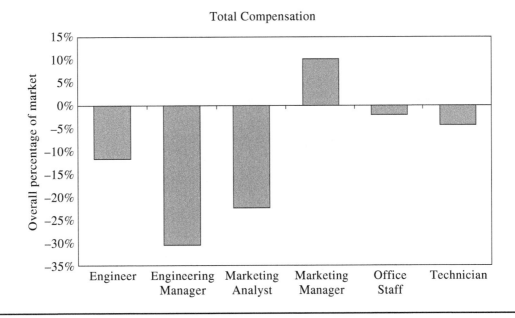

The exhibit, based on actual company data, makes two points. First, companies often set different pay level policies for different job families. Second, how a company looks in comparison to the market depends on the companies they compare to and the pay forms included in the comparison. It is not clear whether this company deliberately chose to emphasize marketing managers and deemphasize engineering in its pay plan, or if it is paying the price for not hiring one of you readers to design their plan.[6] Either way, the point is that even though people love to talk about "market rates," there is no single "going rate" in the marketplace.

There is no single "going mix" of pay forms, either. Exhibit 7.2 compares the mix of pay forms for the same job (marketing manager) at two companies in the same geographic area. Both companies offer about the same total compensation. Yet the percentages allocated to base, bonuses, benefits, and options are very different.

EXHIBIT   **7.2**   Two Companies, Same Total Compensation, Different Mixes ──────────────

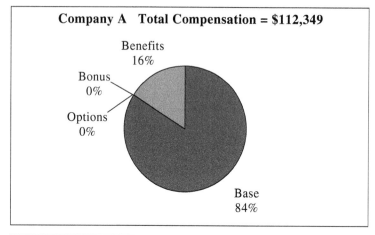

Company A   Total Compensation = $112,349

Benefits 16%
Bonus 0%
Options 0%
Base 84%

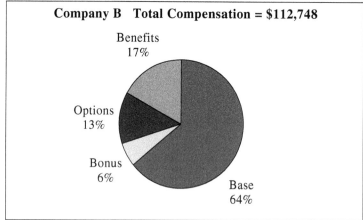

Company B   Total Compensation = $112,748

Benefits 17%
Options 13%
Bonus 6%
Base 64%

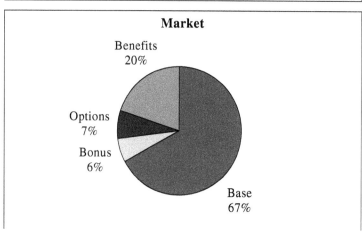

Market

Benefits 20%
Options 7%
Bonus 6%
Base 67%

■ WHAT SHAPES EXTERNAL COMPETITIVENESS?

Exhibit 7.3 shows the factors that affect a company's decision on pay level and mix. The factors include (1) competition in the labour market for people with various skills; (2) competition in the product and service markets, which affects the financial condition of the organization; and (3) characteristics unique to each organization and its employees, such as its business strategy, technology, and the productivity and experience of its workforce. These factors act in concert to influence pay level and mix decisions.

■ LABOUR MARKET FACTORS

Economic theories of labour markets usually begin with four basic assumptions:

1. Employers always seek to maximize profits.
2. People are homogeneous and therefore interchangeable; e.g., a business school graduate is a business school graduate is a business school graduate.
3. The pay rates reflect all costs associated with employment (e.g., base wage, bonuses, holidays, benefits, even training).
4. The markets faced by employers are competitive, so there is no advantage for a single employer to pay above or below the market rate.

Although these assumptions oversimplify reality, they provide a framework for understanding labour markets. Organizations often claim to be "market driven," that is, they pay competitively with the market or even are market leaders. Understanding how markets work requires analysis of the demand and supply of labour. The demand side focuses on the actions of the employer: how many employees they seek and what they are able and willing to pay. The supply side looks at potential employees: their qualifications and the pay they are willing to accept in exchange for their services.[7]

Exhibit 7.4 shows a simple illustration of demand and supply for business school graduates. The vertical axis represents pay rates from $25,000 to $100,000 a year. The horizontal axis is the number of business school graduates in the market, ranging from 100 to 1,000. The line labelled "demand" is the sum of all employers' hiring preferences for business graduates at various pay

---

EXHIBIT 7.3 | What Shapes External Competitiveness?

LABOUR MARKET FACTORS
Nature of Demand
Nature of Supply

PRODUCT MARKET FACTORS
Degree of Competition
Level of Product Demand

ORGANIZATION FACTORS
Industry, Strategy, Size
Individual Manager

EXTERNAL COMPETITIVENESS

EXHIBIT **7.4** | Supply and Demand for Business School Graduates in the Short Run

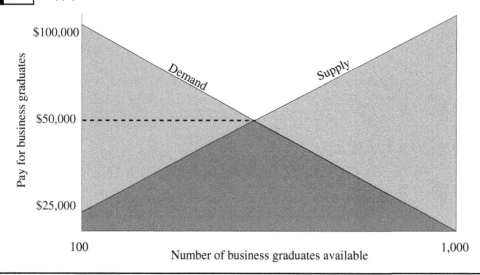

levels. At $100,000, only 100 business graduates will be hired, because only a few firms will be able to afford them. At $25,000, companies can afford to hire 1,000 business graduates. However, the line labelled "supply" indicates that there aren't 1,000 business graduates willing to be hired at $25,000. In fact, only 100 are willing to work for $25,000. As pay rates rise, more graduates become interested in working, so the labour supply line slopes upward. The market rate is the point where the lines for labour demand and labour supply cross. In this illustration, the interaction among all employers and all business graduates determines the $50,000 market rate. Because any single employer can hire all the business graduates it wants at $50,000, and all business graduates are of equal quality (assumption #2), there is no reason for any wage other than $50,000 to be paid.

So, if $50,000 is the market-determined rate for business graduates, how many business graduates will a specific employer hire?

Labour Demand

marginal product of labour

the additional output associated with the employment of one additional human resources unit, with other production factors held constant

Assume that two business graduates form a consulting firm that provides services to 10 clients. The firm hires a third person who brings in four more clients. The **marginal product of labour** (the change in output associated with the additional unit of labour) of employing the third business graduate is four. But adding a fourth business graduate generates only two new clients. This diminishing marginal productivity results from the fact that each additional graduate has a progressively smaller share of the other factors of production such as office space, number of computers, and telephone lines, which are fixed. As more business graduates are brought into the firm without changing other production factors, the marginal productivity must eventually decline.

marginal revenue of labour

the additional revenue generated when the firm employs one additional unit of human resources, with other production factors held constant

The **marginal revenue of labour** is the money generated by the sale of the marginal product—the additional output from the employment of one additional person. In the case of the consulting firm, it is the revenues generated by each additional business graduate. If each new client generates $25,000 in revenue, then the third employee's four new clients will generate $100,000. But the fourth employee's two new clients will generate only $50,000. This $50,000 is exactly the wage that must be paid to that fourth employee. So the consulting firm will break even on the fourth employee but will lose money if it hires more than that. Recall that the first labour market theory assumption is that employers seek to maximize profits. Therefore, the employer will continue to hire graduates until the marginal revenue generated by that last hire is equal to the costs associated with employing that graduate. Because other potential costs will not change in the short run, the level of demand that maximizes profits is that level at which the marginal revenue of the last hire is equal to the wage rate for that hire.

Exhibit 7.5 shows the connection between the labour market model and conditions facing a single employer. On the left is the same supply and demand model from Exhibit 7.4 showing that pay level ($50,000) is determined by the interaction of all employers' demand for business graduates. The right side of the exhibit shows supply and demand for an individual employer. At the market-determined rate ($50,000), the individual employer can hire as many business graduates as it wants. Therefore, supply is now an unlimited horizontal line. However, the demand line still slopes downward. The two lines intersect at 4. So for this employer, the market-determined wage rate ($50,000) equals the marginal revenues of the fourth hire. The marginal revenue of the fifth graduate is less than $50,000 and so will not add enough revenue to cover costs. The point on the graph at which the incremental income generated from an additional employee equals the wage rate is the marginal revenue product.[8]

A manager using the marginal revenue product model must do only two things: (1) determine the pay level set by market forces and (2) determine the marginal revenue generated by each new hire. This will tell the manager how many people to hire. Simple? Of course not.

The model provides a valuable analytical framework, but it oversimplifies the real world. In most organizations, it is almost impossible to quantify the goods or services produced by an individual employee, because most production is through joint efforts of employees with a variety of skills. Even in settings that use piece rates (e.g., 50 cents for each soccer ball sewn), it is hard to separate the contributions of labour from those of other resources (e.g., efficient machinery, sturdy materials, good lighting, ventilation).

So neither the marginal product nor the marginal revenue is directly measurable. However, managers do need some measure that reflects value. In the preceding two chapters, compensable factors, skill, and competencies were discussed. If compensable factors define what organizations value in work, then job evaluation reflects the job's contribution to the organization and may be viewed as a proxy for marginal revenue product. However, compensable factors are usually defined by organizations as input (e.g., skills required, problem solving required, responsibilities) rather than as the value of the output. This same logic applies to skills and competencies.

Labour Supply

A closer look at the assumptions about the behaviour of potential employees shows that this model assumes that many people are seeking jobs, that they possess accurate information about all job openings, and that no barriers to mobility exist (discrimination, licensing provisions, or union membership requirements) between jobs.[9]

EXHIBIT 7.5 Supply and Demand at the Market and Individual Employer Level

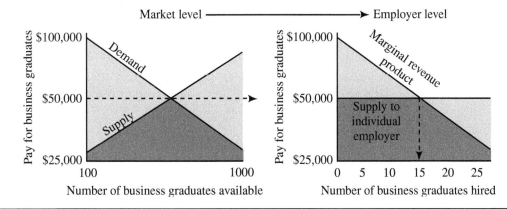

As in the analysis of labour demand, these assumptions greatly simplify the real world. As the assumptions change, so does the supply. For example, the upward-sloping supply assumes that as pay increases, more people will be willing to take a job. But if unemployment rates are low, offers of higher pay may not increase supply—everyone who wants to work is already working. If competitors quickly match a higher offer, the employer may face a higher pay level but no increase in supply, so that it ends up paying more for the employees it already has, but is still shorthanded.

An employer who dominates the local labour market, such as Algoma Steel in Sault Ste. Marie, Ontario, may also find that raising wages doesn't necessarily attract more applicants, simply because the supply has dried up. People who are conveniently located to Algoma Steel and interested in work are already there. Any additional applicants must be induced to enter the labour supply, perhaps from schools, retirement, or more distant areas. So a dominant employer has a relatively free hand in determining pay levels, because few local labour market competitors exist. However, once the local labour supply is exhausted, small increases in the pay levels may not attract more applicants. The supply still slopes upward, but it may take on the shape of a "step" function due to the large pay increases needed to attract additional people. Although many firms find lowering the job requirements and hiring less-skilled workers a better choice than raising wages, this choice incurs increased training costs (which were included in assumption #3).

MODIFICATIONS TO THE DEMAND SIDE

The story is told of the economics professor and the student who were strolling through campus. "Look," the student cried, "there's a $100 bill on the path!"

"No, that cannot be," the wiser head replied. "If there were a $100 bill, someone would have picked it up."

The point of the story is that economic theories frequently must be revised to account for reality. When we change our focus from all the employers in an economy to a particular employer, models must be modified to help us understand what actually occurs.

A particularly troublesome issue for economists is why an employer would pay more than what theory states is the market-determined rate. Exhibit 7.6 looks at three modifications to the model that address this phenomenon: compensating differentials, efficiency wage, and signalling.

EXHIBIT   **7.6**   Labour Demand Theories and Implications

Theory	Prediction	So What?
Compensating differentials	Work with negative characteristics requires higher pay to attract workers.	Job evaluation and compensable factors must capture these negative characteristics.
Efficiency wage	Above-market wages will improve efficiency by attracting workers who will perform better and be less willing to leave.	Staffing programs must have the capability of selecting the best employees; work must be structured to take advantage of employees' greater efforts.
Signalling	Pay policies signal the kinds of behaviour the employer seeks.	Pay practices must recognize desired behaviours with more pay, larger bonuses, and other forms of compensation.

Compensating Differentials Theory

compensating differentials theory

higher wages must be offered to compensate for negative features of jobs

More than 200 years ago, Adam Smith argued that individuals consider the "whole of the advantages and disadvantages of different employments" and make decisions based on the alternative with the greatest "net advantage."[10] **Compensating differentials theory** says that if a job has negative characteristics, that is, if the necessary training is very expensive (medical school), job security is tenuous (stockbrokers), working conditions are disagreeable (highway construction), or chances of success are low (professional sports), then employers must offer higher wages to compensate for these negative features.

Such compensating differentials explain the presence of various pay rates in the market. Although the notion is appealing, it is hard to document, due to the difficulties in measuring and controlling all the factors that go into a net advantage calculation.

Efficiency Wage Theory

efficiency wage theory

high wages may increase efficiency and lower labour costs by attracting higher-quality applicants who will work harder

Efficiency wage theory says that sometimes high wages may increase efficiency and actually lower labour costs if they:

1. Attract higher-quality applicants,
2. Lower turnover,
3. Increase worker effort,
4. Reduce "shirking" (what economists say when they mean "slacking off"), and
5. Reduce the need to supervise employees.

So basically, efficiency increases by hiring better employees or motivating present employees to work smarter or harder. The underlying assumption is that pay level determines effort—again, an appealing notion that is difficult to document.

There is some research on efficiency wage theory.[11] One study looked at shirking behaviour by examining employee discipline and wages in several auto plants. Higher wages were associated with lower shirking, measured as the number of disciplinary layoffs. Shirking was also lower when high unemployment made it more difficult for fired or disciplined employees to find another job. So, although the higher wages cut shirking, the authors were unable to say whether it was cut enough to offset the higher wage bill.[12]

Research shows that higher wages actually do attract more qualified applicants.[13] But they also attract more unqualified applicants. Few companies evaluate their recruiting programs well enough to show whether they do in fact choose only superior applicants from the larger pool. So an above-market wage does not guarantee a more productive workforce.

Does an above-market wage allow an organization to operate with fewer supervisors? Some research evidence says yes. For example, a study of hospitals found that those that paid high wages to staff nurses employed fewer nurse supervisors.[14] The researchers did not speculate on whether the higher wages attracted better nurses or caused average nurses to work harder, nor whether the hospital was able to reduce its overall nursing costs.

An organization's ability to pay is related to the efficiency wage model. Firms with greater profits than competitors are able to share this success with employees. One study found that pay levels at more profitable firms were about 15 percent greater than at firms with lower profits.[15]

Notice that all the discussion so far has dealt with pay level. What forms to pay, the mix question, is virtually ignored in these theories. The simplifying assumption is that the pay level includes the value of different forms. Abstracted away is the distinct possibility that some people find more performance-based bonus pay or better health insurance more attractive. Signalling theory is more useful in understanding pay mix.

Signalling Theory

Signalling theory says that employers deliberately design pay levels and mix as part of a strategy that signals to both prospective and current employees what kinds of behaviours are sought.[16] Viewed through a marketing lens, how much to pay and what pay forms are offered establishes a "brand" that sends a message to prospective employees, just like brands of competing products and services.[17]

A policy of paying below the market for base pay yet offering generous bonuses or training opportunities sends a different signal, and presumably attracts different people, than a policy of matching market wage with no performance-based pay. An employer who combines lower base with high bonuses may be signalling that it wants employees who are risk takers. The proportion of people within the organization who are eligible for bonuses signals whether the same pay system is geared to all employees or to managers only and helps to communicate performance expectations.

Another look at Exhibit 7.2 shows a breakdown of forms of pay for two competitors, as well as their relationship to the market. The pay mix at Company A emphasizes base (84 percent) more than at Company B (64 percent) or the market average (67 percent). Company A pays no bonus, no stock options, and somewhat lighter benefits. Company B's mix is closer to the market average. What is the message that A's pay mix is communicating? The astute reader will note that at A, one can earn the $112,349 with very little apparent link to performance. Whereas for B, earning the $112,748 requires performance bonuses and options as well. Why would anyone work at B without extra returns for the riskier pay? Without a premium, how is B able to attract and retain employees? Perhaps with more interesting projects, flexible schedules, or more opportunity for promotion—all part of B's "total pay brand."

A study of university students approaching graduation found that both pay level and mix affected their job decisions.[18] Students wanted jobs that offered high pay, but they also showed a preference for individual-based (rather than team-based) pay, fixed (rather than variable) pay, job-based (rather than skill-based) pay, and flexible benefits. Job seekers were rated on various personal dimensions—materialism, confidence in their abilities, and risk aversion—which were related to pay preferences. Pay level was most important to materialists and less important to those who were risk averse. So applicants appear to select among job opportunities based on the perceived match between their personal dispositions and the nature of the organization, as signalled by the pay system. Both pay level and pay mix send a signal.

Signalling works on the supply side of the model, too, as suppliers of labour signal to potential employers. People who are better trained, have higher grades in relevant courses, and/or have related work experience signal to prospective employers that they are likely to be better performers. (Presumably they signal with the same degree of accuracy as employers.) So both characteristics of the applicants (degrees, grades, experience) and organization decisions about pay level (lead, match, lag) and mix (higher bonuses, benefit choices) act as signals that help communicate.

■ MODIFICATIONS TO THE SUPPLY SIDE

Two theories shown in Exhibit 7.7—reservation wage and human capital—focus on understanding employee behaviour rather than employers—the supply side of the model.

Reservation Wage Theory

Economists are renowned for their great sense of humour. So it is not surprising that they describe pay as "non-compensatory," as **reservation wage theory** says that job seekers have a reservation wage level below which they will not accept a job offer, no matter how attractive the other job attributes.[19] If pay level does not meet their minimum standard, no other job attributes can make up (i.e., compensate) for this inadequacy. Other theorists go a step further and say that some job

EXHIBIT 7.7 | Supply Side/ Theories and Implications ───────────────

Theory	Prediction	So What?
Reservation wage	Job seekers will not accept jobs when pay is below a certain wage, no matter how attractive other job aspects are.	Pay level will affect ability to recruit
Human capital	The value of an individual's skills and abilities is a function of the time and expense required to acquire them.	Higher pay is required to induce people to train for more difficult jobs.

seekers—satisfiers—take the first job offer they get where the pay meets their reservation wage. A reservation wage may be above or below the market wage. The theory seeks to explain differences in workers' responses to offers.

Human Capital Theory

human capital theory
higher earnings are made by people who improve their potential productivity by acquiring education, training, and experience

Human capital theory, perhaps the most influential economic theory for explaining pay level differences, is based on the premise that higher earnings flow to those who improve their potential productivity by investing in themselves (by acquiring additional education, training, and experience).[20] The theory assumes that people are in fact paid at the value of their marginal product. Improving productive abilities by investing in training or even in one's physical health will increase one's marginal product. The value of an individual's skills and abilities is a function of the time, expense, and resources expended to acquire them. Consequently, jobs that require long and expensive training (engineers, physicians) should receive higher pay levels than jobs that require less investment (clerical workers, elementary school teachers).

A number of additional factors affect the supply of labour. Geographic barriers to mobility between jobs, union requirements, lack of information about job openings, the degree of risk involved, and the degree of unemployment also influence labour markets.

■ PRODUCT MARKET FACTORS AND ABILITY TO PAY

The supply and demand for labour are major determinants of an employer's pay level. However, any organization must generate, over time, enough revenue to cover expenses, including compensation. It follows that an employer's pay level is constrained by its ability to compete in the product/service market. So product market conditions determine to a large extent what the organization can afford to pay.

Product demand and the degree of competition are the two key product market factors. Both affect the ability of the organization to change what it charges for its products and services. If prices cannot be changed without decreasing sales, then the ability of the employer to set a higher pay level is constrained.

Product Demand   Although labour market conditions (and legal requirements) put a floor on the pay level required to attract sufficient employees, the product market puts a lid on the maximum pay level that an employer can set. If the employer pays above the maximum, it must either pass on the higher pay level to consumers through price increases or hold prices fixed and allocate a greater share of total revenues to cover labour costs.

Degree of Competition   Employers in highly competitive markets such as manufacturers of automobiles or generic drugs are less able to raise prices without loss of revenues. At the other extreme, single sellers of a Lamborghini or the drug Viagra are able to set whatever price they choose. However, too high a price often invites the eye of political candidates and government regulators.

Other factors besides product market conditions affect pay level. Some of these have already been discussed. The productivity of labour, the technology employed, the level of production relative to plant capacity available—all affect compensation decisions. These factors vary more across than within industries. The technologies employed and consumer preferences may vary between auto manufacturers, but the differences are relatively small when compared to the technologies and product demand of auto manufacturers versus the oil or financial industry.

A Dose of Reality: What Managers Say

Discussions with managers provide insight into how all of these economic factors translate into actual pay decisions. In one study, a number of scenarios were presented in which unemployment, profitability, and labour market conditions varied.[21] The managers were asked to make wage adjustment recommendations for several positions. Level of unemployment made almost no difference. One manager was incredulous at the suggestion: "You mean take advantage of the fact that there are a lot of people out of work?" The company's profitability was considered a factor for higher management in setting the overall pay budget but not something managers consider for individual pay adjustments. What it boiled down to was, "Whatever the chief financial officer says we can afford!" They thought it shortsighted to pay less, even though market conditions would have permitted lower pay. In direct contradiction to efficiency wage theory, managers believed that problems attracting and keeping people were the result of poor management rather than inadequate compensation. They offered the opinion that, "supervisors try to solve with money their difficulties with managing people."[22]

More Reality: Segmented Supply of Labour

Observing managers' actual responses to shifting economic pressures also gives insight into how economic pressures translate into actual pay decisions. Significant differences in wages paid around the world and the ease of outsourcing work overseas has led many companies to cut pay.[23]

People Flow to the Work   Hospitals can staff nursing positions from four sources: regular full-time, part-time, temporary help agencies specializing in nurses, and "travellers"—nurses employed by agencies that send them to hospitals around the country for extended periods, e.g., six months. This segmented labour supply means using multiple sources of nurses from multiple locations with multiple employment relationships. The level and mix of cash and benefits paid to each nurse depends on the source. Regular employees get pay and benefits; part-timers get pay but no benefits; agency nurses get pay and benefits from the agency; and "travellers" get pay, benefits, and living expenses from the agency. The hospital pays a fee to the agency in addition to the nurses' compensation. The segmented supply results in nurses working the same jobs side by side but earning different pay. This is a case of people flowing to the work, because a hospital cannot send its nursing tasks off-site to other cities or offshore to other nations.[24]

Work Flows to the People—On-site, Off-site, Offshore   A computer software design company can staff a project with employees who are on-site in their Canadian head office, off-site (contract employees throughout Canada), or offshore in India or other countries. To bid on projects, the company needs to know pay levels and mixes of forms not only in Canada, but other locations including Long Beach, California; Krakow, Poland; Shanghai, China; and Bangalore, India.

There are three important points here:

1. Reality is complex; theory abstracts. It is not that our theories are useless. They simply abstract away the detail, clarifying the underlying factors that help us understand how reality works. Theories of market dynamics, the interaction of supply and demand, form a useful foundation.

2. The segmented sources of labour mean that determining pay levels and mix increasingly requires understanding market conditions in different locations worldwide.

3. Managers also need to know the jobs required to do the work, the tasks to be performed, and the knowledge and behaviours required to perform them (sound like job analysis?) so that they can bundle the various tasks to send to different locations.

◼ ORGANIZATION FACTORS

Although product and labour market conditions create a range of possibilities within which managers create a policy on external competitiveness, organizational factors influence pay level and mix decisions, too.[25]

Industry and Technology

The industry in which an organization competes influences the technologies used. Labour-intensive industries such as education and services tend to pay lower than technology-intensive industries such as petroleum or pharmaceuticals. In addition to differences in technology *across* industries, the introduction of new technology *within* an industry also influences pay levels. For example, the use of universal product codes, scanners, scales built into the counter, and self-checkout lanes have reduced the skills required of cashiers. As a result, their average pay has declined by over 8 percent since 1984.[26]

The importance of qualifications and experience tailored to particular technologies is often overlooked in theoretical analysis of labour markets. But machinists and millwrights who build cars for General Motors in Oshawa, Ontario, have very different qualifications from machinists and millwrights who build airplanes for Bombardier in Quebec.[27]

Employer Size

There is consistent evidence that large organizations tend to pay more than small ones. A study of manufacturing firms found that firms with 100 to 500 workers paid 6 percent higher wages than did smaller firms; firms of more than 500 workers paid 12 percent more than did the smallest firms.[28] This relationship between organization size, ability to pay, and pay level is consistent with economic theory. It says that talented individuals have a higher marginal value in a larger organization because they can influence more people and decisions, which leads to more profits. Compare the advertising revenue that David Letterman can bring to CBS versus the potential revenue to station CHEX if his late-night show were seen only in Peterborough, Ontario. No matter how cool he is in Peterborough, CHEX could not generate enough revenue to be able to afford to pay Mr. Letterman $31.5 million; but CBS can. However, theories are less useful for explaining why practically everyone at bigger companies such as CBS, including janitors and compensation managers, is paid more. It seems unlikely that everyone has Letterman's impact on revenues.

Employees' Preferences

What pay forms (health insurance, eye care, bonuses, pensions) do employees really value? What forms should be changed (or started) to improve their value to employees? Better understanding of employee preferences is increasingly important in determining external competitiveness. Markets, after all, involve both employers' and employees' choices.[29] However, there are substantial difficulties in reliably measuring preferences. Who among us would be so crass as to (publicly) rank money over cordial co-workers or challenging assignments in response to the survey question, "What do you value most in your work?"

Organization Strategy

A variety of pay level and mix strategies exists. Some employers adopt a low-wage, no-mix strategy; they compete by producing goods and services with as little total compensation as possible. Nike and Reebok reportedly do this. Others select a low-base, high-services strategy. The Marriotts and McDonald's of the world do this. Still others use a high-base, high-services approach. Medtronic's "Fully present at work" approach is an example of the high-base, high-services approach. Obviously, these are extremes on a continuum of possibilities.

■ RELEVANT MARKETS

Economists take "the market" for granted, as in, "the market determines wages." This strikes compensation managers as bizarrely abstract. They consider defining the relevant market a big part of figuring out how much to pay.

Although the notion of a single homogeneous labour market may be an interesting analytical device, each organization operates in many labour markets, each with unique demand and supply. Consequently, managers must define the markets that are relevant for pay purposes and establish the appropriate competitive positions in these markets. The three factors usually used to determine the relevant labour markets are the occupation (skill/knowledge required), geography (willingness to relocate and/or commute), and competitors (other employers in the same product/service and labour markets).

Defining the Relevant Market

How do employers choose their relevant market? Surprisingly little research has been done on this issue. But if the markets are incorrectly defined, the estimates of competitors' pay rates will be incorrect and the pay level and mix inappropriately established.

Two studies do shed some light on this issue.[30] They conclude that managers look at both their competitors—their products, location, and size—and the jobs—the skills and knowledge required, and their importance to the organization's success (e.g., lawyers in law firms, software engineers at Microsoft). So, depending on its location and size, a company may be deemed a relevant comparison even if it is not a product market competitor. For example, an accounting firm in Sault Ste. Marie, Ontario, would be foolish to set pay rates for new accountants without knowing what Algoma Steel is paying its accountants.

The data from product market competitors (as opposed to labour market competitors) are likely to receive greater weight when:

1. Employee skills are specific to the product market (recall the differences in Bombardier millwrights versus GM millwrights);
2. Labour costs are a large share of total costs;
3. Product demand is responsive to price changes—that is, people won't pay $4.50 for a bottle of Leinenkugel; they'll have Molson's instead; and
4. The supply of labour is not responsive to changes in pay (recall the earlier low-wage, low-skill example).

Compensation theories offer some help in understanding the variations in pay levels we observe between employers. They are less helpful in understanding differences in the mix of pay forms. Relevant markets are shaped by pressures from the labour and product markets and the organization. But so what? How, in fact, do managers set pay level and pay mix policy, and what difference does it make? In the remainder of this chapter, these two issues will be discussed.

COMPETITIVE PAY POLICY ALTERNATIVES

Recall that pay level is the average of the array of rates inside an organization. There are three conventional pay level policies: to lead, to meet, or to follow competition. Newer policies emphasize flexibility: among policies for different employee groups, among pay forms for individual employees, and among elements of the employee relationship they wish to emphasize in their external competitiveness policy.

What difference does the pay level policy make? The basic premise is that the competitiveness of pay will affect the organization's ability to achieve its compensation objectives, which in turn will affect the organization's performance. The probable effects of alternative policies are shown in Exhibit 7.8 and discussed in more detail below. The problem with much pay level research is that it focuses on base pay and ignores bonuses, incentives, options, employment security, benefits, or other forms of pay. Yet the exhibits and discussion in this chapter should have convinced you that base pay represents only a portion of compensation. Comparisons on base alone can mislead. In fact, managers seem to believe they get more bang for the buck by allocating dollars away from base pay and into variable forms that more effectively shape employee behaviour.[31]

Pay with Competition (Match)

Given the choice to match, lead, or lag, the most common policy is to match rates paid by competitors.[32] Managers historically justify this policy by saying that failure to match competitors' rates would cause dissatisfaction among present employees and limit the organization's ability to recruit. Many non-unionized companies tend to match or even lead competition to head off unions.[33] A pay-with-competition policy tries to ensure that an organization's wage costs are approximately equal to those of its product competitors and that its ability to attract applicants will be approximately equal to its labour market competitors. Although this policy avoids placing an employer at a disadvantage in pricing products, it may not provide an employer with a competitive advantage in its labour markets. Classical economic models predict that employers will meet competitive wages.

EXHIBIT 7.8 Probable Relationships between External Pay Policies and Objectives

	Compensation Objectives				
Policy	Ability to Attract	Contain Ability to Retain	Labour Costs	Reduce Pay Dissatisfaction	Increase Productivity
Pay above market (lead)	+	+	?	+	?
Pay with market (match)	=	=	=	=	?
Pay below market (lag)	–	?	+	–	?
Hybrid policy	?	?	+	?	+
Employer of choice	+	+	+	–	?

Lead Policy

A lead policy maximizes the ability to attract and retain quality employees and minimizes employee dissatisfaction with pay. It also may offset less attractive features of the work, à la Adam Smith's "net advantage." Combat pay premiums paid to military personnel offset some of the risk of being killed. The higher pay offered by brokerage firms offsets the risk of being fired when the market tanks.

As noted earlier, sometimes an entire industry can pass high pay rates on to consumers if pay is a relatively low proportion of total operating expenses or if the industry is highly regulated. But what about specific firms within a high-pay industry? Do any advantages actually accrue to them? If all firms *in the industry* have similar technologies and operating expenses, then the lead policy must provide some competitive advantage that offsets the higher costs.

A number of researchers have linked high wages to ease of attraction, reduced vacancy rates and training time, and better-quality employees.[34] Research also suggests that high pay levels reduce turnover and absenteeism. Several studies found that the use of variable pay (bonuses and long-term incentives) is related to an organization's improved financial performance, but that pay level is not.[35]

A lead policy can have negative effects, too. It may force the employer to increase the wages of current employees to avoid internal misalignment and murmuring against the employer. Additionally, a lead policy may mask negative job attributes that contribute to high turnover later on (e.g., lack of challenging assignments or hostile colleagues). Remember the managers' view that high turnover was likely to be a managerial problem rather than a compensation problem.[36]

Lag Policy

A policy to pay below market rates may hinder a firm's ability to attract potential employees. However, if pay level is lagged in return for the promise of higher future returns (e.g., stock ownership in a high-tech startup firm), such a promise may increase employee commitment and foster teamwork, which may increase productivity. Additionally, it is possible to lag competition on pay level but to lead on other returns from work (e.g., hot assignments, desirable location, outstanding colleagues, cool tools, work/life balance).

Flexible Policies

In practice, many employers go beyond a single choice among the three policy options. They may vary the policy for different occupational families, as did the company in Exhibit 7.1. Or they may vary the policy for different forms of pay, as did the companies in Exhibit 7.2. They may also adapt different policies for different business units that face very different competitive conditions.

Limited attention has been devoted to pay mix policies. Some obvious alternatives include *performance driven, market match, work/life balance,* and *security*. Exhibit 7.9 illustrates these four alternatives. Incentives and stock options make up a greater percentage of total compensation in performance driven than in the other three. The *market match* simply mimics the pay mix competitors are paying. How managers actually make these mix decisions is a ripe issue for more research.

How managers position their organization's pay against competitors is changing. Some alternatives that are emerging focus on total returns from work (beyond financial returns) and offering people choices among these returns. Rather than flexible, perhaps a better term would be "fuzzy" policies.

Such pay mix policy alternatives exist among enterprises in other countries, too. Apache Footware, located in Quingyuan, China, offers base plus bonus, which matches local practice. It also offers benefits that include a new medical clinic, housing for married couples, a school, sports facilities, and a shopping mall. Steve Chen, Apache's chief executive, states, "It's not just about

EXHIBIT **7.9** Pay Mix Policy Alternatives

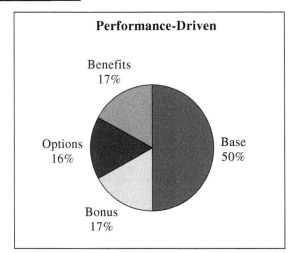

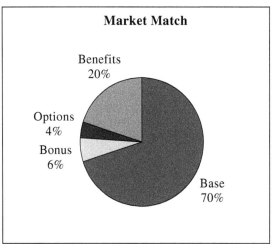

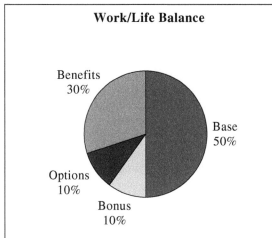

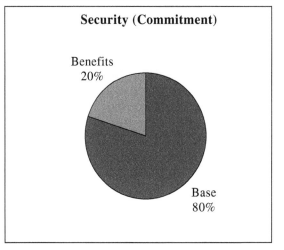

pay, it's about lifestyle. We're building a community so people will stay." In contrast, Top Form Undergarment Wear, located in the same region, phased out its employee housing. It opted to pay employees over 20 percent higher base pay than local practice. Top Form executive Charles Lee says, "Workers need to have a life of their own. They are not children. We pay them more and let each worker decide what is best for them."[37]

Employer of Choice/Shared Choice Some companies compete based on their overall reputation as a place to work, beyond pay level and mix. For example, IBM competes within the information technology marketplace and positions its pay "among the best" in this group. Furthermore, it claims to "strongly differentiate based on business and individual results." It leads the market with its strong emphasis on performance. IBM also offers extensive training opportunities, challenging work assignments, and the like. In a sense, "employer of choice" corresponds to the brand or image the company projects as an employer.

The shared choice approach begins with the traditional alternatives of lead, meet, or lag. But it then adds a second part, which is to offer employees choices (within limits) in the pay mix. This "employee as customer" perspective is not all that revolutionary. Many employers offer choices on health insurance (individual versus dependant coverage), retirement investments (growth or value), and so on.[38] (See information on flexible benefits in Chapter 9.) More advanced software is making the employee-as-customer approach more feasible. Mass customization—being able to select among a variety of features—is routine when purchasing a new laptop or auto. It is now possible with total compensation too. Does offering people choices matter? One risk is that employees might make choices that jeopardize their financial well-being, e.g., inadequate health insurance. Another is the "24 jars of jam" dilemma. Supermarket studies report that offering consumers a taste of just a few different jams increases sales. But offering a taste of 24 different jams decreases sales. Consumers feel overwhelmed by too many choices and simply walk away. Perhaps offering employees too many choices of different kinds of pay will lead to confusion, mistakes, and dissatisfaction.[39]

Pitfalls of Pies

The pie charts in Exhibit 7.9 contrast various pay-mix policies. However, thinking about the mix of pay forms as pieces in a pie chart has limitations. These are particularly clear when the value of options is volatile. The pie charts in Exhibit 7.10 show a well-known software company's mix before and after a major stock market decline (stock prices plummeted 50 percent within a month). Note the effects on the composition of the pay forms. Base pay went from 47 percent to 55 percent of total compensation, whereas the value of stock options fell from 28 percent to 16 percent. (The reverse has happened in this company, too.) But wait, it can get worse. One technology company was forced to disclose that three-quarters of all its stock options were "under water," that is, exercisable at prices higher than their market price. Due to stock market volatility, the options had become worthless to employees. So what is the message to employees? To competitors? Has the compensation strategy changed? Not the company's intended strategy, but in reality, the mix has changed. So possible volatility in the value of different pay forms needs to be anticipated.

Some companies prefer to report the mix of pay forms using a "dashboard," as depicted in Exhibit 7.11. The dashboard changes the focus from emphasizing the relative importance of each form within a single company to comparing each form by itself to the market (many companies).

EXHIBIT 7.10 Volatility of Stock Value Changes Total Pay Mix

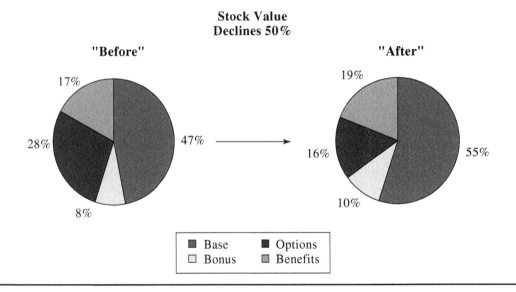

| **EXHIBIT** | **7.11** | Dashboard: Total Pay Mix Breakdown vs. Competitors |

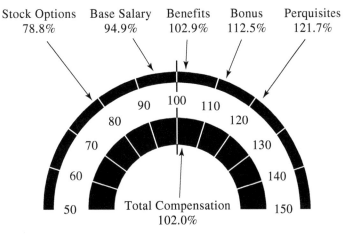

100 = chosen market position, e.g., Market Median

In the example, the value of stock options is 78 percent of competitors' median, base pay is at 95 percent of competitors' median, and overall total compensation is 102 percent of (or 2 percent above) the market median. Pies, dashboards—different focus, both recognizing the importance of the mix of pay forms.

The mix employees receive can also differ at different levels of the internal job structure. Exhibit 7.12 shows the different mix of base, cash incentives, and stock options Merrill Lynch pays at different organizational levels. Executive leadership positions receive less than 10 percent in base, about 20 percent in stock, and the rest in annual incentives. This compares to 50 percent in base, 40 percent in annual incentives, and 10 percent in stock for mid-level manager/professional positions, and 80 percent base, 20 percent incentives, and no stock for entry- and lower-level jobs. Although the percentages vary among organizations, greater emphasis on performance (through incentives and stock) at higher levels is common practice. This is based on the belief that jobs at higher levels in the organization have greater opportunity to influence organizational performance.

| **EXHIBIT** | **7.12** | Pay Mix Varies within the Structure |

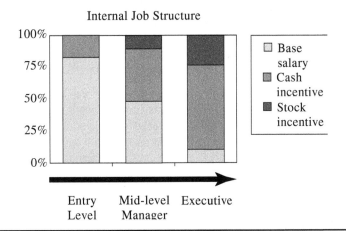

■ CONSEQUENCES OF PAY LEVEL AND MIX DECISIONS

Earlier it was noted that external competitiveness has two major consequences: It affects (1) operating expenses and (2) employee attitudes and work behaviours. Exhibit 7.13 summarizes these consequences, which have been discussed throughout this chapter. The competitiveness policy directly affects the compensation objectives of efficiency, fairness, and compliance. The .Net Worth box summarizes several strategic compensation issues based on a survey of over 200 compensation professionals.

No matter the competitive pay policy, it needs to be translated into practice. The starting point is measuring the market through use of a salary survey. For this, we turn to the next chapter.

.NET WORTH   Compensation Strategy and Market Rates

An organization's compensation strategy should reflect its business strategy. Strategy provides the guideline for various compensation decisions, including how to balance market pricing data and internal equity. A survey of 227 compensation professionals raised four strategic concerns regarding market pricing. The most frequently raised issue was how to decide whether internal or external equity should take precedence and whether this might differ by job family. Many respondents would like guidelines helping them determine what a market-pricing policy should look like, and a means of resolving conflicts between market rate and job evaluation (or other) indicators of job value.

A second critical issue for many respondents was determining which market should be priced against. There is widespread recognition of the existence of different definitions of markets (e.g., geographic breakouts, from local to global; product market competitor or industry breakouts; size breakouts) but much concern about when each might be used. One respondent noted that while the "textbook" answer was available, it didn't seem to match the reality reflected in discussions with colleagues and other professionals.

The third compensation strategy issue raised by respondents was the desire for guidelines on how competitive to be in a variety of different situations, and what a competitiveness strategy that delineated these situations would look like. Different breakout groups (e.g., hot jobs, critical jobs, typical jobs, executive jobs) were the focus of different respondents, but the common thread running through comments in this area is how one should best determine the competitive level of rewards for a set of jobs.

The fourth issue raised with some frequency focused on whether competitiveness in a labour market should be based solely on wages, or whether a broader rewards measure (e.g., total cash compensation, total compensation, compensation plus work/life balance) should be used. There appears to be an unsatisfied need for strategy guidelines on individual- and joint-reward segment competitiveness.

There is a clear recognition that the proper use of market data is a critical issue for organizations that are trying to stay competitive in attracting and retaining human capital while staying competitive in product and service markets. Most respondents noted that no "one best strategy" exists, while at the same time there is a perceived need for best practices in market pricing strategies taking into account industry, organizational, and business strategy characteristics.

Adapted from: C.H. Fay & M. Tare, "Market Pricing Concerns", *WorldatWork Journal*, 16(2), second quarter 2007, pp. 61–69.

| EXHIBIT | 7.13 | Some Consequences of Pay Levels

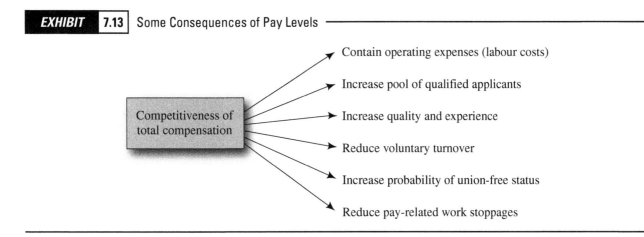

Competitiveness of total compensation

→ Contain operating expenses (labour costs)

→ Increase pool of qualified applicants

→ Increase quality and experience

→ Reduce voluntary turnover

→ Increase probability of union-free status

→ Reduce pay-related work stoppages

CONCLUSION

There are three important conclusions from this chapter. (1) There is no "going rate," and so managers make conscious pay level and pay mix decisions influenced by several factors. (2) There are both product market and labour market competitors that impact the pay level and pay mix decisions. (3) Alternative pay level and pay mix decisions have different consequences.

The pay model used throughout this book emphasizes strategic policy issues: objectives, alignment, competitiveness, contributions, and administration. Policies need to be designed to achieve specific pay objectives. This section is concerned with external competitiveness, or pay comparisons between organizations. Does Research In Motion pay its accountants the same wage that B.C. Hydro pays its accountants? Probably not. Different companies pay different rates; the average of the overall array of rates in an organization constitutes the pay level. Different companies also use different forms of pay to achieve the objectives stipulated for the pay system, both the pay level and mix must be properly positioned relative to competitors. Each integrated job structure or career path within the organization may have its own competitive position in the market. The next chapter considers the decisions involved and the variety of techniques available to implement decisions.

It should be re-emphasized here that the major reason for creating an external competitiveness policy—pay level and mix of forms—is that they have profound consequences on the organization's objectives. Theories and practical experience support this belief, but more research is needed to guide us in making decisions. It has been clearly established that differences between organizations' competitive policies and their pay levels and forms exist, and the factors that determine these differences have been examined. What remains to be better understood is the potential effects of various policies.

CHAPTER SUMMARY

1. External competitiveness refers to the relationship of one organization's pay to that of its competitors. In practice, external competitiveness means (1) setting a pay level that is above, below, or equal to one's competitors; and (2) considering the mix of pay forms relative to those of competitors.

2. The three major factors that shape external competitiveness are: (1) competition in the labour market for people with various skills; (2) competition in the product and service markets, which affects the financial condition of the organization; and (3) characteristics unique to each organization and its employees, such as its business strategy, technology, and the productivity and experience of its workforce.

3. Three labour demand theories are compensating differentials theory, efficiency wage theory, and signalling theory. Compensating differentials theory predicts that work with negative characteristics will require higher pay to attract workers. Efficiency wage theory predicts that above-market wages will improve efficiency by attracting workers who perform better and stay longer. Signalling theory predicts that pay policies will signal the kind of behaviour the employer wants.

4. Two supply-side theories are reservation wage theory and human capital theory. Reservation wage theory predicts that job seekers will not take jobs when pay is below a certain level. Human capital theory predicts that the value of a person's skills and abilities will be related to the time and expense required to acquire them.

5. Three competitive pay alternatives are to match the market/competition, lag the market, and lead the market.

KEY TERMS

REVIEW QUESTIONS

1. Distinguish policies on external competitiveness from policies on internal alignment. Why is external competitiveness so important?
2. What factors shape an organization's external competitiveness?
3. What does marginal revenue product have to do with pay?

EXPERIENTIAL EXERCISES

1. Using efficiency wage theory, find an organization (major league sports teams may make the relevant information publicly available) that offers above-market wages, and investigate whether the theory accurately predicts behaviour such as workers with better performance and lower turnover.

2. What is a relevant market for university professors? For Walmart associates? For politicians? Gather information on market pay for politicians in your municipality.

3. Find a company that follows a lag policy. Why do they believe it pays to pay below market? Can you find any companies that follow performance-driven and/or work/life balance policies?

WEB EXERCISE

External Competitiveness Comparisons

Select three organizations that you believe might be labour market competitors; e.g., Microsoft, IBM, and Oracle; or federal government (http://jobs.gc.ca), government of the Northwest Territories (www.hr.gov.nt.ca/employment), and the Nova Scotia government (www.careerbeacon.com/corpprof/govns/govns.html). Compare their job postings. How many of these organizations list salaries for the job openings? Do they quote a single salary or a range? Do they allow room for salary negotiation? What information is provided about the mix of different pay forms?

CASE

Northern Software

Software engineers directly affect the success of many start-up companies. Suppose that a group of investors is about to create a new start-up, a specialty software company based in Fort McMurray, Alberta. These investors have hired you to help them determine the marketing manager's pay. What would you advise? You will need to get some information on Fort McMurray and on the specialty software industry. Consider the information in Exhibits 7.1, 7.2, and 7.11 in making your recommendation.

1. What policy regarding external competitiveness would you advise? List the options and the pros and cons of each policy option. Offer the rationale for your recommendation.

2. What forms of pay would you recommend? Again, offer your rationale.

3. Consider the theories and research presented in this chapter. Which ones did you use to support your recommendation?

4. List three pieces of additional information you would like to have to refine your recommendation. Explain how this information would help you.

Visit the Online Learning Centre at

www.mcgrawhill.ca/olc/milkovich

DESIGNING PAY LEVELS, MIX, AND PAY STRUCTURES

LEARNING OUTCOMES

- Describe the seven decisions involved in setting externally competitive pay and designing the corresponding pay structure.
- Explain the steps involved in survey design.
- Describe what is meant by "updating" survey data.
- Explain the difference between a market pay line and a pay policy line.
- Discuss how pay grades are created, the relationship of pay ranges to pay grades, and the concept of broadbanding.
- Explain how to adjust a pay structure to balance internal and external pressures.

"Average pay of benchmark jobs set to average pay of similar jobs in comparable companies."—3M

"Pay among the leaders. Base pay will be fully comparable (50th percentile of competitors). Total compensation, including benefits and performance incentives, will bring our compensation to the 75th percentile of competitors."—Colgate-Palmolive

"Our competitive strategy will deliver rewards at the market competitive median for median performance, at the 75th percentile for 75th percentile performance, and so on. We emphasize work-life balance; our benefits insure that every person is fully present and focused when they are at work."—Medtronic[1]

All these statements refer to different organizations' external competitiveness policies—comparison of the compensation offered by an employer relative to its competitors. In Chapter 7, the factors that influenced these policies were discussed. The levels and types of compensation that competitors offer—base salary, bonuses and stock options, benefits—are critical. Market factors that influence policy include the supply of qualified workers and the demand for these workers from other firms. Organizational factors such as the employer's financial condition, technology, size, strategy, productivity, and the influence of unions and employee demographics may also affect a firm's competitive pay policies. In this chapter, we examine managerial techniques to use these factors to design pay levels, mix of forms, and structures.

■ MAJOR DECISIONS

The major decisions involved in setting externally competitive pay policy, obtaining information on market pay rates, and designing the corresponding pay structures are shown in Exhibit 8.1. They include: (1) specify the employer's external pay policy, (2) define the purpose of the compensation survey, (3) choose relevant market competitors to survey, (4) design the survey, (5) interpret survey results and construct the market pay line, (6) construct an internal pay policy line that reflects external pay policy, and (7) balance competitiveness with internal alignment through the use of ranges, flat rates, and/or bands. This is a lengthy list. Think of Exhibit 8.1 as a road map through this chapter. The guideposts are the major decisions in designing a pay structure. In the end, it must be clear how pay structures support business success and ensure fair treatment for employees.

■ SET COMPETITIVE PAY POLICY

compensation survey

the systematic process of collecting and making judgments about the compensation paid by other employers

The first decision, specifying the external competitive pay policy, was covered in the preceding chapter. Employers decide based on whether they want to (1) be a market leader with respect to pay, (2) match the average pay of competitors, or (3) lag behind the average market pay rates. To translate any external pay policy into practice requires information on pay rates in the external market, i.e., comparing with competitors for labour in the same industry or in the same geographic area. **Compensation surveys** provide the data for translating that policy into pay levels, pay mix, and structures.

■ THE PURPOSE OF A COMPENSATION SURVEY

An employer conducts or participates in a compensation survey for a number of reasons: (1) to adjust internal pay level in response to changing competitor pay rates; (2) to set the internal mix of pay forms relative to those paid by competitors; (3) to establish or "price" the internal pay structure; (4) to analyze pay-related problems; or (5) to estimate the labour costs of product market competitors.

EXHIBIT 8.1 Determining Externally Competitive Pay Levels and Structures ————

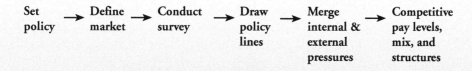

Some Major Decisions in Pay Level Determination
- Determine pay level policy
- Define purpose of survey
- Define relevant market
- Design and conduct survey
- Interpret and apply results
- Design grades and ranges or bands

Adjust Pay Level—How Much to Pay?

Most organizations make adjustments to employees' pay on a regular basis. Such adjustments may be based on the overall upward movement of pay rates caused by the competition for people in the market. Adjustments may also be based on performance, ability to pay, or terms specified in a contract.

Adjust Pay Mix—What Forms?

Adjustments to the different forms of pay competitors use (base, bonus, incentives, benefits) and the relative importance they place on each form occur less frequently than adjustments to overall pay level. The mix of forms and their relative importance makes up the "pay package." Managers today recognize that total compensation involves many types of pay, and some pay forms may affect employee behaviour more than others. So collecting accurate information on total compensation, the mix of pay competitors use, and costs of various forms is increasingly important.

Adjust Pay Structure?

Many employers use market surveys to validate their own job evaluation results. For example, job evaluation may place purchasing assistant jobs at the same level in the job structure as some secretarial jobs. But if the market shows vastly different pay rates for the two types of work, most employers will recheck their evaluation process to see whether the jobs have been properly evaluated. Some may even establish a separate structure for different types of work (e.g., job families such as finance, engineering, law). Thus, the job structure that results from internal job evaluation may not match the pay structures found in the external market. Reconciling these two pay structures is a major issue.

Rather than integrating an internal and external structure, some employers go straight to market surveys to establish their internal structures. Such "market pricing" mimics competitors' pay structures, as will be explained later in the chapter. As organizations move to more generic work descriptions (associate, leader) that focus on the person more than the job, the need for accurate market data increases. Former relationships between job evaluation points and dollars may no longer hold. Informed judgment and accurate information are vital for making all these decisions.

Study Special Situations

Information from specialized surveys may shed light on specific pay-related problems. Many special studies focus on targeted groups, such as patent attorneys, retail sales managers, or software engineers. Unusual increases in an employer's turnover in specific jobs may require focused market surveys to find out if market changes are occurring.[2]

Estimate Competitors' Labour Costs

Increasingly, survey data are used as part of employers' broader efforts to gather "competitive intelligence." To better understand how competitors achieve their market share and price their products/services, companies are also examining competitors' pay practices. As part of their continuous search for ways to squeeze out more costs and become more productive, employers may use salary survey data to benchmark against competitors' product pricing and manufacturing practices. Industry-wide labour cost estimates are reported by Statistics Canada.

■ SELECT RELEVANT MARKET COMPETITORS

To make decisions about pay levels, mix, and structures, a relevant labour market must be defined that includes employers who compete in one or more of the following areas:

1. The same occupation or skills required
2. The same geographic area
3. The same products and services

Exhibit 8.2 shows how qualifications interact with geography to define the scope of relevant labour markets. As the importance and complexity of qualifications increase, the geographic limits also increase. Competition tends to be national for managerial and professional skills, but local or regional for clerical and production skills. However, these generalizations do not always hold true. In areas with high concentrations of scientists, engineers, and managers (e.g., Toronto, Ottawa, or Calgary), the primary market comparison may be regional, with national data used only secondarily.

If the skills are tied to a particular industry, as underwriters, actuaries, and claims representatives are to insurance, it can make sense to define the market on an industry basis.[3] If accounting, sales, or clerical skills are not limited to one particular industry, then industry considerations are less important. From the perspective of cost control and ability to pay, including competitors in the product/service market is crucial.[4] The pay rates of competitors will affect both costs of operations and financial condition (i.e., ability to pay). However, this becomes a problem when the major competitors are based in countries with far lower pay rates, such as China or Mexico. As our discussion in Chapter 7 of segmented labour supplies showed, multiple country comparisons have also become important.[5] This creates additional complexities because legal regulations

EXHIBIT 8.2 | Relevant Labour Markets by Geographic and Employee Groups ——————

Geographic Scope	Production	Office and Clerical	Technicians	Scientists and Engineers	Managerial Professional	Executive
Local: Within relatively small areas such as cities or metropolitan areas	Most likely	Most likely	Most likely			
Regional: Within a particular area of the province or several provinces (e.g., the wheat-producing region of western Canada)	Only if in short supply or critical	Only if in short supply or critical	Most likely	Likely	Most Likely	
National: Across the country				Most likely	Most likely	Most likely
International: Across several countries				Only for critical skills or those in very short supply	Only for critical skills or those in very short supply	Sometimes

and tax policies, as well as customs, vary between countries. For example, because of tax laws, executives in Korea and Spain receive company credit cards that can be used for personal expenses (groceries, clothing). In the United States, these purchases would count as taxable income, but they do not in Korea and Spain.

Although the quality of data available for international comparisons is improving, using the data to adjust pay still requires a lot of judgment. Labour markets are just emerging in some regions (e.g., China, Eastern Europe), where, historically, state agencies set nationwide wage rates, so there was no need for surveys. Japanese companies share information among themselves but not with outsiders, so no surveys were available.[6]

But even if an employer possesses good international survey data, careful judgment is still required. For example, while salaries at international companies in developing economies are low by North American, Western European, and Japanese standards, they are often very high compared to salaries at domestic companies in these developing countries. Pay practices of foreign companies can disrupt emerging local markets.[7] Software engineers working for IBM in India, who are paid very well by Indian standards, feel underpaid compared to IBM engineers in the United States with whom they work on virtual project teams.[8]

Fuzzy Markets

Working in the bays of cubicles at Yahoo are former kindergarten teachers, software engineers, and former sales representatives all collaborating on a single team. Yahoo combines technology, media, and commerce into one company. What is the relevant labour market (skill/geography)? Which firms should be included in Yahoo's compensation surveys?

Even within traditional companies, unique talent is required for unique jobs. West Publishing, the leading provider of legal information to law firms, recently designed the position of Senior Director of Future Vision Services. The holder of this mouthful title is responsible for ensuring that West's customers increase their purchases over the Web and increase their satisfaction with West's services. The job was filled by a software engineer with e-commerce, marketing, and theatre experience. Try finding that job in the market. These new organizations and jobs fuse together diverse knowledge and experience, so "relevant" markets appear more like "fuzzy" markets.[9] Organizations with unique jobs and structures face the double bind of finding it hard to get comparable market data at the same time as they are placing more emphasis on external market data.

■ DESIGN THE COMPENSATION SURVEY

Consulting firms such as Mercer and Towers Watson offer a wide choice of ongoing compensation surveys covering almost every job family and industry group imaginable. Increasingly, consultants offer clients the option of electronically accessing the consultants' survey database. The client then does the special analysis it desires. General Electric conducts most of its market analysis in this manner. Hay PayNet permits organizations to tie into Hay's vast survey data 24/7.[10]

Designing a compensation survey requires answering the following questions: (1) Who should be involved in the survey design? (2) How many employers should be included? (3) Which jobs should be included? and (4) What information should be collected?

Who Should Be Involved?

In most organizations, the responsibility for managing the survey lies with the compensation manager. But because compensation expenses have a powerful effect on profitability, including employees and managers on task forces makes sense. Hiring a third-party consultant instead of managing the survey internally buys expertise but may trade off some control over the decisions that determine the quality and usefulness of the data.

How Many Employers to Survey?

There are no firm rules about how many employers to include in a survey.[11] Large firms with a lead policy may exchange data with only a few top-paying competitors. Recall IBM's policy to pay "the best of the best IT companies." A small organization in an area dominated by two or three employers may decide to survey only smaller competitors. National surveys conducted by consulting firms such as Towers Watson, PricewaterhouseCoopers, and KPMG often include more than 100 employers. Clients of these consultants often stipulate special analyses that report pay rates by selected industry groups, geographic region, and/or pay levels (e.g., top 10 percent).

Publicly Available Data   In Canada, Statistics Canada is the major source of publicly available compensation data. It publishes extensive information on pay for various occupations and industries.

"Word-of-Mouse"   Individual employees used to have a hard time accessing salary data. Confidentiality (secrecy) was the policy of the land, and salary data with which to compare one's own salary was gathered via word of mouth. Today, a click of the mouse makes a wealth of data available to everyone. Employees are comparing their compensation to data from Statistics Canada or salary.monster.ca.[12] This ease of access means that managers must be able to explain and defend the salaries paid to employees compared to those a mouse click away. Unfortunately, the quality of much salary data on the Web is highly suspect. Few of the sites offer any information about how the data were collected, what pay forms were included, and so on. Exhibit 8.3 shows the level of detail provided by salary.monster.ca.

Where Are the Standards?   No systematic study of differences in market definition, participating firms, types of data collected, quality of data, analysis performed, and/or results is available. Issues of sample design and statistical inference are seldom considered. For other HR responsibilities such as staffing decisions, employment test designers report the test's performance against a set of standards (e.g., reliability, validity, etc.). The reliability and validity of job evaluation has been studied. Yet, similar indices and standards do not exist for market surveys and analysis.[13]

Which Jobs to Include?

A general guideline is to keep things as simple as possible. Select as few employers and jobs as necessary to accomplish the purpose. The more complex the survey, the less likely other employers are inclined to participate. There are several approaches to selecting jobs for inclusion.

Benchmark Jobs Approach   In Chapter 5, it was noted that benchmark jobs have stable job content and are common across different employers. If the company's purpose in conducting the survey is to price the entire structure, then benchmark jobs can be selected.

Low-High Approach   If an organization is using skill/competency-based structures or generic job descriptions, it may not be able to match jobs with competitors who use a traditional job-based approach. Job-based market data must be converted to fit the skill or competency structure. The simplest approach is to identify the lowest- and highest-paid benchmark jobs for the relevant skills in the relevant market and to use the wages for these jobs as anchors for the skill-based structures. Work at various levels within the structure then can be slotted between the anchors.

Benchmark Conversion Approach   An alternative approach to job-matching difficulties is to apply the job evaluation plan used to create internal alignment to the descriptions of survey jobs. The magnitude of difference between job evaluation points for internal jobs and survey jobs provides guidance for adjusting the market data.

| EXHIBIT | 8.3 | Salary Data on the Web |

Salary Wizard

A Compensation and Benefits Manager working in Vancouver earns a median total cash compensation of $97,336. The top half of earners are paid an average of $117,171, and the lower half of earners are paid an average of $87,720 *(data as of March 2009)*.

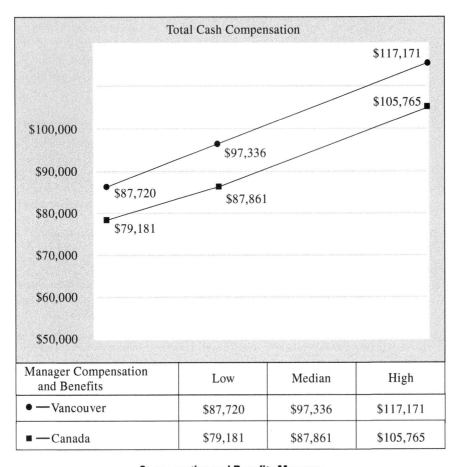

Total Cash Compensation

Manager Compensation and Benefits	Low	Median	High
● —Vancouver	$87,720	$97,336	$117,171
■ —Canada	$79,181	$87,861	$105,765

Compensation and Benefits Manager

Designs, plans, and implements corporate benefits and compensation programs, policies, and procedures. Requires a bachelor's degree in a related area and at least seven years of experience in the field. Generally manages a group of compensation and/or benefits analysts. Relies on experience and judgment to plan and accomplish goals. Typically reports to an executive.

What Information to Collect?

Three basic types of data typically are requested: (1) information about the nature of the organization, (2) information about the total compensation system, and (3) specific pay data on each incumbent in the jobs under study. Exhibit 8.4 lists the basic data elements and the logic for including them. No survey includes all the data that will be discussed. Rather, the data collected depend on the purpose of the survey and the jobs and skills included.

EXHIBIT | **8.4** | Data Elements to Consider for Surveys and Their Rationale

Basic Elements	Examples	Rationale
Nature of Organization		
Identification	Company, name, address, contact person	Further contacts
Financial performance	Assets, sales, profits (after taxes), cash flow	Indicates nature of the product/service markets, the ability to pay, size, and financial viability
Size	Profit centres, product lines	Importance of specific job groups to business success
	Total number of employees	Impact on labour market
Structure	Organizational charts	Indicates how business is organized and how important managerial jobs are
Nature of Total Compensation System		
Cash forms used	Base pay, pay increase schedules, long- and short-term incentives, bonuses, cost of living adjustments, overtime, and shift differentials	Indicate the mix of compensation offered; used to establish a comparable base
Non-cash forms used	Composition of benefits and services, particularly the degree of coverage and contributions to medical and health insurance and pensions	
Incumbent and Job		
Date	Date survey data in effect	Need to update rates to current date
Job	Match generic job description	Indicates degree of similarity with survey's key jobs
	Number of employees supervised and reporting levels	Describes scope of responsibilities
Individual	Years since degree, education, date of hire	Indicates training and tenure of incumbents
Pay	Actual rates paid to each individual, total earnings, last increase, bonuses, incentives	

Organization Data   This information assesses the similarities and differences between survey users. Surveys for executive and upper-level positions include more detailed financial and reporting relationships data, as compensation for these jobs is more directly related to the organization's financial performance. More often than not, the financial data are simply used to group firms by size expressed in terms of sales or revenues rather than considering the performance of competitors.

Total Compensation Data   All the basic forms of pay need to be covered in a survey to assess the similarities and differences in the total pay packages and to accurately assess competitors' practices.[14] The list shown in Exhibit 8.4 reveals the range of forms that could be included in each company's definition of total compensation. As a practical matter, it can be hard to include all the pay forms. Too much detail on benefits, such as medical coverage deductibles and flexible schedules, can make a survey too cumbersome to be useful. Alternatives range from a brief description of a benchmark benefit package to including only the most expensive and variable benefits or asking for an estimate of total benefit expenses as a percentage of total labour costs.

Three alternatives—(1) base pay, (2) total cash (base, profit sharing, bonuses), and (3) total compensation (total cash plus benefits and stock-based incentives)—are the most commonly used. Exhibit 8.5 draws the distinction between these three alternatives and highlights the usefulness and limitations of each one as a survey measure. Exhibit 8.6 shows some results of survey analysis using these three different measures on a sample of seven jobs from an internal job structure. The "going market rate" varies, depending on what forms are included.

A. *Base pay.* This is the amount of cash the competitors decided each job is worth. A company might use this information for its initial observations of how well the data appear to fit a range of jobs. In Exhibit 8.6, Line A is a market line based on base pay.
B. *Total cash is base plus bonus.* This reflects the cash value of the job plus bonuses paid to incumbents
C. *Total compensation includes total cash and benefits plus stock-based incentives.* Total compensation reflects the total overall value of the employee (e.g., performance, experience, skills, etc.) plus the value of the work itself.

For all seven jobs, total compensation is higher than base pay alone or base plus bonus, but the variability and magnitude of the difference is noteworthy: from $7,842 ($30,831 – $22,989, or 34 percent) for the job of Technician A, to $244,104 (182 percent) for the Manager 3. Base pay is, on average, only 35 percent ($134,173/$378,277) of total compensation for the Manager 3s in this survey. So what kinds of compensation to include is an important decision in designing a survey design. Misinterpreting competitors' pay practices can lead to costly mispricing of pay levels and structures.

■ INTERPRET SURVEY RESULTS AND CONSTRUCT A MARKET LINE

After the survey data are all collected, the next step is to analyze the results and use statistics to construct a market line. Twenty years ago, researcher David Belcher interviewed compensation professionals to discover how survey data are actually analyzed. He reported:

EXHIBIT 8.5 | Advantages and Disadvantages of Measures of Compensation ————————————

Base Pay	Tells how competitors are valuing the work in similar jobs	Fails to include performance incentives and other forms, so will not give true picture if competitors offer low base but high incentives
Total Cash (base + bonus)	Tells how competitors are valuing work; also tells the cash pay for performance opportunity in the job	All employees may not receive incentives, so it may overstate the competitors' pay; plus, it does not include long-term incentives
Total Compensation (base + bonus + stock options + benefits)	Tells the total value competitors place on this work	All employees may not receive all the forms. Be careful; don't set base equal to competitors' total compensation. Risks high fixed costs.

EXHIBIT | **8.6** | Salary Graphs Using Different Measures of Compensation

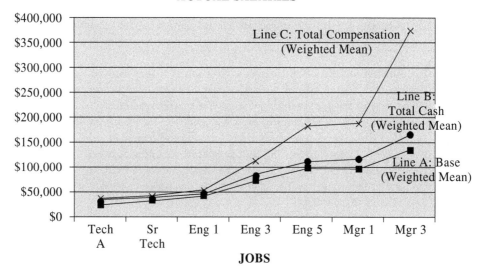

ACTUAL SALARIES

	A: Base, Weighted Mean	B: Total Cash, Weighted Mean	C: Total Compensation, Weighted Mean
Tech A	$22,989	$24,555	$30,831
Sr Tech	$37,749	$42,510	$51,482
Eng 1	$46,085	$48,290	$56,917
Eng 3	$73,135	$81,286	$112,806
Eng 5	$102,415	$112,587	$179,450
Mgr 1	$95,260	$115,305	$188,510
Mgr 3	$134,173	$171,031	$378,277

Every organization uses its own methods of distilling information from the survey; uses different surveys for different purposes; and uses different methods for company surveys. I could find no commonality in these methods of analysis by industry, by firm size, or by union presence. For example, some did nothing except read the entire survey, some emphasized industry data, others geographic competitors (commuting distances), some made comparisons with less than five competitors, some emphasized only large firms, others throw out the data from large firms.[15]

His conclusion still holds today. Diversity rules in analyzing survey data. It is hoped that this diversity reflects flexibility in dealing with a variety of circumstances rather than a lack of business- and work-related logic.

Verify Data

A common first step is to check the *accuracy* of the job matches, then check for anomalies (i.e., an employer whose data are substantially out of line with those from others), age of data, level of abstractness (i.e., standard occupations versus job descriptions), and the nature of the organizations (e.g., Algoma Steel versus Research in Motion). Exhibit 8.7 is an excerpt from the survey used to prepare Exhibit 8.6. Although there were a number of jobs included in the survey, information for just one job—Engineer 1—is used to illustrate. Surveys do not make light reading, but they contain a wealth of information.

survey levelling

multiplying survey data by a numerical factor to adjust for differences between the company job and the survey job

Accuracy of Match   Part A of the survey contains the job description for which survey participants were asked to report data. Does the description match a job at the user organization? If the job is similar but not identical, some companies use **survey levelling,** that is, they multiply the survey data by some numerical factor that corresponds to the analyst's judgment of the differences between the company and survey job. Levelling is another example of the use of judgment in the survey analysis process. It clearly leaves the objectivity of the decisions open to challenge.

Anomalies   Part B of the survey gives actual salaries received by actual Engineer 1s (not all of the 585 Engineer 1s in the survey have been included in the exhibit). Perusal of actual salary data gives the analyst an initial sense of the nature and quality of the data and helps identify any areas for additional consideration. For example, Part B of Exhibit 8.7 shows that no Engineer 1s at Company 1 receive stock options, and five receive no bonuses. The bonuses that are paid range from $500 to $4,000. Individual-level data provide a wealth of information about specific practices. Understanding minimums, maximums, and what percentage actually receive bonuses and/or options is essential. Unfortunately, many surveys provide only summary information such as company averages.

Part C of Exhibit 8.7 provides company data. Again, the first step is to look for anomalies.

- *Does any one company dominate?* For example, Company 57 employs 226 Engineer 1s, much more than any of the others. A separate analysis of the largest company's data will isolate that employer's pay practices and clarify the nature of its influence.
- *Do all employers show similar patterns?* The base pay for a single job at Company 1 ranges from $36,500 to $79,000. This raises the possibility that this company might use broad bands (discussed later in this chapter). Although several of the companies have a bonus-to-base pay ratio of around 2 to 3 percent, Company 15 pays an average bonus of $8,254, for a bonus-to-base ratio of over 6 percent.
- *Outliers?* Company 51 gives one of its engineers options valued at $74,453 on top of base pay. Because they are such outliers (anomalies) compared to other companies, the user analyst might consider dropping these companies. What difference will it make if Company 15 or 51 is dropped? What difference will it make if they are included?

One way to answer questions or anomalies is to analyze them alone. Some firms may be deliberately differentiating themselves with pay as part of their strategy. Other firms may simply match. Learning more about competitors that differentiate can offer valuable insight. Part D at the bottom of Exhibit 8.7 contains summary data: five different measures of base pay, cash, and total compensation, as well as the percentage of engineers who receive bonuses (93%) and options (8.4%). The data suggest that most competitors use bonuses but are less likely to use options for this particular job. Summary data help reduce all the survey information into a smaller number of measures for further statistical analysis. *Statistics help us get from pages of raw data (Exhibit 8.7) to graphs of actual salaries (Exhibit 8.6) and from there to a market line that reflects a competitive pay policy.*

Statistical Analysis

All the statistics necessary to analyze survey data, including regression, are covered in any basic statistics class or textbook. Understanding regression analysis is necessary to make sound compensation judgments. A useful first step in our analysis is to look at a frequency distribution of the pay rates.

Frequency Distributions   Exhibit 8.8 shows a frequency distribution created from the data in the Exhibit 8.7 survey, illustrating the distribution of the base wages for the 585 Engineer 1s. The horizontal axis shows base wages in increments of $1,000, ranging from $36,000 to $79,000. Frequency distributions help visualize the information in the survey and may highlight

EXHIBIT 8.7 | Survey Data

A. Job Description: Engineer 1

Participates in development, testing, and documentation of software programs. Performs design and analysis tasks as a project team member. Typical minimum requirements are a bachelor's degree in a scientific or technical field or the equivalent and up to two years of experience.

B. Individual Salary Data (partial data; for illustration only)

Job	Base	Bonus	Total Cash	Stock Option	Benefits	Total Comp
Engineer 1					*JE Points:*	50
					Number of Incumbents:	585
Company 1						
Engineer 1	$79,000	$500	$79,500	$0	$8,251	$87,751
Engineer 1	$65,500	$2,500	$68,000	$0	$8,251	$76,251
Engineer 1	$65,000	$0	$65,000	$0	$8,251	$73,251
Engineer 1	$58,000	$4,000	$62,000	$0	$8,251	$70,251
Engineer 1	$57,930	$3,000	$60,930	$0	$8,251	$69,181
Engineer 1	$57,200	$2,000	$59,200	$0	$8,251	$67,451
Engineer 1	$56,000	$1,100	$57,100	$0	$8,251	$65,351
Engineer 1	$54,000	$0	$54,000	$0	$8,251	$62,251
Engineer 1	$52,500	$0	$52,500	$0	$8,251	$60,751
Engineer 1	$51,500	$1,500	$53,000	$0	$8,251	$61,251
Engineer 1	$49,000	$3,300	$52,300	$0	$8,251	$60,551
Engineer 1	$48,500	$0	$48,500	$0	$8,251	$56,751
Engineer 1	$36,500	$0	$36,500	$0	$8,251	$44,751
Company 2						
Engineer 1	$57,598	$0	$57,598	$28,889	$8,518	$95,004
Engineer 1	$57,000	$0	$57,000	$31,815	$8,518	$97,332
Engineer 1	$55,000	$0	$55,000	$20,110	$8,518	$83,628

C. Company Data (partial data; for illustration only)

	# Incumbents		Base	Short Term	Total Cash	LTI	Benefits	Total Comp
Company 1								
	13	Avg.	56,202	1,377	57,579	0	8,251	65,830
		Min.	36,500	0	36,500	0	8,251	44,751
		Max.	79,000	4,000	79,500	0	8,251	87,751
Company 2								
	13	Avg.	52,765	1,474	54,238	21,069	8,518	83,825
		Min.	47,376	0	50,038	4,879	8,518	65,417
		Max.	57,598	3,717	58,494	31,815	8,518	97,332
Company 15								
	71	Avg.	49,686	8,254	57,940	1,763	8,404	68,106
		Min.	44,900	0	49,022	0	8,404	57,426
		Max.	57,300	14,132	68,357	63,639	8,404	125,471
Company 51								
	4	Avg.	46,194	1,400	47,594	41,954	7,641	97,189
		Min.	42,375	0	44,989	20,518	7,641	75,159
		Max.	48,400	2,985	51,385	74,453	7,641	133,479

EXHIBIT 8.7 Survey Data (*continued*)

Company 57

226	Avg.	44,092	1,262	45,354	0	6,812	52,166
	Min.	38,064	0	39,372	0	6,812	46,184
	Max.	60,476	2,179	62,655	0	6,812	69,467

Company 59

71	Avg.	44,914	1,153	46,066	0	6,812	52,878
	Min.	39,156	407	40,473	0	6,812	47,285
	Max.	57,000	1,639	57,407	0	6,812	64,219

D. Summary Data for Engineer 1

Base Salary		Total Cash		Total Compensation		Bonuses	Stock Options
Wtd Mean:	$46,085	*Wtd Mean:*	$48,290	*Wtd Mean:*	$56,918	*Avg:* $2,371	*Avg:* $16,920
50th:	$45,000	*50th:*	$46,422	*50th:*	$53,271	*5.2% of base*	*34% of base*
25th:	$42,600	*25th:*	$43,769	*25th:*	$50,593	*93% receive*	*8.4% receive*
75th:	$48,500	*75th:*	$51,854	*75th:*	$60,751		

outlier

a data point that falls outside the majority of the data points

non-conformities. For example, the one base wage of $79,000 may be considered an **outlier**—an extreme that falls outside the majority of the data points. Is this a unique person? Or an error in reporting the data? Whether or not to include outliers is a judgment call.

Central Tendency   A measure of central tendency reduces a large amount of data to a single number. Exhibit 8.7 defines commonly used measures. The *weighted mean* is calculated by adding the base wages for all 585 engineers in the survey and then dividing by the number of engineers (585). A weighted mean gives equal weight to each individual employee's wage.

EXHIBIT 8.8 Frequency Distribution

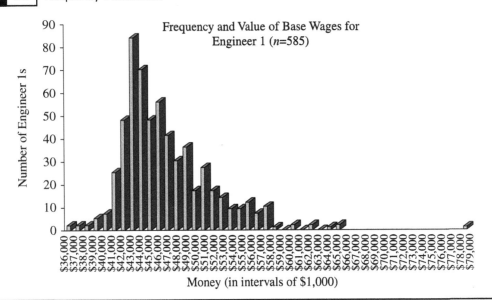

Variance   The distribution of rates around a measure of central tendency is called *variance*. The standard deviation is probably the most common statistical measure of variance, although its use in salary surveys is rare. *Standard deviation* refers to how far from the mean (or weighted mean) each of the items in a frequency distribution is located.

Quartiles and percentiles are more common measures of variance in salary survey analysis. Recall from the chapter introduction a policy "to be in the 75th percentile nationally." A 75th percentile means that 75 percent of all pay rates are at or below that point, and 25 percent are above. The 25th, 50th, and 75th percentiles (also called "quartiles") are commonly used to set pay ranges.

Age/Trend the Survey Data

Because pay reflects decisions of employers, employees, unions, and government agencies, competitors' pay rates are constantly changing. Even though these changes do not occur smoothly and uniformly throughout the year, as a practical matter it is common practice to assume that they do. Therefore, a survey that requires three months to collect, code, and analyze is probably outdated before it becomes available. Consequently, the pay data usually are updated in a process often called **aging/trending survey data** to adjust the data to represent pay at the current or future date when the pay decisions will be implemented.

aging/trending survey data

adjusting survey data to represent pay at the current or future date when the pay decisions will be implemented

The amount to adjust is based on several factors, including historical trends in market economic forecasts, prospects for the economy in which the employer operates, and the manager's judgment, among others.

As an example, a base pay rate of $45,000 collected in the survey was in effect at January 1 of the current year—already in the past. The compensation manager will use these data for pay decisions that will go into effect on January 1 of the next year. Assuming that base pay has been increasing by approximately 5 percent annually, and assuming that the future will be like the past, then the market data are increased by 5 percent (multiplied by 1.05), to account for the rise in pay that is expected to occur by the end of the current year. The $45,000 this past January 1 is updated to $47,250 to estimate pay at January 1 next year.

Construct a Market Pay Line

Turn back and look again at Exhibit 8.6. It shows the results of the compensation analyst's decisions on which benchmark jobs to include (seven jobs on the horizontal axis), which companies to include, and which statistics to use to measure pay. Three different compensation metrics are included: base wage, total cash, and total compensation. For each of these metrics, a line has been drawn connecting the rates for the seven jobs. The seven jobs are arranged in this order on the graph because the ordering on the graph reflects the internal structure at the user company. Jobs are ordered on the horizontal axis according to their position in the internal structure. Consequently, a **market pay line** links a company's benchmark jobs on the horizontal axis (internal structure) with market rates paid by competitors (market survey), which are on the vertical axis.

market pay line

links a company's benchmark jobs on the horizontal axis (internal structure) with market rates paid by competitors (market survey) on the vertical axis

A market line may be drawn freehand by connecting the data points, as was done in Exhibit 8.6, or statistical techniques such as regression analysis may be used. Exhibit 8.9 shows the market pay lines based on regression using the same data as in Exhibit 8.6. Regression generates a straight line that best fits the data by minimizing the variance around the line. Regression provides a statistical summary of the distribution of going rates paid by competitors in the market—in this case, the market pay line. The appendix to this chapter contains more information about regression analysis.

Exhibit 8.9 shows the job evaluation points for the user company jobs that match each of these seven survey jobs, and the regression's prediction of the market pay for each job. The actual base wage for the survey job Tech A is $22,989 (Exhibit 8.6). The regression line based on market data

EXHIBIT	8.9	Market Pay Line (from Regression Analysis)

JOBS

Job	Job Evaluation Points	Predicted Base, Weighted Mean	Predicted Cash, Weighted Mean	Predicted Total Compensation
Tech A	10	$23,058	$20,544	−$1,330*
Sr Tech	25	$34,361	$35,117	$31,172
Eng 1	50	$53,200	$59,405	$85,343
Eng 3	75	$72,038	$83,693	$139,514
Eng 5	100	$90,877	$107,981	$193,685
Mgr 1	125	$109,715	$132,269	$247,856
Mgr 3	150	$128,554	$156,557	$302,027

* This amount is negative because the slope of the line takes it below zero at low levels of job evaluation points.

predicts base pay of $23,058 (Exhibit 8.9). Why use the regression results rather than the actual survey data? Regression "smooths" large amounts of data while minimizing variations in it.

Before finishing this section on survey data analysis, it is important to emphasize that not all survey results look like those in this chapter, and not all companies use the statistical and analytical techniques discussed in this chapter. There is no one "right way" to analyze survey data. The intent here is to provide some insight into the kinds of calculations that are useful and the assumptions that underlie salary surveys.

Combine Internal Structure and External Market Rates

At this point, two parts of the total pay model have merged. Their relationship to each other can be seen in Exhibit 8.10. In Exhibit 8.10, the diamonds are the actual results of the survey, and the solid line is the regression result.

- The *internally aligned structure* developed in Part I of this book is shown on the horizontal axis. For this illustration, the structure consists of the seven benchmark jobs that have been matched in the compensation survey.
- The salaries paid by relevant competitors for those benchmark jobs, as measured by the survey—the *external competitive data*—are shown on the vertical axis.

These two components—internal alignment and external competitiveness—come together in the pay structure. The pay structure has two aspects: the *pay policy line*, and *pay ranges*.

▩ FROM POLICY TO PRACTICE: THE PAY POLICY LINE

pay policy line
pay line representing an adjustment to the market pay line to reflect the company's external competitive position in the market (i.e., lead, match, lag)

The next major decision is to set the external competitive position by adjusting the market pay line in order to construct a **pay policy line**. This line reflects the firm's competitive position in the market. The previous chapter discussed why employers might choose different external competitive pay policies. Here, the organization must put its chosen competitive pay policy (lead, match, or lag) into effect.

Choice of Measure   If Colgate practises what it claims at the beginning of the chapter, then we would expect Colgate to use the 50th percentile for base pay and the 75th percentile for total compensation.

| **EXHIBIT** | **8.10** | Combining Internal Job Structure and External Market Rates: Regression Analysis of Survey Rates — |

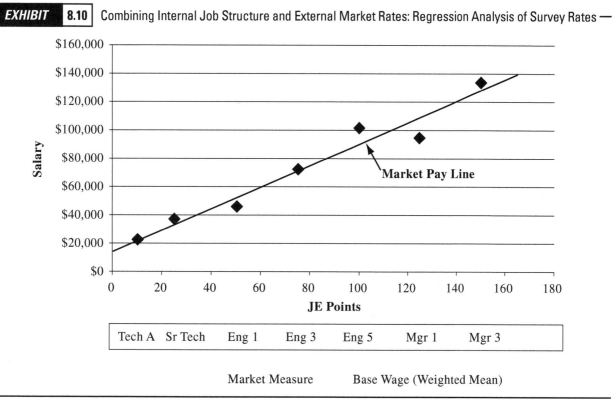

Market Pay Line

| Tech A | Sr Tech | Eng 1 | Eng 3 | Eng 5 | Mgr 1 | Mgr 3 |

Market Measure   Base Wage (Weighted Mean)

Updating   The survey data at the beginning of the plan year (following aging/trending) may be updated again depending on the firm's pay level policy, as shown in Exhibit 8.11. Using the survey data that was previously aged to January 1 of the next year and keeping this rate ($47,250 for Engineer 1 in the earlier example) for the year will constitute a *lag* policy (solid line on Exhibit 8.11).

If the company chooses a *match* policy, but then uses the survey data that was previously aged to January 1 of the next year and keeps this rate ($47,250 in the earlier example) in effect throughout the plan year, it will match its desired market pay level only at the beginning of the plan year. The market rates continue to rise throughout the year; the company's rates do not. Updating the market data to a point halfway through the plan year (dotted line on Exhibit 8.11) is called *lead/lag*. The original survey rates are aged to January 1 of the next year, then updated again by half of the projected increase for the next year ($48,431, calculated as $47,250 × 1.025, assuming the 5 percent increase still holds).

An employer with a *lead* policy will update the aged data at the beginning of the plan year to the end of the plan year ($49,613 calculated as $47,250 × 1.05), and then pay at this rate throughout the plan year (starred line on Exhibit 8.11).

Policy Line as a Percentage of Market Line   A third approach to translate pay level policy into practice is simply to specify a percentage above or below the regression line (market line) that an employer intends to match, and then draw a new line at this higher (or lower) level. This would carry out the policy statement, "We lead the market by 10 percent." Other possibilities exist. An employer might lead by including only a few top-paying competitors in the analysis and then matching them. Or lead for some job families and lag for others. The point is that just as there are alternatives among competitive pay policies (lead, match, lag, etc.), so there are alternative ways to translate policy into practice. If the practice does not match the policy (i.e., saying one thing but doing another), then employees receive the wrong message.

EXHIBIT 8.11 | Updating Market Pay Line to Create Pay Policy Line

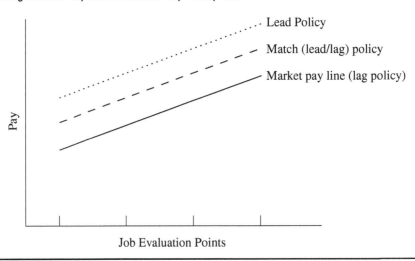

FROM POLICY TO PRACTICE: GRADES AND RANGES

pay grade

grouping of jobs considered substantially equal for pay purposes

The first step in building flexibility into the pay structure is to group different jobs that are considered substantially equal for pay purposes into a **pay grade**. Base pay data are used here because base pay reflects the basic value of the work (or relevant skill sets). Grades enhance an organization's ability to move people between jobs within a grade with no change in pay. In Exhibit 8.12 the jobs are grouped into five grades on the horizontal axis.

The question of which jobs are substantially equal and therefore slotted into one grade requires the analyst to reconsider the original job evaluation results. Each grade will have its own pay range, and *all the jobs within a single grade will have the same pay range.* Jobs in different grades (e.g., jobs C, D, E, and F in Grade 2) should be dissimilar to those in other grades (Grade 1 jobs A and B) and will have a different pay range.

Although grades permit flexibility, they are challenging to design. The objective is that all jobs that are similar for pay purposes be placed within the same grade. If jobs with relatively close job evaluation point totals fall on either side of grade boundaries, the magnitude of difference in salary treatment may be out of proportion to the magnitude of difference in the value of the job content. Resolving such dilemmas requires an understanding of the specific jobs, career paths, and workflow in the organization. Designing the grade structure that fits each organization involves the use of trial and error until one structure is found to fit best. Considerable judgment is involved.

Why Bother with Grades and Ranges?

Grades and ranges offer managers the flexibility to deal with pressures from external markets and within the organization. External market pressures include many already discussed such as those created by supply and demand. Beyond this, ranges permit managers to recognize other differences. These include:

1. *Differences in quality* (skills, abilities, experience) between individuals applying for work (e.g., Microsoft may have stricter hiring requirements for engineers than others, even though job descriptions appear identical).
2. *Differences in the productivity or value of these quality variations* (e.g., the value of the results from a software engineer at Microsoft probably differs from the results of a software engineer at Best Buy).

EXHIBIT 8.12 Develop Pay Grades

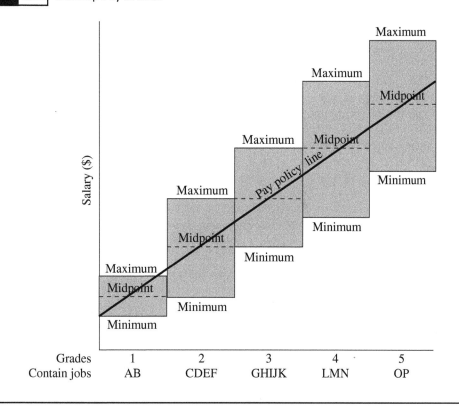

Grades	1	2	3	4	5
Contain jobs	AB	CDEF	GHIJK	LMN	OP

3. *Differences in the mix of pay forms competitors use* (e.g., Oracle uses more stock options than IBM, so IBM managers may need to offer more base pay when competing with Oracle).

In addition to offering flexibility to deal with these external differences in rates, an organization may desire differences in rates paid to employees performing the same job. A pay range exists whenever two or more rates are paid to employees performing the same job. Hence, ranges provide managers the opportunity to:

1. Recognize individual performance differences with pay.
2. Meet employees' expectations that their pay will increase over time, even while holding the same job.
3. Encourage employee commitment to remain with the organization.

From an internal alignment perspective, the range reflects the differences in performance or experience the employer wishes to pay for a given level of work. From an external competitiveness perspective, the range also acts as a control device. A range maximum sets the ceiling on what the employer is willing to pay for that work; the range minimum sets the floor.

Not all employers use ranges. Skill-based plans establish single flat rates for each skill level regardless of performance or seniority. And many collective bargaining contracts establish single flat rates for each job (e.g., all Senior Machinists II receive $14.50 per hour regardless of performance or seniority). This flat rate is often set to correspond to some midpoint on a survey of that job. And increasingly, broad bands (really big ranges) are being adopted. Broad bands offer employers even greater flexibility to treat employees differently and to deal with external pressures. Broadbanding is discussed further below.

Establish Range Midpoints, Minimums, and Maximums

pay range

an upper and lower limit on pay for all jobs in a pay grade

Grades group job evaluation data on the horizontal axis; ranges group salary data on the vertical axis. **Pay ranges** set an upper and lower limit between which all wages for all jobs in a particular grade are expected to fall. A range has three salient features: a midpoint, a minimum, and a maximum. The midpoints for each range usually correspond to the points where the pay policy line crosses each grade. The competitive pay level for each grade, established earlier, becomes the midpoint of the pay range for that grade. If the midpoint for Grade 2 in Exhibit 8.13 is $54,896, then this is the point where the pay policy line crosses the centre of the grade. The maximum and minimum for this grade have been set at 20 percent above and 20 percent below the midpoint. Thus, all engineers are supposed to receive a salary between $43,917 and $65,875. The **range spread** is expressed as a percentage above the minimum of the range, e.g., 30 percent increase from the minimum to the maximum, such as where the minimum is $30,000 and the maximum is $39,000.

What Size Should the Range Be?   The size of the range is based on some judgment about how the ranges support career paths, promotions, and other organization systems. Top-level management positions commonly have ranges of 30 to 60 percent; entry to midlevel professional and managerial positions, between 15 and 30 percent; office and production work, 5 to 15 percent. The underlying logic is that larger ranges in the managerial jobs reflect the greater opportunity for individual discretion and performance variations in the work.

Some compensation managers use the actual rates paid, particularly the 75th and 25th percentiles in the survey data, as their maximums and minimums. Others examine alternatives to ensure that the proposed spread includes at least 75 percent of the rates in the survey data. Still others establish the minimum and maximum separately. The amount between the minimum and the midpoint can be a function of the amount of time it takes a new employee to become fully competent. Jobs quickly learned may have minimums much closer to the midpoints. The maximum becomes the amount above the midpoint that the company is willing to pay for sustained performance on the job. In the end, the size of the range is based on judgment that weighs all these factors.

Overlap

Exhibit 8.13 shows two extremes in the degree of overlap between adjacent grades. The high degree of overlap and low midpoint differentials in Figure A indicate small differences in the value of jobs in the adjoining grades. Being promoted from one grade to another may include a title change but not much change in pay. On the other hand, the smaller ranges in Figure B create less overlap, which permits the manager to reinforce a promotion into a new grade with a larger pay increase. The downside is that there may be fewer opportunities for promotion.

EXHIBIT 8.13 Range Overlap

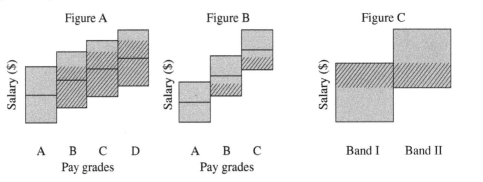

Promotion Increases Matter The size of pay differentials between grades should support career movement though the structure. A managerial job typically would be at least one pay range higher than the jobs it supervises. However, large range overlap and possible overtime in some jobs but not in managerial jobs can make it difficult to maintain manager-employee differentials. The optimal overlap between grades is large enough to induce employees to seek promotion to a higher grade. However, there is virtually no research to indicate how much of a differential is necessary to influence employees to do so.

■ FROM POLICY TO PRACTICE: BROADBANDING

broadbanding
a large band of jobs containing several pay grades

Figure C in Exhibit 8.13 collapses salary grades into only a few broad bands, each with a sizable range. This technique, known as **broadbanding**, consolidates as many as four or five traditional grades into a single band with one minimum and one maximum. Because the band encompasses so many jobs of differing values, a range midpoint usually is not used.[16]

Contrasts between ranges and broad bands are highlighted in Exhibit 8.14. Supporters of broad bands list several advantages over traditional approaches. First, broad bands provide flexibility to define job responsibilities more broadly. They support redesigned, downsized, or boundaryless organizations that have eliminated layers of managerial jobs. They foster cross-functional growth and development in these new organizations. Employees can move laterally across functions within a band in order to gain depth of experience. Companies with global operations use bands to aid in moving managers among worldwide assignments. The emphasis on lateral movement with no pay adjustments tied to such movement helps manage the reality of fewer promotion opportunities in flattened organization structures. The flexibility of banding eases mergers and acquisitions because there are not many levels to argue over.[17]

Bands may result in less time being spent judging fine distinctions between jobs and building barriers. On the other hand, the time saved by not judging jobs may instead will be spent judging individuals, a prospect managers already try to avoid. How will an organization avoid the appearance of salary treatment based on personality and politics rather than objective criteria?[18] Ideally, with a strong performance-based system.

Broadbanding takes two steps:

1. ***Set the number of bands.*** Surveys report companies are using three to eight bands for pay purposes. Merck uses six bands for its entire structure, with titles ranging from contributor to executive. A unit of General Electric replaced 24 levels with five bands. Usually bands are established at the major "breaks," or differences in work or skill/competency requirements.

EXHIBIT 8.14 Contrasts between Ranges and Bands

Ranges Support	Bands Support
Some flexibility within controls	Emphasis on flexibility within guidelines
Relatively stable organization design	Global organizations
Recognition via titles or career progression	Cross-functional experience and lateral progression
Midpoint controls, comparatives	Reference market rates, shadow ranges
Controls designed into system	Controls in budget, few in system
Give managers "freedom with guidelines"	Give managers "freedom to manage" pay
To 150 percent range-spread	100–400 percent spreads

Titles used to label each band reflect these major breaks, such as "associates" (entry-level individual contributor), "professional" (experienced, knowledgeable team member), "leader" (project or group supervisor), "director," or "coach."

2. ***Price the bands' reference rates.*** The four bands in Exhibit 8.15 (associates, professionals, lead professionals, senior professionals) include multiple job families within each band. Each band might include jobs from finance, purchasing, software development and engineering, marketing, and so on. The challenge is how much to pay people who are in the same band but in different functions performing different work. As the bottom of Exhibit 8.15 depicts, the three job families (purchasing, finance, and engineering) in the professionals band have different **reference rates** drawn from survey data.

reference rates

pay rates from market data used in pricing broad bands

This may seem a lot like grades and ranges within each band, which is correct. The difference is that ranges traditionally serve as controls, whereas reference rates act as guides. Today's guides grow into tomorrow's bureaucracy. Further discussion on this point is provided in the .Net Worth box.

Flexibility—Control   Broadbanding encourages employees to move cross-functionally (e.g., purchasing to finance, between development and systems design) to increase the cross-fertilization of ideas. Hence, a career move is more likely within a band and less likely between bands.

EXHIBIT   8.15   Four Bands

.NET WORTH

Second-Generation Banded Salary Systems

The broad band salary systems that were highly acclaimed in the early 1990s addressed a number of problems with traditional salary structures, including locking organizations into job hierarchies that got out of sync with what was happening in labour markets. However, the early model fell into disfavour when companies realized there was no mechanism to control salaries. The bands were often twice as wide as in more traditional salary structures, and that contributed to inflated payroll costs. Another problem was the reliance on market surveys that were based simplistically on job titles and very short job descriptions. The validity of many such surveys is questionable.

Therefore, companies have developed second-generation systems to address these concerns. Two new models provide for close, job-specific market pricing while retaining the advantages inherent with banded systems. The first model establishes separate bands for different occupational groups, using market data specific to these job families. This method has been used in the past by companies with large technology or research groups. The second model uses a single set of bands, but defines job-specific "ranges" within the bands based on survey data.

These new second-generation broadbanding models enable managers to manage salaries to be consistent with market levels while still retaining control over their payroll costs.

Source: Adapted from H. Risher, "Second Generation Banded Salary Systems," *WorldatWork Journal* 16(1), First Quarter 2007, pp. 20–28.

According to supporters, the principal payoff of broadbanding is flexibility. Flexibility is one side of the coin; chaos and favouritism the other. Banding presumes that managers will manage employee pay to accomplish the organization's objectives (and not their own) and will treat employees fairly. Historically, this is not the first time greater flexibility has been given to managers and employees. Indeed, the rationale underlying the use of ranges and grades was to reduce the inconsistencies and favouritism that were destructive to employee relations in previous generations.[19] The challenge today is to take advantage of flexibility without increasing labour costs or leaving the organization vulnerable to charges of favouritism and inconsistent or illegal practices.

■ BALANCING INTERNAL AND EXTERNAL PRESSURES: ADJUSTING THE PAY STRUCTURE

Up until now, a distinction has been made between the job structure and the pay structure. A *job structure* orders jobs on the basis of internal organizational factors (reflected in job evaluation or skill certification). The *pay structure*, on the other hand, is anchored by the organization's external competitive position, reflected in its base pay policy lines.

Reconciling Differences

The problem with using two bases (internal and external) to create a structure is that they are likely to result in two different structures. The order in which jobs are ranked on internal and external factors probably will not agree completely. Differences between market structures/rates and job evaluation rankings warrant a review of the basic decisions in evaluating and pricing that particular job. This may entail a review of the job analysis, the job description, and the evaluation of the job, or the market data for the job in question. Often this re-analysis solves the problem. Sometimes, however, discrepancies persist; sometimes survey data are discarded; sometimes benchmark job matches are changed.

One study of how differences are actually reconciled found that managers weigh external market data more heavily than internal job evaluation data. In light of all the judgments that go into internal evaluation, market data often are considered to be more objective.[20] Yet this chapter and recent research show that market data are also based on judgments.

Sometimes differences arise because a shortage of a particular skill has driven up the market rate. But reclassifying a "hot" job (one in which a supply-and-demand imbalance exists) into a higher salary grade, where it will remain long after the imbalance has been corrected, creates additional problems. Creating a special range that is clearly designated as market responsive may be a better approach. However, decisions made on the basis of expediency run the risk of undermining the integrity of the pay decisions.

■ MARKET PRICING

market pricing

establishing pay structure by relying almost exclusively on external market pay rates

Many organizations in Canada are adopting pay strategies that emphasize external competitiveness and deemphasize internal alignment. Called **market pricing**, this approach sets pay structures by relying almost exclusively on rates paid by competitors in the external market. Organizations that fill a large proportion of their job vacancies with hires from the outside may also become market pricers. Market pricers match a large percentage of their jobs with market data and collect as much market data as possible.[21] They rank to market to determine the pay for jobs unique to their firms. The competitive rates for positions for which external market data are available are first calculated, then the remaining (non-benchmark) jobs are blended into the pay hierarchy created, based on external rates. Pfizer, for example, begins with job analysis and job descriptions. These are immediately followed by labour market analysis and market pricing for as many jobs as possible. After that, the remaining jobs are blended in and the internal job relationships are reviewed to be sure they are "reasonable in light of organization workflow and other uniqueness." The final step is pricing those jobs not priced directly in the market. This is done by comparing the value of these jobs to the Pfizer jobs already priced in the market.

Market pricing goes beyond the use of benchmark jobs and then slotting non-benchmarks. The objective of market pricing is to base most if not all of the internal pay structure on external rates paid by competitors, breaking down the boundaries between the internal organization and external market forces. Some companies even match all forms of pay for each job to their competitors in the market. For example, if the average rate paid by competitors for a controller job is $150,000, then the company pays $150,000. If 60 percent of the $150,000 is base pay, 20 percent is annual bonus, 5 percent is stock options, and 15 percent is benefits, the company matches not only the amount but also this mix of pay forms. Another $150,000 job, say director of marketing, may have a different pattern among market competitors, which is also matched.

Pure market pricing carried to this extreme deemphasizes internal alignment completely. Gone is any attempt to align internal pay structures with the business strategy and the work performed. Rather, the internal pay structure is aligned with competitors' decisions that are reflected in the market. In a very real sense, the decisions of its competitors determine an organization's pay structure.

This approach raises several issues. Among them: Just how valid are the market data?[22] Do they really lend themselves to such decisions? Why should competitors' pay decisions be the sole or even primary determinant of another company's pay structure? If they are, then how much or what forms a company pays no longer constitute a competitive advantage. They are not unique, nor are they difficult to imitate. The premise is that little value is added through internal alignment.

Any unique or difficult-to-imitate aspects of the organization's pay structure, which may have been based on its unique technology or its unique flow of work, are deemphasized by market pricers. Fairness is presumed to be reflected by market rates; employee behaviour is presumed to be reinforced by totally market-priced structures, which are the very same as those of competitors.

In sum, the process of balancing internal and external pressures is a matter of judgment, made with an eye to the strategic perspectives and objectives established for the pay system.[23] Deemphasizing pay alignment within an organization may lead to feelings of unfair treatment among employees and inconsistency with the fundamental culture of the organization. Neglecting external competitive pay practices, however, will affect both the ability to attract applicants and the ability to hire applicants who match the organization's needs. External pay relationships also impact labour costs and hence the ability to compete in the product/service market.

CONCLUSION

This chapter has detailed the basic decisions and techniques involved in setting pay levels and mix and designing pay structures. Most organizations survey other employers' pay practices to determine the rates competitors pay. An employer using survey results considers how it wishes to position its total compensation in the market: to lead, to match, or to follow competition. This policy decision may be different for different business units and even for different job groups within a single organization. The policy on competitive position is translated into practice by setting pay policy lines; they serve as reference points around which pay grades and ranges or bands are designed.

The use of grades and ranges recognizes both external and internal pressures on pay decisions. No single "going rate" for a job exists in the market; instead, an array of rates exists. This array results from conditions of demand and supply, variations in the quality of employees, and differences in employer policies and practices. It also reflects the fact that employers differ in the value they attach to the jobs and people. And, very importantly, it reflects differences in the mix of pay forms different companies emphasize.

Internally, the use of ranges is consistent with variations in the discretion present in jobs. Some employees will perform better than others; some employees are more experienced than others. Pay ranges permit employers to value and recognize these differences with pay.

Managers increasingly are interested in broadbanding, which offers even greater flexibility than grades and ranges to deal with the continuously changing work assignments required in many successful organizations. Broadbanding offers freedom to adapt to changes without requiring approvals, but risks self-serving and potentially inequitable decisions on the part of the manager. Recently, the trend has been toward approaches with greater flexibility to adapt to changing conditions. Such flexibility also makes mergers and acquisitions easier and global alignment possible.

Let us step back for a moment to review what has been discussed and preview what is coming. Two strategic components of the total pay model have been examined. A concern for internal alignment meant that analysis and perhaps descriptions and evaluation were important for achieving a competitive advantage and fair treatment. A concern for external competitiveness required competitive positioning, survey design and analysis, setting the pay policy line (how much and what forms), and designing grades and ranges or broad bands. The next part of the book is concerned with employee contributions—paying the people who perform the work. This is perhaps the most important part of the book. All that has gone before is mere prelude, setting up the pay levels, mix, and structures by which people are to be paid. Now it is time to pay the people.

Chapter Summary

1. The seven decisions involved in setting externally competitive pay and designing the corresponding pay structure are: (1) specify the employer's external pay policy, (2) define the purpose of the compensation survey, (3) choose relevant market competitors to survey, (4) design the survey, (5) interpret survey results and construct the market pay line, (6) construct an internal pay policy line that reflects external pay policy, and (7) balance competitiveness with internal alignment through the use of ranges, flat rates, and/or bands.

2. The steps involved in survey design are deciding: a) whether to do the survey in-house or to involve consultants, b) how many employers to survey, c) which jobs to include in the survey, and d) what specific compensation information to collect.

3. Survey data reported will change after they are collected when pay is increased at various organizations at various points throughout the year. Therefore, data are updated to forecast competitive rates for the date when the pay decisions will be implemented.

4. A market pay line links a company's benchmark jobs on the horizontal axis (internal structure) with market rates paid by competitors (market survey) on the vertical axis. A pay policy line represents external competitive position in the market (i.e., lead, match, lag).

5. Pay grades are created by grouping jobs considered substantially equal for pay purposes. Pay ranges provide an upper and lower limit for pay for all jobs in a pay grade. Broadbanding is the practice of establishing large bands of jobs containing several pay grades.

6. Differences between market structures and rates and job evaluation rankings warrant a review of the basic decisions in evaluating and pricing jobs. Pay structures often are adjusted to balance these internal and external pressures by reviewing job analysis, the job description, and the job evaluation or market data for the job in question. Market data often are weighted more heavily than internal job evaluation data when making adjustments to pay structures.

Key Terms

Review Questions

1. What are the three main categories of employers in the relevant market for pay surveys?
2. Describe three approaches to selecting jobs for inclusion in a survey.
3. What do surveys have to do with pay discrimination?
4. Contrast pay ranges and grades with bands. Why would you use either? Does their use assist or hinder the achievement of internal alignment? External competitiveness?

EXPERIENTIAL EXERCISES

1. Determine the relevant market for a survey of university professors. Explain the factors you considered in order to arrive at this determination. Why is the definition of the relevant market so important?

2. Draft a recommendation regarding a competitive pay policy for Walmart. Explain why this particular recommendation has been made. Does it depend on circumstances faced by the employer? Which ones? What policy would you recommend to your provincial government?

3. Design a survey for setting pay for welders and another for financial managers. Do the issues differ? Will the techniques used and the data collected differ? Why or why not?

WEB EXERCISE

Compensation Comparisons

Click on the Web site http://salary.monster.ca. This site provides pay data on hundreds of jobs in many different industries in cities all over Canada. Identify several jobs of interest to you, such as Compensation and Benefits Manager, Training Manager, Marketing Manager, or Financial Analyst. Select specific cities or use the Canadian national average. Obtain the median, the 25th percentile, and the 75th percentile for base pay, and total cash compensation rates for each job. Then consider the following questions:

1. Which jobs are paid more or less? Is this what you would have expected? Why or why not? What factors could explain the differences in salaries?

2. Do the jobs have different bonuses as a percentage of their base salaries? What could explain these differences?

3. Do the data include the value of stock options? What are the implications of this?

4. How could you use this information in negotiating your salary in your job upon graduation? What data would you provide to support your "asking price"? What factors will influence whether you might get what you ask for?

5. What is the relevant labour market for these jobs? How big are the differences between salaries in different locations?

6. For each job, compare the median base pay to the 25th and 75th percentile base pay. How much variation exists? What factors might explain this variation in pay rates for the same job?

7. Look for a description of how these salary data are developed. Do you think there is enough information? Why or why not? Discuss some of the factors that might impair the accuracy of these data. What are the implications of using inaccurate salary data for individuals or companies?

8. With this information available free, why would you bother with consultants' surveys?

CASE

Calculating Pay Ranges

The market pay regression line (after aging) is $y = 900 + 0.5x$. Your company's pay policy is to lead the market by 5 percent. You are a compensation analyst and your manager has asked you to calculate the pay range maximums, midpoints, and minimums for all four pay grades.

1. Calculate the formula for the pay policy line.

2. Complete the following table (the range spread for each pay grade is indicated in the table).

Pay Grade	Job Evaluation Points	Range Minimum	Range Midpoint	Range Maximum	Range Spread (above and below midpoint)
1	1–249				10%
2	250–499				15%
3	500–749				20%
4	750–1000				30%

3. Draw a graph of the pay policy line including the ranges for each pay grade.

Visit the Online Learning Centre at
www.mcgrawhill.ca/olc/milkovich

■ APPENDIX 8–A: Statistics to Calculate a Market Line Using Regression Analysis

Using the mathematical formula for a straight line,

$$y = a + bx$$

where

> y = dollars
> x = job evaluation points
> a = the y value (in dollars) at which $x = 0$ (i.e., the straight line crosses the y-axis)
> b = the slope of the line

If $b = 0$, the line is parallel to the x-axis and all jobs are paid the same, regardless of job evaluation points. Using the dollars from the market survey data and the job evaluation points from the internal job structure, solving this equation enables the analyst to construct a line based on the relationship between the internal job structure and market rates. An upward sloping line means that more job evaluation points are associated with higher dollars. The market line can be written as

> Pay for job A = a + (b × Job evaluation points for job A)

> Pay for job B = a + (b × Job evaluation points for job B), etc.

The issue is to estimate the values of a and b in an efficient manner so that errors of prediction are minimized. This is what "least squares" regression analysis does.

Example

Regression line for monthly wages is y = \$950 + 0.8x
Monthly pay for job A with 435 job evaluation points = \$950 + 0.8(435) = \$1,298
Monthly pay for job B with 825 job evaluation points = \$950 + 0.8(825) = \$1,610

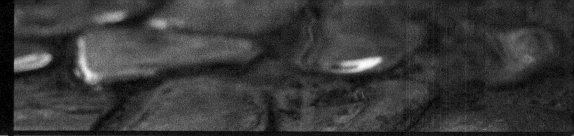

CHAPTER 9

EMPLOYEE BENEFITS

LEARNING OUTCOMES

- Explain why employee benefits are a significant component of total compensation.
- Discuss key issues in benefits planning, design, and administration.
- Describe three important functions in benefits administration.
- Summarize i) the legally required benefits in Canada and ii) the other common employee benefits offered by organizations.
- Explain the difference between defined benefit and defined contribution pension plans.
- Describe the two general strategies for controlling medical benefit costs.

Consider the kinds of benefits that are common in companies described in the book *Canada's Top 100 Employers* (2009).[1] These companies recognize the importance of taking care of employees' needs as a key factor in attracting and retaining the best employees. A first-class benefits plan includes some mix of the following benefits: education reimbursement and employee training; on-site child care services, financial counselling, and concierge services; retirement benefits; and no-cost benefits such as casual dress policies. Some examples from specific companies include:[2]

- Research in Motion in Waterloo, Ontario, provides each employee with a free BlackBerry and tries to find unique "fun" activities for employees, such as ice cream on summer Fridays or a private concert by Barenaked Ladies and Aerosmith.
- Next Level Games in Vancouver, whose employees can tend to get caught up in their creative projects and pull all-nighters, tries to encourage work/life balance by requiring everyone to attend a meeting at 9:30 a.m. They believe that people who get excited about snowboarding and playing with their kids will make good decisions about creative products. One employee's wife e-mailed his boss and thanked him for "giving Ted back to me."
- HOK, a global architectural firm with five offices in Canada, eliminated sugar packets, bleached coffee filters, certain glues, and contact cement when employees said they wanted to be more environmentally friendly. The locations feature state-of-the-art "green offices" with sensor-operated lighting, energy-efficient windows, and low toxic paints. Showers are provided to encourage walking and biking to work. Along with flexible work hours, employees can work summer hours and the offices are closed between Christmas and New Year's. Backup child care and eldercare are also provided.

■ INTRODUCTION TO EMPLOYEE BENEFITS

Clearly the firms mentioned above would argue that these extra services are important benefits of employment, perhaps making attraction, retention, and motivation of employees just that much easier. We know that employee satisfaction with benefits is positively associated with job satisfaction, but we are not sure about more specific payoffs.[3] Until we can clearly identify the advantages of employee benefits, we need to find ways to control their costs. There has been a rapid rise in employee benefit costs, moving from about 15 percent of payroll costs in 1953 to the 40 percent range today.[4]

employee benefits

■ part of the total compensation package, other than pay for time worked, provided to employees in whole or in part by employer payments, such as life insurance, pension plan, workers' compensation, vacation, and so on

However, think about what we know that is fact—not faith—in the benefits area. Which of the issues covered in the pay model, for example, can we answer with respect to benefits? Does effective **employee benefits** administration facilitate organization performance? The answer is unclear. We know that benefit costs can be cut, and this affects the bottom line (admittedly an important measure of organization performance). But what about other design and administrative efforts? Do they complement organization strategy and performance? We don't know. Or do employee benefits impact upon an organization's ability to attract, retain, and motivate employees? Conventional wisdom says employee benefits can affect retention, but there is little research to support this conclusion. A similar lack of research surrounds each of the other potential payoffs to a sound benefits program. Is it any wonder, then, that firms are increasingly paying attention to this reward component? It represents a labour cost with no proven returns.

Compounding this concern is the ever-present entitlement problem. Employees perceive benefits as a right, independent of how well they or the company perform. Efforts to reduce benefit levels or eliminate parts of the package altogether meet with employee resistance and dissatisfaction.

What is clear is that employee benefits are costly. As an example, visualize a $20,000 car rolling down the assembly line at General Motors. A cost accountant would tell you that $1,300 of this cost is due to the cost of health care coverage for pensioners (well above the steel cost). Now compare this to much lower pension costs for foreign automakers in their North American factories (with their younger, healthier workers and hardly any retirees), and the global implications of benefit costs are all too frightening.[5]

Over one 20-year period (1955–1975), employee benefit costs rose at a much greater rate than employee wages or the consumer price index.[6] A similar comparison for the period 1963–1987 showed that the rate of growth had slowed somewhat. Organizations must control the cost of benefits, particularly with the aging, and increasingly costly, baby boomer generation.

■ WHY THE GROWTH IN EMPLOYEE BENEFITS?

Government Impetus

The government has played an important role in the growth of employee benefits. The three government-mandated employment-related benefits are: workers' compensation (provincial), Employment Insurance (federal), and Canada/Quebec Pension Plan (federal and Quebec). In addition, most other employee benefits are affected by such laws as the *Income Tax Act*, human rights acts, pension benefits acts, and so on. For example, Canadian human rights laws require that family and survivor benefits be offered to an employee's unmarried partner, whether of the same or opposite sex, wherever they are provided to a legal spouse. Mandatory retirement at age 65 has been outlawed in most provinces. Many pension and benefit plans have been revised to permit continued pension accrual and continuing benefits coverage for those working past age 65.

Unions

Unions have fought for the introduction of new benefits and the improvement of existing benefits. Largely through the efforts of unions, most notably the auto and steelworkers unions, several benefits common today were given their initial impetus: pension plans, supplementary unemployment benefits, and retiree benefits.[7]

Employer Impetus

Many of the benefits in existence today were provided at employer initiative. Much of this initiative can be traced to pragmatic concerns about employee satisfaction and productivity. Rest breaks often were implemented in the belief that fatigue increased accidents and lowered productivity. Savings and profit-sharing plans (e.g., Procter & Gamble's profit-sharing plan was initiated in 1885) were implemented to improve performance and provide increased security for worker retirement years. Indeed, many employer-initiated benefits were designed to create a climate in which employees perceived that management was genuinely concerned for their welfare. Notice, though, that these supposed benefits were taken on faith. But their costs were quite real. And, absent hard data about payoffs, employee benefits slowly became a costly entitlement of the North American workforce.

Cost Effectiveness of Benefits

Another important and sound impetus for the growth of employee benefits is their cost-effectiveness in three situations. The first cost advantage is that most employee benefits are not taxable. Provision of a benefit rather than an equivalent increase in wages avoids payment of personal income tax. A second cost-effectiveness component of benefits arises because many group-based benefits (e.g., life and health insurance) can be obtained at a lower rate than could be obtained by employees acting on their own. Group insurance also has relatively easy qualification standards, giving security to a set of employees who might not otherwise qualify. Finally, benefit premiums and pension contributions are tax deductible up to limits specified in the *Income Tax Act*.

■ THE VALUE OF EMPLOYEE BENEFITS

Most studies of the relative importance employees attached to different types of benefits show fairly consistent results. For example, medical payments regularly are listed as one of the most important benefits employees receive. These rankings have added significance when we note over the past two decades that health care costs are the most rapidly growing and most difficult to control of all the benefit options offered by employers.[8]

These costs would not seem nearly so outrageous if we had evidence that employees place high value on the benefits they receive. Unfortunately, there is evidence that employees frequently are unaware of, or undervalue, the benefits provided by their organization.[9]

The lack of knowledge about the value of employee benefits inferred from these studies can be traced to both attitudinal and design problems. Looming largest is the attitude problem. Benefits are taken for granted. Employees view them as a right, with little comprehension of, or concern for, employer costs.[10]

One possible salvation from this money pit comes from recent reports that employees are not necessarily looking for more benefits, but rather greater choice in the benefits they receive.[11] In fact, up to 70 percent of employees in one study indicated they would be willing to pay more out of pocket for benefits if they were granted greater choice in designing their own benefits package. Better benefits planning, design, and administration may offer an opportunity to improve benefits effectiveness. Indeed, preliminary evidence indicates employers are making serious efforts to increase employee awareness of benefits.[12]

KEY ISSUES IN BENEFITS PLANNING, DESIGN, AND ADMINISTRATION

Benefits Planning and Design Issues

First and foremost, the benefits planning process must address the vital question: "What is the role of benefits in a total compensation package?"[13] For example, if a major compensation objective is to attract good employees, the question is, "What is the best way to achieve this?" The answer is not always, nor even frequently, "Let's add another benefit."

Consider a company that needs to fill some clerical and administrative jobs. One temptation might be to set up a day-care centre to attract more mothers with preschool children. Certainly this is a popular response today, judging from all the press that day-care centres are receiving. A more prudent compensation policy would ask the question: "Is day care the most effective way to achieve my compensation objective?" Can the necessary workers be attracted to the company using some other compensation tool that better meets company needs? For example, we know that day care is relatively popular in the insurance industry. If we went to compensation experts in that industry they might say (and we would be impressed if they did), "Seventy-five percent of our workforce is female, and one-third have preschool children. Surveys of this group indicate day care is an extremely important factor in the decision to accept a job." If we heard this kind of logic it would certainly illustrate the kind of care firms should use before adopting expensive benefit options.

As a second example, how do we deal with undesirable turnover? It may be tempting to design a benefits package that improves progressively with seniority, thus providing a reward for continuing service. This would only be the preferred option, though, if other compensation tools, such as increasing wages or introducing incentive compensation, were less effective.

In addition to integrating benefits with other compensation components, the planning process also should include strategies to ensure external competitiveness and adequacy of benefits. Competitiveness requires an understanding of what other firms in your product and labour markets offer as benefits. Firms conduct benefits surveys much as they conduct salary surveys. Either our firm must have a package comparable to survey participants, or there should be a sound justification explaining why deviation makes sense for the firm.

By contrast, ensuring that benefits are adequate is a somewhat more difficult task. Most organizations evaluating adequacy consider the financial liability of employees with and without a particular benefit (e.g., employee medical expenses with and without medical benefits). There is no magic formula for defining benefits adequacy.[14] In part, the answer may lie in the relationship between benefits adequacy and the third plan objective, cost-effectiveness. More organizations need to consider whether employee benefits are cost justified. All sorts of ethical questions arise when we start asking this question. How far should we go with eldercare? Can we justify a $50,000 expense for a new drug treatment that will likely buy only a few months more of life? Companies face these impossible questions when designing a benefits system.

Benefits Administration Issues

Three major administration issues arise in setting up a benefits package: (1) Who should be protected or benefited? (2) How much choice should employees have among an array of benefits? (3) How should benefits be financed?[15]

The first issue—who should be covered—ought to be an easy question. Employees, of course. But every organization has a variety of employees with different employment statuses. Should these individuals be treated equally with respect to benefits coverage? Companies often differentiate treatment based on employment status. The dollar value of benefits is much lower, even when the difference in hours worked for part-time versus full-time employees is factored in.

Another example: Should retired automobile executives be permitted to continue purchasing cars at a discount price, a benefit that could be reserved solely for current employees? In fact, a whole series of questions needs to be answered:

1. What probationary periods (for eligibility of benefits) should be used for various types of benefits? Does the employer want to cover employees and their dependants immediately upon employment or to provide such coverage for employees who have established more or less permanent employment with the employer? Is there a rationale for different probationary periods with different benefits?
2. Which dependants of active employees should be covered?
3. Should retirees (as well as their spouses and perhaps other dependants) be covered, and for which benefits?
4. Should survivors of deceased active employees (and/or retirees) be covered? If so, for which benefits? Are benefits for surviving spouses appropriate?
5. What coverage, if any, should be extended to employees who are suffering from disabilities?
6. What coverage, if any, should be extended to employees during layoff, leaves of absence, strikes, and so forth?
7. Should coverage be limited to full-time employees?[16]

The answers to these questions depend on the policy decisions regarding adequacy, competition, and cost effectiveness discussed in the last section.

The second administrative issue concerns choice (flexibility) in plan coverage. In the traditional benefits package, employees typically have not been offered a choice among employee benefits. Rather, a package is designed with the average employee in mind, and any deviations in needs simply go unsatisfied. The other extreme (discussed in greater detail later) is represented by flexible benefit plans.

Even companies that are not considering a flexible benefits program are offering greater flexibility and choice. Such plans might provide, for example, (1) optional levels of group term life insurance; (2) the availability of death or disability benefits under pension or profit-sharing plans; or (3) choices of covering dependants under group medical expense coverage. The level at which an organization finally chooses to operate on this choice/flexibility dimension really depends on its evaluation of the relative advantages and disadvantages of flexible plans.[17]

The final administrative issue involves the question of financing benefits plans. Alternatives include the following:

1. Non-contributory (employer pays total costs)
2. Contributory (costs shared between employer and employee)
3. Employee financed (employee pays total costs for some benefits, e.g., long-term disability)

In general, organizations prefer to make benefits options contributory, reasoning that anything free, no matter how valuable, is less valuable to an employee. Furthermore, employees have no personal interest in controlling the cost of a free good.

■ FACTORS INFLUENCING BENEFIT PLANNING

Exhibit 9.1 outlines a model of the factors influencing benefits planning, from both the employer and employee perspective. We will now briefly examine each of these factors.

Employer Preferences

As Exhibit 9.1 indicates, a number of factors affect employer preference in determining desirable components of a benefits package.

Relationship to Total Compensation Costs   A good compensation manager considers employee benefit costs as part of a total package of compensation costs. Frequently employees think that just because an employee benefit is attractive, the company should provide it. A good compensation

| **EXHIBIT** | **9.1** | Factors Influencing Choice of Benefits Package |

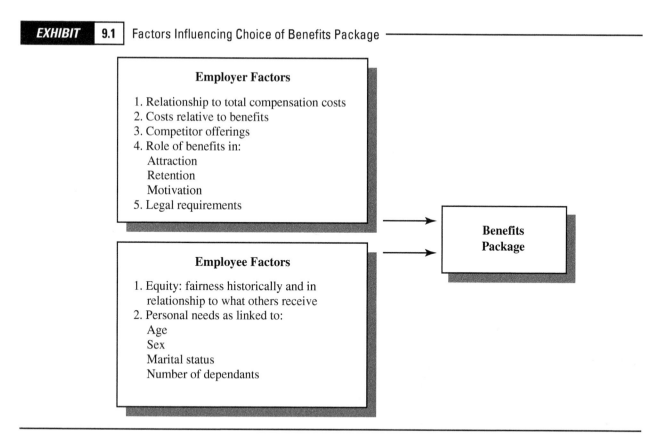

manager thinks somewhat differently: "Is there a better use for this money? Could we put the money into some other compensation component and achieve better results?" Benefit costs are only one part of a total compensation package. Decisions about outlays have to be considered from this perspective.

Costs Relative to Benefits   A major reason for the proliferating cost of benefits programs is the narrow focus of benefits administrators. Too frequently the costs/advantages of a particular benefit inclusion are viewed in isolation, without reference to total package costs or forecasts of rising costs in future years. To control spiralling benefit costs, administrators should adopt a broader, cost-centred approach. As a first step, this approach would require policy decisions on the level of benefit expenditures that are acceptable both in the short and long run. Historically, benefits managers negotiated or provided benefits on a package basis rather than a cost basis. The current cost of a benefit would be identified and, if the cost seemed reasonable, the benefit would be provided for or negotiated with employees.

A cost-centred approach would require benefits administrators, in cooperation with insurance carriers and armed with published forecasts of anticipated costs for particular benefits, to determine the cost commitments for the existing benefits package. Budget dollars not already earmarked might then be allocated to new benefits that best satisfy organizational goals. Factors affecting this decision include an evaluation of benefits offered by other firms and the competitiveness of the existing package. Also important is compliance with various legal requirements as they change over time (see Chapter 12). Finally, the actual value of a new benefit option must be explored in relation to employee preferences. Benefits that top the list of employee preferences should be evaluated in relation to current and future costs. Because future cost estimates may be difficult to project, it is imperative that benefits administrators reduce uncertainty.

If a benefit forecast suggests that future cost containment may be difficult, the benefit should be offered to employees on a cost-sharing basis only. Management determines what percentage of cost it can afford to bear within budget projections, and the option is offered to employees on a cost-sharing basis, with projected increases in both employer and employee costs communicated openly. In the negotiation process, then, employees or union representatives can evaluate their preference for the option against the forecasted cost burden. In effect, this approach defines in advance the contribution an employer is willing to make. And it avoids the constraints of a defined benefit strategy that burdens the employer with continued provision of that defined benefit level despite rapidly spiralling costs.

Competitor Offerings   Benefits must be externally equitable, too. This raises the question: What is the absolute level of benefits payments relative to important product and labour market competitors? A policy decision must be made about the position (that is, market lead, market lag, or competitive) that the organization wants to maintain in its absolute level of benefits relative to the competition. One of the best strategies to determine external equity is to conduct a benefits survey. Alternatively, many consulting organizations, professional associations, and interest groups collect benefits data that can be purchased.

Role of Benefits in Attraction, Retention, and Motivation   Given the rapid growth in benefits and the staggering cost implications, it seems only logical that employers would expect to derive a fair return on this investment. In fact, there is at best only anecdotal evidence that employee benefits are cost-justified. This evidence falls into three categories.[18] First, employee benefits are widely claimed to help in the retention of workers. Benefit schedules are specifically designed to favour longer-term employees. For example, retirement benefits increase with years of service. Also, amount of vacation time increases with years of service; and finally, employees' savings plans, profit-sharing plans, and stock purchase plans frequently provide for increased participation or benefits as company seniority increases. By tying these benefits to seniority, it is assumed that workers will be more reluctant to change jobs.

There is also some research to support this common assumption that benefits increase retention. Two studies found that higher benefits reduced mobility.[19] More detailed follow-up studies, though, found only two specific benefits curtailed employee turnover: pensions and medical coverage.[20] Virtually no other employee benefit had a significant impact on turnover.

It has been assumed here that turnover is bad and stability is good. In fact, there are times when an organization may not want to discourage turnover. Some employees may stay in a job they want to leave simply because the pension plan is so generous. This job lock probably is not a desirable outcome for employers.

Employee benefits also might be valued if we could prove that they increase employee satisfaction. However, benefits satisfaction falls as cost-cutting companies attempt to reduce coverage and to shift more of the costs to employees.[21] A more pessimistic view argues that benefits plans fail to meet either employer or employee needs. In this view, simply pumping more money into benefits is inappropriate. Rather, employers must make fundamental changes in the way they approach the benefits planning process. Companies must realize that declining satisfaction with benefits is a result of long-term changes in the workforce. Ever-increasing numbers of women in the labour force, coupled with increasing numbers of dual-career families and higher educational attainments, suggest changing values of employees.[22] Changing values, in turn, necessitate a re-evaluation of benefits packages.

Finally, employee benefits also are valued because they may have an impact on the bottom line. Although supporting evidence is slim, there are some glimmers of potential. For example, employee stock ownership plans (discussed in more detail in Chapter 11), according to some reports, improve company productivity.[23] Presumably, owning stock motivates employees to be more productive. After all, part of the reward returns to them in the form of dividends and increased stock value. Similar productivity improvements are reported for employee assistance programs (for addiction, mental health, and family problems), with reports of up to 25 percent jumps in productivity after their implementation.[24]

vesting

waiting period for entitlement to the employer-paid portion of pension benefits

Legal Requirements   Employers obviously want a benefits package that complies with all aspects of the law. For example, **vesting** of pension benefits, which occurs when employees become entitled to the employer-paid portion of pension benefits upon termination of employment, is required by Canadian law after no more than two years of employment. There is an increasingly complex web of legislation in the benefits area. Greater detail on legally mandated benefits including Workers' Compensation, Canada/Quebec Pension Plan, and Employment Insurance are provided later in this chapter.

Absolute and Relative Compensation Costs   Any evaluation of employee benefits must be placed in the context of total compensation costs. Cost competitiveness means the total package must be competitive—not just specific segments. Consequently, decisions about whether to adopt certain options must be considered in light of the impact on total costs and in relationship to expenditures of competitors as determined in benefits surveys.

Employee Preferences

Employee preferences for various benefit options are determined by individual needs. Benefits perceived to best satisfy individual needs are most highly desired. In part these needs arise from feelings of perceived fairness.

Fairness   To illustrate the impact of fairness, consider the example of single employees versus employees with a family. Family coverage for benefits often means that more benefit dollars are paid out for the second group as claims for themselves, their spouses, and their children are all paid, rather than just claims relating to the employee. The higher benefit payouts for families might seem unfair to single employees. A Canadian study found that in some circumstances, this sort of self-interest does affect perceptions of fairness, but that overall, the need criterion is still a strong impact on perceptions of fairness in employee benefits.[25]

Occasionally comparison processes result in new benefits offered by a competitor being adopted without careful consideration, simply because the employer wants to avoid hard feelings. This phenomenon is particularly apparent for employers with a strong commitment to maintaining a totally or partially non-union workforce. Benefits obtained by a unionized competitor or a unionized segment of the firm's workforce are frequently passed along to non-union employees. Although the effectiveness of this strategy in thwarting unionization efforts has not been demonstrated, many non-union firms prefer to provide the benefit as a safety measure.

Personal Needs of Employees   A major assumption in empirical efforts to determine employee preferences is that preferences are somehow systematically related to what are termed demographic differences. The demographic approach assumes that demographic groups (e.g., young versus old, married versus unmarried) can be identified for which benefits preferences are fairly consistent across members of the group. Furthermore, this approach assumes that meaningful differences exist between groups in terms of benefit preferences.

There is evidence that these assumptions are only partially correct. In an extensive review of employee preference literature, Glueck traced patterns of group preferences for particular benefits.[26] As one might expect, older workers showed a stronger preference than younger workers for pension plans.[27] Also, families with dependants had stronger preferences for health/medical coverage than did families with no dependants.[28] Beyond these conclusions though, most preference studies have shown wide variation in individuals with respect to benefits desired.

The weakness of this demographic approach has led some organizations to undertake a second and more expensive empirical method of determining employee preferences: surveying individuals about needs. One way of accomplishing this requires development of a questionnaire on which employees evaluate various benefits.

FLEXIBLE BENEFITS PLANS

flexible benefit plans

benefit plans in which the employee is provided with a specified amount of money and then chooses which benefits to spend the money on, according to their attractiveness and cost

Administrative concerns about employee choice, and planning issues related to cost and competitor offerings resulted in gradual growth in the number of Canadian employers offering flexible benefit plans, which had increased to over 40 percent by 2005.[29] In a **flexible benefit plan**, employees are allotted a fixed amount of money and permitted to spend that amount in the purchase of benefit options. Some plans are completely flexible, but others require that "core" benefits (such as basic life insurance) be included, with the remainder being at the employee's choice. A third approach is to offer different modules (packages) of benefits that employees choose from. Exhibit 9.2 illustrates a typical choice among modules (or packages) offered to employees under a flexible benefits system. Imagine an employee whose spouse works and already has family coverage for health, dental, and vision. The temptation might be to select package A. Another employee with retirement in mind might select option B with its contributions to a pension plan. Thus, employees are permitted great flexibility in choosing the benefits options of greatest value to them.

Exhibit 9.3 summarizes some of the major advantages and disadvantages of flexible benefits. Judging from increased adoption of flexible benefits over the past decade, it seems that employers consider that the advantages noted in Exhibit 9.3 far outweigh the disadvantages. Many companies cite the cost savings from flexible benefits as a primary motivation. Companies also offer flexible plans in response to cost pressures related to the increasing diversity of the workforce. Flexible benefits plans, it is argued, increase employee awareness of the true costs of benefits, and therefore, increase employee recognition of benefits value.[30]

From a theoretical perspective, this approach to benefits packaging is ideal. Employees directly identify the benefits of greatest value to them, and, by constraining the dollars employees have to spend, benefits managers are able to control benefits costs. New Brunswick Power saved millions of dollars in health care benefits by implementing a flexible benefits plan and working together with their union on disability management.[31] NCR has adopted a variant on flexible benefits where employees who wish to can exchange some of their base salary for greater coverage on desired benefits, as illustrated in Exhibit 9.4.

EXHIBIT 9.2 | Example of Possible Options in a Flexible Benefits Package

	Package			
	A	B	C	D
Health Care	No	Basic Coverage	Enhanced Coverage	Premium Coverage
Dental Care	No	Basic Coverage	Enhanced Coverage	Premium Coverage
Vision Care	No	No	No	Yes
Life Insurance	$1 \times$ AE*	$2 \times$ AE	$2 \times$ AE	$3 \times$ AE
Family/Dependant Care	Yes	No	No	No
Pension	No	Basic	Enhanced Coverage	Premium Coverage

*AE = Annual Earnings

| **EXHIBIT** | **9.3** | Advantages and Disadvantages of Flexible Benefit Programs |

Advantages

1. Employees choose packages that best satisfy their unique needs.
2. Flexible benefits help firms meet the changing needs of a changing workforce.
3. Increased involvement of employees and families improves understanding of benefits.
4. Flexible plans make introduction of new benefits less costly. The new option is added merely as one among a wide variety of elements from which to choose.
5. Cost containment: Organization sets dollar maximum. Employee chooses within that constraint.

Disadvantages

1. Employees make bad choices and find themselves not covered for predictable emergencies.
2. Administrative burdens and expenses increase.
3. Adverse selection. Employees pick only benefits they will use. The subsequent high benefit utilization increases costs.

ADMINISTERING THE BENEFITS PROGRAM

Benefits administration involves three functions requiring further discussion: (1) communicating the benefits program, (2) claims processing, and (3) cost containment.[32]

Employee Benefits Communication

Much of the effort to achieve benefit goals focuses on identifying methods of communication. Benefits communication, particularly regarding retirement plans, is increasingly important because a large number of employees are approaching retirement. Accurate information must be provided to these employees in a timely manner. Pension legislation across Canada specifies the information that must be disclosed to plan members and their spouses/domestic partners. Court challenges concerning erroneous information on benefit statements are more and more frequent, as employees' awareness of their right to information increases.[33]

 The most frequent method for communicating employee benefits is still the employee benefits handbook. A typical handbook contains a description of all benefits, including levels of coverage and eligibility requirements. The benefits handbook is often supplemented with personalized benefits statements generated by computer. These tailor-made reports provide a breakdown of package components and list selected cost information about the options.[34]

An effective communications package must have three elements. First, an organization must spell out its benefit objectives and ensure that any communications achieve these objectives. Second, the message must be matched with the appropriate medium. In today's corporations, many benefits administrators are providing total rewards statements summarizing the total cost of benefits provided to employees. With the advent of self-service capabilities in employee information systems, these statements have expanded from an annual offering to timely, online statements with each payroll, providing an almost up-to-the-minute value statement of compensation and benefits.[35]

And finally, element three: The content of the communications package must be complete, clear, and free of the complex jargon that so readily invades benefits discussions. The amount of time/space devoted to each issue should vary closely with both the perceived importance of the benefit to employees and with the expected difficulty in communicating option alternatives.[36]

EXHIBIT 9.4   Flexible Benefits at NCR

A. Costs. Please modify this "base" benefit package into another which you would most prefer, bearing in mind that selecting different levels will impact your cash pay (see box to right).

Base Benefit Package	$11,460
Chosen Benefit Package (shaded)	$11,760
Change in Cash Pay	$–300

ALTERNATIVE LEVELS

FEATURE					
Medical Plan	Opt Out –$4,800	Traditional-Basic Current A Base	HMO –$800	Traditional-Enhanced +$1,000	PPO +$1,300
Long-Term Disability Plan	Opt Out –$840	50% of Your Salary Current A Base	60% of Your Salary +$240	70% of Your Salary +$480	
Life Insurance	None A Base	1 Times Your Salary +$240	2 Times Your Salary Current +$480	3 Times Your Salary +$720	4 Times Your Salary +$960
401(k) Plan	None –$1,800	3% Match 5-Year Vesting +$1,200	6% Match 5-Year Vesting Current A Base	6% Match 1-Year Vesting $900	10% Match No Vesting $2,400
Paid Parental/ Family Leave	None Current –$180	3-Day Leave A Base	12-Week Leave 1/2 Salary +$540	12-Week Leave Full Salary +$1,800	

Source: "Employee a Customer" by Lynn Gaughan and Jorg Kasparek, NCR Corp., and Jeff Hagens and Jeff Young, Workspan, September 2000, pp. 31–37.

Claims Processing

Claims processing arises when an employee asserts that a specific event (such as disability or hospitalization) has occurred, and requests that the employer fulfill a promise of payment.[37] If multiple insurance companies are liable for payment (e.g., working spouses covered by different insurers), a good claims processor can save from 10 to 15 percent of claims cost by ensuring that the liability is paid jointly.[38] The major challenges in this area come from the approximately 10 percent of all claims in which payment is denied. A benefits administrator must then become a counsellor, explaining the equitable and consistent procedures used.

Cost Containment

Increasingly, employers are auditing their benefits options for cost containment opportunities. The most prevalent practices include:

1. ***Probationary periods.*** Excluding new employees from benefits coverage until some term of employment (e.g., three months) is completed.
2. ***Benefit maximums.*** It is not uncommon to limit disability income payments to some maximum percentage of income, and to limit medical/dental coverage for specific procedures to a certain fixed amount. Lifetime maximum payouts are sometimes used.
3. ***Coinsurance.*** The employer pays a fixed percentage of insurance premiums; employees pay the remainder.
4. ***Deductibles.*** A specified dollar amount of claims to be paid each year by the employee before the insurance plan begins paying (e.g., $25 deductible means that the employee pays the first $25 in claims submitted each year).
5. ***Coordination of benefits.*** When two spouses both have employee benefits coverage, benefits are reduced by any benefits payable under the spouse's plan (i.e., both spouses cannot receive benefits to cover the same expenses).
6. ***Administrative cost containment.*** Includes such things as seeking competitive bids for program delivery.

coinsurance

percentage of insurance premiums paid for by the employer

deductible

specified dollar amount of claims paid by the employee each year before insurance benefits begin

coordination of benefits

reduction of benefits by any amount paid under a spouse's plan

So prevalent is the cost issue today that the terminology of cost containment is becoming a part of every employee's vocabulary. Exhibit 9.5 provides definitions of some common cost-containment terms. Probably the biggest cost-containment strategy in recent years is the movement to outsourcing. By hiring vendors to administer their benefits programs, many companies have achieved greater centralization, consistency, and control of costs and benefits.[39] Companies such as the Bank of Montreal and Home Depot Canada outsource so that they can focus on their core business and leave benefits to the benefits experts.[40]

Given continuing escalation in the cost of employee benefits, organizations would do well to evaluate the effectiveness of their benefits adoption, retention, and termination procedures. Specifically, how does an organization go about selecting appropriate employee benefits? Are the decisions based on sound evaluation of employee preferences, balanced against organizational goals of legal compliance and competitiveness? Do the benefits chosen serve to attract, retain, and/or motivate employees? Or are organizations paying for indirect compensation without any tangible benefit? The benefits determination process identifies major issues in selecting and evaluating particular benefit choices. Next, the various types of benefits available will be reviewed and some of the decisions confronting a benefits manager will be discussed.

■ TYPES OF BENEFITS

Sometimes the number of different benefits can be overwhelming. A widely accepted categorization of employee benefits is shown in Exhibit 9.6.

| *EXHIBIT* | **9.5** | A Basic Primer of Cost-Containment Terminology |

- **Deductibles.** An employee claim for insurance coverage is preceded by the requirement that the first $x dollars claimed be paid by the claimant.
- **Coinsurance.** The proportion of insurance premiums paid by the employer.
- **Benefit cutbacks.** Wage concessions some employers are negotiating with employees to eliminate or reduce employer contributions to selected options.
- **Defined-contribution pension plans.** Employers establish the limits of their responsibility for employee benefits in terms of a dollar contribution maximum.
- **Defined-benefit pension plans.** Employers establish the limits of their responsibility for employee benefits in terms of a specific benefit and the options included. As the cost of these options rises in future years, the employer is obligated to provide the benefit as negotiated, despite its increased cost.
- **Coordination of benefits.** In families where both spouses work, benefits are reduced by any amount payable under the spouse's plan.
- **Benefit maximums.** Establishing a maximum payout for specific health-related claims.

Legally Required Benefits

Workers' Compensation

a mandatory, government-sponsored, employer-paid, no-fault insurance plan that provides compensation for injuries and diseases that arise out of, and while in the course of, employment

Virtually every employee benefit is somehow affected by law (many of the limitations are imposed by tax laws). In this section the primary focus will be on benefits that are required by law: Workers' Compensation, Canada/Quebec Pension Plan, and Employment Insurance.

Workers' Compensation   **Workers' Compensation** is a form of no-fault insurance (employees are eligible even if their actions caused the accident) that covers injuries and diseases that arise out of, and while in the course of, employment. Workers' Compensation is legislated by each province and territory, but the variations in benefits and costs are relatively minor. The focus of Workers' Compensation has been shifting from the provision of compensation to injured workers to prevention of accidents through promoting occupational health and safety and facilitating recovery and return to work for injured workers.

| *EXHIBIT* | **9.6** | Categorization of Employee Benefits |

Type of Benefit

1. **Legally required payments**
   a. Canada/Quebec Pension Plan (C/QPP)
   b. Employment Insurance (EI)
   c. Workers' Compensation
   d. Government-sponsored medical plans
2. **Retirement and savings plan payments**
   a. Defined-benefit pension plan contributions
   b. Defined-contribution pension plan payments
   c. Profit-sharing
   d. Employee stock ownership plans (ESOP)
   e. Administrative and other costs
3. **Life insurance and death benefits**
4. **Medical insurance**
   a. Employer-sponsored medical plans
   b. Dental insurance
   c. Vision care

5. **Income security**
   a. Short-term disability
   b. Sick leave
   c. Long-term disability
6. **Payments for time not worked**
   a. Paid rest periods, coffee breaks, lunch periods, wash-up time, travel time, clothes-change time, get-ready time, etc.
   b. Payments for vacations
   c. Payments for holidays
7. **Miscellaneous benefits**
   a. Parental leave
   b. Child care services
   c. Eldercare services
   d. Employee assistance plans (EAP)
   e. Other

All jurisdictions provide benefits for:

- Loss of earnings due to temporary disability (total or partial);
- Loss of earnings due to permanent disability (total or partial);
- Health care expenses (including those normally paid under provincial health care plans); and
- Survivor benefits for fatal injuries.

The amount of compensation varies by jurisdiction from 75 percent to 90 percent of net earnings, with two jurisdictions providing 75 percent of gross earnings. Workers' Compensation benefits are non-taxable. The complete cost of administering and paying out compensation for work-related injuries and illnesses is borne by employers under a collective liability fund. Employers are placed in different rate groups, or classes, according to the nature of their business, and all members of the class pay the same assessment rates, based on a percentage of payroll, into the fund. Some jurisdictions offer "experience rating" plans that partially link assessment rates to a company's level of claims.

In 2007, there were 973,462 Workers' Compensation claims reported in Canada. Just over 317,500 were lost-time claims, and 1,055 were fatalities.[41] Workers' Compensation costs are an ongoing concern for employers, who bear the entire cost, but have limited control over administration. The continuing increase in medical costs, together with an aging workforce experiencing longer claims duration, means that no relief can be expected for some time. Some progress has been made in controlling costs in Ontario, where the $11.5 billion unfunded liability for future benefit payments faced in the mid-1990s was decreased to $8 billion by 2007.[42]

Canada/Quebec Pension Plan (C/QPP)

a mandatory, government-sponsored pension plan for all employed Canadians, funded equally by employers and employees

Canada/Quebec Pension Plan (C/QPP) The **Canada/Quebec Pension Plan** is designed to replace employment income in case of retirement, death, or disability. All employees and self-employed persons must contribute to the plan, and employers match their employees' contributions. Both contributions and benefits are calculated on earnings between the Year's Basic Exemption (YBE), now fixed at $3,500, and the Year's Maximum Pensionable Earnings (YMPE), set at $46,300 in 2009, approximately the average Canadian wage. Employers and employees each contribute 4.95 percent of pensionable earnings to the plan.

The retirement pension benefit beginning at age 65 is 25 percent of average pensionable earnings over the retiree's working life, adjusted for inflation up to the average inflation rate during the last five years prior to retirement. Plan members can choose to begin receiving benefits at any time between the ages of 60 and 70. Benefits are reduced upon retirement prior to age 65 and increased upon retirement after age 65. Disability benefits are payable to contributors who sustain a severe, prolonged mental or physical disability and are payable until age 65 when the retirement pension begins. If a plan member dies, a lump sum death benefit is payable to the survivor, and a survivor pension benefit is payable to the surviving spouse/partner. An additional death benefit in the form of a pension is also payable to any dependant children until they reach the age of 18. All benefits are indexed to the Consumer Price Index and are taxable.[43]

The Canada Pension Plan Investment Board is responsible for investing the money contributed to the CPP. A maximum of 30 percent of the funds are permitted to be invested outside of Canada, and the fund cannot own more than 30 percent of any single company.[44]

Employment Insurance (EI)

a mandatory, government-sponsored plan for all employed Canadians that provides workers with temporary income replacement as a result of employment interruptions due to circumstances beyond their control; funded by employer and employee contributions

Employment Insurance **Employment Insurance (EI)** provides workers with temporary income replacement as a result of employment interruptions due to work shortages, sickness, non-occupational accidents, maternity leave, parental or adoption leave, or compassionate care leave. It does not apply to workers who are self-employed. Benefits are not payable when an employee is terminated for just cause or quits without good reason.

Minimum eligibility criteria for employment insurance benefits decrease as the regional unemployment rate increases. The maximum insurable earnings is $42,300 for 2009, and this earnings level provides the basis for the calculation of contributions and benefits. The EI program is funded entirely by contributions from employees and employers. The employee contribution is made on earnings up to the maximum insurable earnings, and varies over time, depending on the funded status of the program. In 2009, the employee contribution was $1.73 per $100 of weekly insurable earnings ($1.38 in Quebec, where parental benefits are provided by the provincial government.) Employers contribute 1.4 times their employees' contributions. Employers who provide a wage loss replacement plan for illness that pays at least as much as the EI benefit qualify for a rate reduction.

The basic benefit is 55 percent of the individual's average insured earnings, and is included in taxable income. A waiting period of two weeks applies before the first benefit payment is made. EI benefits are payable for a maximum of 45 weeks (up to 50 weeks for combined sickness, maternity, and parental leave). In 2009, the maximum weekly benefit was $447. Low-income claimants with children receive a Family Supplement, but their total benefit cannot exceed the maximum weekly benefit. The EI plan provides up to six weeks of compassionate leave benefits to employees who need time off work to care for a dying family member. Many provinces have amended their employment laws to permit such leaves (unpaid by the employer).

Supplementary Unemployment Benefit (SUB) Plans and Work Sharing Programs   SUB plans are voluntary, self-insured employer plans to supplement benefits received under the EI plan. Maternity, parental, and compassionate care SUB plans can supplement up to 100 percent of earnings, and all other SUB plans can supplement up to 95 percent of earnings. EI benefits are not reduced by any SUB benefits received. Work-sharing programs are an arrangement by which employees work a reduced workweek and receive EI benefits for the remainder of the week. The EI Commission must approve SUB plans and work-sharing programs.[45]

Retirement Pension Plans

pension plan

plan that provides income to an employee at retirement as compensation for work performed now

There is a strong relationship between employee age and preference for a **pension plan**. Although this need for retirement security may become more pronounced as workers age, it is evident among younger workers as well. Approximately 40 percent of paid workers in Canada are covered by an employer-provided pension plan.[46]

Pension programs provide income to an employee at retirement as compensation for work performed now. The security motive and certain tax advantages have also fostered this growth in pension programs. The importance of employer-provided retirement plans is demonstrated by one recent study, which showed that employees with employer-provided retirement plans are more likely to have sufficient savings for a comfortable retirement than are others who do not have these plans.[47]

Two types of pension plans will be discussed to varying degrees here: (1) defined-benefit and (2) defined-contribution plans. A third type of plan is a hybrid of the first two.

defined-benefit plan

pension plan in which an employer agrees to provide a specific level of retirement pension, the exact cost of which is unknown

Defined-Benefit Plans   In a **defined-benefit plan**, an employer agrees to provide a specific level of retirement pension, which is expressed either as a fixed dollar or percentage-of-earnings amount that may vary (increase) with years of seniority in the company. The firm finances this obligation by following an actuarially determined benefits formula and making current payments that will yield the future pension benefit for a retiring employee.[48]

Defined-benefit plans generally follow one of three different formulas. The most common approach is to calculate average earnings over the last (or best) three to five years of service for a prospective retiree and to offer a pension of about one-half this amount, adjusted for years of seniority. The second formula for a defined-benefits plan uses average career earnings rather than earnings from the last few years: Other things being equal, this would reduce the level of benefit for pensioners. The final formula commits an employer to a fixed (flat) dollar amount that is not dependent on earnings data. This figure generally rises with seniority level.

The level of pension a company chooses to offer depends on the answer to several questions. First, what level of retirement compensation would a company like to set as a target, expressed in relation to pre-retirement earnings? Second, should Canada/Quebec Pension Plan payments be considered when planning the level of income an employee should have during retirement? Third, should other post-retirement income sources (e.g., savings plans that are partially funded by employer contributions) be integrated with the pension payment? Fourth, a company must decide how to factor seniority into the payout formula. The larger the role played by seniority, the more important pensions will be in retaining employees. The traditional approach has been that the maximum pension payout for a particular level of earnings should be achieved only by employees who have spent an entire career with the company. As Exhibit 9.7 vividly illustrates, employees who change jobs frequently are hurt financially by this type of strategy. In our example—a very plausible scenario —frequent job changes cuts final pension amounts in half.

defined-contribution plan

pension plan in which an employer agrees to provide specific contributions, but the final benefit is unknown

Defined-Contribution Plans   **Defined-contribution plans** require specific contributions by an employer. In some cases, contributions may be required from employees or offered on an optional basis. The final benefit received by employees is unknown, depending on the investment success of those charged with administering the pension fund (in some plans, employees select investments).

Advantages and Disadvantages of Defined-Benefit and Defined-Contribution Plans   The advantages and disadvantages of these two generic categories of pensions (defined-benefit and defined-contribution) are outlined in Exhibit 9.8. Possibly the most important of the factors noted in Exhibit 9.8 is the differential risk borne by employers on the cost dimension. Defined contribution plans have known costs from year one. The employer agrees to a specific level of payment that only changes through negotiation or through some voluntary action. This allows for quite realistic cost projections. In contrast, defined-benefit plans commit the employer to a specific level of benefit. Variations from actuarial projections (regarding pension fund investment returns and other factors) can add or reduce costs over the years and make the budgeting process much more uncertain. Perhaps for this reason, defined-contribution plans have been more popular for the past 15 years or more.[49] As well, some defined benefit plans have been redesigned to become hybrid defined benefit/defined contribution plans or have been changed completely to defined contribution plans.[50] However, concerns have arisen for defined-contribution plan sponsors regarding the employer's potential liability for investment information and education provided to employees about investing their pension plan money.[51]

EXHIBIT 9.7   The High Cost of Frequent Job Changes

		Years in Company	Percentage of Salary for Pension	×	Salary at Company (final)		Annual Pension
Sam's Career History	Job 1	10	10%	×	$ 35,817	=	$ 3,582
	Job 2	10	10%	×	$ 64,143	=	$ 6,414
	Job 3	10	10%	×	$114,870	=	$11,487
	Job 4	10	10%	×	$205,714	=	$20,571
				Sam's Total Pension		=	$42,054
Ann's Career History	Job 1	40	40%	×	$205,714	=	$82,286
				Ann's Total Pension		=	$82,286

Assumptions: 1. Starting salary of $20,000 with 6 percent annual inflation rate. 2. Both employees receive annual increases equal to inflation rate. 3. Pensions based on one percentage point (of salary) for each year of service multiplied by final salary at time of exit from company.
Source: Federal Reserve Bank of Boston.

EXHIBIT | **9.8** | Relative Advantages of Different Pension Alternatives

Defined-Benefit Plan	Defined-Contribution Plan
1. Provides an explicit benefit which is easily communicated	Unknown benefit level is difficult to communicate
2. Company absorbs risk associated with changes in inflation and interest rates which affect cost	Employees assume these risks
3. More favourable to long-service employees	More favourable to short-term employees
4. Employer costs unknown	Employer costs known up front
5. Pension fund surplus, but not deficit, must be shared with employees if plan is wound up	No surplus or deficit in pension fund to manage

---

Pension Legislation   Each province across Canada (except Prince Edward Island) as well as the federal government has legislation regarding pension benefits. In addition, the *Income Tax Act* has detailed requirements regarding pension plans that must be met in order for employer and employee contributions to be tax deductible up to the limits provided in the Act. Pension plans must be registered both with the Canada Revenue Agency (CRA) and with the applicable provincial pension commission. Some of the areas covered by these laws include eligible service, maximum contributions, early and late retirement benefits, pre-retirement and post-retirement death benefits, vesting on termination of employment, portability of pension benefits between plans, regulations regarding investment of pension fund assets, and so on.[52]

Plans covering employees in more than one jurisdiction must comply with the legal requirements of the jurisdiction of registration, but must also apply the rules of each other jurisdiction for employees working in that jurisdiction. This patchwork of legislation creates very complex plan administration for large employers with employees in several provinces/territories. For many years, pension regulators have been trying to agree on one pension regulatory system for all jurisdictions, but many experts think it is unrealistic to expect that this will happen.[53]

Life Insurance

One of the most common employee benefits offered by organizations is some form of life insurance. Typical coverage is a group insurance policy with a face value of one to two times the employee's annual salary. In most cases, premiums are paid completely by the employer. Some employers provide additional life insurance on an optional employee-paid basis. Others provide retirees with life insurance at little or no cost.

Two other common forms of life insurance are dependant life and accidental death and dismemberment insurance. Dependant life insurance provides benefits in the event of the death of the spouse or child of an employee. Accidental death and dismemberment insurance pays double the regular life insurance benefit if the employee dies in an accident, and also pays a percentage of the death benefit for accidental paralysis, or loss of limbs, eyesight, speech, or hearing.

Medical Insurance

Employer-sponsored medical insurance provides coverage for expenses not payable under provincial/territorial plans. Canadian employees consider drug plans to be their most important employee benefit, and they are willing to pay more to ensure that coverage is not diminished.[54] Dramatic increases in health care costs, particularly prescription drugs (which represent 75 percent of employer medical benefit costs in Canada), are the biggest issue facing benefits managers in Canada today.[55]

A survey of Canadian CEOs found that 66 percent ranked the costs of employee stress, burnout, and other physical and mental health issues as the top-ranked factors affecting the future productivity of the workforce.[56] The main reasons for these increases are increased use of expensive new drugs, rising drug utilization by an aging population, and reductions in coverage under provincial/territorial health care plans.[57] Many Canadian employers that provide health care benefits to retirees are considering eliminating these benefits due to rising costs.[58]

Health Care: Cost Control Strategies There are two general strategies available to benefit managers for controlling the rapidly escalating costs of health care.[59] First, organizations can motivate employees to change their demand for health care through changes in either the design or the administration of health insurance policies.[60] Included in this category of control strategies are: (1) deductibles (the first x dollars of health care cost are paid by the employee); (2) coinsurance rates (the percentage of premium payments paid by the company); (3) maximum benefits (defining a maximum payout schedule for specific health problems); and (4) coordination of benefits (ensuring no double payment when coverage exists under the employee's plan and a spouse's plan).

The second cost strategy involves promotion of preventive health, or *wellness,* programs. Incentives for quitting smoking are popular inclusions here. But there is also increased interest in healthier food in cafeterias and vending machines, on-site physical fitness facilities, and early screening to identify possible health problems before they become serious. A review of physical fitness programs found that fitness led to better mental health and improved resistance to stress; there also was some evidence of increased productivity and commitment, as well as decreased absenteeism and turnover.[61] Popular wellness initiatives in Canada are shown in Exhibit 9.9.

One senior benefits consultant recommends that as chronic diseases associated with aging increase, employers need to invest in programs that address poor health behaviour, non-compliance with treatment protocols, and health promotion. Resources devoted to finding illnesses and aggressively engaging patients in their own health outcomes will, over time, reduce the costs associated with avoidable complications of manageable chronic diseases.[62]

EXHIBIT 9.9 Wellness Initiatives in Canada

First aid/CPR courses and employee assistance plans (EAPs) were the most commonly offered wellness initiatives by employers, according to a survey of 512 organizations across Canada. The least popular were child care (11.5 percent) and eldercare (9.0 percent). Here's a look at the top 10 programs and the percentage of respondents offering them:

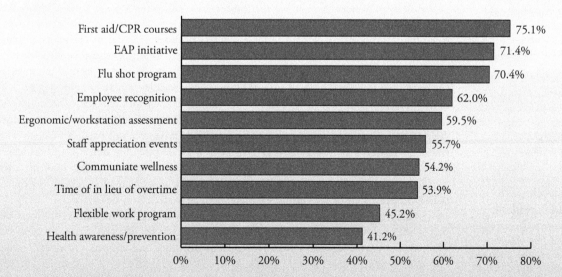

Source: *National Wellness Survey Report 2006,* Buffett & Company Worksite Wellness Ltd. (adapted from *Canadian HR Reporter,* April 9, 2007, p. 23).

As an example, one Ontario employer decided to take aggressive action in dealing with obesity by choosing to subsidize healthy foods in the company cafeteria such as salads, fresh fruits, and vegetables, but not subsidizing fries, chips, and pop. In its Windsor, Ontario, plant, DaimlerChrysler Canada ran a pilot program in cooperation with Pfizer Canada, the Canadian Auto Workers, the Windsor and Essex County Health Unit, and Solutions in Health Inc. that focused on reducing the risk of heart disease among employees. The two-part, 12-month program produced dramatic results with participants reducing their 10-year outlook for risk of heart disease from "moderate" at the launch of the program to "low risk."[63]

Dental Insurance   Dental care plans typically cover the full cost of basic preventive maintenance such as checkups and fillings; 50 to 80 percent of major restorative work such as bridges and crowns; and sometimes orthodontics, usually at 50 percent coverage. Benefits payable are usually linked to the dental fee guide in each province for the current year or a previous year (when fees were lower so that employer costs can be controlled—employees pay any additional charge up to the current fee level).

Vision Care   Vision care dates back only to the 1976 contract between the Auto Workers and the Big Three automakers. Since then, this benefit has spread throughout the private and public sectors. Most plans are non-contributory and cover part or all of the costs of eye examinations, lenses, frames, and contact lenses.

Income Security: Disability Plans

The rate of employee absence from work due to sickness has been slowly but steadily increasing in Canada, according to Statistics Canada figures. For example, the 10,000 employees at the Canadian Broadcasting Corporation took 68,000 sick days in 2006–2007, costing the organization $15.3 million, compared to $13.6 million the previous year.[64] **Short-term disability plans** (also known as **salary continuation plans**) provide a continuation of all or part of an employee's earnings when the employee is absent from work due to an illness or injury that is not work-related. Usually a medical certificate is required if the absence extends beyond two or three days. These plans typically provide full pay for some period of time (often two or three weeks) and then gradually reduce the percentage of earnings paid as the period of absence lengthens. The benefits cease when the employee returns to work or when the employee qualifies for long-term disability (often after 26 weeks of absence).

short-term disability plans/salary continuation plans

employer-sponsored plans that provide a continuation of all or part of an employee's earnings when the employee is absent from work due to an illness or injury that is not work-related

Sick leave plans operate quite differently from short-term disability plans. Most sick leave policies grant full pay for a specified number of paid sick days per month or per year (usually about one per month). A common problem with sick leave is that, although many employees use their sick days only when they are legitimately sick, others simply use their sick leaves as extra vacation days, whether they are sick or not. Worse still, seriously ill or injured employees get no pay once their sick days are used up until long-term disability benefits, if any, begin.

sick leave plans

employer-sponsored plans that grant a specified number of paid sick days per month or per year

Employers have tried several tactics to eliminate or reduce the use of sick leave days by employees who are not sick. Some buy back unused sick leave at the end of the year by paying their employees a daily equivalent pay for each sick leave day not used, a practice which can encourage legitimately sick employees to come to work despite their illness.[65] Others have experimented with holding monthly lotteries in which only employees with perfect monthly attendance are eligible to win a cash prize. Still others aggressively investigate all absences (for example, by calling the absent employees at their homes when they are off on sick leave).

long-term disability plans

employer-sponsored plans that provide income protection due to long-term illness or injury that is not work-related

Long-term disability plans provide income protection due to long-term illness or injury that is not work-related (work-related injuries are covered by Workers' Compensation benefits). The payments typically begin after 26 weeks of disability and continue to age 65 (when pension plan benefits begin) or for life. Benefits usually range from 50 percent to 75 percent of the employee's base pay, and are not taxable if the employee pays the full cost of the plan (any employer contributions result in taxable benefits for the disabled employee).

The number of long-term disability claims in Canada is rising sharply. Psychiatric disabilities are the fastest growing of all occupational disabilities, with depression being the most common. The 2007 *Staying@Work Canada* study by Watson Wyatt Worldwide consultants found that mental health issues are the leading cause of both long- and short-term disability claims (72 percent and 82 percent respectively).[66] The World Health Organization estimates that by 2020, depression will rank second as a leading cause of disability in the world.[67] Due to the rising numbers of disability claims, disability management programs with a goal of returning disabled employees safely back to work are becoming a priority in many organizations.

Pay for Time Not Worked

Included within this category are several self-explanatory benefits:

1. Paid rest periods, lunch periods, wash-up time, travel time, clothes-change time, and get ready time benefits
2. Paid vacations
3. Paid holidays (statutory and other)
4. Other (jury duty allowances, bereavement pay, paid personal leave, paid time for community volunteer work)

Judging from employee preferences discussed in the last chapter and from analysis of negotiated union contracts, pay for time not worked continues to be a high-demand benefit. Twenty years ago it was relatively rare to grant time for anything but vacations, holidays, and sick leave. Now, many organizations have a policy of ensuring payments for civic responsibilities and obligations. Any outside pay for such civic duties usually is nominal, so companies often supplement this pay, frequently to the level of 100 percent of wages lost.

EMPLOYEE ASSISTANCE PLANS (EAPS)

employee assistance plan (EAP)

employer-sponsored program that provides employees with confidential counselling and/or treatment programs for personal problems including addiction, stress, and mental health issues

An **employee assistance plan** is a formal employer program that provides employees with confidential counselling and/or treatment programs for problems such as mental health issues, marital/family problems, work/career stress, legal problems, and substance abuse. These programs are particularly important for helping employees who suffer workplace trauma ranging from harassment to physical assault.[68] The number of EAPs in Canada is growing because they are a proactive way to reduce absenteeism and disability costs. The percentage of employees using EAPs is difficult to determine due to confidentiality, but is estimated to be in the order of 6 to 7 percent.[69]

The largest EAP provider in Canada, Shepell-FGI, has called for tax credits for EAP providers because they are increasingly shouldering the burden of mental health treatment for employees.[70] A 2007 Canadian study found that 41 percent of working Canadians frequently experience stress in the workplace; 53 percent experience physical symptoms such as headaches, indigestion, and fatigue; 55 percent experience psychological symptoms including anxiety, irritability, anger, and mood swings; and 52 percent say that stress affects their behaviour in ways such as impatience, procrastination, neglecting responsibility, and performing poorly.[71] The challenge of supporting and returning those with mental health issues to productive work is discussed further in the .Net Worth box.

OTHER BENEFITS

Child Care Services   Companies increasingly are offering child care services to their employees as a paid benefit. Working is often not optional for women with preschool children—most contribute significantly to their household earnings. Many employers are offering some form of child care benefits to their employees, including resource and referral services, sick or emergency child care programs, and on-site day-care centres.

.NET WORTH

Mental Health Issues a Top Priority for Canadian HR Professionals

The World Health Organization estimates that by 2020, depression will rank second as a leading cause of disability around the world. A Watson Wyatt Worldwide survey found that 82 percent of employers indicated that psychological conditions were the leading cause of short-term disability and 72 percent of long-term disability claims. In light of the growing evidence of the significance of mental health issues in the workplace, it is not surprising that a 2008 Mercer/Canadian Alliance on Mental Illness and Mental Health survey found that concern over mental health issues was a top priority for Canadian HR professionals.

There are many risk factors for mental illness, some of which have workplace components, including lack of social supports at work, increased job demands, and being treated unfairly by supervisors, co-workers, and others. Suggestions for managing mental health challenges in the workplace include:

1. Educate all employees about mental health issues to reduce the stigma.
2. Determine how best to support and accommodate employees with mental health issues at work.
3. Take steps to prevent situations that can lead to or exacerbate mental illness.
4. Provide an EAP or other formal supports for employees who need them.

Source: L.J. Blake, "Fighting the Mental Health Stigma in the Workplace," *Workplace,* November/December 2008.

One fast-growing employee benefit is emergency child care. Companies can lose significant working-hours as a result of last-minute child care problems, and, therefore, more and more companies are offering this low-cost benefit. Emergency child care services generally are offered either at on-site child care centres or at centres that are near the workplace, or through company-paid babysitters. The CIBC expanded its backup child care across the country after a two-year pilot program produced nearly $1.4 million in productivity savings.[72] VanCity Credit Union, Husky Injection Molding Systems, and RBC Financial Group are just some of the employers who also offer emergency child care.[73]

Eldercare   Given longer life expectancy than ever before and the aging of the baby-boom generation, one benefit that will become increasingly important is eldercare assistance. Members of the aging workforce are increasingly assuming caregiver roles for their elderly parents. Most programs that are available so far provide only referral services, but Great-West Life in Winnipeg has an eldercare specialist on staff.[74] This trend is likely to continue: The number of Canadians age 65 and over is predicted to double by the year 2026.[75]

■ BENEFITS FOR CONTINGENT WORKERS

Contingent work relationships include working through a temporary help agency, working for a contract company, working on call, and working as an independent contractor. Contracting offers a viable way to meet rapidly changing environmental conditions, both by reducing costs and by permitting easier expansion and contraction of production/services.

Contingent workers cost less primarily because the benefits offered, if any, are lower than for regular employees. As Exhibit 9.10 shows, the fewer hours employees work in a week, the more severe is the benefits' penalty.

EXHIBIT	**9.10**	Benefits Received: Full-Time versus Contingent Employees

	Small Companies		Medium Companies		Large Companies	
	Full Time	**Contingent**	**Full Time**	**Contingent**	**Full Time**	**Contingent**
Vacation	98%	40%	100%	100%	100%	80%
Health Insurance	96	21	100	56	100	67
Holidays	97	48	100	77	100	67
Life Insurance	85	21	100	47	100	67
Pension	89	43	98	91	100	71
Sick Leave	70	26	83	53	96	58

CONCLUSION

Since the 1940s, employee benefits have been the most volatile area in the compensation field. From 1940 to 1980, these dramatic changes came in the form of more and better forms of employee benefits. The result should not have been unexpected. Employee benefits are now a major—and many believe prohibitively expensive—component of doing business. In the new millennium, cost-savings efforts to improve the competitive position of North American industry are widespread. A part of these cost savings will come from tighter administrative controls on existing benefit packages. But another part may come from a reduction in existing benefits packages. If this does evolve as a trend, benefits administrators will need to develop a mechanism for identifying employee preferences and use these as a guideline to meet agreed-upon savings targets.

CHAPTER SUMMARY

1. Employee benefits have been increasing in cost for the last 50 years, and now constitute a significant amount of compensation expense in all Canadian organizations, in the order of 40 percent of payroll.
2. Key issues in benefits planning, design, and administration are: (i) the relative role of benefits in a compensation package, (ii) external competitiveness, (iii) benefits adequacy and cost justification, (iv) who should be included in these plans, (v) level of choice for employees, and (vi) employee–employer cost sharing.
3. Three important functions in benefits administration are communication, claims processing, and cost containment.
4. There are three legally required benefits in Canada, in addition to government-sponsored health care plans: Workers' Compensation, Canada/Quebec Pension Plan, and Employment Insurance. Workers' Compensation provides compensation for injuries and diseases that arise out of, and while in the course of, employment. The Canada/Quebec Pension Plan is a pension plan for all employed Canadians. Employment Insurance provides workers with temporary income replacement as a result of employment interruptions due to circumstances such as work shortages, sickness, maternity leave, and so on.
5. In a defined-benefit pension plan, the employer agrees to provide a specific level of retirement pension, the exact cost of which is unknown. In a defined-contribution pension plan, the employer agrees to provide specific contributions, but the final benefit is unknown.

6. The two general strategies for controlling medical benefit costs are: (i) motivating employees to change their demand for health care through changes in the design or administration of the plan, and (ii) the promotion of preventive health programs.

KEY TERMS

REVIEW QUESTIONS

1. How does the concept of external equity differ when discussing pay versus benefits?
2. Describe how a flexible benefits plan might increase worker satisfaction with benefits at the same time that costs are being reduced.
3. Explain how an employee assistance plan could reduce costs for several other benefits.

EXPERIENTIAL EXERCISES

1. Your CEO is living proof that a little bit of knowledge is a dangerous thing. He just read in the *Globe and Mail* that employee benefits cost, on average, 38 percent of payroll. To save money, he suggests that the company fire its two benefits administrators, do away with all benefits, and give employees a 38 percent pay raise. What arguments could you provide to persuade the CEO that this is not a good idea?

2. Your company has a serious turnover problem among employees with fewer than five years' seniority. The CEO wants to use employee benefits to lessen this problem. What might you do, specifically in the areas of pension vesting, vacation and holiday allocation, and life insurance coverage, in an effort to reduce turnover?

3. Assume you are politically foolhardy and decide to challenge your CEO's decision in the previous question to use benefits as a major tool for reducing turnover. Before she fires you, what arguments might you use to try to persuade her? (Hint: Are there other compensation tools that might be more effective in reducing turnover? Might the changes in benefits have unintended consequences for older or long-service employees?)

WEB EXERCISE

Certified Employee Benefits Specialist Program (CEBS)

The Certified Employee Benefits Specialist Program is sponsored by the International Foundation of Employee Benefits Plans in Wisconsin (www.ifebp.org). In Canada, CEBS is co-sponsored by Dalhousie University (www.ifebp.org/CEBSDesignation/Overview/Dalhousie). Review these two sites and then go to the Canadian CEBS calendar at www.ifebp.org/pdf/cebs/AcademicCalendar.pdf. What are the course requirements? Where are CEBS courses offered in Canada? What is the difference between the CEBS designation and the three other designations—Group Benefits Associate, Retirement Plans Associate, and Compensation Management Specialist? Would you recommend CEBS to your classmates who are interested in a career in employee benefits?

CASE

Lightning Industries

Lightning Industries manufactures lamps for residential homes. The president of the company, Lewis Jacobs, is convinced that he must get concessions from the workers if Lightning is to compete effectively with increasing foreign competition. In particular, Jacobs is displeased with the cost of employee benefits. He doesn't mind conceding a competitive wage increase (maximum 3 percent), but he wants the total compensation package to cost 3 percent less. The current costs are shown in Table 1.

Your assistant has surveyed other companies that are obtaining concessions from employees. You also have data from a consulting firm that indicates employee preferences for different forms of benefits (Table 2). Based on all this information, you have two possible concession packages that you can propose, labelled "Option 1" and "Option 2" (Table 3).

1. Cost out these packages given the data in Tables 1 and 2 and the information obtained from various insurance carriers and other information sources (Table 4).

2. Which package should you recommend to Jacobs? Why?

3. Which of the strategies do you think will require less input from employees in terms of their reactions?

TABLE   1   Current Compensation Costs

Average yearly wage	$36,769
Average hourly wage	$17.68
Dollar value of yearly benefits, per employee	$12,923
Total compensation (wages plus benefits)	$49,692
Daily average number of hours paid	8

Benefits	Average Employer Cost/ Employee/Year
1. Legally required benefits	$3,472
a. Canada Pension Plan	$1,647
b. Employment Insurance	$891
c. Workers' Compensation	$934
2. Pension, group insurance, disability	$3,446
a. Pension plan contributions	$2,460
b. Group insurance (life, health, dental)	$523
c. Short-term disability	$83
d. Long-term disability	$129
e. Discounts on goods and services purchased from company by employees	$127
f. Miscellaneous payments (termination pay allowances, moving expenses, etc.)	$124
3. Payments for time not worked	$3,324
a. Paid vacations (16 days average)	$1,558
b. Paid statutory holidays (9 days)	$973
c. Paid rest periods, lunch periods, wash-up time, clothes-change time, get-ready time, etc. (60 minutes)	$727
d. Payments for jury/witness duty, voting time, leave for bereavement, or other personal reasons	$66
4. Other items	$2,681
a. Contributions to employee savings plan	$1,064
b. Tuition reimbursement plan (50%)	$804
c. EAP	$687
d. Special wage payments ordered by courts, payments to union stewards, etc.	$126
Total	$12,923

TABLE   2   Benefit Preferences

Benefit Type or Method of Administering	Importance to Workers	Benefit Type or Method of Administering	Importance to Workers
Pensions	87	Paid rest periods, lunch breaks, etc.	55
Health care plan	86	Dental plan	51
Holidays	79	Profit sharing	21
Paid vacation	82	Contributions to savings plan	15
Life insurance	82	Discount on goods	5
Long-term disability	72	Fair treatment in administration	100
Short-term disability	69		

Note: 0 = unimportant; 100 = extremely important.

| **TABLE** | **3** | Two Possible Packages for Cutting Benefit Costs |

Option 1

Implement deductible ($50 annually) for:
- Health care plan
- Dental plan

Reduction of benefit:
- Eliminate 10-minute paid break

Coordination with legally required benefit:
- Integrate CPP with Lightning Industries pension plan (subtract CPP payout from pension benefit)

Option 2

Improved claims processing for:
- Short-term disability
- Long-term disability

Require probationary period (one year) before eligible for:
- Discounts on goods
- Contributions to employee savings plan

Coinsurance (80%):
- Health care plan

| **TABLE** | **4** | Analysis of Cost Implications for Different Cost-Cutting Strategies: Lightning Industries |

Cost-Saving Strategy	**Savings as % of Benefit Cost**
Deductible ($50 annually):	
■ Health care plan	10
■ Dental plan	15
Require probationary period before eligible (one year):	
■ Discount on goods and services	10
■ Contributions to employee savings plan	10
Improved claims processing:	
■ Short-term disability	20
■ Long-term disability	5
Coordination with legally required benefits:	
■ Integrate CPP with Lightning Industries pension plan	15

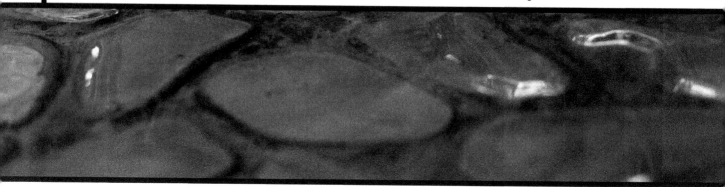

PART III

Employee Contributions: Determining Individual Pay

Thus far the first two components of the pay model have been discussed (Exhibit III.1). Both components essentially deal with fairness. Alignment (Part I) is all about internal fairness. Job analysis and job evaluation provide guidance in relating jobs to one another in terms of the content of the work and the relative contribution to the organization's objectives. External competitiveness (Part II) extended fairness to the external labour market. This raises issues of proper survey definitions, setting policy lines, and arriving at competitive pay levels and equitable pay structures.

Part III finally brings people into the pay equation. How should a pay system be designed so that individual contributions are rewarded according to their value to the organization? How much should one employee be paid relative to another when they both hold the same job in the same organization? If this question is not answered satisfactorily, all prior efforts to evaluate and price jobs will have been in vain. For example, the compensation manager determines that all systems analysts should be paid between $49,000 and $60,000. But where in that range is each individual paid? Should a good performer be paid more than a poor performer? If the answer is yes, how should performance be measured and what should be the differential reward? Similarly, should the systems analyst with more years' experience (i.e., higher seniority) be paid more than a co-worker with less time on the job? Again, if the answer is yes, what is the trade-off between seniority and performance in assigning pay raises? As Exhibit III.1 suggests, all these questions involve the concept of employee contribution. In the next two chapters we will be discussing different facets of employee contribution.

Chapter 10 considers how pay affects performance. Is there evidence that companies should invest in pay-for-performance plans? Does paying for performance result in higher performance? The answer may seem obvious, but there are many ways to complicate this elegant notion. We acknowledge that performance can't always be measured objectively. What do we do to ensure that subjective appraisal procedures are as free from error as possible? Much progress has been made here. Finally, key design issues in pay for performance are reviewed.

Chapter 11 looks at actual pay-for-performance plans. The compensation arena is full of programs that promise to link pay and performance. We identify these plans and discuss their relative advantages and disadvantages. Pay for special groups that require the design of compensation programs that differ from more traditional designs is also discussed.

EXHIBIT **III.1** The Pay Model

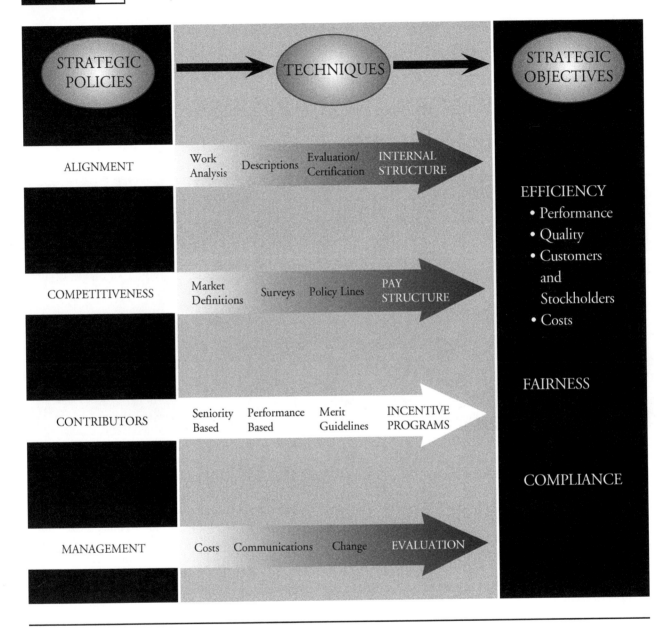

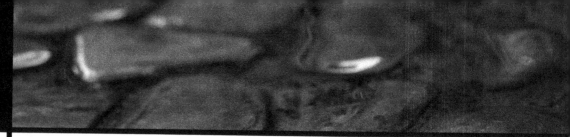

CHAPTER 10

PAY FOR PERFORMANCE: PERFORMANCE APPRAISAL AND PLAN DESIGN

LEARNING OUTCOMES

- Explain why employee performance depends on three factors—skill, knowledge, and motivation.
- Briefly describe the difference between motivation theories that focus on content, those that focus on the nature of the exchange, and those that focus on desired behaviour.
- Discuss the ways in which compensation motivates behaviour.
- Describe at least five common errors in the appraisal process.
- Explain three strategies to better understand and measure job performance.
- Discuss the key elements of an effective performance appraisal process.
- Explain the three factors that determine the effectiveness of a pay-for-performance plan.

pay-for-performance plan

a pay plan that links individual pay to some measure of performance on the job

The primary focus of the last section was to determine the worth of jobs, independent of who performed those jobs. Job analysis, job evaluation, and job pricing all have a common theme. They are techniques to identify the value a firm places on its jobs. Now we introduce people into the equation. Now we declare that different people performing the same job may have different value to the organization. Jim is a better programmer than Sam. Sally knows more programming languages than John. Companies often link individual pay to performance through a **pay-for-performance plan**—in this case, paying Sally more than John, and Jim more than Sam.

Entering people into the compensation equation greatly complicates the compensation process. There is growing evidence that the way we design HR practices, like performance management, strongly affects the way employees perceive the company. The simple (or not so simple) process of implementing a performance appraisal system that employees find acceptable goes a long way toward increasing trust in top management.[1] So there are other important outcomes that also depend on building good performance measurement tools.

In Chapter 1, it was noted that compensation objectives complement overall human resources objectives, and both of these help an organization to achieve its overall strategic objectives. But this raises the question, "How does an organization achieve its overall strategic objectives?" In this section of the book, we will argue that organizational success ultimately depends on human behaviour. Our compensation decisions and practices should be designed to increase the likelihood that employees will behave in ways that help the organization achieve its strategic objectives. This chapter is organized around employee behaviours. First, we identify the four kinds of behaviours in which organizations are interested. Then we review theoretical perspectives about the ability to motivate these behaviours. And finally, we discuss our success, and sometimes lack thereof, in designing compensation systems to elicit these behaviours.

■ WHAT BEHAVIOURS DO EMPLOYERS CARE ABOUT? LINKING ORGANIZATION STRATEGY TO COMPENSATION AND PERFORMANCE MANAGEMENT

The simple answer is that employers want employees to perform in ways that lead to better organizational performance. The focus in this chapter, then, is on employee performance. There is growing evidence that employee performance depends on three general factors:[2]

Employee performance = f (S,K,M) where

S = Skill and ability to perform task
K = Knowledge of facts, rules, principles, and procedures
M = Motivation to perform

Wanting to succeed isn't enough. Having the ability without the desire also isn't enough. For an organization to succeed, it needs employees who perform well. And, as was noted in Chapter 2, this involves not only good compensation strategy and practice, but also other well-developed HR practices.[3] Organizations need to hire people with skill and ability (S). They need to make sure the good employees (high S) stay with the company. If they can succeed at these first two things, we can then concentrate on building further knowledge and skills (K & S). And finally, it is necessary to find ways to motivate (M) employees to perform well on their jobs—to take their knowledge and abilities and apply them in ways that contribute to organizational performance.

Apparent through all of this is the need to accurately measure performance. Performance must be measured if it is to be rewarded. As a simple example, think about where piece-rate systems are used to pay people. Why do many sales jobs use commissions (a form of piece rate) as the primary compensation vehicle? Conventional wisdom has always been that performance in a sales job is relatively easy to measure—dollar sales. There is little ambiguity in the measure of performance, and this makes it easy to create a strong link between units of performance and amount of compensation. One of the biggest recent advances in compensation strategy has been to document and extend this conventional wisdom. Initial evidence suggests that the way compensation systems are designed is intimately linked to the stability of performance measures. Exhibit 10.1 builds on the results of two studies to speculate about the following relationship.[4]

Think about what each of the cells suggests in terms of compensation practices under different performance conditions. First, what might cause wide swings in corporate performance—often this occurs when something in the external environment fluctuates widely also (e.g., exchange rate with a major foreign customer, raw material costs). It probably wouldn't be fair, and employees would certainly object, if a large part of pay were incentive based in this kind of environment.

EXHIBIT 10.1 Performance Measurement Related to Compensation

Variability/ease of measurement in individual performance	Variability in Organizational Performance	
	Low variability: few swings in overall corporate performance	*High variability: regular and large swings in overall corporate performance*
Unstable, unclear, and changing objectives	Cell A—provide wide range of rewards beyond just money. Include significant incentive component.	Cell B—provide wide range of rewards beyond just money. Emphasize base pay with low incentive portion.
Stable and easily measured	Cell C—emphasize monetary rewards with large incentive component.	Cell D—emphasize monetary rewards. Large base pay with low incentive portion.

Things the employees don't control (in the external environment) would be dictating a big part of pay. Lack of employee control translates into perceptions of unfair treatment. Cells B and D both suggest that a low incentive component is appropriate in organizations with highly variable annual performance. Conversely, as cells A and C indicate, larger incentive components are appropriate in companies with stable annual performance.

Employee performance also can vary. Some employees have jobs that are fairly stable, with fairly consistent expectations across time. In other jobs, though, there might be a great deal of fluctuation in the kinds of things expected of employees, requiring employees who are willing to be flexible and adjust to changing demands. Evidence suggests that companies are best able to get employees to adjust, be flexible, and show commitment when a broader array of rewards, rather than just money, is part of the compensation package.[5]

What can be concluded from all this? The response depends on the answers to the following four questions:

- How can good employee prospects be attracted to *join* the company?
- How can these good employees be *retained* once they join?
- How can employees *develop skills* for current and future jobs?
- How can employees *perform* well on their current job?

First, how can good people be attracted to join their company? How did Ford get Wayne Gretzky to serve as corporate spokesperson? Part of the answer is rumoured to be a contract worth millions of dollars. The long-run success of any company depends on getting good people to accept employment. And the compensation challenge is to figure out which components of the compensation package are likely to influence this decision to join.

Second, the obvious complement to the decision to join is the decision to stay. How can employees be retained? Once compensation practices get a good employee in the door, what can be done to ensure that it's not a revolving door.

Third, it is important to recognize that what employees are required to do today could change literally overnight. A fast-changing world requires employees who can adjust quickly. How can employees, traditionally resistant to change, be motivated to willingly develop skills today that may not be vital on the current job but which are expected to become critical as the company's strategic plan adjusts to change? Another compensation challenge!

Finally, it is important for employees to do well on their current jobs. This means performing, and performing well, tasks that support strategic objectives. What motivates employees to succeed? The compensation challenge is to design rewards that enhance job performance.

■ WHAT DOES IT TAKE TO GET THESE BEHAVIOURS? WHAT THEORY AND RESEARCH SAY

motivation

a process involving the determination of what is important to a person, and offering it in exchange for desired behaviour

Another way of asking the same question is, "What motivates employees?" In the simplest sense, **motivation** involves three elements: (1) what's important to a person, and (2) offering it in exchange for some (3) desired behaviour. On the first question, there are data that suggest that employees prefer pay systems that recognize individual performance, changes in the cost of living, seniority, and the market rate, to name the most important factors.[6] To narrow down specific employee preferences, though, there has been some exciting new work on what's important to employees. The new idea is called flexible total compensation—a takeoff on flexible benefits, described in Chapter 9. Flexible compensation develops the idea that only the individual employee knows which package of rewards would best suit his or her personal needs. The key ingredient in this yet-to-be-tried program—careful cost analysis to make sure the dollar cost of the package an employee selects meets employer budgetary limits.[7]

Exhibit 10.2 briefly summarizes some of the important motivation theories. Pay particular attention to the last column where the implications for employee behaviour are discussed.

EXHIBIT **10.2** Motivation Theories ———————————————————————

Theory	Essential Features	Predictions about Performance-Based Pay	So What?
Maslow's Need Hierarchy	People are motivated by inner needs. Needs form a hierarchy from most basic (food and shelter) to higher-order (e.g., self-esteem, love, self-actualization). Needs are never fully met; they operate cyclically. Higher-order needs become motivating after lower-order needs have been met. When needs are not met, they become frustrating.	1. Base pay must be set high enough to provide individuals with the economic means to meet their basic living needs. 2. An at-risk program will not be motivating since it restricts employees' ability to meet lower-order needs. 3. Success-sharing plans may be motivating to the extent they help employees pursue higher-order needs.	A. Performance-based pay may be demotivating if it impinges upon employees' capacity to meet daily living needs. B. Incentive pay is motivating to the extent it is attached to achievement, recognition, or approval.
Herzberg's 2-Factor Theory	Employees are motivated by two types of motivators: hygiene factors and satisfiers. Hygiene or maintenance factors, in their absence, prevent behaviours, but in their presence cannot motivate performance. These are related to basic living needs, security, and fair treatment. Satisfiers, such as recognition, promotion, and achievement motivate performance.	1. Base pay must be set high enough to provide individuals with the economic means to meet hygiene needs, but it cannot motivate performance. 2. Performance is obtained through rewards; payments in excess of that required to meet basic needs. 3. Performance-based pay is motivating to the extent it is connected with meeting employees' needs for recognition, pleasure attainment, achievement, and the like. 4. Other factors such as interpersonal atmosphere, responsibility, type of work, and working conditions influence the efficacy of performance-based pay.	A. Pay level is important—must meet minimum requirements before performance-based pay can operate as motivator. B. Security plans will induce minimum, but not extra, performance. Success-sharing plans will be motivating. At-risk plans will be demotivating. C. Other conditions in the working relationship influence the effectiveness of performance-based pay.
Expectancy	Motivation is the product of three perceptions: expectancy, instrumentality, and valence. Expectancy is employees' assessment of their ability to perform required job tasks. Instrumentality is employees' beliefs that requisite job performance will be rewarded by the organization. Valence is the value employees attach to the organization rewards offered for satisfactory job performance.	1. Job tasks and responsibilities should be clearly defined. 2. The pay-performance link is critical. 3. Performance-based pay returns must be large enough to be seen as rewards. 4. People choose the behaviour that leads to the greatest reward.	A. Larger incentive payments are better than smaller ones. B. Line-of-sight is critical—employees must believe they can influence performance targets. C. Employee assessments of their own ability are important—organizations should be aware of training and resource needs required to perform at target levels.

continued

EXHIBIT | **10.2** | Motivation Theories (*continued*)

Theory	Essential Features	Predictions about Performance-Based Pay	So What?
Equity	Employees are motivated when perceived outputs (i.e., pay) are equal to perceived inputs (e.g., effort, work behaviours). A disequilibrium in the output-to-input balance causes discomfort. If employees perceive that others are paid more for the same effort, they will react negatively (e.g., shirk) to correct the output-to-input balance.	1. The pay-performance link is critical; increases in performance must be matched by commensurate increases in pay. 2. Performance inputs and expected outputs must be clearly defined and identified. 3. Employees evaluate the adequacy of their pay via comparisons with other employees.	A. Performance measures must be clearly defined and employees must be able to affect them through work behaviours. B. If payouts do not match expectations, employees will react negatively. C. Fairness and consistency of performance-based pay across employees in an organization is important. D. Since employees evaluate their pay-effort balance in comparison to other employees, relative pay matters.
Reinforcement	Rewards reinforce (i.e., motivate and sustain) performance. Rewards must follow directly after behaviours to be reinforcing. Behaviours which are not rewarded will be discontinued.	1. Performance-based payments must follow closely behind performance. 2. Rewards must be tightly coupled to desired performance objectives. 3. Withholding payouts can be a way to discourage unwanted behaviours.	A. Timing of payouts is very important.
Goal Setting	Challenging performance goals influence greater intensity and duration in employee performance. Goals serve as feedback standards to which employees can compare their performance. Individuals are motivated to the extent that goal achievement is combined with receiving valued rewards.	1. Performance-based pay must be contingent upon achievement of important performance goals. 2. Performance goals should be challenging and specific. 3. The amount of the incentive reward should match the goal difficulty.	A. Line-of-sight is important; employees must believe they can influence performance targets. B. Performance targets should be communicated in terms of specific, difficult goals. C. Feedback about performance is important. D. Performance-based payouts should be contingent upon goal achievement.
Agency	Pay directs and motivates employee performance. Employees prefer static wages (e.g., a salary) to performance-based pay. If performance can be accurately monitored, payments should be based upon satisfactory completion of work duties. If performance cannot be monitored, pay should be aligned with achieving organizational objectives.	1. Performance-based pay must be tightly linked to organizational objectives. 2. Employees dislike risky pay and will demand a wage premium (e.g., higher total pay) in exchange for accepting performance-based pay. 3. Performance-based pay can be used to direct and induce employee performance.	A. Performance-based pay is the optimal compensation choice for more complex jobs where monitoring employees' work is difficult. B. Performance targets should be tied to organizational goals. C. Use of performance-based pay will require higher total pay opportunity.

Some of the theories in Exhibit 10.2 focus on content—identifying what is important to people. Maslow and Herzberg, for example, both fall in this category. People have certain needs, such as physiological, security, and self-esteem, that influence behaviour. Presumably, if rewards that satisfy one or more needs are offered, employees will behave in desired ways. These theories often drive compensation decisions about the breadth and depth of compensation offerings. Flexible pay, whereby employees choose from a menu of pay and benefit choices, clearly is driven by the issue of needs. Who best knows what satisfies needs? The employee!

A second set of theories, best exemplified by expectancy theory, equity theory, and agency theory, focuses less on need states and more on the second element—the nature of the exchange. Many compensation practices recognize the importance of a fair exchange. Jobs are evaluated using a common set of compensable factors in part to let employees know that an explicit set of rules governs the evaluation process. Salary survey data is collected in order for the exchange to be fair compared to external standards. Incentive systems are designed to align employee behaviour with the needs of the organization. All these pay decisions, and more, owe much to understanding how the employment exchange affects employee motivation.

expectancy theory

motivation theory stating that people cognitively evaluate potential behaviours in relation to rewards offered in exchange

equity theory

motivation theory stating that people are concerned about fairness of the reward outcomes exchanged for employee inputs

agency theory

motivation theory stating that employees and management/owners both will act opportunistically to obtain the most favourable exchange possible

Expectancy theory argues that people behave as though they cognitively evaluate what behaviours are possible (e.g., the probability that they can complete the task) in relation to the value of rewards offered in exchange. According to this theory, employees choose behaviours that yield the most satisfactory exchange. Equity theory focuses also on what goes on inside an employee's head. **Equity theory** argues that people are highly concerned about equity, or fairness of the exchange process. Employees look at the exchange as a ratio between what is expected and what is received. Some theorists say employees judge transactions as fair when others around them do not have a more (or less) favourable balance between the give and get of an exchange.[8] Even greater focus on the exchange process occurs in the last of this second set of theories, **agency theory**.[9] Here employees are depicted as agents who enter an exchange with principals—the owners or their designated managers. It is assumed that both sides to the exchange seek the most favourable exchange possible, and will act opportunistically if given a chance (e.g., try to "get by" with doing as little as possible to satisfy the contract). Compensation is a major element in this theory, because it is used to keep employees in line: Employers identify important behaviours and important outcomes and pay specifically for achieving desired levels of each. Such incentive systems penalize employees who try to shirk their duties by giving them proportionately lower rewards.

Finally, at least one of the theories summarized in Exhibit 10.2 focuses on the third element of motivation: desired behaviour. A review of this literature indicates that the vast majority of studies on goal setting find a positive impact of goal setting on performance. Workers assigned "hard" goals consistently do better than workers told to "do your best."[10]

■ WHAT DOES IT TAKE TO GET THESE BEHAVIOURS? WHAT COMPENSATION PEOPLE SAY

In the past, compensation people didn't ask this question very often. Employees learned what behaviours were important as part of the socialization process or as part of the performance management process.[11] If it was part of the culture to work long hours, they quickly learned this. If the performance appraisal at the end of the year stressed certain types of behaviours, or if the boss said certain things were important to her, then the signals were pretty clear: Do these things! Compensation might have rewarded people for meeting these expectations, but usually the compensation package wasn't designed to be one of the signals for expected performance. Now compensation people talk about pay in terms of a neon arrow flashing: "Do these things." Progressive companies ask the question, "What do we want our compensation package to do? How, for example, do we get our product engineers to take more risks?" Compensation then is designed to support this risk-taking behaviour. In the next section, different types of reward components will be discussed, acknowledging that pay isn't the only reward that influences behaviour.

■ TOTAL REWARD SYSTEM: OTHER REWARDS BESIDES MONEY INFLUENCE BEHAVIOUR!

Compensation is but one of many rewards that influence employee behaviour. Depending on which survey is consulted, workers highly value such other job rewards as empowerment, recognition, and opportunities for advancement.[12] Please note that at least 13 general categories of rewards are provided by organizations (Exhibit 10.3) as part of their **total reward system**.

total reward system

all rewards (in at least 13 general categories) provided by organizations

Now consider an example that demonstrates that compensation decisions have to be integrated with total reward system decisions. If the presence or absence of rewards other than money in an organization is not considered, it may seem like the compensation process is producing unintended consequences. In a team-based work environment where the culture of the organization strongly supports empowerment of workers, empowerment is a form of reward. Exhibit 10.3 identifies the dimensions of empowerment (see #9) as authority to make decisions, some control over factors that influence outcomes, and the autonomy to carry out decisions without overregulation by upper management. Some people find empowerment a very positive inducement, making coming to work each day a pleasure. Others may view empowerment as just added responsibility—legitimizing demands for more pay. In the first case, adding extra compensation may not be necessary. Some have even argued it can lessen motivation.[13] In the second case, extra compensation may be a necessity. Is it any wonder that companies are having trouble finding one right answer to the team compensation question?

Exhibit 10.4 outlines the different types of wage components, ordered from least risky to most risky for employees. Risky is defined in terms of stability of income, or the ability to accurately predict income level from year to year. Over the last several decades, companies have been moving more towards compensation programs higher on the risk continuum. New forms of pay are less entitlement-oriented and more linked to the uncertainties of individual, group, and corporate performance.[14] Employees increasingly are expected to bear a share of the risks that businesses have borne solely in the past. It's not entirely clear what impact this shifting of risk will have in the long run, but some authors are already voicing concerns that efforts to build employee loyalty and commitment may be an early casualty of these new pay systems.[15]

Some research suggests that employees may need a risk premium (higher pay) to stay and perform in a company with pay-at-risk.[16] To explore the impact of these new forms of pay, a summary of what is known about the ability of different compensation components to motivate the four general behaviours noted earlier is now presented.

EXHIBIT   10.3   Components of a Total Reward System ─────────────────

1.	Compensation	Wages, commissions, and bonuses
2.	Benefits	Vacations, health insurance
3.	Social interaction	Friendly workplace
4.	Security	Stable, consistent position and rewards
5.	Status/recognition	Respect, prominence due to work
6.	Work variety	Opportunity to experience different things
7.	Workload	Right amount of work (not too much, not too little)
8.	Work importance	Is work valued by society
9.	Authority/control/autonomy	Ability to influence others; control own destiny
10.	Advancement	Chance to get ahead
11.	Feedback	Receive information helping to improve performance
12.	Work conditions	Hazard free
13.	Development opportunity	Formal and informal training to learn new knowledge/skills/abilities

EXHIBIT 10.4 Wage Components ───────────────────────

Wage Component	Definition	Level of Risk to Employee
Base pay	The guaranteed portion of an employee's wage package.	As long as employment continues, this is the secure portion of wages.
Across-the-board increase	Wage increase granted to all employees, regardless of performance. Size related to some subjective assessment by employer about ability to pay. Typically an add-on to base pay in subsequent years.	Some risk to employee becaise at discretion of employer. But not tied to performance differences, so risk lower in that respect.
Cost-of-living increase	Same as across-the-board increase, except magnitude based on change in cost of living (e.g., as measured by CPI).	Same as across-the-board increase.
Merit pay	Wage increase granted to employee as function of some assessment of employee performance. Adds on to base pay in subsequent years.	Two types of risk faced by employees. Size of total merit pool at discretion of employer (risk element), and individual portion of pool depends on performance, which also is not totally predictable.
Lump-sum bonus	As with merit pay, granted for individual performance. Does not add into base pay, but is distributed as a one-time bonus.	Three types of risks faced here. Both types mentioned under merit pay, plus not added into base—requires annually "re-earning" the added pay
Individual incentive	Sometimes this variable pay is an add-on to a fixed base pay. The incentive component ties increments in compensation directly to extra individual production (e.g., commission systems, piece rate). Although measures of performance typically are subjective, with merit and lump-sum components, this form of variable pay differs because measures of performance are objective (e.g., sales volume).	Most risky compensation component if sole element of pay, but often combined with a base pay. No or low fixed base pay means each year employee is dependent upon number of units of performance to determine pay.
Group incentive	Variable pay that is tied to some measure of group performance, not individual performance. Not added into base pay. Distinguished from risk-sharing plans below because employees share in any success—performance above standard—but are not penalized for performance below standard.	All group incentive plans have risks noted in above pay components plus the risk associated with group performance measures. Now individual worker is also dependent upon the performance of others included in the group.
Gain-sharing plans	Differs from profit sharing in that goal to exceed is not financial performance of organization, but some cost index (e.g., labour cost is most common, might also include scrap costs, utility costs).	Less risk to individual than profit sharing because performance measure is more controllable.
Profit-sharing plans	Add-on linked to group performance (team, division, total company) relative to exceeding some financial goal.	Profit measures are influenced by factors beyond employee control (e.g., economic climate, accounting write-offs). Less control means more risk.
Risk-sharing plans	Variable pay where employees not only share in the successes but also are penalized during poor performance years. Penalty is in form of lower total compensation in poor corporate performance years. Reward, though, is typically higher than for group incentive programs in high performance years.	Greater risk than group incentive plans. Typically, employees absorb a "temporary" cut in base pay. If performance targets are met, this cut is neutralized by one component of variable pay. Risk to employee is increased, though, because even base pay is no longer totally predictable.

■ DOES COMPENSATION MOTIVATE BEHAVIOUR? GENERAL COMMENTS

Although there are exceptions, generally, linking pay to behaviours of employees results in better individual and organizational performance.[17] One particularly good study looked at the HR practices of over 3,000 companies.[18] One set of questions asked: (1) whether the company had a formal appraisal process, (2) was the appraisal tied to the size of pay increases, and (3) did performance influence who would be promoted. Organizations significantly above the mean (by one standard deviation) on these and other "High Performance Work Practices" had annual sales that averaged $27,000 more per employee. So, rewarding employees for performance pays off.

In a more comprehensive review, Heneman reports that 40 of 42 studies looking at merit pay claim performance increases when pay is tied to performance.[19] Gerhart and Milkovich took the performance-based pay question one step further. They found, across 200 companies, there was a 1.5 percent increase in return on assets for every 10 percent increase in the size of a bonus.[20] Furthermore, they found that the variable portion of pay had a stronger impact on individual and corporate performance than did the level of base pay.

■ DOES COMPENSATION MOTIVATE BEHAVIOUR? SPECIFIC COMMENTS

This section looks at the role of compensation in motivating the four types of behaviour outlined earlier: the decision to join, to stay, to develop skills, and to perform well.

Do People Join a Firm Because of Pay?

That level of pay and pay system characteristics influence a job candidate's decision to join a firm shouldn't be too surprising.[21] Pay is one of the more visible rewards in the whole recruitment process. Job offers spell out level of compensation and may even include discussions about kinds of pay such as bonuses and profit participation. Other rewards are subjective and tend to require actual time on the job before we can decide whether they are positive or negative features of the job. Not so for pay. Being objective, it's easily communicated in the employment offer.

Recent research suggests job candidates look for organizations with reward systems that fit their personalities.[22] Outlined below are some of the ways that "fit" is important.

Person Characteristics	Preferred Reward Characteristic
Materialistic	Relatively more concerned about pay level[23]
Low Self-Esteem	Low self-esteem individuals want large, decentralized organization with little pay for performance[24]
Risk Takers	Want more pay based on performance[25]
Individualists ("I control my destiny")	Want pay plans based on individual performance, not group performance[26]

None of these relationships is particularly surprising. People are attracted to organizations that fit their personalities. Evidence suggests talented employees are attracted to companies that have strong links between pay and performance.[27]

It's not a big jump, then, to suggest organizations should design their reward systems to attract people with desired personalities and values. For example, if risk takers are required, then reward systems that have elements of risk built into them should be designed.

Do People Stay in a Firm (or Leave) Because of Pay?

There is clear evidence that poor performers are more likely to leave an organization than good performers.[28] How does pay affect this relationship? Equity theory research has documented that workers who feel unfairly treated in pay react by leaving the firm for greener pastures.[29] This is particularly true under incentive conditions. Turnover is much higher for poor performers when pay is based on individual performance. Conversely, group incentive plans may lead to more turnover of better performers—clearly an undesirable outcome. When AT&T shifted from individual to team-based incentives a number of years ago, star performers either reduced their output or quit. Out of 208 above-average performers, only one continued to report performance increases under the group incentive plan. The rest felt cheated because the incentives for higher individual performance were now spread across all group members.[30]

Recent efforts to use different types of compensation as a tool for retaining workers have focused on what is called *scarce talent*. For example, information technology employees have been scarce for the past decade, at least. One way to retain these workers is to develop a variable pay component for each project. For example, reports of variable pay linked to individual length of stay on a project, to peer ratings, and to project results, suggest that this pay-for-performance combination might appeal to scarce talent.[31]

Do Employees More Readily Agree to Develop Job Skills Because of Pay?

The answer to this question is not clear. Skill-based pay (Chapter 6) is intended, at least partially, to pay employees for learning new skills—skills that hopefully will help employees perform better on current jobs and adjust more rapidly to demands on future jobs. Whether this promise is fulfilled is unclear. Evidence is starting to accumulate that pay for skill may not increase productivity, but that it does focus people on believing in the importance of quality and in turning out products of significantly higher quality.[32]

Do Employees Perform Better on Their Jobs Because of Pay?

Substantial evidence exists that management and workers alike believe pay should be tied to performance. Dyer and colleagues found that workers believed the most important factor for salary increases should be job performance. Following close behind is a factor that presumably would be picked up in job evaluation (nature of job) and a motivational variable (amount of effort expended).[33]

Other research supports these findings.[34] Outside the managerial ranks, though, other groups express a different view of the pay–performance link. The role that performance levels should assume in determining pay increases is less clear-cut for blue-collar workers.[35] Unionized workers prefer seniority rather than performance as a basis for pay increases.[36] Part of this preference may stem from a distrust of subjective performance measurement systems. Unions ask, "Can management be counted on to be fair?" In contrast, seniority is an objective index for calculating increases. Some evidence also suggests that women might prefer allocation methods not based on performance.[37]

In general, workers believe pay should be tied to performance, because it appears to help the bottom line. Numerous studies indicate that tying pay to individual performance has a positive impact on employee performance.[38] One recent study of over 3,000 companies provided convincing evidence that linking pay to performance has a positive impact on the bottom line. Over a five-year period such practices can increase per-employee sales by as much as $100,000.[39] A number of recent studies provide strong evidence that pay for performance has a direct and, at times substantial, impact on firm performance. Companies that pay for performance have stronger corporate earnings!.[40]

Most well-controlled studies in which companies base part of pay on some measure of corporate or division performance report increases in performance of about 4 to 6 percent per year.[41] Typical of these studies is a utility company that placed one division on an experimental group incentive plan and left the other division with no pay changes (the control group).[42] The goal in the experimental division was to lower unit cost of electricity. After implementing this variable pay plan (or group incentive plan), performance improved significantly over the control division on 11 of 12 objective performance measures. As an example, unit production costs fell 6 percent.

Compensation experts estimate that every dollar spent on any performance-based pay plan yields $2.34 in organizational earnings.[43] Put differently, there is further documented evidence that every 10 percent increase in bonus paid yields a 1.5 percent increase in return on assets (ROA) to the firm.[44]

Before rushing out and developing a variable pay component for the compensation package, though, it should be recognized that such plans can, and do, fail. Sometimes the failure arises, ironically, because the incentive works too well, leading employees to exhibit rewarded behaviours to the exclusion of other desired behaviours. But often the problem relates to the definition and measurement of performance.

THE ROLE OF PERFORMANCE APPRAISALS IN COMPENSATION DECISIONS

performance appraisal

process of evaluating or appraising an employee's performance on the job

Performance must be measured if it is to be rewarded. Clearly, a key element of pay-for-performance plans is some measure of performance obtained through a **performance appraisal** process. Sometimes this measure is objective and quantifiable, and sometimes it is not. Objective performance standards may not be feasible. Either job output is not readily quantifiable or the components that are quantifiable do not reflect important job dimensions.

Just because something is quantifiable, though, doesn't mean it is an objective measure of performance. As any accounting student knows, financial measures are arrived at through a process that involves some subjective decision-making. Such potential for subjectivity has led some experts to warn that so-called objective data can be deficient and may not tell the whole story.[45] Despite these concerns, most HR professionals probably would prefer to work with objective data.

The end result, all too often, is a performance appraisal process that is plagued by errors. Edwards Deming, the grandfather of the quality movement here and in Japan, launched an attack of appraisals because, he contended, the work situation (not the individual) is the major determinant of performance.[46] Variation in performance arises many times because employees don't have the necessary information, technology, or control to adequately perform their jobs.[47] Furthermore, Deming argued, individual work standards and performance ratings rob employees of pride and self-esteem.

Some experts argue that total quality management principles should be applied to improving the process.[48] A first step, of course, is recognition that performance is influenced by both the work environment and by employee behaviours. A second step in this direction concerns identifying strategies to understand and measure job performance better. This may help to reduce the number and types of rating errors illustrated in Exhibit 10.5.

COMMON ERRORS IN APPRAISING PERFORMANCE

Suppose a manager supervised 1,000 employees. How many would he or she rate at the highest level? How many would be average or below? An argument that the distribution should look something like a normal curve might get an A in statistics, but fail Reality 101. One survey of 1,816 organizations reported the following distribution of performance ratings (Exhibit 10.6) for its managers.

| **EXHIBIT** | **10.5** | Common Errors in the Appraisal Process |

Halo error	An appraiser giving favourable ratings to all job duties based on impressive performance in just one job function. For example, a rater who hates tardiness rates a prompt subordinate high across all performance dimensions *exclusively because of this one characteristic.*
Negative halo error	The opposite of a halo error. Downgrading an employee across all performance dimensions *exclusively because of poor performance on one dimension.*
First impression error	Developing a negative or positive opinion of an employee early in the review period and allowing that to influence negatively or positively all later perceptions of performance.
Recency error	The opposite of first impression error. Allowing performance, either good or bad, at the end of the review period to play too large a role in determining an employee's rating for the entire period.
Leniency error	Consistently rating someone higher than is deserved.
Strictness error	The opposite of leniency error. Rating someone consistently lower than is deserved.
Central tendency error	Avoiding extremes in ratings across employees.
Similar-to-me error	Giving better ratings to individuals who are like the rater in behaviour and/or personality.
Spillover error	Continuing to downgrade an employee for performance errors in prior rating periods.

The truth is that human raters tend to make mistakes. Their ratings differ from what would occur if it was possible, in a moment of clarity, to divine the truth. Recognizing and understanding the errors are the first steps in communicating and building a more effective appraisal process. Additional factors such as the cultural background of employees can also make performance appraisal more complex, as discussed in the .Net Worth box.

| **EXHIBIT** | **10.6** | Ratings of Managers |

Rating Received	**Percentage of Managers Receiving Rating**
Above average employee	46.4
Average employee	49.0
Below average	4.6

.NET WORTH — Performance Appraisal in a Diverse Workforce

The performance appraisal, with its goal-setting procedures and inherent feedback process, is a Western concept that can be a cultural disconnect with individuals from some countries. In Asian corporations, an employee's appraisal (and prospects for promotion) is as likely to deal with attributes such as cooperation and sociability as achievement of results. And because status within these cultures is so crucial to an individual's sense of worth and contribution, it is important to navigate this cultural minefield with sensitivity so that the employee does not become insulted or lose face.

In hierarchical cultures such as India and China, managers provide explicit directions, and employees are far more deferential to their superiors than in more participative countries like Canada. Employees from participative countries seek new responsibilities as a way to achieve promotion. In contrast, in hierarchical countries, initiative is seen only at the most senior level, while the employee performs current tasks with great care. For them, improving their technical expertise is the proven path to promotion.

In individualistic cultures such as Canada and the United States, individual effort is recognized and rewarded. However, in collectivist cultures such as Pakistan, recognition and rewards are normally assigned for strong group performance. The individual is expected to work for the good of the group.

Procter & Gamble Canada is aware that the Western practice of performance appraisal can be hard to understand for employees from other cultures. Therefore, managers are trained to help them create appraisals where clearly defined expectations are linked with performance measures. Then this process is clearly communicated to all employees, especially those from different cultures. A quality audit of all appraisals is conducted to ensure that the desired results are achieved.

Source: R. Singer, "Watch for Cultural Biases in Assessing Employees," *Canadian HR Reporter,* June 19, 2006, pp. 15, 17.

Not surprisingly, the potential for error causes employees to lose faith in the performance appraisal process. There are several factors that lead raters to give inaccurate appraisals: (1) guilt, (2) embarrassment about giving praise, (3) taking things for granted, (4) not noticing, (5) halo effect, (6) dislike of confrontation, or (7) spending too little time on preparation of the appraisal.[49] To counter such problems, companies and researchers alike have expended considerable time and money to identify ways to improve performance ratings.

■ STRATEGIES TO BETTER UNDERSTAND AND MEASURE JOB PERFORMANCE

Efforts to improve the performance rating process have taken several forms.[50] First, researchers and compensation people traditionally focused on evaluation formats—the methods used to rank or rate performance. Second, more recent attention has focused less on the rating format and more on the raters themselves. Several possible categories of raters (supervisor, peers, subordinates, customers, self) have been studied to determine whether a given category leads to more or less accurate ratings. Third, attempts are being made to identify how raters process information about job performance and translate it into performance ratings. Fourth, research results also suggest that raters can be trained to increase the accuracy of their ratings. The following sections discuss each of these four approaches to better understand and measure performance.

Strategy One: Improve Evaluation Formats

evaluation format

the method used to evaluate an employee's performance, either ranking against other employees or rating on one or more performance criteria

alternation ranking

ranking the best employee, then the worst employee, then the next best and worst, and so on

paired comparison performance ranking

ranking each employee against all other employees, one pair at a time

Types of Formats   **Evaluation formats** can be divided into two general categories: ranking and rating.[51] *Ranking* formats require the rater to compare employees to one another to determine the relative ordering of the group on some performance measure (usually some measure of overall performance). Exhibit 10.7 illustrates three different methods of ranking employees.

The straight ranking procedure is just that: Employees are ranked relative to one another. **Alternation ranking** recognizes that raters are better at ranking people at extreme ends of the distribution. Raters are asked to indicate the best employee and then the worst employee. **Paired comparison performance ranking** simplifies the ranking process by forcing raters to make ranking judgments about discrete pairs of people.

The second category of appraisal formats, *ratings*, is generally more popular than ranking systems. The various rating formats have two elements in common. First, in contrast to ranking formats, rating formats require raters to evaluate employees on some absolute standard rather than relative to other employees. Second, each performance standard is measured on a scale on which appraisers can check the point that best represents the employee's performance. In this way, performance variation is described along a continuum from good to bad. The types of descriptors used in anchoring this continuum provide the major difference in rating scales. These descriptors may be adjectives, behaviours, or outcomes. When *adjectives* are used as anchors, the format is called a *standard rating scale*. Exhibit 10.8 shows a typical rating scale with adjectives as anchors ("well above average" to "well below average").

EXHIBIT   10.7   Three Ranking Formats ———————————————————————

Straight Ranking Method

Rank	Employee's Name
Best	1. _____
Next Best	2. _____
Next Best	3. _____
etc.	

Alternation Ranking

Rank	Employee's Name
Best performer	1. _____
Next best	2. _____
Next best	3. _____
etc.	4. _____
Next worst	3. _____
Next worst	2. _____
Worst performer	1. _____

(alternate identifying best then worst, next best then next worst, etc.)

Paired Comparison Performance Ranking Method

	John	Pete	Sam	Tom	# times ranked higher
Bill	x	x	x	x	4
John		x	x	x	3
Pete			x	x	2
Sam				x	1

x indicates person in row ranked higher than person in column. Highest ranking goes to person with most "ranking wins."

| **EXHIBIT** | **10.8** | Rating Scales Using Absolute Standards |

Standard Rating Scale with Adjective Anchors

| **Communications skills:** | Written and oral ability to clearly and convincingly express thoughts, ideas, or facts in individual or group situations. |

| *Circle the number that best describes the level of employee performance* | 1
well above
average | 2
above
average | 3
average | 4
below
average | 5
well below
average |

---

behaviourally anchored rating scale (BARS)

performance rating scales using behavioural descriptions as anchors for different levels of performance on the scale

Behaviourally anchored rating scales (BARS) seem to be the most common *behavioural* format. BARS help to rate an employee's performance more completely. By anchoring scales with concrete behaviours, firms adopting a BARS format hope to make evaluations less subjective. When raters try to decide on a rating, they have a common definition (in the form of a behavioural example) for each of the performance levels. Exhibit 10.9 illustrates a behaviourally anchored rating scale. In both the standard rating scale and BARS, overall performance is calculated as some weighted average (weighted by the importance the organization attaches to each dimension) of the ratings on all dimensions.

As a brief illustration, though, consider Exhibit 10.10. The employee evaluated in Exhibit 10.10 is rated slightly above average. An alternative method for obtaining the overall rating would be to allow the rater discretion not only in rating performance on the individual dimensions but also in assigning an overall evaluation. Then the weights (shown in the far right column of Exhibit 10.10) would not be used, and an overall evaluation would be based on a subjective and internal assessment by the rater.

In addition to adjectives and behaviours, *outcomes* also are used as a standard. The most common form is **management by objectives (MBO)**. As a first step, organization objectives are identified from the strategic plan of the company. Each successively lower level in the organizational hierarchy is charged with identifying work objectives that will support attainment of organizational goals. Exhibit 10.11 illustrates a common MBO objective. Notice that the emphasis is on outcomes achieved by employees. At the beginning of a performance review period, the employee and supervisor discuss performance objectives (column 1).[52] Months later, at the end of the review period, the two meet again to record results formally (of course, multiple informal discussions should have occurred before this time). Results are then compared to objectives, and a performance rating is then determined based on how well objectives were met. Exhibit 10.12 shows some of the common components of an MBO format and the percentage of experts who judge this component vital to a successful evaluation effort.

management by objectives (MBO)

performance rating method based on meeting objectives set at the beginning of the performance review period

Evaluating Performance Evaluation Formats   Evaluation formats are generally evaluated against employee development potential (amount of feedback about performance that the format offers), administrative value, cost, and validity.[53] Different organizations will attach different weights to these criteria. These criteria are explained below.

- **Employee Development.** Does the method communicate the goals and objectives of the organization? Is feedback to employees a natural outgrowth of the evaluation format so that employee developmental needs are identified and can be attended to readily?
- **Administrative Value.** How easily can evaluation results be used for administrative decisions concerning wage increases, promotions, demotions, terminations, and transfers? Comparisons between individuals require some common denominator for comparison.

EXHIBIT 10.9 Standard Rating Scale with Behavioural Scale Anchors

Teamwork:		Ability to contribute to group performance, to draw out the best from others, to foster activities building group morale, even under high pressure situations.
Exceeds Standards	1	Seeks out or is regularly requested for group assignments. Groups this person works with inevitably have high performance and high morale. Employee makes strong personal contribution and is able to identify strengths of many different types of group members and foster their participation. Wards off personality conflicts by positive attitude and ability to mediate unhealthy conflicts, sometimes even before they arise. Will make special effort to insure credit for group performance is shared by all.
	2	Seen as a positive contributor in group assignments. Works well with all types of people and personalities, occasionally elevating group performance of others. Good ability to resolve unhealthy group conflicts that flare up. Will make special effort to insure strong performers receive credit due them.
Meets Standards	3	Seen as a positive personal contributor in group assignments. Works well with most types of people and personalities. Is never a source of unhealthy group conflict and will encourage the same behaviour in others.
	4	When group mission requires skill this person is strong in, employee seen as strong contributor. On other occasions will not hinder performance of others. Works well with most types of people and personalities and will not be the initiator of unhealthy group conflict. Will not participate in such conflict unless provoked on multiple occasions.
	5	Depending on the match of personal skill and group mission, this person will be seen as a positive contributor. Will not be a hindrance to performance of others and avoids unhealthy conflict unless provoked.
Does Not Meet Standards	6	Unlikely to be chosen for assignments requiring teamwork except on occasions when personal expertise is vital to group mission. Not responsive to group goals, but can be enticed to help when personal appeals are made. May not get along with other members and either withdraw or generate unhealthy conflict. Seeks personal recognition for team performance and/or may downplay efforts of others.
	7	Has reputation for noncontribution and for creating conflicts in groups. Cares little about group goals and is very hard to motivate towards and goal completion unless personal rewards are guaranteed. May undermine group performance to further personal aims. Known to seek personal recognition and/or downplay efforts of others.
Rating:		Documentation of Rating (optional except for 6 and 7):

Typically this is a numerical rating of performance. Evaluation forms that do not produce numerical ratings cause administrative headaches.

- **Cost.** Does the evaluation form require a long time to develop initially? Is it time-consuming for supervisors to use in rating their employees? Is it expensive to use? All these factors increase the format cost.
- **Validity.** By far the most research on formats in recent years has focused on reducing error and improving accuracy. Success in this pursuit would mean that decisions based on performance ratings (e.g., promotions, merit increases) could be made with increased confidence. Although a perfect format that eliminates rating errors and provides complete accuracy does not exist, BARS appears to be the strongest format among those commonly used at the present time.[54]

EXHIBIT 10.10 An Example of Employee Appraisal

Employee: Kelsey T. Mahoney
Job Title: Supervisor, Shipping and Receiving

Performance Dimension	Dimension Rating					Dimension Weight	Rating × Weight
	Well Below Average 1	Below Average 2	Average 3	Above Average 4	Well Above Average 5		
Leadership Ability				X		0.2	0.8
Job Knowledge					X	0.1	0.5
Work Output				X		0.3	1.2
Attendance			X			0.2	0.6
Initiative			X			0.2	0.6

Sum of Rating 3 Weight = 3.7
Overall Rating = 3.7

Exhibit 10.13 provides a report card on the four most common rating formats relative to the criteria just discussed. Which of these appraisal formats is the best? Unfortunately, the answer is a murky "it depends," in large part on the type of tasks being performed.

Strategy Two: Select the Right Raters

A second way that firms have tried to improve the accuracy of performance ratings is to focus on who might conduct the ratings and which of these sources is most likely to be accurate. To lessen the impact of one reviewer and to increase participation in the process, a method known as **360-degree feedback** has grown more popular in recent years. Generally, this system is used in conjunction with supervisory reviews.[55] This method assesses employee performance from five points of view: supervisor, peer, self, customer, and subordinate. Let's take a closer look at the role and benefit of each of these raters.

360-degree feedback
performance appraisal method including feedback from up to five sources: supervisor, peers, self, customers, and subordinates

Supervisors as Raters   Some estimates indicate that more than 80 percent of the input into performance ratings comes from supervisors.[56] Supervisors are knowledgeable about the job and the dimensions to be rated. Also, supervisors frequently have considerable prior experience in

EXHIBIT 10.11 Example of MBO Objective for Communications Skill

1. Performance objective	2. Results
By July 1 of this year, Asad will complete a report summarizing employee reactions to the new performance appraisal system. An oral presentation will be prepared and delivered to all non-exempt employees in groups of 15–20. All oral presentations will be completed by August 31, and reactions of employees to this presentation will average at least 3.0 on a 5-point scale.	Written report completed by July 1. All but one oral presentation completed by August 31. Last report not completed until September 15 because of unavoidable conflicts in vacation schedules. Average rating of employees (reaction to oral presentation) was 3.4, exceeding minimum expectations.

EXHIBIT | **10.12** | Example of MBO Objective for Communications Skill

	Total Number of Responses*	Percentage of Authorities in Agreement
1. Goals and objectives should be specific.	37	97%
2. Goals and objectives should be defined in terms of measurable results.	37	97
3. Individual goals should be linked to overall organization goals.	37	97
4. Objectives should be reviewed "periodically."	31	82
5. The time period for goal accomplishment should be specified.	27	71
6. Wherever possible, the indicator of the results should be quantifiable; otherwise, it should be at least verifiable.	26	68
7. Objectives should be flexible; changed as conditions warrant.	26	68
8. Objectives should include a plan of action for accomplishing the results.	21	55
9. Objectives should be assigned priorities of weights.	19	50

*In this table the total number of responses actually represents the total number of authorities responding; thus, percentages also represent the percentage of authorities in agreement with the statements made.
Source: Mark L. McConkie, "A Clarification of the Goal Setting and Appraisal Process in MBO," *Academy of Management Review* 4, no. 1 (1979), pp. 29–40. © 1979, Academy of Management Review.

rating employees, thus giving them some pretty firm ideas about what level of performance is required for any given level of performance rating.[57] Supervisor ratings also tend to be more reliable than those from other sources.[58] On the negative side, though, supervisors are particularly prone to halo and leniency errors.[59]

Peers as Raters   One of the major strengths of using peers as raters is that they work more closely with the ratee and probably have an undistorted perspective of typical performance. Balanced against this positive are at least two powerful negatives. First, peers may have little or no experience in conducting appraisals, leading to rather mixed evidence about the reliability of this rating source. Second, in a situation in which teamwork is promoted, placing the burden of rating peers on co-workers either may create group tensions (in the case of low evaluations) or yield ratings second only to self-ratings in level of leniency.[60]

Self as Rater   Some organizations have experimented with self-ratings. Obviously self-ratings are done by someone who has the most complete knowledge about the ratee's performance. Unfortunately, though, self-ratings are generally more lenient and possibly more unreliable than ratings from other sources.[61] One compromise in the use of self-ratings is to use them for developmental rather than administrative purposes.

Customer as Rater   This is the era of the customer. The drive for quality means that more companies are recognizing the importance of customers. One logical outcome of this increased interest is ratings from customers. For example, Burger King surveys its customers, sets up toll-free numbers to get feedback, and hires mystery customers to order food and report back on the service and treatment they receive.

Subordinate as Rater   The notion of subordinates as raters is appealing because most employees want to be successful with the people who report to them. Research shows that subordinates prefer, not surprisingly, to give their feedback to managers anonymously. If their identity is known, subordinates give artificially inflated ratings of their supervisors.[62]

EXHIBIT 10.13   An Evaluation of Performance Evaluation Formats

	Employee Development Criterion	Administration Criterion	Research Criterion	HR Economic Criterion	Validity Criterion
Ranking	Poor—ranks typically based on overall performance, with little thought given to feedback on specific performance dimensions.	Poor—comparisons of ranks across work units to determine merit raises are meaningless. Other administrative actions similarly hindered.	Average—validation studies can be completed with rankings of performance.	Good—inexpensive source of performance data. Easy to develop and use in small organizations and in small units.	Average—good reliability but poor on rating errors, especially halo.
Standard Rating Scales	Average—general problem areas identified. Some information on extent of developmental need is available, but no feedback on necessary behaviours/outcomes.	Average—ratings valuable for merit increase decisions and others. Not easily defended if contested.	Average—validation studies can be completed, but level of measurement contamination unknown.	Good—inexpensive to develop and easy to use.	Average—content validity is suspect. Rating errors and reliability are average.
Behaviourally Anchored Rating Scales	Good—extent of problem and behavioural needs are identified.	Good—BARS good for making administrative decisions. Useful for legal defence because job relevant.	Good—validation studies can be completed and measurement problems on BARS less than many other criterion measures.	Average—expensive to develop but easy to use.	Good—high content validity. Some evidence of inter-rater reliability and reduced rating errors.
Management by Objectives	Excellent—extent of problem and outcome deficiencies are identified.	Poor—MBO not suited to merit income decisions. Level of completion and difficulty of objectives hard to compare between employees.	Poor—nonstandard objectives across employees and no overall measures of performance make validity studies difficult.	Poor—expensive to develop and time-consuming to use.	Excellent—high content validity. Low rating errors.

Strategy Three: How Raters Process Information

A third way to improve job performance ratings is to understand how raters think. When performance is observed and evaluated, other factors influence ratings besides an employee's performance.[63] For example, feelings, attitudes, and moods influence raters. Whether the rater is generally cheerful or grumpy could influence the employee's evaluation.[64]

Researchers continue to explore how raters process information about the performance of the people they rate. In general, it appears that the following kinds of processes occur. First, the rater observes behaviour of a ratee. Second, the rater encodes this behaviour as part of a total picture of the ratee. Third, the rater stores this information in memory, which is subject to both short- and long-term decay. Fourth, when it comes time to evaluate a ratee, the rater reviews the performance dimensions and retrieves stored observations/impressions to determine their relevance to the performance dimensions. Finally, the information is reconsidered and integrated with other available information as the rater decides on the final ratings.[65] This process can produce information errors quite unintentionally, and they can occur at any stage.

Errors in the Rating Process   Ideally raters should notice only performance-related factors when they observe employee behaviour. Unless a behaviour affects performance, it should not influence performance ratings. Fortunately, studies show that performance actually does play an important role, perhaps the major role, in determining how a supervisor rates a subordinate.[66] On the negative side, though, performance-irrelevant factors appear to influence ratings, and they can cause errors in the evaluation process.[67]

Errors in Observation (Attention)   Generally, researchers have varied three types of input information to see what raters pay attention to when they are collecting information for performance appraisals. First, it appears that raters are influenced by general appearance characteristics of the ratees.[68] In general, it seems that if supervisors see ratees as similar to themselves, there is a positive influence on performance ratings, independent of actual performance.[69]

Researchers also look at change in performance over time to see if this influences performance ratings. Both the pattern of performance (performance gets better vs. worse over time) and the variability of performance (consistent vs. erratic) influence performance ratings, even when the overall level of performance is controlled.[70]

Errors in Storage and Recall   Research suggests that raters store information in the form of traits.[71] More importantly, people also tend to recall information in the form of trait categories, such as laziness. Specific instructions to recall information about the ratee, as for a performance review, elicit the trait—lazy. The entire rating process, then, may be heavily influenced by the trait categories the rater adopts, regardless of their accuracy. Errors in storage and recall also appear to arise from memory decay. Some research suggests that memory decay can be avoided if raters keep a diary and record information about employee performance as it occurs.[72]

Errors in the Actual Evaluation   The context of the actual evaluation process also can influence evaluations.[73] For example, performance appraisals sometimes serve a political end. Supervisors have been known to deflate performance to send a signal to an employee: You're not wanted here.[74] Supervisors also tend to weigh negative attributes more heavily than positive attributes; employees are likely to receive a much lower score if they perform poorly than they are to receive a proportionally higher score if they perform well.[75]

If the purpose of evaluation is to divide up a fixed pot of merit increases, ratings also tend to be less accurate. Supervisors who know that ratings will be used to determine merit increases are less likely to differentiate among subordinates than when the ratings will be used for other purposes.[76] Being required to provide feedback to subordinates about their ratings also yields less accuracy than a secrecy policy.[77] However, when raters must justify their scoring of subordinates in writing, the rating is more accurate.[78]

Strategy Four: Training Raters to Rate More Accurately

Most research indicates that rater training is an effective method for reducing appraisal errors.[79] Rater-training programs can be divided into three distinct categories:[80] (1) Rater-error training, in which the goal is to reduce psychometric errors (e.g., leniency, severity, central tendency, halo) by familiarizing raters with their existence; (2) performance dimension training, which exposes supervisors to the performance dimensions to be used in rating; and (3) performance-standard training, which provides raters with a standard of comparison or frame of reference for making appraisals.

The greatest success has come from efforts to reduce halo errors and improve accuracy. Leniency errors are the most difficult form of error to eliminate because giving inflated ratings avoids complaints and, possibly, reduced employee morale.

■ PUTTING IT ALL TOGETHER: THE PERFORMANCE EVALUATION PROCESS

There are several key elements of the total process, from day one, that make for a good outcome in the appraisal process.[81] First, performance dimensions should be relevant to the strategic plan of the company. If an employee doesn't know what is expected of him or her, how can he or she possibly perform well?[82] Second, it is important to involve employees in every stage of developing performance dimensions and building scales to measure how well they perform on these dimensions. Third, raters need to be trained in use of the appraisal system and all employees need to understand how the system operates and what it will be used for. Fourth, raters must be motivated to rate accurately. Fifth, raters should maintain a diary of employee performance, both as documentation and to jog the memory.[83] Sixth, raters should attempt a performance diagnosis to determine in advance whether performance problems arise because of motivation, skill deficiency, or external environmental constraints.[84] Lastly, the actual appraisal process should provide:

1. A clear sense of direction.
2. An opportunity for employees to participate in setting the goals and standards for performance.
3. Prompt, honest, and meaningful feedback.
4. Immediate and sincere reinforcement.
5. Coaching and suggestions for improving future performance.
6. Fair and respectful treatment.
7. An opportunity for employees to understand and influence decisions that affect them.

Only when the performance evaluation system is working satisfactorily can attention be focused on designing a pay-for-performance plan.

■ DESIGNING A PAY-FOR-PERFORMANCE PLAN

As the pay model suggests, the effectiveness of reward systems is dependent on three things: efficiency, fairness, and legislative compliance.

Efficiency

Efficiency involves three general areas of concern—strategy, structure, and standards.

Strategy   Does the pay-for-performance plan support corporate objectives? For example, does the plan help to improve quality of service? The plan also should link well with HR strategy and objectives. If other elements of the total HR plan are geared to select, reinforce, and nurture risk-taking behaviour, then the compensation component must not reward the status quo.

The most difficult question is: How much of an increase makes a difference? What does it take to motivate an employee? Is 3 percent, the recent average pay increase, really enough to motivate higher performance? Although there are few hard data on this question, most experts agree that employees don't begin to notice incentive payouts unless they are at least 10 percent, with 15 to 20 percent more likely to evoke the desired response.[85]

Structure   Is the structure of the organization sufficiently decentralized to allow different operating units to create flexible variations on a general pay-for-performance plan? Different operating units may have different competencies and different competitive advantages. It is not advisable to have a rigid pay-for-performance system that detracts from these advantages, all in the name of consistency across divisions. For example, efforts by IBM to adapt performance reviews to the different needs of different units and the managers in them resulted in a very flexible system. In this new system, managers get a budget, some training on how to conduct reviews, and a philosophical mandate: Differentiate pay for stars relative to average performers, or risk losing stars. Managers are given a number of performance dimensions. Which dimensions are used for which employees is totally a personal decision. Indeed, managers who don't like reviews at all can input merit increases directly, anchored only by a brief explanation for the reason.[86]

Standards   Operationally, the key to designing a pay-for-performance plan rests in setting performance standards. Specifically, performance *objectives* must be specific, yet flexible. Can employees see that their behaviour influences the ability to achieve company objectives (called the "line-of-sight" issue in industry)? Do employees know what *measures* (individual appraisals, peer reviews of team performance, corporate financial measures, etc.) will be used to assess whether performance is sufficiently good to merit a payout? How far down the organization will *eligibility* for the plan extend? Companies such as PepsiCo believe all employees should be included. Others think only top management can see how their decisions affect the bottom line. Will the program *funding* come from extra revenue generated above and beyond some preset standard? If so, what happens in a bad year? Many employees become disillusioned when they feel they have worked harder, but economic conditions or poor management decisions conspire to cut or eliminate bonuses.

Fairness

The second design objective is to ensure that the plan is fair to employees. Two types of fairness are concerns for employees. The first type is fairness in the amount that is distributed to employees. This type of fairness is labelled **distributive justice**.[87] Perceptions of fairness here depend on the amount of compensation actually received relative to input (e.g., productivity) compared to some relevant standard. Notice that several of the components of this equity equation are frustratingly removed from the control of the typical supervisor or manager working with employees. A manager has little influence over the size of an employee's paycheque. This is influenced more by external market conditions, pay policy decisions of the organization, and the occupational choice made by the employee.

| **distributive justice** |
| perceived fairness of pay or other work outcomes received |

Managers do have somewhat more control, though, over the second type of fairness. Employees also are concerned about the fairness of procedures used to determine the amount of rewards they receive. Employees expect **procedural justice**. Evidence suggests that organizations that use fair procedures and supervisors who are viewed as fair in the means they use to allocate rewards are perceived as more trustworthy and command higher levels of commitment.[88] A key element in fairness is communication. Employees want to know in advance what is expected of them. They want the opportunity to provide input into these standards or expectations, too. And if performance is judged lacking relative to these standards, they want a mechanism for appeals. In a union environment, this is the grievance procedure. Something similar needs to be set up in a non-union environment.[89]

| **procedural justice** |
| perceived fairness of the procedures used to determine pay or other work outcomes |

Legislative Compliance

Finally, the pay-for-performance plan must comply with existing laws in order to maintain and enhance the reputation of the firm. Think about the companies that visit a university campus. Some of them students naturally gravitate to—the interview schedule fills very quickly indeed. Why? Because of reputation. The reward value of a good reputation tends to be undervalued. To guard this reputation, it is important to be sure to comply with compensation laws.

■ LINKING PAY WITH SUBJECTIVELY APPRAISED PERFORMANCE

Think, for a moment, about what it really means to give employees merit performance increases. Manuel Rojas makes $40,000 per year. He gets a merit increase of 3 percent, the approximate average increase over the past few years. Manuel's take-home pay increase (adjusted for taxes) is a measly $16 per week more than he used to make. Consider Fatima Khan, who is a better performer than Manuel, and receives a 6 percent merit increase. Should she be thrilled by this pay-for-performance differential and be motivated to continue as a high achiever? Probably not. After taxes, her paycheque (assuming a base salary similar to Manuel's) is only $15 dollars per week more than Manuel's.

The central issue involving merit pay is that organizations frequently grant increases that are not designed or communicated to be related to performance. Perhaps the biggest reason for this is that many companies view raises not as motivational tools to shape behaviour, but as budgetary line items to control costs.[90] Frequently, this results in pay increase guidelines with little motivational impact.[91]

One type of pay increase guideline with low motivation potential provides equal increases to all employees regardless of performance, e.g., across-the-board increases and cost-of-living increases. These are typically found in unionized firms. A second form of guideline comes somewhat closer to tying pay to performance. Seniority increases tie pay increases to a preset progression pattern based on seniority. To the extent that performance improves with time on the job, this method has the rudiments of paying for performance.

By far the most prevalent form of pay guideline is one intended to link pay and performance.[92] Of course, the first problem is: What is the measure of performance? If the measure is objective, the ability to link pay to performance is a bit easier. But the measures are often subjective. One set of subjective measures, as discussed in Chapter 6, involves the competencies that people possess or acquire. Increasingly, companies assert that corporate performance depends on having employees who possess key competencies, and merit increases may be linked to employee ability and willingness to demonstrate key competencies.

In practice, tying pay to performance requires three things. First, some definition of performance; second, some continuum that describes different levels from low to high on the performance measure; and third, decisions regarding how much of a merit increase will be given for different levels of performance. Decisions about these three questions lead to some form of merit pay guide. In its simplest form, a guideline specifies pay increases permissible for different levels of performance (see Exhibit 10.14).

A more complex guideline ties pay not only to performance but also to position in the pay range. Exhibit 10.15 illustrates such a system for a food market firm. The percentages in the cells of Exhibit 10.15 are changed yearly to reflect changing economic conditions. Despite these changes, though, two characteristics remain constant. First, as would be expected in a pay-for-performance system, lower performance is tied to lower pay increases. In fact, in many organizations the poorest performers receive no merit increases. The second relationship is that pay increases at a decreasing rate as employees move through a pay range. For the same level of performance, employees low in the pay range will receive higher percentage increases than employees who have progressed farther through the range. In part, this design forestalls the time when employees reach the salary maximum and have salaries frozen. However, it is also a cost-control mechanism tied to budgeting procedures, as discussed in Chapter 13.

Performance- and Position-Based Guidelines

Given a salary increase matrix, merit increases are relatively easy to determine. As Exhibit 10.15 indicates, an employee at the top of his pay grade who receives a "competent" rating would receive a 4 percent increase in base salary. A new trainee starting out below the minimum of a pay grade would receive a 10 percent increase for a "superior" performance rating.

Designing Merit Guidelines

Designing merit guidelines involves answering four questions. First, what should the poorest performer be paid as an increase? Notice that this figure is seldom negative. Wage increases are, unfortunately, considered an entitlement. Wage cuts tied to poor performance are very rare. Most organizations, though, are willing to give no increases to very poor performers.

The second question involves average performers. How much should they be paid as an increase? Most organizations try to ensure that average performers are kept whole (wages will still have the same purchasing power) relative to the cost of living. This dictates that the midpoint of the merit guidelines equal the percentage change in the local or national consumer price index (CPI). Following this guideline, the 6 percent increase for an average performer in the second quartile of Exhibit 10.15 would reflect the change in CPI for that area. In a year with lower inflation, all the percentages in the matrix probably would be lower.

EXHIBIT 10.14 Performance-Based Guideline

	1	2	3	4	5
Performance Level	Very Outstanding	Satisfactory	Marginally Satisfactory	Unsatisfactory	Unsatisfactory
Merit Increase	6–8%	5–7%	4–6%	2–4%	0 %

EXHIBIT 10.15 Performance Rating Salary Increase Matrix

Position in Range	Unsatisfactory	Needs Improvement	Competent	Commendable	Superior
Fourth quartile	0%	0%	4%	5%	6%
Third quartile	0	0	5	6	7
Second quartile	0	0	6	7	8
First quartile	0	2	7	8	9
Below minimum of range	0	3	8	9	10

Third, how much should the top performers be paid? In part, budgetary considerations answer this question. But there is also growing evidence that employees do not agree on the size of increases that they consider meaningful. Continuation of this research may help determine the approximate size of increases needed to make a difference in employee performance.

Finally, matrices can differ in the size of the differential between different levels of performance. Exhibit 10.15 basically rewards successive levels of performance with 1 percent increases (at least in the portion of the matrix in which any increase is granted). A larger jump between levels would signal a stronger commitment to recognizing performance with higher pay increases. Most companies balance this, though, against cost considerations. Larger differentials cost more. When money is tight this option is less attractive.

■ PROMOTIONAL INCREASES AS A PAY-FOR-PERFORMANCE TOOL

It must be kept in mind that firms have methods of rewarding good performance other than raises. One of the most effective is a promotion accompanied by a salary increase, generally reported as being in the 8 to 12 percent range. This method of linking pay to performance has at least two characteristics that distinguish it from traditional annual merit pay increases. First, the size of the increment is approximately double a normal merit increase. A clearer message is sent to employees, both in the form of money and promotion, that good performance is valued and tangibly rewarded. Second, promotion increases represent, in a sense, a reward to employees for commitment and exemplary performance over a sustained period of time. Promotions generally are not annual events. They complement annual merit rewards by showing employees that there are benefits to both single-year productivity and to the continuation of such desirable behaviour.

CONCLUSION

Employee performance depends upon some blend of skill, knowledge, and motivation. Absent any of these three ingredients, performance is likely to be sub-optimal. Rewards must help organizations attract and retain employees, make high performance an attractive option for employees, encourage employees to build new skills, and foster commitment to the organization. There are a wide variety of different things that can serve as rewards to motivate employees.

The process of appraising employee performance can be both time-consuming and stressful. Development of sound appraisal systems requires an understanding of organizational objectives balanced against the relative merits of each type of appraisal system. For example, despite its inherent weaknesses, an appraisal system based on ranking of employee performance may be appropriate in small organizations which, for a variety of reasons, choose not to tie pay to performance; a sophisticated MBO or BARS appraisal system may not be appropriate for such a company.

Training supervisors effectively to appraise performance requires an understanding of organizational objectives. Relatively little is known about the ways raters process information and evaluate employee performance. However, a thorough understanding of organizational objectives combined with knowledge of common errors in evaluation can make a significant difference in the quality of appraisals.

Designing a pay-for-performance plan involves (1) efficiency in supporting corporate objectives, being sufficiently flexible to adapt to decentralized organizations, and setting clear standards regarding objectives, measures, eligibility, and funding; (2) equity/fairness, including distributive justice and procedural justice; and (3) legislative compliance. Merit guidelines, often performance- and position-based, are then designed to link pay to performance appraisal. Promotional increases are another form of pay-for-performance.

CHAPTER SUMMARY

1. The three factors on which employee performance depends are: (1) skill and ability to perform the task; (2) knowledge of facts, rules, principles, and procedures; and (3) motivation to perform.
2. Content theories focus on human needs that influence behaviour. Motivation theories that focus on the nature of the exchange look at the cognitive processes used to assess a situation and choose behaviour that yields the most satisfactory exchange. Goal-setting theory focuses on desired behaviour.
3. Compensation motivates behaviour because it affects decisions about whether to join a firm, to stay or leave, to agree to develop job skills, and to perform better.
4. Common errors in the performance appraisal process include the halo error (overall high rating due to one characteristic), the negative halo error (overall low rating due to one characteristic), first-impression error (rating based only on first impression), recency error (rating based only on most recent impression), leniency error, strictness error, central tendency error (rating all employees as average), similar-to-me error (high ratings for individuals similar to the rater), and spillover error (low ratings related to poor performance in a prior rating period).
5. Three strategies to better understand and measure job performance are: (1) improving the appraisal format, (2) selecting the right raters, and (3) understanding why raters make mistakes.
6. The key elements of an effective performance appraisal process are: (1) a sound basis for establishing performance dimensions, (2) involving employees in developing performance dimensions and building measurement scales, (3) ensuring that raters are trained and motivated to rate accurately, (4) ensuring that raters maintain a diary of employee performance, (5) having raters attempt a performance diagnosis to identify solutions for performance problems, and (6) following established guidelines for the actual appraisal process between the supervisor and the employee.
7. Three factors that determine the effectiveness of a pay-for-performance plan are: (1) efficiency in supporting corporate objectives, (2) fairness, and (3) legal compliance.

KEY TERMS

REVIEW QUESTIONS

1. If you wanted workers to perceive their compensation package as secure, which components would you include and which would you avoid?
2. How does procedural justice differ from distributive justice? Defend the position that supervisors have considerable control over procedural justice in their departments, but little control over distributive justice. How might you use the principle of procedural justice to avoid having an employee quit because she believes her boss gave her an unfair evaluation?
3. Shaw Corporation manufactures specialty equipment for the auto industry (e.g., seat frames). One job involves operation of machines that form heat-treated metal into various seat shapes. The job is fairly low-level and routine. Without any further information, which of the five types of appraisal formats do you think would be most appropriate for this job? Justify your answer.
4. Employees in your department have formed semi-autonomous work teams (they determine their own production schedule and individual work assignments). Individual performance is assessed using four performance dimensions: quantity of work, quality of work, interpersonal skills, and teamwork. Should the supervisor have a role in the rating process? What role, if any, should other members of the work team have in the assessment process?

EXPERIENTIAL EXERCISES

1. Roycroft Industries makes DVD cases that are particularly well received on the international market. Because of currency fluctuations, the profits Roycroft generates vary widely from year to year. Jim McVeigh, who works for Roycroft, is in charge of a large product development group in which the emphasis is on flexible performance, creativity, and "doing whatever it takes to get the job done." What kind of reward system would you recommend for this group of employees? In particular, should there be a large incentive component? Should rewards focus mostly on money, or should Roycroft work hard to incorporate the other 12 rewards noted in this chapter?

2. Think about the last group project you worked on. Describe that project and identify three performance criteria you think would be appropriate for evaluating the team members. Should each team member rate each other team member on all these dimensions? Should the team member ratings be used for feedback only or for feedback as well as for part of the overall grade (assuming the instructor agrees)? Should the instructor rate each team member on performance (all three criteria) in the group assignment? How are these questions relevant to setting up a 360-degree performance review?

WEB EXERCISE

360-Degree Performance Appraisal Online

Several Web-based products have been developed in order to reduce the administrative burden associated with 360-degree performance appraisal. Go to The Learning Curve site at www.thelearningcurve.co.uk and take the guided tour (or go to its subsidiary www.click-360.com). Next, go to the Halogen Software site at www.halogensoftware.com and under "Products," select Halogen e-360 and take the online tour. Compare and contrast these two 360-degree appraisal products. What are the strengths and weaknesses of each? Which would you select for employee development purposes? Why? Would you select one of these products for performance appraisal purposes? If so, which one? Explain.

CASE

Burger Boy

This is a true case. Jerry Newman (second author of this book) spent 14 months working in 7 fast-food restaurants (two McDonald's, two Burger Kings, one each of Wendy's, Arby's, and Krystal (a southern U.S. chain). I write about my experiences in the book *My Secret Life on the McJob* (McGraw-Hill, 2007). This is a description of events in one store . . . labelled here Burger Boy.

Person	Job Title	Base Salary	Overtime Eligibility	Avg Hrs/Wk
Otis	Assistant Store Manager	34k	No	55
Leon	Shift Supervisor	23k	Yes	55
Marge	Crew Member (fries)	$6.25/hr	Yes	30
Me	Cook	$6.50/hr	Yes	20
Chuck	Drive-thru Window	$7.00/hr	Yes	30
Lucy	Sandwich Assembler	$7.00/hr	Yes	35

It's a hot Friday in Florida, and lunch rush is just beginning. Chuck is working the pay window and is beginning to grouse about the low staffing for what is traditionally the busiest day of the week. "Where the heck is LaVerne," he yells to no one. Chuck has only worked here for six weeks, but has prior experience at another Burger Boy. Marge, typically working the fries station (the easiest job at this Burger Boy), has been pressed into service on the front drive-thru window because two of ten scheduled workers have called in sick. She can handle the job when business is slow, but she clearly is getting flustered as more cars enter the drive-thru line. I'm cooking, my third day on the job, but my first one alone. I've worked the grill for 10 years as a volunteer at Aunt Rosie's Womens Fastpitch Softball Tournament, but nothing prepared me for the volume of business we will do today. By 11:30 I've got the grill full of burgers. Lucy is going full speed trying to keep up with sandwich assembly and wrapping. She's the best assembler the place has, and would be a supervisor if she could just keep from self-destructing. Yesterday she lit a can of vegetable spray with a lighter and danced around the floor, an arc of flame shooting out from the can. She thinks this is funny. Everyone else thinks she's nuts. But she's rumoured to be a friend of the manager, Nancy, so everyone keeps quiet.

"Marge, you've got to get moving girl. The line's getting longer. Move girl, move," shouts Otis, unfazed by the fact that Marge really isn't good enough to work the window, and clearly is showing signs of heavy stress. "I'll help her," chimes in Chuck. "I can work the pay window, then run up front to help Marge when she gets way behind." Otis says nothing and goes back to the office where he begins to count the morning receipts for the breakfast rush.

My job as cook also includes cooking baked potatoes in the oven and cooking chicken in the pressure cooker, so I have little time to do anything besides stay on top of my job. Finally, at noon, in comes Leon. He will replace Otis at three, but for now he is a sorely needed pair of hands on the second sandwich assembly board. Leon looks over at me and shouts above the din, "Good job, Jerry. Keeping up with Friday rush on your third cooking day. Good job." That's the first compliment I've received in the two weeks I've worked here, so I unexpectedly smile at the recognition. By 12:30 we're clearly all frazzled. Even with Chuck's help, Marge falls farther behind. She is now making mistakes on orders in efforts to get food out the drive-thru window quickly. Otis comes barreling up front from the office and shouts for everyone to hear: "We're averaging 3:05 on drive time. Someone's in trouble if we don't get a move on." He says this while staring directly at Marge. Everyone knows that drive times (the amount of time from an order being placed until the customer receives it) should be about 2:30 (two minutes, thirty seconds). In my head I do some mental math. The normal staffing for a Friday is 13 people (including management). Because of absenteeism we're working with eight, including Otis and Leon. By noon Marge is crying, but she stays at it. And finally things begin to slow at 1 p.m. We know rush is officially over when Lucy tells Leon she's "going to the can." This starts a string of requests for rest breaks that are interrupted by Otis, "All right, for God's sake. Here's the order of breaks." He points to people in turn, with me being next to last, and Marge going last. After Lucy, Chuck is second, and the others fill in the gap ahead of me. When my turn finally comes I resolve to break quickly, taking only 6 minutes instead of the allotted 10. When I return Otis sneers at me and chides, "What was that, about a half hour?" I snap, I'm angry, and let him know it. "If I could tell time, would I be working fast food?" Now I realize I've done the unforgivable, sassing my boss. But I'm upset, and I don't care. My only care is I've just claimed fast food is work for dummies, and I absolutely don't believe this. But as I said, I was mad. Otis looks me over, staring at my face, and finally decides to let out a huge bellow, "You're OK, Newman. Good line!"

It's now 2:10 and Marge has told Otis twice that she has to leave. Her agreement with the store manager at the time of hire was that she would leave no later than 2:30 every day. Her daughter gets off the school bus at 2:45, and she must meet her at that time. Otis ignores her first request, and is nowhere to be seen when, at 2:25, Marge looks around frantically and pleads to no one in particular, "What should I do? I have to leave." I look at her and declare, "Go. I will tell Otis when he comes out again." Marge leaves. Ten minutes later we have a mini surge of customers. Leon yells, "Where the hell is Marge? That's it; she's out of here tomorrow. No more chances for her." When he's done ranting, I explain the details of Marge's plight. Angrily, Leon stomps back to the manager's office and confronts Otis. The yelling quickly reaches audible levels. Everyone in the store, customers included, hear what is quickly broadening into confrontations about other unresolved issues:

Leon: "I'm sick of coming in here and finding nothing stocked. Otis, it's your job to make sure the lunch shift (roughly 10 a.m–2 p.m.) stocks items in their spare time. It never happens and I'm sick of it. Now you tell me you're leaving and sticking me with a huge stocking job."

Otis: "I'm sick of your whining, Leon. I work 50 to 60 hours a week. I'm sick of working 10 to 12 hours a day for crappy wages. You want things stocked . . . you do it. I'm going home and try to forget this place."

With that Otis drops what he has in his hands, a printout of today's receipts so far, and walks out the door. Leon swears, picks up the spreadsheet, and storms back to the office. I finish my shift, and happily go home. No more Burger Boy for this burger boy.

1. What appear to be the problems at this Burger Boy?

2. How many of these problems could be explained by compensation issues?

3. How many other problems could be lessened with diligent use of rewards other than pay?

4. Are hours of work a reward? What might explain why I was happy to be working 20 hours per week, but Chuck was unhappy with 30 hours per week? How might schedules be used as a reward?

Visit the Online Learning Centre at

www.mcgrawhill.ca/olc/milkovich

PAY-FOR-PERFORMANCE PLANS

What's in a name? The answer is … confusion, at least when it comes to pay-for-performance/variable pay plans. Listen long enough and there will be talk of incentive plans, variable pay plans, compensation at risk, earnings at risk, gain-sharing, and others. Sometimes these names are used interchangeably. They shouldn't be. The major thing all these names have in common is a shift in thinking about compensation. Pay used to be viewed as primarily an entitlement—if a person went to work and did well enough to avoid being fired, he or she was entitled to the same size paycheque as everyone else.

WHAT IS A PAY-FOR-PERFORMANCE PLAN?

Pay-for-performance plans signal a movement away from entitlement—sometimes a very slow movement—toward pay that varies with some measure of individual or organizational performance. Of the pay components discussed in Chapter 10, only base pay and across-the-board increases don't fit the pay-for-performance category. Curiously, though, many of the surveys on pay-for-performance tend to omit the grandfather of all these plans, merit pay. Merit pay is still a pay-for-performance plan used for more than three-quarters of all managerial, clerical, and administrative employees.[1] Although more innovative pay-for-performance plans may get more and better press, there is still no widespread evidence of their adoption.

A wide variety of variable pay plans is in use today. What used to be primarily a compensation tool for top management is gradually becoming more prevalent for lower-level employees too. The *2009 Compensation Planning Outlook* report from the Conference Board of Canada reported that 92 percent of private sector employers and 54 percent of public sector employers have at least one variable pay plan.[2] Exhibit 11.1 shows the types of variable pay plans used by Canadian employers.

EXHIBIT **11.1** Variable Pay Plans in Canada ⎯⎯⎯⎯⎯⎯⎯⎯⎯⎯⎯⎯⎯⎯

(*n* = 320; percent; based on organizations with at least one annual variable pay plan in place)

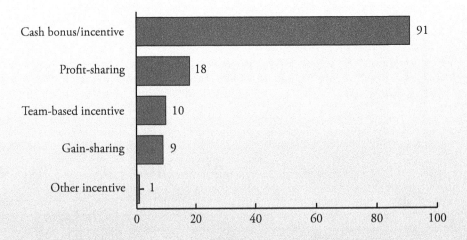

Note: Figures do not add to 100 because some respondents have more than one plan.
Source: Adapted from A. Cowan, *Compensation Planning Outlook 2009*. Ottawa ON: The Conference Board of Canada.

The strong interest in variable pay can be traced to two trends. First, increasing competition from foreign producers forces North American producers to cut costs and/or increase productivity. Well-designed variable pay plans have a proven track record of motivating better performance and helping cut costs. Second, today's fast-paced business environment means that workers must be willing to adjust what they do and how they do it. There are new technologies, new work processes, new work relationships. All these require workers to adapt in ways and with a speed that is unparalleled. Failure to move quickly means market share goes to competitors. If this happens, workers face possible layoffs and terminations. To avoid this scenario, compensation experts are focusing on ways to design reward systems so that workers will be able and willing to move quickly into new jobs, and new ways of performing old jobs. The ability and incentive to do this come partially from reward systems that more closely link worker interests with the objectives of the company.

As the evidence pointed out in Chapter 10, pay-for-performance plans—those that introduce variability into the level of pay received—seem to have a positive impact on performance when designed well. The .Net Worth box explains in more detail why it is necessary to qualify the statement that variable pay plans *can* be effective—provided they are designed well. The next sections will discuss issues in design and the impacts they can have.

SPECIFIC PAY-FOR-PERFORMANCE PLANS: SHORT TERM

Merit Pay

merit pay
increase in base pay
related to performance

A **merit pay** system links increases in base pay (called merit increases) to how highly employees are rated on a subjective performance evaluation. Chapter 10 covers performance evaluation, but as a simple illustration, consider the following merit pay setup.

.NET WORTH

Employee Understanding of Variable Pay Is Crucial to Plan Success

Employers are finding that creating and implementing a variable pay program may be harder than it seems. Two-thirds of the 411 employers who participated in a 2008 Hewitt Associates survey reported difficulty in designing pay programs that give employees a clear line of sight between their achievements and their rewards. In addition, 61 percent cited enabling managers to have effective pay conversations with their employees as a challenge.

"Successful variable pay programs have the ability to help employers drive business objectives, as well as keep employees focused on their goals in order to realize their earning potential," said Jeff Vathje, a senior compensation consultant in Hewitt's Calgary office. "The program must, of course, be designed appropriately and administered properly. However, it is also crucial that employees understand how the variable compensation plan works. Without a clear grasp of what they need to accomplish in order to help the organization succeed and be rewarded themselves, the program isn't going to work. Employers run the risk of losing key talent to competitors that appear to pay more when that happens."

Source: 2008–2009 Canada Salary Increase Survey. Toronto ON: Hewitt Associates.

	Well Above Average	Above Average	Average	Below Average	Well Below Average
Performance Rating	1	2	3	4	5
Merit Pay Increase	6%	5%	3%	0%	0%

At the end of a performance year, the employee is evaluated, usually by the direct supervisor. The performance rating, 1 to 5 in the above example, determines the size of the increase added into base pay. This last point is important. In effect, what the employee does this year in terms of performance is rewarded every year he or she remains with the employer. By building into base pay, the dollar amount, just like the Energizer bunny, keeps on going! With compounding, this can amount to tens of thousands of dollars over an employee's work career.[3]

Merit pay has its detractors, who argue that it is expensive and that it doesn't achieve the desired goal: improving employee and corporate performance.[4] In a thorough review of merit pay literature, though, researcher Robert Heneman concludes that merit pay does have a small, but significant, impact on performance.[5]

If merit pay is going to live up to its potential, it needs to be managed better.[6] This requires a complete overhaul of the way raises are allocated: improving the accuracy of performance ratings, allocating enough merit money to truly reward performance, and making sure the size of the merit increase differentiates across performance levels. To illustrate this latter point, consider the employee who works hard all year, earns a 6 percent increase as our guidelines above indicate, and compares himself with the average performer who coasts to a 3 percent increase. First, take out taxes on that extra 3 percent. Then spread it out over 52 paycheques. It's only a slight exaggeration to suggest that the extra money won't pay for a good cup of coffee. Unless the reward difference is larger for every increment in performance, many employees are going to say, "Why bother?"

Lump-Sum Bonuses

Lump-sum bonuses are used by most Canadian organizations.[7] Based on employee or company performance; employees receive an end-of-year bonus that does not build into base pay. Because employees must earn this increase every year, it is viewed less as an entitlement than is merit pay. As Exhibit 11.2 indicates, lump-sum bonuses also can be considerably less expensive than merit pay over the long run.

Notice how quickly base pay rises under a merit pay plan. After just five years, base pay is almost $14,000 higher than under a lump-sum bonus plan. It should be no surprise that cost-conscious firms report switching to lump-sum bonuses. It also should be no surprise that employees aren't particularly fond of lump-sum bonuses. After all, the intent of lump-sum bonuses is to cause shock waves in an entitlement culture. By giving lump-sum bonuses for several years, a company is essentially freezing base pay. Gradually this results in a repositioning relative to competitors. The message becomes loud and clear: "Don't expect to receive increases in base pay year after year—new rewards must be earned each year."

Individual Spot Awards

Technically, spot awards should fall under pay-for-performance plans. About 30 percent of all companies use spot awards.[8] Usually these payouts are awarded for exceptional performance, often on special projects or for performance that so exceeds expectations as to be deserving of an add-on bonus. The mechanics are simple. After the fact, someone in the organization alerts top management to the exceptional performance. If the company is large, there may be a formal mechanism for this recognition, and perhaps some guidelines on the size of the spot award (so named because it is supposed to be awarded on the spot). Smaller companies may be more casual about recognition and more subjective about deciding the size of the award. One creative user of spot awards is Mary Kay Cosmetics. Top saleswomen get pink Cadillacs, mink coats, and diamond rings.[9]

Individual Incentive Plans: Types

These plans differ from the above because they offer a promise of pay for some objective, pre-established level of performance. A standard is established against which worker performance is compared in order to determine the magnitude of the incentive pay. For individual incentive systems, this standard is compared to individual worker performance. From this basic foundation,

---

EXHIBIT 11.2   Relative Cost Comparisons

	Merit Pay	Lump-Sum Bonus
Base pay	$50,000	$50,000
Year 1 payout (5%)	2,500	2,500
New base pay	52,500	50,000
Extra cost total	2,500	2,500
Year 2 payout (5%)	$2,625 (.05 × 52,500)	$2,500 (.05 × 50,000)
New base pay	55,125 (52,500 + 2,625)	50,000
Extra cost total	5,125	5,000
After 5 years. . . .		
Year 5 payout	3,039	2,500
New base pay	63,814	50,000

a number of seemingly complex and divergent plans have evolved. Before discussing the more prevalent of these plans, however, it is important to note that each varies along two dimensions and can be classified into one of four cells, illustrated in Exhibit 11.3.

The first dimension on which incentive systems vary is in the method of rate determination. Plans either set up a rate based on units of production per time period or on time period per unit of production. On the surface, this distinction may appear trivial but, in fact, the deviations arise because tasks have different cycles of operation.[10] Short-cycle tasks, those that are completed in a relatively short period of time, typically have as a standard a designated number of units to be produced in a given time period. For long-cycle tasks, this would not be appropriate. It is entirely possible that only one task or some portion of it may be completed in a day. Consequently, for longer cycle tasks, the standard is typically set in terms of time required to complete one unit of production. Individual incentives are based on whether workers complete the task in the designated time period.

The second dimension on which individual incentive systems vary is the specified relationship between production level and wages. The first alternative is to tie wages to output on a one-to-one basis so that wages are some constant function of production. By contrast, some plans vary wages as a function of production level. For example, one common alternative is to provide higher dollar rates for production above the standard than for production below the standard.

Each of the plans discussed in this section has as a foundation a standard level of performance determined by some form of time study or job analysis completed by an industrial engineer or trained human resources administrator. The variations in these plans occur either in the way the standard is set or in the way wages are tied to output. As shown in Exhibit 11.3, there are four general categories of plans.

1. *Cell 1.* The most frequently implemented incentive system is a straight piecework system (Exhibit 11.4). Rate determination is based on units of production per time period, and wages vary directly as a function of production level. The major advantages of this type of system are that it is easily understood by workers and, perhaps consequently, more readily accepted than some of the other incentive systems.

2. *Cell 2.* Another relatively common plan, called a standard hour plan, sets standards based on time per unit and ties incentives directly to level of output. A common example can be found in any neighbourhood gasoline station or automobile repair shop. Assume that a car needs a new transmission and the estimate for labour costs is based on the mechanic's hourly rate of pay multiplied by a time estimate for job completion derived from a book listing average time estimates for a wide variety of jobs. If the mechanic receives $60 per hour and a transmission is listed as requiring four hours to remove and replace, the labour cost would

---

EXHIBIT 11.3 Individual Incentive Plans

Relationship between Production Level and Pay	Method of Rate Determination	
	Units of production per time period	*Time period per unit of production*
Pay constant function of production level	(1) Straight piecework plan.	(2) Standard hour plan.
Pay varies as function of production level	(3) Taylor differential piece rate system. Merrick multiple piece rate system.	(4) Halsey 50–50 method.

| **EXHIBIT** | **11.4** | Illustration of a Straight Piece Rate Plan |

Piece rate standard (e.g., determined from time study): 10 units/hour
Guaranteed minimum wage (if standard is not met): $5/hour
Incentive rate (for each unit over 10 units): $.50/unit

Examples of Worker Output	**Wage**
10 units or less	$5.00/hour (as guaranteed)
20 units	20 × $.50 = $10/hour
30 units	30 × $.50 = $15/hour

be $240. All this is determined in advance of any actual work. Of course, if the mechanic is highly experienced and fast, the job may be completed in considerably less time than indicated in the book. However, the job is still charged as if it took the quoted time to complete. Standard hour plans are more practical than a straight piecework plan for long-cycle operations and jobs that are non-repetitive and require numerous skills for completion.[11]

3. *Cell 3.* The two plans included in cell 3 provide for variable incentives as a function of units of production per time period. Both the Taylor plan and the Merrick plan provide different piece rates, depending on the level of production relative to the standard. The Taylor plan establishes two piecework rates. One rate goes into effect when a worker exceeds the published standard for a given time period. This rate is set higher than the regular wage incentive level. A second rate is established for production below standard, and this rate is lower than the regular wage.

The Merrick system operates in the same way, except that three piecework rates are set: (1) high—for production exceeding 100 percent of standard; (2) medium—for production between 83 and 100 percent of standard; and (3) low—for production less than 83 percent of standard. Exhibit 11.5 compares these two plans.

4. *Cell 4.* Plans included in cell 4 provide for variable incentives linked to a standard expressed as time period per unit of production, such as the Halsey 50–50 method. This plan features a shared split between worker and employer of any savings in direct cost. An allowed time for a task is determined via time study. The savings resulting from completion of a task in less than the standard time are allocated 50–50 (the most frequent division) between the worker and the company.

| **EXHIBIT** | **11.5** | Illustrations of the Taylor and Merrick Plans |

Piece rate standard: 10 units per hour
Standard wage: $5.00/hour
Piecework rate:

Output	Taylor Rate per Unit	Taylor Wage	Merrick Rate per Unit	Merrick Wage
7 units/hour	$.50/unit	$3.50	$.50/unit	$3.50
8 units/hour	$.50/unit	$4.00	$.50/unit	$4.00
9 units/hour	$.50/unit	$4.50	$.60/unit	$5.40
10 units/hour	$.50/unit	$5.00	$.60/unit	$6.00
11 units/hour	$.70/unit	$7.70	$.70/unit	$7.70
12 + units	Calculations at same rate as for 11 units.			

Individual Incentive Plans: Advantages and Disadvantages

A common problem with incentive plans is that employees and managers end up in conflict because the incentive system often focuses only on one small part of what it takes for the company to be successful.[12] Employees, being rational, do more of what the incentive system pays for. Exhibit 11.6 outlines some of the other problems, as well as advantages, of individual incentive plans.

Even though incentive systems are less popular than they used to be, there are still notable successes. Of course, most sales positions have some part of pay based on commissions, a form of individual incentives. Perhaps the longest running success with individual incentives, going back to before World War I, belongs to a company called Lincoln Electric in Cleveland, Ohio. The compensation package for factory jobs at Lincoln Electric is described in Exhibit 11.7. Notice how the different pieces fit together. This is not a case of an incentive plan operating in a vacuum. All the pieces of the compensation and reward package fit together. Lincoln Electric's success is so striking that it is the subject of many case analyses.[13]

Group Incentive Plans

group incentive plans

incentive pay for meeting or exceeding team performance standards

When the focus shifts away from individual incentive systems and moves to people working together, **group incentive plans** are used. The group might be a work team, a department, a division, or the whole company. The basic concept is still the same, though. A standard is established against which team performance is compared to determine the magnitude of the incentive pay. As Exhibit 11.8 suggests, the range of performance measures for different types of corporate objectives is indeed impressive.[14] Historically, financial measures have been the most widely used

---

EXHIBIT 11.6 Advantages and Disadvantages of Individualized Incentive Plans ————

Advantages

1. Substantial contribution to raise productivity, to lower production costs, and to increase earnings of workers.
2. Less direct supervision is required to maintain reasonable levels of output than under payment by time.
3. In most cases, systems of payment by results, if accompanied by improved organizational and work measurement, enable labour costs to be estimated more accurately than under payment by time. This helps costing and budgetary control.

Disadvantages

1. Greater conflict may emerge between employees seeking to maximize output and managers concerned about deteriorating quality levels.
2. Attempts to introduce new technology may be resisted by employees concerned about the impact on production standards.
3. Reduced willingness of employees to suggest new production methods for fear of subsequent increases in production standards.
4. Increased complaints that equipment is poorly maintained, hindering employee efforts to earn larger incentives.
5. Increased turnover among new employees discouraged by the unwillingness of experienced workers to cooperate in on-the-job training.
6. Elevated levels of mistrust between workers and management.

Source: T. Wilson, "Is It Time to Eliminate the Piece Rate Incentive System?" *Compensation and Benefits Review* 24, no. 2 (1992), pp. 43–49; and Pinhas Schwinger, *Wage Incentive Systems* (New York: Halsted, 1975).

| **EXHIBIT** | **11.7** | Lincoln Electric's Compensation System |

Description of Culture:	Reservoir of trust. Long history of employment stability even under severe economic downturns. Employees with 3+ years seniority are guaranteed (on one-year renewable basis) at least 75 percent full-time work for that year. In exchange, employees agree to flexible assignment across jobs.
Base Wages:	Market rate determined. Time study department sets piece rate so average worker can earn market rate.
Bonus (short term):	Board of directors sets year-end bonus pool as function of company performance. Employee's share in pool is function of semi-annual performance review (see below).
Incentive (long term):	Employees share in long-term company successes/failures in form of employee stock ownership plan (ESOP). Employees now own 28 percent of outstanding stock shares.
Performance Review:	Employees rated on four factors: 1) dependability, 2) quality, 3) output, 4) ideas and cooperation in comparison to others in department. To ensure against rating inflation, the average score in department cannot exceed 100.

| **EXHIBIT** | **11.8** | A Sampling of Performance Measures |

Customer-Focused Measures

Time-to-Market Measures
- On-time delivery
- Cycle time
- New product introductions

Customer Satisfaction Measures
- Market share
- Customer satisfaction
- Customer growth and retention
- Account penetration

Financially Focused Measures

Value Creation
- Revenue growth
- Resource yields
- Profit margins
- Economic value added

Shareholder Return
- Return on invested capital
- Return on sales/earnings
- Earnings per share
- Growth in profitability

Capability-Focused Measures

Human Resources Capabilities
- Employee satisfaction
- Turnover rates
- Total recruitment costs
- Rate of progress on developmental plans
- Promotability index
- Staffing mix/head-count ratio

Other Asset Capabilities
- Patents/copyrights/regulations
- Distribution systems
- Technological capabilities

Internal Process-Focused Measures

Resource Utilization
- Budget-to-actual expenses
- Cost-allocation ratios
- Reliability/rework
- Accuracy/error rates
- Safety rates

Change Effectiveness
- Program implementation
- Teamwork effectiveness
- Service/quality index

performance indicator for group incentive plans. Increasingly, though, top executives express concern that these measures do a better job of communicating performance to stock analysts than to managers trying to figure out how to improve operating effectiveness.[15]

One of the refinements designed in part to address this concern is called the *balanced scorecard*. Mount Sinai Hospital in Toronto, for example, looks at outcomes in the four key areas of efficiency and growth, safety, patient- and family-centred care, and learning and innovation, in addition to the traditional financial measures.[16] The balanced scorecard forces discussions about priorities among these different measures. But dissent is viewed positively. A picture begins to emerge about what is most important and what the necessary trade-offs are to achieve the different objectives. What evolves is a series of objectives with different weights in terms of importance. These objectives send clear signals to managers, and then to their employees, about what is important.

Comparing Group and Individual Incentive Plans

In this era of heightened concern about productivity, a frequent question is whether setting up incentive plans really boosts performance. As noted in Chapter 10, the answer is yes, although recent evidence suggests that firms high on business risk—those with uncertain outcomes—will have higher corporate performance if they do not have incentive plans.[17] As Exhibit 11.9 illustrates, it is necessary to decide whether a group incentive plan is a better choice than an individual plan. Factors such as the type of task, the organizational commitment to teams, and the type of work environment may preclude one or the other. When forced to answer the question anyway, experts agree that individual incentive plans have better potential, and probably better track records, in delivering higher productivity.

Group plans suffer from what is called the "free-rider" problem where at least one person doesn't carry his or her share of the load. Top-performing employees quickly grow disenchanted with having to carry free riders and leave. Recent research on free riders suggests that the problem can be lessened through use of good performance measurement techniques. Specifically, free riders have a harder time loafing when there are clear performance standards. Rather than being given instructions to "do your best," when asked to deliver specific levels of performance at a specific time, the poorer performers actually showed the most performance improvement.[18]

Problems can arise from at least five other causes.[19] First, one of the problems with group compensation is that teams come in many varieties. Thus it is hard to find one best type of incentive plan, and it is often necessary to look at different compensation approaches for different types of teams. A second problem with rewarding teams is called "the level problem." If teams are defined at a very broad level, much of the motivational impact of incentives can be lost. A member of a 1,000-person team is unlikely to be convinced that his or her extra effort will significantly affect the team's overall performance. Conversely, if teams get too small, other problems arise. Teams may hoard star performers, refusing to allow transfers even for the greater good of the company. Teams may be reluctant to take on new employees for fear that time lost to training will hurt the team—even when the added employees are essential to long-run success.[20]

The last three major problems with team compensation involve the three Cs: complexity, control, and communications. Some plans are simply too complex. The second C is control. Praxair, a worldwide provider of gases (including oxygen) extracted from the atmosphere, works hard to make sure all its team pay comes from performance measures under the control of the team. If Mother Nature ravages a construction site, causing delays and skyrocketing costs, workers aren't penalized with reduced team payouts. Such uncontrollable elements are factored into the process of setting performance standards. Indeed, experts assert that this ability to foretell sources of problems and adjust for them is a key element in building a team pay plan.[21] Key to the control issue is the whole question of fairness. Are the rewards fair, given the team's ability to produce results? The final C is communication. Team-based pay plans simply are not well communicated. Employees asked to explain their plans often flounder because more effort is devoted by the design team to the mechanics than to explaining the plan.

EXHIBIT **11.9** | Different Types of Variable Pay Plans: Advantages and Disadvantages

Plan Type	What It Is	Advantages	Disadvantages	Why?
Cash Profit Sharing	▪ Award based on organizational profitability ▪ Shares a percentage of profits (typically above a target level of profitability) ▪ Usually an annual payout ▪ Can be cash or deferred	▪ Simple, easily understood ▪ Low administrative costs	▪ Profit influenced by many factors beyond employee control ▪ May be viewed as an entitlement ▪ Limited motivational impact	▪ To educate employees about business operations ▪ To foster teamwork or "one-for-all" environment
Stock Ownership or Options	▪ Award of stock shares or options	▪ Option awards have minimal impact on the financial statements of the company at the time they are granted ▪ If properly communicated, can have powerful impact on employee behaviour ▪ Tax deferral to employee	▪ Indirect pay/performance link ▪ Many factors outside individual influence affect stock price ▪ Employees may be required to put up money to exercise grants	▪ To recruit top quality employees when organization has highly uncertain future (e.g., startups, high-tech, or biotech industries) ▪ To address employee retention concerns ▪ To focus employees on need to increase shareholder value
Productivity/Gain-Sharing	▪ Awards that share economic benefits of improved productivity, quality, or other measurable results ▪ Focus on group, plant, department, or division results ▪ Designed to capitalize on untapped knowledge of employees	▪ Clear performance–reward links ▪ Productivity and quality improvements ▪ Employee's knowledge of business increases ▪ Fosters teamwork, cooperation	▪ Can be administratively complicated ▪ Unintended effects, such as a drop-off in quality ▪ Management must "open the books" ▪ Payouts can occur even if company's financial performance is poor	▪ To support a major productivity/quality initiative (such as TQM or re-engineering) ▪ To foster teamwork environment ▪ To reward employees for improvements in activities that they control
Team/Group Incentives	▪ Awards determined based on team/group performance goals or objectives ▪ Payout can be more frequent than annual and can also extend beyond the life of the team ▪ Payout may be uniform for team/group members	▪ Reinforces teamwork and team identity/results ▪ Effective in stimulating ideas and problem-solving ▪ Minimizes distinctions between team members ▪ May better reflect how work is performed	▪ May be difficult to isolate impact of team ▪ Not all employees can be placed on a team ▪ Can be administratively complex ▪ May create team competition ▪ Difficult to set equitable targets for all teams	▪ To demonstrate an organizational commitment to teams ▪ To reinforce the need for employees to work together to achieve results

Gain-Sharing Plans

gain-sharing plan
group incentive plan where employees share in cost savings

Gain-sharing plans are a common type of group incentive plan, used by about 10 percent of Canadian employers.[22] Most employees feel that, realistically, there is little they alone can do to affect profits—that's something top management decisions influence more. So gain-sharing looks at cost components and identifies savings over which employees have more impact (e.g., reduced scrap, lower labour costs, reduced utility costs).

The following issues are key elements in designing a gain-sharing plan:

1. *Strength of reinforcement.* What role should base pay assume relative to incentive pay? Incentive pay tends to encourage only those behaviours that are rewarded.
2. *Productivity standards.* What standard will be used to calculate whether employees will receive an incentive payout? Almost all group incentive plans use a historical standard. A historical standard involves the choice of a prior year's performance to use for comparison with current performance. But which baseline year should be used? If too good (or too bad) a comparison year is used, the standard will be too hard (or too easy) to achieve, with obvious motivational and cost effects. One possible compromise is to use a moving average of several years (for example, the average for the past five years, with the five-year block changing by one year on an annual basis). It is also important that environmental influences on performance, those not controllable by plan participants, be factored out when identifying incentive levels.
3. *Sharing the gains—split between management and workers.* Part of the plan must address the relative share paid to management and workers of any profit or savings generated. This also includes discussion of whether an emergency reserve (gains withheld from distribution in case of future emergencies) will be established in advance of any sharing of profits.
4. *Scope of the formula.* Formulas can vary in the scope of inclusions for both the labour inputs in the numerator and productivity outcomes in the denominator.[23] Because organizations are complex and require more complex measures, performance measures have expanded beyond traditional financial measures to include retention of customers, customer satisfaction, delivery performance, safety, absenteeism, turnaround time, and number of suggestions submitted. Great care must be exercised with these alternative measures, though, to ensure that the behaviours reinforced actually affect the desired bottom-line goal.
5. *Perceived fairness of the formula.* One way to ensure that the plan is perceived as fair is to let employees vote on whether implementation should go forward. This and union participation in program design are two elements in plan success.[24]
6. *Ease of administration.* Sophisticated plans with involved calculations of profits or costs can become too complex for existing company information systems. Increased complexities also require more effective communications and higher levels of trust among participants.
7. *Production variability.* One of the major sources of problems in group incentive plans is failure to set targets properly. A good plan ensures that environmental influences on performance, not controllable by plan participants, should be factored out when identifying incentive levels. One alternative would be to set standards that are relative to industry performance. The obvious advantage of this strategy is that economic and other external factors hit all firms in the industry equally. If the company performs better, relatively, it means that employees are doing something to help achieve success.

The three primary types of gain-sharing plans, differentiated by their focus on either cost savings (the numerator of the equation) or some measure of revenue (the denominator of the equation), are noted below.

Scanlon Plan Scanlon plans are designed to lower labour costs without lowering the level of a firm's activity. Incentives are derived as a function of the ratio between labour costs and sales value of production (SVOP).[25] The SVOP includes sales revenue and the value of goods in inventory. To illustrate how these two figures are used to derive incentives under a Scanlon plan, consider Exhibit 11.10.

EXHIBIT 11.10 Examples of a Scanlon Plan

Data (base year)		
SVOP	=	$10,000,000
Total wage bill	=	4,000,000
Total wage bill ÷ SVOP	=	4,000,000 ÷ 10,000,000 = .40, or 40%

Operating Month (March)		
SVOP	=	$950,000
Allowable wage bill	=	.40 ($950,000) = $380,000
Actual wage bill (August)	=	$330,000
Savings	=	$50,000

$50,000 available for distribution as a bonus.

In practice, the $50,000 bonus in Exhibit 11.10 is not all distributed to the workforce. Rather, 25 percent is distributed to the company, 75 percent of the remainder is distributed as bonus, and 25 percent of the remainder is withheld and placed in an emergency fund to reimburse the company for any future months when a "negative bonus" is earned (i.e., when the actual wage bill is greater than the allowable wage bill). Any excess remaining in the emergency pool is distributed to workers at the end of the year.

Rucker Plan   The Rucker plan involves a somewhat more complex formula than a Scanlon plan for determining worker incentive bonuses. Essentially, a ratio is calculated that expresses the value of production required for each dollar of total wage bill. Consider the following illustration:[26]

1. Assume accounting records show the company expended $0.60 worth of electricity, materials, supplies, and so on, to produce $1.00 worth of product. The value added is $0.40 for each $1.00 of sales value. Assume also that 45 percent of the value added was attributable to labour; a productivity ratio (PR) can be allocated from the formula:
2. PR (labour) × 0.40 × 0.45 = 1.00. Solving yields PR = 5.56.
3. If the wage bill equals $100,000, the expected production value is the wage bill ($100,000) × PR (5.56) = $555,556.
4. If actual production value equals $650,000, then the savings (actual production value minus expected production value) is $94,444.
5. Because the labour contribution to value added is 45 percent, the bonus to the workforce should be 0.45 × $94,444 = $42,500.
6. The savings are distributed as incentive bonuses according to a formula similar to the Scanlon formula—75 percent of the bonus is distributed to workers immediately and 25 percent is kept as an emergency fund to cover poor months. Any excess in the emergency fund at the end of the year is then distributed to workers.

Implementation of the Scanlon/Rucker Plans   There are two major components vital to the implementation and success of a Rucker or Scanlon plan: (1) a productivity norm and (2) development of effective worker committees. Development of a productivity norm requires both effective measurement of base year data and acceptance by workers and management of this standard for calculating bonus incentives.

The second ingredient of Scanlon/Rucker plans is a series of worker committees (also known as productivity committees or bonus committees). The primary function of these committees is to evaluate employee and management suggestions for ways to improve productivity and/or cut costs. It is not uncommon for the suggestion rate to be above that found in companies with standard suggestion incentive plans.[27] This climate that the Scanlon/Rucker plans foster is probably the element most vital to success.

Improshare   Improshare (IMproved PROductivity through SHARing) is a gain-sharing plan that has proven easy to administer and to communicate.[28] First, a standard is developed that identifies the expected hours required to produce an acceptable level of output. This standard comes either from time and motion studies conducted by industrial engineers or from a base period measurement of the performance factor. Any savings arising from production of the agreed-upon output in fewer than the expected hours is shared by the firm and by the worker.[29] So, for example, if 100 workers can produce 50,000 units over 50 weeks, this translates into 200,000 hours (40 hours × 50 weeks) for 50,000 units, or 4 hours per unit. If we implement an Improshare plan, any gains resulting in less than 4 hours per unit are shared 50–50 between employees and management (wages times number of hours saved).[30]

One survey of 104 companies with an Improshare plan found a mean increase in productivity during the first year of 12.5 percent.[31] By the third year, the productivity gain rose to 22 percent. A significant portion of this productivity gain was traced to reduced defect rates and downtime (e.g., repair time).

Profit-Sharing Plans

profit-sharing plans
variable pay plans requiring a profit target to be met before any payouts occur

Profit-sharing plans are used by about 20 percent of Canadian organizations.[32] These plans require some profit target to be met before any payouts occur. Profit sharing continues to be used because the focus is on the measure that matters most to the most people: some index of profitability. When payoffs are linked to these measures, employees spend more time learning about financial measures and the business factors that influence them.

On the downside, most employees don't feel their jobs have a direct impact on profits. Furthermore, even if workers are able to improve operating efficiency, there is no guarantee that profits will automatically increase. Strength of the market, global competition, even the way we enter accounting information into the balance sheet all can affect profits and serve to disenchant workers.

The trend in recent variable pay design is to combine the best of gain-sharing and profit-sharing plans.[33] The organization specifies a funding formula for any variable payout that is linked to some profit measure. As experts say, the plan must be self-funding. Dollars going to workers are generated by additional profits gained from operational efficiency. Along with the financial incentive, employees feel they have a measure of control. For example, an airline might give an incentive for reductions in lost baggage, with the size of the payout dependent on hitting profit targets. Such a program combines the need for fiscal responsibility with the chance for workers to affect something they can control.

Earnings-at-Risk Plans

earnings-at-risk plan
incentive plan that includes reductions in base pay in unsuccessful years

In an incentive scheme that includes an **earnings-at-risk plan**, base pay is reduced if the company does poorly. For example, base pay could be reduced 15 percent across the board in year one. That 15 percent could be replaced with a 0.5 percent increase in base pay for every 1 percent increase in productivity beyond 70 percent of the prior year's productivity. This figure would leave workers whole (no decline in base pay) if they only matched the prior year's productivity. Each additional percentage of improvement in productivity could yield a 1.5 percent increase in base wages.

Clearly, at-risk plans shift some of the risk of doing business from the company to the employee. The company hedges against the devastating effects of a bad year by mortgaging some of the profits that would have accrued during a good year. Experience has produced mixed results. DuPont terminated its plan in the second year because of lacklustre performance and the expectation of no payout. At-risk plans appear to be met with decreases in satisfaction with both pay in general and with the process used to set pay.[34] It's clear that the long-term success of at-risk plans depends on employee acceptance.

One of the reasons for the separation of the United Auto Workers (UAW) in Canada from the international union in 1984 was the UAW's decision to enter into an earnings-at-risk plan with General Motors. The Canadian autoworkers rejected this approach to compensation and instead preferred a known, fixed-increment compensation package. The Canadian workers left the UAW and formed the Canadian Auto Workers (CAW) union because of this issue.

Group Incentive Plans: Advantages and Disadvantages

Clearly, group pay-for-performance plans are becoming more common, while the number of individual plans is stable or declining. In 2005, Statistics Canada reported that the number of workplaces offering individual incentives had declined to 24 percent and that the number offering group incentives had increased to 9 percent.[35] Why? A big part of the reason is the changing nature of work processes. Teams as the basic work unit are now the norm. The interdependence of jobs and the need for cooperation mean compensation must reinforce working together. Efforts to reinforce these group efforts with compensation generally have been successful (as discussed in Chapter 10). Exhibit 11.11 outlines some of the general positive and negative features of group pay-for-performance plans.[36]

◼ EXPLOSIVE INTEREST IN LONG-TERM INCENTIVE PLANS

Long-term incentives (LTIs) focus on performance beyond the one-year timeline used as the cutoff for short-term incentive plans. Recent explosive growth in long-term plans appears to be spurred in part by a desire to motivate longer-term value creation.[37] In fact, studies indicate that when top management has greater ownership (usually more stock), there is significantly more

---

EXHIBIT 11.11   Advantages and Disadvantages of Group Incentive Plans

Advantages

1. Positive impact on organization and individual performance of about 5–10 percent per year.
2. Easier to develop performance measures than for individual plans.
3. Signal that cooperation, both within and across groups, is a desired behaviour.
4. Teamwork meets with enthusiastic support from most employees.
5. May increase participation of employees in decision-making process.

Disadvantages

1. Line of sight may be lessened, i.e., employees may find it more difficult to see how their individual performance affects their incentive payouts.
2. May lead to increased turnover among top individual performers who are discouraged because they must share with lesser contributors.
3. Increases compensation risk to employees because of lower income stability. May influence some applicants to apply for jobs in firms where base pay is larger compensation component.

investment in research and development (an indicator of long-term value creation). Stock ownership also is likely to increase internal growth, rather than more rapid external diversification.[38]

Stock Options

stock options
the right to purchase stock at a specified (exercise) price for a fixed time period

Stock options provide an employee with the right to purchase stock at a specified (exercise) price for a fixed time period. They are the most common type of long-term incentive used in Canada.[39] The exercise price is usually close to the current stock price at the time options are awarded; when stock prices are rising, these options can be worth a lot, but in declining markets, there can be negative effects. If the options have exercise prices higher than the current market value, the options become worthless. Due to the market volatility, Canadian companies are increasingly adopting a range of long-term incentives to supplement stock option programs.[40]

Broad-Based Option Plans (BBOPs)

broad-based option plans (BBOPs)
stock options provided to employees at all levels

The latest trend in long-term incentives is **broad-based option plans (BBOPs)**, where stock options are granted to a wide variety of employees rather than just senior executives. The strength of BBOPs is their versatility. Depending on the way they are distributed to employees, they can either reinforce a strong emphasis on performance (performance culture) or inspire greater commitment and retention (ownership culture) of employees. For example, Starbucks has a stock grant program called Beanstock, and all employees who work at least 500 hours per year, up to the level of vice president, are eligible (broad-based participation). If company performance goals are reached, all employees receive equal stock options worth somewhere between 10 and 14 percent of their earnings. The options vest 20 percent each year, and the option expires 10 years after the grant date. This program exists to send a clear signal that all employees, especially the two-thirds who are part-timers, are business partners. This effort to create a culture of ownership is viewed as the primary reason Starbucks has turnover that is only a fraction of the usual high turnover in the retail industry.

Microsoft's program shares one common feature with Starbucks in that the stock option program is broad based. By rewarding all employees, Microsoft hopes to send a strong signal to all employees that reinforces its culture: Take reasoned risks that have long-run potential for contributing to the company. Microsoft's BBOP is targeted at all permanent employees. Unlike Starbucks' plan, though, the size of the stock option grant is linked to individual performance and estimated long-run contribution to the company. Starting 12 months after the stock grant date, 12.5 percent is vested every 6 months.

Employee Stock Ownership Plans (ESOPs)

employee stock ownership plan (ESOP)
plan offering employees the opportunity to purchase company stock, often partially or fully matched by employer-paid stock for the employee

Some companies believe that employees can be linked to the success or failure of a company in yet another way—through **employee stock ownership plans (ESOPs)**.[41] WestJet has one of Canada's most generous ESOP plans. Employees can contribute up to 20 percent of their salary to purchase WestJet shares and the company matches these contributions. Over 80 percent of employees participate. WestJet believes that the plan is largely responsible for employees thinking and acting like owners.[42]

Only 7 percent of Canadian workers participate in ESOP plans,[43] as these plans are not particularly effective incentives. First, the effects are generally long term. It is difficult to predict what makes stock prices rise—and this is the central ingredient in the reward component of ESOPs. So the performance measure is too complex to figure out how to control one's own destiny. But ESOPs do foster employee willingness to participate in the decision-making process.[44] And a company that takes advantage of that willingness (such as WestJet) can harness a considerable resource—the creative energy of its workforce.

In conclusion, pay-for-performance plans can work, but the design and effective administration of these plans is key to their success. Having a good idea is not enough. The good idea must be followed up by sound practices that recognize that rewards, if used properly, can shape employee behaviour.

PAY-FOR-PERFORMANCE FOR SPECIAL EMPLOYEE GROUPS

Open any newspaper to see that some jobs and some people are singled out for special compensation treatment in an organization. Why do professional sports players regularly make millions per year? Why does Frank Stronach (CEO of Magna International Corp.) regularly make over $10 million per year? Is the value of these jobs determined in the same way that compensation is determined for other jobs in a company? The answer is generally no. But why? To answer this question it is useful to work backwards. What jobs get special compensation treatment in a company? Are they basically the same kinds of jobs across companies? If they are the same kinds of jobs, are there any common characteristics the jobs share that would cause companies to devise special compensation packages?

Special treatment tends to focus on a few specific groups of employees that share two characteristics. First, special groups tend to be placed in positions that have built-in conflict, conflict that arises because different factions place incompatible demands on members of the group. And second, simply facing conflict is not sufficient; the way that this conflict is resolved has important consequences for the success of the company.

When both of these characteristics are present, distinctive compensation practices adopted to meet the needs of these special groups are often found. Exhibit 11.12 describes the nature of the conflicts faced by such special groups as supervisors, top management, boards of directors, scientists and engineers, salespeople, and contingent workers.

Compensation Strategy for Supervisors

Supervisors are caught between the demands of upper management in terms of production and the needs of employees in terms of rewards and reinforcements. The major challenge in compensating supervisors centres on equity. Some incentive must be provided to entice hourly employees to accept the challenges of being a supervisor. For many years, the strategy was to treat supervisors like lower-level managers. But in so doing, the existing job evaluation system sometimes left these supervisors making less money than the top paid employees they supervised, and this reality created little incentive to take on the extra work involved.

More recently, organizations have devised several strategies to attract workers to supervisory jobs. The most popular method is to key the base salary of supervisors to some amountexceeding the top paid subordinate in the unit (5 percent to 30 percent represents the typical size of the differential). Another method to maintain equitable differentials is simply to pay supervisors for scheduled overtime. The current trend in supervisory compensation centres on increased use of variable pay.

Compensation Strategy for Corporate Directors

A typical board of directors consists of 10 outside and 3 inside directors, each having a term averaging three years. Outside members now include unaffiliated business executives and major shareholders. Outside directors usually are paid higher compensation, probably because it takes a greater incentive to get them to participate. Direct compensation includes an annual retainer, attendance fees, and fees for participation on subcommittees.

In 2006, median cash compensation for Canadian corporate directors was $55,600.[45] Directors' compensation is rising because of the increased workloads and the exposure to financial, reputation, and personal risks as scrutiny of board decisions increases following the 2008

EXHIBIT 11.12 Conflicts Faced by Special Groups

Special Group	Type of Conflict Faced
Supervisors	Caught between upper management and employees. Must balance need to achieve organization's objectives with importance of helping employees satisfy personal needs. If unsuccessful, either corporate profit or employee morale suffers.
Top management	Stockholders want healthy return on investment. Government wants compliance with laws. Executive must decide between strategies that a) maximize short-run gains at the expense of long-term outcomes versus b) maximize long-term results but may involve lower returns in the short term.
Board of directors	Face possibility that disgruntled stockholders may sue over corporate strategies that don't pan out.
Professional employees	May be torn between goals, objectives, and ethical standards of their profession (e.g., should an engineer leak information about a product flaw, even though that information may hurt corporate profits?) and demands of an employer concerned more with the profit motive.
Salespeople	Often go for extended periods in the field with little supervision. Challenge is to stay motivated and continue making sales calls even in the face of limited contact or scrutiny from manager.
Contingent workers	Play an important "safety valve" role for companies. When demand is high, more are hired. When demand drops, these are the first workers downsized. Employment status is highly insecure and challenge is to find low cost ways to motivate.

market meltdown and subsequent recession. As well, companies are having difficulty finding board members with the required knowledge and technical expertise.[46]

In addition to cash compensation, there is an increasing emphasis on director rewards that link to corporate performance. Ninety percent of Canadian companies provide stock compensation to directors. The most common forms are restricted stock grants (prohibited from being sold or transferred for a certain period of time) and stock options. In 2007, the median value of restricted stock grants was $50,000 and the median value of the stock options was $22,500.[47]

Compensation Strategy for Executives

Jim Balsillie, co-CEO of Research in Motion, made $54,709,465 in total compensation in 2006. Mr. Balsillie's base salary was $561,032, his annual bonus was zero, and his stock option gains were $54,148,433.[48] Stock options play a big role in executive compensation!

Exhibit 11.13 shows total compensation for the top 10 executives in Canada in 2008. Notice that most highly paid executives reap the greatest rewards from long-term incentives, usually by exercising stock options. Many critics argue that this level of compensation for executives is excessive.[49] Are the critics right? One way to answer the question is to look at the different ways people say executive compensation is determined and ask, "Does this seem reasonable?"

Possible Explanations for CEO Compensation   One approach to explaining why executives receive such large sums of money involves social comparisons.[50] In this view, executive salaries bear a consistent relative relationship to the compensation of lower-level employees. When salaries of lower-level employees rise in response to market forces, top executive salaries also rise to

EXHIBIT 11.13	Compensation for Executives in Canada, 2008

Rank	Name	Company	Base Salary	Total
1	Thomas Glocer	Thomson Reuters Corp.	$1,598,223	$39,010,519
2	Ted Rogers	Rogers Communications Inc.	1,592,067	21,484,708
3	George Cope	BCE Inc.	959,327	19,551,345
4	William Doyle	Potash Corp. of Saskatchewan	1,164,072	18,150,052
5	Edward Sampson	Niko Resources Ltd.	608,000	14,084,992
6	Hunter Harrison	Canadian National Railway Co.	1,790,880	13,350,260
7	Dominic D'Alessandro	Manulife Financial Corp.	1,361,540	13,251,199
8	Mike Lazaridis	Research in Motion Ltd.	1,167,102	12,785,157
9	James Balsillie	Research in Motion Ltd.	1,167,102	12,785,157
10	Jean Claude Gandur	Addax Petroleum Corp.	1,921,966	11,906,263

Source: "Beyond Salary: How the Money Stacks Up," *The Globe and Mail,* June 23, 2009, p. B10.

maintain the same relative relationship. In general, managers who are in the second level of a company earn about two-thirds of a CEO's salary, while the next level down earns slightly more than half of a CEO's salary.[51] Much of the criticism of this theory, and an important source of criticism about executive compensation in general, is the gradual increase in the spread between executives' compensation and the average salaries of the people they employ, particularly in the United States, where in 1980, CEOs received about 42 times the average salary of workers. By 1999, U.S. top executives were paid 475 times the average factory worker.[52] As a point of reference, the corresponding differential in Japan is under 20.[53] Both these pieces of information suggest that a social comparison explanation is not sufficient to explain why executive wages are as high as they are.

A second approach to understanding executive compensation focuses less on the difference in wages between executive and other jobs, and more on explaining the level of executive wages. The premise in this economic approach is that the worth of a CEO should correspond closely to some measure of company success, such as profitability or sales. Intuitively, this explanation makes sense. There is also empirical support. Numerous studies over the past 30 years demonstrate that executive pay bears some relationship to company success.[54] An article analyzing the results from over 100 executive pay studies found empirical evidence that firm size (sales or number of employees) is by far the best predictor of CEO compensation. The size variables are nine times better at explaining executive compensation than are any of the performance measures. How big the firm is explains what the boss gets paid better than how well he or she performs![55]

Some evidence contradicts this, however. One recent study combined both social comparison and economic explanations to try to better understand CEO salaries. Both of these explanations turned out to be significant. Size and profitability affected level of compensation. But social comparisons did also. In this study, the social comparison was between CEOs and the wages of the board of directors. It seems that CEO salaries rose, on average, 51 percent for every $100,000 more that was earned by directors on the board.[56] Recognizing this, CEOs sometimes lobby to get a board loaded with directors who are highly paid in their primary jobs.

A third view of CEO salaries, based on agency theory, incorporates the political motivations that are an inevitable part of the corporate world. Sometimes, this argument runs, CEOs make decisions that aren't in the economic best interest of the firm and its shareholders. One variant of this view suggests that the normal behaviour of a CEO is self-protective—CEOs make decisions to solidify their position and to maximize the rewards they personally receive.[57]

On the other hand, responsible executive behaviour was demonstrated in early 2009 when CEOs of two large Canadian banks voluntarily turned down long-term incentives because their organizations failed to meet profit targets. RBC chairman Gord Nixon voluntarily turned down nearly $5 million in deferred shares and stock options; and BMO chief William Downe gave up mid- and long-term compensation worth $4.21 million. The Bank of Nova Scotia cut CEO Rick Waugh's bonus by almost 70 percent compared to 2007. However, this action may have been more about self-protection as all three banks were facing a proposal to give shareholders a vote on executive compensation and a separate resolution calling for a comprehensive review of executive pay.[58]

Agency theory argues that executive compensation should be designed to ensure that executives have the best interests of stockholders in mind when they make decisions. The outcome has been to use some form of long-term incentive plan, most commonly stock options. There is a built-in incentive for an executive to increase the value of the firm. Stock prices rise; the executive exercises the option to buy the stock at the agreed-upon price. Because the stock price has risen in the interim, the executive profits from the stock sale.

Although this sounds like an effective tool to motivate executives, there still are many critics.[59] The major complaint is that stock options don't have a downside risk. If stock prices rise, the stock options are exercised. If stocks don't improve, the executive suffers no out-of-pocket losses. Some argue that executive compensation should move more toward requiring executives to own stock, and not just the option to buy.[60] With the threat of possible financial loss and the hopes of possible substantial gains, motivation might be higher. Some early evidence supports this position. In three industries in which executives had large stock holdings, firms outperformed other industries in which executives had little or no current stock investment.

The second trend in response to complaints about excessive executive compensation is increasing government regulation. For example, the Ontario Securities Commission has rules regarding disclosure of executive compensation for companies listed on the TSX. The chief executive officer's pay always must be disclosed, as well as that of the next four highest paid employees. Furthermore, boards of directors must disclose how they make executive compensation decisions. In the public sector, the Ontario government requires that salaries for provincial government employees earning $100,000 or more be publicly disclosed. The law also applies to employees in the broader public sector, including hospitals, universities, school boards, Crown agencies, and municipalities.

Components of Executive Compensation Packages   There are five basic elements of most executive compensation packages: (1) base salary, (2) short-term (annual) incentives or bonuses, (3) long-term incentives and capital appreciation plans, (4) employee benefits, and (5) perquisites. Because of the changing nature of tax legislation, each of these at one time or another has received considerable attention in designing executive compensation packages. Companies are now placing more and more emphasis on incentives at the expense of base salary. Such a change in emphasis signals the growing importance attached to making decisions that ensure the survival and profitability of a company.

1. Base Salary.   As noted earlier, being competitive is a very important factor in the determination of executive base pay. Although formalized job evaluation still plays an occasional role in determining executive base pay, other sources are much more important. Particularly important is the opinion of a compensation committee of the company's board of directors.[61] Frequently, this compensation committee will take over some of the data analysis tasks previously performed by the chief human resources officer, even going so far as to analyze salary survey data and performance records for executives of comparably sized firms.[62] One empirical study suggests the most common behaviour (60 percent of the cases) of executive compensation committees is to identify major competitors and set the CEO's compensation at a level between the best and worst of these comparison groups.[63]

2. Bonuses.   Annual bonuses play a major role in executive compensation and are primarily designed to motivate better performance. Today, bonuses are given to 90 percent of executives. The types of organizations relying almost exclusively on base salary for total direct compensation typically have one or more of the following characteristics: (1) tight control of stock ownership, (2) not-for-profit institutions, or (3) firms operating in regulated industries.

3. Long-Term Incentive and Capital Appreciation Plans.   By far the most common long-term incentive remains the executive stock option. Because many of the highest reported executive pay packages can be traced to stock options, critics have focused on their use and abuse. One clear complaint is that stock options don't pay for performance of the executive. In a stock market that is rising on all fronts, executives can exercise options at much higher prices than the initial grant price—and the payouts likely will be attributable to general market increases rather than to any specific action by the executive. Efforts to counter this undeserved reward are linked to the rise of other types of long-term incentives, some of which require the executive to "beat the market" or hit certain performance targets specifically linked to firm performance. Exhibit 11.14 identifies other types of long-term incentives and generally describes their main features.[64] Clearly, in today's more turbulent stock market, stock options are not the "mother lode" they were in earlier times. Options granted at one price quickly become poor motivational tools when the stock price drops far below that figure. Many companies then scramble to grant new options at lower prices, reflecting better the realities of a declining market.

4. Executive Benefits.   Because many benefits are tied to income level (e.g., life insurance, disability insurance, pension plans), executives typically receive higher benefits than most other exempt employees. Beyond the typical benefits outlined in Chapter 9, however, many executives also receive additional life insurance, exclusions from deductibles for health care costs, and supplementary pension income exceeding the maximum limits permissible under legal guidelines for registered (eligible for tax deductions) pension plans.

EXHIBIT 11.14 Long-Term Incentives for Executives

Type	Description
I. Appreciation-Based Plans	
Stock Options	Option to purchase of stock at a stipulated price in a given time period.
Stock Appreciation Rights	Stock award determined by increase in stock price during any time chosen (by the executive) in the option period.
II. Full-Share Plans	
Restricted Stock Plans	Grant of stock with the condition it may not be sold before a specified date.
Restricted Stock Units/Phantom Stock Plans	Grant of notional shares/units with the condition that they may not be sold before a specified date.
Deferred Share Units	Restricted stock units/phantom stock payable upon retirement, termination, or death.
III. Performance-Based Plans	
Performance Share/Unit Plans	Any stock award vested when specific performance goals achieved.

Source: L. Moate and M. Ng, "There's More to Long-Term Incentives Than Stock Options," *Canadian HR Reporter,* October 9, 2006.

5. Executive Perquisites.   Perquisites, or "perks," probably have the same genesis as the expression "rank has its privileges." Indeed, life at the top has its rewards, designed to satisfy several types of executive needs. One type of perk could be classified as internal, providing a little something extra while the executive is inside the company: luxury offices, executive dining rooms, special parking. A second category also is designed to be company-related, but for business conducted externally: company-paid membership in clubs/associations, payment of hotel, resort, airplane, and auto expenses.

The final category of perquisites should be totally isolated from the first two because of the differential tax status. This category, called personal perks, includes such things as low-cost loans, personal and legal counselling, free home repairs and improvements, personal use of company property, and expenses for vacation homes.[65]

Compensation Strategy for Scientists and Engineers

The compensation of scientists and engineers focuses on rewarding them for their special scientific or intellectual training. Here lies one of the special compensation problems that scientists and engineers face. Consider the freshly minted electrical engineer who graduates with all the latest knowledge in the field. For the first few years after graduation this knowledge is a valuable resource for engineering projects in which new applications of the latest theories are a primary objective. Gradually, though, this engineer's knowledge starts to become obsolete. Team leaders begin to look to newer graduates for fresh ideas. There is a close relationship between pay increases and knowledge obsolescence. Early years bring larger-than-average (relative to employees in other occupations) increases. After 10 years, increases drop below average, and become downright puny in the 15- to 20-year time frame. Partly because salary plateaus arise, many scientists and engineers make career changes such as moving into management or temporarily leaving business to update their technical knowledge. In recent years, some firms have tried to deal with the plateau effect and also accommodate the different career motivations of mature scientists and engineers.

dual career track

career progression on either a managerial path or a professional path

The result has been the creation of **dual career tracks**. Exhibit 11.15 shows a typical dual career track. Notice that dual tracks provide exactly that: two different ways of progressing in an organization, each reflecting different types of contributions to the organization's mission. The first, or managerial track, ascends through increasing responsibility for supervision or direction of people. The professional track ascends through increasing contributions of a professional nature, which do not mainly entail the supervision of employees. Scientists and engineers have the opportunity at some stage in their careers to consider a management track or to continue along the scientific track. Not only do dual tracks offer greater advancement opportunities for scientists and engineers but also maximum base pay in the technical track can approximate that of upper-management positions.

A second problem in designing the compensation package of scientists and engineers centres on the question of equity. The very nature of technical knowledge and its dissemination requires the relatively close association of scientists and engineers across organizations. In fact, scientists and engineers tend to compare themselves for equity purposes with other graduates who entered the labour market during the same time period. Partly because of this, and because of the volatile nature of both jobs and salaries in these occupations, organizations rely heavily on external market data in pricing their base pay.[66] This has resulted in the use of maturity curves.

Maturity curves reflect the relationship between scientist/engineer compensation and years of experience in the labour market. Generally, surveying organizations ask for information about salaries as a function of years since the incumbent(s) last received a degree. This is intended to measure the half-life of technical obsolescence. In fact, a plot of these data, with appropriate smoothing to eliminate aberrations, typically shows curves that are steep for the first five to seven years and then rise more gradually as technical obsolescence erodes the value of jobs. Exhibit 11.16 illustrates such a graph with somewhat greater sophistication built into it, in that different graphs are constructed for different levels of performance.

EXHIBIT 11.15 IBM Dual Ladders

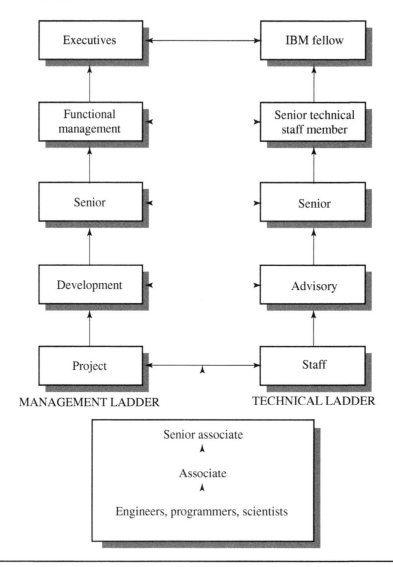

Most scientists and engineers also receive performance-based incentives such as profit sharing and stock ownership incentives.[67] Other incentives link payment of specific cash amounts to completion of specific projects on or before agreed-upon deadlines. Post-hiring bonuses are also paid for such achievements as patents, publications, election to professional societies, and attainment of professional licences.

Finally, organizations provide perks that satisfy the unique needs of scientists and engineers, such as flexible work schedules, large offices, campus-like environments, and lavish athletic facilities. The strategic importance of these groups dictates that both mind and body be kept active.

Compensation Strategy for Salespeople

Salespeople span the all-important boundary between the organization and consumers of the organization's goods or services. Salespeople must be sensitive to changing consumer tastes, and therefore, there is a growing trend toward linking sales compensation to customer satisfaction

EXHIBIT 11.16 Maturity Curve Showing Years since Last Degree Relative to Salary

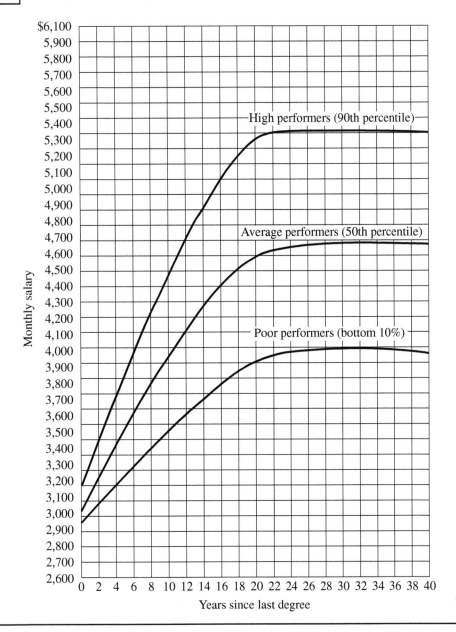

measures, with about one-third of all companies reporting use of such quality-based measures.[68] The role of interacting in the field with customers requires individuals with high initiative who can work under low supervision for extended periods of time, so there is much more reliance on incentive payments tied to individual performance. Thus, even when salespeople are in the field—and relatively unsupervised—there is always a motivation to perform. Most sales employees at every organization level have some component of pay, usually a large one, that is an incentive tied to performance.

There are four major factors that influence the design of sales compensation packages: (1) the nature of people who enter the sales profession, (2) organizational strategy, (3) competitor practices, and (4) the product to be sold.

People Who Enter the Sales Profession   Salespeople are often characterized as heavily motivated by financial compensation. One study supports this perception, with salespeople ranking pay significantly higher than five other forms of reward.[69] These values virtually dictate that the primary focus of sales compensation should be on direct financial rewards (base pay plus incentives).

Organizational Strategy   A sales compensation plan should link desired behaviours of salespeople to organizational strategy.[70] This is particularly true in the Internet age. As more sales dollars are tied to computer-based transactions, the role of sales personnel also will change.[71] Salespeople must know when to stress customer service and when to stress volume sales. And when volume sales are the goal, which products should be pushed hardest? Strategic plans signal which behaviours are important. For example, emphasis on customer service to build market share, or movement into geographic areas with low potential, may limit sales volume. Alternatively, an organization may want to motivate aggressive sales behaviour. A straight commission-based incentive plan will focus sales efforts in this direction, to the possible exclusion of supportive tasks such as processing customer returns.

Competitor Practices   The very nature of sales positions means that competitors will cross paths, at least in their quest for potential customers. This provides the opportunity to chat about relative compensation packages, an opportunity which salespeople frequently take. To ensure that the comparison is favourable, the organization should identify a compensation level strategy that explicitly indicates target salaries for different sales groups and performance levels.

Product to Be Sold   Consider a product which, by its very technical nature, takes time to understand and thus to fully develop an effective sales presentation. Such products are said to have high barriers to entry, meaning considerable training is needed to become effective in the field. Compensation in this situation usually includes a large base pay component, minimizing the risk a sales representative will face, and encouraging entry into the necessary training program. At the opposite extreme are products with lower barriers to entry, where the knowledge needed to make an effective sales presentation is relatively easy to acquire. These product lines are sold more often using a higher incentive component, thus paying more for actual sales than for taking the time to learn the necessary skills.

Base compensation tends to be more important with easily sold products, but incentives become more important when willingness to work hard may make the difference between success and failure. One recent study argues convincingly that setting sales targets or quotas is the most important, and most difficult, part of sales compensation. Several clues help to indicate whether quotas are reasonable: (1) Can the salespeople explain how the quotas are set? (2) In periods when the company hits its business plan, does 60 to 70 percent of the salesforce hit quota? (3) Do high performers hit their target consistently? (4) Do low performers show improvement over time?[72]

Most jobs do not fit the ideal specifications for either of the two extremes, represented by straight salary or straight commission plans. A combination plan is intended to capture the best of both these plans. A guaranteed straight salary can be linked to performance of non-sales functions such as customer service, while a commission for sales volume yields the incentive to sell. A plan combining these two features signals the intent of the organization to ensure that both types of activities occur.

Compensation Strategy for Contingent Workers

Contingent workers now constitute one-third of the workforce in Canada. These employees work through a temporary help agency, on an on-call basis, through a contract company, or as an independent contractor. Why the move to contingent workers? Part of the answer may be cost savings. Employee benefit costs are rarely provided to contingent workers.[73] The real reason for contingent workers may be the added flexibility such employment offers the employer. In today's fast-paced marketplace, lean and flexible are desirable characteristics. In fact, recent evidence suggests that the most rapidly growing segment of contingent workers is "technical experts," added to assist in efforts to build virtual corporations.[74]

A major compensation challenge for contingent workers, as with all our special group employees, is identifying ways to deal with fairness and equity problems. Contingent workers may work alongside permanent workers, yet may receive either higher or lower wages and benefits for the same work. Employers deal with this potential source of inequity in two ways. One response is to view contingent workers as a pool of candidates for more permanent hiring status. High performers may be moved off contingent status and afforded more employment stability. A second way to look at contingent workers is to champion the idea of boundaryless careers.[75] At least for high-skilled contingent workers, it is increasingly popular to view careers as a series of opportunities to acquire valuable increments in knowledge and skills. Sometimes these opportunities arise in one organization through transfers across different jobs. But knowledge acquisition may be even faster for employees willing to forgo traditional job security and accept temporary assignments that quickly enhance their skill repertoire. In this framework, for employees who accept the idea of boundaryless careers, contingent status isn't a penalty or cause of dissatisfaction but rather part of a fast-track developmental sequence. Lack of benefits is offset by opportunities for rapid development of skills—opportunities that might not be so readily available in more traditional employment arrangements.

CONCLUSION

Pay-for-performance plans can work, but the design and effective administration of these plans is key to their success. Having a good idea is not enough. The good idea must be followed up by sound practices that recognize that rewards can, if used properly, shape employee behaviour.

Special groups share two common characteristics: They all have jobs with high potential for conflict, and resolution of this conflict is central to the goals of the organization. Probably because of these characteristics, special groups receive compensation treatment that differs from other employees. Unfortunately, most of this compensation differentiation is prescriptive in nature, and little is known about the specific roles assumed by special groups and the functions compensation should assume in motivating appropriate performance. Future practice and research should focus on answering these questions.

CHAPTER SUMMARY

1. Three short-term, individual pay-for-performance plans are: merit pay, lump sum bonuses, and individual spot awards.
2. Five causes of problems with team compensation systems are: the need for different compensation programs for different types of teams, the loss of motivational impact if the team is very large, overly complex team compensation plans, lack of control by teams over what they are measured on, and poor communication of team-based plans.
3. Seven key issues in designing a gain-sharing plan are: strength of reinforcement, productivity standards, sharing the gains between management and workers, scope of the formula, perceived fairness of the formula, ease of administration, and production variability.
4. Employee stock ownership plans offer employees the opportunity to purchase company stock, often partially or fully matched by employer-paid stock for the employee. Stock options provide an employee with the right to purchase stock at a specified price for a fixed time period. Broad-based option plans are stock grants to employees over a specified time frame.

5. Three possible explanations for extremely high levels of CEO compensation are: social comparisons to salaries of lower-level employees, the desirability of a relationship between pay and company success, and the agency theory suggestion that CEOs act with a self-protecting, political motivation.

6. The five basic elements of executive compensation packages are: base salary, short-term (annual) incentives or bonuses, long-term incentives and capital accumulation plans, employee benefits, and perquisites.

7. Dual career ladders are two different ways of progressing in an organization, one through a managerial ladder, the other through a scientific ladder. This approach helps to deal with the plateauing effect of gradual technological obsolescence, and accommodates the opportunity for mature scientists and engineers to switch to the management ladder. Maturity curves reflect the relationship between scientist/engineer compensation and years of experience in the labour market, as pay increases sharply for the first five to seven years and then rises more gradually due to the effect of technological obsolescence.

Key Terms

Review Questions

1. How is an earnings-at-risk plan different from an ordinary gain-sharing or profit-sharing plan? How might earnings-at-risk plans affect attraction and retention of employees?

2. Why are firms shifting away from stock options and moving to different types of long-term incentives for executives?

3. For each of the special groups discussed in this chapter, explain how the issue of equity is especially important. To which comparison groups might special group members compare themselves to determine if their compensation is fair?

EXPERIENTIAL EXERCISES

1. As VP of HR at Senior Sam's Bakery (a regional baker of wraps and pitas), you are experiencing turnover problems with the employees who package the products after coming from the bakery. Plant Manager Gail Foy has asked you to fix the problem. While your primary emphasis might be on having a competitive base pay, you need to decide if there is anything you can do in the incentive department. Before you can make this decision, what information would you like about base pay and incentives at major competitors, and about the reasons for the turnover?

2. Your boss had lunch yesterday with a CEO in the same town who just implemented a gain-sharing plan. You guessed it—he wants to see if it would work in your company. What conditions would you like to see exist before you would be comfortable making a positive recommendation?

3. You own Higgins Tool Coating Company, a high-tech firm specializing in coating of cutting tools (e.g., drill bits, cutting blades) that provides longer life before re-sharpening is needed. You are concerned that the competition is continuing to develop new coating methods and new applications of this coating in different industries. If you wanted to create a work environment in which employees offered more new product suggestions and suggested new industries where these suggestions might be applied, what type of compensation plan might you recommend? What are some of the problems you need to be aware of?

WEB EXERCISE

ESOP Feasibility

ESOP Builders Inc. is a company that assists small- and medium-sized businesses in implementing employee stock ownership plans. The first step is to assess whether such a plan would be feasible, and ESOP Builders has prepared a feasibility questionnaire to assist with this process. Go to the ESOP Builders Web site at www.esopbuilders.com and click on "free feasibility survey." Complete the questionnaire for a small- or medium-sized company that you are familiar with. Submit the questionnaire for analysis and then review the response you get back. Given the material in the chapter, do you agree with the response from ESOP Builders? Explain why or why not.

CASE

Understanding Stock Options

Information regarding calculations and data can be found online at http://mgt.buffalo.edu/departments/ohr/jmnewman, including links to sites displaying current share prices.

Exercise 1

After graduation you and a friend both got great jobs, you with Dell and your friend with Microsoft. You both started at the same salary and bonus and got 2,000 non-qualified stock options as a signing bonus (good negotiating!). You received 2,000 stock options at July 28, 1996, and the grant price was $43.69. Your options vest over four years, 25 percent a year, and they expire in 10 years. Your friend's information is exactly the same, except the grant price is $69.69. Compare your friend's gain to yours. Whose stock options appreciated more? Did you earn money? If the stocks climbed 40 percent, what would be the gain? Was it reasonable for you to reject an offer of 1,000 more options at the price of $3,000? How much would you (in hindsight) pay for those 1,000 stock options?

Exercise 2

You are sales manager of American Express Co. Today you have been granted 8,000 non-qualified stock options. The exercise price was chosen so that the options would only be in the money if the stock price increased by more than 10 percent in each of the following years. What will be the exercise price for each of the next five years? At what stock price could you take home $1,000,000 after taxes? What would be your gain if the stock price increased by 15 percent per year? *Hint:* Assume for convenience that all shares vest today.

Exercise 3

You have been chosen to set up a stock option program at a new Canadian airline. The CEO and co-founder holds only 63 percent of the shares. He does not want to lose control over the company, so the number of options you can offer is limited. In order to retain control, the CEO needs 50 percent of the shares plus one more share. There are 10,000 shares authorized and outstanding, and current share price is $10. Considering that the company will give out new shares to the option holders and not buy back the stock in the market, how many stock options can be granted to employees? You would like the stock price to rise within the first three years at an average of 20 percent a year. Which grant price should you select to make sure that the employees will only get rich when the stock outperforms the 20 percent offset?

You decided to give 5,000 non-qualified stock options to each of the 100 top employees. Imagine the share price rose to $60. How much would a grantee earn from exercising his options? What would be the cost to the company if the money had been paid as a bonus after the third year?

The CEO earned $10,000,000 (before taxes) from exercising stock options this year. How many options did he get if the exercise price was at $10? As in the last exercise, assume all shares vest at once.

Financial Background: Stock Options

Making money with shares is pretty easy: One buys shares at a certain price and sells the shares at a different price. The win (or loss) can be calculated by multiplying the number of shares with the difference between the buying price and selling price. For example, buying 5,000 shares at $20 and selling them for $15 will generate a loss of ($20 − $15) x 5,000 = $25,000. The only problem is that nobody knows what the share price will be in the future.

A stock option entitles the owner to buy shares of a company at a certain price (the grant price). If you have an option to buy one share of a company for $10 and the stock price is at $20, you will buy the share for $10 and then sell it for $20 and make a gain of $10 exercising this option. You cannot lose any money with an option, because you don't need to exercise the option when the stock price is below the exercise price (this is why it is called an option). Yet if the share price rises, the option will be worth more and more, as the gain for exercising the option will increase even faster.

Example: Company X has a stock price of $500. You have an option to buy this stock at $480. Therefore the option is worth $500 − $480 = $20. If the stock price rises by 10 percent, one share will be worth $550 ... the option is now worth $550 − $480 = $70, equivalent to a price increase of 350 percent. This effect is also called leverage effect.

The exercise of stock options is usually limited to a certain period of time (e.g., 10 years after issuance). Therefore, it is reasonable to exercise options before that date if they are "in the money."

Visit the Online Learning Centre at

www.mcgrawhill.ca/olc/milkovich

PART IV

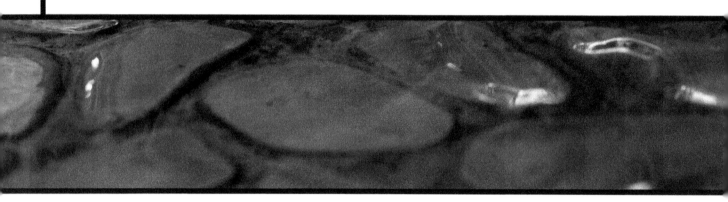

Managing the System

The last part of the total pay model is management. Some aspects of management have been touched on already—the use of budgets in merit increase programs, the "message" that employees receive from their variable pay bonuses, communication and cost control in benefits, and the importance of employee involvement in designing the total compensation system.

Several important issues remain. The first is the significant role that government plays in managing compensation. Laws and regulations are the most obvious government intervention. In Canada, employment standards legislation, pay equity acts, and human rights laws, among others, regulate pay decisions. Government is more than a source of laws and regulations, however. As a major employer, as a consumer of goods and services, and through its fiscal and monetary policies, government affects the supply and demand for labour. Unions also impact wage determination. These issues are covered in Chapter 12.

Chapter 13 covers three aspects of managing compensation: costs, communication, and change. One of the key reasons for being systematic about pay decisions is to manage the costs associated with pay decisions. As Chapter 13 will show, a total compensation system is really a device for allocating money in a way that is consistent with the organization's objectives.

Communication and change are linked. What is to be communicated to whom is an important, ongoing issue. In addition to communication, the system must be constantly evaluated to judge its effectiveness. Is it helping the organization achieve the objectives? What information can help us make these judgments? If it is not doing what it should be doing, how do we change it? Any system will founder if it is ineffectively implemented, managed, and communicated.

Chapter 13 also discusses how to organize the compensation department. Which activities should be done in-house and which may be candidates for digitizing and outsourcing are among the issues discussed.

EXHIBIT **IV.1** The Pay Model

CHAPTER 12

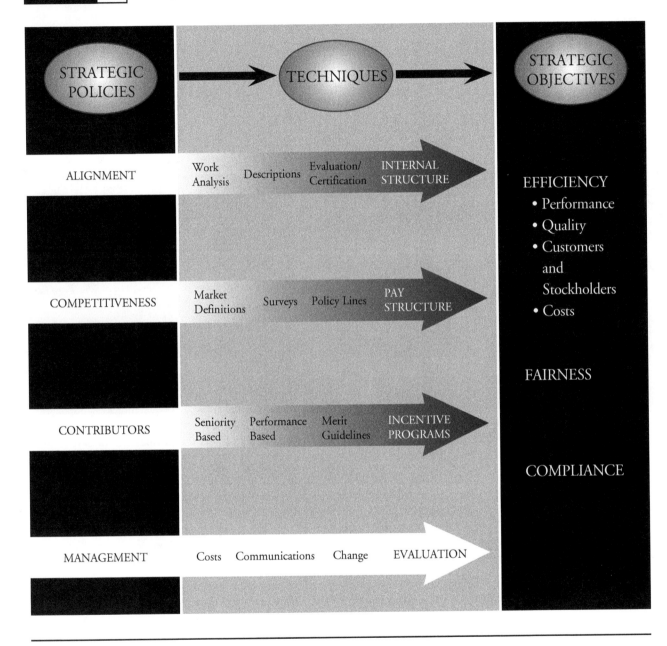

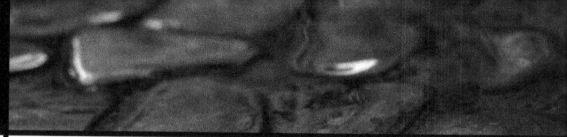

THE ROLE OF GOVERNMENT AND UNIONS IN COMPENSATION

LEARNING OUTCOMES

■ Explain the role of government in compensation.

■ Describe the major compensation-related provisions of employment standards legislation.

■ Explain the impact of human rights legislation on compensation.

■ Discuss the causes of the male-female wage gap and explain what pay equity legislation is intended to accomplish.

■ Describe four ways in which unions have an impact on wage determination.

■ Explain why union attitudes regarding pay-for-performance have gradually become more favourable.

A 1939 pay policy handbook for a major corporation outlines this justification for paying different wages to men versus women working on the same jobs:[1]

> The . . . wage curve . . . is not the same for women as for men because of the more transient character of the former, the relative shortness of their activity in industry, the differences in environment required, the extra services that must be provided, overtime limitations, extra help needed for the occasional heavy work, and the general sociological factors not requiring discussion herein. Basically then we have another wage curve . . . for women below and not parallel with the men's curve.

The presumption that people should be paid different wages based on "general sociological factors" was still evident in the 1960s, in newspaper help-wanted ads that specified "perky gal Fridays." The women's movement and subsequent legislation ended such practices. However, legislation does not always achieve what it intends. Nor does it always intend what it achieves. Consequently, compliance and fairness are continuing compensation issues.

In democratic societies, the legislative process begins when a problem is identified (not all citizens are receiving fair treatment in the workplace) and corrective legislation is proposed (human rights, employment equity, and pay equity). If enough support develops, often as a result of compromises and trade-offs, the proposed legislation becomes law. Employers, along with other stakeholders, attempt to influence the form any legislation will take.

Once passed, laws are enforced by agencies through rulings, regulations, inspections, and investigations. Companies respond to legislation by auditing and perhaps altering their practices, and perhaps again lobbying for legislative change. The laws and regulations issued by governmental agencies created to enforce the laws have a significant influence on compensation decisions throughout the world.

GOVERNMENT AS PART OF THE EMPLOYMENT RELATIONSHIP

The exact role that government should play in the contemporary workplace depends in part on one's political ideology. Some call for organizations and the government to act in concert to carry out a public policy that protects the interests of employees.[2] Others believe that the best opportunities for employees are created by the constant change and reconfiguring that is inherent in market-based economies; the economy ought to be allowed to adapt and transform, undistorted by government actions.[3] All countries throughout the world must address these issues. However, different countries and cultures have different perspectives. Government is a key stakeholder in compensation decision making.

Governments' usual interests are whether procedures for determining pay are fair (e.g., pay equity), safety nets for the unemployed and disadvantaged are sufficient (e.g., minimum wage, unemployment compensation), and employees are protected from exploitation (e.g., overtime pay, child labour). Consequently, company pay practices set the context for national debates on minimum wage, the security and portability of pensions, even the quality of public education and the availability of training. So, in addition to individuals and employers, government is a key party in pay decisions.

Government policy decisions also affect compensation by affecting the supply and demand for labour.

Supply   Legislation aimed at protecting specific groups also tends to restrict that group's participation in the labour market. For example, compulsory schooling laws restrict the supply of children available to sell hamburgers or to assemble soccer balls. Licensing requirements for certain occupations (plumbers, taxi drivers, psychologists) restrict the number of people who can legally offer a service.

Demand   Government affects demand for labour most directly as a major employer. A government also indirectly affects labour demand through its purchases (military aircraft, computer systems, paper clips) as well as its public policy decisions. For example, lowering interest rates generally boosts manufacturing of everything from cars to condominiums. Increased business activity translates into increased demand for labour and upward pressure on wages.

This chapter will examine the most important Canadian regulations concerning wages. Because our society continues to wrestle with the issue of discrimination, we will go into some depth about how pay discrimination has been defined and the continuing earnings gap between men and women.

EMPLOYMENT STANDARDS ACTS

Each of the 14 jurisdictions regulating employment across Canada (ten provinces, three territories, and the federal jurisdiction) has enacted legislation, usually named "employment standards acts," specifying minimum terms and conditions of employment.[4] Although there are differences in specific requirements, these laws all specify a minimum hourly wage, paid vacations, paid holidays, standard hours of work and overtime pay, pay for employees who are terminated by the company, minimum age of employment, and equal pay for equal work by men and women. Administrative rules regarding record keeping, statement of wages, and deductions from wages are also prescribed.

Minimum Wage

Minimum wage laws are intended to provide an income floor for workers in society's least productive jobs. The minimum hourly wage varies by jurisdiction, and is increased regularly as the cost of living rises. Workers who are paid slightly above minimum wage often benefit as well when these increases are mandated. As legislation forces pay rates at the lowest end of the scale to move up, pay rates above the minimum often increase to maintain differentials. This shift in pay structure does not affect all industries equally. For example, the lowest rates paid in the software, chemical, oil, and pharmaceutical industries already are well above minimum; any legislative change would have little direct impact in these industries. In contrast, retailing and service firms tend to pay at or near minimum wage for many clerks and sales personnel. When legislation results in substantially higher labour costs for these firms, they may consider substituting non-human forms of capital by using robots or by reducing the number of jobs available.

Minimum wage discussion is also relevant to the social good of the people who are not faring well in the market economy.[5] Some make the case that continuing a low minimum wage permits the continuation of boring, dead-end jobs that ought to be modernized. If employers are forced to pay higher wages, they will find it worthwhile to offer training to employees to increase their economic value.

So the topic stirs endless debate. What is certain is that people working at or near the minimum wage who continue to work definitely do benefit from mandated minimum wage increases, and other workers in higher-level jobs in those same companies may also benefit. Yet fewer workers will be hired or hours will be cut if the increased costs cannot be passed on to consumers or offset by increased productivity.

Paid Vacation

Each jurisdiction recognizes that vacations are necessary to ensure continued employee health and productivity. The specific amounts of minimum vacation vary across jurisdictions, but the basic structure and philosophy of the laws regarding vacations are similar across the country. In most cases, the minimum amount of vacation is either two weeks or three weeks per year.

Paid Holidays

Each jurisdiction recognizes that there are days of special significance that citizens celebrate together, and provide for paid days off from work to observe these holidays. The number of paid holidays varies from five to nine across the country, but all jurisdictions include New Year's Day, Good Friday, Canada Day, Labour Day, and Christmas Day.

Standard Hours of Work and Overtime Pay

Employment standards legislation sets out the standard hours of work for employees, and provides for overtime pay when an employee is required to work more than these standard hours. Standard hours of work vary between 40 hours per week and 48 hours per week across jurisdictions, and overtime pay is one-and-one-half times regular pay in almost all cases. Meal breaks and rest periods also are required during working hours, but do not have to be paid. Sometimes counting the hours of work becomes a contest, as shown in Exhibit 12.1.

The original intent of overtime pay laws was to share available work by making hiring additional workers a less costly option than scheduling overtime for current employees. However, the workplace has changed considerably over the years. Today, overtime pay is often the least costly option. Contemporary employers face (1) an increasingly skilled workforce with higher training costs per employee and (2) higher benefit costs, often a fixed cost per employee. These factors have lowered the break-even point at which it pays employers to schedule longer hours and pay the overtime premium, rather than hire, train, and pay benefits for more employees. Additionally, in times of low unemployment, hiring new employees is a difficult and expensive process.

EXHIBIT | **12.1** | There's No Such Thing As a Free ...

Gainers Workers Must Pay to Use Bathroom

EDMONTON—Employees at Gainers Inc. are now docked pay for every bathroom break visit made outside of breaks and lunch hour under regulations brought in last week by company owner Burns Meats Ltd.

A notice posted in the meat-packing plant tells employees that abusing washroom visits has lowered productivity. If employees need to use the bathroom outside of breaks, they must report to a supervisor, who records the time of departure and return. The time is tabulated at the end of the week and pay cheques are deducted based on an employee's hourly wage.

"How can they charge you for going to the washroom?" asked one angry employee.

The man said one worker at the plant had a kidney transplant and has to use the washroom often.

"Because of this system, he had to hold it in [between breaks] for a whole week. He went once for three minutes and was charged 43 cents."

Such washroom rules are rare but there is nothing in the Alberta employment standards code that requires a person to be paid when they don't work, said Kathy Lazowski, a public affairs officer with Alberta Labour.

—Canadian Press

Pay on Termination of Employment

In the event that the company terminates the employment of one of its workers, certain payments are required. The employer must provide a minimum notice of termination during which time the employee continues to be paid or else receives the same payment in lieu of notice. This notice period varies from one week to eight weeks, depending on the employee's length of service. Two jurisdictions (Ontario and federal) require additional severance pay to be provided, in certain circumstances, to an individual employee who is terminated.

In situations where a group of employees are terminated, such as when a business closes or downsizes, employment standards legislation across the country (other than in Prince Edward Island) requires special additional notice (or pay in lieu thereof) to be provided to the workers affected. The minimum number of employees considered a group for this purpose varies between 10 and 50, and the amount of additional notice varies from 4 weeks to 18 weeks, depending on the number of employees being terminated. Some jurisdictions require the employer to take responsibility for organizing a joint planning committee to consider how terminations could be avoided, or to help employees find alternative employment.

Minimum Age of Employment

Restriction of child labour was one of the primary reasons for the creation of employment laws, in recognition of the importance of ensuring that children have access to education, and of protecting their safe and normal development. All jurisdictions have established a minimum age for employment, ranging from 14 to 17. These rules are qualified by exemptions for specified occupations such as certain types of agricultural work and vocational training programs.

Equal Pay for Equal Work by Men and Women

All jurisdictions require that men and women who are doing similar work be paid equally. The legislation also applies to men and women doing substantially the same work, based on an assessment of skill, effort, responsibility, and working conditions required in each case. For example, if the only difference between the work of a male orderly and a female nursing assistant is that the orderly occasionally does heavy lifting, then the work is considered to be substantially the same.

■ HUMAN RIGHTS LAWS

Canada is a world leader in the protection of basic human rights, and a Charter of Rights and Freedoms forms part of its Constitution.[6] As the Canadian workforce has become more diverse, the issue of workplace discrimination has become increasingly important. The Charter specifically permits the development of programs to relieve the situation of historically disadvantaged groups. For example, employment equity programs designed to increase the number of women, visible minorities, Aboriginal people, and people with disabilities in positions where they have been underrepresented in the past are mandated by law in the federal jurisdiction.

Human rights legislation has been enacted in every jurisdiction in Canada, and guarantees every person equal treatment in regard to employment and opportunity for employment regardless of race, colour, creed/religion, sex, sexual orientation, marital status, age, or mental or physical disability. Employment applications and interviews are in violation of the law if they ask for any information in these areas. Hiring, firing, training, and promotion decisions based on these grounds are prohibited. Compensation decisions based on any of these grounds are also illegal. Employers must ensure that their compensation systems treat all groups neutrally, compensating for merit rather than membership in a particular group.

Enforcement of human rights legislation is complaint-based. Employees who believe they have been discriminated against must make a complaint to the appropriate human rights commission, which will then launch an investigation and assess penalties if discrimination is deemed to have occurred.

■ PAY EQUITY

wage gap

the amount by which the average pay for female workers is less than the average pay for male workers

Across North America, Europe, and Australia, gender remains the best predictor of wages, a factor surpassing in importance education, experience, or unionization. As shown in Exhibit 12.2, in 2004, Canadian women working full-time earned approximately 70 percent of the amount that full-time male workers earned.[7] This 30 percent difference is called the "**wage gap**."

EXHIBIT 12.2 | Male/Female Average Earnings Ratio* for Full-Year, Full-Time Workers

Year	Women	Men	Earnings Ratio
1998	$39,500	$55,000	71.9%
1999	$38,000	$55,600	68.4%
2000	$39,300	$55,600	70.6%
2001	$39,600	$56,700	69.9%
2002	$39,900	$56,800	70.2%
2003	$39,700	$56,600	70.2%
2004	$41,000	$58,700	69.9%
2005	$40,900	$58,000	70.5%
2006	$42,200	$58,700	71.9%
2007	$43,000	$60,300	71.4%

* Earnings stated in constant year 2007 dollars.
Source: Statistics Canada Web site and Statistics Canada CANSIM database,
Table 202-0102; http://www40.statcan.gc.ca/l01/cst01/labor01b-eng.htm (accessed August 16, 2009)

The Wage Gap

A variety of factors contribute to the wage gap. Some of the more important factors include the following:

1. Differences in occupation
2. Differences in number of hours worked
3. Differences among industries and firms
4. Differences in union membership
5. The presence of discrimination

occupational segregation

the historical segregation of women into a small number of occupations such as clerical, sales, nursing, and teaching

Differences in Occupation   One of the most important factors in the pay gap is differences in jobs held by men and women. Traditionally, female workers were segregated in occupations such as clerical, sales, nursing, and teaching. Over the last 20 years, not that much has changed, other than an increase in women holding managerial jobs, as shown in Exhibit 12.3. Thus occupational segregation is a persistent phenomenon.

Currently, more women than men graduate from Canadian universities. The choice of major is the single strongest factor affecting income of university graduates.[8] Gender differences in choice of major continue, although those differences are diminishing. Men are more likely to enroll, graduate, and continue working in engineering and scientific specialties. A study of women in science and engineering professions found that women scientists and engineers are almost twice as likely as males to leave these occupations.[9]

Differences in Number of Hours Worked   On average, male full-time workers put in 6 percent more hours per week than women full-time workers. By the time men and women have been out of school for 6 years, women on average have worked 30 percent less than men. After 16 years out of school, women average half as much labour market experience as men.[10] A study of middle-aged law school graduates concluded that the women lawyers did work fewer hours—about 91 percent as long as men.[11] However, they were paid substantially (not proportionately) less; they earned only 61 percent of what men earned. Even with differences in work history accounted for, male lawyers continue to enjoy a considerable earnings advantage as well as a higher rate of growth earnings. Women's record of working hours is continuing to grow closer to that of men, but small initial discriminatory differences in wages affect women's decisions about their future, including their willingness to stay in the workforce.[12]

The relatively small wage gap among younger cohorts (i.e., recent university graduates) tends to increase as the cohort ages. A 2004 Statistics Canada research study that followed three cohorts of university graduates from bachelor's degree programs in 1982, 1986, and 1990 for the first five years of their careers found that the gender wage gap had decreased to an almost negligible level by 1990 for new graduates. However, the gap widened as time went on, and female earnings quickly began to trail behind those of their male classmates, returning to virtually the same gap as for prior cohorts after five years in the workforce. Much of the narrowing of the initial wage gap and of the widening of wage gap as the years progressed was "unexplained," meaning it was not explained by job characteristics, experience, or individual characteristics. The one factor that did explain some of the wage gap was hours of work—women have been working fewer hours than men, particularly women with children.[13]

Differences in Industries and Firms   Other factors that affect earnings differences between men and women are the industry and the firms in which they are employed. The study of middle-aged lawyers revealed large differences between men and women lawyers in the types of firms that employed them. Men were much more likely than women to be in private practice, and they were twice as likely to practise in large firms (over 50 lawyers). In contrast, men are much less likely than women to be in the relatively low-paying areas of government and legal services. Clearly,

EXHIBIT 12.3 Male/Female Employment by Occupation, 1987, 1996, and 2006

	1987			1996			2006		
	Women	*Men*	*Women as percentage of total employed*	*Women*	*Men*	*Women as percentage of total employed*	*Women*	*Men*	*Women as percentage of total employed*
Managerial									
Senior management	0.3	0.8	21.0	0.3	0.7	27.2	0.3	0.8	26.3
Other management	5.7	9.7	30.7	7.8	10.9	37.5	6.7	10.2	36.9
Total management	6.0	10.5	30.1	8.2	11.6	37.0	7.1	11.0	36.3
Professional									
Business and finance	1.9	2.3	38.3	2.8	2.7	46.9	3.3	2.8	51.6
Natural sciences/engineering/mathematic	2.3	7.0	19.6	2.3	8.0	19.1	3.2	10.1	22.0
Social sciences/religion	4.3	2.0	61.4	6.0	2.3	68.8	6.7	2.4	71.3
Teaching	3.8	2.6	52.3	5.1	2.8	60.1	5.6	2.8	63.9
Doctors/dentists/other health	0.9	0.9	43.1	1.2	1.1	48.1	1.4	1.0	55.3
Nursing/therapy/other health-related	8.3	0.9	87.1	8.3	1.0	87.0	8.9	1.1	87.4
Artistic/literary/recreational	2.7	2.1	48.4	3.1	2.4	51.5	3.4	2.6	54.1
Total professional	24.1	18.0	50.4	28.8	20.3	54.2	32.5	22.9	55.9
Clerical and administrative	29.7	7.9	73.9	25.6	7.2	74.9	24.1	7.1	75.0
Sales and service	30.0	18.4	55.2	28.6	19.2	55.4	28.6	19.3	56.8
Primary	2.3	7.2	19.7	2.1	6.5	20.9	1.5	5.3	20.5
Trades, transport, and construction	2.1	28.9	5.2	2.1	26.4	6.1	2.1	26.3	6.5
Processing, manufacturing, and utilities	5.8	9.1	32.4	4.7	8.8	30.6	4.1	8.1	31.1
Total[1]	100.0	100.0	43.0	100.0	100.0	45.4	100.0	100.0	47.1
Total employed (000s)	5,307.7	7,025.3	—	6,099.0	7,322.4	—	7,757.2	8,727.1	—

[1] Includes occupations that are not classified.

Source: *Women in Canada: Work Chapter Updates, 2006.* Statistics Canada Catalogue no. 89F0133XWE. www.statcan.gc.ca/pub/89f0133x/89f0133x2006000-eng.pdf (accessed March 2, 2009).

these differences are related to pay: The most highly paid legal positions are in private practice law firms, and the larger the law firm, the greater the average rate of pay.[14]

Differences in the firm's compensation policies and objectives within a specific industry constitute another factor that accounts for some of the earnings gap. As noted in Chapters 7 and 8, some firms within an industry adopt pay strategies that place them among the leaders in their industry; other firms adopt policies that may offer more employment security coupled with bonuses and gain-sharing schemes. The issue here is whether within an industry some firms are more likely to employ women than other firms and whether that likelihood leads to earnings differences.

It is also known that the size of a firm is related systematically to differences in wages. Female employment is more heavily concentrated in small firms. Wages of men in large firms are 54 percent higher than wages of men in small firms. That gap was only 37 percent for women in small versus large firms. Other studies report that employees in some jobs can get about a 20 percent pay increase simply by switching industries in the same geographic area while performing basically similar jobs.[15] On the other hand, recent studies conclude that this pay premium associated with changing jobs is only enjoyed by white males. Women and minorities who were MBA graduates from five universities did not obtain the same pay increases as their white male classmates when they switched jobs.[16] The authors speculate that the reason that women and minorities did not receive a comparable premium is that they lack the well-developed social networks that provide "inside information" on job opportunities. A weaker network may hurt them in the pay bargaining process, too.

To the extent that these differences are the result of industry and firm practices that steer women and minorities into certain occupations and industries, or lower-paying parts of a profession, they may reflect discrimination. At a minimum, they require thoughtful exploration.

Differences in Union Membership   As discussed later in this chapter, it is well known that belonging to a union will affect differences in earnings. Belonging to a union increases wages.

Presence of Discrimination   Finally, a study of MBAs found that 10 to 15 years after graduation, in addition to a pay gap there is also a gender-based chasm in such subjective measures as career satisfaction, boss appreciation, and feelings of discrimination.[17] Fully 46 percent of women said they had experienced discrimination; only 9 percent of men said they had. The most common problem women reported was that less qualified men were chosen for promotions over them. Additionally, they felt that at higher levels discrimination was subtler and harder to prove. Clearly, many professional women and minorities believe they operate in less supportive work environments than their white male colleagues.[18]

So it is clear that many factors affect pay, and discrimination appears to be one of them.[19] But there is little agreement as to what constitutes evidence of discrimination. Although 15 to 20 percent of the wage gap that remains after the effects of the above factors are removed is the most frequently cited example, closer inspection reveals the weaknesses in this statistic. A 2002 Statistics Canada analysis of the wage gap concluded, "While earning differences between men and women have narrowed since the 1970s, they continue to be remarkably persistent. Measurement and methodological issues play important roles in studying these differences.[20] However, significant progress has been made in reducing the wage gap in New Brunswick, as detailed in the .Net Worth box.

Pay Equity Legislation

pay equity
legislation intended to redress the unexplained portion of the wage gap assumed to be due to gender discrimination

Pay equity legislation has been introduced in several Canadian jurisdictions, often for public sector employees only, but also for private sector employees in Ontario, Quebec, and federally regulated workplaces. The laws are intended to address the effects of occupational segregation and the historical undervaluing of work done by women by requiring that female-dominated jobs be compensated in the same way as male-dominated jobs of the same value. Thus, pay equity legislation is proactive, rather than complaint-based.[21]

.NET WORTH

New Brunswick Closing Gender Wage Gap

Women around the world, including Canada, continue to earn less than men. But at least one province is making some inroads. Since New Brunswick implemented its wage gap action plan in 2005, it experienced the largest drop in the wage disparity of any Canadian province.

The biggest part of the government's strategy has been educating employers, employees, and students about the wage gap, said Cindy Lanteigne, director of the province's wage gap reduction intiative.

"When you say 'wage gap,' people don't know what it is, especially the youth," she said. "They can't believe there's a wage gap."

The national wage gap between men and women, based on average hourly earnings, remained the same in 2005 and 2006 at 19.3 percent, according to Statistics Canada. However, New Brunswick's wage gap dropped 3.1 percentage points from 16.7 percent to 13.6 percent.

New Brunswick's wage gap action plan includes 4 goals and 13 concrete measures to determine whether those goals have been met:

1. Change social attitudes
   - Women's right to work outside the home
   - Sharing of domestic responsibilities
   - Percentage of women in decision-making structures and bodies

2. Increase sharing of family responsibilities
   - Number of licensed day-care spaces and centres
   - Number of employer-sponsored day-care services
   - Number of hours spent on family duties
   - Number of employers with family-friendly practices

3. Reduce job clustering of women
   - Percentage of women employed in gender-clustered jobs
   - Number of female journeypersons
   - Wage gap for community college grads
   - Percentage of women decision makers in the workplace

4. Increase use of pay equity practices
   - Percent of employees paid under gender-neutral pay systems
   - Wage gap between gender-clustered jobs

The government also has on online toolkit for employers with a seven-step process to reduce the wage gap. It includes fact sheets on the wage gap; assessments to measure the organization's wage gap, employee retention, satisfaction and absenteeism; and workshops to help organizations develop and implement a wage gap plan.

Source: S. Klie, "New Brunswick Closing Gender Wage Gap," *Canadian HR Reporter*, June 18, 2007.

The pay equity process is detailed, technical, and complex, and varies to some extent between jurisdictions. However, the following steps are the basic components of a pay equity process:

- Identify the unit for which the pay equity plan will be developed.
- Identify job classes with similar duties and responsibilities.
- Identify male and female job classes.
- Assess the value of jobs using a gender-neutral (free of gender bias) job evaluation system based on the criteria of:
  - Skill, including intellectual and physical qualifications acquired by experience, training, education, or natural ability, but not considering the methods by which skills are acquired;
  - Effort, including both physical and intellectual effort;
  - Responsibility, for technical, financial, and human resources; and
  - Working conditions, including both the physical and psychological conditions, such as noise, temperature, isolation, physical danger, health hazards, and stress.
- Compare male and female job classes using one of the following (varies by jurisdiction):
  - The **job-to-job method** where each female job class is compared to each male job class of equal or comparable value.
  - The **proportional value/wage line method**, for female job classes with no appropriate male comparators under the job-to-job system, where the wage line for male job classes is applied when setting pay for female classes (see Exhibit 12.4).
  - The **proxy comparison method**, when pay equity cannot be achieved through job-to-job or proportional value methods, where female job classes are compared to similar female job classes that have achieved pay equity with another employer. This method has been quite controversial.

- Identify where compensation adjustments are required due to disparities in compensation between male and female job classes of equal value.
- Develop a pay equity plan that sets out how the differences in compensation that were discovered through the pay equity process will be remedied, containing:
  - A description of the unit for which the pay equity plan has been developed;
  - An identification of all the job classes that formed the basis of comparisons, including which were female and which were male;
  - A description of the gender-neutral job evaluation system used;
  - Where more than one method of comparison was permissible, the method of comparison used for each job class;
  - The results of the comparisons;
  - An identification of those job classes where permissible differences in compensation existed;
  - For those job classes where differences in compensation exist which are not permissible, a description of how the compensation will be adjusted to achieve pay equity; and
  - A schedule of the payout of compensation adjustments.
- Make compensation adjustments, up to limits prescribed in the legislation.

Most pay equity legislation requires that pay equity be maintained over time. Employers must update or revise their pay equity plans when there are significant changes in circumstances, such as the creation or elimination of job classes, changes to the value of job classes, changes to job comparison processes, and mergers or acquisitions.

Pay Equity Conclusions

Governments around the world play varying roles in the workplace. Legislation in any society

---

job-to-job method

method of comparing pay for male- and female-dominated job classes where each female job class is compared to a male job class of equal or comparable value

proportional value/ wage line method

method of comparing pay for male- and female-dominated job classes when female job classes have no appropriate male comparators under the job-to-job system, where the wage line for male job classes is applied when setting pay for female job classes

proxy comparison method

method of comparing pay for male- and female-dominated job classes when pay equity cannot be achieved through job-to-job or proportional value methods, where female job classes are compared to similar female job classes that have achieved pay equity with another employer

EXHIBIT 12.4 Proportional Value/Wage Line Method: Job Evaluation Points and Salary

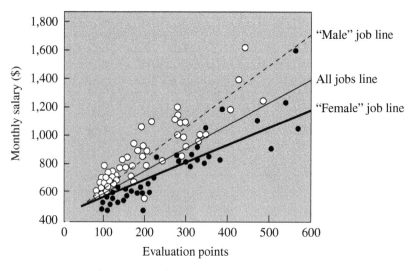

• Female-dominated jobs   ○ Male-dominated jobs

reflects people's expectations about the role of government. Beyond direct regulation, government affects compensation through policies and purchases that affect the supply and demand for labour.

In Canada, legislation reflects the changing nature of work and the workforce. In the 1930s, legislation was concerned with correcting the harsh conditions and arbitrary treatment facing employees, including children. In the 1980s, legislation turned to the issue of human rights. Such legislation has had a profound impact on Canadian society. Nevertheless, discrimination in the workplace, including pay discrimination, remains an unresolved issue.

Pay equity laws require special attention for several reasons. These laws regulate the design and administration of pay systems. Many of the provisions of these laws simply require sound pay practices that should have been employed in the first place. Achieving compliance with these laws rests in large measure on the shoulders of compensation managers. It is their responsibility to ensure that the pay system is properly designed and managed.

Is all this detail on pay equity really necessary? Yes. Without understanding legislation, compensation managers risk violating the law, exposing their employers to considerable liability and expense, and losing the confidence and respect of all employees when a few are forced to turn to the Pay Equity Commission to gain non-discriminatory treatment.

THE IMPACT OF UNIONS ON WAGE DETERMINATION

Unions assume an important role in wage determination. Even in a non-union firm, the protective actions taken by wage and salary administrators are influenced by external union activity. The general factors affecting wages in unionized firms include the impact of the union on: (1) general wage and benefit levels, (2) the structure of wages, (3) non-union firms (also known as spillover), and (4) wage and salary policies and practices in unionized firms.

Union Impact on General Wage Levels

Do unions raise wages? Are unionized employees better off than they would be if they were non-union? Unfortunately, comparing what is versus what might have been is no easy chore. Several measurement problems are difficult to overcome. The ideal situation would be to compare numerous organizations that are identical except for the presence or absence of a union.[22] Any wage differences between these organizations could then be attributed to unionization.

Unfortunately, few such situations exist. One alternative strategy adopted has been to identify organizations within the same industry that differ in level of unionization. For example, consider company A that is unionized, and company B that is not. It is difficult to argue with assurance that wage differences between the two firms are attributable to the presence or absence of a union. First, the fact that the union has not organized the entire industry weakens its power base (strike efforts to shut down the entire industry could be thwarted by non-union firms). Consequently, any assessment of union impact in this example might underestimate the role of unions in an industry where the percentage of unionization is greater. A second problem in measuring union impact is apparent from this example. What if company B grants concessions to employees as a strategy to avoid unionization? These concessions, indirectly attributable to the presence of a union, would lead to underestimation of union impact on wages.

Another strategy in estimating union impact on wages is to compare two different industries that vary dramatically in level of unionization.[23] This strategy suffers because non-unionized industries (e.g., agriculture, service) are markedly different from unionized industries in the types of labour employed and their general availability. Such differences have a major impact on wages independent of the level of unionization and make any statements about union impact difficult to substantiate.

Another situation in which unions affect general wage levels occurs when wage cuts are negotiated. This usually happens in extreme situations where the only other alternative is job loss. Canadian auto workers faced wage cuts in 2009 due to a severe economic recession.[24]

Perhaps the best conclusion about union versus non-union wage differences comes from a summary analysis of 114 different studies.[25] Two important points emerged:

1. *Unions do make a difference in wages.* Union workers earn approximately 10 percent more than their non-union counterparts.
2. *The size of the gap varies from year to year.* During periods of higher unemployment, the impact of unions is greater. During strong economies the union–non-union gap is smaller.

The Structure of Wage Packages

The second compensation issue involves the structuring of wage packages. One dimension of this issue concerns the division between direct wages and employee benefits. Research indicates that the presence of a union adds about 20 to 30 percent to employee benefits.[26] Whether because of reduced management control, strong union–worker preference for benefits, or other reasons, unionized employees also have a greater percentage of their total wage bill allocated to employee benefits.[27] Typically, the higher costs show up in the form of higher pension expenditures or higher insurance benefits.[28] One particularly well-controlled study found unionization associated with a 217 percent higher level of pension expenditures and 127 percent higher insurance expenditures.[29]

A second dimension of the wage structure issue is the evolution of two-tier pay plans. With two-tier pay plans, basically a phenomenon of the union sector, a contract is negotiated which specifies that employees hired after a given target date will receive lower wages than their higher seniority peers working on the same or similar jobs. From management's perspective, tiers can be used as a cost-control strategy to allow expansion or investment, or as a cost-cutting device to allow economic survival.[30] Two-tier pay plans spread initially because unions viewed them as less painful than wage freezes and staff cuts among existing employees, even though they represent a radical departure from the most basic precept of unionization—the belief that all members are equal. Two-tier plans are obviously at odds with this principle. Lower-tier employees, those hired after the contract is ratified, may receive wages significantly lower than employees in the higher tier.[31] The contract may specify that the wage differential be permanent, or that the lower tier may be scheduled ultimately to catch up with the upper tier. Eventually, the inequity resulting from receiving different pay for the same level may cause employee dissatisfaction.[32] Consider the Roman emperor who implemented a two-tier system for his army in AD 217.[33] He was assassinated by his disgruntled troops shortly thereafter. Although such expressions of dissatisfaction are unlikely today, Canadian unions are reluctant to accept a two-tier structure, and may view it as a strategy of last resort.[34]

Union Impact: The Spillover Effect

spillover effect

employers seeking to avoid unionization offer workers the wages, benefits, and working conditions won in rival unionized firms

The impact of unions in general would be understated if we did not account for what is termed the **spillover effect**. Specifically, employers seek to avoid unionization by offering workers the wages, benefits, and working conditions won in rival unionized firms. A classic example is Dofasco, which pays their non-unionized workforce based on the union pay rates at their heavily unionized competitor, Stelco. The non-union management continues to enjoy freedom from union "interference" in decision making, and the workers receive the spillover of rewards already obtained by their unionized counterparts. Several studies document the existence of this phenomenon (although smaller as union power diminishes), providing further evidence of the continuing role played by unions in wage determination.[35]

Role of Unions in Wage and Salary Policies and Practices

Perhaps of greatest interest to current and future compensation administrators is the role unions play in administering wages. The role of unions in administering compensation is outlined primarily in the contract. For example, collective agreements often require union representation on job evaluation committees. The following sections provide further illustrations of this role.

Basis of Pay   The vast majority of contracts specify that one or more jobs are to be compensated on an hourly basis and that overtime pay will be paid beyond a certain number of hours. Notice the specificity of the language in the following contract clause:

A.   Overtime pay is to be paid at the rate of one and one-half (1½) times the basic hourly straight-time rate.
B.   Overtime shall be paid to employees for work performed only after eight (8) hours on duty in any one service day or forty (40) hours in any one service week. Nothing in this Section shall be construed by the parties or any reviewing authority to deny the payment of overtime to employees for time worked outside of their regularly scheduled workweek at the request of the Employer.
C.   Penalty overtime pay is to be paid at the rate of two (2) times the basic hourly straight-time rate. Penalty overtime pay will not be paid for any hours worked in the month of December.
D.   Excluding December, part-time flexible employees will receive penalty overtime pay for all work in excess of ten (10) hours in a service day or fifty-six (56) hours in a service week.

Furthermore, many contracts specify that a premium be paid above the worker's base wage for working non-standard shifts. Alternatively, agreements may specify a fixed daily, weekly, biweekly, or monthly rate. In addition, agreements often indicate a specific day of the week as payday, and sometimes require payment on or before a certain hour. Much less frequently, contracts specify some form of incentive system as the basis for pay. The vast majority of clauses specifying incentive pay occur in manufacturing (as opposed to non-manufacturing) industries.

Occupation–Wage Differentials   Most contracts recognize that different occupations should receive different wage rates. Within occupations, though, a single wage rate prevails, such as:

Occupation	Hourly Wage
Production Line Operator	$ 10.28
Packing Clerk	$ 10.38
QC Inspector	$ 10.48

Experience/Merit Differentials   Single rates are usually specified for workers within a particular job classification. Single-rate agreements do not differentiate wages on the basis of either seniority or merit. Workers with varying years of experience and output receive the same single rate. Alternatively, agreements may specify wage ranges. The following example is fairly typical:

Job Title	Start	2 mo	6 mo	1 yr	2 yr	5 yr	7 yr	10 yr
Packing Clerk	$10.02	$10.47	$11.90	$11.38	$12.01	$12.22	$12.56	$12.76
QC Inspector	10.12	10.57	11.00	11.48	12.11	12.32	12.66	12.86

The vast majority of contracts, as in the example above, specify seniority as the basis for movement through the range. Automatic progression is an appropriate name for this type of movement through the wage range, with the contract frequently specifying the time interval between movements. This type of progression is most appropriate when the necessary job skills are within the grasp of most employees.

A second strategy for moving employees through wage ranges is based exclusively on merit. Employees who are evaluated more highly receive larger or more rapid increments than average or poor performers. Within these contracts, it is common to specify that disputed merit appraisals may be submitted to grievance. If the right to grieve is not explicitly excluded, the union has the implicit right to grieve.

The third method for movement through a range combines automatic and merit progression in some manner. A frequent strategy is to grant automatic increases up to the midpoint of the range and to permit subsequent increases only when merited on the basis of performance appraisal.

Vacations and Holidays   Vacation and holiday entitlements are among clauses frequently found in labour contracts. They, too, use very specific language, as the following example illustrates:

Observance

The following holidays will be observed

New Year's Day—First day in January

Canada Day—First day of July

Labour Day—First Monday in September

Thanksgiving Day—Second Monday in October

Christmas Day—Twenty-fifth day of December

When a holiday falls on a Sunday, the holiday is observed on the following Monday. When a holiday falls on a Saturday, the holiday is observed on the preceding Friday. For employees whose work assignment is to a seven (7) day operation, the holiday shall be celebrated on the day it actually falls. A holiday shall start at 12:01 a.m. or with the work shift that includes 12:01 a.m.

Work on Holidays

Employees required to work on a holiday will be compensated at their discretion either at the rate of one and one-half (1 1/2) times their regular rate of pay, or granted compensatory time at the rate of one and one-half (1 1/2) times, plus straight time pay for the holiday. The choice of compensatory time or wages will be made by the employee.

Wage Adjustment Provisions   Frequently in multi-year contracts, some provision is made for wage adjustment during the term of the contract. There are three major ways these adjustments might be specified: (1) deferred wage increases, (2) reopener clauses, and (3) cost-of-living adjustments (COLA) or escalator clauses. A deferred wage increase is negotiated at the time of initial contract negotiations, with the timing and amount specified in the contract. A reopener clause specifies that wages, and sometimes such non-wage items as pension and benefits, will be renegotiated at a specified time or under certain conditions. Finally, a COLA clause, as noted earlier, involves periodic adjustments based typically on changes in the consumer price index.

▨ UNIONS AND ALTERNATIVE REWARD SYSTEMS

International competition causes a fundamental problem for unions. If a unionized company settles a contract and the company raises prices to cover the increased wage costs, there is always the threat that an overseas competitor with lower labour costs will capture market share. Eventually, enough lost market share means the unionized company will be out of business. To keep this from happening, unions have become more receptive in recent years to alternative reward systems that link pay to performance. After all, if worker productivity rises, product prices can remain relatively stable, even with wage increases.

Alternative reward systems include lump sum, piece rate, gain sharing, profit sharing, and skill-based pay.[36] Willingness to try such plans is greater when the firm faces extreme competitive pressure.[37] In unionized firms that do experiment with these alternative reward systems, though, the union usually insists on safeguards that protect both the union and its workers. The union insists on group-based performance measures with equal payouts to members. This equality principle cuts down strife and internal quarrels among the members and reinforces the principles of equity that are at the very foundation of union beliefs. To minimize bias by the company, performance measures tend to be objective in unionized companies. Most frequently the measures rely on past performance as a gauge of realistic targets, rather than some time study or other engineering standard that might appear more susceptible to tampering.[38]

CONCLUSION

Governments around the world play varying roles in the workplace. Legislation in any society reflects people's expectations about the role of government. Beyond direct regulation, government affects compensation through policies and purchases that affect the supply of and demand for labour.

In Canada, legislation reflects society's concern for justice and fair treatment. Human rights laws prohibit discrimination in employment and pay equity laws prohibit discrimination in compensation. Pay equity laws require special attention because they regulate the design and administration of pay systems.

Unions understand that other countries continue to make inroads in producing goods that were traditionally made only by Western companies. The impact of this increased competition has been most pronounced in the compensation area. Labour costs must be cut in order to improve the competitive stance of Western companies.

Alternative compensation systems to achieve this end are being devised regularly. Unions face a difficult situation: How should they respond to these attacks on traditional compensation systems? Many unions believe that the crisis demands changing attitudes from both management and unions. Labour and management identify compensation packages that both parties can agree on. Sometimes these packages include cuts in traditional forms of wages in exchange for compensation tied more closely to the success of the firm. The future is expected to be dominated by more innovation in compensation design and increased exploration between unions and management for ways to improve the competitive stance of Western business.

Chapter Summary

1. The role of government in compensation is to assess whether procedures for determining pay are fair, whether safety nets for the unemployed and disadvantaged are sufficient, and whether employees are protected from exploitation. Governments also affect the supply and demand for people.

2. The major compensation-related provisions of employment standards legislation are minimum wage, paid vacation, paid holidays, standard hours of work and overtime pay, pay on termination of employment, minimum age of employment, and equal pay for equal work by men and women.

3. Human rights legislation affects compensation in that compensation decisions based on any of the prohibited grounds for discrimination are illegal. Employers must ensure that their compensation systems treat all groups neutrally, compensating for merit rather than membership in a particular group.

4. The persistent wage gap between men and women can be partially, but not fully, explained by factors such as differences in i) occupations, ii) hours worked, iii) types of industries and firms where they are employed, and iv) union membership. Pay equity legislation is intended to redress the unexplained portion of the wage gap assumed to be due to gender discrimination. The laws are intended to address the effects of occupational segregation and the historical undervaluing of work done by women by requiring that female-dominated jobs be compensated in the same way as male-dominated jobs of the same value.

5. Unions affect wage determination through their impact on (1) general wage and benefit levels, (2) the structure of wages, (3) spillover effect on non-union firms, and (4) wage and salary policies and practices in unionized firms.

6. Union attitudes regarding pay-for-performance have gradually become more favourable because of the threat of overseas competitors with lower labour costs taking so much market share from unionized companies that they go out of business.

Key Terms

REVIEW QUESTIONS

1. Consider compensation practices such as skill/competency-based pay, broadbanding, market pricing, and pay-for-performance plans. What are some of the issues related to pay equity that arise when using these practices? How can these issues be resolved?
2. Could the pay objective of regulatory compliance ever conflict with other pay objectives such as consistency, competitiveness, or employee perceptions of fairness? If so, how would you deal with such situations?
3. What factors help account for the male–female wage gap?
4. Most union contracts do not include provisions for merit pay. Given what you have learned here and in Chapter 10, explain why unions oppose merit pay.

EXPERIENTIAL EXERCISE

1. Assume that, as local union president, you have just received valid information that the grocery chain employing your workers is close to bankruptcy. What types of wage concessions might your union be able to make? Which of these are likely to have the least negative impact on your union workers' wages in the short run (one year)? Which is most likely to create internal dissension between different factions of the union?

WEB EXERCISE

Pay Equity Quizzes

The Ontario Pay Equity Commission Web site at www.payequity.gov.on.ca contains a wide variety of information about pay equity in general and on the Ontario pay equity legislation in particular. To find pay equity quizzes, start by going to the Pay Equity Office (PEO) section of the Web site (www.payequity.gov.on.ca/peo/english/about_us.html). Once there, click on "Library," then "user groups," and then "employers." Scroll down to the "Tools" section and complete the *Pay Equity Quiz* and the *Women and Work Quiz*. How did you score? How much/how little did you know in these areas? Which of the answers did you find most surprising?

CASE

Garfield Technology

The Company

Garfield Technology (GT) is an international producer of burglar alarm systems. To crack the international market, GT must comply with quality standards as set by the International Organization for Standardization (ISO). Compliance requires that all products and processes pass a series of 17 strict criteria, the so-called ISO 9000 audit.

The Union

The Technology Workers of Canada organized GT in 2004. In the last contract, both parties agreed to have a three-person panel listen to all disputes between union and management concerning the proper classification of jobs.

Your Role

You are the neutral third party hired to hear the dispute described below. The union representative has voted in the union's favour, and management has sided with management's position. You will break the tie.

The Grievance

A job titled Technical Review Analyst I with responsibility for ISO 9000 audits is slotted as a tier 3 job. (Note: Tier 1 is the low end and tier 5 is the high end for all skilled craft jobs. Different evaluation systems are used for management and for clerical employees.)

Union believes that this job should be evaluated as a tier 4 job. Management contends that both this job and its counterpart in tier 4 (Senior Technical Review Analyst) should be graded in tier 3.

Summary of Important Points in the Union Case

The union asserts, and management agrees, that the only difference historically between auditors classified as Technical Review Analysts I (tier 3) and those classified as Senior Technical Review Analysts (tier 4) was the presence or absence of one task. That task was the performance of systems tests. Only tier 4 personnel performed this work, and this yielded the higher tier classification. With the introduction of ISO 9000 audits, the systems test component of the tier 4 job eventually was phased out, and both tier 3 and tier 4 auditors were asked to perform the ISO 9000 audit. The union and management agree that the systems test work previously performed by tier 4 employees was easier (and less valuable to the company) than the new ISO 9000 work now being performed.

However, the union maintains that this added responsibility from the ISO 9000 audit, which involves about 150 hours of training, is sufficiently complex to warrant tier 4 classification. As partial support, the union provided a list of attendees to one ISO 9000 training session and noted that many of the attendees from other companies are managers and engineers, asserting this as evidence of the complexity involved in the audit material and the importance attached to this job by other firms.

The union also presented evidence to support the assertion that tier 3 personnel performing ISO 9000 audits are doing work of substantially the same value as the old grade 310 work. (Note: The former job evaluation system broke jobs down into many more grades. As of the last contract, jobs are now classified into one of five tiers or grades.)

This grade, as agreed by both the union and the company, is equivalent to the new tier 4.

Summary of Important Points in Management Case

Management's case includes four major points. First, management argues that a Technical Review Analyst performing ISO 9000 audits has a job that is similar in complexity, responsibility, and types of duties to jobs previously classified as grade 308 and 309. Jobs in these old grades are now slotted into tier 3, per the contract.

Second, management presented evidence that many of the duties performed in the ISO 9000 audits were performed in a series of prior audits, variously labelled Eastcore MPA, QSA 1981, and QPS 1982. This long and varied history of similar duties, management contends, is evidence that ISO 9000 does not involve higher level or substantially different (and hence no more valuable) duties than have been performed historically.

Third, management presented both notes and a memorandum from W. P. Salkrist (the company job evaluation expert) in support of its argument that the audit job with ISO 9000 responsibilities should be classified as a tier 4 job. Prior to introduction of the ISO 9000 audit, neither the union nor management had found any reason to complain about the existing prior job evaluations of the tier 3 and tier 4 review analysts.

Fourth, management provided evidence that these jobs at other facilities, with other local contract provisions and conditions, were all classified as tier 3. (Note: Union strongly contests the introduction of this information. In the past, management has vehemently argued that conditions at other facilities should not be introduced because local contracts were negotiated, with different trade-offs being made by the different parties. Union believes that this same logic should now apply if a consistent set of rules is to evolve.)

Questions

1. How would you vote and why?

2. Some experts would argue that enough evidence is presented here for you to make a decision. See if you can figure out what the logic was that led to this conclusion.

3. Also list what other information you would like to have and how that might influence your decision.

COMPENSATION BUDGETS AND ADMINISTRATION

LEARNING OUTCOMES

- Explain the three components of labour cost and how they are mathematically combined to create total labour cost.
- Describe how salary level can be controlled by a top-down approach and a bottom-up approach.
- Identify four inherent controls in compensation design techniques.
- Explain the six stages in the compensation communication cycle.
- Discuss the various issues regarding how organizations structure the compensation function.

Today, managers of compensation are business partners. The financial status of the organization, the competitive pressures it faces, and budgeting are integral to managing compensation. The cost implications of decisions such as updating the pay structure, merit increases, or gain-sharing proposals are critical for making sound decisions. Consequently, budgets are an important part of managing compensation. They are also part of managing human resources and the total organization.[1]

Creating a compensation budget involves trade-offs among the basic pay policies—how much of the increase in external market rates should be budgeted according to employee contributions to the organization's success compared to automatic across-the-board increases. Trade-offs also occur over short- versus long-term incentives, over pay increases contingent on performance versus seniority, and over direct pay (cash) compared to benefits. Budgeting also involves trade-offs between how much to emphasize compensation compared to other aspects of human resource management.

Managers must decide on the financial resources to deploy toward compensation compared to staffing (e.g., workforce size and job security), compared to training (e.g., workforce skills), and so on. The human resource budget implicitly reflects the organization's human resource strategy; it becomes an important part of the human resource plan. Finally, budgeting in the total organization involves allocating financial resources to human resources and/or technology, capital improvements, and the like. Today's managers of compensation need to demonstrate how compensation decisions help achieve organization success while treating employees fairly.

The management of pay involves how the pay systems are used by managers.

ADMINISTRATION AND THE TOTAL PAY MODEL

Consider making pay decisions without a formal system. Each manager could pay whatever seemed to work at the moment. Total decentralization of compensation decision making would result in a chaotic array of rates. Employees could be treated inconsistently and unfairly. Managers might use pay to motivate behaviours that achieved their own objectives, not necessarily those of the organization.

This was the situation in Canada in the early 1900s. The "contract system" made highly skilled workers managers as well as workers. The employer agreed to provide the "contractor" with floor space, light, power, and the necessary raw or semi-finished materials. The contractor hired and paid labour. Pay inconsistencies for the same work were common. Some contractors demanded kickbacks from employees' paycheques; many hired their relatives and friends. Dissatisfaction and grievances became widespread, resulting in legislation and an increased interest in unions.

Now consider the current use of outsourcing. Outsourcing means that organizations secure a range of services from independent, external vendors. Payroll processing and benefits administration are two popular areas to outsource. The danger is that if everything is outsourced, the organization becomes a network of individual contractors.[2] Look back to the early 1900s, replace contracting with outsourcing, and the similarities emerge. Will dissatisfaction, unfair treatment, cost sharing, and risk shifting to employees again be the result? Some see the litigation over the pay of contract workers as history repeating itself.

To avoid this result, any management system must be goal directed. Compensation is managed to achieve the three pay model objectives: efficiency, fairness, and compliance. Properly designed pay techniques help managers achieve these objectives. Rather than goal-directed tools, however, pay systems often degenerate into bureaucratic burdens whose administrators blindly follow the fads and fashions of the day. Techniques become ends in themselves rather than focusing on objectives. Operating managers may complain that pay techniques are more a hindrance than a help. So any discussion of administration must again raise the questions: What does this technique do for us? How does it help us better achieve our objectives? Although it is possible to design a system that includes internal alignment, external competitiveness, and employee contributions, it will not achieve its objectives without competent administration.

Although many pay administration issues have been discussed throughout the book, a few remain to be called out explicitly. Therefore, this chapter covers a variety of compensation administration issues, including (1) managing labour costs, (2) variable pay as a cost control, (3) inherent controls, (4) communication, and (5) structuring the compensation function.

MANAGING LABOUR COSTS

The factors that affect labour costs are shown in Exhibit 13.1.

$$\text{Labour costs} = \text{Employment} \times (\text{Average cash compensation} + \text{Average benefit cost})$$

Using this model, there are three main factors to control in order to manage labour costs: employment (e.g., number of employees and the hours they work), average cash compensation (e.g., wages, bonuses), and average benefit costs (e.g., health and life insurance, pensions). The cash and benefits factors are this book's focus. However, if the objective is to better manage labour costs, it should be clear that all three factors need attention.

Controlling Employment: Number of Employees and Hours

Managing the number of employees and/or the hours worked is the most obvious and perhaps most common approach to managing labour costs. Paying the same wages to fewer employees is

EXHIBIT **13.1** Managing Labour Costs ——————————————————

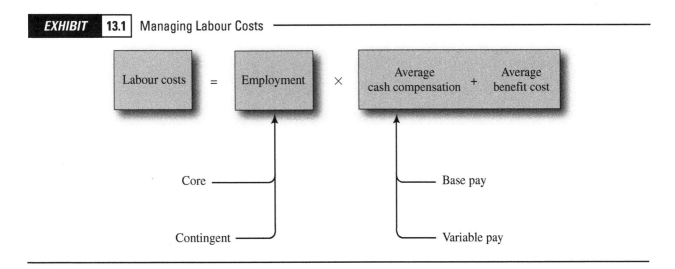

less expensive. However, as part of their social contracts, many European countries have legislation that makes it very difficult to reduce the number of employees. Managing labour costs is a greater struggle in such circumstances.

Announcements of layoffs and plant closings often have favourable effects on stock prices, as investors anticipate improved cash flow and lower costs. However, it doesn't always work out that way. Other evidence suggests that the adverse effects of workforce reduction, such as the loss of trained employees and unrealized productivity, often cause the financial gains of the reductions to be less than anticipated.[3]

To manage labour costs better, many employers attempt to buffer themselves and employees by establishing different relationships with different groups of employees. As Exhibit 13.2 depicts, the two groups are commonly referred to as core employees, with whom a strong and long-term relationship is desired, and contingent workers, whose employment agreements may cover only short, specific time periods.[4] Rather than expand or contract the core workforce, many employers achieve flexibility and control labour costs by expanding or contracting the contingent workforce.[5] Hence, the fixed portion of labour costs becomes smaller and the variable portion larger. And the contingent labour force can be expanded or contracted more easily than the core.

Contingent workers have many and varied compensation packages. It is common to pay more cash (base) but no benefits. Hence, contractors tend to be less expensive. So in the labour cost model, contingent workers' average salary may be greater, but there may be no additional benefits, which can run to one-third or more of total compensation costs.[6] Other issues of contingent worker compensation were covered in the section in Chapter 11 on special groups.

Hours Rather than defining employment in terms of the number of employees, hours of work often are used. For non-management employees, hours over 40 per week are more expensive (1.5 × regular wage). Hence, another approach to managing labour costs is to examine overtime hours rather than adding to the workforce.

Note that the three factors—employment, cash compensation, and benefits costs—are not independent. Overtime hours require higher wages but avoid the benefits cost of hiring a new employee. Other examples of interdependence are the apparent lower wages (and lack of benefits) for some contingent workers, or a program that sweetens retirement packages to make early retirement attractive. Sweetened retirements drive head count down and usually affect the most expensive employees—older, more experienced ones. Hence, the average wage and health care costs for the remaining (younger) workforce probably will be lowered too.[7]

EXHIBIT 13.2 | Core and Contingent Employees

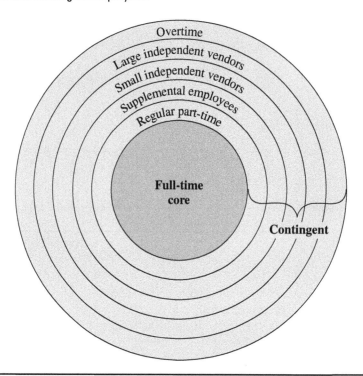

Controlling Average Cash Compensation

Exhibit 13.1 indicates that controlling the average cash compensation includes managing average salary level and variable compensation payments such as bonuses, gain-sharing, or profit sharing. Two approaches to help manage adjustments to average salary level are: (1) top down, in which upper management determines pay and allocates it "down" to each subunit for the plan year, and (2) bottom up, in which individual employee's pay for the next plan year is forecast and summed to create an organization salary budget.

■ CONTROL SALARY LEVEL: TOP DOWN

top-down budgeting

top management of each organizational unit estimates the pay-increase budget for that unit

Top-down budgeting requires top management of each organizational unit to estimate the pay-increase budget for that unit. Once the total budget is determined, it is then allocated to each manager, who plans how to distribute it among employees. There are many approaches to unit-level budgeting in use. A typical one, controlling the planned pay-level rise, will be considered. A planned pay-level rise is simply the percentage increase in average pay for the unit that is planned to occur.

Exhibit 13.3 lists several factors that influence the decision about how much to increase the average pay level for the next period: how much the average level was increased this period, ability to pay, competitive market pressures, turnover effects, and cost of living.

Current Year's Rise

This is the percentage by which the average wage changed in the past year; mathematically:

$$\text{Percentage level rise} = 100 \times \frac{(\text{Average pay at year end} - \text{Average pay at year beginning})}{\text{Average pay at the beginning of the year}}$$

EXHIBIT | **13.3** | What Drives Level Rise?

Current year's rise
Ability to pay
Competitive market   } Percentage increase
Turnover effects   in average pay
Cost of living   in plan year

Ability to Pay

The decision regarding how much to increase the average pay level is in part a function of financial circumstances. Financially healthy employers may wish to maintain their competitive position in the labour market or even to share outstanding financial success through bonuses and profit sharing.

Conversely, financially troubled employers may not be able to maintain competitive market positions. The conventional response in these circumstances has been to reduce employment. However, another option is to reduce the rate of increase in average pay by controlling adjustments in base pay and/or variable pay. Rapidly eroding economic conditions in late 2008 caused many Canadian employers to decrease their previously determined salary budgets for 2009, as described in the .Net Worth box.

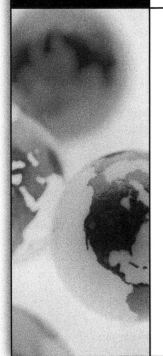

.NET WORTH | Salary Budgets Decline as Economy Worsens

The Conference Board of Canada's annual *Compensation Planning Outlook* for 2009, based on questionnaires completed by 395 Canadian companies in June through August 2008, predicted that "turmoil in the financial markets and the possibility of a global economic turndown will put downward pressures on pay increases in 2009" (pg. i). The average non-union pay increase for 2009 was predicted to be 3.9 percent nationally, down from the actual 4.2 percent increases experienced in 2008.

Following the collapse of equity markets in October 2008, the Conference Board of Canada conducted a winter update survey asking for revised data in December 2008 and January 2009. The update survey was completed by 220 of the original 395 organizations. These results showed that salary-increase predictions for non-union employees had decreased from 3.9 percent to 2.9 percent.

Fifty-seven percent of organizations had not yet finalized their salary budgets for 2009. Overall salary budget increase predictions fell from 4.1 to 3.2 percent and predicted average increases to salary ranges/structures dropped from 2.8 to 2 percent. It was predicted that the economic downturn would spark continued uncertainty and revisions to salary budgets.

Source: A. Cowan, *Compensation Planning Outlook 2009: Economic Uncertainty Spells Caution Ahead*, (October 2009) and *Compensation Planning Outlook 2009: Winter Update* (February 2009). Ottawa ON: The Conference Board of Canada.

Competitive Market Rates

How managers determine an organization's competitive position in relation to their competitors was discussed in Chapter 8. A distribution of market rates for benchmark jobs was collected and analyzed into a single average wage for each benchmark. This "average market wage" became the "going market rate." It then was compared to the average wage paid by the organization for its benchmark jobs.[8] The market rates adjust differently each year in response to a variety of pressures.

Turnover Effects

turnover effect

decreased budget required as lower-paid workers replace employees who leave, calculated as annual turnover rate times planned average increase

The **turnover effect** recognizes the fact that when people leave (through layoffs, quitting, or retiring), they typically are replaced by workers earning a lower wage. Depending on the degree of turnover, the effect can be substantial. Turnover effect can be calculated as annual turnover times planned average increase. For example, assume that an organization whose labour costs equal $1 million a year has a turnover rate of 15 percent and a planned average increase of 6 percent. The turnover effect is 0.9 percent, or $9,000 (0.009 × $1,000,000). So, instead of budgeting $60,000 to fund a 6 percent increase, only $51,000 is needed. The lower average pay also will reduce those benefit costs linked to base pay, such as pensions.

Cost of Living

Although there is little research to support this conclusion, employees undoubtedly compare their pay increases to changes in their costs of living. Unions consistently argue that increasing living costs justify adjustments in pay.[9]

It is important to distinguish between three related concepts: the cost of living, changes in prices in the product and service markets, and changes in wages in labour markets. As Exhibit 13.4 shows, changes in wages in labour markets are measured by pay surveys. These changes are incorporated into the system through market adjustments in the budget and by updating the policy line and range structure. Price changes for goods and services in the product and service markets are measured by several government indexes, one of which is the Consumer Price Index. The third concept, the cost of living, refers to the expenditure patterns of individuals for goods and services. The cost of living is more difficult to measure because employees' expenditures depend on many things: marital status, number of dependants and ages, personal preferences, and so on. Different employees experience different costs of living, and the only accurate way to measure them is to examine the personal expenditures of each employee.

The three concepts are interrelated. Wages in the labour market are part of the cost of producing goods and services, and changes in wages create pressures on prices. Similarly, changes in the prices of goods and services create needs for increased wages in order to maintain the same lifestyle.

Consumer Price Index (CPI)

index that measures changes in prices over time

Consumer Price Index (CPI)   Many people refer to the CPI as a "cost of living" index, and many employers choose, as a matter of pay policy or in response to union pressures, to tie wages to it. However, the CPI does not necessarily reflect an individual employee's cost of living. Instead, it measures changes in prices over time. Changes in the CPI indicate only whether prices have increased more or less rapidly in an area since the base period. For example, a CPI of 110 in Halifax and 140 in Vancouver does not necessarily mean that it costs more to live in Vancouver. It does mean that prices have risen faster in Vancouver since the base year than they have in Halifax, as both cities started with bases of 100.

The index is based on a survey of the actual buying habits of Canadians. Categories of major expenditures are derived, and weights assigned based on each category's percentage of total

EXHIBIT	**13.4**	Three Distinct but Related Concepts and Their Measures

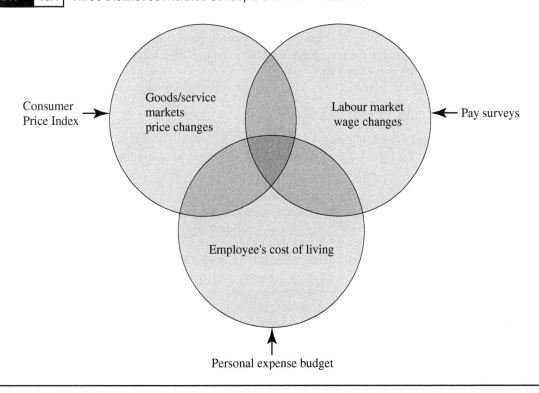

Consumer Price Index → Goods/service markets price changes

Labour market wage changes ← Pay surveys

Employee's cost of living

↑ Personal expense budget

expenditures. For example, a weighting of 5.02 percent for auto purchases means that of the total money spent by all the people in the study, 5.02 percent of it was spent to buy new cars. This weighting plan measures both the price of cars and the frequency of new car purchases.

The CPI is of public interest because changes in it trigger changes in labour contracts, Old Age Security payments, federal and military pensions, and social assistance eligibility, as well as employers' pay budgets.[10] Tying budgets or payments to the CPI is called *indexing*. Note that the cost of living is included in Exhibit 13.3 as an influence on the percentage increase of average salary level. It also may affect cost of benefits, either through health insurance coverage or pension costs.

Rolling It All Together

Managers take into account all these factors—current year's rise, ability to pay, market adjustments, turnover effects, changes in the cost of living, and geographic differentials—and decide what the planned rise in average salary for the next period should be—say 2.9 percent. This means that the organization has set a target of 2.9 percent as the increase in average salary that will occur in the next budget period. It does not mean that every employee's increase will be 2.9 percent. It means that at the end of the budget year, the average salary calculated to include all employees will be 2.9 percent higher than it is now.

The next issue is, how to distribute that 2.9 percent budget in a way that accomplishes management's objectives for the pay system and meets the organization's goals. A variety of methods exists to determine what percentage of the salary budget each manager should receive. Some firms use a uniform percentage, in which each manager gets an equal percentage of the budget, based on the salaries of each subunit's employees. Others vary the percentage allocated to each manager based on pay-related problems, such as turnover or performance, which have been identified in that subunit.

Once salary budgets are allocated to each subunit manager, they become a constraint: a limited fund of money that each manager has to allocate to their employees. Typically, merit increase guidelines are used to help managers make these allocation decisions. Merit increase grids help ensure that different managers grant consistent increases to employees with similar performance ratings and in the same position in their ranges. Additionally, grids help control costs. Examples of grids are included in Chapter 10.

■ CONTROL SALARY LEVEL: BOTTOM UP

bottom-up budgeting

managers forecast the pay increases they will recommend in the coming year

Bottom-up budgeting requires managers to forecast the pay increases they will recommend during the upcoming plan year. Exhibit 13.5 shows the process involved. Each of the steps within this compensation forecasting cycle is described here.

1. Instruct managers in compensation policies and techniques. Train managers in the concepts of a sound pay-for-performance policy and in standard company compensation techniques such as the use of pay increase guidelines and budgeting techniques. Also communicate the salary ranges and market data.
2. Distribute forecasting instructions and worksheets. Furnish managers with the forms and instructions necessary to pre-plan increases. Each employee's performance rating history, past raises, training background, and past incentives are all included. Guidelines for increases based on merit, promotion, and equity adjustments are provided, and all the worksheets are linked so that the manager can model pay adjustments for each employee and see the budgetary effects of those adjustments immediately.

   Some argue that providing such detailed data and recommendations to operating managers makes the system too mechanical. Pay histories ensure that managers are at least aware of this information and that pay increases for any one period are part of a continuing message to individual employees, not some ad hoc response to short-term changes.

EXHIBIT 13.5 Compensation Forecasting and Budgeting Cycle

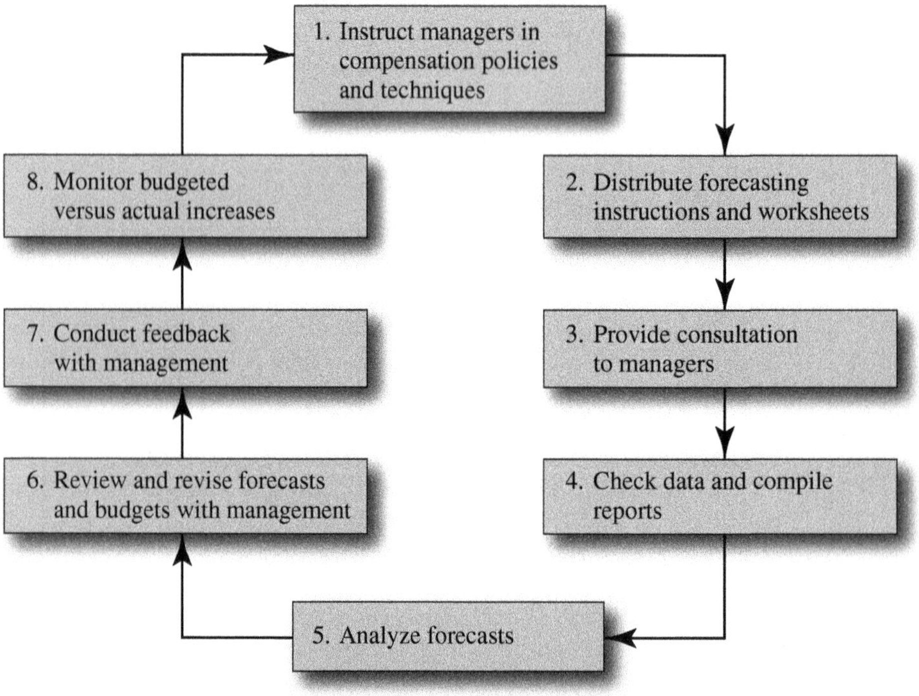

3. Provide consultation to managers. Offer advice and salary information services to managers upon request. An online approach makes it much easier to request and apply such guidance.
4. Check data and compile reports. Audit the increases forecasted to ensure that they do not exceed the pay guidelines and are consistent with appropriate ranges. Then use the data to feed back the outcomes of pay forecasts and budgets.
5. Analyze forecasts. Examine each manager's forecast and recommend changes based on noted inequities between different managers.
6. Review and revise forecasts and budgets with management. Consult with managers regarding the analysis and recommended changes. Obtain top-management approval of forecasts.
7. Conduct feedback with management. Present statistical summaries of the forecasting data by department and establish unit goals.
8. Monitor budgeted versus actual increases. Control the forecasted increases versus the actual increases by tracking and reporting periodic status to management.

The result of the forecasting cycle is a budget for the upcoming plan year for each organization's unit as well as estimated pay treatment for each employee. The budget does not lock in the manager to the exact pay change recommended for each employee. Rather, it represents a plan, and deviations due to unforeseen changes such as performance improvements, unanticipated promotions, and the like are common.

This approach to pay budgeting requires managers to plan the pay treatment for each of their employees. It places the responsibility for pay management on the managers. The compensation manager takes on the role of advisor to operating management's use of the system.[11]

Managing or Manipulating?

Budgeting average compensation costs is increasingly complicated, for two reasons. First is the increased use of variable forms of pay (i.e., gain-sharing, performance bonuses, and stock options). The second is the use of generally accepted accounting practices that permit earnings to be "managed."

Labour costs associated with performance-based pay typically are included in the budget process by estimating the anticipated profits and then the expected profit-sharing pool. Many organizations seek to ensure that these variable incentive plans are "self-funded," i.e., the bonuses (increase in labour costs) are offset by productivity gains (output/costs).

However, controlling variable pay costs may have a "smoke and mirrors" feel to it. At one organization's compensation strategy session, the chief financial officer observed that it was possible to "manage our reported earnings within several percentage points of the target. We can exceed analysts' and shareholder expectations by 1 to 10 percent." This was relatively easy for this company as about one-third of its earnings came from liquid investments in other companies. The remainder was revenue from its products and services. The implication of managing earnings for employees' profit-sharing payouts was not ignored, but clearly it was a secondary concern. Goodbye "pay for performance strategy," hello managed earnings to "meet or slightly exceed analysts' expectations." The point is that measures of financial performance do not provide an immutable "gold standard." They can be "managed."[12]

Clearly, these accounting practices have implications for managing labour costs, especially costs associated with variable pay programs. Compensation managers need to become active players and knowledgeable about the accounting practices used in their organizations.

■ INHERENT CONTROLS

Pay systems have two basic processes that serve to control pay decision making: (1) those inherent in the design of the techniques and (2) the formal budgeting process. Many of the basic techniques already discussed, such as job analysis and evaluation, skill/competency-based plans, policy lines, range minimums and maximums, broad bands, performance evaluation, gain-sharing, and salary increase guidelines, also regulate managers' pay decisions by guiding what managers do. Controls are embedded in the design of these techniques to ensure that decisions are directed toward the pay system's objectives. A few of these controls are examined below.

Range Maximums and Minimums

These ranges set the maximum and minimum dollars to be paid for specific work. The maximum is an important cost control. Ideally, it represents the highest value the organization places on the output of the work. Under job-based structures, skills and knowledge possessed by employees may be more valuable in another job, but the range maximum represents all that the work produced in a particular job is worth to the organization. For example, the job of airline flight attendant is in a pay range with a maximum that is the highest an airline will pay a flight attendant, no matter how well the attendant performs the job.

red circle rates
pay rates above the range maximum

Pressures to pay above the range maximum occur for a number of reasons—for example, when employees with high seniority reach the maximum or when promotion opportunities are scarce. If employees are paid above the range maximum, these rates are called **red circle rates**. Most employers "freeze" red circle rates until the ranges are shifted upward by market update adjustments so that the rate is back within the range again.

green circle rates
pay rates below the range minimum

Range minimums are just that: the minimum value placed on the work. Often rates below the minimum are used for trainees. Rates below minimum may also occur if outstanding employees receive a number of rapid promotions and rate adjustments have not kept up. **Green circle rates** are those that are below the range minimum; they are usually swiftly increased to the range minimum. If red and/or green circle rates become common throughout an organization, the design of the ranges and the evaluation of the jobs should be reexamined.

Broad Bands   Broad bands are intended to offer managers greater flexibility than a grade-range design. Usually, broad bands are accompanied by external market "reference rates" and "shadow ranges" that guide managers' decisions. Bands may be more about career management than pay decisions. From the perspective of managing labour costs, broad bands really don't play a role. Rather, the control is in the salary budgets given to managers. The manager has flexibility in pay decisions, as long as the total pay comes in under the budget.

Compa-Ratios

Range midpoints reflect the pay policy line of the employer in relationship to external competition. To assess how managers actually pay employees in relation to the midpoint, an index called a **compa-ratio** is often calculated.

compa-ratio
ratio of average rates actually paid to range midpoint

$$\text{Compa-ratio} = \frac{\text{Average rates actually paid}}{\text{Range midpoint}}$$

A compa-ratio of less than 1.00 means that, on average, employees in that range are paid below the midpoint. Translated, this means that managers are paying less than the intended policy. There may be several valid reasons for such a situation. The majority of employees may be new or recent hires; they may be poor performers; or promotion may be so rapid that few employees stay in the job long enough to get to the high end of the range.

A compa-ratio greater than 1.00 means that, on average, the rates exceed the intended policy. The reasons for this are the reverse of those mentioned above: a majority of workers with high seniority, high performance, low turnover, few new hires, or low promotion rates. Compa-ratios may be calculated for individual employees, for each range, for organization units, or for functions.

One control designed into pay techniques is the mutual sign-off on job descriptions required of supervisors and subordinates. Another is slotting new jobs into the pay structure via job evaluation, which helps ensure that jobs are compared on the same factors.

Similarly, an organization-wide performance management system is intended to ensure that all employees are evaluated on similar factors.

Variable Pay

Variable pay depends on performance and is not added to employees' base pay. Thus, the compounding effects of merit pay and across-the-board increases do not occur. The essence of variable pay is that it must be re-earned each period, in contrast to conventional merit pay increases or across-the-board increases that are added to base pay each year and that increase the base on which the following year's increase is calculated.

Increases added into base pay have compounding effects on costs, and these costs are significant. For example, $15 a week take-home pay added onto a $40,000 base compounds into a cash flow of $503,116 over 10 years. In addition, costs for many benefits also increase. By comparison, the organization could use that same $503,000 to keep base pay at $40,000 a year and pay a 26.8 percent bonus every single year. As the example shows, the greater the ratio of variable pay to base pay, the more variable (flexible) the organization's labour costs. The general labour cost model in Exhibit 13.1 shows that the greater the ratio of contingent to core workers and variable to base pay, the greater the variable component of labour costs, and the greater the options available to managers to control these costs.

But a caution: Although variability in pay and employment may be an advantage for managing labour costs, it may be less appealing from the standpoint of managing fair treatment of employees. The inherent financial insecurity built into variable plans may adversely affect employees' financial well-being and subsequently their behaviours at work and attitudes toward their employers. Managing labour costs is only one objective of managing compensation; other objectives in the pay model include sustaining competitive advantage (productivity, total quality, customer service, and costs) and equitable treatment of employees.

Analyzing Costs

Costing out wage proposals is commonly done prior to recommending pay increases. It is also used in preparation for collective bargaining. For example, it is useful to bear in mind the dollar impact of a 1-cent-per-hour wage change or a 1 percent change in payroll when one goes into bargaining. Knowing these figures, negotiators can quickly compute the impact of a request for a 5 percent wage increase. Commercial computer software is available to analyze almost every aspect of compensation information, providing analysis and data that improve the administration of the pay system. Spreadsheet programs can simulate alternate wage proposals and compare their potential effects. Software also can evaluate salary survey data and simulate the cost impact of incentive and gain-sharing options. However, trained compensation decision makers are still required to make decisions based on the results.

Analyzing Value Added   Only a few organizations calculate the cost and value added by their pay programs, because most compensation specialists consider their tools "ineffective" to determine the value added. However, a handful of companies, supported by consultants and researchers, are beginning to analyze the value added (or return on investments) of pay decisions. This analysis requires a shift in how compensation is viewed. Compensation becomes an investment as well as an expense. Decisions are based on analysis of the return on this investment. The hope is to answer questions such as, "So what" returns are expected from spending more on the top 25 percent of performers (as does General Electric), or on a new incentive plan based on a balanced scorecard (as does Citigroup)? Measuring the value gained from various programs is like the search for life on Mars: Both processes require an awful lot of assumptions, and both are susceptible to hope and hype.

Exhibit 13.6 illustrates the approach to assessing value gained. The company in this exhibit has already done an analysis that suggests that the top 10 percent of employees improve returns by about 2 to 5 percent of their average salary. Now the company is considering two actions:

1.   Implement a bonus plan based on balanced scorecards for individual managers.
2.   Increase the differentiation between top performers and average performers.

The exhibit shows the analysis of potential value added by these two options. The returns are grouped into four types: recruiting and retaining top talent, reducing turnover of top performers, revenue enhancement, and productivity gains. The logic, assumptions, measures, and estimates of gains are described in the exhibit. The cautious reader will immediately see that the assumptions are critical and based on research evidence, best estimates, and judgments.

The practice of analyzing the returns from compensation decisions is in its early stages. The promise is that it will direct thinking beyond treating compensation as only an expense to considering the returns gained as well. Nevertheless, managers still must use their heads as well as their models. Treating compensation as an investment and employees as human capital risks losing sight of them as people. The fairness objective must not get lost in the search for return on investment.

Making Information Useful—Compensation Enterprise Systems   Most managers find themselves overwhelmed with too much information. The challenge is to make the information useful. Compensation software transforms data into useful information and guides decision making. Many software packages that serve a variety of purposes are available. Some of them support *employee self-service,* by which employees can access their personal information, make choices about which benefits coverage they prefer, access vacation schedules, or check out a list of child care or eldercare service providers. *Manager self-service* helps managers pay their employees appropriately. *Communication portals,* designed for employees or managers, explain compensation policies and practices, answer frequently asked questions, and explain how these systems affect their pay. Other software *processes transactions.* It standardizes forms, performs some analysis, and creates reports at the click of the mouse. The advantage is that all employees at all locations are on the same system.

While compensation software is proliferating, what remains a scarcer resource is the intellectual capital: the compensation knowledge and judgment required to understand which information, analyses, and reports are useful. This intellectual capital includes analytical skills and knowledge of the business. A shortage of this knowledge among compensation managers not only limits the usefulness of compensation software but also limits the contribution of compensation management.

■ COMMUNICATION: MANAGING THE MESSAGE

Compensation communicates. It signals what is important and what is not. If a pay increase is provided for one more year of experience on the job, then one more year is important. If the pay increase is equal to any change in the CPI, then cost of living is important. If the increase is for moving to a bigger job or for outstanding performance, then a bigger job or outstanding performance is important. Pay sends a powerful message about what matters. Therefore, managing that message is important.

Earlier in the book, it was stressed that employees must believe that the pay system is fair. Employees' perceptions of fairness of the pay system are shaped through formal communication programs about their pay and performance and through participation in the design of the system.

EXHIBIT 13.6 Illustration of Value-Added Analysis

Description of Value	Assumptions	Measure	Value Added — Low Estimate	Value Added — High Estimate
		Recruiting/Retaining Top Talent		
Increase pool of top people applying; Increase percent accepting offers; decrease time to fill position	Top performers improve returns by 2% to 5% of average salary ($68,000)	Increase top talent yield ratios and turnover rates	Increases revenues by $1,400/top person	Improves revenues by $3,400/top person
		Reduced Turnover/Replacement Costs		
Reduction of recruiting costs due to lower turnover of top performers	Reduction in turnover of one top performer results in a savings of $25,000 (based on an average salary of $68,000)	Savings of $25,000/top performer. Productivity savings reflected in "loss of revenue" section	$100,000 for a reduction of four "resigned" top employees	$500,000 for a reduction of 10 "resigned" top employees
		Revenue Enhancers		
Reduced loss of revenue due to faster time to fill key customer-facing (sales, technical support) and other key positions	Revenue will increase by some percentage (e.g., 5%). Head count remains constant	Revenue increase. Assume current revenue of $2 billion	2% or $40 million	5% or $100 million
Greater revenue because of focus on revenue and customer goals as driven by the balanced scorecard				
Increased revenue because of stronger and longer-lasting customer relationships due to retention of key/top performers through market competitiveness and pay differentiation				
		Productivity Gains		
Increased productivity by retaining top performers through significant pay differentiation and market-competitive base pay	Retaining and engaging more of the top employees results in significant productivity gains and revenue generation because top employees are 25% to 50% more productive than the average employee	Increased revenue (reflected in revenue gains–above). Head-count reduction (need fewer employees or grow slower)	A reduction in 10 head count results in a savings of $900,000 ($68,000 employee + benefit cost)	A reduction in 50 head count results in a savings of $4.5 million
Increased productivity of all employees because of greater perception of "internal alignment" and "market competitiveness" resulting from paying competitively with the market and common programs	Increasing the productivity of all results in increased revenue, customer satisfaction, or fewer head count			
Terminating low-productivity employees and replacing them with high-productivity employees result in significant productivity gains and revenue generation		Head-count reduction because fewer top performers achieve the same results as more lower performers	A reduction in 1 head count results in a savings of $90,000	A reduction in 5 head count results in a savings of $450,000

WorldatWork, an international group of compensation and human resources professionals, recommends a six-stage process of communication, shown in Exhibit 13.7.[13]

Step one is, not surprisingly, defining the objectives of the communication program. Perhaps the objective is to ensure that employees fully understand all the components of the compensation system; perhaps it is to change expectations, or to better capitalize on the motivational aspects built into the compensation systems. Although specifying objectives as a first step seems obvious, it is often overlooked in the rush to design an attractive brochure.

Step two is to collect information from executives, managers, and employees concerning their current perceptions, attitudes, and understanding of the compensation programs in effect. Information may be gathered through opinion survey questionnaires, focus groups, or formal or informal interviews. Some research concludes that employees typically misperceive the pay system by overestimating the pay of those with lower-level jobs and underestimating the pay of those in higher-level jobs. If differentials are underestimated, their motivational value is diminished.

 Furthermore, there is evidence to suggest that the goodwill engendered by the act of being open about pay may affect employees' attitudes toward pay. Interestingly, the research also shows that employees in companies with open pay communication policies are as inaccurate in estimating pay differentials as those in companies in which pay secrecy prevails. However, employees under open pay policies tend to express higher satisfaction with their pay and with the pay system.

After the information on current attitudes and perceptions is analyzed, *step three* is to develop a communication strategy that will accomplish the original objectives. There is no standard approach about what to communicate to individuals about their own pay or that of their colleagues. Some organizations adopt a *marketing approach* that includes consumer attitude surveys about the product, snappy advertising about the pay policies, and elaborate videotapes

---

EXHIBIT   13.7 | The Compensation Communication Cycle

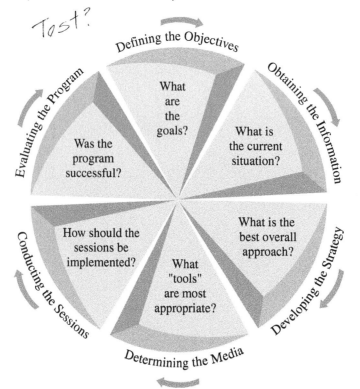

expounding policies and strengths. The objective is to manage expectations and attitudes about pay. In contrast, the *communication approach* tends to provide technical details. The marketing approach focuses on the quality and advantages of overall policies and is silent on specifics such as range maximums, increase guides, and the like.

Steps four and five of the communication process are to determine the most effective media, in light of the message and the audience, and to conduct the campaign. Exhibit 13.8 recommends designing the message in terms of detail and emphasis according to the audience. Executives, for example, will be interested in how the compensation programs fit the business strategy (Chapter 2).

Managers will need to know how to use the development and motivation aspects of the compensation program for the people they supervise. Employees may want to know the process and policy (procedural justice) as well as specifics about how their pay is determined.

Reach versus Richness   A trade-off in any communication program is what should they know, and when should they know it. A "richness" approach tailors information to the individual employee on a number of employment-related topics. The danger is overload—information so detailed that employees don't bother sorting through it to find out what they really wanted to know.

EXHIBIT 13.8 Conducting Formal Communication Sessions for Various Audiences

Compensation Components Communicated to All Audiences

- Job Descriptions
- Job Evaluation
- Market Data Collection and Analysis
- Pay Structure Development
- Incentive Plan Design
- Performance Appraisal System
- Salary Management Administration Procedures
- Benefit Plans

The Level of Detail and Emphasis Varies Depending upon the Audience

Executives	Managers	Employees
Components explained in a general way. Emphasis on strategic implications of the compensation system. Executive compensation explained in detail in one-on-one meetings	Components thoroughly explained throughout the communication process; reviewed at the formal sessions. Emphasis on development and motivation of employees using salary management, performance appraisal, and incentive plan	Fairly detailed explanation of components. Emphasis on both process and policy information. Particular attention paid to the workings of the incentive plan

Intended and Unintended Consequences   *Step six* of the communication process suggests that the program be evaluated. Did it accomplish its goals? Pay communication can have unintended consequences. For example, providing accurate pay information may cause some initial short-term concerns among employees. Over the years, employees may have rationalized a set of relationships between their pay and the perceived pay and efforts of others. Receiving accurate data may require that those perceptions be adjusted.

Amount of Information to Communicate

If the pay system is not based on work-related or business-related logic, then the wisest course probably is to avoid formal communication until the system is put in order. However, avoiding formal communication is not synonymous with avoiding communication. Employees are constantly receiving intended and unintended messages through the pay treatment they receive.

Many employers communicate the range for an incumbent's present job and for all the jobs in a typical career path or progression to which employees reasonably can aspire. Some also communicate the typical pay increases that can be expected for poor, satisfactory, and top performance. The rationale is that employees exchange data (not always factual) and/or guess at normal treatment, and the rumour mills are probably incorrect. One potential danger in divulging increase schedule data is the inability to maintain that schedule in the future for reasons outside the control of the compensation department (e.g., economic or product market conditions). Nevertheless, providing accurate data may have a positive effect on employee work attitudes and behaviours.

Opening the Books   There are some who advocate sharing all financial information with employees.[14] All of it. For 10 years, employees at Springfield Remanufacturing, a rebuilder of engines, have been given weekly peeks at everything from revenues to labour costs. The employees, who own 31 percent of the company stock, and others argue that this "open book" approach results in high commitment and an understanding of how to maintain competitiveness. Many employers don't share information with such gusto, but they are increasingly disclosing more to their employees. Some are even providing basic business and financial training to help employees better understand the information.

Devotees of opening the books and financial training believe that these methods will improve attitudes and performance, but there is no research to support this conclusion. Web sites increasingly are being used as part of communicating compensation and "opening the books." With salary data available on the Internet (albeit often inaccurate and misleading data), developing in-house compensation sites has appeal.

At a minimum, perhaps the most important information to be communicated is the work-related and business-related rationale on which pay systems are based. Some employees may not agree with this rationale or with the results, but at least it will be made clear that pay is determined by something other than the whims or biases of their supervisors.

Participation: Beliefs, Payoffs, and Practices

An often-unchallenged premise of this book has been that employee (and manager) participation in the design and administration of pay systems pays off through increased understanding and commitment. As one might expect, research on the effects of employee participation in general shows mixed results. Overall, the evidence suggests that participation does have positive effects, but that they are not overwhelming. Generally, employees seem to have input into aspects that are directly related to them (i.e., job descriptions), but not into overall policies, structure, or competitor salary surveys.

PAY: CHANGE AGENT IN RESTRUCTURING

Compensation often plays a singular role when organizations restructure. Strategic changes in the business strategy mean that the compensation strategy must be realigned as well.[15] Pay is a powerful signal of change; changing people's pay captures their attention.

Pay changes can play two roles in any restructuring: Pay can be a leading catalyst for change or a follower of the change. Shifts from conventional across-the-board annual increases to profit sharing, or from narrow job descriptions and ranges to broad roles and bands signal major change to employees. To signal yet another major restructuring, one company shifted the measures it used to trigger its bonus plan from 25 percent based on corporate earnings and 75 percent on individual performance, to 75 percent on corporate earnings and 25 percent on individual performance. Managers were meant to "understand" the need to focus on improving performance. Unfortunately, two years later the company restructured again. So it is not clear whether pay alone can be a sufficient catalyst.

Whether pay is a leading catalyst for change or a follower of change, compensation managers need to learn how to implement and manage change. Not only do they need to know the strategic and technical aspects of compensation, they also need to learn how to bargain, resolve disputes, empower employees, and develop teams.

STRUCTURING THE COMPENSATION FUNCTION

Compensation professionals seem to be constantly reevaluating where the responsibility for the design and administration of pay systems should be located within the organization. The organizational arrangements of the compensation function vary widely.

Centralization–Decentralization

An important issue related to structuring the function revolves around the degree of decentralization (or centralization) in the overall organization structure. Decentralized refers to a management strategy of giving separate organization units the responsibility to design and administer their own systems. This contrasts with a centralized strategy, which locates the design and administration responsibility in a single corporate unit.

Some firms, such as 3M and Xerox, have relatively large corporate staffs whose responsibility it is to formulate pay policies and design the systems. Administration of these policies and systems falls to those working in various units, often human resources generalists. Such an arrangement runs the risk of formulating policies and practices that are well tuned to overall corporate needs, but less well tuned to each unit's particular needs and circumstances. The use of task forces, with members drawn from the generalists in the affected units, to design new policies and techniques helps to diminish this potential problem.

More decentralized organizations have relatively small corporate compensation staffs (three or four professionals). Their primary responsibility is to manage the systems by which executives and the corporate staff are paid. These professionals operate in a purely advisory capacity to other organization subunits. The subunits, in turn, may employ compensation specialists. Or the subunits may choose to employ only human resources generalists rather than compensation specialists, and may turn to outside compensation consultants to purchase the expertise required on specific compensation issues.

Compensation could even be handled completely by teams of managers rather than compensation specialists. Decentralizing certain aspects of pay design and administration has considerable appeal. Pushing these responsibilities (and expenses) close to the units, managers, and employees affected by them may help to ensure that decisions are business related. However, decentralization is not without problems. For example, it may be difficult to transfer employees from one business unit to another. Problems crop up as a result of designing pay systems that support a subunit's objectives but run counter to the overall corporate objectives. So, too, does the potential for pay discrimination.

Flexibility within Corporate-wide Principles

The answer to these and related problems of decentralization can be found in developing a set of corporate-wide principles or guidelines that all must meet. These principles may differ for each major pay technique. For example, GE's business units worldwide have the flexibility to design incentive plans tailored to each unique business unit's strategies and cultures. The only guidance is to ensure that the plans adhere to GE's basic beliefs, improve financial and business objectives, and maintain or enhance GE's reputation.

The pay system is one of many management systems used in the organization. Consequently, it must be congruent with these other systems. For example, it may be appealing, on paper at least, to decentralize some of the compensation functions. However, if financial data and other management systems are not decentralized also, the pay system may not fit and may even be at odds with other systems.

Reengineering and Outsourcing

Reengineering the compensation function involves changing the process of paying people. It means reshaping the compensation function to make it more client- or customer-focused. Clients may include employees, managers, owners, and perhaps even real customers of the organization. The basic question asked during reengineering is, "Does each specific activity (technique) directly contribute to our objectives (i.e., to our competitive advantage)?" If some added value isn't apparent, then the technique should be dropped. The next question, directed at those pay activities that do contribute to achieving objectives is, "Should we be doing the specific activity in-house, or can others do it more effectively? That is, should we outsource it?"

Outsourcing is a viable alternative in the compensation (and benefits) field as organizations struggle to cease doing activities that do not directly contribute to strategic objectives.[16] In a recent survey, about 33 percent of over 1,000 firms reported that they already outsourced major responsibilities for their pay (e.g., market surveys and structure design) and benefits administration.

Cost savings is the apparent major short-term advantage of outsourcing. All those compensation experts can be laid off or retrained. Major disadvantages of outsourcing include less responsiveness to unique and specific employee–manager problems, less control over decisions that are often critical to all employees (i.e., their pay), and information leaks to rivals and competitors.[17]

CONTROLS AS GUIDELINES: LET (THOUGHTFUL) MANAGERS BE FREE

One of the major attacks on traditional compensation plans is that they often degenerate into bureaucratic nightmares that interfere with the organization's ability to respond to competitive pressures. Some recommendations for reducing the controls and guidelines inherent in any pay plan are as follows: broadbanding eliminates or at least reduces the impact of range maximums and minimums; replacing merit grids with awards and bonuses eliminates the link between the pay increase and the employees' salary position in the range and performance rating; and replacing job evaluation with skill-based plans opens up the freedom to assign employees to a wider variety of work, regardless of their pay and the value of the work they perform.

Yet permitting managers to be free to pay employees as they judge best rests on a basic premise: Managers will use pay to achieve the organization's objectives—efficiency, fairness, and compliance with regulations—rather than their own objectives. Clearly, some balance between strict controls and chaos is required to ensure that pay decisions are directed at the organization's goals, yet permit sufficient flexibility for managers and employees to respond to unique situations. Achieving the balance becomes part of the art of managing compensation.

CONCLUSION

The discussion of the pay administration process is now complete. Administration includes control: control of the way managers decide individual employees' pay as well as control of overall costs of labour. As was noted, some controls are designed into the fabric of the pay system (inherent controls, range maximums and minimums, etc.). The salary budgeting and forecasting processes impose additional controls. The formal budgeting process focuses on controlling labour costs and generating the financial plan for the pay system. The budget sets the limits within which the rest of the system operates.

It was also noted that with continuous change in organizations, compensation managers must understand how to manage change and be knowledgeable business partners.

Other aspects of administration we examined in this chapter included the fair treatment of employees in communications and participation. The basic point was that pay systems are tools, and like any tools, they need to be evaluated in terms of usefulness in achieving an organization's objectives.

CHAPTER SUMMARY

1. The three components of labour cost are employment (number of employees and hours they work), average cash compensation, and average benefit cost. Average cash compensation and average benefit cost are added together and then multiplied by employment levels in order to create total labour cost.
2. Salary levels can be controlled by a top-down budgeting approach by requiring top management of each unit to estimate the pay increase budget for the entire unit, and then allocating it to each manager, who plans how to distribute it among subordinates. The bottom-up budgeting approach requires each manager to forecast the pay increases he or she will recommend during the upcoming plan year, which are then reviewed by top management for approval.
3. Four inherent controls on pay decision making in compensation design techniques are range maximums and minimums, compa-ratios, variable pay, and costing of wage proposals.
4. The six stages in the compensation communication cycle are: (1) defining the objectives and goals of the communication program; (2) obtaining information on the current compensation program; (3) developing the strategy for the best overall communication approach—a marketing (sales) approach or a more technical communication approach; (4) determining the media and tools that are most appropriate; (5) conducting communication sessions; and (6) evaluating the success of the program.
5. Various issues regarding how organizations structure their compensation function include: decisions on centralization versus decentralization of compensation management, level of flexibility for compensation management decisions within corporate-wide principles for all systems, and consideration of reengineering or outsourcing the compensation function.

KEY TERMS

REVIEW QUESTIONS

1. What are some of the approaches used to control labour costs, based on Exhibit 13.1? Based on budgeting methods? Based on the design of the pay system?
2. Which activities in administering the pay system are likely candidates to be outsourced? Why?
3. How do employee communication and participation influence the effectiveness of the pay system?

EXPERIENTIAL EXERCISES

1. Find a news article or information about the impact of layoffs some time after the cuts were made. Was the layoff successful in reducing costs? In achieving corporate objectives?

2. Calculate the compounding effect of an annual 5 percent merit pay increase on a salary of $60,000 over five years. How much less money would be paid out if the merit pay increase of 5 percent were not added to base pay and had to be re-earned each year?

3. Consider the top-down and bottom-up approaches to controlling salary levels. Which one do you think would be more effective in a small entrepreneurial company? In a large government department?

WEB EXERCISE

Salary Budgeting at Athabasca University

Some organizations make their salary budgeting process public. Go to the Athabasca University Web site for information on their policy regarding annual merit increments: www.athabascau.ca/policy/humanresources/070_004.htm. Read the policy carefully. Does Athabasca University use a top-down or bottom-up salary budgeting process? Explain.

CASE

Two Harbours Teachers

Private school teachers typically are paid according to salary schedules that include:

1. "Steps" that pay for accumulating experience.

2. "Lanes" that pay for extra university credits.

Steps and lanes operate to boost pay even if the school does not grant any across-the-board or cost-of-living increases.

Critics of such schedules say that they guarantee steadily climbing costs, even in times when the school's finances do not permit increases.

Exhibit 1 shows a simplified salary schedule at Two Harbours, a private school that employs 100 teachers and whose enrolment is growing at about 3 percent a year.

A. Calculate the change in salary in year 2 under the following conditions:

1. Six teachers earning an average salary of $43,444 resign.

2. Nine teachers are hired at an average of $25,666.

EXHIBIT 1 Two Harbours Salary Schedule Showing Distribution of 100 Teachers ————

Year One

Total salaries for 100 teachers $3,110,000
Average salary $ 31,100

	B.A. degree	B.A. and credits	M.A. degree	M.A. and credits
Step 5	7 teachers	18 teachers	14 teachers	11 teachers
	$29,000	$33,000	$36,000	$41,000
Step 4	4 teachers	6 teachers	5 teachers	1 teacher
	$27,000	$30,000	$34,000	$38,000
Step 3	6 teachers	4 teachers	3 teachers	1 teacher
	$25,000	$28,000	$31,000	$35,000
Step 2	6 teachers	2 teachers	2 teachers	0 teachers
	$23,000	$26,000	$28,000	$32,000
Step 1	8 teachers	1 teacher	1 teacher	0 teachers
	$22,000	$24,000	$26,000	$28,000

Each step represents four years of service; the vertical columns show levels of university credits. In year 2, the faculty moves from an average of 3.86 steps to 3.93, and the proportion of teachers with master's degrees increases from 38 to 39 percent.

Visit the Online Learning Centre at

www.mcgrawhill.ca/olc/milkovich

◾ APPENDIX 13–A
COMPENSATION WEB SITES

Consulting Firms

Consulting Firms	WWW Address	What Does Web Site Offer?
Hay Group	www.haygroup.com/ca www.haygrouppaynet.com	▪ News releases, legislative and regulatory updates, and survey data ▪ Hay PayNet allows organization to tap into Hay's customized compensation databases
Hewitt Associates	www.hewitt.com/canada	▪ Provides press releases, full text articles, and brief items on laws and regulations
Runzheimer International	www.runzheimer.com	▪ Information on salary differentials living costs, and travel and moving benefits
Sibson Consulting	www.sibson.ca	▪ Case studies drawn from client experiences ▪ Items on compensation design, organization development, etc.
Towers Watson	www.towerswatson.com/canada-english	▪ Information on international pay and benefits ▪ New legislation, regulations, and new issues in major countries ▪ Global news service, including reports and surveys from all over the world
Mercer	www.mercer.ca	▪ Surveys on salaries, performance pay, assessment, compensation committees, and executive pay

Broad Listing for Compensation

Employee Compensation	WWW Address	What Does Web Site Offer?
WorldatWork	www.worldatwork.org	▪ Information on seminars and organization certification programs ▪ Listings of publications
Canadian Management Centre	www.cmctraining.org	▪ Information about training and programs, publications, and other resources
Canadian Council of Human Resources Assocations	www.cchra-ccarh.ca	▪ HR news and wide range of links, including compensation and benefits ▪ A number of links to human resources service providers

Benefits

Benefits	WWW Address	What Does Web Site Offer?
Employee Benefit Research Institute (EBRI)	www.ebri.org	• Lists of health care providers and links to other benefits and business Web sites • A list of links to other benefits sources on the Web • EBRI reports on benefit issues
International Foundation of Employee Benefit Plans (IFEBP)	www.ifebp.org	• Industry news • Reports on benefit issues • Full listing of IFEBP services and resources

Pensions and Retirement

Pensions and Retirement	WWW Address	What Does Web Site Offer?
Association of Canadian Pension Management	www.acpm.com	• Canada's pension portal • Pension consultants • Industry organizations • Industry publications • Regulation
Canadian Pension & Benefits Institute	www.cpbi-icra.ca	• Seminars • Conferences

APPENDIX

INTERNATIONAL PAY SYSTEMS

Around the world, global competitive forces have changed the way people work and the way they get paid. Toyota is dismantling its seniority-based pay system for managers and replacing it with a merit-based system.[1] Toshiba is offering stock awards, which were not even legal in Japan only a few years ago.[2] Deutsche Bank, Nokia, Siemens, and other European countries are shifting to variable pay and performance-based (rather than personality-based) appraisal in their search for ways to improve productivity and control labour costs.[3]

Global acquisitions of former competitors change international pay systems. As part of its takeover and restructuring of Tungsram Electric in Hungary, General Electric changed from a rigid seniority-based pay system to broad bands, market-based wage rates, and performance bonuses. India's leading software companies, such as Tata Consultancy Services, Wipro, and Infosystems all use performance-based plans for their software engineers.

Sometimes the changes in pay are directly tied to larger, cataclysmic sociopolitical change, as in China, Russia, and Eastern Europe where government authorities had long dictated pay rates.[4] Now companies in these countries face the challenge of devising pay systems responsive to business and market pressures while maintaining a sense of social justice among the people. In China, the only hope for profitability is to cut the massively bloated numbers of employees. Yet an army of unemployed people without social support threatens stability and even government survival.[5] Some state-owned enterprises, such as Baogang, the country's largest steelmaker, have moved to more "market and performance-based" systems, even though labour markets are just emerging in many regions in China. Shanghai Shenyingwanguo Security Company and Shanghai Bank have implemented job-based structures to help them retain key employees and increase pay satisfaction. Most surprising of all is that some town-owned enterprises are using stock awards as part of their employee compensation.[6]

However, too much change and experimentation can have a dark side that threatens social unrest. Following the breakup of the USSR, workers in some of the former socialist countries reported going unpaid for months. At one point, over half the Russian workers said they were owed back wages, with the average wait to be paid 4.8 months.[7] In Russia, a friend maintains that "the most effective pay delivery system is a brown bag under the table."

So it is a time of unprecedented global change, but some historical perspective may help.

> … There is hardly a village or town anywhere on the globe whose wages are not influenced by distant foreign markets, whose infrastructure is not financed by foreign capital, whose engineering, manufacturing, and even business skills are not imported from abroad, or whose labor markets are not influenced by the absence of those who had emigrated or by the presence of strangers who had immigrated.[8]

This is not a description of the 21st century. Rather, it is from 100 years ago. In the late 1800s, trade barriers were reduced, free trade was promoted, and mass migration of people was underway. Thanks to transoceanic telegraphic cables, the speed of communication increased dramatically, and investment capital flowed between nations. Yet by 1917 these global links had been replaced by a global war. Citizens desired security rather than face the greater risks and uncertainty of globalization. Nations began to raise tariffs to protect domestic companies hurt by foreign competitors. Immigrants were accused of "robbing jobs." Historians conclude that "globalization is neither unique nor irreversible; it has and can again sow seeds of its own destruction."[9]

MANAGING PAY VARIATIONS: THE GLOBAL GUIDE

Understanding international compensation begins with recognizing variations (differences and similarities) and figuring out how best to manage them. How people get paid around the world depends on differences (and similarities) in the factors in the global guide depicted in Exhibit A-1. Four general ones are listed: *economic, institutional, organizational, and employee.* These factors have been discussed throughout the book; now they can be applied globally. But when shifting from a

EXHIBIT **A-1** Guide to International Compensation

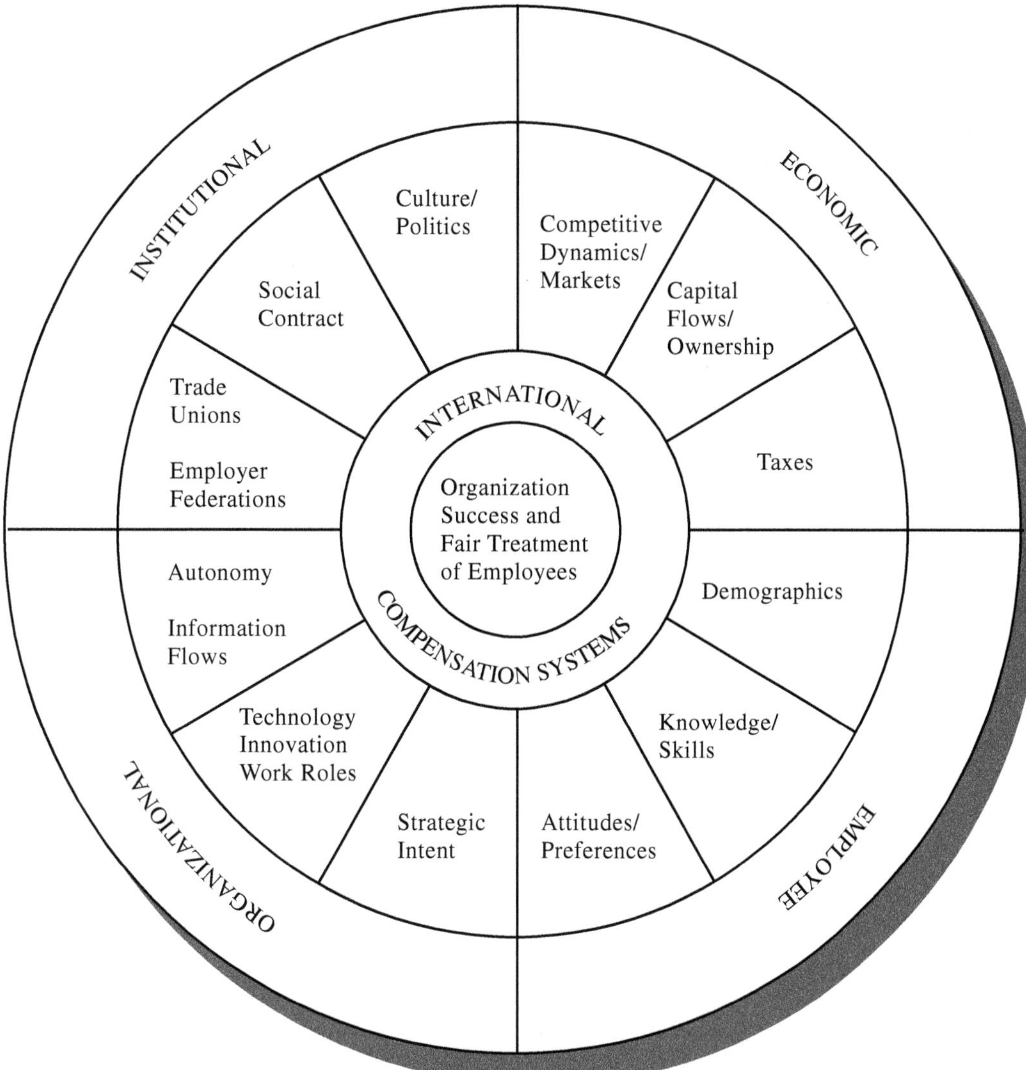

domestic to an international perspective, additional factors become important. Institutional factors such as cultural traditions and political structures, and economic factors such as differences in ownership of enterprises and the development of capital and labour markets come into play. Furthermore, social contracts and the roles of trade unions must be reconsidered.

The DaimlerChrysler example illustrates the usefulness of the global guide. Prior to Daimler's acquisition of Chrysler, the pay for the 10 top Daimler executives equaled the pay of Chrysler's CEO alone. As little as 25 percent of Chrysler managers' total compensation was in the form of base pay, whereas Daimler managers' base pay accounted for up to 60 percent of their total compensation. The merged DaimlerChrysler adopted a Chrysler-like approach to executive compensation.

The Daimler and Chrysler managerial pay systems are contrasted in Exhibit A-2, using the specific factors in the global guide in Exhibit A-1. At Daimler, the roots of today's pay system reach back to post-war Germany and efforts to rebuild an economy devastated by two world wars. Rather than aggressive wage competition that risked inflation, trade union federations, employer associations, government agencies, and financial institutions participated in centralized negotiations. The result was industry-wide negotiated pay systems called tariff agreements. They included predictable annual increases, government-provided social welfare programs, and well-defined internal structures. All companies competing in the same product markets (e.g., Daimler, Volkswagen, and Opel) used the same pay structures. Daimler could pay above these negotiated rates but had little reason to do so. Instead, it competed for employees based on its reputation as a place to work, its quality of training, and the like. As a result, managers were less likely to consider pay as an instrument of strategy. Instead, pay looked more like a constraint to them, determined by people and processes outside the organization.

German tax policies and labour regulations supported this approach. A typical Daimler employee's marginal tax rate (percentage tax on each additional Euro earned) is 30 percent higher than a Chrysler employee's tax rate on an additional dollar in the United States. As a result, the financial returns for working smarter (and longer and harder) in order to receive performance bonuses are significantly smaller at Daimler. Additionally, broad-based stock options for employees were illegal until very recently. In exchange for their higher taxes, Daimler employees receive generous welfare and unemployment payments, plus subsidized college and apprenticeship programs.

Applying the global guide to Chrysler, it can be seen that Chrysler reflects the competitive dynamics in North American labour and product markets as well as the social contract in North America, which values individual choice. Pay setting is highly decentralized; government involvement is limited to ensuring conformance with minimum wage, overtime, tax, and discrimination laws. Chrysler's managerial pay system arguably is aligned with its business strategy, sensitive to market conditions, and includes significant performance bonus and stock ownership. The pay system is considered a strategic tool intended to competitively attract, retain, and motivate managers, and to support business objectives.

So the global guide serves as a tool kit.[10] By examining each of the factors, an increased understanding of the variation in international pay can be gained. Five factors are particularly salient: (1) social contracts, (2) cultures, (3) trade unions, (4) ownership and capital markets, and (5) managers' autonomy. Although the factors are separated here for clarification, they do not separate so easily in reality. Instead, they overlap and interact.

■ THE SOCIAL CONTRACT

Viewed as part of the social contract, the employment relationship is more than an exchange between an individual and an employer. It includes the government, all enterprise owners (sometimes acting individually and sometimes in trade unions). The relationships and expectations of

| **EXHIBIT** | **A-2** | Applying the Global Guide |

Pressures	Daimler	Chrysler
ECONOMIC		
Competitive markets	Moderately competitive	Highly competitive
Capital/ownership	Few shareholders	Many shareholders
Taxes	High taxes	Moderate taxes
INSTITUTIONAL		
Culture/politics	Centralized process	Decentralized process
Regulations	Strong government/trade union involvement	Limited government involvement
Trade union/employer federations	Tripartate-based social contract	Individual/employer-based social contract
ORGANIZATIONAL		
Strategic intent	High margins/high-end vehicles	Lower-margin passenger vehicles, higher-margin SUVs, minivans
Autonomy	Lower autonomy	Moderate autonomy
Work roles	Defined roles	More flexible roles
EMPLOYEE		
Skill/knowledge	Continuous learning	On-the-job
Attitudes/behaviours	High commitment	Committed but contentious
Demographics	Older, experienced	Older, experienced
TOTAL PAY SYSTEM	Sensitive to social contract; hierarchical; well-defined jobs	Aligned with strategy, sensitive to competitive markets
	Base and benefits; annual increase	Base/performance bonuses, stock ownership
	Focus on commitment and continuous learning	Focus on performance and cost control

these parties form the social contract. As you think about how people get paid around the world, it will be clear that different people in different countries hold differing beliefs about the role of government, employees, unions, and employers. Understanding how to manage employee compensation in any country requires an understanding of the social contract in that country. Efforts to change employee compensation systems—for example, to make them more responsive to customers, encourage innovative and quality service, or control costs—require changing the mutual expectations of parties to the social contract.

Centralized–Localized Decision Making   Perhaps the most striking example of the social contract's effects on pay systems is shown in Exhibit A-3, which contrasts the degree of centralization of pay setting among countries.[11] The United States, the United Kingdom, Canada, Hong Kong, and Brazil use a highly decentralized approach with very little government involvement. Japan, Singapore, Germany, Belgium, and Slovakia are moderately centralized by industry section. Sweden, Denmark, and Austria use highly centralized approaches that create a national pay system.

EXHIBIT **A-3** | Social Contracts and Pay Setting

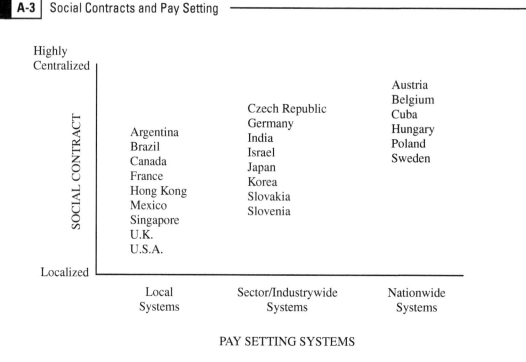

CULTURE

Culture is often defined as shared mental programming.[12] It is rooted in the values, beliefs, and assumptions shared in common by a group of people, and it influences how information is processed. How critical is culture in managing international pay? Some would say that it is very important. The assumption that pay systems must be designed to fit different national cultures is based on the belief that most of a country's inhabitants share a national character. Therefore, the job of the global manager is to search for national characteristics whose influence is assumed to be critical in managing international pay systems.

Typical of this thinking is the widely used list of national cultural attributes proposed by Hofstede (power distance, individualism–collectivism, uncertainty avoidance, and masculinity–femininity).[13] According to this view, "it is crucial that companies adjust their compensation practices to the cultural specifics of a particular host country."[14] Accordingly, in nations where the culture emphasizes respect for status and hierarchy (high power distance, attributed to Malaysia and Mexico), more hierarchical pay structures are appropriate. In "low power distance" nations (Australia and the Netherlands), more egalitarianism is called for.[15]

Advice can be even more specific. Companies operating in nations with "collectivistic" cultures, such as Singapore, Japan, Israel, and Korea, should use egalitarian pay structures (small differences between levels of work), equal pay increases, and group-based rather than individual-based performance incentives. Employers in the more "individualistic" national cultures such as the United States, United Kingdom, and Hong Kong prefer individual-based pay and increases that are proportional to contributions.

But such thinking risks stereotyping.[16] So the issue to resolve is not, What are the cultural differences between nations? Rather, the question is: Whose culture matters?[17] Any group of people may exhibit a culture, a shared set of beliefs—in any university or workplace—engineers, lawyers, accountants, technicians may each hold unique shared mindsets. Employees of organizations may, too. A university's culture probably differs from Microsoft's, Toshiba's, or the London Symphony Orchestra's. In fact, individuals are likely part of many cultures—workplace; family; social, political, interest groups; region, province, or country; and so on. Cultures may be similar or different among all these categories.

Culture Matters, but So Does Cultural Diversity

The United States is considered a country of risk takers who rank high on the individualistic (rather than collectivist) scale. In contrast, the country of Slovenia has been classified as more collectivist and security-conscious (as opposed to risk taking).[18] Slovenia was the first country to break off from the former Yugoslavia. It has a population of under three million, and by most standards would be considered very homogeneous. So you would expect Slovenian managers to be very different from U.S. managers. However, a study found that Slovenian managers tended on average to be more risk taking and individualistic than U.S. managers. The most striking finding, as shown in Exhibit A-4, was that the degree of variation among managers on cultural dimensions was virtually the same in both the Slovenian and U.S. data. Thus, one can find risk-averse collectivists and risk-taking individualists in both nations.

So how useful is the notion of a national culture when managing international pay? In the absence of better data on variations such as in Exhibit A-4, it may offer a starting point. However, it is only a starting point. National culture can be thought of as the "average" in Exhibit A-4. It provides some information about what kinds of pay attitudes and beliefs are likely to be found in an area. But over-reliance on the "average" can be misleading. This point is critical for managing international pay. To claim that all organizations and people in Germany or Japan or Canada use the same shared mindset ignores variations and differences within each nation. Considerable diversity exists between companies and people within any country. The Chinese company Lenovo, which purchased IBM's PC division, illustrates the point. Throughout its short history, Lenovo has relied heavily on government support. Yet Lenovo's approach to compensating employees does not reflect the widely held beliefs about Chinese national culture. For example, the CEO uses 20 percent of the company's profits to award high-performing employees with merit bonuses. Pay differentials between jobs, which in 1990 were 2 to 1, are now up to 30 to 1. The benefits plan allows individual employees to select the specific benefits that best meet their personal preferences. The variation in compensation is unexpected given that the Chinese government still owns controlling interest in the company.

EXHIBIT A-4 Understanding the "Full House" of Variation within a Culture ———

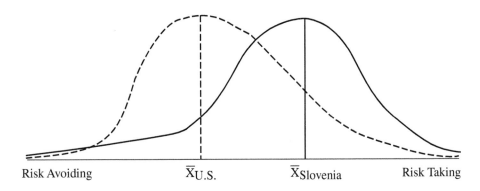

U.S. MBAs = – – – – –
Slovenian MBAs = ———

Thus the interplay between economic, institutional, organizational, and individual conditions within each nation or region, taken as a whole, forms distinct approaches to total comparisons. Understanding these factors in the global guide is useful for managing employee compensation. However, rather than assuming uniformity (the average) within a country, it is important to understand the full range of individuals within nations when managing international pay.

■ TRADE UNIONS AND EMPLOYEE INVOLVEMENT

Europe remains highly unionized: In Sweden, 91 percent of the workforce belongs to unions; in the United Kingdom, 33 percent; and in Italy, 44 percent. Asia is less heavily unionized. Japan's unionization rate is 24 percent and South Korea's is around 11 percent. In some countries, workers' pay is set by collective agreements, even though they may not be union members. In France, for example, 90 percent of workers are covered by collective agreements, even though only 10 percent are members of unions.[19] In addition to having higher rates of unionization, Belgium and Germany require the establishment of worker councils that must be involved in any changes to a pay plan.

The European Union (EU) is trying to provide common labour standards in all its member countries. The purpose of standards is to avoid "social dumping," or the relocation of a business in a country with lower standards and labour costs. At present, hourly labour costs and productivity vary substantially between the EU countries. Often, the higher labour costs are offset by greater productivity.[20] Social legislation also varies among European countries. Britain specifies the fewest requirements, with no minimum wage, no maximum hours, and no formal methods for employee participation. France and Germany have the most generous social insurance. According to the German federal labour agency, monthly unemployment benefits for a couple with two children can reach 1,600 Euros ($2,450).[21]

■ OWNERSHIP AND FINANCIAL MARKETS

Ownership and financing of companies differ widely around the world. These differences are also important to understanding and managing international pay. Fifty percent of American households own stock in companies either directly or indirectly through mutual funds and pension funds.[22] Direct stock ownership is only a few mouse clicks away. In Korea, six conglomerates control a significant portion of the Korean economy, and the six are closely linked to specific families.[23] In Germany, the national Bundesbank and a small number of other influential banks have ownership interests in most major companies. These patterns of ownership make certain types of pay systems almost nonsensical because ownership in the companies is not readily available for individual investors. For example, linking performance bonuses to increased shareholder value or offering stock options to employees makes little sense in the large conglomerates in Germany, Korea, or Japan. However, ownership in small start-ups in these nations is outside these traditional channels, so they are offering stock options to attract new employees.[24] Recent tax law changes in these countries have made options more attractive, but limited ownership of many companies remains the rule.

The most vivid illustrations of the importance of ownership occur in China and in Eastern Europe (Poland, Hungary, Slovenia, Czech Republic, and Slovakia), where a variety of forms are emerging. Although state-owned enterprises still employ two-thirds of all workers in China, township enterprises, wholly privately owned enterprises, joint ventures with foreign companies, and wholly-owned foreign enterprises (WOFEs) account for 50 percent of the profits. Chinese employees switching from government-owned enterprises to these newer organizations find that both the pay and the employer expectations (i.e., the social contract) are substantially different.[25] Individuals attracted to work in these various enterprises have different values and expectations. One study found that those working for local or town-owned enterprises prefer more performance-based pay than those working in federal-owned enterprises.[26] Many families find it makes sense to have one wage earner working at a safe but low-paying government enterprise and another wage earner working at a private enterprise where expectations and pay are high. So it is clear that ownership differences may influence what forms of pay make sense. It is misleading to assume that everyplace is like home.

MANAGERIAL AUTONOMY

Managerial autonomy, an organizational factor in the global guide in Exhibit A-1, refers to the degree of discretion managers have to make the choices that make total compensation a strategic tool. Managerial autonomy is inversely related to the degree of centralization discussed earlier. Thus, most U.S.- and U.K.-based organizations have relatively greater freedom to change employee pay practices than do most European companies. As already noted, centralized pay settings found in European Union countries limit organizations' autonomy to align pay to business strategies and changing market conditions.[27] Volkswagen AG, which is trying to reduce labour costs to better compete with Toyota and others, must negotiate changes with IG Metall, a powerful trade union, and also with a federal labour agency.[28] In contrast, in Singapore the National Wage Council issues voluntary guidelines, e.g., "wage freezes for most companies," "emphasize variable and performance-based pay." Most government organizations adhere to these guides; private organizations do so to varying degrees.[29]

Governments and trade unions are not the only institutions to limit managerial autonomy. Corporate policies often do as well.[30] Compensation decisions made in the home country corporate offices and exported to subunits around the world may align with the corporate strategy but discount local economic and social conditions. Although IBM corporate in Armonk, New York, expects all its worldwide operations to "differentiate people on performance" with total compensation, some IBM units in Tokyo remain convinced that local Japanese IBMers prefer more egalitarian practices. Nevertheless, managers in IBM Japan are expected to comply with Armonk.

In sum, as the global guide depicts, international compensation is influenced by economic, institutional, organizational, and individual conditions. Globalization really means that these conditions are changing—hence international pay systems are changing as well.

COMPARING COSTS

In Chapter 8, the importance of obtaining accurate information about what competitors pay in domestic markets was discussed. Similar comparisons of total compensation between nations can be misleading. Even if wage rates appear the same, expenses for health care, living costs, and other employer-provided allowances for such expenses as housing and commuting all complicate the picture. Health care and benefits are examples. Most industrialized nations other than the United States offer some form of national health care. An organization may pay indirectly for it through payroll taxes, but its value as part of total compensation is diminished, as all people in a nation may share similar coverage.

Comparisons between a specific Canadian firm and a specific foreign competitor may be even more misleading. While consulting firms are improving their global databases, much of their data are still from Western companies' operations in global locations. Other foreign and local–national companies' data often are not available. Thus international data may be biased toward Western practices.

Standard of Living: Basket of Goods versus Big Mac

If comparing total compensation is difficult, comparing living costs and standards is even more complex. *The Economist* takes a Big Mac approach. Rather than pricing a complex basket of goods and services, the magazine uses the price of a Big Mac in different locations.[31] According to Exhibit A-5, the average price of a Big Mac in the United States is $3.10 (average of four cities), in China 10.5 yuan (US$1.31), in Canada $3.52 (US$3.14), and in South Korea 2,500 won (US$2.62).

So what does a Big Mac have to do with compensation? Companies use cost comparisons in adjusting pay for employees who transfer between countries. The objective is to maintain *purchasing power parity.*[32] There are several ways to calculate purchasing power. A common approach is to divide hourly wages by the cost of a standard basket of goods and services. Another approach is to calculate the working time required to buy an item such as a one-kilogram loaf of bread: 7 minutes in London, 15 minutes in Tokyo, 27 minutes in Montreal, and 12 minutes in Chicago. Or to buy a Big Mac: 14 minutes in Chicago, 36 minutes in London, and 90 minutes in Mexico City. The Big Mac (plus fries) attains luxury status in Nairobi, Caracas, and Lagos; an employed person must toil three hours (Nairobi), four hours (Caracas), or almost two days (Lagos) to afford it.

EXHIBIT A-5 The Hamburger Standard

	Big Mac Prices	
	In Local Currency	In US Dollars
United States*	$3.10	$3.10
Argentina	Peso 7.00	2.29
Australia	A$ 3.25	2.44
Brazil	Real 6.40	2.78
Britain	£ 1.94	3.65
Canada	C$ 3.52	3.14
Chile	Peso 1,560	2.94
China	Yuan 10.5	1.31
Czech Republic	Koruna 59.05	2.67
Denmark	DKr 27.75	4.77
Egypt	Pound 9.50	1.65
Euro area	2.94	3.77
Hong Kong	HK$ 12.00	1.55
Hungary	Forint 560	2.71
Indonesia	Rupiah 14,600	1.57
Japan	¥ 250	2.23
Malaysia	Ringgit 5.50	1.52
Mexico	Peso 29.00	2.57
New Zealand	NZ$ 4.45	2.75
Peru	New Sol 9.50	2.91
Philippines	Peso 85.00	1.62
Poland	Zloty 6.50	2.10
Russia	Ruble 48.00	1.77
Singapore	S $3.60	2.27
South Africa	Rand 13.95	2.11
South Korea	Won 2,500	2.62
Sweden	SKr 33.00	4.53
Switzerland	SFr 6.30	5.21
Taiwan	NT$ 75.00	2.33
Thailand	Baht 60.00	1.56
Turkey	Lire 4.20	2.72
Venezuela	Bolivar 5,701	2.17

*Average of New York, Chicago, San Francisco, and Atlanta.
Source: "McCurrencies," *The Economist*, May 25, 2006, www.economist.com.

COMPARING SYSTEMS

The point that pay systems differ around the globe has been made. Those differences relate to variations in economic pressures, socio-political institutions, and the diversity of organizations and employees. In this section we compare several compensation systems. The caution about stereotyping raised earlier applies here as well. Even in nations described by some as homogeneous, pay systems differ from business to business. For example, two well-known Japanese companies, Toyota and Toshiba, have designed different pay systems. Toyota places greater emphasis on external market rates, uses far fewer levels in its structure, and places greater emphasis on individual-based merit and performance pay than does Toshiba. So, as "typical" pay systems are discussed, it must be remembered that differences exist, and change in these systems is occurring everywhere.

The Total Pay Model: Strategic Choices

The total pay model used throughout the book guides our discussion of pay systems in different countries. We have already examined how all organizations face similar strategic issues, but that the relative importance among them differs. You will recognize the basic choices, which seem universal:

- Objectives of pay systems
- External competitiveness
- Internal alignment
- Employee contributions
- Management

Although the choices are universal, the results are not.

NATIONAL SYSTEMS: COMPARATIVE MINDSET

A national system mindset assumes that most employers in a company adopt similar pay practices; analysis then consists of comparing Japanese, German, North American, and other systems.[33] This approach is most useful in nations with centralized approaches (see Exhibit A-4) or where homogeneous economic and cultural conditions exist (e.g., Sweden). Some writers abstract even more and describe broader regional systems, as in the "European Way," the "Asian Way," or the "North American Way."[34] The Japanese and German national systems will be described below, but it must be remembered that the national or regional mindset overlooks variations among organizations within each nation.

Japanese National System

Traditionally, Japan's employment relationships were supported by "three pillars":

1. Lifetime security within the company
2. Seniority-based pay and promotion systems
3. Enterprise unions (decentralized unions that represent workers within a single company)

Japanese pay systems tend to emphasize the person rather than the job; seniority and skills possessed rather than job or work performed; promotions based upon supervisory evaluation of trainability, skill/ability levels, and performance rather than performance alone; internal alignment over competitors' market rates; and employment security based on the performance of the organization and the individual (formerly lifetime security). Japanese pay systems can be described in terms of three basic components: base pay, bonuses, and allowances/benefits.[35]

Base Pay   Base pay accounts for 60 to 80 percent of an employee's monthly pay, depending on the individual's rank in the organization. Base pay is not based on job evaluation or market pricing (as predominates in North America), nor is it attached to specific job titles. Rather, it is based on a combination of employee characteristics: career category, years of service, and skill/performance level.

Career Category   Five career categories prevail in Japan: (1) general administration, (2) engineer/scientific, (3) secretary/office, (4) technician/blue collar job, and (5) contingent.

Years of Service   Seniority remains a major factor in determining base pay. Management creates a matrix of pay and years of service for each career category. Exhibit A-6 shows a matrix for general administration work. Companies meet periodically to compare their matrices, which accounts for the similarity among companies. In general, salary increases with age until 50 years of age and then is reduced. Employees can expect annual increases no matter what their performance level until age 50, though the amount of increase varies according to individual skills and performance.

Skills and Performance   Each skill is defined by its class (usually 7–13) and rank (1–9) within the class. Exhibit A-7 illustrates a skill salary chart for the General Administration career category. Classes 1 and 2 typically include associate (entry) and senior associate work; 2, 3, and 4, supervisor and managerial; 5, 6, and 7, managerial, general director, and so on. Employees advance in rank as a result of their supervisor's evaluation of their:

■ Effort (e.g., enthusiasm, participation, responsiveness).
■ Skills required for the work (e.g., analytical, decision making, leadership, planning, process improvement, teamwork).
■ Performance (typical MBO-style ratings).

To illustrate how the system works, consider graduates fresh from university who enter at class 1, rank 1. After one year, all those hired are evaluated by their supervisors on their effort, abilities, and performance. Early in their career (the first three years), effort is more important; in later years abilities and performance receive more emphasis. The number of ranks an employee moves each year (and therefore the increase in base pay) depends on this supervisory rating (e.g., receiving an A on the appraisal form lets an employee move up three ranks within the class, a B moves the employee up two ranks, and so on).

EXHIBIT   A-6   Salary and Age Matrix for General Administration Work in a Japanese Company

*Age	†Salary	Age	Salary	Age	Salary	Age	Salary
		31	$1,900	41	$2,900	51	$3,800
22	$1,000	32	2,000	42	3,000	52	3,700
23	1,100	33	2,100	43	3,100	53	3,600
24	1,200	34	2,200	44	3,200	54	3,500
25	1,300	35	2,300	45	3,300	55	3,400
26	1,400	36	2,400	46	3,400	56	3,300
27	1,500	37	2,500	47	3,500	57	3,200
28	1,600	38	2,600	48	3,600	58	3,100
29	1,700	39	2,700	49	3,700	59	3,000
30	1,800	40	2,800	50	3,800	60	2,900

Notes: *Age 22 is typical entry with college degree.
†Monthly salary, converted to dollars.

| **EXHIBIT** | **A-7** | Skill Chart for General Administration Work |

	Associate	Associate	Supervisor		Senior Manager	General Director	
	Class 1	*Class 2*	*Class 3*	*Class 4*	*Class 5*	*Class 6*	*Class 7*
Rank 1	$ 600	$1,600	$2,600	$3,100	$3,600	$4,500	$5,500
Rank 2	700	1,700	2,650	3,150	3,750	4,700	6,000
Rank 3	800	1,800	2,700	3,200	3,800	4,900	
Rank 4	900	1,900	2,750	3,250	3,900	5,100	
Rank 5	1,000	2,000	2,800	3,300	4,000		
Rank 6	1,100	2,100	2,850	3,350	4,100		
Rank 7	1,200	2,200	2,900	3,400			
Rank 8	1,300	2,300	2,950	3,450			
Rank 9	1,400	2,400	3,000	3,500			

Theoretically, a person with an A rating could move up three ranks in class each year and shift to the next class in three years. However, most companies require both minimum and maximum years of service within each class. So, even if the employee receive four straight A ratings, the employee would still remain in class 1 for the minimum of six years. Class 2 may also have a six-year minimum time, and so on. Conversely, if the employee received four straight D grades, the employee would still get promoted to the next skill class after spending the maximum of 10 years in class 1. On the one hand, setting a minimum time in each class helps ensure that the employee knows the work and returns value to the company. On the other hand, the system also slows the progress of high-potential performers. Even the weakest performers eventually advance to the top of the pay structure, although they do not get the accompanying job titles or responsibility. The system reflects the traditional Japanese saying, "A nail that is standing too high will be pounded down." An individual employee will not want to stand out. Employees work to advance the performance of the group or team rather than themselves.

Under the traditional Japanese system, increases in annual base pay are relatively small (7 percent in our example of superior performance, compared to 10 to 12 percent for star performers in good economic times in many Canadian merit systems), though they compound over time just as conventional merit and across-the-board increases in Canada. However, because the Japanese system is so seniority based, labour costs increase as the average age of the workforce increases. In fact, a continuing problem facing Japanese employers is the increasing labour costs caused by the cumulative effects of annual increases combined with lifetime employment security. Early retirement incentives and "new jobs" with lower salaries are programs being used to contain these costs.[36]

Bonuses   Bonuses account for between 20 and 40 percent of annual salary, depending on the level in the organization. Generally, the higher up the employee is, the larger the percentage of annual salary received as bonus. Typical Japanese companies pay bonuses twice a year (July and December). The bonuses as an *expectable* additional payment to be made twice a year, even in bad financial times. They are not necessarily related to performance.

The amount of bonuses is calculated by multiplying employees' monthly base pay by a multiplier. The size of the multiplier is determined by collective bargaining between employers and unions in each company. Sometimes the multiplier may also vary according to an employee's performance evaluation. In a recent year, the average multiplier was 4.8 (2.3 in summer and 2.5 in winter) for white-collar workers. A worker whose monthly base pay was $4,500 would receive a bonus of $10,350 in July and $11,250 in December.

According to the Japan Institute of Labour, for most employees (managers excepted), bonuses are in reality variable pay that helps control the employers' cash flow and labour costs but that are not intended to act as a motivator or to support improved corporate performance. Japanese labour laws encourage the use of bonuses to achieve cost savings by omitting bonuses from calculations of many other benefits costs, i.e. pension plan, overtime pay, severance pay, and early retirement allowances.

The timing of the bonuses is very important. In Japan both the summer festival and the new year are traditional gift-giving times; in addition, consumers tend to make major purchases during these periods. Employees use their bonuses to cover these expenses. Thus, the tradition of the bonus system is deeply rooted in Japanese life and is still considered an indispensable form of pay.

Benefits and Allowances   The third characteristic of Japanese pay systems, the allowance, comes in a variety of forms: family allowances, commuting allowances, housing and geographic differential allowances, and so on. Company housing in the form of dormitories for single employees or rent or mortgage subsidies is a substantial amount. Life-passage payments are made when an employee marries or experiences a death in the immediate family. Commuting allowance is also important. One survey reported that employees who took public transportation received about 9,000 yen (approximately $90 per month) for commuting. Family allowances vary with the number of dependants. Toyota provides about 17,500 to 18,000 yen ($200 to $205) a month for the first dependant and about 4,500 to 5,500 yen ($52 to $63) for additional dependants. Some employers even provide matchmaking allowances for those who tire of life in company dorms.

Legally Mandated Benefits   Legally mandated benefits in Japan include social security, unemployment, and workers' compensation. Although these three are similar to Canada, Japanese employers also pay premiums for mandated health insurance, preschool child support, and employment of the handicapped.

The slow economic growth that Japan has been experiencing over the last decade, coupled with its heavy emphasis on seniority-based pay, means that Japanese labour costs have climbed faster than those of their global competitors. Faced with these pressures, many companies are trying to maintain *long-time* (rather than lifetime) employment while they look for other ways to reward younger and more flexible employees. These younger employees, who have been paid relatively poorly under the seniority-based pay system, are finding the pay in non-Japanese firms operating in Japan more attractive. Their willingness to move is creating a more active labour market. Western firms are succeeding in hiring such young Japanese by offering them more competitive base pay plus performance-based pay. In order to retain younger employees, many Japanese firms such as Toyota, Toshiba, and Mitsubishi are increasingly using performance-based pay. As a result, considerable variation in pay systems is beginning to emerge between traditional Japanese companies.[37]

German National System

The social contract in which traditional German pay systems are embedded in a social partnership between business, labour, and government creates a generous *vater staat*, or "nanny state."[38] *Vergutung* is the most common German word for compensation. Pay decisions are highly regulated; over 90 different laws apply. Different *tariff agreements* (pay rates and structures) are negotiated for each industrial sector (e.g., banking, chemicals, metals manufacturing) by the major employers and unions. Thus, the pay rates at Adam Opel AG, a major car company, are quite similar to those at Daimler, Volkswagen, and any other German car company. Methods for job evaluation (non-managerial jobs) and career progression are included in the tariff agreements. Even small organizations that are not legally bound by tariffs tend to use them as guidelines.

Base Pay   Base pay accounts for 70 to 80 percent of German employees' total compensation, depending on their job level. Base pay is based on job descriptions, job evaluations, and employee age. The tariff agreement applicable to Adam Opel AG, for example, sets the following *tariff groups* (similar to job families and grades):

Wage earners	8 groups (L2–L9)
Salary earners	6 office/administrative (K1–K6)
	6 technical (T1–T6)
	4 supervisory (M1–M4)

Generally, a rate will be negotiated for one of the levels, for example K2, and the other levels in that group will be calculated as a percentage of the negotiated rate.

Bonuses   Although there is a trend to increase variable-performance-based bonuses, they have not been part of a traditional German pay system for unionized workers. However, Adam Opel AG's tariff agreement stipulates that an average 13 percent of the total base wages must be paid as "efficiency allowances." Systems to measure this efficiency are negotiated with the works councils for each location. In reality, these efficiency allowances become expected annual bonuses. Performance bonuses for managerial positions not included in tariffs are based on company earnings and other company objectives. Currently only about one-third of top executives receive stock options.

Allowances and Benefits   Germany's social contract includes generous social benefits. These nationally mandated benefits, paid for through taxes on employers and employees, include liberal social security, unemployment protection, health care, nursing care, and other programs. Employer and employee contributions to the social security system can add up to more than one-third of wages. Additionally, companies commonly provide additional benefits and services such as pension plans, savings plans, building loans, and life insurance. Company cars are always popular. The make and model of the car and whether or not the company provides a cellphone are viewed as signs of status in an organization. German workers also receive 30 working days of vacation plus about 13 national holidays annually (compared to an average of nine or ten days in Canada).

Trends   Germany today is not all traditional manufacturing, machine tools, and Mercedes vehicles. It has over half of the top Internet companies in Europe. And nearly one in five German adults own stock, double the rate in the late 1990s. Many of the changes are the result of global competitive pressures and technological changes. However, the picture today is not as bright as it once was. An aging population, low birth rates, earlier retirement ages, and high pension and unemployment benefits are pushing up the costs of the social support system.[39] A relatively inflexible labour market means that employers are finding it easier to move to other EU countries as well as to Asia. All these factors are causing a rethinking of the traditional German social contract and the resulting total compensation systems. Companies are asking for greater autonomy in negotiating tariff agreements to better reflect their economic conditions, the use of performance-based pay, and ways to link job security to company performance.

Strategic Comparisons: Japan, Germany, Canada

Japanese and German traditional systems appear to have different strategic approaches than Canadian pay systems. Exhibit A-8 uses the basic strategic choices outlined in the total pay model—objectives, internal alignment, competitiveness, contribution, and administration—as a basis for comparisons. Both the Japanese and German systems constrain organizations' use of pay as a strategic tool. German companies face pay rates, job evaluation methods, and bonuses identi-

EXHIBIT	A-8	Strategic Similarities and Differences: An Illustrated Comparison

	Japan	**Canada**	**German**
Objectives	Long-term focus High commitment Egalitarian—internal fairness Flexible workforce Control cash flow with bonuses	Short/intermediate focus High commitment Performance—market—meritocratic Flexible workforce Cost control; varies with performance	Long term High commitment Egalitarian—fairness Highly trained Cost control through tariff negotiations
Internal alignment	Person based: age, ability, performance determines base pay Many levels Small pay differences	Work based: jobs, skills, accountabilities Fewer levels Larger pay differences	Work based: jobs and experience Many levels Small pay differences
External competitiveness	Monitor age–pay charts Consistent with competitors	Market determined Compete on variable and performance-based pay	Tariff based Same as competitors
Employee contribution	Bonuses vary with performance only at higher levels in organization Performance appraisal influences promotions and small portion of pay increases	Bonuses an increasing percentage of total pay Increases based on individual, unit, and corporate performance	Tariff negotiated bonuses Smaller performance bonuses for managers
Advantages	Supports commitment and security Greater predictability for companies and employees Flexibility—person based	Supports performance—competitor focus Costs vary with performance Focus on short-term payoffs (speed to market)	Supports commitment and security Greater predictability for companies and employees Companies do not compete with pay
Disadvantage	High cost of aging workforce Discourages unique contributors Discourages women and younger employees	Skeptical workers, less security Fosters "What's in it for me?" No reward for investing in long-term projects	Inflexible; bureaucratic High social and benefit costs Not a strategic tool

cal to those of their competitors, set by negotiated tariff agreements. The basic strategic premise, that competitive advantage is sustained by aligning with business strategy, is limited by laws and unions. Japanese companies do not face pay rates fixed industry-wide; rather, they voluntarily meet to exchange detailed pay information. So the end result appears to be the same: similar pay structures across companies competing within an industry. In contrast, managers in Canadian companies possess considerable flexibility to align pay systems with business strategies. As a result, greater variability exists among companies within and across industries.

The pay objectives in traditional German systems include long-term commitment, greater egalitarianism, and cost control through the negotiation of tariff agreements, which apply to competitors' labour costs, too. Japanese organizations set pay objectives that focus on the long term (age and security), support high commitment (seniority/ability-based), are more egalitarian (smaller pay differences), signal the importance of company and individual performance (company bonuses, individual promotions), and encourage flexible workers (person-based pay). Canadian companies, in contrast, focus on the shorter term (less job security); are market sensitive (competitive total pay); emphasize cost control (variable pay based on performance); reward performance improvement (bonuses, options, etc.), meritocracy, and innovation (individual rewards); and encourage flexibility (broadbanding and skill-based).

In Japan, person-based factors (seniority, ability, and performance) are used to set base pay. Market comparisons are monitored in Japan, but internal alignment based on seniority remains far more important. Job-based factors (job evaluation) and seniority are also used in Germany. Labour markets in Germany remain highly regulated, and tariff agreements set pay for union workers. So, like the Japanese system, the German system places much greater emphasis on internal alignment than on external markets.

Each approach has advantages and disadvantages. Clearly, the Japanese approach is consistent with low turnover/high commitment, greater acceptance of change, and the need to be flexible. Canadian firms face higher turnover (which is not always a disadvantage) and greater skepticism about change (i.e., "What's in it for me?"). Canadian firms encourage innovation; they also recognize the enormous talent and contributions to be tapped from workforce diversity. German traditional systems tend to be more bureaucratic and rule-bound. Hence, they are more inflexible. However, they also offer more predictability and stability for people. The Japanese national system faces challenges from the high costs associated with an aging white-collar workforce, its limited use of women's capabilities, and emerging efforts to reward innovative individuals. The Canadian challenges include the impact of increased uncertainty and risk among employees, a short-term focus, and employees' stress and skepticism about continuous change.

■ STRATEGIC MARKET MINDSET

A global study of pay systems used by companies with worldwide operations identified three general compensation strategies that capture the different approaches: (1) localizer, (2) exporter, and (3) globalizer. These approaches reflect the company's business strategy.[40]

Localizer: "Think Global, Act Local"

If a localizer operates in 150 countries, it may have 150 different systems. The company's business strategy is to seek competitive advantage by providing products and services tailored to local customers. Localizers operate independently of the corporate headquarters. One manager compared his company's pay system to McDonald's. "It's as if McDonalds used a different recipe for hamburgers in every country. So, too, for our pay system." Another says, "We seek to be a good citizen in each nation in which we operate. So should our pay system." The pay system is consistent with local conditions.

Exporter: "One Size Fits All"

Exporters are the virtual opposites of localizers. Exporters design a total pay system at headquarters and export it worldwide for implementation at all locations. Exporting a basic system (with some adjustments for national laws and regulations) makes it easier to move managers and professionals among locations or countries without having to change how they are paid. It also communicates consistent corporate-wide objectives. Managers say that "one plan from headquarters gives all managers around the world a common vocabulary and a clear message about what the leadership values." Common software used to support compensation decisions and deployed around the world makes uniform policies and practices feasible. On the other hand, not everyone likes the idea of simply implementing what others have designed. One manager complained that headquarters rarely consulted managers in the field: "There is no notion that ideas can go both ways. It's a one-way bridge."

Globalizer: "Think and Act Globally and Locally"

Similar to exporters, globalizers seek a common system that can be used as part of the "glue" to support consistency across all global locations. But headquarters and the operating units are heavily networked to shared ideas and knowledge. Managers in these companies said:

- "No one has a corner on good ideas about how to pay people. We need to get them for all our locations."
- "Home country begins to lose its meaning; you measure performance where it makes sense for the business and you design pay structures to support the business."
- "Compensation policy depends more on tax policies and the dynamics of our business than it does on 'national' culture. The culture argument is something politicians hide behind."

Some believe the globalizer is the business model for the 21st century. IBM, for example, calls itself a "globally integrated enterprise." The aim is for all its operations, from production to marketing to R&D to be integrated around the world.[41] They continue to compete as multinationals. The point is that rather than emphasizing national pay systems as the key to international compensation, the three strategic global approaches focus first on the global business strategy and then adapt to local conditions.

■ EXPATRIATE PAY

Multinationals operate, by definition, in many nations. They segment their workforces into subgroups based on home country.

- Expatriates ("expat": someone whose citizenship is that of the employer's base country; for example, a Japanese citizen working for Sony in Toronto)
- Third-country nationals (TCN: someone whose citizenship is neither the employer's base country nor the location of the subsidiary; for example, a German citizen working for Sony in Toronto)
- Local country nationals (LCN: citizens of the country in which the subsidiary is located; for example, Canadian citizens working for Sony in Toronto). LCNs are also known as host country nationals (HCNs).

Hiring LCNs has advantages. The company saves relocation expenses and avoids concerns about employees adapting to the local culture. Employment of LCNs satisfies nationalistic demands for hiring locals. Only rarely do organizations decide that hiring LCNs is inappropriate.

Expats or TCNs may be brought in for a number of reasons.[42] The foreign assignment may represent an opportunity for selected employees to develop an international perspective; the position may be sufficiently confidential that information is entrusted only to a proven domestic veteran; the particular skills required for a position may not be readily available in the local labour pool. Exhibit A-9 catalogues a number of reasons for asking employees to take work assignments in another country. Designing expatriate pay systems is a challenge. A company that sends a Canadian employee (base salary of $80,000) with a spouse and two children to London for three years can expect to spend $800,000 to $1,000,000. Obviously, the high cost of expatriate assignments needs to be offset by the value of the contributions the employee makes.[43]

| EXHIBIT | A-9 | Why Expatriates Are Selected |

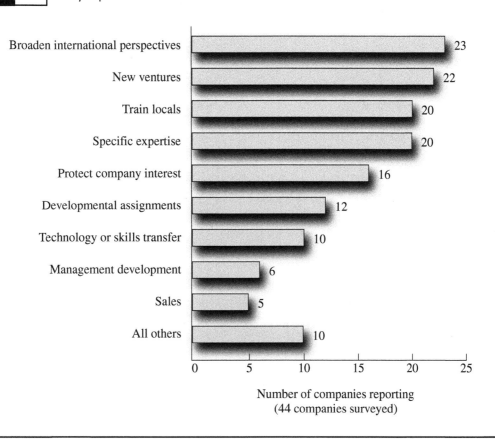

Number of companies reporting
(44 companies surveyed)

Elements of Expatriate Compensation

"We are becalmed. There has been little real innovation in the expatriate compensation field in years," according to a leading consultant.[44] Exhibit A-10 is a shopping list of items that can make up expatriate compensation, including everything from household furnishing allowances to language and culture training, spousal employment assistance, and rest and relaxation leaves for longer-term assignments. Usually such lists are organized into four major components: salary, taxes, housing, and allowances and premiums.[45]

Salary The base salary plus incentives (merit, eligibility for profit sharing, bonus plans, etc.) for expatriate jobs is usually determined via job evaluation or some system of "job levelling."[46] 3M applies a global job evaluation plan for its international assignments. Common factors describe different 3M jobs around the world. With this system, the work of a regional human resource manager in Brussels can be compared to the work of a human resource manager in Vancouver or Singapore.

Beyond salaries and incentives, the intent of the other components is *to help keep expatriate employees financially whole and minimize the disruptions of the move.* This basically means maintaining a standard of living about equal to their peers in their home or base country. This is a broad standard that has often resulted in very costly packages.

Taxes Income earned in foreign countries has two potential sources of income tax liability.[47] With few exceptions (Saudi Arabia is one), foreign tax liabilities are incurred on income earned

---

EXHIBIT   **A-10**   Common Allowances in Expatriate Pay Packages ───────────────

Financial Allowances
   Reimbursement for tax return preparation
   Tax equalization
   Housing differential
   Children's education allowance
   Temporary living allowance
   Goods and services differential
   Transportation differential
   Foreign service premium
   Household furnishing allowance
   Currency protection
   Hardship premium
   Completion bonus

Family Support
   Language training
   Assistance locating schools for children
   Training for local culture's customs (family)
   Child care providers
   Assistance locating spousal employment

Social Adjustment Assistance
   Emergency leave
   Home leave
   Company car/driver
   Assistance with locating new home
   Access to Western-style health care
   Club membership
   General personal services (e.g., translation)
   Personal security (manager and family)
   General culture-transition training (manager)
   Social events
   Career development and repatriation planning
   Training for local culture customs (manager)
   Orientation to community (manager and
     family)
   Counselling services
   Rest and relaxation leave
   Domestic staff (excluding child care)
   Use of company-owned vacation facilities

---

in foreign countries. For example, money earned in Japan is subject to Japanese income tax, whether earned by a Japanese or a Korean citizen. The other potential liability is the tax owed in the employees' home country. The United States is the only developed country that taxes its citizens for income earned in another country, even though that income is taxed by the country in which it was earned. Most employers pay whatever income taxes are due in the host country and/or the home country via *tax equalization*.[48] Taxes are deducted from employees' earnings up to the same amount of taxes they would pay had they remained in their home country.

This allowance can be a substantial amount. For example, the marginal tax rates in Belgium, the Netherlands, and Sweden can run between 70 and 90 percent. So, if a Swedish expatriate is sent to a lower-tax country, say, Great Britain, the company keeps the difference. If a British expatriate goes to Sweden, the company makes up the difference in taxes. The logic here is that if the employee kept the windfall from being assigned to a low-tax country, getting this person to accept assignments elsewhere would become difficult.

Housing   Appropriate housing has a major impact on an expatriate's success. Most international companies pay allowances for housing or provide company-owned housing for expatriates. "Expatriate colonies" often grow up in sections of major cities where many different international companies group their expatriates.

Allowances and Premiums   Visitors to Moscow are cautioned that when taking the famed Moscow subway, they should pay the fare at the beginning of the ride. Inflation is so high there that if they wait to pay until the end of the ride, they won't be able to afford to get off! Cost of living allowances, club memberships, transportation assistance, child care and education, spousal employment, local culture training, and personal security are some of the many service allowances and premiums expatriates receive. The logic supporting these allowances is that foreign assignments require the expatriate to (1) work with less direct supervision than a domestic counterpart, (2) often live and work in strange and sometimes uncongenial surroundings, and (3) represent the employer in the host country. The size of the premium is a function of both the expected hardship and hazards in the host country and the type of job. So an assignment in London will probably yield fewer allowances than one in Tehran, where Death to Americans Day is still a national holiday.

The Balance Sheet Approach

Most North American, European, and Japanese global firms combine these elements of pay in a *balance sheet approach*.[49] The name stems from accounting, where credits and debits must balance. It is based on the premise that employees on overseas assignments should have the same spending power as they would in their home country. Therefore, the home country is the standard for all payments. The objective is to:

1. Ensure mobility of people to global assignments as cost effectively as is feasible.
2. Ensure that expatriates neither gain nor lose financially.
3. Minimize adjustments required of expatriates and their dependants.

Notice that none of these objectives links to performance.

Exhibit A-11 depicts the balance sheet approach. Home country salary is the first column. A person's salary (based on job evaluation, market surveys, merit, and incentives) must cover taxes, housing, goods and services, plus other financial obligations (a "reserve"). The proportions set for each of the components in the exhibit are norms (i.e., assumed to be "normal" for the typical

EXHIBIT　A-11　Balance Sheet Approach

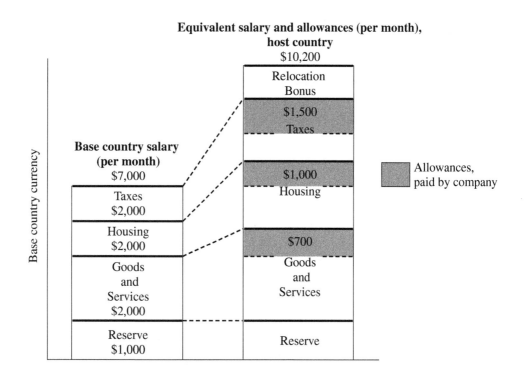

expatriate) set to reflect consumption patterns in the home country for a person at that salary level with that particular family pattern. They are not actual expenditures. These norms are based on surveys conducted by consulting firms. Using these norms is supposed to avoid negotiating with each individual, though substantial negotiation still occurs.

Assume that the norms suggest that a typical manager with a spouse and one child, earning $84,000 in Canada, will spend $2,000 per month on housing, $2,000 on taxes, $2,000 on goods and services, and put away a reserve of $1,000 per month. The next building block is the equivalent costs in the host country where the assignment is located. For example, if similar housing costs $3,000 in the host country, the expatriate is expected to pay the same $2,000 paid in Canada, and the company pays the employee the difference (in this example, the extra $1,000 per month). In the illustration, taxes, housing, and goods and services components are all greater in the host country than in the home country. The expatriate bears the same level of costs as at home. The employer is responsible for the additional costs. (Changing exchange rates among currencies complicate these allowance calculations.)

However, equalizing pay may not motivate an employee to move to another country, particularly if the new location has less personal appeal. Therefore, many employers also offer some form of financial incentive or bonus to encourage the move. Column 2 of Exhibit A-11 includes a relocation bonus. Four out of five multinational corporations pay relocation bonuses to induce people to take expatriate assignments.

If gaining international experience is really one of the future competencies required by organizations, then the need for such bonuses ought to be reduced, because the expatriate experience should increase the likelihood of future promotions. Either the experience expatriates obtain is unique to each situation and therefore not transferrable, or companies simply do not know how to value it. Whatever the reason, research reveals that North American expatriates feel that their organizations still do not value their international expertise.[50] So the rhetoric of the value of global competencies has yet to match the reality; hence the need for relocation incentives.

Alternatives to Balance Sheet Approach   Employers continue to explore alternatives to the balance sheet approach, due primarily to the cost. *Negotiation* simply means that the employer and employee find a mutually agreeable package. The arrangements tend to be relatively costly (or generous, depending on your point of view), create comparability problems when other people are asked to locate overseas ("but Mike and Sarah got . . ."), and need to be renegotiated with each transfer.

Another alternative, *localization*, ties salary to the *host* (local) country salary scales and provides some cost of living allowances for taxes, housing, and dependants. The allowances tend to be similar to those under the balance sheet, but the salary can vary. The downside is that individual salaries vary with the location (average rate for an engineer in Geneva is $55,000, compared to $41,300 in Rome and $32,000 in Bristol) rather than with the job or performance.

While the balance sheet approach ties salary to the home country; the *modified balance sheet* ties salary to a *region* (Asia-Pacific, Europe, North America, Central America, and South America). The logic is that if an employee of a global business who relocates from Winnipeg to Halifax receives only a moving allowance, why should all the extras be paid for international moves of far less distance (e.g., from Germany to Spain)? In Europe, many companies no longer view those European managers who work outside their home country as expats. Instead, they are Europeans running their European businesses. And the use of a common currency, the Euro, makes this easier.

Another common modification is to decrease allowances over time. The logic is that the longer the employee is in the host country, the closer the standard of living should come to that of a local employee. For example, if Canadians eat a $10 pizza twice a week at home, should they eat a $30 pizza twice a week in Tokyo, at the employer's expense? More typically, after a couple of months, the expatriate will probably learn where the nationals find cheaper pizza or switch to sushi. The main purpose of the modified balance sheet seems to be to reduce costs; it pays little attention to performance, ensuring fairness, or satisfying preferences of expats.

The *lump-sum/cafeteria approach* offers expats more choices. This approach sets salaries according to the home-country system and simply offers employees lump sums of money to offset differences in standards of living. For example, a company will still calculate differences in cost of living, but instead of breaking them into housing, transportation, goods and services, and so on, the employee simply receives a total allowance. Perhaps one employee will trade less spacious housing for private schooling and tutors for the children; another employee will make different choices. We know of one expatriate who purchased a villa and a winery in Italy with his allowance. He has been reassigned to Chicago, but still owns and operates his winery.

Expatriate Systems Objectives? *Quel Dommage!*

Experts in international compensation focus on the complexities of taxes, exchange rates, housing differences, and the like rather than how the expatriate pay system affects competitive advantage, customer satisfaction, quality, or other performance concerns. It does emphasize maintaining employee purchasing power and minimizing disruptions and inequities. But the lack of attention to improving performance or ensuring that the expatriate assignment is consistent with organization objectives is glaring. Sadly, the major innovation in expat pay over the past decade seems to have been to re-label expats and TCNs as "international assignees."

Expatriate compensation systems are forever trying to be not too high, not too low, but just right. The expatriate pay must be sufficient to encourage the employee to take the assignment, yet not so attractive that local nationals will feel unfairly treated or that the expatriate will refuse any future reassignments. These systems also presume that expats will be repatriated to their home country. However, the relevant standard for judging fairness may not be home-country treatment. It may be the pay of other expats, that is, the expat community, or it may be local nationals. And how do local nationals feel about the allowances and pay levels of their expat co-workers? Very little research tells us how expats and those around them judge the fairness of expat pay.

Employee Preferences Beyond work objectives, costs, and fairness, an additional consideration is employees' preferences for international assignments. For many Europeans, working in another country is just part of a career. Yet many Canadian employees may feel that leaving Canada means leaving the action. They may worry that expatriate experience will sidetrack rather than enhance their career. Employees undoubtedly differ in their preferences for overseas jobs, and preferences can vary over time. Having children in high school or elderly parents to care for, divorce, working spouses, and other life factors exert a strong influence on whether an offer to work overseas is a positive or negative opportunity. Research does inform us of the following:

- 68 percent of expatriates do not know what their jobs will be when they return home.
- 54 percent return to lower-level jobs. Only 11 percent are promoted.
- Only 5 percent believe their company values overseas experience.
- 77 percent have less disposable income when they return home.
- Only 13 percent of expatriates are women (approximately 50 percent of all North American managers and professionals are women).
- More than half of returning expatriates leave their company within one year.[51]

Unfortunately, although research does highlight the problem, it does not offer much guidance for designers of expat pay systems, leading to reliance on conjecture and beliefs.[52]

■ BORDERLESS WORLD → BORDERLESS PAY? GLOBALISTS

Some corporations, particularly those attempting to become "globally integrated enterprises," are creating cadres of globalists: managers who operate anywhere in the world in a borderless manner. They expect that during their career, they will be located in and travel from country to country.

According to a former CEO of General Electric, "The aim in a global business is to get the best ideas from everyone, everywhere."[53] To support this global flow of ideas and people, some are also designing borderless or at least regionalized pay systems. One testing ground for this approach is the European Union. As the global guide, discussed earlier, points out, one difficulty with borderless pay is that base pay levels and the other components depend too much on differences in each nation's laws and customs.[54]

Focusing on expatriate compensation may blind companies to the issue of appropriate pay for employees who are seeking global career opportunities. Ignoring such employees causes them to focus only on local operations and pay less attention to the broader goals of the global firm. It is naive to expect commitment to a long-term global strategy in which local managers have little input and receive limited benefits. Paradoxically, attempts to localize top management in subsidiaries may reinforce the gap in focus between local and global management.

CONCLUSION

Studying employee compensation only in the home neighbourhood, city, or country is like being a horse with blinders. Removing the blinders by adopting a global perspective will deepen the understanding of local or national issues. Anyone interested in compensation needs to adopt a global perspective. The globalization of businesses, financial markets, trade agreements, and even labour markets is affecting every workplace and every employment relationship. And employee compensation, so central to the workplace, is embedded in the different political–socio-economic arrangements found around the world. Examining employee compensation with the factors in the global pay model offers insights into managing total compensation internationally.

The basic premise of this book has been that compensation systems have a profound impact on individual behaviour, organization success, and social well-being. This premise also holds true within and across all national boundaries.

ENDNOTES

Chapter 1

1 E. E. Lawler, III, *Treat People Right! How Organizations and Individuals Can Propel Each Other Into a Virtuous Spiral of Success.* San Francisco: Jossey-Bass, 2003; D. Ulrich and W. Brockbank, *The HR Value Proposition.* Boston: Harvard Business School Press, 2005.

2 Statistics Canada, http://www40.statcan.gc.ca/l01/cst01/labor01b-eng.htm (August 16, 2009).

3 M. Drolet, "The Male-Female Wage Gap," *Perspectives,* Spring 2002, pp. 29–35. Statistics Canada Catalogue No. 75-001-XPE.

4 Bureau of Labor Statistics, *International Comparisons of Hourly Compensation Costs for Production Workers in Manufacturing 2006,* USDL 08-0093, January 25, 2008; *OECD Compendium of Productivity Indicators 2008,* p. 69.

5 S. Greenhouse, "Anti-Sweatshop Movement Is Achieving Gains Overseas," *New York Times,* January 26, 2000, p. A10; S. Greenhouse, "Activism Surges at Campuses Nationwide, and Labor Is at Issue," *New York Times,* March 29, 1999, p. A14.

6 D. Olive, "Many CEOs Richly Rewarded for Failure," *Toronto Star,* August 25, 2002, pp. A1, A10, A11; E. Raymer, "Executive Compensation under Scrutiny," *Globe and Mail,* April 1, 2003, p. E8.

7 *Industry Total Labor Cost Studies* (Philadelphia: The Hay Group, 1997); J. E. Triplett, *An Essay on Labor Costs* (Washington, D.C.: Office of Research and Evaluation, U.S. Bureau of Labor Statistics, 1997).

8 K. Bartol and E. Locke, "Incentives and Motivation," Chapter 4 in S. Rynes and B. Gerhart (eds.), *Compensation in Organizations,* San Francisco: Jossey-Bass, 2000, pp. 104–150.

9 E. E. Lawler III, *Rewarding Excellence* (San Francisco: Jossey-Bass, 2000); B. E. Becker and M. Huselid, "High Performance Work Systems and Firm Performance: A Synthesis of Research and Management Implications," in G. Ferris (ed.), *Research in Personnel and Human Resources* (Greenwich, CT: JAI Press, 1998).

10 G. T. Milkovich and M. Bloom, "Rethinking International Compensation: From National Cultures to Markets and Strategic Flexibility," *Compensation and Benefits Review,* January 1998, pp. 1–10; M. Bloom and G. Milkovich, "A SHRM Perspective on International Compensation and Reward Systems," *Research in Personnel and Human Resources Management,* Supplement 4 (Greenwich, CT: JAI Press, 1999), pp. 283–303.

11 E. E. Lawler, *Rewarding Excellence* (San Francisco: Jossey-Bass, 2000).

12 D. Rousseau, *Psychological Contracts in Organizations* (Thousand Oaks, CA: Sage, 1995).

13 *Compensation Planning Outlook 2009* (Ottawa, ON: Conference Board of Canada).

14 S. Kerr, "The Best Laid Incentive Plans," *Harvard Business Review,* January 2003.

15 Some believe greater stock ownership motivates performance; others argue that the link between individual job behaviours and the vagaries of the stock market are tenuous at best. D. Kruse and J. Blasi, "Employee Ownership, Employee Attributes and Firm Performance," *Journal of Employee Ownership, Law, and Finance,* April 2000, pp. 37–48; "Web Sites for Employees with Stock Options," *Employee Ownership Report,* November/December 2000, p. 11.

16 Employee Benefits Research Institute's Web site at http://www.ebri.org. See also the *EBRI's Fundamentals of Employee Benefits* (Washington, D.C.: EBRI, 1997) and *EBRI Health Benefits Databook* (1999).

17 www.buffetttaylor.com (September 10, 2008).

18 *2007–2008 Global Workforce Study.* Towers Perrin.

19 Further information on each company's philosophy and way of doing business can be deduced from their Web sites: www.medtronic.com and www.aesc.com. Readers of earlier editions of this book will note that fairness is substituted for equity. Equity has taken on several meanings in compensation, e.g., stock ownership, and pay discrimination. We decided that fairness better conveyed our meaning in this book.

20 J. Brockner, Y. Chen, K. Leung, and D. Skarlicki "Culture and Procedural Fairness: When the Effects of What You Do Depend on How You Do It," *Administrative Science Quarterly* 45 (2000), pp. 138–159; M. P. Miceli, "Justice and Pay System Satisfaction" in *Justice in the Workplace: Approaching Fairness in Human Resource Management* (Lawrence Erlbaum Associates, 1993).

21 F. W. Cook, "Compensation Ethics: An Oxymoron or Valid Area for Debate?" Featured Speech at ACA International Conference Workshop, 1999; S. P. Green, *Lying, Cheating, and Stealing: A Moral Theory of White-Collar Crime.* Boston: Oxford University Press, 2006.

22 M. Gibbs and W. Hendricks, "Do Formal Pay Systems Really Matter?" *Industrial and Labor Relations Review,* October 2004, pp. 71–93; J. Boudreau and P. Ramstad, *Beyond Cost-Per-Hire and Time to Fill: Supply Chain Measurement for Staffing.* Los Angeles: Center for Effective Organizations, 2006.

[23] M. Graham et al., "In the Land of Milk and Honey: One Dairy Farm's Strategic Compensation System," *Journal of Agribusiness*, 15(2), 1997, pp. 171–188.

Chapter 2

[1] Timothy M. Gardner, "Interfirm Competition for Human Resources: Evidence from the Software Industry," *Academy of Management Journal* 48(2), pp. 237–256; Yoshio Yanadori and Janet Marler, "Compensation Strategy: Does Business Strategy Influence Compensation in High Technology Firms?" *Strategic Management Journal*, June 2006, pp. 559–570; Patrick Wright, Timothy Gardner, Lisa Moynihan, and Matthew Allen, "The Relationship Between HR Practices and Firm Performance: Examining Causal Order," *Personnel Psychology*, Summer 2005, pp. 409–446.

[2] R. Herbolt, "Inside Microsoft," *Harvard Business Review*, January 2002; Rich Karlgaard, "Microsoft's IQ Dividend," *The Wall Street Journal*, July 28, 2004, p. A13; Holman W. Jenkins Jr., "Stock Options Are Dead, Long Live Stock Options," *The Wall Street Journal*, July 16, 2003, p. A15; Sarah Kershaw, "For Newer Microsoft Employees, A Sense of Redress," *New York Times*, July 10, 2003. An *option* is the opportunity to buy stock at a set price. If the value of shares increases, then the option has value (market price minus the set option price). Awards grant employees stock whose value is its market price. Later chapters discuss stock options and awards in detail. Kevin F. Hallock and Craig A. Olson, "The Value of Stock Options to Non-Executive Employees," Working paper, Institute of Labor and Industrial Relations, University of Illinois Urbana/Champaign, January 2006.

[3] "SAS Institute," Stanford Business School case; also, "SAS: The Royal Treatment," *60 Minutes*, October 13, 2002.

[4] Rich Karlgaard, "Microsoft's IQ Dividend," *The Wall Street Journal*, July 28, 2004, p. A13; Holman W. Jenkins Jr., "Stock Options Are Dead, Long Live Stock Options," *The Wall Street Journal*, July 16, 2003.

[5] M. Treacy and F. Wiersma, *The Discipline of Market Leaders* (Reading, MA: Addison-Wesley, 1997).

[6] M. Porter, "What Is Strategy?" *Harvard Business Review*, November–December 1996, pp. 61–78.

[7] Yoshio Yanadori and Janet Marler, "Compensation Strategy: Does Business Strategy Influence Compensation in High Technology Firms?" *Strategic Management Journal*, June 2006, pp. 559–570; B. Gerhart, "Pay Strategy and Firm Performance," in *Compensation in Organizations: Current Research and Practice*, eds. S. L. Rynes and B. Gerhart (San Francisco: Jossey-Bass, 2000); Barry Gerhart and Sara Rynes, *Compensation: Theory, Evidence, and Strategic Implications* (Thousand Oaks, CA: Sage, 2003).

[8] *Strategic Rewards in Canada: Gaining Momentum, Room for Improvement*. Watson Wyatt Worldwide, 2006.

[9] A. Richter, "Paying the People in Black at Big Blue," *Compensation and Benefits Review*, May/June 1998, pp. 51–59;

Thomas Fleming, *Compensating a Global Workforce at IBM*, presentation at Cornell University, February 21, 2003.

[10] Charles Fishman, "The Anarchist's Cookbook," *Fast Company*, July 2004, *pf.fastcompany.com/magazine/84/wholefoods.html*.

[11] H. Mintzberg, "Crafting Strategy," *Harvard Business Review*, July–August 1970, pp. 66–75.

[12] M. Brown, M. C. Sturman, and M. Simmering, "Compensation Policy and Organizational Performance: The Efficiency, Operational, and Financial Implications of Pay Levels and Pay Structure," *Academy of Management Journal* 46 (2003), pp. 752–762; Yoshio Yanadori and Janet Marler, "Compensation Strategy: Does Business Strategy Influence Compensation in High Technology Firms?" *Strategic Management Journal*, June 2006, pp. 559–570; Patrick Wright, Timothy Gardner, Lisa Moynihan, and Matthew Allen, "The Relationship Between HR Practices and Firm Performance: Examining Causal Order," *Personnel Psychology*, Summer 2005, pp. 409–446.

[13] S. Chatterjee, "Core Objectives: Clarity in Designing Strategy," *California Management Review* 47(2) (2005).

[14] M. Bloom and G. Milkovich, "Strategic Perspectives on International Compensation and Reward Systems," in *Research and Theory in Strategic HRM: An Agenda for the Twenty-First Century*, eds. Pat Wright et al. (Greenwich, CT: JAI Press, 1999); M. Bloom, G. Milkovich, and A. Mitra, "International Compensation: Learning from How Managers Respond to Variations in Local Host Contexts," *International Journal of Human Resource Management* special issue, 2003; Allen D. Engle, Sr., and Mark Mendenhall, "Transnational Roles and Transnational Rewards: Global Integration in Executive Compensation," presentation at International HR conference, Limerick, Ireland, June 2003; Paul Evans, Vlado Pucik, and Jean-Louis Barsoux, *The Global Challenge* (New York: McGraw-Hill, 2002); *Global Rewards: A Collection of Articles from WorldatWork* (Scottsdale, AZ: WorldatWork, 2005).

[15] Yoshio Yanadori, "Minimizing Competition? Entry-Level Compensation in Japanese Firms," *Asia Pacific Journal of Management* 21 (December 2004), pp. 445–467.

[16] Sanford Jacoby, *The Embedded Corporation: Corporate Governance and Employment Relations in Japan and the United States* (Princeton, NJ: Princeton University Press, 2004).

[17] *www.jnj.com/our_company/our_credo* in over 50 languages!

[18] See the Web site for Federation of European Employers, at *www.fedee.com*. Also, Watson Wyatt Worldwide, "Strategic Rewards: Managing through Uncertain Times," survey report, 2001/2002.

[19] Jason Shaw, Michelle Duffy, Atul Mitra, Daniel Lockhart, and Matthew Bowler, "Reactions to Merit Pay Increases: A Longitudinal Test of a Signal Sensitivity Perspective," *Journal of Applied Psychology* 88 (2003), pp. 538–544; Loretta Chao, "For Gen Xers, It's Work to Live," *The Wall Street Journal*, November 29, 2005, p. B6; Eduardo Porter, "Choice Is Good. Yes, No, or Maybe?" *New York Times*, March 27, 2005, p. WK12; Melissa Barringer and George Milkovich, "Employee Health Insurance

Decisions in a Flexible Benefit Environment," *Human Resource Management* 35 (1996), pp. 293–315; M. P. Patterson, "Health Benefit Evolutions for the 21st Century: Vouchers and Other Innovations?" *Compensation and Benefits Review* 32(4) (July/August 2000), pp. 6–14.

[20] Eduardo Porter, "Choice Is Good. Yes, No or Maybe?" *New York Times,* March 27, 2005, p. WK12.

[21] S. S. Iyengar, R. E. Wells, and B. Schwartz, "Doing Better but Feeling Worse: Looking for the 'Best' Job Undermines Satisfaction," *Psychological Science* 17(2) (2003), pp. 143–150; R. Chua, S. S. Iyengar, "Empowerment through Choice?: A Critical Analysis of the Effects of Choice in Organizations" in *Research on Organizational Behavior*, eds. B. Staw and M. Kramer, (Oxford, UK: Elsevier, in press).

[22] Morris M. Kleiner, Jonathan S. Leonard, and Adam M. Pilarski, "How Industrial Relations Affects Plant Performance: The Case of Commercial Aircraft Manufacturing," *Industrial and Labor Relations Review* 55(2) (January 2002), pp. 195–218; Sean Karimi and Gangaram Singh, "Strategic Compensation: An Opportunity for Union Activism," *Compensation and Benefits Review,* March/April 2004, pp. 62–67; Henry S. Faber, "Union Success in Representation Elections: Why Does Unit Size Matter?" *Industrial and Labor Relations Review* 54(2) (2001), pp. 329–348.

[23] "Wage Cuts at Loblaw," *HR Professional*, February/March 2007, 88.

[24] B. Aldridge, "Innovative Workplace Practices — 1st Quarter 2008," *Workplace Bulletin (HRSDC)*, May 29, 2008, p. 2.

[25] Richard B. Freeman and Lawrence F. Katz, eds., *Differences and Changes in Wage Structures* (Chicago: University of Chicago Press, 1995); M. Mendenhall and G. Oddou, *Readings and Cases in International HRM*, 3rd ed. (Cincinnati: Southwest, 2000).

[26] Paul Osterman, "The Wage Effects of High Performance Work Organization in Manufacturing," *Industrial and Labor Relations Review,* January 2006, pp. 187–204; Patrick Wright, Timothy Gardner, Lisa Moynihan, and Matthew Allen, "The Relationship Between HR Practices and Firm Performance: Examining Causal Order," *Personnel Psychology*, Summer 2005, pp. 409–446. Rosemary Batt, Virginia Doellgast, and Hyunji Kwon, *The U.S. Call Center Industry 2004: National Benchmarking Report—Strategy, HR Practices, and Performance* (Ithaca, NY: Industrial and Labor Relations School, 2005).

[27] J. Barney, "Firm Resources and Sustained Competitive Advantage," *Journal of Management* 17 (1997), pp. 99–120; P. M. Wright, G. C. McMahan, and A. McWilliams, "Human Resources and Sustained Competitive Advantage: A Resource-Based Perspective," *International Journal of Human Resource Management* 5 (1994), pp. 301–326.

[28] L. Bossidy, R. Charman, and C. Burck, *Execution: The Discipline of Getting Things Done,* (New York: Crown Business Publishers, 2002); R. Preston McAffee, *Competitive Solutions: The Strategist's Toolkit* (Princeton, NJ: Princeton University Press, 2005).

[29] Samir Raza, "Optimizing Human Capital Investments for Superior Shareholder Returns," *Valuation Issues,* 2006 (*www. valuationissues.com*); M. Huselid and B. Becker, "Improving HR Analytical Literacy: Lessons from Moneyball," Chapter 32 in M. Losey, S. Meisinger, and D. Ulrich, *The Future of Human Resource Management* (Hoboken, NJ: Wiley, 2005); Lindsay Scott, "Managing Labor Costs Using Pay-for-Performance," *Lindsay Scott & Associates, Inc.*, www.npktools.com, 2006; Thomas Stewart, *Intellectual Capital: The New Wealth of Organizations* (New York: Currency, 1997); D. Scott, D. Morajda, and T. McMullen, "Evaluating Pay Program Effectiveness," *WorldatWork Journal,* First Quarter 2006; and D. Scott, T. McMullen and R. Sperling, "Evaluating Pay Program Effectiveness: A National Survey of Compensation and Human Resource Professionals," *WorldatWork Journal* 15(2) (Second Quarter 2006), pp. 50–59. See also John Boudreau and Pete Ramstad, "Beyond Cost-per-Hire and Time to Fill: Supply-Chain Measurement for Staffing," Working Paper T04–16 (468), Los Angeles: Center for Effective Organizations, 2006.

[30] Richard Donkin, "Measuring the Worth of Human Capital," *Financial Times,* November 7, 2002; Peter F. Drucker, "They're Not Employees, They're People," *Harvard Business Review,* February 2002, pp. 70–77; Stephen Gates, *Value at Work: The Risks and Opportunities of Human Capital Measurement and Reporting* (New York: Conference Board, 2002).

[31] Connie Willis, *Bellwether* (London: Bantam Books 1996); M. Gladwell, *The Tipping Point: The Next Big Thing* (Boston: Little, Brown, 2000).

[32] J. Purcell, "Best Practices and Best Fit: Chimera or Cul-de-Sac?" *Human Resources Management Journal* 9(3), pp. 26–41.

[33] B. Gerhart, "Pay Strategy and Firm Performance," in *Compensation in Organizations: Current Research and Practice,* eds. S. Rynes and B. Gerhart (San Francisco: Jossey-Bass, 2000); B. Gerhart and G. Milkovich, "Employee Compensation" in *Handbook of Industrial and Organization Psychology 3,* eds. M. Dunnette and L. Hough (Palo Alto, CA: Consulting Psychologists Press, 1992).

[34] J. Shaw, M. Duffy, A. Mitra, D. Lockhart, and M. Bowler, "Reactions to Merit Pay Increases: A Longitudinal Test of a Signal Sensitivity Perspective," *Journal of Applied Psychology* 88 (2003), pp. 538–544; C. O. Trevor and D. L. Wazeter, "A Contingent View of Reactions to Objective Pay Conditions: Interdependence among Pay Structure Characteristics and Pay Relative to Internal and External Referents," *Journal of Applied Psychology*, in press; M. Brown, M. C. Sturman and M. Simmering, "Compensation Policy and Organizational Performance: The Efficiency, Operational, and Financial Implications of Pay Levels and Pay Structure," *Academy of Management Journal* 46 (2003), pp. 752–762.

[35] B. Gerhart and G. Milkovich, "Organization Differences in Managerial Compensation and Financial Performance," *Academy of Management Journal* 33 (1990), pp. 663–691; K. Murphy and M. Jensen, "It's Not How Much, but How You Pay," *Harvard Business Review,* January–February 1993, pp. 32–45.

36 Patrick Wright, Timothy Gardner, Lisa Moynihan, and Matthew Allen, "The Relationship Between HR Practices and Firm Performance: Examining Causal Order," *Personnel Psychology*, Summer 2005, pp. 409–446. Deepak K. Datta, James P. Guthrie, and Patrick M. Wright, "Human Resource Management and Labor Productivity: Does Industry Matter?" *Academy of Management Journal* 48(5), pp. 135–145; S. Werner and H. Tosi, "Other People's Money: The Effects of Ownership on Compensation Strategy," *Academy of Management Journal* 38(6), pp. 1672–1691; Brian Becker and Mark Huselid, "High Performance Work Systems and Firm Performance: A Synthesis of Research and Managerial Implications," in *Research in Personnel and Human Resource Management,* ed. G. R. Ferris (Greenwich, CT: JAI Press, 1997); Stephen H. Wagner, Christopher P. Parker, and Neil D. Christiansen, "Employees that Think and Act Like Owners: Effects of Ownership Beliefs and Behaviors on Organizational Effectiveness," *Personnel Psychology,* Winter 2003, pp. 847–871; M. C. Sturman, C. O. Trevor, J. W. Boudreau, and B. Gerhart, "Is It Worth It to Win the Talent War? Evaluating the Utility of Performance-Based Pay," *Personnel Psychology* 56 (2003), pp. 997–1035; A. D. Stajkovic, and F. Luthans, "Differential Effects of Incentive Motivators on Work Performance," *Academy of Management Journal* (44) (2001), pp. 580–590; Jeffrey B. Arthur and Christopher L. Huntley, "Ramping Up the Organizational Learning Curve: Assessing the Impact of Deliberate Learning on Organizational Performance under Gainsharing," *Academy of Management Journal* 48(6) (2005), pp. 1159–1170.

37 Edilberto F. Montemayor, "Congruence between Pay Policy and Competitive Strategy in High-Performing Firms," *Journal of Management* 22(6) (1996), pp. 889–908; L. R. Gomez-Mejia and D. B. Balkin, *Compensation, Organization Strategy, and Firm Performance* (Cincinnati: Southwestern, 1992); Charlie Trevor, Barry Gerhart, and Greg Reilly, "Decoupling Explained and Unexplained Pay Dispersion to Predict Organizational Performance," presentation at Academy of Management meetings, Atlanta, Georgia, August 11–16, 2006; Jeffrey Pfeffer and Robert Sutton, "Management Half-Truth and Nonsense: How to Practice Evidence-Based Management," *California Management Review,* Spring 2006.

38 Mark A. Huselid, Brian E. Becker, and Richard W. Beatty, *The Workforce Scorecard* (Boston: Harvard Business School Press, 2005); David Ulrich and Wayne Brockbank, *The HR Value Proposition* (Boston: Harvard Business School Press, 2005); John Boudreau and Peter M. Ramstad, "Measuring Intellectual Capital: Learning from Financial History," *Human Resource Management* 36(3) (Fall 1997), pp. 343–356; Watson Wyatt Worldwide, "Human Capital Index: Human Capital as a Lead Indicator of Shareholder Value" (*www.watsonwyatt.com),* 2001; Brian Becker, Mark Huselid, and Dave Ulrich, *The HR Scorecard: Linking People, Strategy, and Performance* (Boston: Harvard Business School Press, 2001); Rosemary Batt, Virginia Doellgast, and Hyunji Kwon, *The U.S. Call Center Industry 2004: National Benchmarking Report—Strategy, HR Practices, and Performance* (Ithaca, NY: Industrial and Labor Relations School, 2005); D. Scott, D. Morajda, and T. McMullen, "Evaluating Pay Program Effectiveness," *WorldatWork Journal,*

First Quarter 2006; and D. Scott, T. McMullen, and R. Sperling, "Evaluating Pay Program Effectiveness: A National Survey of Compensation and Human Resource Professionals," *WorldatWork Journal* 15(2) (Second Quarter 2006), pp. 50–59.

39 Deepak K. Datta, James P. Guthrie, and Patrick M. Wright, "Human Resource Management and Labor Productivity: Does Industry Matter?" *Academy of Management Journal* 48(5), pp. 135–145.

Chapter 3

1 Matthew 20: 1–16.

2 For a history of the different standards for pay, see Thomas Mahoney, *Compensation and Reward Perspectives* (Burr Ridge, IL: Richard D. Irwin, 1979); G. Milkovich and J. Stevens, "From Pay to Rewards: 100 Years of Change" *ACA Journal* 9 9(1), (2000) pp. 6–18; D. F. Schloss, *Methods in Industrial Remuneration* (New York: G. P. Putnam's Sons, 1892).

3 S. G. Cohen and D. E. Bailey, "What Makes Teams Work: Group Effectiveness Research from the Shop Floor to Executive Suite," *Journal of Management* 23 (1997), pp. 239–291; M. Apgar, "The Alternative Workplace: Changing Where and How People Work," *Harvard Business Review*, May–June 1998, pp. 125–137; R. A. Guzzo and M. W. Dickson, "Teams in Organizations: Recent Research in Performance and Effectiveness," *Annual Review of Psychology* 47 (1996), pp. 307–338; N. Nohria and S. Ghoshal, *The Differential Network: Organizing Corporations for Value Creation* (San Francisco: Jossey-Bass, 1998).

4 S. Rynes and G. Gerhart, *Compensation in Organizations: Current Research and Practice* (San Francisco: Jossey-Bass, 2000); R. H. Thaler, "From Homo Economicus to Homo Sapiens," *Journal of Economic Perspectives* 14(1), Winter 2000, pp. 133–141; and P. Milgrom and J. Roberts, "An Economic Approach to Influence Activities in Organizations," *American Journal of Sociology* 94 (1988), pp. S154–S179.

5 C. W. Hill, M. A. Hitt, and R. E. Hoskisson, "Cooperative Versus Competitive Structures in Related and Unrelated Diversified Firms," *Organization Science* (1992), pp. 501–521.

6 D. M. Cowherd and D. I. Levine, "Product Quality and Pay Equity between Lower-Level Employees and Top Management: An Investigation of Distributive Justice Theory," *Administrative Science Quarterly* 37 (1992), pp. 302–320; M. Bloom and G. Milkovich, "Money, Managers, and Metamorphosis," in *Trends in Organizational Behavior*, 3rd ed., eds. D. Rousseau and C. Cooper (New York: John Wiley & Sons, 1996).

7 E. E. Lawler III, "From Job-Based to Competency-Based Organizations," *Journal of Organization Behavior* 15 (1994), pp. 3–15.

8 C. Tucker, ed., *The Marx-Engels Reader* (New York: W. W. Norton, 1978).

[9] Allan M. Cartter, *Theory of Wages and Employment* (Burr Ridge, IL: Richard D. Irwin, 1959); P. Milgrom and J. Roberts, *Economics, Organization, and Management* (Englewood Cliffs, NJ: Prentice Hall, 1992).

[10] M. Bloom, G. Milkovich, and A. Mitra, *"Toward a Model of International Compensation"* (Ithaca, NY: CAHRS Working Paper, 2000); S. Finkelstein and D. Hambrick, *Strategic Leadership: Top Executives and Their Effects on Organizations* (St. Paul: West Publishing, 1996); S. Brown and K. Eisenhardt, *Competing on the Edge: Strategy and Structured Chaos* (Boston: Harvard Business Press, 1998).

[11] M. Bloom, G. Milkovich, and A. Mitra, "Toward a Model of International Compensation" (Ithaca, NY: CAHRS Working Paper, 2000); M. Mendenhall and G. Oddou, *Readings and Cases in International HRM* (Cincinnati: Southwestern Publishing, 2000).

[12] G. Hoefstede, *Culture's Consequences: International Differences in Work Relationships and Values* (Thousand Oaks, CA: Sage Publications, 1980); M. Bloom, G. Milkovich, and A. Mitra, "Toward a Model of International Compensation" (Ithaca, NY: CAHRS Working Paper, 2000); F. Trompenaars, *Riding the Waves of Culture: Understanding Diversity in Global Business* (Burr Ridge, IL: Irwin,1995); J. Brockner, Y. Chen, K. Leung, and D. Skarlick, "Culture and Procedural Fairness: When the Effects of What You Do Depend on How You Do It," *Administrative Science Quarterly* 45 (2000), pp. 138–159.

[13] Yoshio Yanadori, "Minimizing Competition? Entry-Level Compensation in Japanese Firms," *Asia Pacific Journal of Management* 21 (December 2004), pp. 445–467.

[14] D. Levine, D. Belman, G. Charness, E. Groshen, and K. C. O'Shaughnessy, *The New Employment Contract: How Little Wage Structures at U.S. Employers Have Changed* (Kalamazoo: Upjohn, 2001).

[15] R. Batt, "Explaining Wage Inequities, Customer Segmentation, HR Practices, and Unions," *Industrial and Labor Relations Review*, in print; P. Milgrom and J. Roberts, *Economics, Organization, and Management* (Englewood Cliffs, NJ: Prentice Hall, 1992).

[16] Pui-Wing Tam, "Hurd's Big Challenge at H-P: Overhauling Corporate Sales," *The Wall Street Journal,* April 3, 2006, pp. A1, A13.

[17] Rosemary Batt, Alexander J. S. Colvin, and Jeffrey Keefe, "Employee Voice, Human Resource Practices, and Quit Rates: Evidence from the Telecommunications Industry," *Industrial and Labor Relations Review* 55(4) (July 2002), pp. 573–594; Wayne F. Cascio, "Strategies for Responsible Restructuring," *Academy of Management Executive* 19(4) (2005), pp. 39–50.

[18] Paul Schumann, Dennis Ahlburg, and Christine B. Mahoney, "The Effects of Human Capital and Job Characteristics on Pay," *The Journal of Human Resources* XXIX (2), pp. 481–503.

[19] Specialized studies of competitors' pay structures are conducted by some consulting firms. These are discussed in Chapter 8.

[20] Thomas A. Mahoney, "Organizational Hierarchy and Position Worth," *Academy of Management Journal*, December 1979, pp. 726–737.

[21] E. Robert Livernash, "The Internal Wage Structure," in *New Concepts in Wage Determination*, eds. G. W. Taylor and F. C. Pierson (New York: McGraw-Hill, 1957), pp. 143–172.

[22] T. Judge and H. G. Heneman, III, "Pay Satisfaction," in S. Rynes and G. Gerhart, *Compensation in Organizations: Current Research and Practice* (San Francisco: Jossey-Bass, 2000); Robert Folger and Mary Konovsky, "Effects of Procedural and Distributive Justice on Reactions to Pay Raise Decisions," *Academy of Management Journal*, March 1989, pp. 115–130; Jerald Greenberg, "Looking Fair vs. Being Fair: Managing Impressions of Organizational Justice," in *Research in Organizational Behavior*, Vol. 12, eds. B. M. Staw and L. L. Cummings (Greenwich, CT: JAI Press, 1990).

[23] Frederick P. Morgeson, Michael A. Campion, Carl P. Maertz, "Understanding Pay Satisfaction: The Limits of a Compensation System Implementation," *Journal of Business & Psychology* Fall 16(1) (2001), pp. 133–163.

[24] Frederick P. Morgeson, Michael A. Campion, Carl P. Maertz, "Understanding Pay Satisfaction: The Limits of a Compensation System Implementation," *Journal of Business & Psychology* Fall 16(1) (2001), pp. 133–163.

[25] "Federal Uniformed Police: Selected Data on Pay, Recruitment, and Retention at 13 Police Forces in the Washington, D.C. Metropolitan Area," GAO-03-658, June 13, 2003.

[26] Elliot Jaques, "In Praise of Hierarchies," *Harvard Business Review*, January–February 1990, pp. 32–46; M. Bloom and J. Michel, *"Understanding the Causes and Consequences of Pay Structures: The Importance of Organization Context"* (Notre Dame working paper, 2000).

[27] R. D. Bretz and S. L. Thomas, "Perceived Equity, Motivation, and Final-Offer Arbitration in Major League Baseball," *Journal of Applied Psychology* 77 (1992), pp. 280–287; M. Bloom and J. Michel, *"Understanding the Causes and Consequences of Pay Structures: The Importance of Organization Context"* (Notre Dame working paper, 2000).

[28] Charlie O. Trevor and David L. Wazeter, "A Contingent View of Reactions to Objective Pay Conditions: Interdependence among Pay Structure Characteristics and Pay Relative to Internal and External Referents," *Journal of Applied Psychology*, in press; E. Lawler III, *Treat People Right! How Organizations and Individuals Can Propel Each Other into a Virtuous Spiral of Success* (San Francisco: Jossey-Bass, 2003).

[29] J. Shaw and N. Gupta, "Pay System Characteristics and Quit Rates of Good, Average, and Poor Performers," University of Kentucky working paper, May 2006.

[30] G. Milkovich and P. H. Anderson, "Management Compensation and Secrecy Policies," *Personnel Psychology* 25 (1972), pp. 293–302.

31 B. E. Becker and M. A. Huselid, "The Incentive Effects of Tournament Compensation Systems," *Administrative Science Quarterly* 37 (1992), pp. 336–350; E. Lazear and S. Rosen, "Rank-Order Tournaments as Optimum Labor Contracts," *Journal of Political Economy* 89 (1981), pp. 841–864; Matthew C. Bloom, "The Performance Effects of Pay Structures on Individuals and Organizations," *Academy of Management Journal* 42(1) (1999), pp. 25–40.

32 R. G. Ehrenberg and M. L. Bognanno, "The Incentive Effects of Tournaments Revisited: Evidence from the European PGA Tour," *Industrial and Labor Relations Review* 43 (1990), pp. 74S–88S.

33 R. D. Bretz and S. L. Thomas, "Perceived Equity, Motivation, and Final-Offer Arbitration in Major League Baseball," *Journal of Applied Psychology* 77 (1992), pp. 280–287.

34 M. Bloom and J. Michel, *"Understanding the Causes and Consequences of Pay Structures: The Importance of Organization Context"* (Notre Dame working paper, 2000); W. Jurgens, "Look Out Below," *Wall Street Journal*, April 1, 2000, p. R3.

35 P. S. Tolbert and L. G. Zucker, "Institutionalization of Institution Theory," in *Handbook of Organization Studies*, eds. G. Glegg, C. Hardy, and W. Lord (London: Sage, 1996), pp. 175–199; M. Barringer and G. Milkovich, "A Theoretical Exploration of the Adoption and Design of Flexible Benefit Plans: A Case of HR Innovation," *Academy of Management Review* 23(2) (1998), pp. 305–324; Y. Yanadori, "Organization Variations in Stock Option Designs: Insights of Organization Theory," Working Paper, CAHRS, Ithaca, NY, 2004.

36 M. Brown, M. C. Sturman, and M. Simmering, "Compensation Policy and Organizational Performance: The Efficiency, Operational, and Financial Implications of Pay Levels and Pay Structure," *Academy of Management Journal* 46 (2003), pp. 752–762.

37 Edward Lazear, "Labor Economics and Psychology of Organization," *Journal of Economic Perspectives* 5 (1991), pp. 89–110; David Wazeter, *"Determinants and Consequences of Pay Structures"* (Ph.D. Dissertation, Cornell University, 1991).

38 E. Robert Livernash, "The Internal Wage Structure," in *New Concepts in Wage Determination*, eds. G. W. Taylor and F. C. Pierson (New York: McGraw-Hill, 1957), pp. 143–172.

39 Elliot Jaques, "In Praise of Hierarchies," *Harvard Business Review*, January–February 1990, pp. 32–46.

Chapter 4

1 Peter Cappelli, *The New Deal at Work: Managing the Market-Driven Workforce* (Boston, MA: Harvard Business School Press, 1999).

2 Most human resource management texts discuss these multiple uses of job analysis information. See, for example, Chapter 3 in G. Milkovich and J. Boudreau, *Human Resource Management* (Burr Ridge, IL: Irwin, 1997).

3 E. J. McCormick, "Job and Task Analysis," in *Handbook of Industrial and Organizational Psychology*, ed. M. D. Dunnette (Chicago: Rand McNally, 1976), pp. 651–96; E. J. McCormick, *Job Analysis: Methods and Applications* (New York: AMACOM, 1979).

4 Robert J. Harvey, "Job Analysis," in *Handbook of Industrial and Organizational Psychology*, Vol. 2, ed. M. D. Dunnette and L. Hough (Palo Alto, CA: Consulting Psychologists Press, 1991), pp. 72–157.

5 Steven G. Allen, Robert L. Clark, and Sylvester J. Schieber, "Has Job Security Vanished in Large Corporations?" *NBER Working Paper 6966* (1999).

6 Treasury Board of Canada Secretariat, www.tbs-sct.gc.ca/gui/ncls-eng.asp (August 16, 2009).

7 Much of the developmental and early applications of the PAQ was done in the 1960s and 1970s. See, for example, McCormick, "Job Analysis"; McCormick, "Job and Task Analysis"; McCormick et al., "A Study of Job Characteristics and Job Dimensions as Based on the Position Analysis Questionnaire" (West Lafayette, IN: Occupational Research Center, Purdue University, 1969). The PAQ is distributed by the University Book Store, 360 West State St., West Lafayette, IN 47906. For more recent discussions, see PAQ Newsletters.

8 V. L. Huber, S. Crandall, and G. B. Northcraft, *"A Rose by Any Other Name Is Not as Sweet: Effects of Job Titles and Upgrade Requests on Job Evaluation and Wage Decisions"* (unpublished manuscript, University of Washington, 1992).

9 Robert Harvey, *"Incumbent vs. Superior Perception of Jobs,"* Presentation at SIOP Conference, Miami, FL, 1990.

10 Link Group Consultants, Limited, Chester, U.K.

11 Juan I. Sanchez and Edward L. Levine, "Accuracy or Consequential Validity: Which Is the Better Standard for Job Analysis Data?" *Journal of Organizational Behavior* 21 (2000), pp. 809–818; W. C. Borman, D. Dorsey, and L. Ackerman, "Time-Spent Responses and Time Allocation Strategies: Relations with Sales Performance in a Stockbroker Sample," *Personnel Psychology* 45 (1992), pp. 763–777.

12 Richard Arvey, Emily M. Passino, and John W. Lounsbury, "Job Analysis Results as Influenced by Sex of Incumbent and Sex of Analyst," *Journal of Applied Psychology* 62(4) (1977), pp. 411–416.

13 K. C. O'Shaughnessy, David Levine, and Peter Cappelli, "Changes in Management Pay Structures, 1986–1992 and Rising Returns to Skill," *University California at Berkeley Institute of Industrial Relations Working Paper*, Berkeley, CA, 1998.

14 S. G. Cohen and D. E. Bailey, "What Makes Teams Work: Group Effectiveness Research from the Shop Floor to Executive Suite," *Journal of Management* 23 (1997), pp. 239–291.

[15] Ronald A. Ash and Edward L. Levine, "A Framework for Evaluating Job Analysis Methods," *Personnel* 57, (6) (November–December 1980, pp. 53–59; R. A. Ash, E. L. Levine, and F. Sistrunk, "The Role of Jobs and Job Based Methods in Personnel and Human Resources Management," *Research in Personnel and Human Resources Management 1* (1983), pp. 45–84; Edward L. Levine, Ronald A. Ash, Hardy Hall, and Frank Sistrunk, "Evaluation of Job Analysis Methods by Experienced Job Analysts," *Academy of Management Journal* 26 (2) (1983), pp. 339–348.

[16] M. D. Dunnette, L. M. Hough, and R. L. Rosse, "Task and Job Taxonomies as a Basis for Identifying Labor Supply Sources and Evaluating Employment Qualifications," in *Affirmative Action Planning*, ed. George T. Milkovich and Lee Dyer (New York: Human Resource Planning Society, 1979), pp. 37–51.

Chapter 5

[1] Donald P. Schwab, "Job Evaluation and Pay Setting: Concepts and Practices," in *Comparable Worth: Issues and Alternatives*, ed. E. Robert Livernash (Washington, DC: Equal Employment Advisory Council, 1980), pp. 49–77.

[2] Alvin O. Bellak, "Comparable Worth: A Practitioner's View," in *Comparable Worth: Issue for the 80's*, Vol. 1 (Washington, DC: U.S. Civil Rights Commission, 1985).

[3] M. A. Konovsky, "Understanding Procedural Justice and Its Impact on Business Organizations," *Journal of Management* 26 (3) (2000), pp. 489–511; R. Cropanzano, *Justice in the Workplace, Volume 2: From Theory to Practice.* (Mahwah, NJ: Lawrence Erlbaum Associates, 2000); R. Folger, R. and R. Crepanzano, *Organizational Justice and Human Resource Management* (Thousand Oaks, CA: Sage, 1998); R. B. Foreman and J. Rogers, *What Workers Want* (Ithaca, NY: ILR/Cornell University Press, 1999); B. H. Sheppard, R. J. Lewicki, and J. W. Minton, *Organizational Justice: The Search for Fairness in the Workplace* (New York: Macmillan, 1992).

[4] M. S. Viteles, "A Psychologist Looks at Job Evaluation," *Personnel* 17 (1941), pp. 165–176.

[5] Vandra Huber and S. Crandall, "Job Measurement: A Social-Cognitive Decision Perspective," in *Research in Personnel and Human Resources Management*, Vol. 12, ed. Gerald R. Ferris (Greenwich, CT: JAI Press, 1994).

[6] R. L. Heneman and P. V. LeBlanc, "Developing a More Relevant and Competitive Approach for Valuing Knowledge Work," *Compensation & Benefits Review*, July/August 2002, pp. 43–47; R. L. Heneman and P. V. LeBlanc, "Work Valuation Addresses Shortcomings of Both Job Evaluation and Market Pricing," *Compensation & Benefits Review*, January/February 2003, pp. 7–11.

[7] Tjarda Van Sliedregt, Olga F. Voskuijl, and Henk Thierry, "Job Evaluation Systems and Pay Grade Structures: Do They Match?" *International Journal of Human Resource Management* 12(8) (December 2001), pp. 1313–1324; E. Jane Arnault et al., "An Experimental Study of Job Evaluation and Comparable Worth,"

Industrial and Labor Relations Review 54(4) (July 2001), pp. 806–815; Judith M. Collins and Paul M. Muchinsky, "An Assessment of the Construct Validity of Three Job Evaluation Methods: A Field Experiment," *Academy of Management Journal* 36(4) (1993), pp. 895–904.

[8] Factor comparison, another method of job evaluation, bears some similarities to the point method in that compensable factors are clearly defined and the external market is linked to the job evaluation results. However, factor comparison is used by less than 10 percent of employers who use job evaluation. The method's complexity makes it difficult to explain to employees and managers, which limits its usefulness.

[9] M. K. Mount and R. A. Ellis, "Investigation of Bias in Job Evaluation Ratings of Comparable Worth Study Participants," *Personnel Psychology* 40 (1987), pp.85–96; H. Remick, *"Strategies for Creating Sound, Bias-Free Job Evaluation Plans,"* Paper presented at the I.R.C. Colloquium, Atlanta, GA, September 1978.

[10] D. F. Harding, J. M. Madden, and K. Colson, "Analysis of a Job Evaluation System," *Journal of Applied Psychology* 44 (1960), pp. 354–357.

[11] R. Nisbett, D. Krantz, C. Jepson, and A. Kunda, "The Use of Statistical Heuristics in Everyday Intuition," *Psychological Review* 90 (1983), pp. 339–363.

[12] See a series of studies conducted by C. H. Lawshe and his colleagues published in the *Journal of Applied Psychology* from 1944–1947. For example, C. H. Lawshe, "Studies in job evaluation: II. The adequacy of abbreviated point ratings for hourly paid jobs in three industrial plans," *Journal of Applied Psychology* 29 (1945), pp. 177–184.

[13] Charles Fay and Paul Hempel, *"Whose Values? A Comparison of Incumbent, Supervisor, Incumbent-Supervisor Consensus and Committee Job Evaluation Ratings"* (Working paper, Rutgers University, 1991); John Doyle, Rodney Green, and Paul Bo Homley, "Judging Relative Importance: Direct Rating and Point Allocation Are Not Equivalent," *Organizational Behavior and Human Decision Processes*, April 1997, pp. 65–72.

[14] Paul M. Edwards, "Statistical Methods in Job Evaluation," *Advanced Management* (December 1948), pp. 158–163.

[15] Donald J. Treiman, "Effect of Choice of Factors and Factor Weights in Job Evaluation," in *Comparable Worth and Wage Discrimination*, ed. H. Remick (Philadelphia: Temple University Press, 1984), pp. 79–89.

[16] M. K. Mount and R. A. Ellis, "Investigation of Bias in Job Evaluation Ratings of Comparable Worth Study Participants," *Personnel Psychology* 40 (1987); Tjarda Van Sliedregt, Olga F. Voskuijl, and Henk Thierry, "Job Evaluation Systems and Pay Grade Structures: Do They Match?" *International Journal of Human Resource Management* 12(8), (December 2001), pp. 1313–1324; Judith M. Collins and Paul M. Muchinsky, "An Assessment of the Construct Validity of Three Job Evaluation Methods: A Field

Experiment," *Academy of Management Journal* 36(4) (1993), pp. 895–904; Robert M. Madigan and David J. Hoover, "Effects of Alternative Job Evaluation Methods on Decisions Involving Pay Equity," *Academy of Management Journal* 29 (1986), pp. 84–100.

[17] The importance of appropriate criterion pay structure is particularly relevant in "pay equity studies" to assess gender bias. (*Canadian Telephone Employees Association et al v. Bell Canada; Canada Equal Wages Guidelines*, 1986).

[18] One of the key findings of a National Academy of Science report that examined virtually all research on pay was that the process used to design pay plans is vital to achieving high commitment. George Milkovich and Alexandra Wigdor, eds., *Pay and Performance* (Washington, DC: National Academy Press, 1991). Also see Carl F. Frost, John W. Wakely, and Robert A. Ruh, *The Scanlon Plan for Organization Development: Identity, Participation, and Equity* (East Lansing: Michigan State Press, 1974); E. A. Locke and D. M. Schweiger, "Participation in Decision Making: One More Look," *Research in Organization Behavior* (Greenwich, CT: JAI Press, 1979); G. J. Jenkins, Jr. and E. E. Lawler III, "Impact of Employee Participation in Pay Plan Development," *Organizational Behavior and Human Performance* 28 (1981), pp. 111–128.

[19] B. Carver and A. A. Vondra, "Alternative Dispute Resolution: Why It Doesn't Work and Why It Does," *Harvard Business Review*, May–June 1994, pp. 120–129.

[20] Theresa M. Welbourne and Charlie O. Trevor, "The Roles of Departmental and Position Power in Job Evaluation," *Academy of Management Journal* 43 (2000), pp. 761–771.

[21] A. G. P. Elliott, *Staff Grading* (London: British Institute of Management, 1960); N. Gupta and G. D. Jenkins, Jr., *"The Politics of Pay,"* Paper presented at the annual meeting of the Society for Industrial and Organizational Psychology, Montreal, 1992.

[22] Vandra Huber and S. Crandall, "Job Measurement: A Social-Cognitive Decision Perspective" in *Research in Personnel and Human Resources Management*, Vol. 12, ed. Gerald R. Ferris (Greenwich, CT: JAI Press, 1994).

Chapter 6

[1] Gupta, N., and Shaw, J. D., "Successful skill-based pay plans," in ed. C. H. Fay, *Executive Handbook on Compensation: Linking Strategic Rewards to Business Performance* (New York: Free Press, 2001), pp. 513–526.

[2] Diana Southall and Jerry Newman, *Skill-Based Pay Development* (Buffalo NY: HR Foundations, Inc., 2000).

[3] G. Douglas Jenkins, Jr., Gerald E. Ledford, Jr., Nina Gupta, and D. Harold Doty, *Skill-Based Pay* (Scottsdale, AZ: American Compensation Association, 1992).

[4] D. Southall and J. Newman, *Skill-Based Pay Development* (Buffalo, NY: HR Foundations, 2000).

[5] Gerald E. Ledford, Jr., "Three Case Studies of Skill-Based Pay: An Overview," *Compensation and Benefits Review* (March/April 1991), pp. 11–23.

[6] B. Murray and B. Gerhart, "An Empirical Analysis of a Skill-Based Pay Program and Plant Performance Outcomes," *Academy of Management Journal* 41 (1998), pp. 68–78.

[7] N. Fredric Crandall and Marc J. Wallace, Jr., "Paying Employees to Develop New Skills," in *Aligning Pay and Results*, ed. Howard Risher (New York: American Management Association 1999).

[8] Cynthia Lee, Kenneth S. Law, and Philip Bobko, "The Importance of Justice Perceptions on Pay Effectiveness: A Two-Year Study of a Skill-Based Pay Plan," *Journal of Management* 25 (6) (1999), pp. 851–873.

[9] K. Parent and C. Weber, "Case Study: Does Paying for Knowledge Pay Off?" *Compensation and Benefits Review*, September–October 1994, pp. 44–50; B. Murray and B. Gerhart, "An Empirical Analysis of a Skill-Based Pay Program and Plant Performance Outcomes," *Academy of Management Journal* 41 (1998), pp. 68–78.

[10] Kenneth Mericle and Dong-One Kim, *"Determinants of Skill Acquisition and Pay Satisfaction under Pay-for-Knowledge Systems"* (Working Paper, Institute of Industrial Relations, University of California Berkeley, 1996).

[11] J. D. Shaw, N. Gupta, G. E. Ledford Jr., and A. Mitra, *"Survival of Skill-Based Pay Plans,"* paper presented at the annual meetings of the Academy of Management, Toronto, 2000.

[12] E. E. Lawler, III, S. A. Mohrman, and G. E. Ledford, Jr., *Strategies for High Performance Organizations* (San Francisco: Jossey-Bass, 1998); B. Gerhart, C. O. Trevor, and M. E. Graham, "New Directions in Compensation Research: Synergies, Risk, and Survival," *Research in Personnel and Human Resources Management* 14, 1996, pp. 143–203.

[13] Lyle M. Spencer, Jr. and Signe M. Spencer, *Competence at Work* (New York: John Wiley and Sons, 1993).

[14] N. Jagmin, *"Assessing and Rewarding Competencies: The Ten-Year Tune-Up at Frito-Lay,"* Presentation for Center for Organizational Effectiveness, April 2003, Marina del Rey, California.

[15] James T. Kochanski and Howard Risher, "Paying for Competencies: Rewarding Knowledge, Skills, and Behaviors," in *Aligning Pay and Results*, ed. Howard Risher (New York: American Management Association 1999).

[16] C. A. Bartlett and Sumantra Ghoshal, "The Myth of the Generic Manager: New Personal Competencies for New Management Roles," *California Management Review* 40 (1) (1997), pp. 92–105.

[17] Edward E. Lawler III, "From Job-Based to Competency-Based Organizations," *Journal of Organizational Behavior* 15 (1994), pp. 3–15.

[18] R. H. Dorr and Thomas Gresch, *Human Resources Concept: Europe* (General Motors Acceptance Corporation, Wiesbaden,

Germany, 1996); Graham L. O'Neill and David Doig, "Definition and Use of Competencies by Australian Organizations: A Survey of HR Practitioners," *ACA Journal*, Winter 1997, pp. 45–56.

[19] Margaret E. Allredge and Kevin J. Nilan, "3M's Leadership Competency Model: An Internally Developed Solution," *Human Resource Management* 39, Summer/Fall 2000, pp. 133–145.

[20] Zingheim, Ledford, and Schuster, "Competencies and Competency Models," *Raising the Bar: Using Competencies to Enhance Employee Performance* (Scottsdale, AZ: American Compensation Association, 1996).

[21] F. Giancola, "Why People-Based Pay Is Struggling," *Workspan*, April 2008, pp. 35–37.

[22] A. R. Levenson, W. A. Van der Stede, and S. G. Cohen, "Measuring the Relationship Between Managerial Competencies and Performance," *Journal of Management* 32(3) (2006), pp. 360–380.

[23] Scott A. Snell, David P. Lepak, and Mark A. Youndt, "Managing the Architecture of Intellectual Capital," in *Strategic Human Resources Management in the Twenty-First Century, supplement 4*, eds. Patrick M. Wright, Lee D. Dyer, John W. Boudreau, and George T. Milkovich (Stamford, CT: JAI Press, 1999).

[24] This is a variation of the resource dependence ideas discussed in the strategy chapter (Chapter 2).

[25] C. A. Bartlett and S. Ghoshal, "Changing the Role of Top Management (part 3): Beyond Systems to People," *Harvard Business Review* 73, May–June 1995, pp. 132–143.

[26] Edward E. Lawler III, "From Job-Based to Competency-Based Organizations," *Journal of Organizational Behavior* 15 (1994), pp. 3–15.

[27] *HRJob Evaluation Software, Online Job Classification, Web. NPKTools* (part of CompXpert compensation analysis suite) *www. npktools.com.*

[28] S. Davis, "Closing the Assessment Gap," *Canadian HR Reporter*, March 10, 2008.

[29] An exception is the study cited in A. R. Levenson, W. A. Van der Stede, and S. G. Cohen, "Measuring the Relationship Between Managerial Competencies and Performance," *Journal of Management* 32(3) (2006), pp. 360–380.

[30] Tjarda van Sliedregt, Olga F. Voskuijl, and Henk Thierry, "Job Evaluation Systems and Pay Grade Structures: Do They Match?" *International Journal of Human Resource Management* 12(8) (December 2001), pp. 1313–1324.

[31] Erich C. Dierdorff and Mark A. Wilson, "A Meta-Analysis of Job Analysis Reliability," *Journal of Applied Psychology*, August 2003, pp. 635–646; Vandra Huber and S. Crandall, "Job Measurement: A Social-Cognitive Decision Perspective," in *Research in Personnel and Human Resources Management*, Vol. 12, ed. Gerald R. Ferris (Greenwich, CT: JAI Press, 1994), pp. 223–269; Sheila M. Rutt

and Dennis Doverspike, "Salary and Organizational Level Effects on Job Evaluation Ratings," *Journal of Business and Psychology*, Spring 1999, pp. 379–385.

[32] R. M. Madigan and D. J. Hoover, "Effects of Alternative Job Evaluation Methods on Decisions Involving Pay Equity," *Academy of Management Journal*, March 1986, pp. 84–100.

[33] D. Doverspike and G. Barrett, "An Internal Bias Analysis of a Job Evaluation Instrument," *Journal of Applied Psychology* 69 (1984), pp. 648–662; Kermit Davis, Jr., and William Sauser, Jr., "Effects of Alternative Weighting Methods in a Policy-Capturing Approach to Job Evaluation: A Review and Empirical Investigation," *Personnel Psychology* 44 (1991), pp. 85–127.

[34] Judith Collins and Paul M. Muchinsky, "An Assessment of the Construct Validity of Three Job Evaluation Methods: A Field Experiment," *Academy of Management Journal* 36(4) (1993), pp. 895–904; Todd J. Maurer and Stuart A. Tross, "SME Committee vs. Field Job Analysis Ratings: Convergence, Cautions, and a Call," *Journal of Business and Psychology* 14(3), (Spring 2000), pp. 489–499.

[35] Examples abound. A recent one is the pay equity settlement by Bell Canada, discussed in Chapter 17. See Pay Equity Information Centre at www.equityic.ca and "CEP Reaches $104 million pay equity settlement at Bell," www.cep.ca/human_rights/equity/bell/equityrelease_e.pdf.

[36] D. Lipsky and R. Seeber, "In Search of Control: The Corporate Embrace of Alternative Dispute Resolution," *Journal of Labor and Employment Law* 1 (1) Spring 1998, pp. 133–157.

[37] D. J. Treiman and H. I. Hartmann, eds., *Women, Work and Wages: Equal Pay for Jobs of Equal Value* (Washington, DC: National Academy of Sciences, 1981); H. Remick, *Comparable Worth and Wage Discrimination* (Philadelphia: Temple University Press, 1984).

[38] D. Schwab and R. Grams, "Sex-Related Errors in Job Evaluation: A 'Real-World' Test," *Journal of Applied Psychology* 70 (3) (1985), pp. 533–559; Richard D. Arvey, Emily M. Passino, and John W. Lounsbury, "Job Analysis Results as Influenced by Sex of Incumbent and Sex of Analyst," *Journal of Applied Psychology* 62 (4) (1977), pp. 411–416.

[39] Michael K. Mount and Rebecca A. Ellis, "Investigation of Bias in Job Evaluation Ratings of Comparable Worth Study Participants," *Personnel Psychology*, Spring 1987, pp. 85–96.

[40] S. Rynes, C. Weber, and G. Milkovich, "The Effects of Market Survey Rates, Job Evaluation, and Job Gender on Job Pay," *Journal of Applied Psychology* 74 (1989), pp. 114–123.

[41] N. Fredric Crandall and Marc J. Wallace, Jr., "Paying Employees to Develop New Skills," in *Aligning Pay and Results*, ed. Howard Risher (New York: American Management Association 1999); B. Murray and B. Gerhart, "An Empirical Analysis of a Skill-Based Pay Program and Plant Performance Outcomes," *Academy of Management Journal* 41 (1998), pp. 68–78.

[42] Howard Risher, ed. *Aligning Pay and Results* (New York: American Management Association 1999).

Chapter 7

[1] M. Reilly and L. Audi, "Does It Still Make Sense to Use Geographic Pay Rates?" *Workspan*, December 2006, pp. 52–56.

[2] S. L. Rynes and B. Gerhart, eds., *Compensation in Organizations: Current Research & Practice* (San Francisco: Jossey-Bass, 2000); Margaret L. Williams and George Dreher, "Compensation System Attributes and Applicant Pool Characteristics," *Academy of Management Journal*, August 1992.

[3] www.rotman.utoronto.ca/career/employment.htm (January 27, 2009).

[4] The National Association of Colleges and Employers, Bethlehem, PA, publishes a quarterly survey of starting salary offers to college graduates. Data are reported by curriculum, by functional area, and by degree. It is one of several sources employers may use to establish the offers they extend to new graduates (www.naceweb.org).

[5] Adapted from our analysis of CHIPS 2000 data set, by arrangement with Executive Alliance, Boston, Massachusetts.

[6] Barry Gerhart and George Milkovich, "Employee Compensation: Research and Practice," in *Handbook of Industrial and Organizational Psychology*, 2nd ed., eds. M. D. Dunnette and L. M. Hough (Palo Alto, CA: Consulting Psychologists Press, 1992).

[7] Barry Gerhart and Sara Rynes, "Determinants and Consequences of Salary Negotiations by Male and Female MBA Graduates," *Journal of Applied Psychology* 76, (2) (1991), pp. 256–262. Also see S. L. Rynes and B. Gerhart, eds., *Compensation in Organizations: Current Research & Practice* (San Francisco: Jossey-Bass, 2000).

[8] Robert Pindyck and Daniel Rubinfeld, *Microeconomics*, 5th ed. (Upper Saddle River, NJ: Prentice Hall, 2001).

[9] Morris M. Kleiner, *Licensing Occupations: Ensuring Quality or Restricting Competition?* (Kalamazoo, MI: Upjohn Institute, 2006).

[10] Thomas A. Mahoney, *Compensation and Reward Perspective* (Burr Ridge, IL: Richard D. Irwin 1979), p. 123.

[11] David Levine, D. Belman, G. Charness, E. Groshen, and K. C. O'Shaughnessy, *The New Employment Contract: Evidence About How Little Wage Structures Have Changed* (Kalamazoo: Upjohn Institute, 2001); C. Murphy, "Inequality," *Fortune*, September 4, 2000, pp. 253–257; Edward P. Lazear, *Personnel Economics* (New York: John Wiley & Sons, 1998); Carl M. Campbell III, "Do Firms Pay Efficiency Wages? Evidence with Data at the Firm Level," *Journal of Labor Economics* 11, (3) (1993), pp. 442–469.

[12] Peter Cappelli and Keith Chauvin, "An Interplant Test of the Efficiency Wage Hypothesis," *Quarterly Journal of Economics*, August 1991, pp. 769–787.

[13] L. Rynes and J. W. Boudreau, "College Recruiting in Large Organizations: Practice, Evaluation, and Research Implications," *Personnel Psychology* 39 (1986), pp. 729–757.

[14] E. Groshen and A. B. Krueger, "The Structure of Supervision and Pay in Hospitals," *Industrial and Labor Relations Review*, February 1990, pp. 134S–146S.

[15] A. K. G. Hildreth and A. Oswald, "Rentsharing and Wages: Evidence from Company and Establishment Panels," *Journal of Labor Economics* 15 (1997), pp. 318–337.

[16] Allison Barber, *"Pay as a Signal in Job Choice"* (Working paper, Graduate School of Business Administration, Michigan State University); A. VanVinnen, "Person-Organization Fit: The Match Between Newcomers' and Recruiters' Preferences for Organization Cultures," *Personnel Psychology* 53 (2000), pp. 115–125.

[17] Christopher J. Collins and Jian Han, "Exploring Applicant Pool Quantity and Quality: The Effects of Early Recruitment Practice Strategies, Corporate Advertising, and Firm Reputation," *Personnel Psychology*, Autumn 2004, pp. 685–717.

[18] Daniel M. Cable and Timothy A. Judge, "Pay Preferences and Job Search Decisions: A Person-Organization Fit Perspective," *Personnel Psychology*, Summer 1994, pp. 317–348.

[19] C. Brown, "Firms' Choice of Method of Pay," *Industrial and Labor Relations Review*, February 1990, pp. S165–S182.

[20] Gary S. Becker, *Human Capital* (Chicago: University of Chicago Press, 1975); Barry Gerhart, "Gender Differences in Current and Starting Salaries: The Role of Performance, College Major, and Job Title," *Industrial and Labor Relations Review* 43 (1990), pp. 418–433.

[21] David I. Levine, "Fairness, Markets, and Ability to Pay: Evidence from Compensation Executives," *American Economic Review*, December 1993, pp. 1241–1259; B. Klaas, "Containing Compensation Costs: Why Firms Differ in Their Willingness to Reduce Pay," *Journal of Management* 25 (6) (1999), pp. 829–850.

[22] David I. Levine, "Fairness, Markets, and Ability to Pay: Evidence from Compensation Executives," *American Economic Review*, December 1993, p. 1250.

[23] "National Wages Council Recommends the Restructuring of Wage System for Competitiveness—Ministers and Top Civil Servants to Lead with Wage Cuts," *Singapore Straits*, May 22, 2003; Marek Szwejczewski and Sri Srikanthan, "The Risks of Outsourcing: Unexpected Consequences," *Financial Times*, April 14, 2006, p. 8; Thomas Friedman, *The World Is Flat* (New York: Farrar, Straus and Giroux 2006).

[24] Dinah Wisenberg Brin, "Staffing Agencies May See Pickup in Demand for Traveling Nurses," *The Wall Street Journal*, June 22, 2005, p. B2A.

[25] Erica L. Groshen and David Levine, *The Rise and Decline (?) of

Employer Wage Structures (New York: Federal Reserve Bank, 2000); John Haltowanger, *The Creation and Analysis of Employer-Employee Matched Data* (Amsterdam: North Holland, 1999).

[26] John W. Budd and Brian P. McCall, "The Grocery Stores Wage Distribution: A Semi-Parametric Analysis of the Role of Retailing and Labor Market Institutions," *Industrial and Labor Relations Review* 54(2A) (2001), pp. 484–501.

[27] D. M. Raff, "The Puzzling Profusion of Compensation Systems in the Interwar Automobile Industry," *NBER*, 1998. Raff attributes the fantastic diversity of compensation programs for blue-collar employees (firm-based, piece rate, company-wide, team-based) to differences in technology employed among competitors.

[28] J. Abowd and I. Kramarz, *"Interindustry and Firm Size Wage Differentials: New Evidence,"* working paper: ILR-Cornell Institute of Labor Market Policies, July 2000; Walter Oi and Todd L. Idson, "Firm Size and Wages," in *Handbook of Labor Economics*, eds., O. Ashenfelter and D. Card (Amsterdam: North Holland, 1999), pp. 2165–2214.

[29] H. Heneman and T. Judge, "Pay and Employee Satisfaction," in *Compensation in Organizations: Current Research & Practice*, eds. S. L. Rynes and B. Gerhart (San Francisco: Jossey-Bass, 2000); T. R. Mitchell and A. E. Mickel, "The Meaning of Money: An Individual Differences Perspective," *Academy of Management Review* (24) (1999), pp. 568–578; *Playing to Win: Strategic Rewards in the War for Talent* (New York: Watson Wyatt, 2001); Gerry Ledford, Paul Mulvey, and Peter LeBlanc, *The Rewards of Work: What Employees Value* (Scottsdale, AZ: World at Work, 2000).

[30] Charlie Trevor and M. E. Graham, *"Discretionary Decisions in Market Wage Derivatives: What Do Cheeseheads Rely Upon and Does It Really Matter?"* Working paper, University of Wisconsin, Madison, 2000; C. Viswesvaran and M. Barrick, "Decision Making Effects on Compensation Surveys: Implications for Market Wages," *Journal of Applied Psychology* 77, (5) (1992), pp. 588–597.

[31] See, for example, any of the surveys conducted by leading consulting firms. Hewitt, www.hewitt.com; Hay, www.haygroup.com; Mercer, www.mercer.com; Towers Watson, www.towerswatson.com;; Executive Alliance, www.executivealliance.com.

[32] Brian S. Klaas and John A. McClendon, "To Lead, Lag, or Match: Estimating the Financial Impact of Pay Level Policies," *Personnel Psychology* 49 (1996), pp. 121–140.

[33] R. B. Freeman and J. Rogers, *What Workers Want* (Ithaca, NY: Cornell University Press, 1999); P. D. Lineneman, M. L. Wachter, and W. H. Carter, "Evaluating the Evidence on Union Employment and Wages," *Industrial and Labor Relations Review* 44 (1990), pp. 34–53.

[34] M. B. Tannen, "Is the Army College Fund Meeting Its Objectives?" *Industrial and Labor Relations Review* 41 (1987), pp. 50–62; Hyder Lakhani, "Effects of Pay and Retention Bonuses on Quit Rates in the U.S. Army," *Industrial and Labor Relations Review* 41 (1988), pp. 430–438.

[35] B. Gerhart and G. Milkovich, "Organizational Differences in Managerial Compensation and Financial Performance," *Academy of Management Journal* 33 (1990), pp. 663–691; M. Bloom and J. Michel, *"The Relationships among Organization Context, Pay, and Managerial Theories,"* working paper, University of Notre Dame Department of Management, 2000; M. Bloom and G. Milkovich, "Relationships among Risk, Incentive Pay, and Organization Performance," *Academy of Management Journal* 41 (3) (1998), pp. 283–297; B. Hall and J. Liebman, "Are CEOs Really Paid Like Bureaucrats?" *Quarterly Journal of Economics*, August 1998, pp. 653–691. Variable pay is discussed in Chapters 9 through 11. "Variable" indicates that the pay increase (bonus) is not added to base pay; hence, it is not part of fixed costs but is variable, since the amount may vary next year.

[36] David I. Levine, "Fairness, Markets, and Ability to Pay: Evidence from Compensation Executives," *American Economic Review*, December 1993, pp. 1241–1259.

[37] Mei Fong, "A Chinese Puzzle," *The Wall Street Journal*, August 16, 2005, p. B1.

[38] L. Gaughan and J. Kasparek, "Employees as Customers: Using Market Research to Manage Compensation and Benefits," *Workspan* (9) (2000), pp. 31–38; M. Sturman, G. Milkovich, and J. Hannon, "Expert Systems' Effect on Employee Decisions and Satisfaction," *Personnel Psychology* (1997), pp. 21–34; J. Shaw and Schaubrock, *"The Role of Spending Behavior Patterns in Monetary Rewards,"* working paper, University of Kentucky, 2001.

[39] S. J. Dubner, "Calculating the Irrational in Economics," *New York Times*, June 28, 2003.

Chapter 8

[1] Adapted from each company's compensation strategy statements.

[2] Consulting firms' Web sites list their specialized surveys. See, for example, Towers Watson (www.towerswatson.com); Hay (http://www.haypaynet.com); Hewitt www.hewitt.com; or Mercer (www.mercer.com).

[3] Charlie Trevor and Mary E. Graham, *"Discretionary Decisions in Market Wage Derivatives: What Do Managers Rely Upon and Does It Really Matter?"* Working paper, University of Wisconsin, Madison, 2000.

[4] Barry Gerhart and George Milkovich, "Employee Compensation," in *Handbook of Industrial and Organizational Psychology*, 2nd ed., eds. M. D. Dunnette and L. M. Hough (Palo Alto, CA: Consulting Psychologists Press, 1992).

[5] In addition to these consultants, international organizations also do surveys. See Income Data Services Web site (www.incomesdata.co.uk) and their publication Employment Europe Pay Objectives 2000, or Link Group Consultants, Limited, Chester, UK. Also see William M. Mercer's International Compensation Guidelines 2000 (information on 61 nations); Towers Watson's Global Surveys, and Organization Resource Counselors online survey for positions

in countries ranging from Azerbaijan to Yugoslavia (www.orcinc. com). Mercer and Towers Watson Web site addresses are provided in footnote 2.

[6] Y. Yanadori and G. Milkovich, *Minimizing Wage Competition? Entry-Level Compensation in Japanese Firms*, working paper, Center for Advanced HR Studies, Ithaca, NY, 2003.

[7] D. Vaughan-Whitehead, *Paying the Price: The Wage Crisis in Central and Eastern Europe* (Handmill Hampshire, UK: McMilllin Press Ltd., 1998); S. M. Puffer and S. V. Shekshnia, "Compensating Local Employees in Post-Communist Russia: In Search of Talent or Just Looking for a Bargain?" *Compensation and Benefits Review*, September–October 1994, pp. 35–43.

[8] M. Bloom, G. Milkovich, and A. Mitra, *"Toward a Model of International Compensation and Rewards: Learning from How Managers Respond to Variations in Local-Host Conditions,"* Ithaca, NY: ILR-CAHRS Working Paper, 2000.

[9] M. Wanderer, "Dot-Comp: A 'Traditional' Pay Plan with a Cutting Edge," *WorldatWork Journal*, Fourth Quarter 2000, pp. 15–24.

[10] Hay (http://www.haypaynet.com).

[11] Chockalingam Viswesvaran and Murray Barrick, "Decision-Making Effects on Compensation Surveys: Implications for Market Wages," *Journal of Applied Psychology* 77 (5)(1992), pp. 588–97.

[12] "The Value of Pay Data on the Web," *Workspan*, September 2000, pp. 25–28.

[13] *2003–04 Survey Handbook and Directory* (Scottsdale AZ: WorldatWork, 2002).

[14] Joseph R. Rich and Carol Caretta Phalen, "A Framework for the Design of Total Compensation Surveys," *ACA Journal*, Winter 1992–1993, pp. 18–29.

[15] Letter from D. W. Belcher to G. T. Milkovich, in reference to D. W. Belcher, N. Bruce Ferris, and John O'Neill, "How Wage Surveys Are Being Used," *Compensation and Benefits Review*, September–October 1985, pp. 34–51.

[16] Kenan S. Abosch and Beverly L. Hmurovic, "A Traveler's Guide to Global Broadbanding," *ACA Journal*, Summer 1998, pp. 38–47.

[17] "Life with Broadbands," ACA Research Project, 1998; "Broad Banding Case Study: General Electric," *World at Work Journal*, Third Quarter 2000, p. 43.

[18] Hill, "Get Off the Broadband Wagon," *Journal of Compensation and Benefits*, January–February 1993, pp. 25–29; Michael Enods and Greg Limoges, "Broadbanding: Is That Your Company's Final Answer?" *World at Work Journal*, Fourth Quarter 2000, pp. 61–68.

[19] Robert Kanigel, *The One Best Way* (New York: Viking, 1997).

[20] S. Rynes, C. Weber, and G. Milkovich, "Effects of Market Survey Rates on Job Evaluation, and Job Gender on Job Pay," *Journal of Applied Psychology* 74 (1989), pp. 114–123.

[21] Frederic W. Cook, "Compensation Surveys Are Biased," *Compensation and Benefits Review*, September–October 1994, pp. 19–22.

[22] S. Rynes and G. Milkovich, "Wage Surveys: Dispelling Some Myths about the 'Market Wage,'" *Personnel Psychology*, Spring 1986, pp. 71–90; Frederic W. Cook, "Compensation Surveys Are Biased," *Compensation and Benefits Review*, September–October 1994, pp. 19–22.

[23] Vandra Huber and S. Crandall, "Job Measurement: A Social-Cognitive Decision Perspective," in *Research in Personnel and Human Resources Management*, Vol. 12, ed. Gerald R. Ferris (Greenwich, CT: JAI Press, 1994), pp. 223–269.

Chapter 9

[1] R. Yerema, "Canada's Top 100 Employers 2009," Toronto: Mediacorp.

[2] S. Dobson, "Building a Sustainable Culture," *Canadian HR Reporter*, October 20, 2008; L. Young, "Taking Work-Life Balance to 'Next Level,'" *Canadian HR Reporter*, March 24, 2008; and S. Dobson, "BlackBerry Maker Pick of the Crop," *Canadian HR Reporter*, October 22, 2007.

[3] M. L. Williams, S. B. Malos, and D. K. Palmer, "Benefit Systems and Benefit Level Satisfaction: An Expanded Model of Antecedents and Consequences," *Journal of Management*, 28(2) (2002), pp. 195–215.

[4] J. Mackintosh, "GM Pensioner Care Biggest Cost in Vehicle." *National Post*, August 20, 2003, pp. 1, 16.

[5] Rebecca Blumenstein, "Seeking a Cure: Auto Makers Attack High Health-care Bills with a New Approach," *The Wall Street Journal*, December 9, 1996, p. A1.

[6] John Hanna, "Can the Challenge of Escalating Benefits Costs Be Met?" *Personnel Administration* 27(9), 1977, pp. 50–57

[7] McCaffery, *Managing the Employee Benefits Program* (New York: American Management Association, 1983).

[8] N. Pandey and J. J. Martocchio, "Health Care and Retirement Costs in North America Spiralling Uncontrollably: What Are Employers to Do?" *The International Journal of Human Resource Management*, 19(8), August 2008, pp. 1515–1533.

[9] N. Cole, "New Benefits Survey – Employees Still Don't Understand." *Compensation & Benefits Update*, 3(7), July–August 1999, pp. 1–2.

[10] Foegen, "Are Escalating Employee Benefits Self-Defeating?" *Pension World* 14 (9), September 1978, pp. 83–84, 86.

[11] J. Kolysher and C. Westcott, "Emerging Benefits Focus on Flexibility," *Canadian HR Reporter*, December 17, 2007.

[12] Carol Danehower and John Lust, "How Aware Are Employees of Their Benefits?" *Benefits Quarterly* 12(4), pp. 57–61.

[13] Burton Beam, Jr., and John J. McFadden, *Employee Benefits* (Chicago: Dearborn Financial Publishing 1996).

[14] Ibid.

[15] Ibid.

[16] Ibid.

[17] Melissa W. Barringer and George T. Milkovich, "A Theoretical Exploration of the Adoption and Design of Flexible Benefit Plans: A Case of Human Resource Innovation," *Academy of Management Review* 23 (1998) pp. 306–308; Commerce Clearing House, *Flexible Benefits* (Chicago: Commerce Clearing House, 1983); American Can Company, *Do It Your Way* (Greenwich, Conn.: American Can Co., 1978); L. M. Baytos, "The Employee Benefit Smorgasbord: Its Potential and Limitations," *Compensation Review*, First Quarter 1970, pp. 86–90; "Flexible Benefit Plans Become More Popular," *The Wall Street Journal*, December 16, 1986, p. 1; Richard Johnson, *Flexible Benefits: A How To Guide* (Brookfield, WI: International Foundation of Employee Benefit Plans, 1986).

[18] Donald P. Crane, *The Management of Human Resources*, 2nd ed. (Belmont, CA: Wadsworth, 1979); Foegen, "Are Escalating Employee Benefits Self-Defeating?" *Pension World* 14(9) (September 1978), pp. 83–84, 86.

[19] Olivia Mitchell, "Fringe Benefits and Labor Mobility," *Journal of Human Resources* 17(2) (1982), pp. 286–298; Bradley Schiller and Randal Weiss, "The Impact of Private Pensions on Firm Attachment," *Review of Economics and Statistics* 61(3) (1979), pp. 369–380.

[20] Olivia Mitchell, "Fringe Benefits and the Cost of Changing Jobs," *Industrial and Labor Relations Review* 37(1) (1983), pp. 70–78; William E. Even and David A. MacPherson, "Employer Size and Labor Turnover: The Role of Pensions," *Industrial and Labor Relations Review* 49(4) July 1996, p. 707.

[21] George Dreher, Ronald Ash, and Robert Bretz, "Benefit Coverage and Employee Cost: Critical Factors in Explaining Compensation Satisfaction," *Personnel Psychology* 41 (1988), 237–254.

[22] George Dreher, Ronald Ash, and Robert Bretz, "Benefit Coverage and Employee Cost: Critical Factors in Explaining Compensation Satisfaction," *Personnel Psychology* 41 (1988), 237–254.

[23] "ESOPs Key to Performance," *Employee Benefit News* 5 (1987), p. 16.

[24] Lynn Densford, "Bringing Employees Back to Health," *Employee Benefit News* 2 (February 1988), p. 19.

[25] N. D. Cole and D. H. Flint, "Opportunity Knocks: Perceptions of Fairness in Employee Benefits," *Compensation and Benefits Review*, Mar/Apr 2005; 37(2), pp. 55–62.

[26] William F. Glueck, *Personnel: A Diagnostic Approach* (Plano, Tex.: Business Publications, 1978).

[27] Ludwig Wagner and Theodore Bakerman, "Wage Earners' Opinions of Insurance Fringe Benefits," *Journal of Insurance*, June 1960, pp. 17–28; Brad Chapman and Robert Otterman, "Employee Preference for Various Compensation and Benefits Options," *Personnel Administrator* 25 (November 1975), pp. 31–36.

[28] Stanley Nealy, "Pay and Benefit Preferences," *Industrial Relations* (October 1963), pp. 17–28.

[29] B. McKay, "Trends in Flexible Benefits," *HR Professional*, June/July 2008, p. 20.

[30] EBRI, *Employee Benefits Research Institute Databook on Employee Benefits* (Employee Benefits Research Institute, 1995); C. O'Bright, "Flex Benefits Drive Culture Change, Contain Costs at Superior Propane." *Canadian HR Reporter*, September 8, 2003, pp. 16–17.

[31] T. Humber, "The Power to Change," *Canadian HR Reporter*, May 31, 2004.

[32] McCaffery, *Managing the Employee Benefits Program* (New York: American Management Association, 1983).

[33] M. Picard, "Communicating Benefits? Be Cautious," *Canadian HR Reporter*, November 3, 2008.

[34] "Towers Perrin Survey Finds Dramatic Increase in Companies Utilizing the Web for HR Transactions: Two- to Threefold Increase Compared to 1999 Survey." Retrieved October 20, 2000 from the World Wide Web: http://www.towers.com/towers/news; Towers, Perrin, Forster, and Crosby, "Corporate Benefit Communication . . . Today and Tomorrow," 1988.

[35] J. Deniso, "Showing the Whole Benefits Picture," *Canadian HR Reporter*, November 3, 2008

[36] "How Do You Communicate? It May Not Be Nearly as Well as You Think," *Benefits*, December 1988, pp. 13–15; Kevin Greene, "Effective Employee Benefits Communication," in David Balkin and Luis Gomez-Mejia, *New Perspectives on Compensation* (Englewood Cliffs, NJ: Prentice-Hall 1987).

[37] Bennet Shaver, "The Claims Process," in *Employee Benefit Management*, ed. H. Wayne Snider, pp. 141–152.

[38] Thomas Fannin and Theresa Fannin, "Coordination of Benefits: Uncovering Buried Treasure," *Personnel Journal*, May 1983, pp. 386–391.

[39] E. Scott Peterson, "From Those Who've Been There . . . Outsourcing Leaders Talk about Their Experiences," *Benefits Quarterly* 6(1), First Quarter 1997, pp. 6–13.

[40] JF Potvin and A. Mian, "HR Outsourcing Lessons from Home Depot, Devon Canada," *Canadian HR Reporter*, January 28, 2008; U. Vu, "Outsourcing Calls for New HR Skills." *Canadian HR Reporter*, March 22, 2004, pp. 1, 3.

[41] www.awcbc.org/common/assets/ksms/ksms2007kms.pdf (February 1, 2009).

[42] WSIB, *2007 Annual Report — Workplace Safety and Insurance Board*, p. 40.

[43] J. Greenan, *The Handbook of Canadian Pension and Benefits Plans* (12th edition) (Toronto, ON: CCH Canadian Ltd., 2002).

[44] J. Sanford, "Cleaning House." *Canadian Business*, October 11–24, 2004, pp. 38–39.

[45] J. Greenan, *The Handbook of Canadian Pension and Benefits Plans* (12th edition) (Toronto, ON: CCH Canadian Ltd., 2002).

[46] www40.statcan.ca/cbin/fl/cstprintflag.cgi, Statistics Canada Catalogue #74-507-XCB (March 15 2006).

[47] Institute of Management & Administration (IOMA), *"Managing 401(k) Plans,"* Institute of Management & Administration, August 2000.

[48] Employee Benefit Research Institute, *Fundamentals of Employee Benefit Programs* (Washington, DC: EBRI, 1997), pp. 69–73.

[49] Kevin Dent and David Sloss, "The Global Outlook for Defined Contribution Versus Defined Benefit Pension Plans," *Benefits Quarterly*, First Quarter 1996, pp. 23–28.

[50] J. Hobel, "Defined Benefit Pension Plan Sponsors Worry Risk Becoming Too Great." *Canadian HR Reporter*, pp. 5, 10.

[51] F. Giancola, "The Truth About Employee Investment Behavior," *Workspan*, April 2005, pp. 42–45; L. Maldonado, "You Decided to Convert…Now What?" *Canadian HR Reporter*, May 23, 2005, pp. 15, 17; F. Holden and S. Lewis, "The Rules are Changing for Capital Accumulation Plans," *Canadian HR Reporter*, January 16, 2004, pp. 15–16.

[52] B. Cohen and B. Fitzgerald, *The Pension Puzzle: Your Complete Guide to Government Benefits, RRSPs, and Employer Plans.* Toronto, ON: John Wiley & Sons, 2002.

[53] D. Brown, "The Slow March Toward One Pension Law for All." *Canadian HR Reporter*, November 8, 2004, pp. 7, 11.

[54] T*he Aventis Healthcare Survey*, 2004.

[55] 2007 ACS/Buck Canadian Health Care Trend Survey; KPMG, *Employee Benefit Costs in Canada, 1998.*

[56] U. Vu, "CEOs Rank Health Issues as Major Concern: Survey." *Canadian HR Reporter*, July 18, 2005, pp. 1, 3.

[57] S. Lebrun, "Keeping the Lid on Drug Benefit Costs," *Canadian HR Reporter*, December 16, 1996, p. 12.

[58] J. Kolysher, "Has the Death Knell Sounded for Post-retirement Benefits?" *Canadian HR Reporter*, October 24, 2005, p. 16.

[59] Shelly Reese, "Can Employers Halt the Price Hikers?" *Business & Health* 17, December 1999, p. 29; Regina Herzlinger and Jeffrey Schwartz, "How Companies Tackle Health Care Costs: Part I," *Harvard Business Review* 63, July–August 1985, pp. 69–81.

[60] David Rosenbloom, *"Oh Brother, Our Medical Costs Went Up Again."* Paper presented for the Health Data Institute, March 16, 1988.

[61] Nicholas A. DiNubile, MD. and Carl Sherman, "Exercise and the Bottom Line," *Physician and Sportsmedicine* 27, February, 1999, p. 37.

[62] E. A. Kaplan, "Health Care Gets Personal," *Workspan*, May 2007 pp. 98–103.

[63] J. Taggart, "Getting the Most out of Benefit Plans," *Canadian HR Reporter*, December 18, 2006.

[64] "Tallying up the Sick Days and Disability Leave at CBC," *Globe and Mail*, November 7, 2008, p. R3.

[65] R. Bunning, "A Prescription for Sick Leave," *Personnel Journal* 67 (August 1988), pp. 44–49.

[66] *2007 Staying@Work Canada*, Toronto: Watson Wyatt; and "Workers' Mental Health and Stress Affecting Business Results in Canada," *Workplace*, January/February 2008, p. 6.

[67] L. J. Blake, "Fighting the mental health stigma in the workplace," *Workplace*, November/December 2008, pp. 17–18; C. Hall, "Breaking the Silence: Mental Illnesses in the Workplace," *Ultimate HR Manual* 42, November 2008, pp. 1–3; and WHO study at http://www.who.int/mental_health/management/depression/definition/en/.

[68] F. Engel, "Lost Profits, Increased Costs: The Aftermath of Workplace Trauma," *Canadian HR Reporter*, September 7, 1998, pp. 21–22.

[69] U. Vu, "Give Firms EAP Tax Credit, Senate told." *Canadian HR Reporter*, August 11, 2003, pp. 1, 12.

[70] Ibid.

[71] "Canadian Study: Stress Can Limit Emotional Intelligence, Workplace Success," *Workspan Focus*: Work-Life 2007, p. 124.

[72] "CIBC Expands Child-Care Program." *Canadian HR Reporter*, March 14, 2005, p.2.

[73] J. Marvin and N. Spinks, "Backup Child Care: Canada's New Employee Benefit." *Canadian HR Reporter*, November 8, 2004, p. 19.

[74] U. Vu, "At Great-West, There's Elder-Care Help on Staff." *Canadian HR Reporter*, September 13, 2004, p. 18.

[75] B. Healey, "Support for Employees Providing Support." *Canadian HR Reporter*, September 13, 2004, pp. 17–18.

Chapter 10

[1] R. Mayer and J. Davis, "The Effect of the Performance Appraisal System on Trust for Management," *Journal of Applied Psychology* 84(1), (1999), pp. 123–136.

[2] Rodney A. McCloy, John P. Campbell, and Robert Cuedeck, "A Confirmatory Test of a Model of Performance Determinants," *Journal of Applied Psychology* 79(4) (1994), pp. 493–505.

[3] Brian Becker and Barry Gerhart, "The Impact of Human Resource Management on Organizational Performance: Progress and Prospects," *Academy of Management Journal* 39(4) (1996), pp. 779–801.

[4] This table extrapolates the findings from two studies: Matthew C. Bloom and George T. Milkovich, "The Relationship between Risk, Incentive Pay, and Organizational Performance," *Academy of Management Journal*, forthcoming; Anne Tsui, Jone L. Pearce, Lyman W. Porter, and Angela M. Tripoli, "Alternative Approaches to the Employee–Organization Relationship: Does Investment in Employees Pay Off?" *Academy of Management Journal* 40(5) (1997), pp. 1089–121.

[5] Anne Tsui, Jone L. Pearce, Lyman W. Porter, and Angela M. Tripoli, "Alternative Approaches to the Employee-Organization Relationship: Does Investment in Employees Pay Off?" *Academy of Management Journal* 40(5) (1997), pp. 1089–1121.

[6] A. Mamman, M. Sulaiman, and A. Fadel, "Attitude to Pay Systems: An Exploratory Study within and across Cultures," The International Journal of Human Resource *Management* 7(1), February 1996, pp. 101–121.

[7] IOMA, "Are You Ready to Serve Cafeteria Style Comp?" *Pay for Performance Report*, June 2000, pp. 1, 13.

[8] J. S. Adams, "Toward an Understanding of Inequity," *Journal of Abnormal and Social Psychology* 67 (1963), pp. 422–36; J. S. Adams, "Injustice in Social Exchange," *Advances in Experimental Social Psychology*, Vol. 2, ed. L. Berkowitz (New York: Academic Press, 1965); R. Cosier and D. Dalton, "Equity Theory and Time: A Reformulation," *Academy of Management Review* 8 (1983), pp. 311–119.

[9] B. Oviatt, "Agency and Transaction Cost Perspectives on the Manager-Shareholder Relationship: Incentives for Congruent Interests," *Academy of Management Review* 13 (1988), pp. 214–125.

[10] E. A. Locke, K. N. Shaw, L. M. Saari, and G. P. Latham, "Goal Setting and Task Performance: 1969–1980," *Psychological Bulletin* 90 (1981), pp. 125–152.

[11] M. R. Louis, B. Z. Posner, and G. N. Powell, "The Availability and Helpfulness of Socialization Practices," *Personnel Psychology* 36 (1983), pp. 857–866; E. H. Schein, "Organizational Socialization and the Profession of Management," *Industrial Management Review* 9 (1968), pp. 1–16.

[12] Ioma, "Pay for Performance Report," *Ioma Pay for Performance Report*, January 1998, p. 8; P. Stang and B. Laird, "Working Women's Motivators," reported in *USA Today*, February 9, 1999, p. B1 for Nationwide Insurance/Working Women Magazine Survey.

[13] E. L. Deci and R. M. Ryan, *Intrinsic Motivation and Self-Determination in Human Behavior* (New York: Plenum Press, 1985). Note, however, the evidence is not very strong.

[14] J. R. Schuster and P. K. Zingheim, *The New Pay: Linking Employee and Organizational Performance* (New York: Lexington Books, 1992).

[15] E. J. Conlon and J. M. Parks, "Effects of Monitoring and Tradition on Compensation Arrangements: An Experiment with Principal-Agent Dyads," *Academy of Management Journal* 33 (1990), pp. 603–622.

[16] E. J. Conlon and J. M. Parks, "Effects of Monitoring and Tradition on Compensation Arrangements: An Experiment with Principal-Agent Dyads," *Academy of Management Journal* 33 (1990), pp. 603–622.

[17] W. N. Cooke, "Employee Participation Programs, Group Based Incentives, and Company Performance," *Industrial and Labor Relations Review* 47 (1994), pp. 594–610; G. W. Florkowski, "The Organizational Impact of Profit Sharing," *Academy of Management Review* 12 (1987), pp. 622–636; R. Heneman, *Merit Pay: Linking Pay Increases to Performance Ratings* (Reading, MA: Addison-Wesley, 1992); J. L. McAdams and E. J. Hawk, *Organizational Performance and Rewards* (Phoenix, Ariz.: American Compensation Association, 1994); D. McDonaly and A. Smith, "A Proven Connection: Performance Management and Business Results," *Compensation and Benefits Review*, January–February 1995, pp. 59–64; G. T. Milkovich, *"Does Performance-Based Pay Really Work? Conclusions Based on the Scientific Research,"* Unpublished document for 3M, 1994; G. Milkovich and C. Milkovich, "Strengthening the Pay Performance Relationship: The Research," *Compensation and Benefits Review* (1992), pp. 53–62.

[18] Mark A. Huselid, "The Impact of Human Resource Management Practices on Turnover, Productivity, and Corporate Financial Performance," *Academy of Management Journal* 38 (3) (1995), pp. 635–672.

[19] R. Heneman, *Merit Pay: Linking Pay Increases to Performance Ratings* (Reading, MA: Addison-Wesley, 1992).

[20] B. Gerhart and G. Milkovich, "Organizational Differences in Managerial Compensation and Financial Performance," *Academy of Management Journal* 33 (1990), pp. 663–690.

[21] E. E. Lawler, *Pay and Organizational Effectiveness: A Psychological View* (New York: McGraw-Hill, 1971); E. E. Lawler and G. D. Jenkins, "Strategic Reward Systems" in *Handbook of Industrial and Organizational Psychology*, eds. M. D. Dunnette and L. M. Hough (Palo Alto, CA: Consulting Psychologist Press, 1992), pp. 1009–1055; W. Mobley, *Employee Turnover: Causes, Consequences and Control* (Reading, MA: Addison-Wesley, 1982).

[22] D. M. Cable and T. A. Judge, "Pay Preferences and Job Search Decisions: A Person-Organization Fit Perspective," *Personnel Psychology* 47 (1994), pp. 317–348.

23 B. Turban and T. A. Judge, "Pay Preferences and Job Search Decisions: A Person-Organization Fit Perspective," *Personnel Psychology* 47 (1994), pp. 317–348.

24 D. M. Cable and T. L. Keon, "Organizational Attractiveness: An Interactionist Perspective," *Journal of Applied Psychology* 78 (1993), pp. 184–193.

25 D. M. Cable and T. A. Judge, "Pay Preferences and Job Search Decisions: A Person-Organization Fit Perspective," *Personnel Psychology* 47 (1994), pp. 317–348; A. Kohn, *Punished by Rewards: The Trouble with Gold Stars, Incentive Plans, A's, Praise and Other Bribes* (Boston: Houghton-Mifflin, 1993).

26 D. M. Cable and T. A. Judge, "Pay Preferences and Job Search Decisions: A Person-Organization Fit Perspective," *Personnel Psychology* 47 (1994), pp. 317–348.

27 T. R. Zenger, "Why Do Employers Only Reward Extreme Performance? Examining the Relationships Among Performance Pay and Turnover," *Administrative Science Quarterly* 37(1992), pp. 198–219.

28 David A. Harrison, Meghna Virick, and Sonja William, "Working Without a Net: Time, Performance, and Turnover Under Maximally Contingent Rewards," *Journal of Applied Psychology* 81(4) (1996), pp. 331–345.

29 M. R. Carrell and J. E. Dettrich, "Employee Perceptions of Fair Treatment," *Personnel Journal* 55 (1976), pp. 523–524.

30 A. Weiss, "Incentives and Worker Behavior: Some Evidence" in *Incentives, Cooperation and Risk Sharing*, ed. H. R. Nalbantian (Totowa, NJ: Rowan & Littlefield, 1987), pp. 137–150.

31 P. Zingheim and J. R. Shuster, Pay People Right (San Francisco: Jossey-Bass, 2000); J. Boudreau, M. Sturman, C. Trevor, and B. Gerhart, "Is It Worth It to Win the Talent War? Using Turnover Research to Evaluate the Utility of Performance-Based Pay," *Working Paper 99-06* (Center for Advanced Human Resource Studies, Cornell University, 2000).

32 IOMA, "Report on Salary Surveys," May 1997, p. 14; Kevin J. Parent and Caroline L. Weber, "Does Paying for Knowledge Pay Off?" *Compensation and Benefits Review*, September 1994, pp. 44–50.

33 L. Dyer, D. P. Schwab, and R. D. Theriault, "Managerial Perceptions Regarding Salary Increase Criteria," *Personnel Psychology* 29 (1976), pp. 233–242.

34 J. Fossum and M. Fitch, "The Effects of Individual and Contextual Attributes on the Sizes of Recommended Salary Increases," *Personnel Psychology* 38 (1985), pp. 587–603.

35 L. V. Jones and T. E. Jeffrey, "A Quantitative Analysis of Expressed Preferences for Compensation Plans," *Journal of Applied Psychology* 48 (1963), pp. 201–210; Opinion Research Corporation, *Wage Incentives* (Princeton, NJ: Opinion Research Corporation, 1946); Opinion Research Corp., *Productivity from the Worker's Standpoint* (Princeton, NJ: Opinion Research Corporation, 1949).

36 D. Koys, T. Keaveny, and R. Allen, "Employment Demographics and Attitudes That Predict Preferences for Alternative Pay Increase Policies," *Journal of Business and Psychology* 4 (1989), pp. 27–47.

37 B. Major, "Gender, Justice and the Psychology of Entitlement," *Review of Personality and Social Psychology* 7 (1988), pp. 124–148.

38 IOMA, "Incentive Pay Programs and Results: An Overview," *IOMA*, May 1996, p. 11; G. Green, "Instrumentality Theory of Work Motivation," *Journal of Applied Psychology* 53 (1965), pp. 1–25; R. D. Pritchard, D. W. Leonard, C. W. Von Bergen, Jr., and R. J. Kirk, "The Effects of Varying Schedules of Reinforcement on Human Task Performance," *Organizational Behavior and Human Performance* 16 (1976), pp. 205–230; D. P. Schwab and L. Dyer, "The Motivational Impact of a Compensation System on Employee Performance," *Organizational Behavior and Human Performance* 9 (1973), pp. 215–225; D. Schwab, "Impact of Alternative Compensation Systems on Pay Valence and Instrumentality Perceptions," *Journal of Applied Psychology* 58 (1973), pp. 308–312.

39 Mark A. Huselid, "The Impact of Human Resource Management Practices on Turnover, Productivity, and Corporate Financial Performance," *Academy of Management Journal* 38(3), pp. 635–672.

40 Barry Gerhart, "Pay Strategy and Firm Performance" in S. Rynes and B. Gerhart (eds), *Compensation in Organizations: Progress and Prospects.* (San Francisco: New Lexington Press) (1999).

41 W. N. Cooke, "Employee Participation Programs, Group Based Incentives, and Company Performance," *Industrial and Labor Relations Review* 47 (1994), pp. 594–610; D. L. Kruse, Profit Sharing: Does It Make a Difference? (Kalamazoo, Mich.: Upjohn Institute, 1993); G. T. Milkovich, *"Does Performance-Based Pay Really Work? Conclusions Based on the Scientific Research,"* Unpublished document for 3M, 1994; M. M. Petty, B. Singleton, and D. W. Connell, "An Experimental Evaluation of an Organizational Incentive Plan in the Electric Utility Industry," *Journal of Applied Psychology* 77 (1992), pp. 427–436; J. R. Schuster, "The Scanlon Plan: A Longitudinal Analysis," *Journal of Applied Behavioral Science* 20 (1984), pp. 23–28.

42 M. M. Petty, B. Singleton, and D. W. Connell, "An Experimental Evaluation of an Organizational Incentive Plan in the Electric Utility Industry," *Journal of Applied Psychology* 77 (1992), pp. 427–436.

43 McAdams and Hawk, *Organizational Performance and Rewards*, 1994.

44 B. Gerhart and G. Milkovich, "Organizational Differences in Managerial Compensation and Financial Performance," *Academy of Management Journal* 33 (1990), pp. 663–690.

[45] Robert L. Cardy and Gregory H. Dobbins, *Performance Appraisal: Alternative Perspectives* (Cincinnati: Southwestern Publishing, 1994).

[46] W. E. Deming, *Out of the Crisis* (Cambridge, Mass.: MIT Press, 1986).

[47] David Waldman, "The Contributions of Total Quality Management of a Theory of Work Performance," *Academy of Management Review* 19 (1994), pp. 510–536.

[48] David Antonioni, "Improve the Performance Management Process before Discontinuing Performance Appraisals," *Compensation and Benefits Review*, May–June 1994, pp. 29–37.

[49] Timothy D. Schellhardt, "Annual Agony," *The Wall Street Journal*, November 19, 1996, p. A1.

[50] R. Arvey and K. Murphy, "Performance Evaluation in Work Settings," *Annual Review of Psychology* 49 (1998), pp. 141–168.

[51] Daniel Ilgen and Jack Feldman, "Performance Appraisal: A Process Focus," *Research in Organizational Behavior* 5 (1983), pp. 141–197.

[52] Mark L. McConkie, "A Clarification of the Goal Setting and Appraisal Processes in MBO," *Academy of Management Review* 4 (1) (1979), pp. 29–40.

[53] Bruce McAfee and Blake Green, "Selecting a Performance Appraisal Method," *Personnel Administrator* 22 (5) (1977), pp. 61–65.

[54] V. M. Catano, W. Darr, and C. A. Campbell, "Performance Appraisal of Behavior-Based Competencies: A Reliable and Valid Procedure," *Personnel Psychology*, 60(1) (2007), pp. 201–230.

[55] Mark R. Edwards and Ann J. Ewen, *360 Degree Feedback: The Powerful New Model for Employee Assessment and Performance Improvement* (Toronto: American Management Association, 1996).

[56] Susan E. Jackson, Randall S. Schuller, and J. Carlos Rivero, "Organizational Characteristics as Predictors of Personnel Practices," *Personnel Psychology* 42 (1989), pp. 727–786.

[57] E. Pulakos and W. Borman, *Developing the Basic Criterion Scores for Army-wide and MOS-specific Ratings* (Alexandria, VA: U.S. Army Research Institute, 1992).

[58] Deniz S. Ones, Frank L. Schmidt, and Chockalingam Viswesvaran, "Comparative Analysis of the Reliability of Job Performance Ratings," *Journal of Applied Psychology* 81 (5) (1996), pp. 557–574.

[59] F. S. Landy and J. L. Farr, "Performance Rating," *Psychological Bulletin* 87 (1980), pp. 72–107.

[60] M. M. Harris and J. Schaubroeck, "A Meta Analysis of Self-supervisor, Self-peer and Peer-supervisor ratings," *Personnel Psychology* 4 (1988), pp. 43–62.

[61] Harris and Schaubroeck, "A Meta Analysis of Self-supervisor, Self-peer and Peer-supervisor Ratings."

[62] D. Antonioni, "The Effects of Feedback Accountability on Upward Appraisal Ratings," *Personnel Psychology* 47 (1994), pp. 349–356.

[63] K. Murphy and J. Cleveland, *Understanding Performance Appraisal* (Thousand Oaks, CA: Sage, 1995).

[64] G. Alliger and K. J. Williams, "Affective Congruence and the Employment Interview," in *Advances in Information Processing in Organizations*, Vol. 4, eds. J. R. Meindl, R. L. Cardy, and S. M. Puffer (Greenwich, CT: JAI Press).

[65] Landy and Farr, "Performance Rating"; A. S. Denisi, T. P. Cafferty, and B. M. Meglino, "A Cognitive View of the Performance Appraisal Process: A Model and Research Propositions," *Organizational Behavior and Human Performance* 33 (1984), pp. 360–396; Jack M. Feldman, "Beyond Attribution Theory: Cognitive Processes in Performance Appraisal," *Journal of Applied Psychology* 66 (2) (1981), pp. 127–148; and W. H. Cooper, "Ubiquitous Halo," *Psychological Bulletin* 90 (1981), pp. 218–244.

[66] Angelo Denisi and George Stevens, "Profiles of Performance, Performance Evaluations, and Personnel Decisions," *Academy of Management* 24 (3) (1981), pp. 592–602; Wayne Cascio and Enzo Valtenzi, "Relations among Criteria of Police Performance," *Journal of Applied Psychology* 63 (1) (1978), pp. 22–28; William Bigoness, "Effects of Applicant's Sex, Race, and Performance on Employer Performance Ratings: Some Additional Findings," *Journal of Applied Psychology* 61 (1) (1976), pp. 80–84; Dorothy P. Moore, "Evaluating In-Role and Out-of-Role Performers," *Academy of Management Journal* 27 (3) (1984), pp. 603–618; W. Borman, L. White, E. Pulakos, and S. Oppler, "Models of Supervisory Job Performance Ratings," *Journal of Applied Psychology* 76 (6) (1991), pp. 863–872.

[67] H. J. Bernardin and Richard Beatty, *Performance Appraisal: Assessing Human Behavior at Work* (Boston: Kent Publishing, 1984).

[68] G. Dobbins, R. Cardy, and D. Truxillo, "The Effects of Purpose of Appraisal and Individual Differences in Stereotypes of Women on Sex Differences in Performance Ratings: A Laboratory and Field Study," *Journal of Applied Psychology* 73 (3) (1988), pp. 551–558. Edward Shaw, "Differential Impact of Negative Stereotyping in Employee Selection," *Personnel Psychology* 25 (1972), pp. 333–338; Benson Rosen and Thomas Jurdee, "Effects of Applicant's Sex and Difficulty of Job on Evaluation of Candidates for Managerial Positions," *Journal of Applied Psychology* 59 (1975), pp. 511–512; Gail Pheterson, Sara Kiesler, and Philip Goldberg, "Evaluation of the Performance of Women as a Function of Their Sex, Achievement, and Personal History," *Journal of Personality and Social Psychology* 19 (1971), pp. 114–118; W. Clay Hamner, Jay Kim, Lloyd Baird, and William Bignoness, "Race and Sex as Determinants of Ratings by Potential Employers in a Simulated Work Sampling Task," *Journal of Applied Psychology* 59 (6) (1974), pp. 705–711; and Neal Schmitt and Martha Lappin, "Race and Sex as Determinants of the Mean and Variance of Performance

Ratings," *Journal of Applied Psychology* 65 (4) (1980), pp. 428–435.

69 D. Turban and A. Jones, "Supervisor-subordinate Similarity: Types, Effects and Mechanisms," *Journal of Applied Psychology* 73 (2) (1988), pp. 228–234.

70 Angelo Denisi and George Stevens, "Profiles of Performance, Performance Evaluations, and Personnel Decisions," *Academy of Management Journal* 24(3) (1981), 592–602; William Scott and Clay Hamner, "The Influence of Variations in Performance Profiles on the Performance Evaluation Process: An Examination of the Validity of the Criterion," *Organizational Behavior and Human Performance* 14 (1975), pp. 360–70; Edward Jones, Leslie Rock, Kelly Shaver, George Goethals, and Laurence Ward, "Pattern of Performance and Ability Attributions: An Unexpected Primacy Effect," *Journal of Personality and Social Psychology* 10 (4) (1968), pp. 317–340.

71 F. S. Landy and J. L. Farr, *Psychological Bulletin* 87(1980), 72–107; H. J. Bernardin and Richard Beatty, *Performance Appraisal: Assessing Human Behavior at Work* (Boston: Kent Publishing, 1984).

72 B. P. Maroney and R. M. Buckely, "Does Research in Performance Appraisal Influence the Practice of Performance Appraisal? Regretfully Not," *Public Personnel Management* 21 (1992), pp. 185–196.

73 Robert Liden and Terence Mitchell, "The Effects of Group Interdependence on Supervisor Performance Evaluations," *Personnel Psychology* 36 (2) (1983), pp. 289–299.

74 G. R. Ferris and T. A. Judge, "Personnel/Human Resource Management: A Political Influence Perspective," *Journal of Management* 17 (1991), pp. 1–42.

75 Yoav Ganzach, "Negativity (and Positivity) in Performance Evaluation: Three Field Studies," *Journal of Applied Psychology* 80, no. 4 (1995), pp. 491–99.

76 R. Heneman and K. Wexley, "The Effects of Time Delay in Rating and Amount of Information Observed on Performance Rating Accuracy," *Academy of Management Journal* 26 (4), 1983, pp. 677–686.

77 L. L. Cummings and D. P. Schwab, *Performance in Organizations* (Glenview Ill: Scott Foresman, 1973).

78 Neal P. Mero and Stephan J. Motowidlo, "Effects of Rater Accountability on the Accuracy and the Favorability of Performance Ratings," *Journal of Applied Psychology* 80 (4) (1995), pp. 517–524.

79 H. J. Bernardin and M. R. Buckley, "Strategies in Rater Training," *Academy of Management Review* 6 (2) (1981), pp. 205–212; D. Smith, "Training Programs for Performance Appraisal: A Review," *Academy of Management Review* 11 (1) (1986), pp. 22–40; B. Davis and M. Mount, "Effectiveness of Performance Appraisal Training Using Computer Assisted Instruction and Behavioral Modeling," *Personnel Psychology* 3 (1984), pp. 439–452; H. J. Bernardin, "Effects of Rater Training on Leniency and Halo Errors

in Student Ratings of Instructors," *Journal of Applied Psychology* 63 (3) (1978), pp. 301–308; and J. M. Ivancevich, "Longitudinal Study of the Effects of Rater Training on Psychometric Error in Ratings," *Journal of Applied Psychology* 64 (5) (1979), pp. 502–508.

80 Bernardin and Buckley, "Strategies in Rater Training."

81 Robert Heneman, *Merit Pay: Linking Pay Increases to Performance Ratings* (Reading, MA: Addison-Wesley 1992).

82 Ann Podolske, "Creating a Review System That Works," *IOMA's Pay for Performance Report*, March 1996, pp. 2–4.

83 A. DeNisi, T. Robbins, and T. Cafferty. "Organization of Information Used for Performance Appraisals: Role of Diary-keeping," *Journal of Applied Psychology* 74 (1) (1989), pp. 124–129.

84 S. Snell and K. Wexley, "Performance Diagnosis: Identifying the Causes of Poor Performance," *Personnel Administrator*, April 1985, pp. 117–127.

85 IOMA, "When Are Bonuses High Enough to Improve Performance?" *IOMA*, November 1996, p. 12.

86 A. Richter, "Paying the People in Black at Big Blue," *Compensation and Benefits Review*, May/June 1998, pp. 51–59.

87 John Thibaut and Laurens Walker, *Procedural Justice: A Psychological View* (Hillsdale, NJ: John Wiley & Sons, 1975).

88 Robert Folger and Mary Konovsky, "Effects of Procedural and Distributive Justice on Reactions to Pay Raise Decisions," *Academy of Management Journal* 32, 1, (1989) 115–130.

89 G. S. Leventhal, J. Karuza, and W. R. Fry, "Beyond Fairness: A Theory of Allocation Preferences," in *Justice and Social Interaction*, G. Mikula, ed. (New York: Springer Verlag 1980), pp. 167–218.

90 Milkovich and Milkovich, "Strengthening the Pay-for-Performance Relationship. . .," *Compensation and Benefits Review*, May–June 1996, pp. 27–33.

91 *Compensating Salaried Employees During Inflation: General vs. Merit Increases* (New York: Conference Board, Report no. 796, 1981).

92 Jackson, Schuller, and Rivero, "Organizational Characteristics as Predictors of Personnel Practices."

Chapter 11

1 American Management Association, "Merit Raises Remain Popular Among Fortune 1000," *Compflash*, December 1994, p. 1.

2 *Compensation Planning Outlook 2009*, Ottawa: Conference Board of Canada, p. 7.

3 Jerry M. Newman and Daniel J. Fisher, "Strategic Impact Merit Pay," *Compensation and Benefits Review*, July/August 1992, pp. 38–45.

[4] Glenn Bassett, "Merit Pay Increases Are a Mistake," *Compensation and Benefits Review*, March/April, 1994, pp. 20–25.

[5] Robert Heneman, *Merit Pay: Linking Pay Increases to Performance Ratings* (Reading, MA: Addison-Wesley, 1992).

[6] Cincinnati Federation of Teachers, *"Teacher Quality Update"* (August 2000), Cincinnati Federation of Teachers.

[7] *Compensation Planning Outlook 2009*, Ottawa: Conference Board of Canada, p. 7.

[8] American Management Association, "A Growing Trend: Variable Pay for Lower Level Employees," *Compflash* (1992), p. 1.

[9] Bob Nelson, *1001 Ways to Reward Employees* (New York: Workman Publishing, 1994).

[10] Thomas Patten, *Pay: Employee Compensation and Incentive Plans* (New York: Macmillan, 1977).

[11] Thomas Wilson, "Is It Time to Eliminate the Piece Rate Incentive System?" *Compensation and Benefits Review*, March– April 1992, pp. 43–49.

[12] Kenneth Chilton, "Lincoln Electric's Incentive System: A Reservoir of Trust," *Compensation and Benefits Review*, Nov.– Dec. 1994, pp. 29–34.

[13] Jon Katzenbach and Douglas Smith, *The Wisdom of Teams* (New York: Harper Collins, 1993).

[14] F. McKenzie and M. Shilling, "Ensuring Effective Incentive Design and Implementation," *Compensation and Benefits Review*, May–June 1998, pp. 57–65.

[15] Ibid.

[16] S. Singh, "Mount Sinai goes online for performance management," *Canadian HR Reporter*, June 20, 2005, pp. 1, 4.

[17] M. Bloom and G. Milkovich, "Relationships Among Risk, Incentive Pay, and Organizational Performance," *Academy of Management Journal* 11(3) (1998), pp. 283–297.

[18] American Management Association, "Team-Based Pay: Approaches Vary, but Produce No Magic Formulas," *Compflash* (April 1994), p. 4.

[19] Conversation with Thomas Ruddy, Manager of Research, Xerox Corporation, 1997.

[20] John G. Belcher, *Results Oriented Variable Pay System* (New York: AMACOM, 1996); Steven E. Gross, *Compensation for Teams* (New York: AMACOM, 1995).

[21] Theresa M. Welbourne, David B. Balkin, and Luis R. Gomez-Mejia, "Gainsharing and Mutual Monitoring: A Combined Agency-Organizational Justice Interpretation," *Academy of Management Journal* 38(3) (1995), pp. 881–899.

[22] *Compensation Planning Outlook 2009*, Ottawa: Conference Board of Canada, p. 7.

[23] John G. Belcher, "Gainsharing and Variable Pay: The State of the Art," *Compensation and Benefits Review*, May/June 1994, pp. 50–60.

[24] D. Kim, "Determinants of the Survival of Gainsharing Programs," *Industrial and Labor Relations Review* 53(1) (1999), pp. 21–42.

[25] A. J. Geare, "Productivity from Scanlon Type Plans," *Academy of Management Review* 1 (3) (1976), pp. 99–108.

[26] Ibid.

[27] T. Patten, *Pay: Employee Compensation and Incentive Plans* (New York: Macmillan, 1977); Pinhas Schwinger, *Wage Incentive Plans* (New York: Halsted, 1975).

[28] Newman, "Selecting Incentive Plans to Complement Organizational Strategy," in *Current Trends in Compensation Research and Practice*, eds. L. Gomez-Mejia and D. Balkin (Englewood Cliffs, NJ: Prentice Hall, 1987).

[29] Marhsall Fein, "Improshare: A Technique for Sharing Productivity Gains with Employees," *The Compensation Handbook*, eds. M. L. Rock, and L. A. Berger (New York: McGraw-Hill, 1993), pp. 158–175.

[30] R. Kaufman, "The Effects of Improshare on Productivity," *Industrial and Labor Relations Review* 45 (2) (1992), pp. 311–322.

[31] Darlene O'Neill, "Blending the Best of Profit Sharing and Gainsharing," *HR Magazine*, March 1994, pp. 66–69.

[32] *Compensation Planning Outlook 2009*, Ottawa: Conference Board of Canada, p. 7.

[33] K. Brown and V. Huber, "Lowering Floors and Raising Ceilings: A Longitudinal Assessment of the Effects of an Earnings-at-Risk Plan on Pay Satisfaction," *Personnel Psychology* 45 (1992), pp. 279–311.

[34] These observations are drawn from a variety of sources, including: K. Brown and V. Huber, "Lowering Floors and Raising Ceilings: A Longitudinal Assessment of the Effects of an Earnings-at-Risk Plan on Pay Satisfaction," *Personnel Psychology* 45 (1992), pp. 279–311; D. Collins, L. Hatcher, and T. Ross (1993), "The Decision to Implement Gainsharing: The Role of Work Climate, Expected Outcomes and Union Status," *Personnel Psychology* 46 (1993), pp. 77–103; "Team-Based Pay: Approaches Vary but Produce No Magic Formulas," *Compflash*, April 1994, p. 4; W. N. Cooke, "Employee Participation Programs, Group Based Incentives and Company Performance," *Industrial and Labor Relations Review* 47 (1994), pp. 594–610; G. W. Florowski, "The Organizational Impact of Profit Sharing," *Academy of Management Review* 12(4) (1987), pp. 622–636.

[35] *Workplace and Employee Survey Compendium 2005*, Statistics Canada Labour Statistics Division, 2008, p. 53. Catalogue no.71-585-X.

[36] T. H. Hammer and R. N. Stern, "Employee Ownership: Implications for the Or Oganizational Distribution of Power," *Academy of Management Journal* 23 (1980), pp. 78–100.

[37] B. J. Hall, "What You Need to Know About Stock Options," *Harvard Business Review*, March–April 2000, pp. 121–129.

[38] Barry Gerhart, "Pay Strategy and Firm Performance," in S. Rynes and B. Gerhart (eds.), *Compensation in Organizations: Progress and Prospects* (San Francisco: New Lexington Press, 1999).

[39] *Compensation Planning Outlook 2009*, Ottawa: Conference Board of Canada, p. 11.

[40] L. Moate and M. Ng, "There's More to Long-Term Incentives Than Stock Options," *Canadian HR Reporter*, October 9, 2006; and S. Burchman and B. Jones, "Long-Term Performance Plans: Overcoming Design Challenges," *Workspan*, July 2008, pp. 46–50.

[41] Chilton, "Lincoln Electrics' Incentive System: A Reservoir of Trust," *Compensation and Benefits Review*, Nov.–Dec. 1994, pp. 29–34; Howard Rudnitsky, "You Have to Trust the Workforce," *Forbes*, July 19, 1993, pp. 78–81.

[42] N. Cote, "Employee Share Purchase Plans: Do They Really Motivate Employees to Think and Act Like Owners?" *Ultimate HR Manual* 38, July 2008, pp. 1–3.

[43] *Workplace and Employee Survey Compendium 2005*, Statistics Canada Labour Statistics Division, 2008, p. 54. Catalogue no. 71-585-X.

[44] IOMA "Another Pan of Stock Option Plans," *IOMA's Pay for Performance Report*, January 1999, p. 11.

[45] *Directors' Compensation and Board Practices in 2007*, Ottawa: Conference Board of Canada.

[46] "Paying for Board Director Expertise," *Canadian HR Reporter*, December 19, 2005, p. 2.

[47] *Directors' Compensation and Board Practices in 2007*, Ottawa: Conference Board of Canada.

[48] *Top 50 Highest Paid Executives*, Globe and Mail. http://business.theglobeandmail.com/v5/content/tp1000-2007/index.php?view=top_50_execs.

[49] Graef S. Crystal, *In Search of Excess* (New York: W. W. Norton, 1991).

[50] Herbert A. Simon, *Administrative Behavior*, 2nd ed. (New York: MacMillan, 1957).

[51] The Conference Board, *Top Executive Compensation: 1995*.

[52] "Executive Pay," *BusinessWeek*, April 17, 2000, p. 110.

[53] This comparison needs to be interpreted with some caution. One counterargument (the Hay Group, Compflash, April 1992, p. 3) notes that American companies are generally much larger than their foreign counterparts. When compared to like-sized companies in other countries, the U.S. multiple is comparable to the international average.

[54] Marc J. Wallace, "Type of Control, Industrial Concentration, and Executive Pay," *Academy of Management Proceedings* (1977), pp. 284–288; W. Lewellan and B. Huntsman, "Managerial Pay and Corporate Performance," *American Economic Review* 60 (1977), pp. 710–720.

[55] H. L. Tosi, S. Werner, J. Katz, and L. Gomez-Mejia, "A Meta Analysis of CEO Pay Studies," *Journal of Management* 26 (2) (2000), pp. 301–339.

[56] Charles O'Reilly, Brian Main, and Graef Crystal, "CEO Compensation as Tournament and Social Comparison: A Tale of Two Theories," *Administrative Science Quarterly* 33 (1988), pp. 257–274.

[57] Kathryn M. Eisenhardt, "Agency Theory: An Assessment and Review," *Academy of Management Review* 14 (1989), pp. 57–74.

[58] "Bank CEOs Take a Pay Cut," *Canadian HR Reporter*, February 3, 2009.

[59] Nancy C. Pratt, "CEOs Reap Unprecedented Riches While Employees' Pay Stagnates," *Compensation and Benefits Review*, September/October 1996, p. 20.

[60] Ira T. Kay, "Beyond Stock Options: Emerging Practices in Executive Incentive Programs," *Compensation and Benefits Review* 23(6) (1991), pp. 18–29.

[61] C. Daly, J. Johnson, A. Ellstrand, and D. Dalton, "Compensation Committee Composition as a Determinant of CEO Compensation," *Academy of Management Journal* 41(2) (1998), pp. 209–220; H. Barkema and L. Gomez-Mejia, "Managerial Compensation and Firm Performance: A General Research Framework," *Academy of Management Journal* 41(2) (1998), pp. 135–148.

[62] Ernest C. Miller, "How Companies Set the Base Salary and Incentive Bonus Opportunity for Chief Executive and Chief Operating Officers. . . A Compensation Review Symposium," *Compensation Review* 9 (Fourth Quarter, 1976), pp. 30–44; Monci Jo Williams, "Why Chief Executives' Pay Keeps Rising," *Fortune*, April 1, 1985, pp. 66–72, 76.

[63] Daniel J. Miller, "CEO Salary Increases May Be Rational After All: Referents and Contracts in CEO Pay," *Academy of Management Journal* 38(5) (1995), pp. 1361–1385.

[64] Other tax reform issues are discussed in Gregory Wiber, "After Tax Reform, Part I: Planning Employee Benefit Programs," *Compensation and Benefits Review* 19(2) (1987), pp. 16–25; and Irwin Rubin, "After Tax Reform, Part 2," *Compensation and Benefits Review* 20(1) (1988), pp. 26–32.

[65] Michael F. Klein, "Executive Perquisites," *Compensation Review* 12 (Fourth Quarter 1979), pp. 46–50.

[66] Jo C. Kail, "Compensating Scientists and Engineers," in *New Perspectives on Compensation*, eds. David B. Balkin and Luis R. Gomez-Mejia (Englewood Cliffs, NJ: Prentice-Hall, 1987), pp. 247–281.

[67] *Compensation Planning Outlook 2009*, Ottawa: Conference Board of Canada, pp. 7, 10.

[68] "Sales Compensation Is Increasingly Tied to Quality," *Compflash*, July 1995, p. 1.

[69] N. Ford, O. Walker, and G. Churchill, "Differences in the Attractiveness of Alternative Rewards among Industrial Salespeople: Additional Evidence," *Journal of Business Research* 13(2) (1985), pp. 123–138.

[70] Bill O'Connell, "Dead Solid Perfect: Achieving Sales Compensation Alignment," *Compensation and Benefits Review*, March/April 1996, pp. 41–48.

[71] B. Weeks, "Setting Sales Force Compensation in the Internet Age," *Compensation and Benefits Review*, March/April 2000, pp. 25–34.

[72] S. Sands, "Ineffective Quotas: The Hidden Threat to Sales Compensation Plans," *Compensation and Benefits Review*, March/April 2000, pp. 35–42.

[73] *Compensation Planning Outlook 2009*, Ottawa: Conference Board of Canada, p. 49; J. Bernier, *The Scope of Federal Labour Standards and Nontraditional Work Situations* (Submission to the Federal Labour Standards Review), October 2005, pp. 5–13.

[74] Matusik and Hill, "The Utilization of Contingent Workers ..."

[75] Janet H. Marler, George T. Milkovich, and Melissa Barringer, *"Boundaryless Organizations and Boundaryless Careers: A New Market for High Skilled Temporary Work"* (Unpublished paper submitted to 1998 Academy of Management Annual Conference, Human Resource Division).

Chapter 12

[1] The job evaluation manual was introduced as evidence in *Electrical Workers (IUE) v. Westinghouse Electric Corp.*, 632 F.2d 1094, 23 FEP Cases 588 (3rd Cir. 1980), cert. denied, 452 U.S. 967, 25 FEP Cases 1835 (1981).

[2] Bruce Kaufman, ed. *Government Regulation of the Employment Relationship* (Ithaca, NY: Cornell University Press, 1998); Arthur Gutman, *EEO Law and Personnel Practices,* 2nd ed. (Thousand Oaks, CA: Sage Publications, 2000).

[3] *Keeping America Competitive* (Washington, DC: Employment Policy Foundation, 1994).

[4] This section based on T. A. Opie, *You Asked? Your Employment Standards Questions Answered*, 2nd edition. Toronto, ON: CCH Canadian Ltd., 2002, and S. D. Saxe, *Ontario Employment Law Handbook: An Employer's Guide*, sixth edition. Toronto, ON: Butterworths Canada, 2002.

[5] Oren M. Levin-Waldman, "Do Institutions Affect the Wage Structure? Right-to-Work Laws, Unionization, and the Minimum Wage," *No. 57, Public Policy Brief* (Washington, DC: National Academy of Sciences, 1999).

[6] This section based on T. A. Opie, *You Asked? Your Employment Standards Questions Answered*, 2nd edition. Toronto, ON: CCH Canadian Ltd., 2002.

[7] This section based on T. A. Opie, *You Asked? Your Employment Standards Questions Answered*, 2nd edition. Toronto, ON: CCH Canadian Ltd., 2002.

[8] Andrew M. Gill and Duane E. Leigh, "Community College Enrollment, College Major, and the Gender Wage Gap," *Industrial and Labor Relations Review* 54 (1), October 2000, pp. 163–181; Catherine J. Weinberger, "Race and Gender Wage Gaps in the Market for Recent College Graduates," *Industrial Relations* 37 (1) (1998), pp. 67–84; John M. McDowell, Larry D. Singell Jr., and James P. Ziliak, "Cracks in the Glass Ceiling: Gender and Promotion in the Economics Profession," *American Economic Review* 89 (2) (1999), pp. 392–396.

[9] Anne E. Preston, "Why Have All the Women Gone? A Study of Exit of Women from the Science and Engineering Professions," *American Economic Review*, December 1994, pp. 1446–1462.

[10] Francine Blau and Marianne Ferber, "Career Plans and Expectations of Young Women and Men," *Journal of Human Resources* 26 (4) (1991), pp. 581–607.

[11] Robert G. Wood, Mary E. Corcoran, and Paul N. Courant, "Pay Differences among the Highly Paid: The Male–Female Earnings Gap in Lawyers' Salaries," *Journal of Labor Economics* 11 (3) (1993), pp. 417–41.

[12] Barry A. Gerhart and George T. Milkovich, "Salaries, Salary Growth, and Promotions of Men and Women in a Large, Private Firm," *Pay Equity: Empirical Inquiries* (Arlington, VA: National Science Foundation, 1989); Jane Waldfogel, "Understanding the 'Family Gap' in *Pay for Women with Children*," Journal of Economic Perspectives 12 (1) (1998), pp. 157–170; C. Brown, C. and M. Corcoran, "Sex-Based Differences in School Content and the Male–Female Wage Gap," *Journal of Labor Economics* 15 (3) (1997), pp. 431–465.

[13] R. Finnie and T. Wannell, "The Evolution of the Gender Earnings Gap Amongst Canadian University Graduates," *Statistics Canada - 11F0019MIE No. 235*, November 2004; Joy A. Schneer and Frieda Reitman, "The Importance of Gender in Mid-Career: A Longitudinal Study of MBAs," *Journal of Organizational Behavior* 15 (1994), pp. 199–207; F. Blau and L. Kahn, *"Gender Differences in Pay"* (Cambridge, MA: NBER working paper 7732, June 2000).

[14] Robert G. Wood, Mary E. Corcoran, and Paul N. Courant, "Pay Differences among the Highly Paid: The Male-Female Earnings Gap in Lawyers' Salaries," *Journal of Labor Economics* 11 (3) (1993), pp. 417–441.

[15] Jerry Jacobs, "The Sex Segregation of Occupations: Prospects for the 21st Century," in *Handbook of Gender in Organizations*, Gary N. Powell, ed. (Newbury Park, CA: Sage Publications, 1999), pp. 125–141.

[16] George F. Dreher and Taylor H. Cox, Jr., "Labor Market Mobility and Cash Compensation: The Moderating Effects of Race and Gender," *Academy of Management Journal* 43 (5) (2000), pp. 890–900; J. M. Brett and L. K. Stroh, "Jumping Ship: Who Benefits from an External Labor Market Career Strategy?" *Journal of Applied Psychology* 82 (1997), pp. 331–341; G. F. Dreher and T. H. Cox, Jr., "Race, Gender, and Opportunity: A Study of Compensation Attainment and the Establishment of Mentoring Relationships," *Journal of Applied Psychology* 81 (1996), pp. 297–308; J. H. Greenhaus, S. Parasuraman, and W. J. Wormley, "Effects of Race on Organizational Experiences, Job Performance Evaluations, and Career Outcomes," *Academy of Management Journal* 33 (1990), pp. 64–86.

[17] Joy A. Schneer and Frieda Reitman, "The Importance of Gender in Mid-Career: A Longitudinal Study of MBAs," *Journal of Organizational Behavior* 15 (1994), pp. 199–207.

[18] Alison M. Konrad and Kathy Cannings, "Of Mommy Tracks and Glass Ceilings: A Case Study of Men's and Women's Careers in Management," *Relations Industrielles* 49 (2) (1994), pp. 303–333.

[19] Donald J. Treiman and H. J. Hartmann, eds., *Women, Work and Wages* (Washington, DC: National Academy Press, 1981); Gregory Attiyeh and Richard Attiyeh, "Testing for Bias in Graduate School Admissions," *Journal of Human Resources* 32 (3), pp. 524–548.

[20] M. Drolet, "The Male-Female Wage Gap," *Perspectives*, Spring 2002, pp. 29–37. Statistics Canada Catalogue no. 75-001-XPE.

[21] This section based on T. A. Opie, *You Asked? Your Employment Standards Questions Answered*, 2nd edition. Toronto, ON: CCH Canadian Ltd., 2002.

[22] Allan M. Carter and F. Ray Marshall, *Labor Economics* (Homewood, Ill.: Richard D. Irwin, 1982).

[23] Ibid.

[24] G. Keenan and K. Howlett, "Find More Cuts, Premier Tells GM and CAW," *Globe and Mail*, March 31, 2009; and N. Van Praet, "GM Deal a Yardstick Got Union Talks with Chrysler," *Financial Post*, March 17, 2009.

[25] Stephen B. Jarrell and T. D. Stanley, "A Meta Analysis of the Union–Non-Union Wage Gap," *Industrial and Labor Relations Review* 44, (1) (1990), pp. 54–67.

[26] Richard Freeman and James Medoff, *What Do Unions Do?* (New York: Basic Books, 1981).

[27] Bureau of Labor Statistics, *"Employer Costs for Employee Compensation Summary"* (Washington DC: Bureau of Labor Statistics 1999). Retrieved November 3, 2000, from the World Wide Web: http://stats.bls.gov/news.release/ecec.nws.htm.

[28] Bureau of Labor Statistics, *"Table 7: Private Industry, by Region and Bargaining Status"* (Washington DC: Bureau of Labor Statistics 1999). Retrieved November 3, 2000, from the World Wide Web: http://stats.bls.gov/news.release/ecec.t07.htm; Robert Rice, "Skill, Earnings and the Growth of Wage Supplements," *American Economic Review*, Fall 1972, pp. 139–147; William Bailey and Albert Schwenk, "Employer Expenditures for Private Retirement and Insurance Plans," *Monthly Labor Review* 95 (1972), pp. 15–19.

[29] Loren Solnick, "Unionism and Fringe Benefits Expenditures," *Industrial Relations* 17 (1) (1978), pp. 102–107.

[30] James E. Martin and Thomas D. Heetderks, *Two-Tier Compensation Structures: Their Impact on Unions, Employers and Employees* (Kalamazoo, MI: W.E. Upjohn Institute for Employment Research, 1990).

[31] Mollie Bowers and Roger Roderick, "Two-Tier Pay Systems: The Good, The Bad, and The Debatable," *Personnel Administrator* 32(6) (1987), pp. 101–112.

[32] James Martin and Melanie Peterson, "Two-Tier Wage Structures: Implications for Equity Theory," *Academy of Management Journal* 30(2) (1987), pp. 297–315.

[33] "Two-Tier Systems Falter as Companies Sense Workers' Resentment," *The Wall Street Journal*, June 16, 1987, p. 1.

[34] Fehmida Sleemi, "Collective Bargaining Outlook for 1995," *Compensation and Working Conditions* 47 (1), January 1995, pp. 19–39.

[35] Richard B. Freeman and Joel Rogers, *What Workers Want* (Ithaca, NY: ILR Press, 1999); David Neumark and Michael L. Wachter, "Union Effects on Nonunion Wages: Evidence from Panel Data on Industries and Cities," *Industrial and Labor Relations Review* 31(1) (1978), pp. 205–216.

[36] J. L. McAdams and E. J. Hawk, *Organizational Performance and Reward: 663 Experiences in Making the Link* (Scottsdale, AZ: American Compensation Association, 1994).

[37] L. B. Cardinal and I. B. Helbrun, "Union versus Nonunion Attitudes toward Share Agreements," *Proceedings of the 39th Annual Meeting of the Industrial Relations Research Association* (Madison, WI 1987), pp. 167–173.

[38] R. L. Heneman, C. von Hippel, D. E. Eskew, and D. B. Greenberger, "Alternative Rewards in Union Environments," *ACA Journal*, Summer 1997, pp. 42–55.

Chapter 13

[1] Stan Durda, "Total Labor Costs: Overview," 3M presentation, April 2000; Robert H. Meehan, "Analyzing Compensation Program Costs," in *Compensation Guide*, ed. William Caldwell (Boston, MA: Warren Gorham and Lamont, 1994).

[2] "The New World of Work," and "Sixty-Five Years of Work in America," *BusinessWeek*, October 17, 1994, pp. 76–148.

[3] K. P. DeMeuse, P. A. Vanderheiden, and T. J. Bergmann, "Announced Layoffs: Their Effect on Corporate Financial Performance," *Human Resource Management* 33 (4) (1994).

[4] E. A. Lenz, "Flexible Employment: Positive Work Strategies for the 21st Century," *Journal of Labor Research* XVII, no. 4 (1996), pp. 555–565.

[5] Janet H. Marler, George T. Milkovich, and Melissa Barringer, *"Boundaryless Organizations and Boundaryless Careers: A New Market for High-Skilled Temporary Work"* (Ithaca, New York: Center for Advanced Human Resource Studies working paper #98-01, 1998); P. S. Tolbert, "Occupations, Organizations, and Boundaryless Careers," in *Boundaryless Careers*, eds. M. Arthur and D. M. Rousseau (New York: Oxford University Press, 1996), pp. 331–349

[6] L. M. Segal and D. G. Sullivan, "The Growth of Temporary Services Work," *Journal of Economic Perspectives* 11 (2) (1997), pp. 117–136; M. W. Barringer and M. Sturman, *"Exploring The Effects of Variable Work Arrangements on the Organizational Commitment of Contingent Workers"* (Working Paper, University of Massachusetts, Amherst, 1998); Scott Lever, "An Analysis of Managerial Motivations behind Outsourcing Practices in Human Resources," *Human Resource Planning* 20 (2) (1997), pp. 37–47; Leslie King, "Microsoft Rulings and Contingent Workers: What Does It All Mean for Employers?" *Workspan*, October 2000, pp. 79–81.

[7] M. Carnoy, M. Castells, and C. Benner, "Labour Markets and Employment Practices in the Age of Flexibility: A Case Study of Silicon Valley," *International Labour Review* 136 (1) (1997), pp. 27–48.

[8] S. Snell and M. A. Youndt, "Human Resource Management and Firm Performance: Testing a Contingency Model of Executive Controls," *Journal of Management* 4, 1995.

[9] J. Barney, "Organizational Economics: Understanding the Relationship Between Organizations and Economic Analysis," in *Handbook of Organization Studies*, eds. S. Clegg, C. Hardy, and W. Nord (London: Sage Publishers, 1997), pp. 115–147.

[10] For information on the CPI, see the Government of Canada Web site for Statistics Canada; Mary Kokoski, "Alternate CPI Aggregations: Two Approaches," *Monthly Labor Review*, November 2000, pp. 31–39.

[11] Ronald T. Albright and Bridge R. Compton, *Internal Consulting Basics* (Scottsdale, AZ: American Compensation Association, 1996).

[12] Nancy Emmons, *"Managed and Manipulated Earnings: Implications for Compensation Managers"* (working paper, ILR/Cornell University, 2000); Flora Guidry, Andrew J. Leon, and Steve Rock, "Earnings-Based Bonus Plans and Earnings Management by Business-Unit Managers," *Journal of Accounting and Economics* 26 (1999), pp. 113–142

[13] John A. Rubino, *Communicating Compensation Programs* (Scottsdale, AZ: American Compensation Association, 1997).

[14] "Rethinking Ways to Present Financial Information to Employees," *Employee Ownership Report*, March/April 2000, pp. 7, 10.

[15] Michael Beer and Mitin Nohria, "Cracking the Code of Change," *Harvard Business Review*, May–June 2000, pp. 133–141; Dave Ulrich, "A New Mandate for Human Resources," *Harvard Business Review*, January–February 1998, pp. 125–134.

[16] Brian Hackett, *Transforming the Benefit Function* (New York: The Conference Board, 1995); *Outsourcing HR Services* (New York: The Conference Board, 1994).

[17] Robert M. Dodd and Barbara M. Renterghem, "Increasing Benefit Plan Value through Outsourcing," *Benefits Quarterly*, First Quarter 1997, pp. 14–19.

Appendix

[1] A. Harney, "Toyota Plans Pay Based on Merit," *Financial Times*, July 8, 1999, p. 20.

[2] Interviews with Toshiba Managers, included in G. Milkovich, M. Bloom, and A. Mitra, *"Research Report: Rethinking Global Reward Systems,"* working paper, Cornell University, 2000.

[3] Income Data Services, *IDS Employment Europe* January 2000, 457, p. 20.

[4] A. Puffer and S. Shekshnia, "Compensating Local Employees in Post-Communist Russia," *Compensation and Benefits Journal*, September–October 1994, pp. 35–42; D. Soskice, "Wage Determination: The Changing Role of Institutions in Advanced Industrialized Countries," *Oxford Review of Economic Policy* 6 (4), pp. 36–61; *Paying the Price: Crisis in Central and Eastern Europe*, ed. D. Vaughan Whitehead (Geneva: ILO, 1999); L. Bajzikova, "Transition Process of HRM in the Slovak Republic," *Journal of HRM* 2 (2001), in press; N. Zupan, *"HRM in Slovenian Transitional Companies,"* working paper, Faculty of Economics, Ljubljana University, Slovenia, 2000.

[5] D. Dong, K. Goodall, and M. Warner, "The End of the Iron Rice Bowl," *International Journal of Human Resource Management*, April 2, 2000, pp. 217–236; Hesan A. Quazi, *Compensation and Benefits Practices in Selected Asian Countries* (Singapore: McGraw Hill, 2004).

[6] Zhong-Ming Wang, presentation to Cornell University Global HRM Distance Learning seminar, Shanghai China, March 2000;

comments by Ningyu Tang, instructor in Shanghai for Global HRM Distance Learning seminar.

[7] D. Woodruff, "Germany's Ties Among Government, Corporations, and Labor are Unraveling," *Wall Street Journal*, March 11, 1999, p. A18; G. T. Khulikov, "Ukraine Wage Decentralization in a Nonpayment Crisis," Chapter 11 in *Pay the Price* (Geneva: ILO, 2000); R. Yokovlev, "Wage Distortions in Russia," Chapter 9 in *Pay the Price* (Geneva: ILO, 2000).

[8] Kevin O'Rourke and J. G. Williamson, *Globalization and History: The Evolution of a 19th Century Atlantic Economy* (Cambridge, MA: MIT Press, 1999), p. 2.

[9] Kevin O'Rourke and J. G. Williamson, *Globalization and History: The Evolution of a 19th Century Atlantic Economy* (Cambridge, MA: MIT Press, 1999), Chapter 14. Also see D. Rodrik, "Has Globalization Gone Too Far?" *California Management Review* 39 (3), Spring 1997; W. Keller, L. Pauly, and S. Reich, *The Myth of the Global Corporation* (Princeton University Press, 1998); B. Kogut, "What Makes A Company Global? *Harvard Business Review*, January–February 1999, pp. 165–170; "Blaming Immigrants" editorial in *New York Times*, October 14, 2000, p. 18; Deborah Hargreaves, "Europe: Immigration: Rocky Road from Control to Management," *Financial Times*, October 12, 2000, p. 8.

[10] A similar toolkit is used to map the conditions in countries to assess investment potential. See T. Khanna, K. G. Palepu, and J. Sinha, "Strategies that Fit Emerging Markets," *Harvard Business Review*, June 2005, pp. 63–75.

[11] R. Freeman and L. F. Katz, *Differences and Changes in Wage Structures* (University of Chicago Press, 1994); *Income Data Services Employment Europe 2000* monthly newsletter.

[12] F. Trompenaars, *Riding the Waves of Culture: Understanding Diversity in Global Business* (Burr Ridge, IL: Irwin, 1995); H. C. Triandis, "Cross-Cultural Industrial and Organizational Psychology," in M. D. Dunnette and L. M. Hough, eds. *Handbook of Industrial and Organizational Psychology* (Palo Alto, CA: Consulting Psychologists Press, 1994), pp. 103–172, H. C. Triandis, *Individualism and Collectivism* (Boulder, CO: Westview Press, 1995).

[13] G. Hofstede, "Cultural Constraints in Management Theories," *International Review of Strategic Management* 5 (1994), pp. 27–51.

[14] R. Schuler and N. Rogovsky, "Understanding Compensation Practice Variations Across Firms: The Impact of National Culture," *Journal of International Business Studies* 29 (1998), pp. 159–178.

[15] L. R. Gomez-Mejia and T. Welbourne, "Compensation Strategies in a Global Context," *Human Resource Planning* 14 (1994), pp. 29–41.

[16] G. Milkovich and M. Bloom, "Rethinking International Compensation: From Expatriates and National Cultures to Strategic Flexibility," *Compensation and Benefits Review*, April 1998; L. Markoczy, "Us and Them," *Across the Board*, February 1998, pp. 44–48.

[17] F. Trompenaars, *Riding the Waves of Culture: Understanding Diversity in Global Business* (Burr Ridge, IL: Irwin, 1995); G. Hofstede, "Cultural Constraints in Management Theories," *International Review of Strategic Management* 5 (1994), pp. 27–51; P. C. Earley and C. B. Gibson, "Taking Stock in our Progress on Individualism–Collectivism: 100 Years of Solidarity and Community," *Journal of Management* 24 (1998), pp. 265–304; David Landes, *Culture Matters: How Values Shape Human Progress* (New York: Basic Books, 2001).

[18] M. Bloom, G. Milkovich, and N. Zupan, "Contrasting Slovenian and U.S. Employment Relations: The Links Between Social Contracts and Psychological Contracts" *CEMS Business Review* 2 (1997), pp. S95–S109.

[19] H. Katz and Owen Darbishire, *Converging Divergences: Worldwide Changes in Employment Systems* (Ithaca, NY: Cornell University Press, 2000); and Harry Katz and Owen Darbishire, *Converging Divergences: Worldwide Changes in Employment Systems* (Ithaca, NY: Cornell University Press, 2000); George Boyer "Review Symposium: Converging Divergences: Worldwide Changes in Employment System," *Industrial and Labor Relations Review* 54(3) (2001), pp. 647–662.

[20] Christopher L. Erickson and Sarosh Kuruvilla, "Labor Costs and the Social Dumping Debate in the European Union," *Industrial and Labor Relations Review*, October 1994, pp. 28–47; K. Schwab, M. Porter, J. Sachs, A. Warner, and M. Levison, *The Global Competitiveness Report 2000*, World Economic Forum (Harvard University Press, 2000).

[21] Bertrand Benoit, "Benefit Check: Why Germany is Confronted with a Welfare State Fiasco," *Financial Times*, June 26, 2006, p. 13; P. Dowling and R. Schuler, *International Dimensions of Human Resource Management* (Boston: PWS Kent, 2000); Matthew F. Davis, "Global Compensation in the New Economy," *International HR Journal* 9(3) (Fall 2000), pp. 45–50; Mark Fenton-O'Creevy, "HR Practices: Vive La Difference; Part 7: Mastering People Management," *Financial Times*, November 26, 2001.

[22] The Web site for the National Center for Employee Ownership (NCEO) has information and referrals concerning employee stock ownership plans (ESOPs) and other forms of employee ownership: www.esop.org. Worker Ownership around the world is discussed at www.activistnet.org.

[23] Michael Byungnam Lee, "Bonuses, Unions, and Labor Productivity in South Korea," *Journal of Labor Research* (1997); G. R. Ungson, R. J. Steers, and S. H. Park, *Korean Enterprises: The Quest for Globalization* (Boston: Harvard Business School Press, 1997).

[24] Lowell Turner, ed. *Negotiating the New Germany: Can Social Partnership Survive?* (Ithaca, New York: Cornell University Press, 1998); D. Soskice, "Wage Determination: The Changing Role of Institutions in Advanced Industrialized Counties," *Oxford Review of Economic Policy* 6 (4), pp. 36–61.

[25] Zhong-Ming Wang, interview of Shang Gua Gao, President of the Economic Reforms Foundation, *American Management*

Executive 14 (1), February 2000, pp. 8–12; G. Breton, H. Lan, and Yuan Lu, "China's Township and Village Enterprises," *American Management Executive* 14 (1), February 2000, pp. 19–30; W. Van Honacher, "Entering China: An Unconventional Approach," *Harvard Business Review*, March–April 1992, pp. 130–140.

26 J. Zhou and J. J. Martocchio, "Chinese and American Managers' Compensation Award Decisions," *Personnel Psychology* 54 (Spring 2001), pp. 115–145.

27 Giuseppe Fajertag, ed. *Collective Bargaining in Europe 1998–1999* (European Trade Union Institute, Brussels, 2000). The European Trade Union Institute's Web site is at http://www.etuc.org/etui/default.cfm.

28 Stephen Power and Guy Chazan, "Europe Auto Relations Get Testy," *The Wall Street Journal*, June 15, 2006, p. A8.

29 Hesan Ahmed Quazi and Sophia Lee, "A Study of Compensation Strategies of Organizations Operating in Singapore," Nanyang Business School, May 2003.

30 K. Roth and S. O'Donnell, "Foreign Subsidiary Compensation Strategy: An Agency Theory Perspective," *Academy of Management Journal* 39 (3) (1996), pp. 678–703; Ingmar Bjorkman and Patrick Furu, "Determinants of Variable Pay for Top Managers of Foreign Subsidiaries in Finland," *International Journal of Human Resource Management* 11 (4), August 2000, pp. 698–713.

31 "Big Mac Currencies," *Economist*, April 29, 2000, p. 75.

32 J. Abowd and M. Bognanno, "International Differences in Executive & Managerial Compensation," in *Differences and Changes in Wage Structures*, R. B. Freeman and L. Katz, eds. (Chicago: NBER, 1995), pp. 67–103.

33 Hugh Williamson, "IG Metall is the Trend-Setter: What Happened in the Strike Will Have Far-Reaching Implications," *Financial Times*, July 2, 2003, p. 11; B.Benoit, "German Executives May be Forced to Publish Salaries," *Financial Times*, May 20, 2003, p. 6; C. Roads, "In Deep Crisis, Germany Starts to Revamp Vast Welfare State," *Wall Street Journal*, July 10, 2003, pp. 1.A5.

34 D. Brown, "The Third Way: The Future of Pay and Rewards in Europe," *WorldatWork Journal*, Second Quarter 2000, pp. 15–25.

35 C. Hitoshi, S. Osamu, and I. Ryuko, "Salaryman Today and into Tomorrow," *Compensation and Benefits Review*, September–October 1997, pp. 67–75; M. Yashiro, *Human Resource Management in Japanese Companies in the Future* (New York: Organization Resource Counselors, 1996); *International Benefit Guidelines* (New York: William M. Mercer, 2000).

36 T. Kato, "The End of Lifetime Employment in Japan? Evidence from National Surveys and Field Research," *Journal of the Japanese and International Economies* 15 (2002), pp. 489–514; T. Kato and M. Rockell, "Experience, Credentials and Compensation in the Japanese and U.S. Managerial Labor Markets: Evidence from New Micro Data," *Journal of the Japanese and International Economies* 6 (1992), pp. 30–51; V. Pucik, "The Challenge of Globalization:

The Strategic Role of Local Managers in Japanese-Owned U.S. Subsidiaries," paper presented at Cornell Conference on Strategic HRM, Ithaca, New York, October 1997; P. Evans, V. Pucik and J. Barcoux, *The Global Challenge: Frameworks for International HRM* (New York, Irwin, 2002).

37 S. Strom, "In Japan, from Lifetime Job to No Job at All," *New York Times Online*, February 3, 1999; M. Bloom, G. Milkovich, and A. Mitra, *"Toward a Model of International Compensation and Rewards: Learning from How Managers Respond to Local Conditions,"* CAHRS working paper, Cornell University, #2015; Michiyo Wakamoto, "Leaving the Fold," *Financial Times*, April 2000, p. 18.

38 We thank Thomas Gresch and Elke Stedelmann, whose manuscript, *Traditional Pay Systems in Germany* (Ruesselsheim, Germany: Adam Opel AG, 2001), is the basis for this section of the chapter.

39 Andranik Tangian, "Monitoring Flexicurity Policies in Europe From Three Different Viewpoints," WSI-Discussion Paper 145 www.boeckler.de/pdf/p_wsi_diskp_145_e.pdf; S. M. Fuess and M. Millea, "Pay and Productivity in 'Corporatist' Germany," *Journal of Labor Research*, Summer 2006, pp. 397–410.

40 Thomas Friedman, *The World is Flat: A Brief History of the Twenty-first Century* (New York: Farrar, Straus and Giroux, 2006); J. W. Walker, "Are We Global Yet?" *Human Resource Planning*, First Quarter 2000, pp. 7–8; R. Locke and K. Thelen, "Apples and Oranges Revisited: Contextualized Comparisons and Comparative Labor Policies," *Politics and Society* 23(2) (1996), pp. 337–367; M. Mendenhall and Gary Oddou, *Readings and Cases in International Human Resource Management* (Cincinnati: Southwestern, 2000); and M. Bloom, G. Milkovich and A. Mitra, *"Toward a Model of International Compensation and Rewards: Learning from How Managers Respond to Local Conditions,"* CAHRS working paper, Cornell University, #2015. See also N. Napier and Van Tuan Vu, "International HRM in Developing and Transitional Economy Context," *Human Resource Management Review* 8 (1) (1998), pp. 39–71.

41 Samuel Palmisano, "The Globally Integrated Enterprise," *Foreign Affairs*, May/June 2006.

42 C. Reynolds, "Expatriate Compensation in Historical Perspective," *International Human Resource Journal*, Summer 1997, pp. 118–131.

43 *What It Costs to House Expatriates Worldwide* (New York: Runzheimer International, 2000); Orley Ashenfelter and Stepan Jurajda, *"Cross-Country Comparisons of Wage Rates: The Big Mac Index,"* paper presented at Ninth Annual Policy Conference, Labor Markets in Comparative Perspective, Ithaca, New York, October 7, 2000.

44 G. Latta, "The Future of Expatriate Compensation," *WorldatWork*, Second Quarter 2006, pp. 42–49; Cris Prystay and Tom Herman, "Tax Hike Hits Home for Americans Abroad," *The Wall Street Journal*, July 19, 2006, pp. D1, D5.

45 Runzheimer International, *www.runzheimer.com,* publishes monthly newsletters on the costs of relocation.

[46] S. Webster Brown, "Spanning the Globe for Quality Pay Data," in *2003–2004 Survey Handbook and Directory* (Scottsdale AZ: WorldatWork, 2002), pp. 95–100; M. A. Coil, "Salary Surveys in a Blended-Role World," in *2003–2004 Survey Handbook and Directory* (Scottsdale AZ: WorldatWork, 2002), pp. 57–64.

[47] Monica M. Sabo, "Tax-Effective Compensation Planning for International Assignments," *International Compensation and Benefits*, January–February 1995, pp. 24–28; Paul Bailey, "The Role of Cost of Living Data in Creating Cost-Effective Expatriate Assignments," *International HR Journal*, Winter 2001 (9) (4), pp. 27–30.

[48] C. Reynolds, "Expatriate Compensation in Historical Perspective," *International Human Resource Journal*, Summer 1997, pp. 118–131.

[49] International Total Remuneration, certification course T9 (Scottsdale, AZ: WorldatWork, 2000); Cal Reynolds, "International Compensation," in *Compensation Guide*, ed. William A. Caldwell (Boston: Warren, Gorham and Lamont, 1998).

[50] Fred K. Piker, "Attracting, Retaining, Motivating Senior-Level Expatriates: What's Fair to Both Company and Employee," *Innovations in International HR*, Summer 1997, pp. 1–5; Hal B. Gregersen and Linda K. Stroh, "Coming Home to the Arctic Cold: Antecedents to Finnish Expatriate and Spouse Repatriation Adjustment," *Personnel Psychology* 50 (1997), pp. 635–654; Richard A. Guzzo, Katherine A. Noonan, and Efrat Elron, "Expatriate Managers and the Psychological Contract," *Journal of Applied Psychology* 7 (4) (1994), pp. 617–626; "Focusing on International Assignments," *ACA News*, July/August 1999.

[51] *Expatriate Dual Career Survey Report* (New York: Windham International and National Foreign Trade Council, 1997); G. M. Wederspahn, "Costing Failures in Expatriate Human Resources Management," *Human Resource Planning* 15(3), pp. 27–35; M. S. Schell and I. L. Dolins, "Dual-Career Couples and International Assignments," *International Compensation and Benefits*, November–December 1992, pp. 25–29; Soo Min Toh and Angelo deNisi, "Host Country National Reactions to Expatriate Pay Policies: A Model and Implications," *Academy of Management Review*, 28(4), 2003, pp. 606–621.

[52] *Expatriate Dual Career Survey Report* (New York: Windham International and National Foreign Trade Council, 1997); Garry M. Wederspahn, "Costing Failures in Expatriate Human Resources Management," *Human Resource Planning* 15(3), pp. 27–35; Michael S. Schell and Ilene L. Dolins, "Dual-Career Couples and International Assignments," *International Compensation and Benefits*, November–December 1992, pp. 25–29; Carolyn Gould, "Can Companies Cut Costs by Using the Balance-Sheet Approach?" *International Compensation and Benefits*, July–August 1993, pp. 36–41; David E. Molnar, "Repatriating Executives and Keeping Their Careers on Track," *International Compensation and Benefits*, November–December 1994, pp. 31–35; Ken I. Kim, Hun-Joon Park, and Nori Suzuki, "Reward Allocations in the United States, Japan, and Korea: A Comparison of Individualistic and Collectivistic Cultures," *Academy of Management Journal* 33(1) (1990), pp. 188–98; Anne S. Tsui, Jone L. Pearce, Lyman W. Porter, and Angela M. Tripoli, "Alternative Approaches to the Employee-Organization Relationship: Does Investment in Employees Pay Off?" *Academy of Management Journal* 40(5) (1997), pp. 1089–121.

[53] "The Global Company: Series on Global Corporations," *Financial Times*, November 7, 1995.

[54] P. Evans, V. Pucik and J-L Barsoux, *The Global Challenge* (New York: McGraw Hill, 2002); A. D. Engle Sr. and Mark Mendenhall, "Transnational Roles and Transnational Rewards: Global Integration in Executive Compensation," presentation at International HR Conference, Limerick, Ireland, June 2003; M. Chaukar, J. Sovina and C. Tyler, "Globalist Compensation," paper presented at Cornell University seminar on International Compensation, Spring 2003.

GLOSSARY

agency theory—motivation theory stating that employees and management/owners both will act opportunistically to obtain the most favourable exchange possible

aging/trending survey data—adjusting survey data to represent pay at the current or future date when the pay decisions will be implemented

allowances—compensation to provide for items that are in short supply

alternation ranking—ranking the best employee, then the worst employee, then the next best and worst, and so on

alternation ranking method—ranking the highest- and lowest-valued jobs first, then the next highest- and lowest-valued jobs, repeating the process until all jobs have been ranked

behaviourally anchored rating scale (BARS)—performance rating scale using behavioural descriptions as anchors for different levels of performance on the scale

benchmark job—a job whose contents are well-known, relatively stable, and common across different employers

benefit maximums—limitations on benefit payable

bottom-up budgeting—managers forecast the pay increases they will recommend in the coming year

broadbanding—a large band of jobs containing several pay grades

broad-based option plans (BBOPs)—stock options provided to employees at all levels

Canada/Quebec Pension Plan (C/QPP)—a mandatory, government-sponsored pension plan for all employed Canadians, funded equally by employers and employees

central tendency error—avoiding extremes in ratings across employees

classification—job evaluation method based on job class descriptions into which jobs are categorized

coinsurance—percentage of insurance premiums paid for by the employer

compa-ratio—ratio of average rates actually paid to range midpoint

compensable factors—characteristics of the work that the organization values, that help it pursue its strategy and achieve its objectives

compensating differentials theory—higher wages must be offered to compensate for negative features of jobs

compensation—all forms of financial returns and tangible services and benefits that employees receive as part of an employment relationship

compensation survey—the systematic process of collecting and making judgments about the compensation paid by other employers

competencies—underlying, broadly applicable knowledge, skills, and behaviours that form the foundation for successful work performance

competency analysis—a systematic process to identify and collect information about the competencies required for successful work performance

competency-based pay structure—links pay to work-related competencies

competency indicators—observable behaviours that indicate the level of competency within each competency set

competency sets—specific components of a competency

competitive advantage—a business practice or process that results in better performance than one's competitors

Consumer Price Index (CPI)—index that measures changes in prices over time

coordination of benefits—reduction of benefits by any amount paid under a spouse's plan

core competencies—competencies required for successful work performance in any job in the organization

cost-of-living adjustment—percentage increment to base pay provided to all employees regardless of performance

deductible—specified dollar amount of claims paid by the employee each year before insurance benefits begin

defined-benefit plan—pension plan in which an employer agrees to provide a specific level of retirement pension, the exact cost of which is unknown

defined-contribution plan—pension plan in which an employer agrees to provide specific contributions, but the final benefit is unknown

differentials—pay differences between job levels

distributive justice—fairness of a decision outcome

dual career track—career progression on either a managerial path or a professional path

earnings-at-risk plan—incentive plan that includes reductions in base pay in unsuccessful years

efficiency wage theory—high wages may increase efficiency and lower labour costs by attracting higher-quality applicants who will work harder

employee assistance plan (EAP)—employer-sponsored program that provides employees with confidential counselling and/or treatment programs for personal problems including addiction, stress, and mental health issues

employee benefits—part of the total compensation package, other than pay for time worked, provided to employees in whole or in part by employer payments, such as life insurance, pension plan, workers' compensation, vacation, and so on

employee engagement—a level of connection employees feel to their employer that results in them giving full discretionary effort on a sustained basis above and beyond specific job requirements

employee stock ownership plan (ESOP)—plan offering employees the opportunity to purchase company stock, often partially or fully matched by employer-paid stock for the employee

Employment Insurance (EI)—a mandatory, government-sponsored plan for all employed Canadians that provides workers with temporary income replacement as a result of employment interruptions due to circumstances beyond their control; funded by employer and employee contributions

equity theory—motivation theory stating that people are concerned about fairness of the reward outcomes exchanged for employee inputs

evaluation format—the method used to evaluate an employee's performance, either ranking against other employees or rating on one or more performance criteria

expectancy theory—motivation theory stating that people cognitively evaluate potential behaviours in relation to rewards offered in exchange

external competitiveness—comparison of compensation with that of competitors

factor degree/level—description of several different degrees or levels of a factor in jobs; a different number of points is associated with each degree/level

factor weights—weighting assigned to each factor to reflect differences in importance attached to each factor by the employer

first impression error—developing a negative or positive opinion of an employee early in the review period and allowing that to influence negatively or positively all later perceptions of performance

flexible benefit plans—benefit plans in which the employee is provided with a specified amount of money and then chooses which benefits to spend the money on, according to their attractiveness and cost

gain-sharing plan—group incentive plan where employees share in cost savings

green circle rates—pay rates below the range minimum

group incentive plans—incentive pay for meeting or exceeding team performance standards

halo error—an appraiser giving favourable ratings to all job duties based on impressive performance in just one job function; for example, a rater who hates tardiness rates a prompt subordinate high across all performance dimensions exclusively because of this one characteristic

human capital—the education, experience, knowledge, abilities, and skills that people possess

human capital theory—higher earnings are made by people who improve their potential productivity by acquiring education, training, and experience

incentives (variable pay)—one-time payments for meeting previously established performance objectives

internal alignment (internal equity)—pay comparisons between jobs, skill levels, or competencies within a single organization

internal labour markets—rules and procedures that determine the pay for different jobs within a single organization and that allocate employees to those different jobs

job analysis—the systematic process of collecting information about the nature of specific jobs

job description—written summary of a job, including responsibilities, qualifications, and relationships

job evaluation—the process of systematically determining the relative worth of jobs to create a job structure for the organization

job specifications—qualifications required to be hired for a job; may be included in the job description

job structure—hierarchy of all jobs based on value to the organization; provides the basis for the pay structure

job-to-job method—method of comparing pay for male- and female-dominated job classes where each female job class is compared to a male job class of equal or comparable value

leniency error—consistently rating someone higher than is deserved

line-of-sight—link between an individual employee's work and the achievement of organizational objectives

long-term disability plans—employer-sponsored plans that provide income protection due to long-term illness or injury that is not work-related

loosely coupled structure—pay structure for jobs that are flexible, adaptable, and changing

management by objectives (MBO)—performance rating method based on meeting objectives set at the beginning of the performance review period

marginal product of labour—the additional output associated with the employment of one additional human resources unit, with other production factors held constant

marginal productivity theory—unless an employee can produce something of value from his/her job equal to the value received in wages, it will not be worthwhile for an employer to hire that employee

marginal revenue of labour—the additional revenue generated when the firm employs one additional unit of human resources, with other production factors held constant

market pay line—links a company's benchmark jobs on the horizontal axis (internal structure) with market rates paid by competitors (market survey) on the vertical axis

market pricing—establishing pay structure by relying almost exclusively on external market pay rates

merit increase—increment to base pay in recognition of past work behaviour

merit pay—increase in base pay related to performance

motivation—a process involving the determination of what is important to a person, and offering it in exchange for desired behaviour

negative halo error—the opposite of a halo error; downgrading an employee across all performance dimensions exclusively because of poor performance on one dimension

occupational segregation—the historical segregation of women into a small number of occupations such as clerical, sales, nursing, and teaching

outlier—a data point that falls outside the majority of the data points

paired comparison method—listing all jobs across columns and down rows of a matrix, comparing the two jobs in each cell and indicating which is of greater value, then ranking jobs based on the total number of times each is ranked as being of greater value

paired comparison performance ranking—ranking each employee against all other employees, one pair at a time

pay equity—legislation intended to redress the unexplained portion of the wage gap assumed to be due to gender discrimination

pay-for-performance plan—a pay plan that links individual pay to some measure of performance on the job

pay forms—the mix of the various types of payments that make up total compensation

pay grade—grouping of jobs considered substantially equal for pay purposes

pay level—the average of the array of rates paid by an employer: base + bonuses + benefits + options/number of employees

pay policy line—pay line representing an adjustment to the market pay line to reflect the company's external competitive position in the market (i.e., lead, match, lag)

pay range—an upper and lower limit on pay for all jobs in a pay grade

pay structure—the array of pay rates for different work or skills within a single organization; the number of levels, differentials in pay between the levels, and the criteria used to determine these differences create the structure

pension plan—plan that provides income to an employee at retirement as compensation for work performed now

performance appraisal—process of evaluating or appraising an employee's performance on the job

point method—job evaluation method that assigns a number of points to each job, based on compensable factors that are numerically scaled and weighted

Position Analysis Questionnaire (PAQ)—a structured job analysis questionnaire used for analyzing jobs on the basis of 194 job elements that describe generic work behaviours

procedural fairness—fairness of the process used to make a decision

procedural justice—fairness of a process by which a decision is reached

profit-sharing plans—variable pay plans requiring a profit target to be met before any payouts occur

proportional value/wage line method—method of comparing pay for male- and female-dominated job classes when female job classes have no appropriate male comparators under the job-to-job system, where the wage line for male job classes is applied when setting pay for female job classes

proxy comparison method—method of comparing pay for male- and female-dominated job classes when pay equity cannot be achieved through job-to-job or proportional value methods, where female job classes are compared to similar female job classes that have achieved pay equity with another employer

range spread—the specific numerical distance between the minimum and maximum of the pay range

ranking—job evaluation method that ranks jobs from highest to lowest based on a global definition of value

recency error—the opposite of first impression error; allowing performance, either good or bad, at the end of the review period to play too large a role in determining an employee's rating for the entire period

red circle rates—pay rates above the range maximum

reference rates—pay rates from market data used in pricing broad bands

relational returns—psychological returns employees believe they receive in the workplace

reliability—consistency of results from repeated applications of a measure

reservation wage theory—job seekers have a reservation wage level below which they will not accept a job

salary—pay calculated at an annual or monthly rate

short-term disability plans/salary continuation plans—employer-sponsored plans that provide a continuation of all or part of an employee's earnings when the employee is absent from work due to an illness or injury that is not work-related

sick leave plans—employer-sponsored plans that grant a specified number of paid sick days per month or per year

signalling theory—pay levels and pay mix are designed to signal desired employee behaviours

similar-to-me error—giving better ratings to individuals who are like the rater in behaviour and/or personality

skill analysis—a systematic process to identify and collect information about skills required to perform work in an organization

skill-based pay structures—link pay to the depth or breadth of the skills, abilities, and knowledge a person acquires that are relevant to the work

spillover effect—employers seeking to avoid unionization offer workers the wages, benefits, and working conditions won in rival unionized firms

spillover error—continuing to downgrade an employee for performance errors in prior rating periods

stock options—the right to purchase stock at a specified (exercise) price for a fixed time period

strategic objectives—goals identified by an organization as necessary for the achievement of its strategy for success

strategic perspective—a focus on compensation decisions that help the organization gain and sustain competitive advantage

strategy—the fundamental business decisions that an organization has made in order to achieve its strategic objectives, such as what business to be in and how to obtain competitive advantage

strictness error—the opposite of leniency error; rating someone consistently lower than is deserved

survey—the systematic process of collecting and making judgments about the compensation paid by other employers

survey levelling—multiplying survey data by a numerical factor to adjust for differences between the company job and the survey job

tailored structure—pay structure for well-defined jobs with relatively small differences in pay

360-degree feedback—performance appraisal method including feedback from up to five sources: supervisor, peers, self, customers, and subordinates

top-down budgeting—top management of each organizational unit estimates the pay-increase budget for that unit

total rewards—all rewards received by employees, including cash compensation, benefits, and relational returns

total reward system—all rewards (in at least 13 general categories) provided by organizations

turnover effect—decreased budget required as lower-paid workers replace employees who leave, calculated as annual turnover rate times planned average increase

validity—accuracy of a measure

vesting—waiting period for entitlement to employer-paid portion of pension benefits

wage—pay calculated at an hourly rate

wage gap—the amount by which the average pay for female workers is less than the average pay for male workers

workflow—process by which goods and services are delivered to the customer

work/life programs—programs that help employees better integrate their work and life responsibilities

Workers' Compensation—a mandatory, government-sponsored, employer-paid, no-fault insurance plan that provides compensation for injuries and diseases that arise out of, and while in the course of, employment

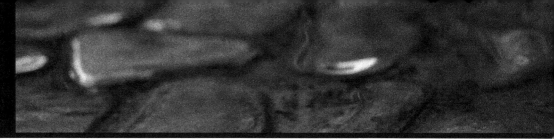

NAME INDEX

SUBJECT INDEX